P9-BIE-782

User Guide

Adobe Illustrator® version 8.0

Adobe Illustrator 8.0 User Guide for Windows and Macintosh

Adobe Systems Incorporated, 345 Park Avenue, San Jose, California 95110, USA

Adobe Systems Europe Limited, Adobe House, Edinburgh EH11 4DU, Scotland, United Kingdom

Adobe Systems Co., Ltd., Yebisu Garden Place Tower, 4-20-3 Ebisu, Shibuya-ku, Tokyo 150, Japan

Adobe Systems Pty. Ltd., P.O. Box 672, 18-20 Orion Road, Lane Cove, New South Wales 2066, Australia

Printed in the U.S.A.

Part Number: 90014246 (12/98)

Contents

Modifying Shapes

Chapter 6

Working with Color

Chapter 7

Using Gradients, Blends, and Patterns

Using Layers

Working with Bitmap Images

Introduction

Welcome to the Adobe® Illustrator® program, the industry-standard illustration program for print, multimedia, and online graphics. Whether you're a novice or an illustration expert, Adobe Illustrator offers you the tools you need to get professional-quality results.

You'll find that Adobe Illustrator excels as an art production tool, whether you are a designer or technical illustrator producing artwork for print publishing, an artist producing multimedia graphics, or a creator of Web pages or online content. The software gives you an unmatched level of precision and control over your artwork and the flexibility to produce anything from small designs to large, complex projects. Adobe Illustrator also provides a consistent work environment with other Adobe applications including Adobe Photoshop® and Adobe PageMaker®.

About this user guide

The *Adobe Illustrator 8.0 User Guide* contains detailed information about the Illustrator tools and commands. It is designed to be used as a reference tool in your everyday work with Adobe Illustrator. This cross-platform user guide provides instructions for using Illustrator on both the Windows® and Mac® OS platforms. Any differences in procedures and commands between platforms are noted in the text.

This guide assumes you have a working knowledge of your computer and its operating conventions, including how to use a mouse and standard menus and commands. It also assumes you know how to open, save, and close files. For help with any of these techniques, please see your Windows or Mac OS documentation.

Learning Adobe Illustrator

Adobe Illustrator 8.0 includes the following printed and online documentation:

The *Adobe Illustrator 8.0 User Guide* Contains complete instructions for using all Adobe Illustrator commands and features.

Online Help for Adobe Illustrator 8.0 Contains all the information in the *Adobe Illustrator 8.0 User Guide*, optimized for use online. In addition, online Help includes Illustrator shortcuts and full-color galleries and illustrations.

Adobe Illustrator movies and tutorials Provide information and step-by-step instructions about Adobe Illustrator 8.0 features. (For a description, see "Contents of the Adobe Illustrator Tour & Training CD" on page 3.)

The *Adobe Illustrator 8.0 Quick Reference Card* Contains basic information about the Adobe Illustrator tools and palettes and shortcuts for using them.

System requirements

To use Adobe Illustrator, you need the following hardware and software:

• A hard drive with at least 50 MB of free space. You'll need additional disk space if you work with very large image files.

• At least 32 MB of random-access memory (RAM) (for Mac OS, with 20 MB available to Adobe Illustrator).

• A CD-ROM drive.

For the best performance, Adobe Systems recommends the following hardware and software:

• 95 MB of hard disk space.

• 64 MB or more of RAM.

• A 24-bit (millions of colors) video display card.

• A PostScript® printer.

Adobe Illustrator performance improves with more RAM, faster CPUs, and faster and larger hard disk drives. (For information on technical support and troubleshooting, see Appendix B, "Troubleshooting.")

For the latest system requirements, see the Read Me file in the Adobe Illustrator 8.0 folder.

Windows system requirements

• A Pentium® or faster Intel® processor.

• Windows 95, Windows 98, or Windows NT® 4.0 or later.

• A video card displaying 800 x 600 pixels of desktop area.

Mac OS system requirements

• An Apple Power Macintosh computer.

• Mac OS version 7.5 or later. (For best performance, Adobe Systems recommends Mac OS version 8.1 or later.)

• 832 x 624 monitor resolution.

The Adobe Illustrator package contents

The Adobe Illustrator software package includes the following software and documentation:

• The Adobe Illustrator CD set consisting of the Application and Tour & Training CDs.

• *Adobe Illustrator 8.0 User Guide.*

• *Adobe Illustrator 8.0 Quick Reference Card.*

• Registration card.

Contents of the Adobe Illustrator Application CD

The Application CD contains the following:

The Adobe Illustrator installer Includes everything needed to install Adobe Illustrator 8.0 on your hard drive—the installer, the Adobe Illustrator program, plug-in modules, the Adobe Illustrator tutorial files, sample brushes, and numerous sample files.

Fonts Include 300 Type 1 fonts from the Adobe Type Library, as well as ATM® Light.

Clip art and images Include many professional clip-art images, stock photographs, and textures for your personal, non-commercial use.

Illustrator extras Include path patterns and textures, brushes, and action sets.

Adobe products and services Let you try out versions of other Adobe applications and learning resources.

Adobe technical notes Provide technical information for advanced users, written by Adobe staff. For updates, visit the Adobe Web site.

Adobe Acrobat Reader software Lets you view PDF files online.

Adobe PostScript (AdobePS™) printer driver An operating system program that lets applications such as Illustrator communicate with printers.

Third-party products Adobe Illustrator plug-in demos and Adobe Photoshop plug-in demos.

QuickTime software (QuickTime for Windows, Apple QuickTime for Mac OS) Enables you to view the movies included in the Adobe Illustrator CD set.

Contents of the Adobe Illustrator Tour & Training CD

The Tour & Training CD contains the following documentation and software:

The Adobe Illustrator 8.0 movies The Quick Tour movie gives a basic overview of the Adobe Illustrator features. A step-by-step description of the techniques shown in this movie is in Chapter 1 of this user guide.

The New Features movie introduces and demonstrates new features in Adobe Illustrator 8.0, including new and enhanced editing tools, type sampling, paintbrush effects, layers, and actions.

The Drawing and Selecting movie teaches you how to use the Illustrator drawing tools and selection tools.

The Adobe Illustrator 8.0 tutorials Provide step-by-step tutorials in PDF format on creating basic shapes, painting, working with type, and drawing with the pen tool. These tutorials are also included in *Adobe Illustrator 8.0 Classroom in a Book*, which is sold separately.

Adobe Illustrator Digital Art Show This digital "slide show" showcases the software's broad range of capabilities through the original work of leading Adobe Illustrator artists. (Please note that any featured artwork may not be copied, modified, or reused without the artist's written permission.)

Adobe Acrobat Reader software Lets you view PDF files online and is required when using the Tour & Training CD.

QuickTime software (QuickTime for Windows, Apple QuickTime for Mac OS) Enables you to view the movies included in the Adobe Illustrator CD set.

Registration

Adobe is confident you will find that the Adobe Illustrator program greatly increases your productivity. So that Adobe can continue to provide you with the highest quality software, offer technical support, and inform you about new Illustrator software developments, please register your copy by filling out and returning the warranty registration card included with your software package.

About Adobe products and services

If you have an Internet connection and a Web browser installed on your system, you can access the Adobe Systems Home Page on the World Wide Web (at http://www.adobe.com) for information on services, products, and tips pertaining to Illustrator.

For more information about Adobe technical support resources, see the notice that came with Illustrator.

To use Adobe Online:

1 Do one of the following:

- Choose File > Adobe Online.
- Click the icon at the top of the toolbox.

2 Click a topic to open the Adobe Home Page.

Classroom in a Book

Classroom in a Book is the official training series for Adobe graphics and publishing software developed by experts at Adobe and published by Adobe Press. For information on purchasing *Adobe Illustrator 8.0 Classroom in a Book*, visit the Adobe Web site at http://www.adobe.com, or contact your local book distributor.

Training & Certification

The Adobe® Training & Certification Programs are designed to help Adobe customers improve and promote their product proficiency skills. The Adobe Certified Expert (ACE) program is designed to recognize the high-level skills of expert users. Adobe Certified Training Providers (ACTP) use only Adobe Certified Experts to teach Adobe software classes either in their own classrooms or at their clients' sites. For worldwide Adobe Training Programs information visit the Training Programs section of http://www.adobe.com, where you can link to the appropriate regional site for your location.

Installing Adobe Illustrator

You must install the application from the Application CD onto your hard drive; you cannot run the program from the CD.

If you're upgrading to Adobe Illustrator 8.0 from an earlier version, the installer creates by default a new folder containing the new Adobe Illustrator files. Your current Adobe Illustrator files are not affected.

(For tips on installing the software, see "Before you call Adobe technical support" on page 403.)

To install the Adobe Illustrator program for Windows:

1 Start Windows, if it is not already running.

2 Insert the Application CD disc into your CD-ROM drive.

3 Follow the on-screen instructions to start the installer, or open the Illustrator folder and double-click the Setup.exe file.

4 Follow the on-screen instructions to install the program files. A message appears when the installation is complete.

The following sections provide more information on the installation procedure.

Installation setup When prompted, specify an installation option:

- Typical installs the complete set of Illustrator program files and system support files.
- Compact installs the minimum options required to use Illustrator.
- Custom lets you choose the options you want to install.

Note: *In the Chinese, Japanese, and Korean versions of Illustrator, the Typical option also installs CMap files that enable the use of double-byte fonts in Illustrator artwork. To install the CMap files in any other version of Illustrator, you must use the Custom option.*

Registration When prompted, enter your name and company information. Type the serial number exactly as it appears—including the hyphen—on the registration card included with your Adobe Illustrator software package.

If you're upgrading from version 7, you may use your old serial number, which you can find on the first page of your original user guide, or by launching Illustrator and choosing Help > About Illustrator.

QuickTime To view the movies in the Adobe Illustrator CD Set and to show previews when opening images in Windows, you also must install QuickTime, located on the CD (if it's not already installed on your computer).

To install the Adobe Illustrator program for Mac OS:

1 Turn off or remove any virus-protection software, and restart your computer.

2 Insert the Application CD disc into your CD-ROM drive.

3 Double-click the Install Adobe Illustrator 8.0 icon.

4 Follow the on-screen instructions to install the program files. A message appears when the installation is complete.

Note: *If you're upgrading from an earlier version of Adobe Illustrator, the installer may ask you to locate the previously installed version, or insert the original CD or floppy diskette for verification. Follow the on-screen instructions.*

The following sections provide more information on the installation procedure.

Installation setup When prompted, specify an installation option:

- Easy Install (Mac OS) installs the complete set of Illustrator program files and system support files.

• Custom Install (Mac OS) lets you choose the options you want to install.

Note: *In the Chinese, Japanese, and Korean versions of Illustrator, the Easy Install option also installs CMap files that enable the use of double-byte fonts in Illustrator artwork. To install the CMap files in any other version of Illustrator, you must use the Custom Install option.*

Registration When prompted, enter your name and company information. Type the serial number exactly as it appears—including the hyphen—on the registration card included with your Adobe Illustrator software package.

If you're upgrading from version 5.0 or later, you may use your old serial number, which you can find on the first page of your original user guide, or by launching Illustrator and choosing About Illustrator under the Apple menu.

QuickTime To view the movies in the Adobe Illustrator CD Set and to show previews when opening images in Mac OS, you also must install QuickTime, located on the CD, if it's not already installed on your computer.

Starting Adobe Illustrator

Follow the steps in this section to start the program.

To start Adobe Illustrator in Windows:

Choose Start > Programs > Adobe > Illustrator 8.0 > Adobe Illustrator 8.0. (If you installed the program in a folder other than Adobe, choose that folder from the Start > Programs menu.)

The Adobe Illustrator window appears, with a new file opened for you. You can now work with the new file or open a different file or artwork and start working.

To start Adobe Illustrator in Mac OS:

Open the Adobe Illustrator 8.0 folder, and double-click the Adobe Illustrator 8.0 program icon.

The Adobe Illustrator window appears, with a new file opened for you. You can now work with the new file or open a different file or artwork and start working.

What's new in Adobe Illustrator 8.0

Adobe Illustrator 8.0 includes many new features that improve creativity, productivity, accessibility, and integration.

Brush effects Enhancements to the paintbrush tool allow you to create various brush effects along a path, simulating a paintbrush stroke or artwork stretched along a path. You can choose from brush effects that appear by default in the Brushes palette, or you can create your own art and save it as a brush in the palette. Choose from Calligraphic, Scatter, Art, and Pattern brushes. You can also import sample brushes from the Window menu or access complete brush libraries from the Illustrator Extras folder on the Application CD. (See "Using the Brush Libraries" on page 98.)

Gradient mesh tool The gradient mesh tool converts an object to a multi colored, mesh object on which colors flow smoothly into one another. You can designate colors at different points inside the fill of a mesh object; the designated color is seamlessly blended from one region of the fill to another. You can also produce airbrush effects such as complex shading, highlighting, and contouring. (See "Creating multicolored objects with the gradient mesh tool" on page 191.)

Photo Crosshatch filter You can now convert a photographic image into a series of hatched layers, to give the appearance of a pen sketch. (See "Using the Photo Crosshatch filter" on page 245.)

Enhanced blend tool With the blend tool, you can now blend two or more selected objects to create intermediate objects and colors, and then have them follow an irregular path, or "spine," which can be updated immediately. You can blend between open paths, closed paths, gradients, colors, and other blends. You can edit any part of a blend, and the artwork will reblend automatically. (See "Blending shapes" on page 195.)

Navigator palette You can view an illustration in reduced size to see different areas of the illustration quickly, locate the area you are viewing, and change the magnification of the illustration. (See "Using the Navigator palette" on page 38.)

Links palette With the Links palette, you can identify, select, monitor, and update objects that are linked to external files and identify embedded files. You can also determine if an object's link to an external file is broken or missing, get information about the link characteristics and paths, and open a linked object's original file and application so you can edit the image. (See "Managing linked and embedded images" on page 58.)

Pathfinder palette You can now choose Pathfinder commands from the new Pathfinder palette. (See "Using the Pathfinder palette to modify shapes" on page 146.)

Actions palette You can now automate tasks by grouping a series of Illustrator commands into a single command—called an action—to reproduce frequently used effects easily. Use one of the actions provided with Illustrator in the Illustrator Extras folder on the Application CD, or create one of your own. (See "Using the Actions palette" on page 383.)

Type sampling Use the eyedropper and paint bucket tools to copy the fill, stroke, character, and paragraph attributes from selected type and copy the attributes to selected type, or apply the copied attributes to text you will type. You can select options for copying and applying type attributes in the Eyedropper/Paint Bucket dialog box. (See "Copying type attributes between objects" on page 268.)

Enhanced text handling You can now view non-printing characters, such as spaces, tabs, and paragraph marks on-screen. Also, improvements in the Character and Paragraph palettes allow you to work more precisely with Japanese text. You now have more flexibility when working with wari-chu text and kinsoku shori. (See Chapter 11, "Using Type.")

Enhanced layers You can create a template layer whenever you want to base a new illustration on an existing piece of artwork and, for example, trace over it or build a new illustration from it. Template layers are locked, dimmed, and nonprintable. Additional layers improvements include more flexibility in showing and printing layers and viewing layers in the Layers palette, and the ability to export Illustrator files as Photoshop layers. (See Chapter 9, "Using Layers.")

Color palette and Swatch palette enhancements Changes to the Color palette and Swatches palette make it even easier to use and create process or spot colors. In addition, Illustrator has improved spot color management when colors are merged from other files. (See Chapter 7, "Working with Color.")

Bounding box editing You can now use the bounding box (which displays when an object is selected) to scale, move, and duplicate objects easily by dragging a handle surrounding the selected objects. (See "Using the bounding box" on page 115.)

Free transform tool You can use the free transform tool to perform transformations on selected objects, such as reflecting, rotating, shearing, and distorting, without selecting the associated transformation tool or using the Transform palette. (See "Transforming selected objects" on page 131.)

Pencil tool Using the new editable pencil tool, you can easily lay down paths and then reshape paths or objects. (See "Drawing and editing freeform paths" on page 66.)

Smooth tool Using the new smooth tool, you can easily smooth out sections of a path or object. (See "Smoothing the path with the smooth tool" on page 68.)

Erase tool Using the new erase tool, you can easily erase segments of paths or objects. (See "Erasing the path with the erase tool" on page 68.)

Smart Guides Use Smart Guides, temporary "snap-to" guides, to help you create, align, and edit objects relative to other objects in a file. The direction, angle, and tolerance of Smart Guides are determined by settings in Preferences. (See "Using Smart Guides" on page 112.)

Registration color You can mark objects with a color that prints on all plates. (See "Specifying printer's marks" on page 371.)

Changed keyboard shortcuts, tools, and commands

The following are some of the Adobe Illustrator 7.0 shortcuts, tools, and commands that have changed for Adobe Illustrator 8.0. For more details about these and other changes, see the *Adobe Illustrator 8.0 Quick Reference Card* or the Adobe Illustrator online Help system.

• In the toolbox, the paint bucket tool is now under the eyedropper tool; the shear tool is under the reflect tool; and the measure tool is under the hand tool.

• To select the pencil tool, press N. This shortcut no longer brings up the ellipse tool. (To select the ellipse tool, press L.)

• To select the paintbrush tool, press B. This shortcut no longer brings up the blend tool.

• To select the blend tool, press W. This shortcut no longer brings up the shear tool. (To select the shear tool, press Shift+O until you see the tool.)

• To add or delete anchor points on a selected path, move the pen tool over the anchor point or selected path. Click when you see a + sign to add an anchor point, or when you see a – sign to delete an anchor point.

• To choose a different unit of measure, right-mouse-click (Windows) or Ctrl-click (Mac OS) the ruler in the document window to open the context-sensitive menu.

• To hide a selection, press Ctrl+3 (Windows) or Command+3 (Mac OS).

• To show all selections, press Alt+Ctrl+3 (Windows) or Command+Option+3 (Mac OS).

• To lock a selected object, press Ctrl+2 (Windows) or Command+2 (Mac OS).

• To unlock all objects, press Alt+Ctrl+2 (Windows) or Command+Option+2 (Mac OS).

• To resize a selected object proportionately, press Shift and drag a handle on the bounding box.

• To resize a selected object from the center, press Alt (Windows) or Option (Mac OS) and drag a handle on the bounding box.

• To resize a selected object proportionately from the center, press Shift+Alt (Windows) or Shift+Option (Mac OS) and drag a handle on the bounding box.

• To select an object that is hidden below another object, position the selection tool on the top object at a point directly above the object below it. Without moving the selection tool, right-click (Windows) or Ctrl-click (Mac OS) to open the context-sensitive menu. Then choose an option from the Select submenu.

• To open the Print Setup or Page Setup dialog box, press Shift+Ctrl+P (Windows) or Command+Shift+P (Mac OS).

1

Chapter 1: A Quick Tour of Adobe Illustrator

This interactive demonstration of Adobe Illustrator is designed to provide an overview of key features of the program in approximately one hour.

For a movie overview of Adobe Illustrator, see the Tour & Training CD. To find complete information about any feature, see the index in this user guide.

Getting started

You'll be working in one art file during this tour, but before you begin you'll need to restore the default preferences for Adobe Illustrator and then you'll open the finished art file for this lesson to see what you'll be creating.

1 To ensure that the tools and palettes function exactly as described in this tour, delete or deactivate (by renaming) the Adobe Illustrator 8.0 preferences file. (See "Restoring default preferences" on page 398.)

2 Start Adobe Illustrator.

3 To open the finished art file, choose File > Open, and open the *AI_01.ai* file located in the Tour folder in the Training folder inside the Adobe Illustrator 8.0 application folder.

4 If you like, choose View > Zoom Out to make the finished artwork smaller, and leave it on your screen as you work. If you don't want to leave the image open, choose File > Close.

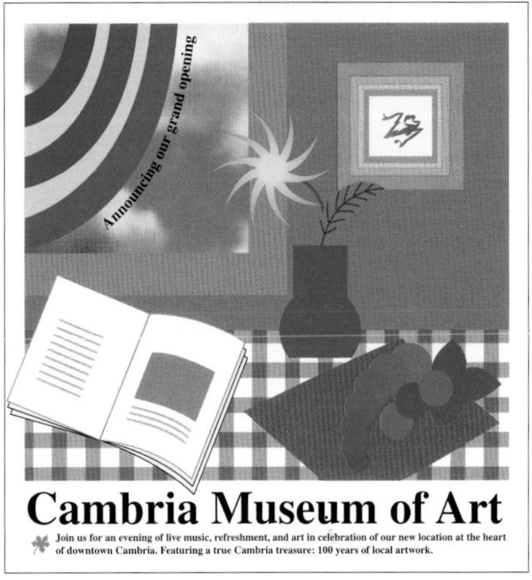
Announcing our grand opening
Cambria Museum of Art
Join us for an evening of live music, refreshment, and art in celebration of our new location at the heart of downtown Cambria. Featuring a true Cambria treasure: 100 years of local artwork.

Now open the start file to begin the tour.

5 To open the start file, choose File > Open, and open the *AI_00.ai* file, located in the Tour folder in the Training folder inside the Adobe Illustrator 8.0 application folder.

Cambria Museum of Art
us for an evening of live music, refreshment, and art in celebration of our new location at the heart of
downtown Cambria. Featuring a true Cambria treasure: 100 years of local artwork.

6 Choose File > Save As, name the file **TourWork.ai**, and then click Save. In the Illustrator Format dialog box, select version 8.0 of Illustrator and click OK.

Creating basic shapes

Adobe Illustrator provides a variety of tools and commands for creating basic geometric shapes, as well as specialized tools for precision drawing and patterns.

You'll begin this tour by adding some basic shapes to the artwork.

Drawing a star

First, you'll draw a star and modify the shape to create the flower.

1 Hold the mouse down on the ellipse tool (○) in the toolbox to display a group of tools. Select the star tool (☆) and then click once at the top left of the flower stem.

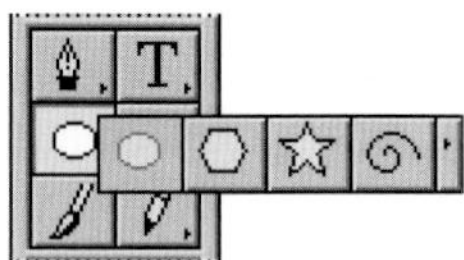

Clicking once with the star tool rather than dragging it in the artwork allows you to precisely specify the shape's dimensions.

2 In the Star dialog box, specify the shape of the star. (We specified 60 points in the Radius 1 text box, 15 points in the Radius 2 text box, and 10 for the number of points on the star.) Click OK.

Now you'll change the direction of the star points.

3 Select the twirl tool ( ) from the same group as the rotate tool ( ) in the toolbox, grab the top point of the star (don't release the mouse), and drag it to the right or left.

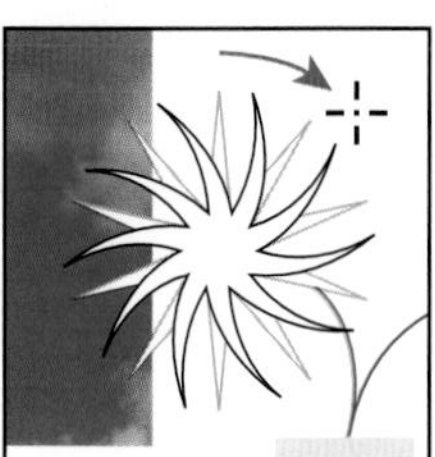

Painting the fill and stroke

In Illustrator, color within an object is called a *fill* and color on a line is called a *stroke*. The current fill and stroke colors are shown in the large Fill and Stroke boxes near the bottom of the toolbox and in the Color palette.

Now you'll paint the flower's fill and remove the stroke.

1 With the star still selected, click the Stroke box in the toolbox and click the None button to remove the stroke. Then, click the Fill box to specify you want to edit the fill of the star.

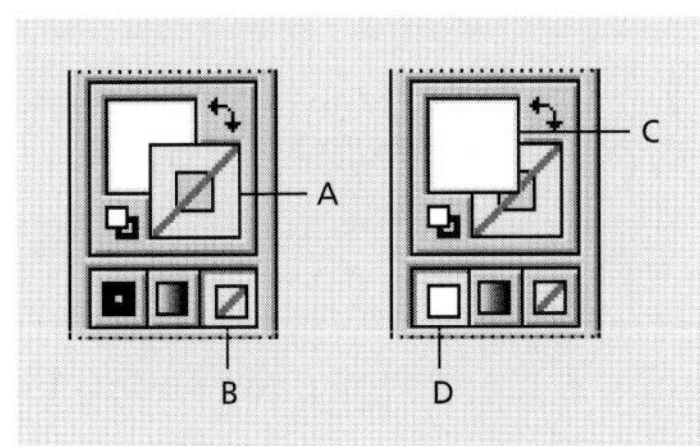

A. Stroke box selected ***B.*** *None button selected*
C. Fill box selected ***D.*** *Color button selected*

2 If the Swatches palette isn't visible, choose Window > Show Swatches.

The Swatches palette provides you with a premade set of colors, gradients, and patterns that you can edit, save, and apply.

3 Click any swatch in the palette to change the flower's color. (We chose the Yellow & Orange Radial gradient.)

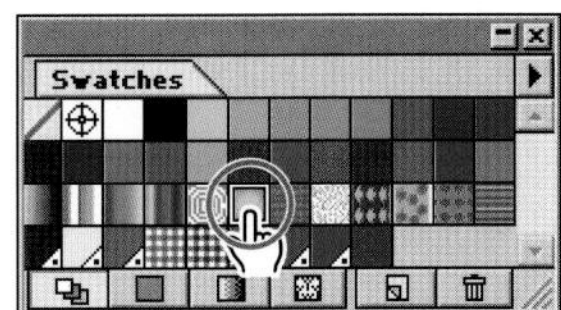

For information on how to create your own gradients, see Chapter 8, "Using Gradients, Blends, and Patterns."

Now, you'll change the stroke weight of the flower stem.

4 Select the selection tool ( ) in the toolbox and then click the left line of the stem to select it. If the Stroke palette is not visible, choose Window > Show Stroke.

5 In the Stroke palette, type a larger value in the Weight text box (we increased it to 3 points) and press Enter or Return to apply the change.

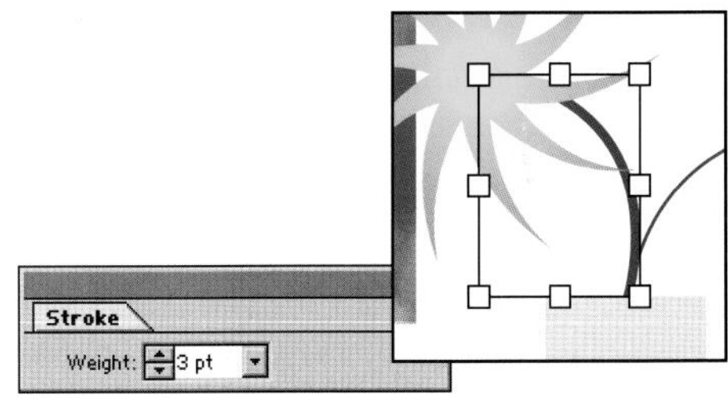

6 Choose File > Save.

Combining shapes

Adobe Illustrator includes numerous tools and commands that let you modify the shapes of objects. The Pathfinder commands change the shapes of objects by adding and subtracting the outlines, or *paths,* around them.

Uniting shapes into one

Now you'll add a circle shape to the rectangular flower vase and unite the shapes into one object.

1 Choose View > Smart Guides to turn them on. Smart Guides give you information about the objects as you point to them.

2 Choose Edit > Deselect All to deselect the artwork and then click the Default Fill and Stroke button in the toolbox to deselect the current settings of the flower stem.

Default Fill and Stroke button

3 Select the ellipse tool (○) from the same group as the star tool (☆) in the toolbox. Hold down Shift+Alt (Windows) or Shift+Option (Mac OS) and drag to draw a circle that's almost as tall as the rectangular flower vase. (Holding down Shift constrains the ellipse to a circle. Holding down Alt/Option draws from the center rather than from the left side.)

4 Click the selection tool (▶) to select the circle, grab the center point (don't release the mouse), and drag the circle to the center of the rectangle. When you release the mouse, the Smart Guides snap the circle's center to the center of the rectangle.

5 Now grab the circle's center point and slowly drag the circle straight down the vertical guide until its center reaches the intersect point of the table, and then release the mouse.

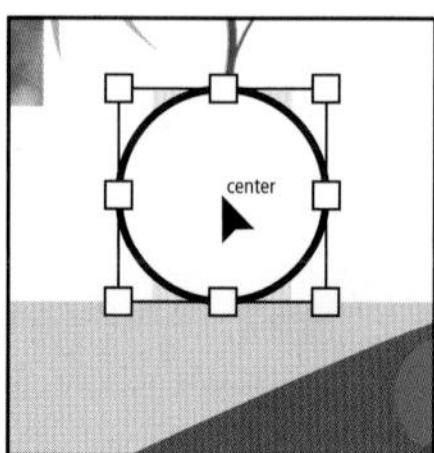

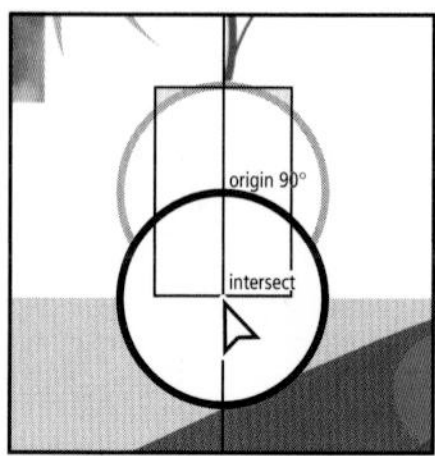

Now you'll unite the circle and rectangle into one object.

6 Using the selection tool (▶), Shift-click the rectangle to select both objects. Choose Window > Show Pathfinder and click the Unite button (■) in the Pathfinder palette.

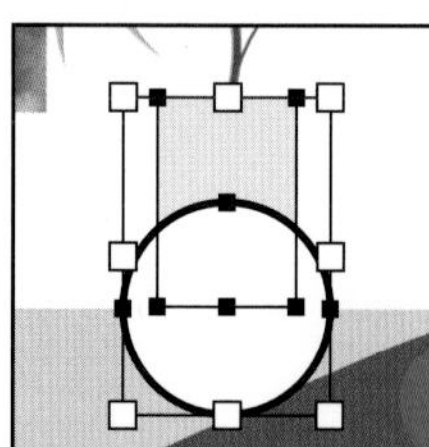

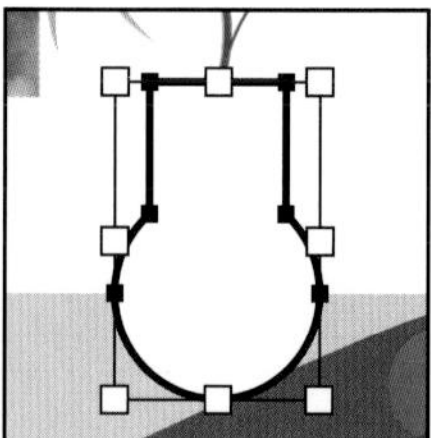

Sampling a color

Now you'll paint the vase with a color from the window curtain.

1 With the vase still selected, select the eyedropper tool (✐) in the toolbox and click the middle stripe of the curtain to pick up, or *sample,* its dark blue color. Sampling a color copies the color's fill and stroke into the Color palette and into any objects that are currently selected.

Subtracting a shape from another

Now you'll use a Pathfinder command to change the shape of the bottom of the flower vase.

1 Select the rectangle tool (□) and draw a rectangle over the bottom portion of the vase.

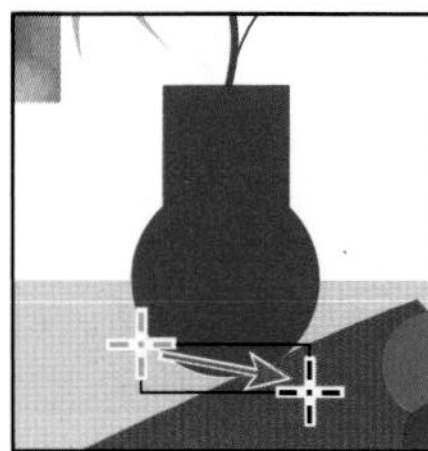

2 Click the selection tool (➤) to select the rectangle and Shift-click the vase to select both objects.

3 In the Pathfinder palette, click the Minus Front button (◰).

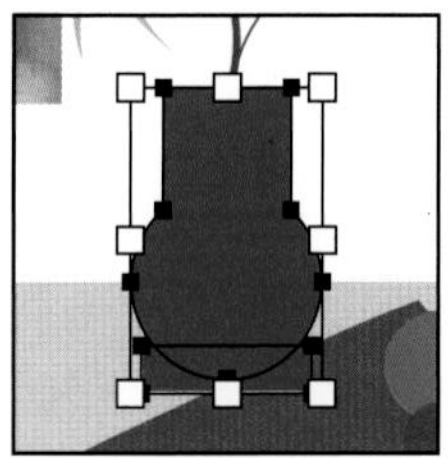

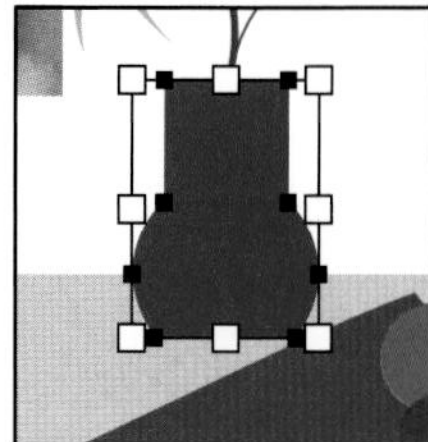

The rectangle shape (the front shape) is subtracted from the round shape of the vase, creating a straight line at the base.

Creating blends

Adobe Illustrator lets you blend shapes and colors of objects together into a new object that you can modify.

Making a path blend

Now you'll blend two different sized and colored circles to create a bunch of grapes.

1 Click the largest circle on the napkin to select it and then Shift-click the smallest circle to select it.

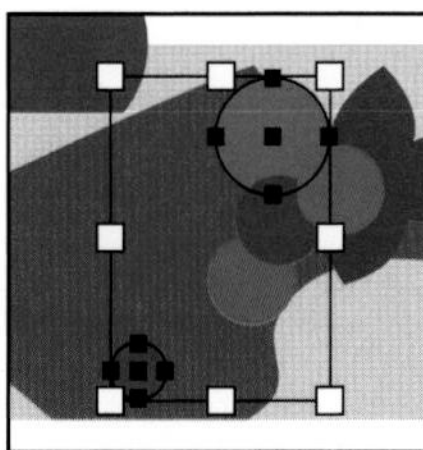

2 Choose Object > Blends > Blend Options. In the Blend Options dialog box, choose Specified Steps from the Spacing menu, type **5** for the number of steps, and click OK.

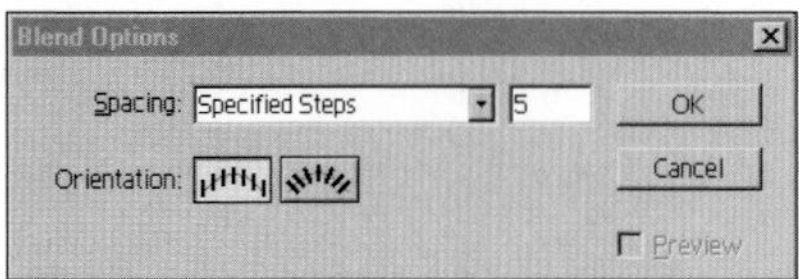

3 Choose Object > Blends > Make to create five intermediate objects that blend the colors and size of the two circles.

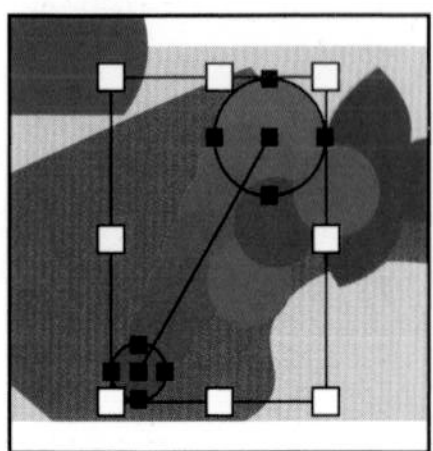

Editing your drawing

Adobe Illustrator provides tools that let you edit, erase, and smooth what you draw and a Navigator palette to help you move around in the artwork as you work.

Zooming in

Now you'll use the Navigator palette to zoom in closer on the blended grapes so you can change the direction of their path.

1 If it isn't visible, choose Window > Show Navigator to display the Navigator palette.

2 In the Navigator palette, move the slider or click the Zoom In button (⛰) to zoom in closer to the artwork (to about 300%) and use the hand pointer to move the red view box over the grapes.

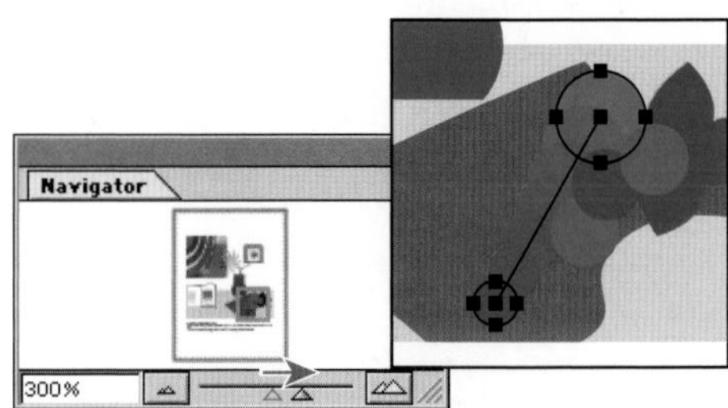

Diverting a path

You can change the straight path of the blended grapes to a curved path by moving the direction points of an anchor on the path.

1 Select the convert-direction-point tool (⌃) from the same group as the pen tool (✒) and experiment with moving the path of the grapes by grabbing an end anchor point and dragging it to the left or right. You can also drag the direction handles on the anchor point.

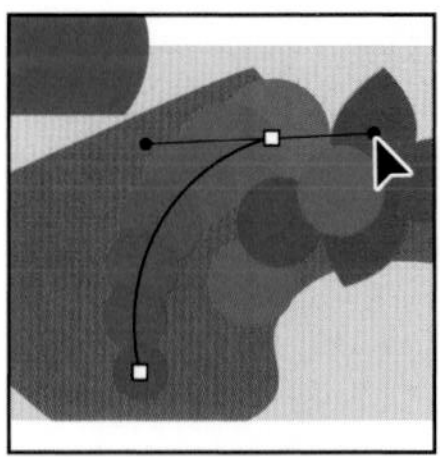

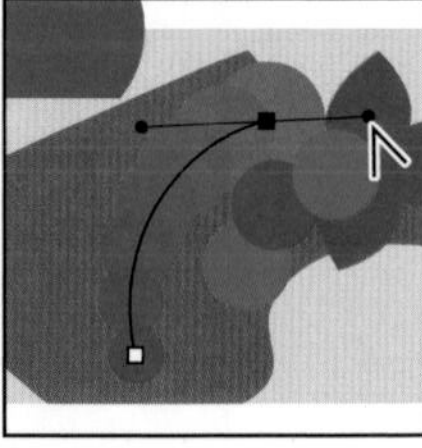

2 Press Shift+Ctrl+A (Windows) or Shift+Command+A (Mac OS) to deselect the artwork and then choose File > Save.

Editing a shape

Now you'll use the pencil tool to change the shape of the table napkin under the grapes.

1 Select the selection tool (↖) in the toolbox and click the napkin to select it.

2 Select the pencil tool (✎) in the toolbox, and position the pointer over the anchor point at the right corner of the napkin. (If necessary, scroll to the right to see it.)

3 Press the mouse and drag the pencil tool down along the right side of the napkin to straighten out the shape starting from the right corner and ending on the bottom corner of the napkin. When you release the mouse, the napkin is reshaped.

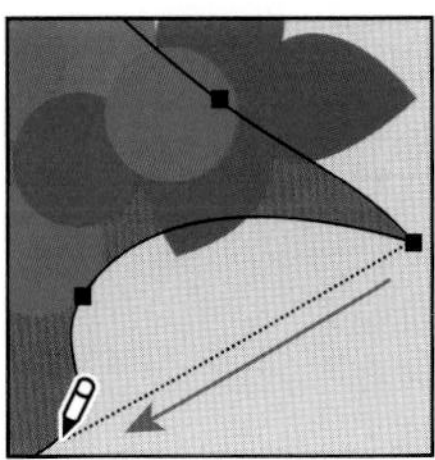

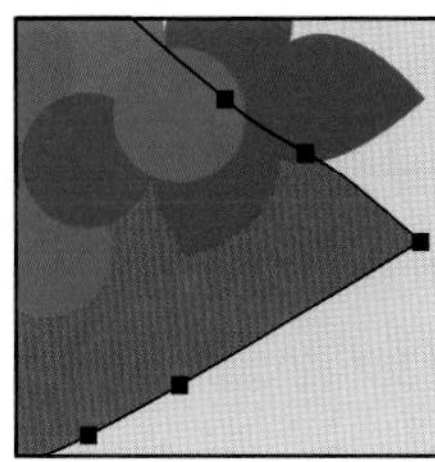

4 If you make a mistake, choose Edit > Undo and then redraw the shape.

5 When you're finished, choose Edit > Deselect All to deselect the napkin.

6 In the Navigator palette, click the Zoom Out button (⏶) a few times to zoom back out to 100%, and then move the view box to the center of the artwork.

Drawing straight lines

Now you'll draw some straight lines to create a window frame on two sides of the window.

1 Click the Default Fill and Stroke button (◳) in the toolbox to deselect the settings of the napkin.

2 Choose View > Artwork and then select the pen tool (✒) from the same group as the convert-direction-point tool (ᐱ) in the toolbox.

3 Be sure the Smart Guides are turned on in the View menu and click the anchor point on the bottom left corner of the window to begin drawing the first straight line. Then hold down Shift and click below the window to end the line.

Each time you click, you create an anchor point and Illustrator connects the anchor points with a straight line. Holding down Shift constrains the line to vertical, horizontal, or diagonal paths.

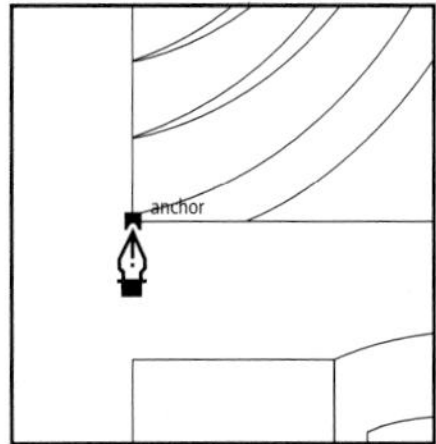

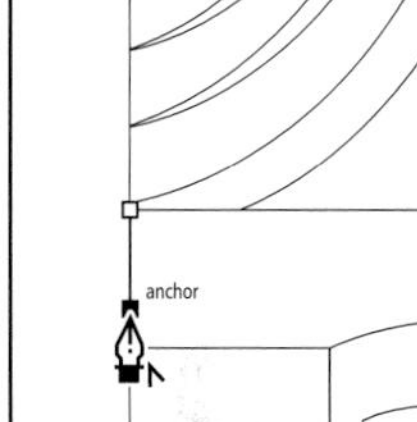

4 Shift-click five more times to draw the window frame, ending with the same anchor point you started with. Notice the pen tool has a small circle on it indicating that your last click will close the object's path.

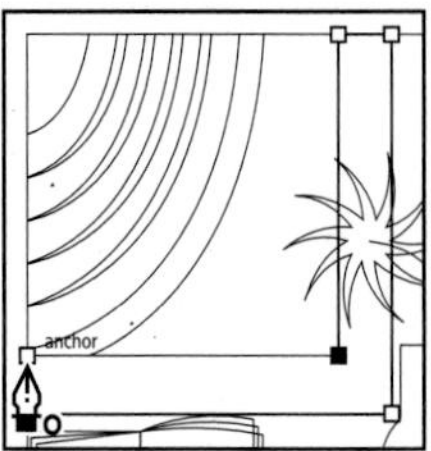

5 Click the selection tool (↖) to select the frame and Shift-click the top of the wall to select it also.

6 Choose View > Preview. Notice the window frame you just drew is on top of the flower. Objects are tiled in the order that they're created with the most current on top.

7 Choose Object > Arrange > Send to Back.

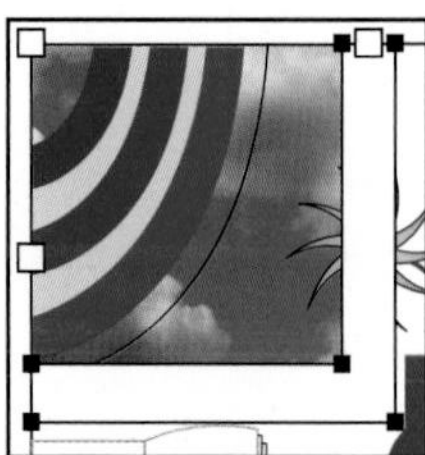

Many of the objects in this illustration were created using the pen tool. For information on drawing with the pen tool, see Chapter 4, "Drawing."

Painting

Adobe Illustrator provides many ways to paint an object. So far, you've painted the flower with a color or gradient from the Swatches palette and copied a color from the curtain to the flower vase using the eyedropper tool. You can paint objects in Illustrator artwork with black, white, shades of gray, process and spot colors, gradients, and patterns. You can also use the Brushes palette to apply patterns to the stroke or path of an object.

Painting with a spot color

Now, you'll paint the wall and the window frame with the same spot color and change the tint.

1 With both the window frame and the wall still selected, make sure the Fill box is selected in the toolbox. (The Fill box appears in front of the Stroke box to indicate that it's selected.)

2 If it's not visible, choose Window > Swatches or click the Swatches tab to bring the Swatches palette to the front.

3 Position the hand pointer over the swatches to see their names, and select the Aqua swatch. You can identify this swatch as a spot color by the triangle and dot in the bottom right corner of the swatch.

In Illustrator, a color swatch can be a predefined spot color (such as a PANTONE® color) or any color you save and name in your artwork. (See Chapter 7, "Working with Color.")

4 Shift-click the wall to deselect it and keep the window frame selected.

5 In the Color palette, drag the Tint slider to the left to lighten the color (we used 65%).

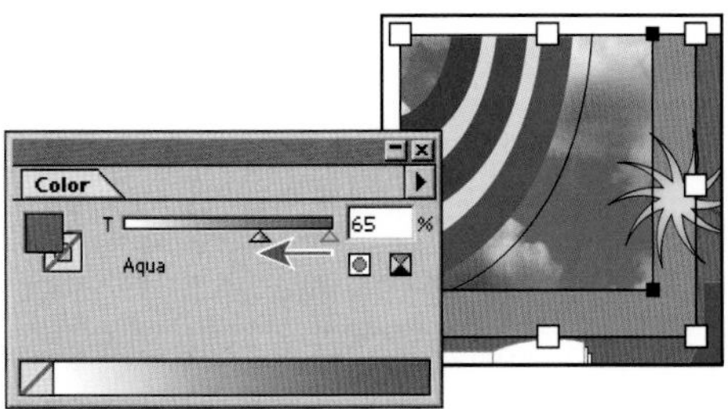

6 Drag the None button up and drop it over the Stroke box in the Color palette to remove the window frame's stroke. (This action allows you to keep the Fill box selected.)

Painting with brushes

You can create your own brushes to draw with or to apply to existing paths. There are four types of brushes: calligraphic, scatter, art, and pattern. You'll apply a custom-made art brush to the flower's stem and a pattern brush to the picture frame on the wall.

1 Click the right side of the flower stem to select it and choose Window > Show Brushes or click the Brushes tab behind the Swatches palette to bring the Brushes palette to the front.

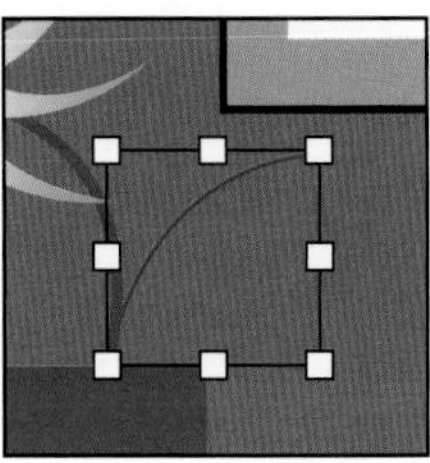

2 Hold the mouse down on the triangle in the top right corner of the Brushes palette and choose View By Name from the pop-up menu. The names of the brushes are grouped by type (calligraphic, scatter, art, or pattern) and then listed alphabetically with each group. Scroll down to the list of art brushes and select the "Leaf" art brush.

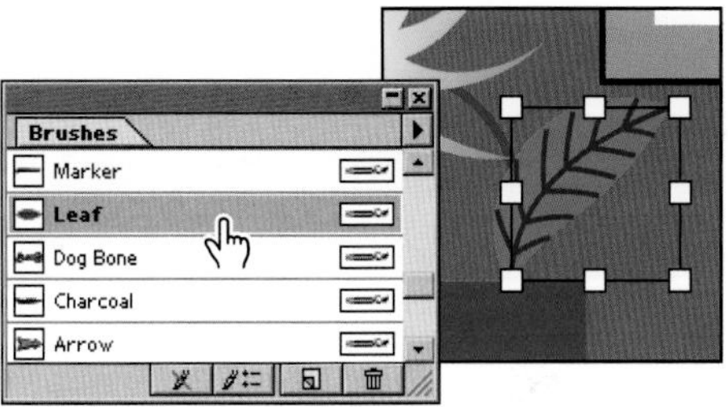

3 Now click the outer edge of the picture frame on the wall to select it and select the Picframe pattern brush in the Brushes palette.

See Chapter 4, "Drawing", for information about creating your own custom brushes and using the Brushes palette.

Painting with a pattern swatch

Now you will use the Swatches palette to add a pattern fill to the tablecloth.

1 Click inside the tablecloth to select it. If necessary, click the Fill box in the toolbox to select the tablecloth's fill.

2 Click the Swatches tab to bring the palette to the front of the Brushes palette, click the Show Pattern Swatches button at the bottom of the Swatches palette, and click the pattern you want. Try out the other different pattern fills for the tablecloth. (We used Tablecloth Pattern #1.)

Scaling and rotating objects

You can easily scale, rotate, and shear objects—either by dragging or by specifying precise values. Now you'll scale and rotate the book to make it bigger and turned at an angle.

1 To scale the book, first click the book to select its bounding box. Then hold down Shift and slowly drag the bottom right corner of the bounding box to about halfway to the napkin.

Holding down Shift as you drag increases the size of the book proportionally while keeping the left side of the book in its original position.

2 To rotate the book, select the free transform tool (⛶) in the toolbox, and position it near the bottom right corner of the book, just outside the bounding box. (The pointer changes from a scale symbol to a rotate symbol.) Press the mouse and drag the pointer down and to the left to rotate the book in a clockwise direction.

3 Choose Edit > Deselect All to deselect the artwork and then choose File > Save.

Using layers

The Layers palette in Adobe Illustrator lets you organize artwork into groups that can be selected, displayed, edited, and printed individually or together.

1 If the Layers palette is not visible, choose Window > Show Layers to display it.

The artwork has been organized into four layers. New objects are created on the layer that is currently selected in the Layers palette.

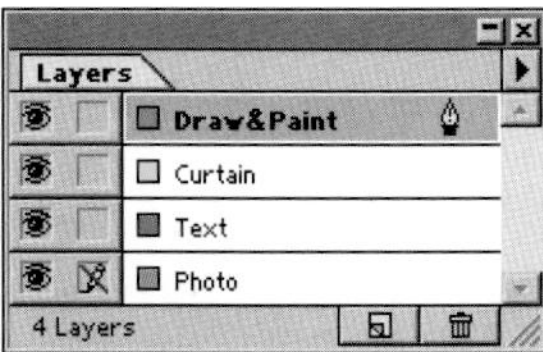

2 Click Photo in the Layers palette to select that layer and then drag the Photo layer up just above the Curtain layer and below the Draw & Paint layer to bring the photo to the front of the window.

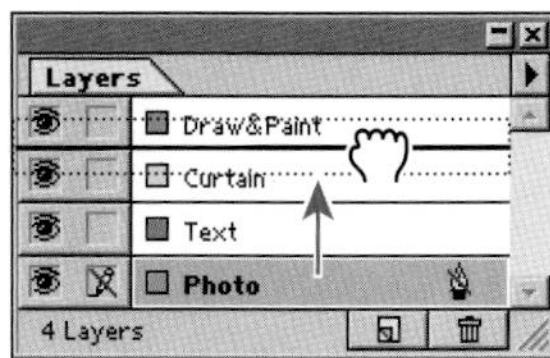

3 Notice how the curtain is hidden behind the clouds in the window. Now drag the Curtain layer back up to just above the Photo layer to bring the curtain to the front of the artwork.

Moving the layers around in the Layers palette changes the order that the objects appear in the artwork, with the layer at the top of the palette containing the frontmost objects.

Applying bitmap image filters

Adobe Illustrator includes special-effects filters you can apply to embedded bitmap images (also known as *raster images*) for a range of effects.

Filtering a bitmap image

Now you'll apply a filter to the embedded bitmap image of the sky to make it look less like a photo.

1 In the Layers palette, click the pencil icon next to the Photo layer to unlock the layer, allowing you to modify artwork on that layer.

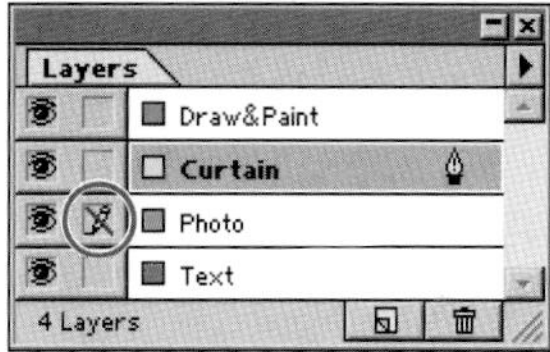

2 Click Photo to select the Photo layer. Hold down Alt (Windows) or Option (Mac OS) and click the eye icon in the column to the left of the Photo layer.

Holding down Alt/Option as you click the eye icon hides all of the other layers. Hiding layers is a useful way to isolate detailed artwork as you work.

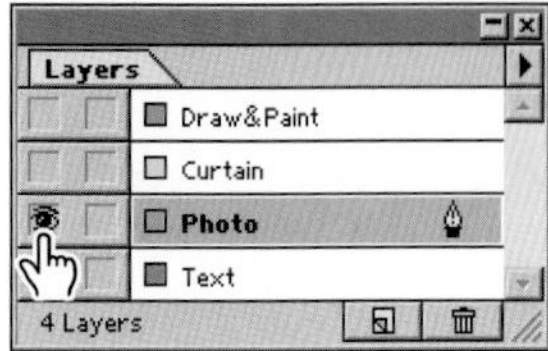

3 Select the selection tool ( ), and click the photo image of the sky to select it.

The image is an imported TIFF file from Adobe Photoshop. You can import artwork in a wide variety of formats from other programs. For information about embedding or linking image files to your artwork, see "Opening and placing artwork" on page 55.

4 Choose Filter > Sketch > Water Paper. Experiment with changing the filter values. When the preview in the Water Paper dialog box appears the way you like, click OK to apply the filter to the bitmap image.

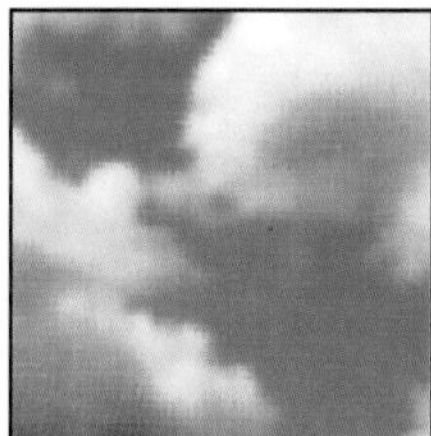

Original, and filter applied

5 In the Layers palette, Alt-click (Windows) or Option-click (Mac OS) the eye icon again to show all the layers.

Rasterizing an object

Now you'll turn the wall into a bitmap image so you can apply a bitmap image filter to it. Converting Illustrator artwork, called *vector artwork,* into a bitmap image is called *rasterizing.* (See Chapter 3, "Setting Up Artwork in Illustrator.")

1 Click the wall to select it and choose Object > Rasterize. In the Rasterize dialog box, choose RGB from the Color Model menu and select the Screen (72 ppi), Anti-Alias, and Create Mask options. Then click OK.

The Create Mask option lets you apply a filter to the selected object without including the background area of the bounding box. The Anti-Alias option will smooth the jagged edges around the wall when it's converted to the bitmap image.

Now you can apply a bitmap image filter to the rasterized object.

2 Choose Filter > Artistic > Rough Pastels. Experiment with different filter values, and then click OK.

Original, and filter applied

3 Choose File > Save to save the changes.

You're now ready to work with type.

Adding type

Adobe Illustrator lets you easily create type on a path or at any point in your artwork, as well as create and import text in columns or in other containers. (See Chapter 11, "Using Type.")

Now you'll add a headline to a path along the edge of the curtain.

1 In the Layers palette, move the Text layer to the top of the palette.

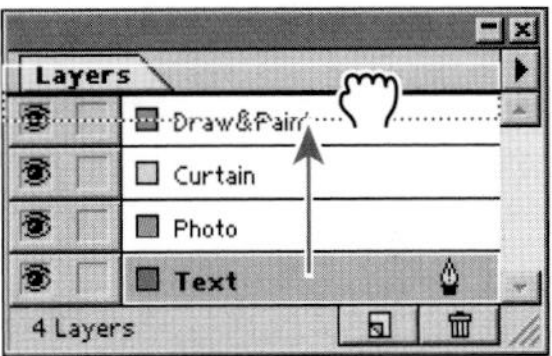

A curved line has been drawn along the edge of the window curtain.

2 Select the Path type tool ( ) in the toolbox, and click once on the bottom end of the curved line to position the insertion point.

When you click on a line with the Path type tool, the line is converted to an invisible path (without any fill or stroke color) and a blinking insertion point appears.

3 Type **Announcing our grand opening**.

The default characteristics of the type are Helvetica* Regular 12 Points.

Sampling type

Now you'll sample the type characteristics of the title at the bottom of the artwork and apply them to the new type.

1 Click the selection tool ( ). Clicking the selection tool after typing automatically selects the entire block of type.

2 Select the eyedropper tool ( ) in the toolbox and click somewhere in the words "Cambria Museum of Art."

Sampling type with the eyedropper tool applies the characteristics to any type objects that are currently selected. It also copies the type characteristics to the Paragraph and Character palettes, and the fill colors to the Color palette.

Changing type characteristics

Now you'll open the Character palette and change the character size of the poster's title to make it bigger.

1 Select the selection tool ( ) and click the title "Cambria Museum of Art" to select the block of type.

2 Choose Type > Character to display the Character palette. Double-click to select 15 pt in the Size box and type **44**. Press Enter or Return to apply the change.

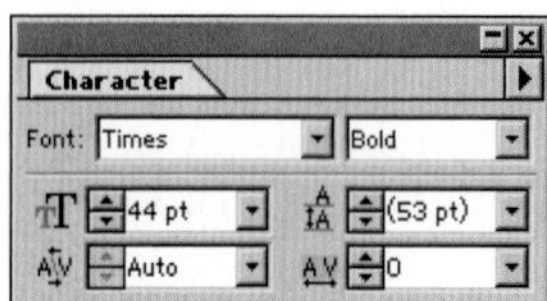

Wrapping text around objects

Now you'll wrap the type at the bottom of the artwork around the linked image of a cloverleaf.

1 Click the cloverleaf image to select it and then Shift-click the text to the right of the image.

2 Choose Type > Wrap > Make to wrap the type around the cloverleaf image.

3 Choose File > Save to save the artwork.

You can save Illustrator files in different formats depending on how you want to use the artwork. (See Chapter 13, "Saving and Exporting Artwork.")

Congratulations! You've completed the Illustrator tour. You're now ready to create your own Illustrator artwork.

2

Chapter 2: Looking at the Work Area

The Adobe Illustrator work area includes the command menus at the top of your screen, the illustration window, and a variety of tools and palettes for editing and adding elements such as masks and layers. You can also add commands and filters to the menus by installing software programs called plug-in modules.

SELECTING TOOLS You can select a tool from the default toolbox by clicking the tool. The toolbox contains several hidden tools that are related to the tools shown. These tools are indicated by arrows to the right of the tool icons. You can select a hidden tool by pressing the current tool in the toolbox and then selecting the tool you want. The Shift key plus the keyboard shortcuts cycle through the hidden keys, except where noted otherwise. You can also tear off the toolbar from the toolbox to display the tools in the work area.

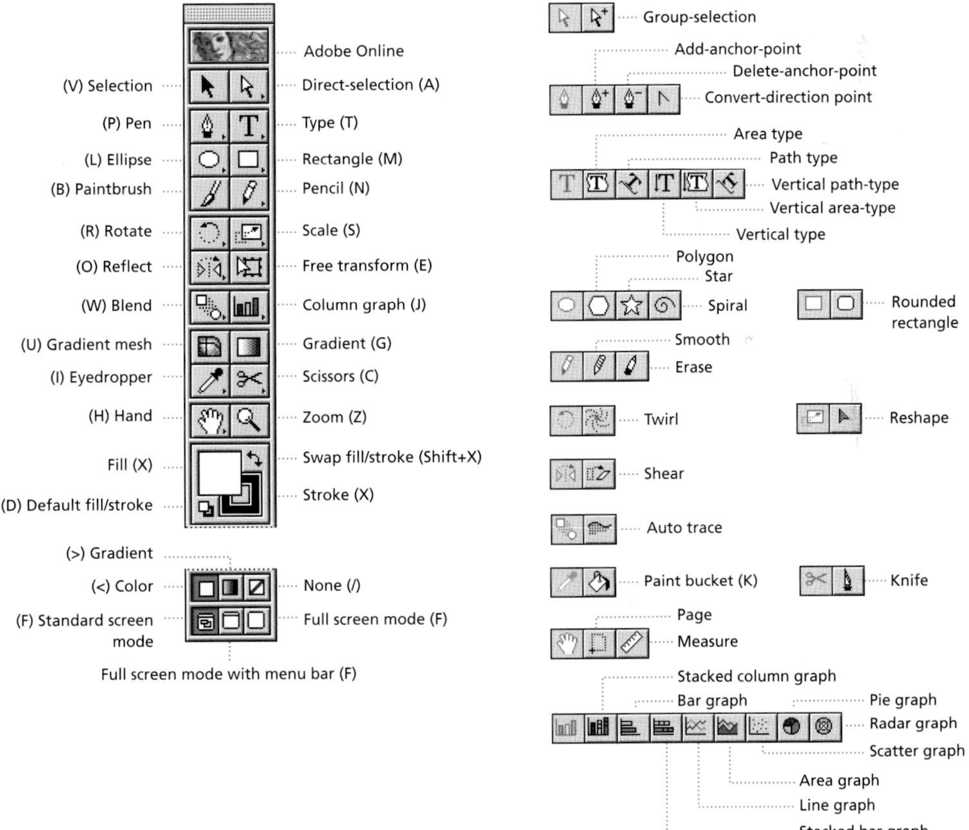

Using the tools

The first time you open a file, the toolbox appears on the left side of the screen. The tools in the toolbox let you create, select, and manipulate objects in Illustrator.

When you select most tools, the mouse pointer matches the tool's icon. For example, choosing the paintbrush tool changes the pointer to a paintbrush. You can also change a tool pointer to a cross hair (×) for greater precision when aligning or working with detailed artwork.

To move the toolbox:

Drag the toolbox by the top bar.

To show or hide the toolbox:

To show the toolbox, choose Window > Show Tools; to hide the toolbox, choose Window > Hide Tools.

To display hidden tools on-screen:

1 Press a tool in the toolbox that has hidden tools underneath it. (Tools that have hidden tools are identified by a triangle in the lower right corner.)

2 When the toolbar of hidden tools appears, hold down the mouse button and drag to the tearoff at the end of the toolbar. The toolbar detaches from the toolbox.

To reattach a detached toolbar to the toolbox:

Click the close box.

To change the pointer to a cross hair:

Do one of the following:

- While the tool is selected, press Caps Lock on the keyboard.
- Choose File > Preferences > General, select Use Precise Cursors, and click OK.

For a gallery demonstrating the use of Illustrator's various tools, see online Help.

Using palettes

Adobe Illustrator includes a number of palettes to help you monitor and modify your work. By default, these palettes appear stacked together in several groups. You can display and hide these palettes as you work. You can also dock palettes so that more than one palette can be viewed at the same time.

To show or hide a palette:

Do one of the following:

- Choose Window > Show or Window > Hide. Show displays the selected palette at the front of its group; Hide conceals the entire group.
- Press Tab to hide or show all palettes and the toolbox.
- Press Shift+Tab to hide all palettes except for the toolbox.

Changing the palette display

You can rearrange your palettes to make better use of your work area by using the following techniques:

• To make a palette appear at the front of its group, click the palette's tab.

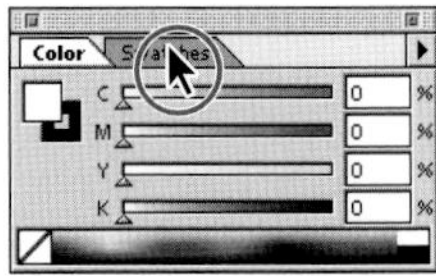

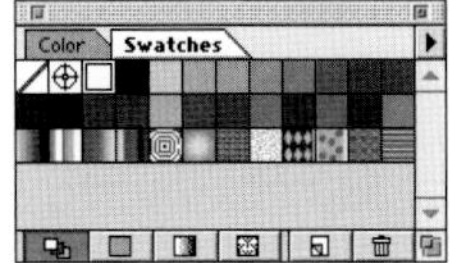

• To move an entire palette group, drag its title bar.

• To rearrange or separate a palette group, drag a palette's tab. Dragging a palette outside of an existing group creates a new group.

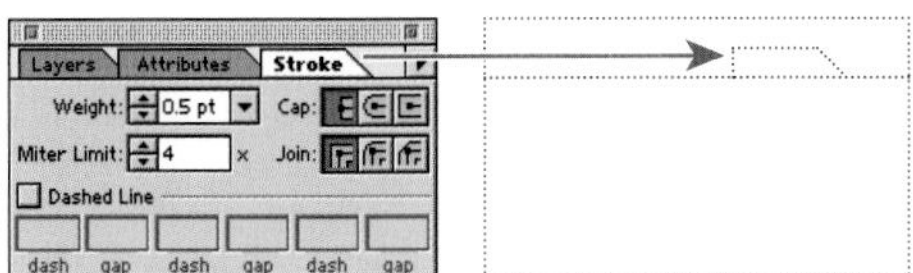

Click the palette tab and drag the palette to a new location.

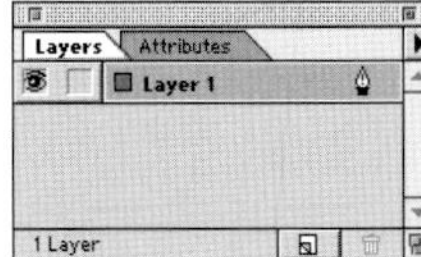

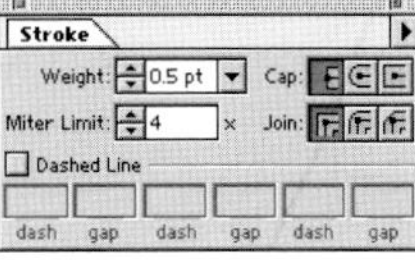

Palettes are separated.

• To move a palette to another group, drag the palette's tab to that group.

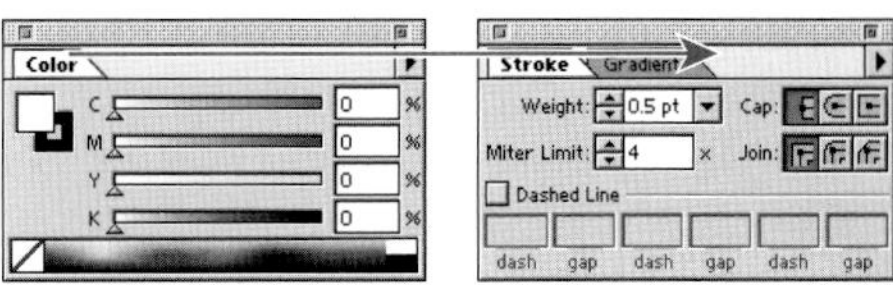

Click the palette tab and drag the palette to another group.

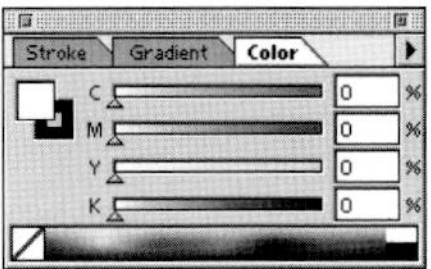

Palettes are merged.

• To dock palettes together so more than one palette is visible at the same time, drag a palette's tab to the bottom of another palette.The bottom of the palette is highlighted.

• To move an entire docked palette group, drag its title bar.

• To display a palette menu, position the pointer on the triangle in the upper right corner of the palette and hold down the mouse button.

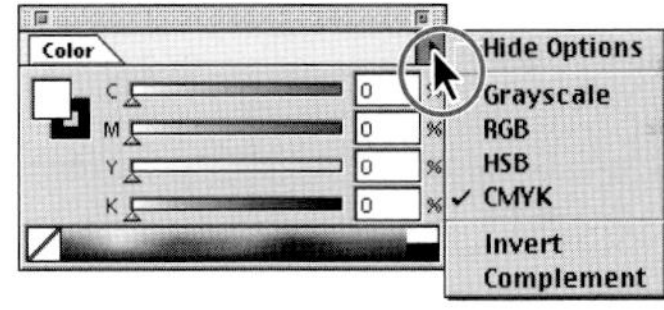

- To change the size of a resizable palette, drag the lower right corner of the palette (Windows) or drag the size box at the lower right corner of the palette (Mac OS).

Note: *Many palettes can be resized in Adobe Illustrator, but a few—such as the Color palette—are a standard unchangeable size.*

- To return the palette to the default size, double-click a palette's tab.

- To collapse a group to the palette titles only, click the minimize/maximize box (Windows) or click the zoom box (Mac OS). You can also double-click a palette's tab, if the palette is already in the default size. You can still open the palette menu from a collapsed palette.

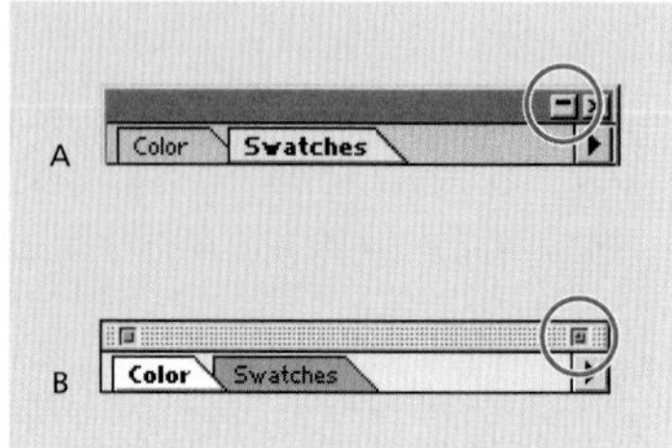

A. *Windows minimize/maximize box*
B. *Macintosh zoom box*

Using the Info palette

The Info palette provides information on the selected tool and the area beneath the pointer. Depending on the tool you're using, you can use the Info palette to measure size, distance, and angle of rotation. In most cases when a tool is in use, the Info palette displays the *x* and *y* coordinates of the pointer's position in the artwork by using the units of measurement you specify.

To display the Info palette:

Choose Window > Show Info. The Info palette displays the following information, depending on the tool or command selected:

- When using a selection tool, the *x* and *y* coordinates of your starting position and of the ending position after you release the mouse button are displayed. If an object is selected, the width (*W*) and height (*H*) of the object are also displayed.

- When using a zoom tool, the magnification factor and the *x* and *y* coordinates are displayed after you release the mouse button.

- When using a pen tool or gradient tool, or when you move a selection, the change in *x* (*W*), the change in *y* (*H*), the distance (*D*), and the angle (∠) as you drag are displayed.

- When using the Scale tool, the percentage change in width (*W*) and height (*H*), and the new width (*W*) and height (*H*) are displayed after the scale is finished.

- When using the Rotate or Reflect tools, the coordinates of the object's center and the angle of rotation (∠) or reflection (∠) are displayed.

- When using the Shear tool, the coordinates of the object's center, the angle of shear axis (∠), and the amount of shear (▱) are displayed.

- When using the Paintbrush tool, the *x* and *y* coordinates and the name of the current brush are displayed.

Using context menus

In addition to the menus that appear at the top of your screen, Adobe Illustrator contains a number of context-sensitive menus. These menus display commands that relate to the active tool, selection, or palette. You can use context menus as a quick way to choose commonly used commands.

To display context menus:

1 Position the pointer over the artwork or palette.

2 Do one of the following:

- In Windows, click with the right mouse button.
- In Mac OS, press Control and hold down the mouse button.

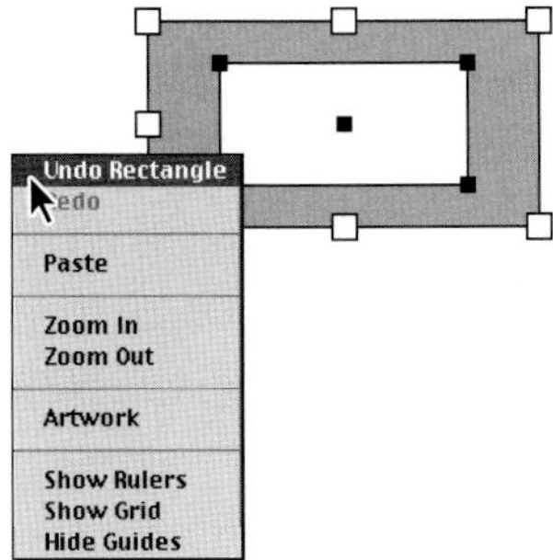

Right-mouse-click (Windows) or Control-click (Mac OS) to bring up context menus.

Using online Help

Adobe Illustrator includes complete documentation in online Help, including all of the information in this user guide, plus keyboard shortcuts, and more.

To get online help in Windows:

Do one of the following:

- Press F1 to display the Help Contents menu.
- Choose Help > Contents (Windows).

To get online help on Mac OS systems:

Choose Help > Contents.

To get context-sensitive help (Windows only):

Press Shift+F1 (a question mark appears next to the pointer), and choose a command or click in a toolbox or palette to display the appropriate help topic.

Viewing artwork

The hand tool, the zoom tools, the Zoom commands, and the Navigator palette let you view different areas of your artwork at different magnifications.

Changing the view

You can open additional windows to display several views at once (such as different magnifications) in the document. For example, you can set one view highly magnified for doing close-up work on some objects and create another view less magnified for laying out those objects on the page.

To change the viewing mode of illustration windows:

Click a window button in the toolbox.

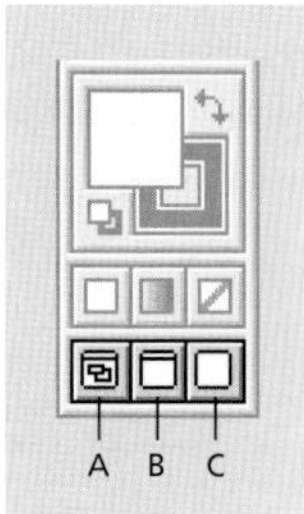

A. Standard screen mode
B. Full screen mode with menu bar
C. Full screen mode

• The left window button displays artwork in a standard window, with a menu bar at the top and scroll bars on the sides.

• The center window button displays artwork in a full-screen window with a menu bar but with no title bar or scroll bars.

• The right window button displays artwork in a full-screen window, but with no title bar, menu bar, or scroll bars.

To open a new window:

Choose Window > New Window.

A new window of the same size appears on top of the previously active window. The two windows are identical except for their window numbers. The title bar in the new window is highlighted, indicating that it is the active window.

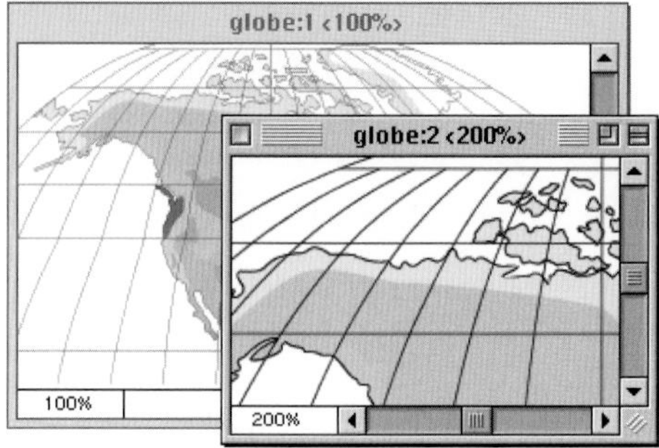

Working in magnified view with 200% view displayed

To close windows:

Do one of the following:

• Choose File > Close to close the active window.

• Press Alt (Windows) or Option (Mac OS) and choose File > Close to close all document windows.

To arrange multiple windows (Windows only):

Do one of the following:

• Choose Window > Cascade to display windows stacked and cascading from the top left to the bottom right of the screen.

• Choose Window > Tile to display windows edge to edge.

• Choose Window > Arrange Icons to arrange minimized windows within the program window.

To create a view:

1 Set up the view that you want.

2 Choose View > New View.

3 Enter a name for the new view, and click OK.

The view names, along with keyboard shortcuts for choosing them, appear at the bottom of the View menu. To retrieve a view, select the name of the view you want to use. It is possible to create and store up to 25 views for each document.

To rename or delete a view:

1 Choose View > Edit Views.

2 Select the view you want to edit, and rename it or click Delete.

To scroll the view with the hand tool:

1 Select the hand tool (✋).

2 Move the pointer onto the artwork, and drag in the direction in which you want the artwork to move.

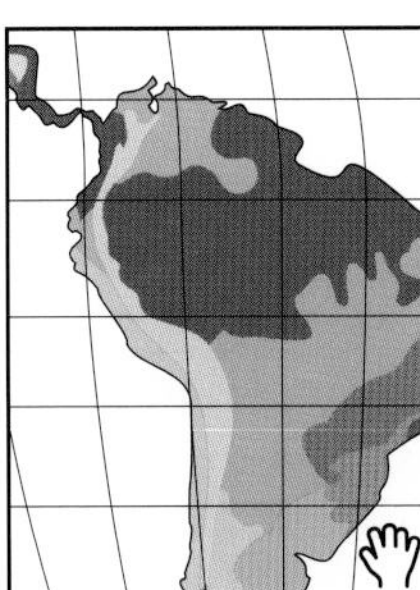

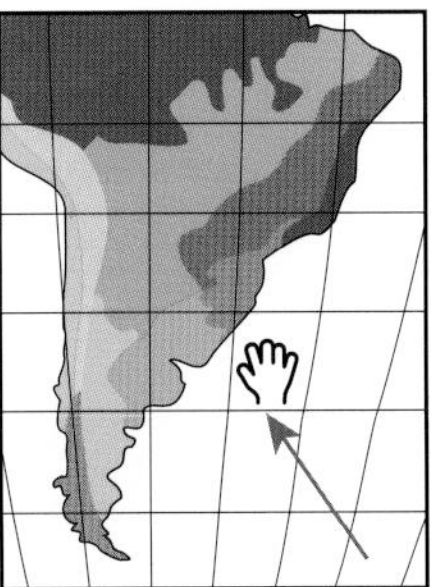

Drag the hand tool to move the view.

To switch to the hand tool when using another tool, hold down the spacebar.

Viewing artwork as paths

Adobe Illustrator sets the view so that all artwork is previewed in color. You can also set the view so that some or all of your artwork is displayed only as paths with all paint attributes hidden. Viewing artwork without paint attributes speeds up the time it takes to redraw the screen when working with complex artwork.

To view the artwork in color or as path outlines:

Choose a viewing option:

- Choose View > Preview to display the artwork as close as possible to how it will be printed, drawn with as much color, shading, and detail as your monitor is capable of displaying.
- Choose View > Artwork to display the artwork as paths, hiding each object's paint attributes. Working in this view speeds up the redraw time when working with complex artwork.

Use the New Window command to preview in one window while editing in Artwork view in another.

• Choose View > Preview Selection to view selected objects in Preview view and unselected objects in Artwork view. Selecting other objects in Preview Selection view displays the newly selected objects with their paint attributes visible. This view increases your speed when working on complex files—you can select portions of the file on which you are working and speed up the redraw time for those portions on which you are not working.

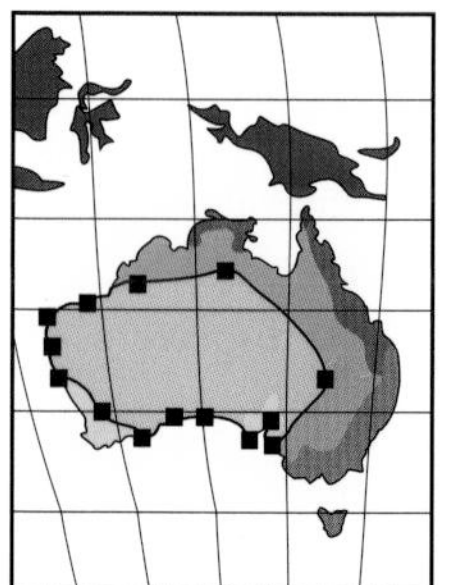

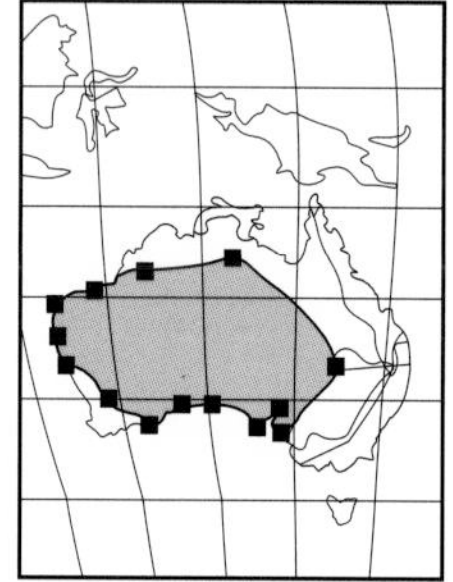

Preview view and Preview Selection view

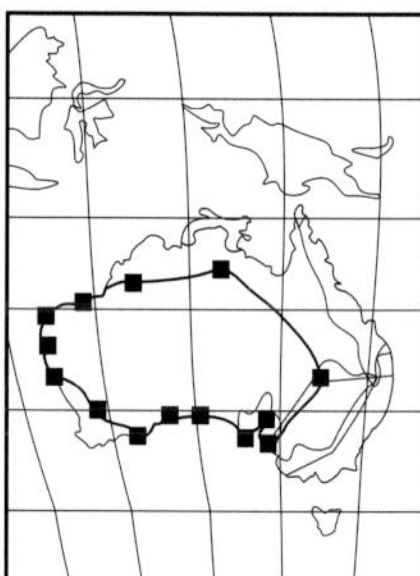

Artwork view

Magnifying and reducing the view

The zoom-in and zoom-out tools and commands let you magnify or reduce the display of any area in the file up to 64 times actual size. Zooming in and out does not change the actual size of the file, only the magnification at which you see it. See "Scaling" on page 134.

You see the current magnification level at the top of the window.

To zoom in:

Do one of the following:

• Select the zoom tool (🔍). The pointer becomes a magnifying glass with a plus sign in its center. Click at the center of the area you want to magnify. Each click magnifies the view to the next preset percentage. When the file has reached its maximum magnification level of 6400%, the magnifying glass appears blank.

• Choose View > Zoom In. Each click magnifies the view to the next preset percentage. When the file has reached its maximum magnification level of 6400%, the command is dimmed.

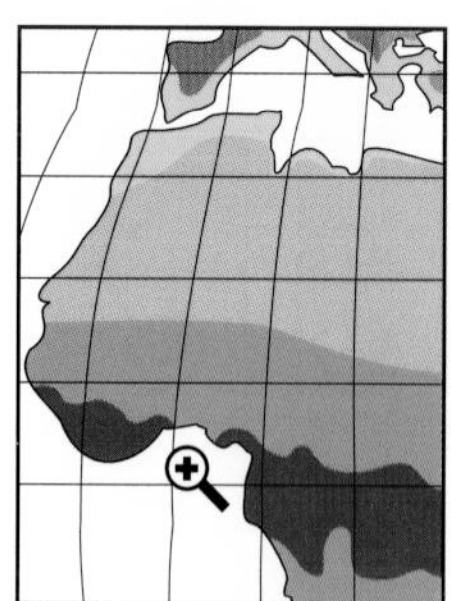

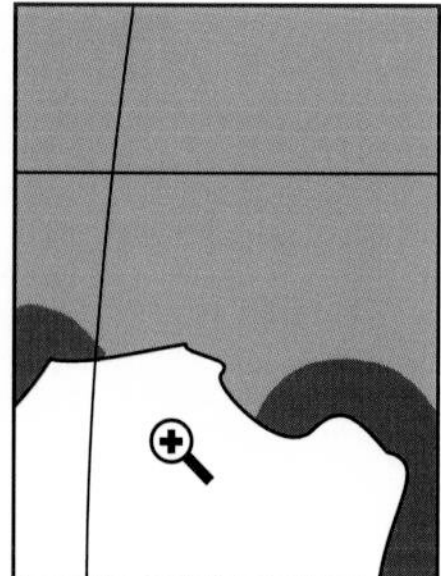

Click to zoom in.

• Enter a magnification level in the Zoom text box at the lower left of the window

• In the Zoom text box, click the right mouse button (Windows) or press Ctrl (Mac OS) and select the magnification level from the pop-up menu.

To zoom out:

Do one of the following:

• Select the zoom tool while holding down Alt (Windows) or Option (Mac OS). The pointer becomes a magnifying glass with a minus sign in its center. Click the center of the area you want to reduce. Each click reduces the view to the previous preset percentage. When the file has reached its maximum reduction level of 3.13%, the magnifying glass appears blank.

• Choose View > Zoom Out. Each click reduces the view to the previous preset percentage. When the file reaches its maximum reduction level of 3.13%, the command is dimmed.

• When no objects are selected, click the right mouse button (Windows) or Ctrl-click (Mac OS) and select the Zoom Out command from the pop-up menu.

• Enter a reduction level in the Zoom text box at the lower left of the window.

• In the Zoom text box, click the right mouse button (Windows) or press Ctrl (Mac OS) and select the magnification level from the pop-up menu.

To choose the zoom-in tool while using another tool, press Ctrl+spacebar (Windows) or Command+spacebar (Mac OS). To choose the zoom-out tool while using another tool, press Ctrl+Alt+spacebar (Windows) or Command+Option+spacebar (Mac OS).

To magnify by dragging:

1 Select the zoom-in tool (🔍).

2 Drag a dotted rectangle, called a *marquee*, around the area you want to magnify. To move the marquee around the artwork, begin dragging a marquee and then hold down the spacebar while dragging the marquee to a new location.

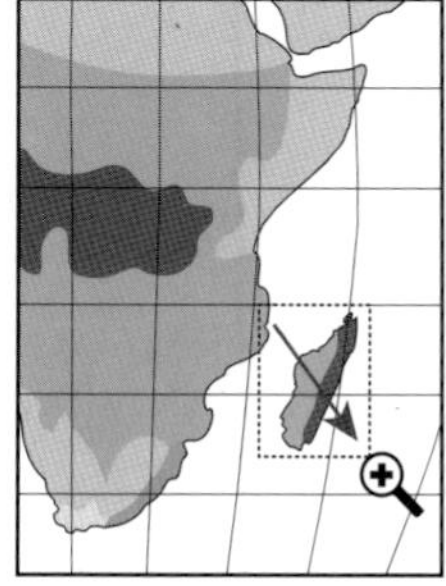

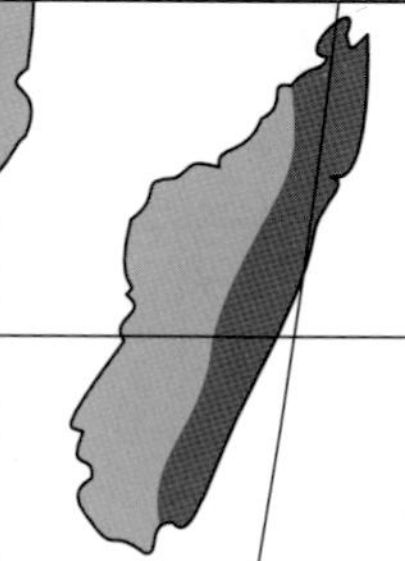

Drag the zoom tool to magnify the view.

To display a file at 100%:

Choose View > Actual Size, or double-click the zoom tool.

To change the view to fit the screen:

Choose View > Fit In Window, or double-click the hand tool.

Using the Navigator palette

The Navigator palette lets you quickly change the view of your artwork using a thumbnail display. By default, the Navigator palette displays all artwork in the Illustrator window; however, you can elect to show only artwork on the Artboard using the View Artboard Only command.

To display the Navigator palette:

Choose Window > Show Navigator.

To display only artwork inside the boundaries of the Artboard:

1 Choose Window > Show Navigator.

2 Choose View Artboard Only from the pop-up menu in the Navigator palette. Any objects outside the border of the Artboard are removed from the Navigator palette thumbnail display. (See "Viewing artwork" on page 33.)

To magnify or reduce the view using the Navigator palette:

Do one of the following:

- Click the zoom in or zoom out button at the bottom of the Navigator palette.
- Drag the zoom slider at the bottom of the palette.
- Enter the percentage of magnification or reduction you want in the zoom text box of the Navigator palette, and press Enter (Windows) or Return (Mac OS).
- Hold down Ctrl (Windows) or Command (Mac OS), and drag over the area of the Navigator palette's thumbnail that you want to magnify.

To move the view of an image using the Navigator palette:

Do one of the following:

- Drag the view box, which represents the boundaries of the illustration window.
- Click in the thumbnail of the image. The new view includes the area you click.

To change the color of the Navigator palette view box:

1 Choose Palette Options from the Navigator palette menu.

2 Choose a color:

- To use a preset color, choose an option for Color.
- To specify a different color, double-click the color box or choose Custom, and choose a color.

3 Click OK.

Using the status bar

At the bottom left edge of the Illustrator window is the status bar. The status line can display information about any of the following topics:

- The current tool in use.
- The date and time.
- The amount of virtual memory (Windows) or free RAM memory (Mac OS) available for your open file.

• The number of undos and redos available.

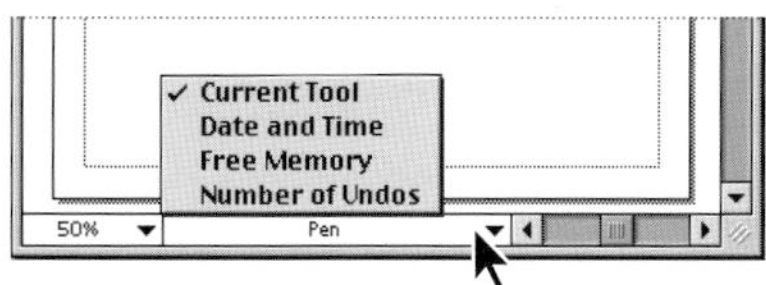

To specify the type of information you want to display in the status line:

1 Position the cursor over the status line bar, and hold down the mouse button.

2 Drag to choose the type of information you want from the pop-up menu.

Previewing placed EPS images

Placed images from other applications can slow performance when previewing and printing artwork.

You can turn off previewing of placed images when you need to work quickly. You can then turn previewing back on when you want to view the finished art.

To determine how placed EPS images appear:

1 Choose File > Document Setup.

2 Select Show Images in Artwork to specify that placed images should display a preview image when seen in Artwork view and click OK. (See "Opening and placing artwork" on page 55.)

Using plug-in modules

Plug-in modules are software programs developed by Adobe Systems, and by other software developers in conjunction with Adobe Systems, to add features to Adobe Illustrator. A number of special effects plug-ins come with your program and are automatically installed in the Plug-Ins folder.

If you change the location of the Plug-ins folder, or if you want to use a different folder as your plug-ins folder, you must use the Plug-ins Preferences command to tell Illustrator about the new location of the plug-ins.

You can also use plug-ins from Adobe Photoshop version 3.0 or later. In addition, you can use any commercial plug-in designed for use with Photoshop or Illustrator.

To avoid duplicating your filters between the two programs, make a shortcut (Windows) or an alias (Mac OS) to your Photoshop plug-in filters in your Illustrator Plug-ins folder.

To specify the location of plug-in modules:

1 Choose File > Preferences > Plug-ins & Scratch Disk.

2 Click Choose and select the folder containing the plug-in modules, then click OK.

3 Quit Illustrator, and then start it again for the plug-in modules to take effect.

To install an Adobe Systems plug-in module:

If an installer is provided, use it to install the plug-in module. Otherwise, drag a copy of the module to the Plug-ins folder inside the Adobe Illustrator folder.

Follow any installation instructions that come with third-party plug-ins.

Developing plug-in modules for Adobe Illustrator

The open architecture of the Adobe Illustrator program allows third-party developers to create features that are accessible from within Adobe Illustrator. If you are interested in creating plug-in modules compatible with Adobe Illustrator, see the Adobe Systems U.S. Web site at http://www.adobe.com.

You can also contact the Adobe Developers Association (ADA) by telephone. In the United States, call 408-536-9000; in Europe, call +44-131-458-6800. In addition, you can reach the ADA by e-mail at ada@adobe.com.

Setting preferences

Numerous program settings are stored in the Adobe Illustrator preference file, called *AIPrefs* (Windows) or *Adobe Illustrator 8.0 Prefs* (Mac OS). The *AIPrefs* file is located inside the Illustrator directory (Windows), and the *Adobe Illustrator 8.0 Prefs* file is located in the Preferences folder in your System folder (Mac OS). The settings stored in this file include display options, separation setup information, tool options, ruler units, and options for exporting information. Most of these options are set in dialog boxes that can be opened through the Preferences submenus in the File menu.

To find an explanation of a particular preferences option or set of options, refer to the index.

To open a preferences dialog box:

1 Choose the desired preference dialog box from the File > Preferences submenu.

2 Switch to a different preference dialog box:

• Choose an option from the menu at the top of the dialog box.

• Click Next to display the next preference dialog box in the menu list; click Prev to display the previous preference dialog box.

3

Chapter 3: Setting Up Artwork in Illustrator

In the Adobe Illustrator program, you can create artwork or import artwork created from other applications. To create effective artwork, you need to understand some basic concepts about vector graphics versus bitmap images, resolution, and color.

About vector graphics and bitmap images

Computer graphics fall into two main categories—vector graphics and bitmap images. Understanding the difference between the two helps as you create, edit, and import artwork.

In Illustrator the type of graphic image can have important effects on your workflow. For example, some file formats only support bitmap images and others only vector graphics. Graphic image types are particularly important when importing or exporting graphic images to and from Illustrator. Linked bitmap images cannot be edited in Illustrator. Graphic formats also affect how commands and filters can be applied to images; some filters in Illustrator will only work with bitmap images.

Vector graphics

Drawing programs such as Adobe Illustrator create vector graphics, made of lines and curves defined by mathematical objects called *vectors*. Vectors describe graphics according to their geometric characteristics. For example, a bicycle tire in a vector graphic is made up of a mathematical definition of a circle drawn with a certain radius, set at a specific location, and filled with a specific color. You can move, resize, or change the color of the tire without losing the quality of the graphic.

A vector graphic is resolution-independent—that is, it can be scaled to any size and printed on any output device at any resolution without losing its detail or clarity. As a result, vector graphics are the best choice for type (especially small type) and bold graphics that must retain crisp lines when scaled to various sizes—for example, logos.

Because computer monitors represent images by displaying them on a grid, both vector and bitmap images are displayed as pixels on-screen.

Bitmap images

Paint and image-editing software, such as Adobe Photoshop, generate bitmap images, also called *raster images.* The images use a grid (also known as a *bitmap* or *raster*) of small squares, known as *pixels*, to represent graphics. Each pixel in a bitmap image has a specific location and color value assigned to it. For example, a bicycle tire in a bitmap image is made up of a collection of pixels in that location, with each pixel part of a mosaic that gives the appearance of a tire. When working with bitmap images, you edit pixels rather than objects or shapes.

Bitmap images are the most common electronic medium for continuous-tone images, such as photographs or images created in painting programs, because they can represent subtle gradations of shades and color. Bitmap images are resolution dependent—that is, they represent a fixed number of pixels. As a result, they can appear jagged and lose detail if they are scaled on-screen or if they are printed at a higher resolution than they were created for.

BITMAP VS. VECTOR A bitmap image is composed of a grid of small squares known as pixels. A vector graphic is defined by mathematical objects called vectors.

Bitmap images *are good at reproducing subtle gradations of color, as in photographs. They can show jagged edges when printed at too large a size or displayed at too high a magnification.*

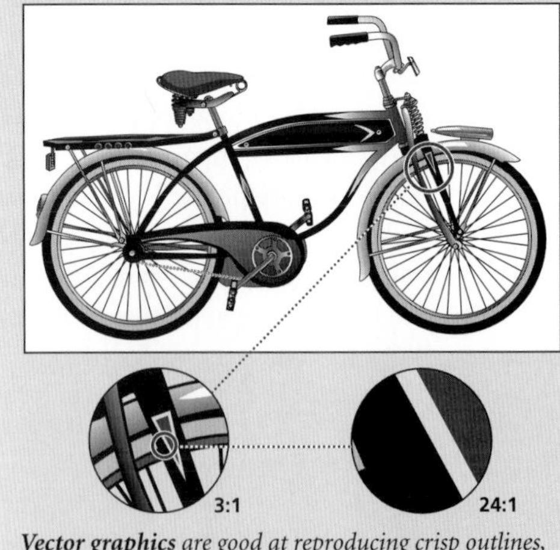

Vector graphics *are good at reproducing crisp outlines, as in logos or illustrations. They can be printed or displayed at any resolution without losing detail.*

About resolution in bitmap images

Resolution is the number of dots or pixels per linear unit used to reproduce artwork and images. Output devices display images as groups of pixels. The resolution of vector graphics, such as Illustrator artwork, depends on the device used to display the artwork. The resolution of bitmap images, such as digital photographs, depends on both the display device and the inherent resolution of the bitmap image.

Pixel dimensions The number of pixels along the height and width of a bitmap image. The display size of an image on-screen is determined by the pixel dimensions of the image plus the size and setting of the monitor. The file size of an image is proportional to its pixel dimensions.

A typical 13-inch monitor displays 640 pixels horizontally and 480 vertically. An image with pixel dimensions of 640 by 480 would fill this small screen. On a larger monitor with a 640 by 480 setting, the same image (with pixel dimensions of 640 by 480) would still fill the screen, but each pixel would appear larger. Changing the setting of this larger monitor to 1152 pixels by 870 pixels would display the image at a smaller size, occupying only part of the screen.

When preparing an image for online display (for example, a Web page that will be viewed on a variety of monitors), pixel dimensions become especially important. Because your image may be viewed on a 13-inch monitor, you'll probably want to limit the size of your image to a maximum of 640 pixels by 480 pixels.

Image resolution The number of pixels displayed per unit of printed length in an image, usually measured in pixels per inch (ppi). An image with a high resolution contains more, and therefore smaller, pixels than an image of the same printed dimensions with a low resolution. For example, a 1-inch-by-1-inch image with a resolution of 72 ppi contains a total of 5184 pixels (72 pixels wide x 72 pixels high = 5184). The same 1-inch-by-1-inch image with a resolution of 300 ppi would contain a total of 90,000 pixels.

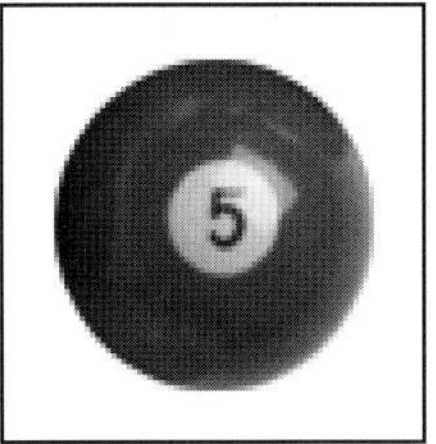

A 72-ppi bitmap image and a 300-ppi bitmap image

Because they use more pixels to represent each unit of area, higher-resolution images usually reproduce more detail and subtler color transitions than lower-resolution images when printed. However, increasing the resolution of an image scanned or created at a lower resolution only spreads the original pixel information across a greater number of pixels and rarely improves image quality.

To determine the image resolution to use, consider the medium of final distribution for the image. If you're producing an image for online display, the image resolution only needs to match the typical monitor resolution (72 or 96 ppi). However, using too low a resolution for a printed image results in *pixelation*—output with large, coarse-looking pixels. Using too high a resolution (pixels smaller than what the output device can produce) increases the file size and slows the printing of the image.

Note: *The Document Setup dialog box lets you define the output resolution for vector drawings. In Illustrator,* output resolution *refers to the number of line segments the PostScript interpreter uses to approximate a curve. (See "Changing the output resolution" on page 352.)*

Monitor resolution The number of pixels or dots displayed per unit of length on the monitor, usually measured in dots per inch (dpi). Monitor resolution depends on the size of the monitor plus its pixel setting. The typical resolution of a PC monitor is about 96 dpi, of a Mac OS monitor 72 dpi. Understanding monitor resolution helps explain why the display size of an image on-screen often differs from its printed size.

Printer resolution The number of ink dots per inch (dpi) produced by an imagesetter or laser printer. For best results, use an image resolution that is proportional to, but not the same as, printer resolution. Most laser printers have output resolutions of 300 dpi to 600 dpi and produce good results with images from 72 ppi to 150 ppi.

High-end imagesetters can print at 1200 dpi or higher and produce good results with images from 200 ppi to 300 ppi.

Screen frequency The number of printer dots or halftone cells per inch used to print grayscale images or color separations. Also known as screen ruling or line screen, screen frequency is measured in lines per inch (lpi)—or lines of cells per inch in a halftone screen.

The relationship between image resolution and screen frequency determines the quality of detail in the printed image. To produce a halftone image of the highest quality, you generally use an image resolution that is from 1.5 to at most 2 times the screen frequency. But with some images and output devices, a lower resolution can produce good results.

Note: *Some imagesetters and 600-dpi laser printers use screening technologies other than halftoning. If you are printing an image on a nonhalftone printer, consult your service provider or your printer documentation for the recommended image resolutions.*

About the work area

In Adobe Illustrator, the work area occupies the entire space within the Illustrator window and includes more than just the printable page containing your artwork. The printable and non-printable areas are represented by a series of solid and dotted lines between the outermost edge of the window and the printable area of the page.

A. Imageable area B. Nonimageable area
C. Edge of the page D. Artboard E. Scratch area

Imageable area The imageable area is bounded by the innermost dotted lines and represents the portion of the page on which the selected printer can print. Many printers cannot print to the edge of the paper.

Nonimageable area The nonimageable area is between the two sets of dotted lines representing any nonprintable margin of the page. This example shows the nonimageable area of an 8.5" x 11" page for a standard laser printer.

Edge of the page The page edge is indicated by the outermost set of dotted lines.

Artboard The artboard is bounded by solid lines and represents the entire region that can contain printable artwork. By default, the artboard is the same size as the page, but it can be enlarged or reduced. The U.S. default artboard is 8.5" x 11", but it can be set as large as 227" x 227".

Scratch area The scratch area is the area outside the artboard that extends to the edge of the 227-inch square window. The scratch area represents a space on which you can create, edit, and store elements of artwork before moving them onto the artboard. Objects placed onto the scratch area are visible on-screen, but they do not print.

Setting up the work area

Once you have created a document, you can then set up your work area to organize your work and streamline the workflow. For example, you can change the size of the artboard, tile your workspace, or move your page boundaries.

To open a new file:

Choose File > New.

To open an existing file:

1 Choose File > Open.

2 Select the name of the file you want to open, and click Open.

To close a file and quit Illustrator:

1 Choose File > Exit (Windows) or File > Quit (Mac OS).

2 If the file has not yet been saved or named, the Save dialog box appears. To save the file, enter a name in the Name text box (if necessary) and then click OK.

To change the size of the artboard:

1 Choose File > Document Setup.

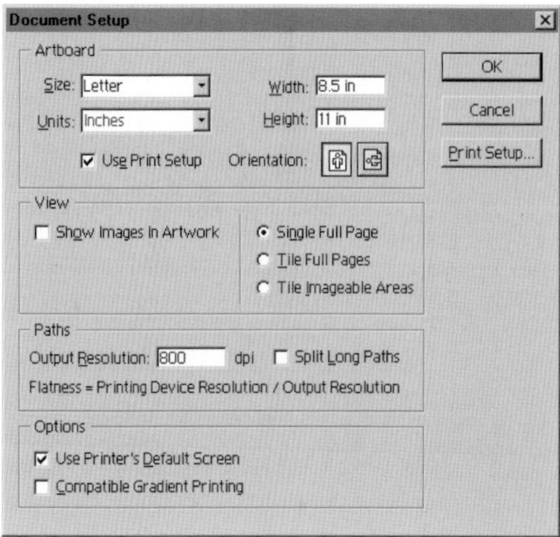

2 Do one of the following:

• Choose a preset size from the Size pop-up menu.

• Choose Custom from the Size pop-up menu, and enter the dimensions you want in the text boxes, up to 227 inches by 227 inches. You can change the units in the document (and therefore of the artboard size) by choosing a different unit from the File > Preferences > Units & Undo dialog box.

• Select Use Print Setup (Windows) or Use Page Setup (Mac OS) to set the size of the artboard to match the page size set in the Print Setup (Windows) or Page Setup (Mac OS) dialog box. The size of the artboard then changes anytime you choose a new page size in the Print/Page Setup dialog box.

3 Click OK.

Note: *The artboard displays the maximum printable area but does not define the size of the printed page. The printable area of the page is derived from the printer driver and ppd of the printing device. You can only change page size settings if your printer will accept custom page sizes. (See Chapter 14, "Printing.")*

To change the size of the page:

Choose File > Print Setup (Windows) or File > Page Setup (Mac OS) and select a page type in the dialog box.

Note: *The imageable area and page size are not limitations when printing to imagesetters that handle large media. Imagesetters can typically print to the edge of the page. The page size used by an imagesetter may be larger than the page size specified in Illustrator, enabling you to print bleeds, for example, that run past the edge of the page.*

Working with tiled artwork

The artboard's dimensions do not necessarily match the paper sizes used by printers. As a result, when you print a file, the program divides the artboard into one or more rectangles that correspond to the page size available on your printer. Dividing the artboard to fit a printer's available page size is called *tiling*.

As you work with tiled artwork, be sure to consider how the artwork relates to the boundaries of the page grid and to the total dimensions of the artboard. For example, if the artwork is tiled onto six pages, part of the artwork will print on a separate sheet of paper that corresponds to page 6. If you specify printing only from pages 1 to 5, the part of the artwork that is on page 6 won't print.

If you have set up the file to view and print multiple pages, the file is tiled onto pages numbered from left to right and from top to bottom, starting with page 1. (The first page is always page 1; there is no way to change the page 1 designation in Adobe Illustrator.) These page numbers appear on-screen for your reference only; they do not print. The numbers enable you to print all of the pages in the file or specify particular pages to print.

The page or set of pages is aligned with the upper left corner of the artboard by default. However, you can reposition pages on the artboard by using the page tool. (See "Moving the page boundaries" on page 51.)

To see whether the tiling format is visible on-screen:

Choose View > Show Page Tiling or View > Hide Page Tiling.

To change the page tiling options:

1 Choose File > Document Setup.

2 Choose from the following options:

• Single Full Page (the default) to view and print one page.

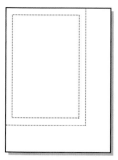

Single Full Page option: 8.5"x 11" page on 11"x 14" artboard

• Tile Full Pages to view and print multiple pages containing separate pieces of artwork. For example, you can use this option to print a two-page brochure.

To view and print multiple pages, the artboard size set in the Document Setup dialog box must be large enough to fit more than one full page at a time.

Note: *With the Tile Full Pages option, any artwork that extends past the imageable area of a given page is not printed.*

Tile Full Pages option: 20"x 14"artboard

• Tile Imageable Areas to view and print a single piece of artwork that is too large to fit on one page. For example, you could use this option to print artwork for a large poster onto several sheets of standard-size paper for proofing.

When you print a file by using this option, the artwork is divided among the imageable areas of the pages.

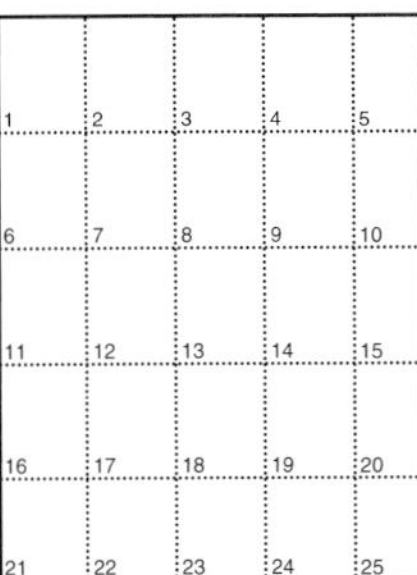

Tile Imageable Areas option: 40"x 60"artboard

3 Click OK.

Adjusting the bounding box when tiling pages

The program may print blank pages if the artwork is tiled so that the *editing bounding box* intersects pages that do not contain any artwork. The *bounding box* is a border that defines the boundaries of your artwork, and can be used to move and transform the artwork. For information about editing artwork with the bounding box, see "Using the bounding box" on page 115.

In the following illustration, the bounding box surrounds the artwork, not its direction lines. (See "About direction lines and direction points" on page 70.)

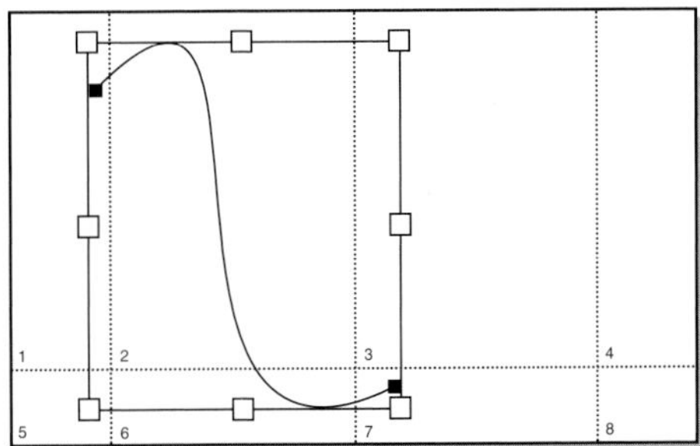

Tile Imageable Areas; bounding box surrounds artwork

Moving the page boundaries

You can adjust the placement of the printable area of the page to control how artwork is printed. This is a good way to avoid having the artwork extend past the boundaries of the current page.

You can adjust the page from any view. You may find it easiest to choose View > Fit In Window so you can see all of your artwork while you adjust the pages.

To adjust a page by using the page tool:

1 Select the page tool ( ). The pointer becomes a dotted cross when you move it to the active window.

2 Drag the page to the new location. As you drag, the page tool responds as if you were moving the page from its lower left corner. Two gray rectangles are displayed. The outer rectangle represents the page size, and the inner rectangle represents the printable area of a page.

Note: *You can move the page anywhere on the artboard; however, any part of a page that extends past the printable area boundary is not printed.*

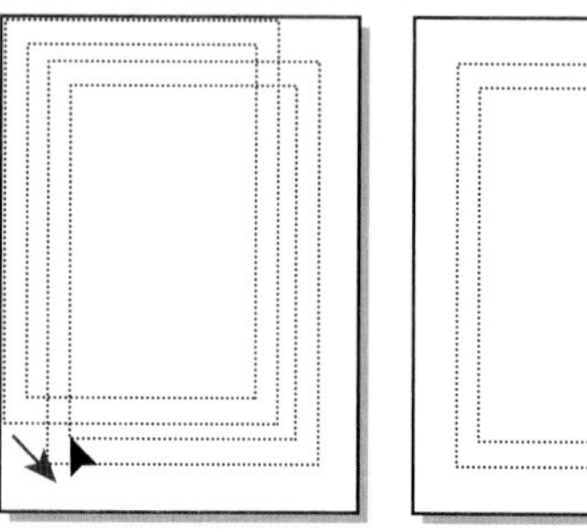

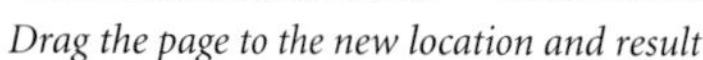

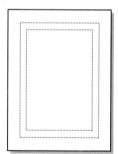

Drag the page to the new location and result

To adjust the placement of artwork by moving it in the printable area:

1 Unlock any locked objects, and display any hidden objects. (See “Locking and hiding objects” on page 127, “Locking layers” on page 226, and “Hiding or displaying layers” on page 219.)

2 Click the selection tool ( ).

3 Choose Edit > Select All.

4 Drag the artwork to the new position within the printable page boundaries.

SETTING UP STANDARD AND CUSTOM PAGES You can use the Document Setup dialog box to create custom-size as well as standard-size artboards. Use the Print Setup (Windows) or Page Setup (Mac OS) dialog box to change printable page sizes. These settings override the dimensions set in the Document Setup dialog box. Also, making the artboard larger than the page leaves room for crop marks, trim marks, and registration marks.

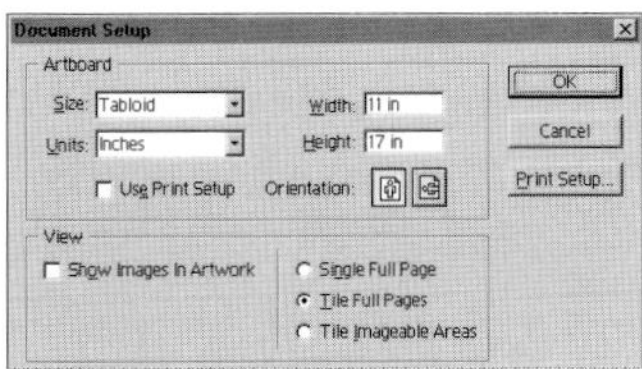

Use the Document Setup dialog box to define the artboard and how pages are tiled on the artboard.

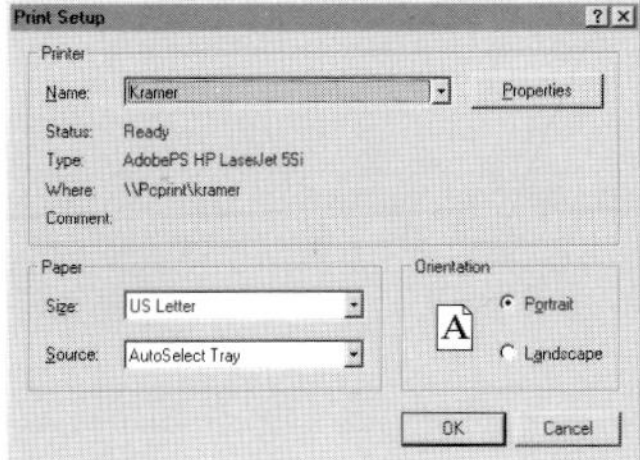

Use the Print Setup (Windows) or Page Setup (Mac OS) dialog box to print with different paper sizes and orientations.

Vertical tabloid page

Document Setup:

- *Use Print Setup (Windows) or Use Page Setup (Mac OS)*

Page Setup:

- *Tabloid paper*
- *Portrait orientation*

Vertical letter page

Document Setup:

- *Use Print Setup/Use Page Setup*

Page Setup:

- *US letter paper*
- *Portrait orientation*

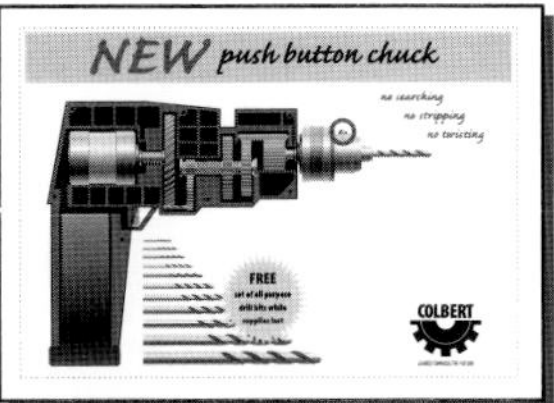

Horizontal A4 page

Document Setup:

- *Use Print Setup/Use Page Setup*

Page Setup:

- *A4 paper*
- *Landscape orientation*

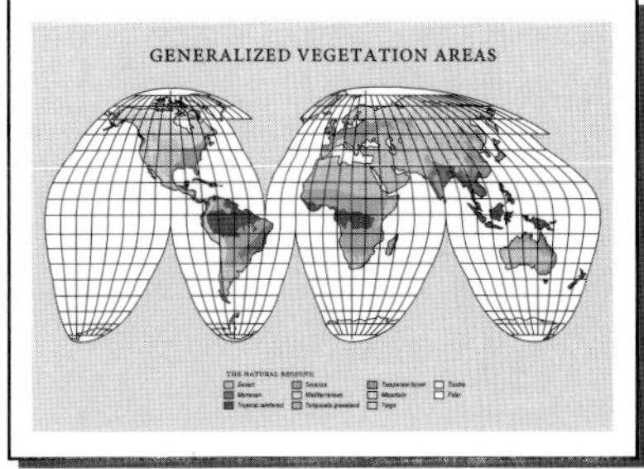

Horizontal A3 page

Document Setup:

- *Use Print Setup (Windows) or Use Page Setup (Mac OS)*

Page Setup:

- *A3 paper*
- *Landscape orientation*

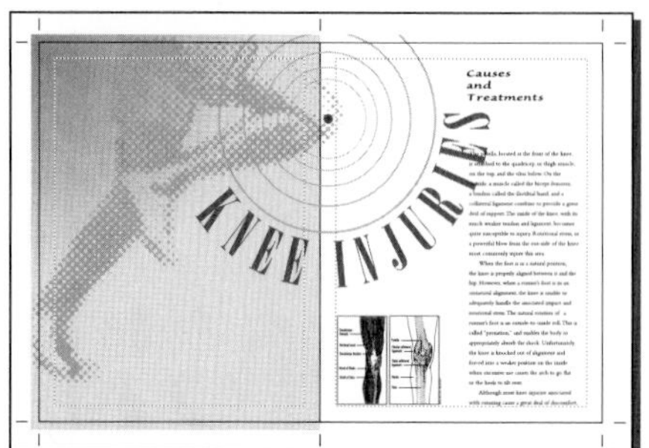

Two-page spread

Document Setup:

- *Custom artboard (19.5" by 13.5")*
- *Landscape orientation*
- *Tile Full Pages view*

Page Setup:

- *US letter paper*
- *Portrait orientation*

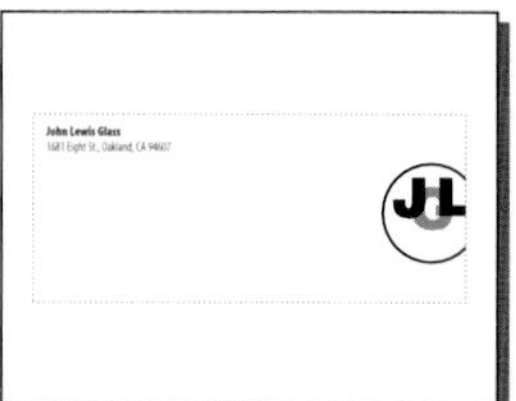

Standard envelope – center fed

Document Setup:

- *Use Print Setup (Windows) or Use Page Setup (Mac OS)*

Page Setup:

- *Envelope paper*
- *Landscape orientation*

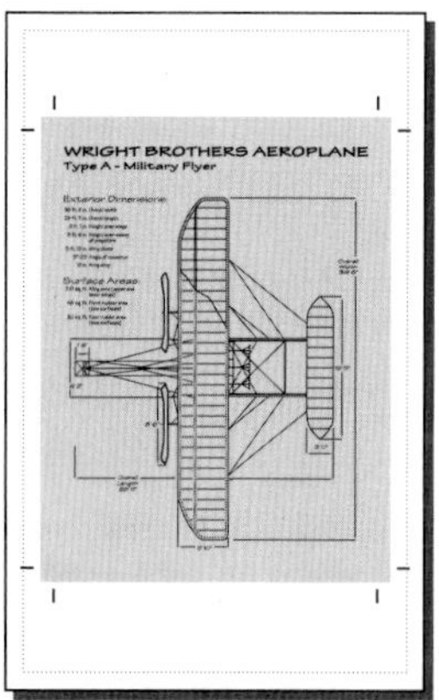

US letter page with bleed

Document Setup:

- *Tabloid paper*
- *Portrait orientation*
- *Single Full Page view*

Page Setup:

- *US letter paper*
- *Portrait orientation*

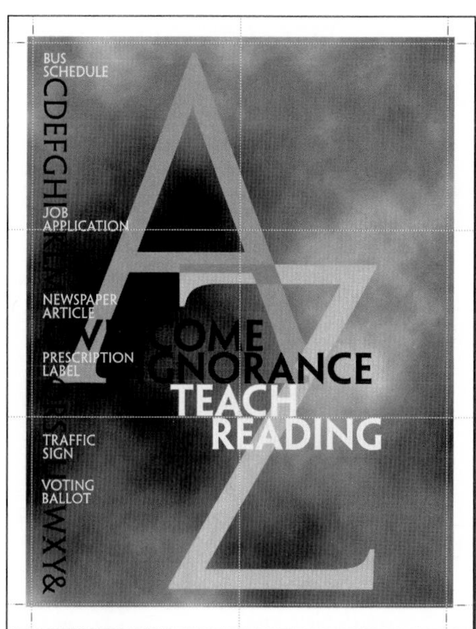

Custom page

Document setup:

- *Custom artboard (19.73" by 25.3375")*
- *Portrait orientation*
- *Tile Imageable Areas view*

Page Setup:

- *US letter paper*
- *Landscape orientation*

Importing artwork

Placing artwork from other applications, such as Adobe Photoshop, into Adobe Illustrator is easily performed using various Adobe Illustrator commands.

Illustrator can import many common graphic file formats, including EPS, CorelDRAW™, FreeHand™, GIF, JPEG, PICT, TIFF, DXF, PDF, and PostScript. In addition to these common graphic file formats, Illustrator can use artwork in any file format supported by an Adobe Photoshop-compatible file format plug-in filter, including Photo CD™, PNG, and TGA.

File Format	Import Methods	Considerations
AI	Open	Opens all Illustrator format files.
EPS	Open, Place	Placed files may be linked or embedded.
PDF	Open, Place	Specify which page of file you want to use. Placed files may be linked or embedded.
Photoshop	Open, Place	Supports Photoshop 2.5 and later. Placed files may be linked or embedded. Drag and drop artwork directly from Photoshop.
PICT	Open, Place	Macintosh only. Placed files may be linked or embedded.
WMF/EMF	Open, Place	Windows only. Placed files will be embedded. Drag and drop artwork directly from Microsoft Office. Supports the import of both the Windows and Aldus WMF formats.
DXF	Open, Place	Supports DXF release 13. Placed files will be embedded.

File Format	Import Methods	Considerations
FreeHand	Open, Place	Supports FreeHand versions 5.0, 5.5, and 7.0. (Japanese version supported to version 5.5.) Placed files will be embedded.
CorelDRAW	Open	Supports CorelDRAW versions 5.0, 6.0, and 7.0. Supports roman language files only.
CMX	Open	
CGM	Open	
All raster formats supported by Photoshop-compatible filters	Open, Place	Supports the following formats: Amiga IFF, BMP, Filmstrip, GIF 89a, JPEG, PCX, PIXAR, PNG, TIFF, and TGA.
Text formats	Open, Place	Supports the following formats: plain text, MS RTF, MS Word 6.0 and 95, Corel WordPerfect (roman only). Vertical Japanese text in RTF and Word files will be imported as horizontal text. Placed files will be embedded.

Opening and placing artwork

You can use the Clipboard and drag-and-drop importing to bring images into Illustrator. (See "Moving, copying, and deleting objects" on page 117.) However, two commands are most commonly used when importing artwork created by other applications:

- The Open command opens a file created by another application as a new Adobe Illustrator file.

- The Place command places an image in an existing Illustrator file in one of two ways. Depending on the file format, the Place command creates a link to an external file by default and does not include a copy of the file in the Illustrator file. You can also deselect the Link option in the Place dialog box, which embeds (includes) a copy of the file in the Illustrator file.

- In addition to the Open and Place commands, you can subscribe to a file created by any application that supports the Mac OS Publish and Subscribe feature. (See "Using the Publish and Subscribe commands (for Mac OS only)" on page 330.)

Opening files

When you open a file created by another application, it becomes a new Adobe Illustrator file. Vector artwork in the file you open is converted to Illustrator paths, which can be modified using any Illustrator tool; bitmap images can be modified using transformation tools, such as scale and rotate, and using image filters from the Illustrator Filter menu. (See "About vector graphics and bitmap images" on page 43.)

Files that have been saved in Portable Document Format (PDF) can be opened as Adobe Illustrator documents, without losing the ability to edit artwork with Illustrator tools and commands. Artwork stored in PDF format can also be placed into Illustrator files, as described in "Importing EPS and PDF files into Illustrator" on page 57.

To open a file created by another application:

1 Choose File > Open.

2 Locate and select the file you want to open. If you don't see the name of the file you want, the file is stored in a format that Illustrator can't read. See "Importing artwork" on page 55 for a complete list of all the file formats you can open.

3 Click Open.

Note: *If you open an EPS file that contains fonts not installed on your system, font substitution will occur when you print.*

To open a file that has recently been used:

Choose File > Recent Files and select the filename from the list.

Placing files

The Place command places files from other applications into Adobe Illustrator. Files can be *embedded*, or included in, the Illustrator file, or they can be linked to the Illustrator file. *Linked* files remain independent of the Illustrator file, resulting in a smaller Illustrator file; when the artwork in the linked file is edited or changed, the linked image in the Illustrator file is automatically changed.

By default, the Link option is selected in the Place dialog box. If you deselect the Link option, the artwork is embedded in the Adobe Illustrator file, resulting in a larger Illustrator file. The Links palette lets you identify, select, monitor, and update objects in the Illustrator artwork that are linked to external files. (See "Managing linked and embedded images" on page 58.)

Placed bitmap images can be modified using transformation tools and image filters; placed vector artwork is converted to Illustrator paths (embedded images only).

To place and link files created by other applications:

1 Open the Illustrator file into which you want to place the artwork.

2 Choose File > Place.

3 Locate and select the file you want to place. If you don't see the name of the file you want, the file has been saved in a format that Illustrator cannot read.

4 Do one of the following:

• To create a link between the artwork file and the Illustrator file, make sure the Link option is selected in the Place dialog box.

• To embed the artwork in the Illustrator file, deselect the Link option in the Place dialog box.

5 Click Place. The artwork is placed into the Illustrator file as either a linked or an embedded image, depending on the option you selected in the Place dialog box.

Importing EPS and PDF files into Illustrator

You can use Adobe Illustrator to edit artwork that was imported as Encapsulated PostScript (EPS) and Portable Document Format (PDF) file types.

You can import PDF and EPS files using these commands:

• The Open command to open a PDF or EPS file as a new Illustrator file.

• The Place command to place a PDF or EPS file in the current layer in an existing Illustrator file.

Important: *To place an EPS image containing a gradient mesh object as an embedded file (that is, the Link option is deselected in the Place dialog box), the file should be saved as an EPS Level 1 PostScript file.*

To open a PDF or EPS file as a new Adobe Illustrator file:

1 Choose File > Open.

2 Select the file you want to open, and click Open. If the file does not appear, for Files of Type, choose All Formats (Windows) or Show All Files (Mac OS).

To place PDF or EPS artwork into an Adobe Illustrator file:

1 Open the Adobe Illustrator file into which you want to place the artwork.

2 Choose File > Place, select the file you want to place, and click Place.

Placing EPS or PDF files in Illustrator with the Link option selected in the Place dialog box does not allow you to modify the linked object within the Illustrator file. To convert the elements in an EPS or PDF file to Illustrator objects that can be modified, deselect the Link option in the Place dialog box. Deselecting the Link option when you place the EPS or PDF file embeds the file and lets you edit each part of the artwork as a discrete object. (See "Editing artwork contained in linked files" on page 61.)

3 If you are placing a page from a PDF file that contains multiple pages, select the page you want to place, and click OK.

4 Adjust the placed artwork as described in Chapter 5, "Working with Objects."

Important: *If you import an EPS color that has the same name as a color in your document but with a different definition, Illustrator displays an alert. Choose Use Linked file's color to replace the color in your document with the EPS color in the linked file. All objects using this color in your document will get updated appropriately. Choose Use document's color to leave the swatch as is and resolve all color conflicts using the document's color. The EPS preview cannot be changed so the preview may be incorrect, but it will print to the correct plates. Checking "Apply to All" will resolve all color conflicts using the definition either of the document or the linked file, depending on which option you choose.*

Turning preview images on or off

If a placed file with the Link option selected was not saved with a preview image in the application that created it, it will not be visible in Adobe Illustrator when it is placed. Instead, an outlined box containing two diagonal lines appears and defines the artwork's dimensions. The box is placed into the center of the active window, in front of all other artwork in the file, and is selected.

If a placed file was saved with a preview image in the application that created it, you can see it in Preview view and you can choose to display a preview image in Artwork view.

To turn on and off the display of preview images in Artwork view:

1 Choose File > Document Setup.

2 Click Show Images in Artwork, and then click OK.

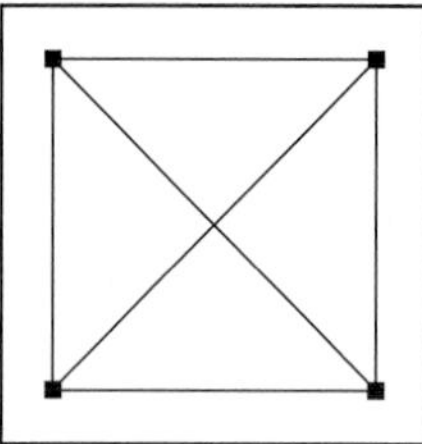
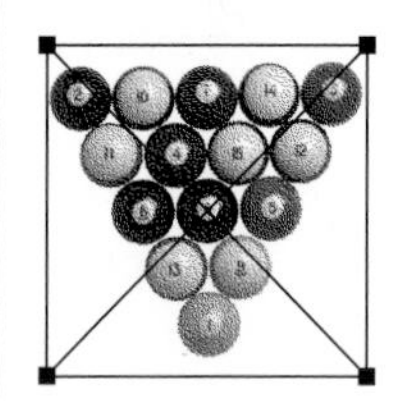

Artwork view with Show Images in Artwork option off and on

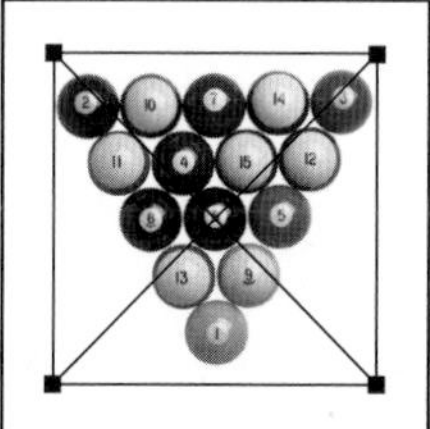
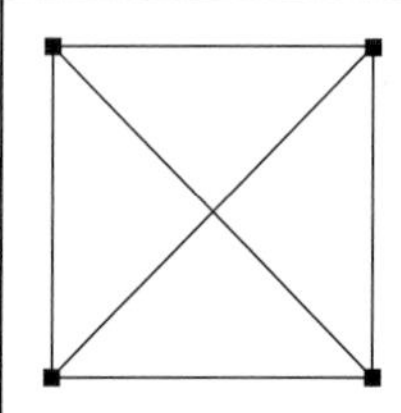

Preview view and image saved with no preview

Note: *Placed images with the appropriate resource always display in Preview view, regardless of the Show Images in Artwork setting.*

Managing linked and embedded images

The Links palette lets you identify, select, monitor, and update images that are linked to external files, or images that are embedded in the Illustrator file. In addition, you can determine if an image's link to an external file is broken or missing, get information about linked or embedded image characteristics, and open a linked image's original file and application to edit the image.

You can also use the Links palette to replace a linked image with another linked image. When you replace a linked image, the new image adopts the size, placement, and transformation status of the original linked image.

If you are color-managing artwork in a document, embedded EPS images are part of the document and therefore color-managed when sent to a printing device. In contrast, linked images are not color-managed, even if color management is turned on for the rest of the document. (See "Ensuring accurate color" on page 178.)

Important: *Occasionally you may encounter a warning when printing an Illustrator document containing embedded EPS images. If the application cannot find the original EPS image, you will be prompted to extract the EPS image. Select the Extract option in the dialog box; the image will be extracted into the same directory as the current document. Although the embedded file does not preview in the document, the file will now print correctly.*

Using the Links palette

All linked or embedded images in the file are listed in the Links palette. Linked images whose originals have been modified since the image was placed are identified with an exclamation point icon; linked images whose original files are missing are identified with a stop sign icon.

You can use the Links palette to quickly convert linked images into embedded images, using the Embed Image command.

To display the Links palette:

Choose Window > Show Links. Each linked or embedded image is identified by name and by a thumbnail display.

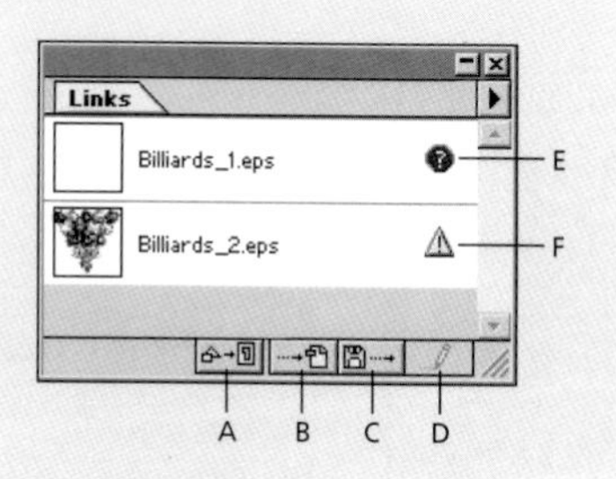

A. *Replace Link* ***B.*** *Go to Link* ***C.*** *Update Link*
D. *Edit Original* ***E.*** *Missing Link*
F. *Modified Link*

To select one or more links:

Choose from the following options:

• Click a link to select it.

• Shift-click to select a continuous range of links.

• Ctrl-click (Windows) or Command-click (Mac OS) to select a non continuous range of links.

• Ctrl+Alt (Windows) or Command+Option (Mac OS) and then click in the palette window to select a link by typing its name.

To display link information:

Do one of the following:

• Double-click a link to bring up the Link Information dialog box.

• Select a link, and choose Information from the Links palette menu.

To go to a linked object and select it:

1 Select a link in the Links palette display.

2 Choose one of the following:

• Click the Go to Link button at the bottom of the palette.

• Choose Go to Link from the Links palette menu.

The page containing the link is displayed, and the linked image is selected.

To replace a link with a new linked image:

1 Select a link in the link palette.

2 Choose one of the following:

• Click the Replace Link button at the bottom of the palette.

• Choose Replace Link from the Links palette menu.

3 Select the file to replace the linked image in the Place dialog box, and click OK. The new image retains the size, placement, and transformation characteristics of the image that it replaced.

To update a link with the most recent data from the linked file:

1 Select one or more links in the Links palette display.

2 Choose one of the following to refresh the link with the most current version of the original file:

• Click the Update Link button at the bottom of the palette.

• Choose Update Link from the Links palette menu.

To change a linked image into an embedded image:

1 Select a linked image in the Links palette display.

2 Choose Embed Image from the Links palette menu.

Modifying the Links palette display

You can change the way that links are displayed in the Links palette using commands in the Links palette menu.

The palette can display icons of the links, or show different sized thumbnail images of the links. In addition, you can sort the display to show only those links that have missing or broken links with the original file, or those links that have been modified since the last update.

To change the links display icons or thumbnails:

1 Choose Palette Options from the Links palette menu.

2 In the Palette Options dialog box, select the type of icon or thumbnail you want displayed.

To sort the links display by name, kind, or status:

1 Select all or some of the links to sort in the Links palette display.

2 Choose one of the following from the Links palette menu to customize the links display by sorting:

• Sort by Names to alphabetize the links display.

• Sort by Kind to sort the display according to the type of file (for example, all JPEG files, all GIF files, all EPS files, and so on).

• Sort by Status to sort the display according to the linked or embedded status. Embedded images are listed first, followed by linked images.

To display links according to link type:

Choose one of the following from the Links palette menu:

• Show All to display all links in the file.

• Show Missing to display only links with missing or broken connections with the original file.

• Show Modified to display only links that have been changed after the last time the link was updated.

• Show Embedded to display only embedded images.

To refresh links in the Links palette:

Choose Refresh List from the palette menu to display the most current version of the links displayed in the Links palette.

Editing artwork contained in linked files

When you make changes to a linked image using the application that created it, the changes are applied to the Illustrator file once you update the link.

Note that if you replace a linked image with another image, any transformation attributes applied to it, such as scaling, rotating, or shearing, are retained and applied to the new image.

To edit a linked object from within the original file:

1 Select a link in the Links palette display.

2 Choose one of the following:

• Click the Edit Original button at the bottom of the palette.

• Choose Edit Original from the Links palette menu.

4

Chapter 4: Drawing

Adobe Illustrator provides a multitude of ways to draw objects, ranging from simulated paintbrush artwork to detailed pen strokes. Used in conjunction with a mouse or a pressure-sensitive drawing tablet, Illustrator drawing tools give you a greater range of control and speed than ever before.

About paths and anchor points

A *path* is any line or shape that you create using the Adobe Illustrator drawing tools. A single straight line, a rectangle, and the outline of a map are all typical examples of paths.

A path consists of one or more segments. *Anchor points,* which define where each segment of a path starts and ends, affix the path in place. By moving anchor points, you modify path segments and change the shape of a path.

A path can be either open or closed. A *closed* path is a path that is continuous and has no beginning or end; a circle is an example of a closed path. An *open* path has distinct endpoints; a wavy line, for example, is an open path.

The first and last anchor points on an open path are called the *endpoints.* If you fill an open path, the program draws an imaginary line between the two endpoints and fills the path.

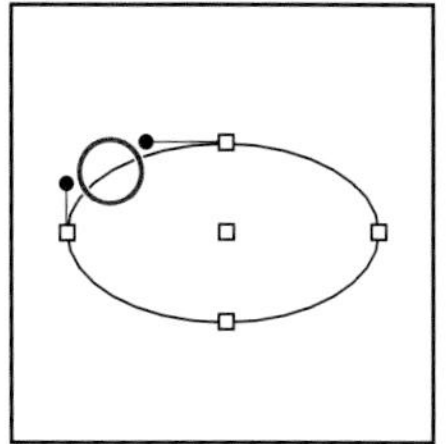
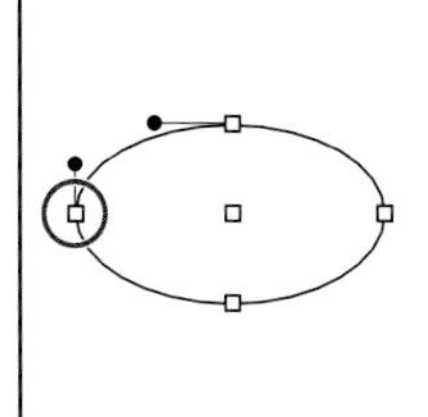

Selected path segment and unselected anchor point

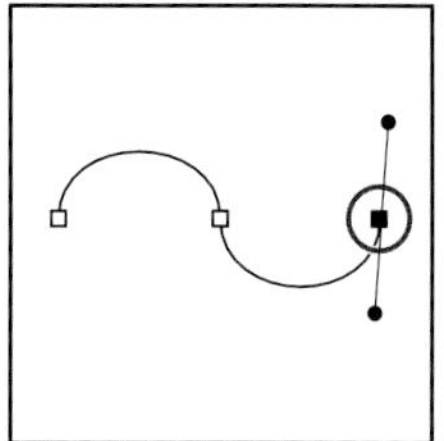
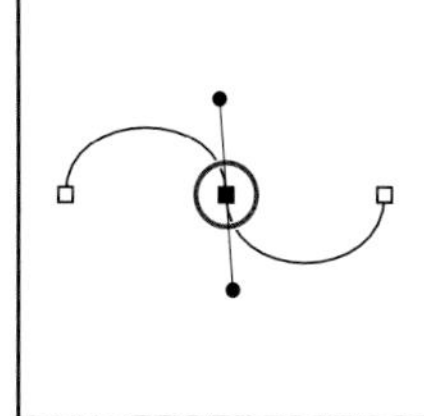

Selected endpoint and selected anchor point

You draw paths with various tools from the toolbox. The pencil tool, pen tool, paintbrush tool, and shape tools all draw paths. Once you draw a path, you can edit it by changing its size, shape, location, and color.

Changing a tool pointer

You can change the appearance of the pointer from the tool pointer to a cross hair for more precise control. When the pointer is a cross hair, more of your artwork is visible. This is convenient when you're doing detailed drawing and editing.

To make a drawing tool pointer appear as a cross hair:

Do one of the following:

• Choose File > Preferences > General. Select Use Precise Cursors, and click OK.

• Press Caps Lock before you begin drawing with the tool.

Drawing and editing freeform paths

When you want to draw and edit freeform paths, use the pencil tool. You can also smooth out and erase segments of a freeform path with the smooth tool and erase tool.

Anchor points are set down as you draw with the pencil tool; you do not determine where they are positioned. However, you can adjust them once the path is complete. The number of anchor points set down is determined by the length and complexity of the path and by the tolerance values set in the Pencil Tool Preferences or Smooth Tool Preferences dialog box for either tool.

Note: *You can draw and edit brushed paths with the paintbrush tool by using the same methods as for paths drawn with the pencil tool.*

Drawing and editing with the pencil tool

The pencil tool lets you draw open and closed paths as if you were drawing with a pencil on paper. It is most useful for fast sketching or creating a hand-drawn look. Once you draw a path, you can immediately change it if needed.

To draw a freeform path with the pencil tool:

1 Select the pencil tool (✎).

2 Position the pointer where you want the path to begin, and drag to draw a path. The pencil tool displays a small *x* to indicate drawing a freeform path.

As you drag, a dotted line follows the pointer. Anchor points appear at both ends of the path and at various points along it. The path takes on the current paint attributes, and the path remains selected by default.

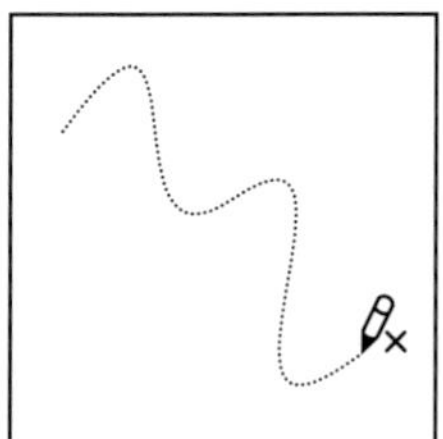

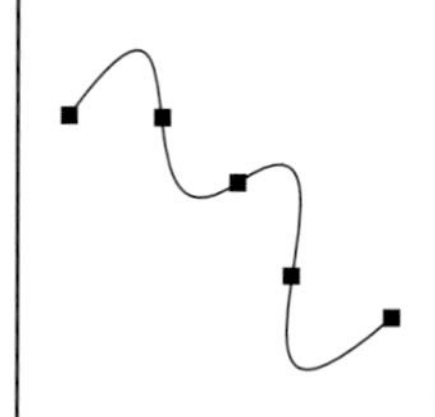

Drag to draw.

3 To continue the existing freeform path, make sure the path is selected, and then position the pencil tip on an endpoint of the path and drag.

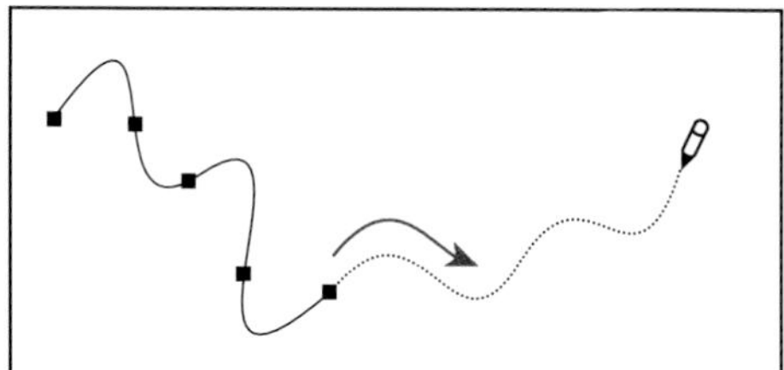

Drag from an endpoint to continue the path.

To draw a closed path with the pencil tool:

1 Select the pencil tool.

2 Position the pointer where you want the path to begin, and start dragging to draw a path.

3 As you drag, hold down Alt (Windows) or Option (Mac OS). The pencil tool displays a small loop, and its eraser is solid, to indicate drawing a closed path.

4 When the path is the size and shape you want, release the mouse button (but not the Alt or Option key). After the path closes, release the Alt or Option key.

To connect a new path to an existing path:

Ctrl-drag (Windows) or Command-drag (Mac OS) from the current path onto the endpoint of the other path. You cannot use this method for brushed paths.

To change a path with the pencil tool:

1 If the path you want to change is not selected, select it with the selection tool (➤). Or Ctrl-click (Windows) or Command-click (Mac OS) the path to select it.

2 Position the pencil tool on or near the path to redraw, and drag the tool until the path is the desired shape.

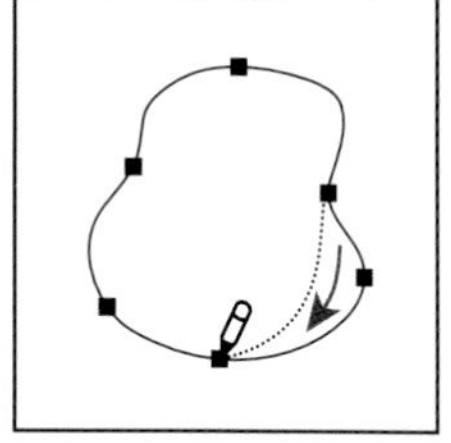
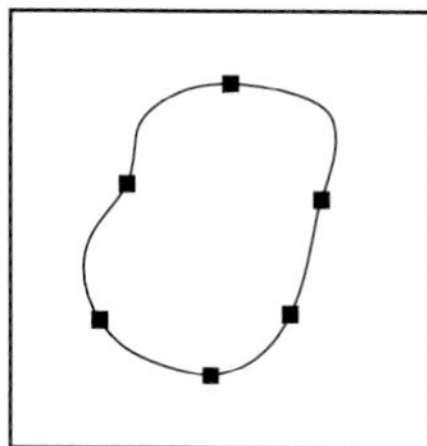

Using the pencil tool to edit a closed shape

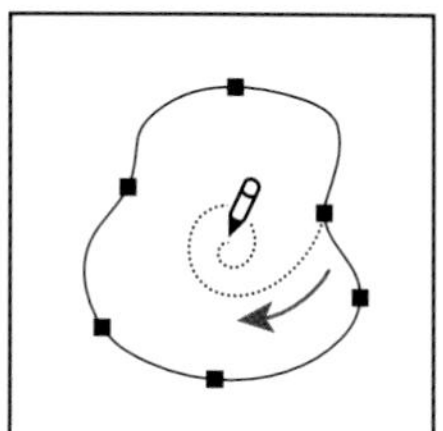
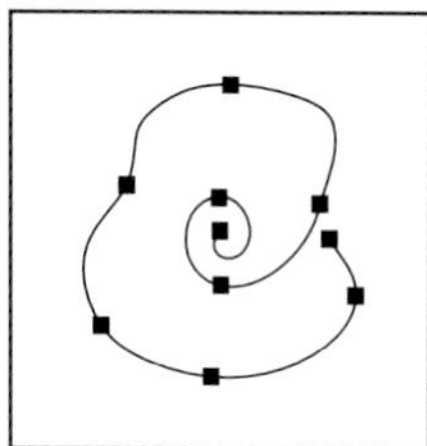

Using the pencil tool to create an open shape

Note: *Depending on where you begin to redraw the path and in which direction you drag, you may get unexpected results. For example, you may unintentionally change a closed path to an open path, change an open path to a closed path, or lose a portion of a shape.*

Smoothing the path with the smooth tool

The smooth tool lets you smooth out an existing stroke or section of a path. The smooth tool retains the original shape of the path as much as possible.

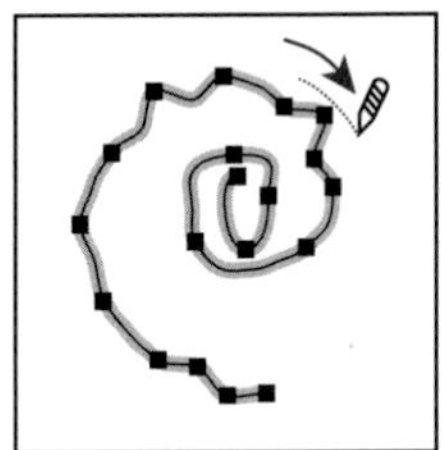

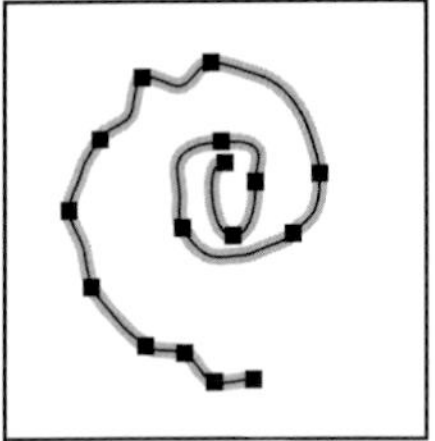

Stroke before and after using the smooth tool

To use the smooth tool:

1 If the path to smooth is not selected, select it with the selection tool ( ). Or Ctrl-click (Windows) or Command-click (Mac OS) the path to select it.

2 Do one of the following:

- Select the smooth tool ( ).
- When the pencil or paintbrush tool is selected, hold down Alt (Windows) or Option (Mac OS) to change the pencil to the smooth tool.

3 Drag the tool along the length of the path segment you want to smooth out. The modified stroke or path may have fewer anchor points than the original.

4 Continue smoothing until the stroke or path is the desired smoothness.

Erasing the path with the erase tool

The erase tool lets you remove a portion of an existing path or stroke. You can use the erase tool on paths (including brushed paths), but not on text or meshes.

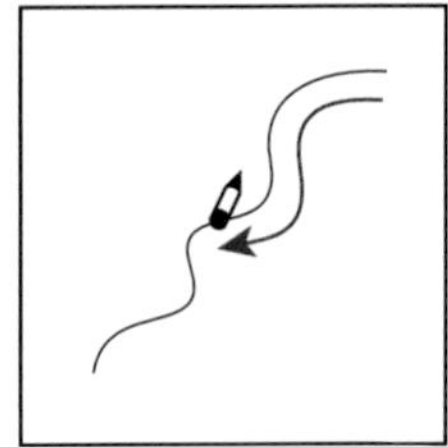

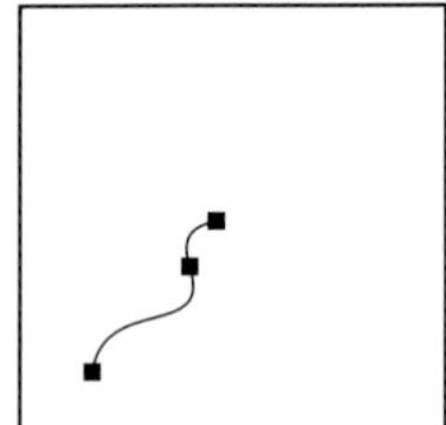

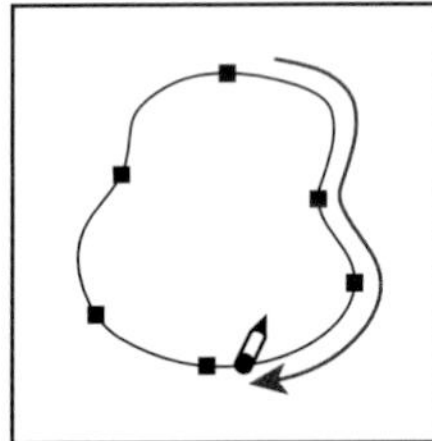

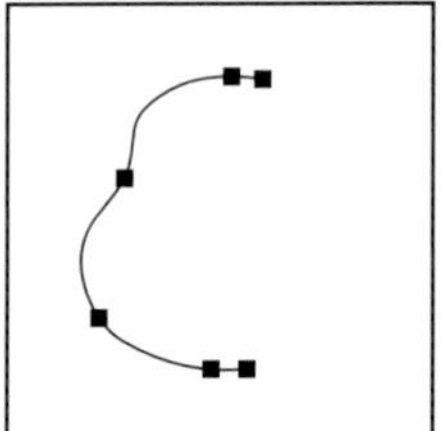

Strokes before and after using the erase tool

To use the erase tool:

1 Select the erase tool ( ).

2 Drag the tool along the length of the path segment you want to erase (not across the path). For best results, use a single, smooth, dragging motion.

Anchor points are added to the ends of the new paths.

Setting preferences for tools

You can set preferences for the pencil tool and smooth tool. The preferences include tolerances that control how sensitive the pencil and smooth tools are to the movement of your mouse or graphics-tablet stylus, and whether you want the path to remain selected after you draw it.

The tolerance is calculated in number of pixels. The larger the number of pixels you specify, the smoother and less complex are the paths.

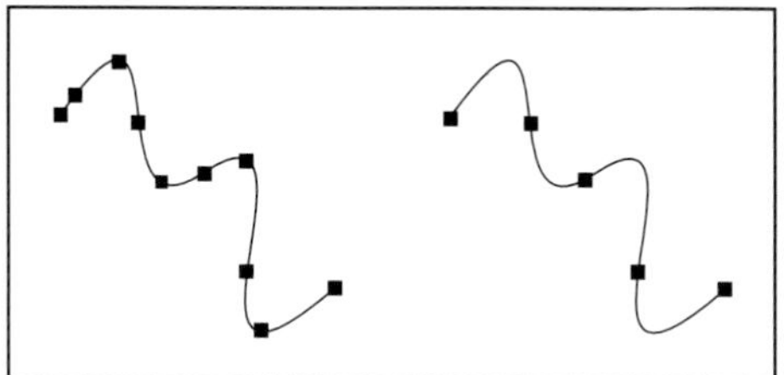

Paths with low fidelity and smoothness (left), and high fidelity and smoothness (right)

Note: *You can also set preferences for the paintbrush tool. (See "Drawing and editing brushed paths" on page 85.)*

To set preferences for the pencil tool and smooth tool:

1 Double-click the pencil tool ( ) or smooth tool ( ).

2 Use the Fidelity and Smoothness sliders or enter values in the text boxes:

• Fidelity controls the distance (in pixels) in which curves can stray from the smoothed mouse or tablet data when using the tool. The lower the fidelity value, the more angular the curves; the higher the value, the smoother the curves.

• Smoothness controls the amount of smoothing (by percentage) applied when you use the tool. The lower the smoothness value, the coarser the path appears; the higher the value, the smoother the path.

3 To keep the path selected after you draw it, select Keep Selected. This option is selected by default.

4 Click OK.

Drawing with the pen tool

The pen tool lets you create straight lines and smooth, flowing curves with great precision. For most users, it is the most powerful and flexible drawing tool in Illustrator, as it provides the best control and greatest accuracy for drawing.

Note: *As you pass the pen tool over selected anchor points or path segments, the tool changes to the add-anchor-point tool ( ) or delete-anchor-point tool ( ). You can override this capability if desired. (See "Adding, deleting, and converting anchor points" on page 74.)*

Drawing straight line paths

The simplest kind of line you can draw with the pen tool is a straight line, made by clicking the pen tool to create anchor points.

To draw straight lines with the pen tool:

1 Select the pen tool ( ).

2 Position the tip of the pen point where you want the straight line to begin, and click to define the first anchor point. The anchor point remains selected (solid) until you define the next point.

3 Click again where you want the first segment of the straight line to end. Shift-click to constrain the tool to multiples of 45 degrees.

4 Continue clicking to create additional straight segments.

The last anchor point added is always a solid square, indicating that it is selected. Previously defined anchor points become hollow squares as you add further anchor points.

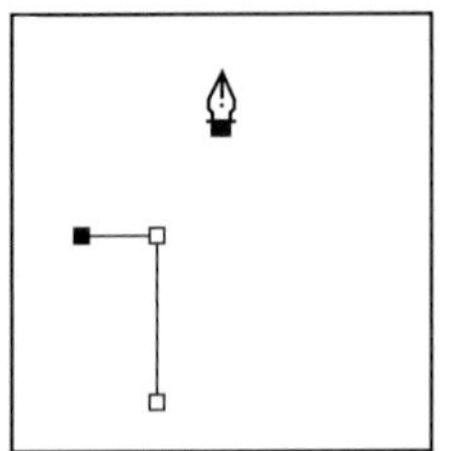
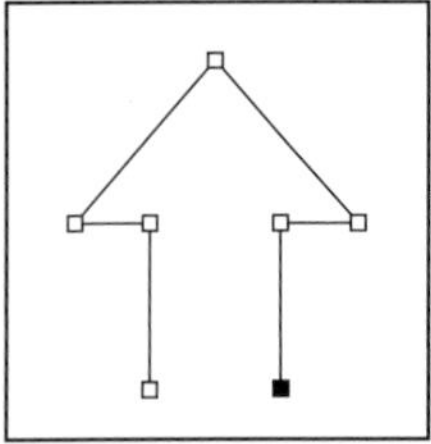

Adding straight lines to a path

To keep the last anchor point active and move its position, continue to hold down the mouse button, and then hold down the spacebar and drag the anchor point to the new position.

5 Complete the path by doing one of the following:

- To end an open path, click the pen tool. Or Ctrl-click (Windows) or Command-click (Mac OS) anywhere away from the path.

- To close a path, position the pen pointer over the first anchor point. A small loop appears next to the pen tip when it is positioned correctly. Click or drag to close the path.

- Choose Edit > Deselect All.

- Select a different tool.

About direction lines and direction points

Before you draw and modify curved lines with the pen tool, it is important to know about two elements that are associated with anchor points on curves. On curved segments, each selected anchor point displays one or two *direction lines,* ending in *direction points.* The positions of direction lines and points determine the size and shape of a curved segment. Moving these elements reshapes the curves in a path.

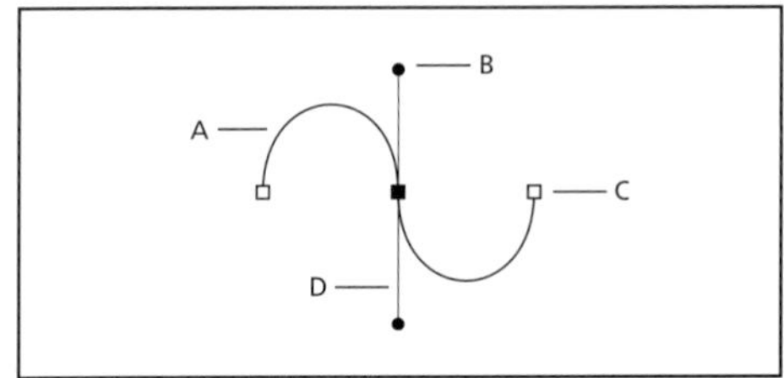

A. *Curved segment* **B.** *Direction point* **C.** *Anchor point* **D.** *Direction line*

The direction lines are always tangent to (touching) the curve at the anchor points. The slope of each direction line determines the slope of the curve, and the length of each direction line determines the height, or depth, of the curve.

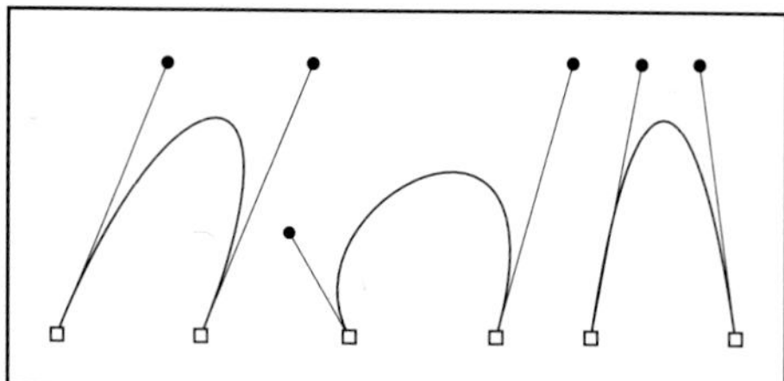

Moving direction lines changes the slope of the curve.

Continuous curved paths—that is, paths along a continuous wave shape—are connected by anchor points called *smooth points*. Noncontinuous curved paths are connected by *corner points*.

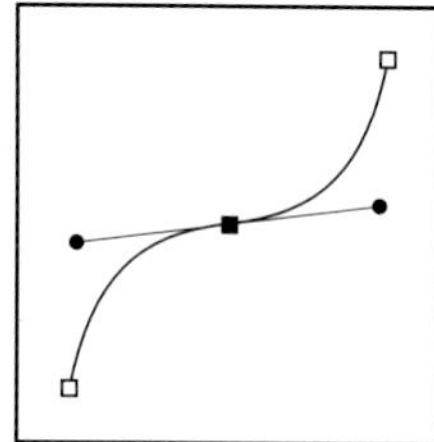

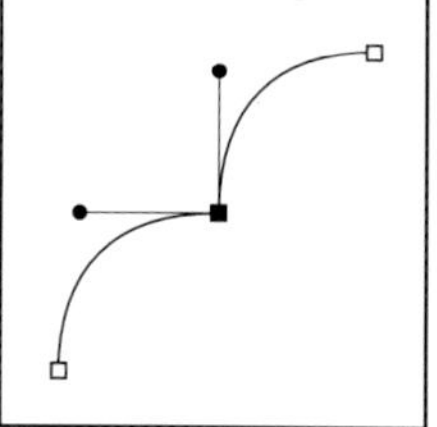

Smooth point and corner point

When you move a direction line on a smooth point, the curves on both sides of the point adjust simultaneously. In comparison, when you move a direction line on a corner point, only the curve on the same side of the point as the direction line is adjusted.

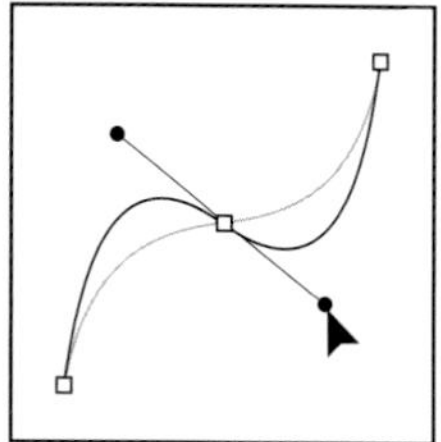

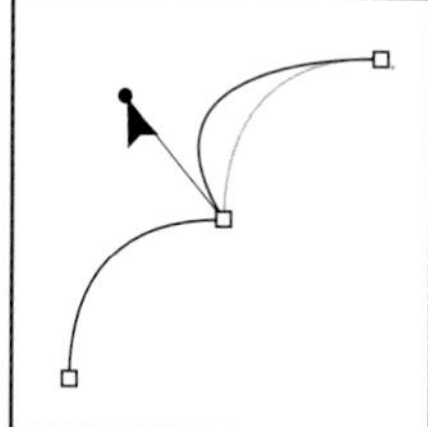

Adjusting smooth point and corner point

Drawing curved paths

You create curves by dragging the pen tool in the direction you want the curve to go.

To draw a curved path:

1 Select the pen tool ( ).

2 Position the pen tip where you want the curve to begin. Hold down the mouse button. The first anchor point appears, and the pen tip changes to an arrowhead.

3 Drag in the direction you want the curve segment to be drawn. As you drag, the pointer pulls one of two direction points. Shift-drag to constrain the tool to multiples of 45 degrees.

4 Release the mouse button.

The length and slope of the direction line determine the shape of the curve segment. You can adjust one or both sides of the direction line later.

5 Position the pointer where you want the curve segment to end, press the mouse button, and drag in the opposite direction to complete the segment. Shift-drag to constrain the tool to multiples of 45 degrees, or to the angle specified by the Constrain Angle text box in the General Preferences dialog box.

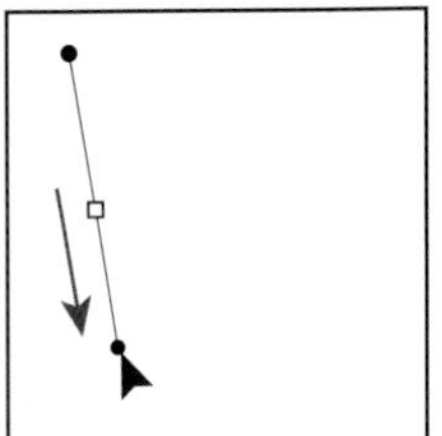

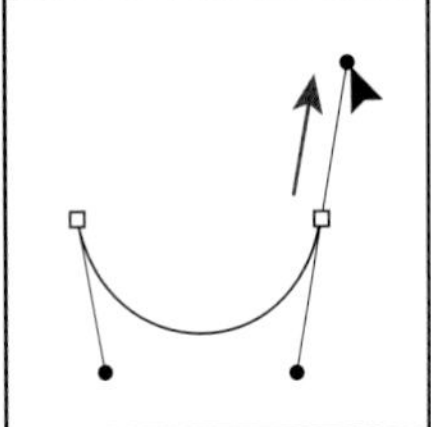

Drag in the direction of the curve to set the first anchor point. Then drag in the opposite direction to complete the curve.

6 Do one of the following:

• To draw the next segment of a continuous curve, position the pointer where you want the next segment to end, and drag away from the curve.

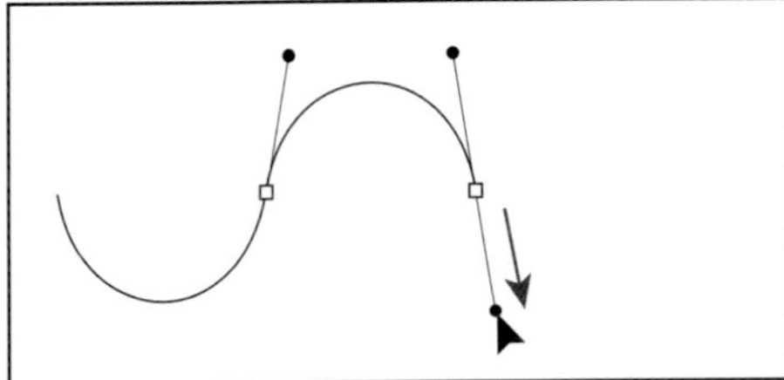

Drag away from curve to create the next segment.

• To move a segment of a curve as you draw, hold down the spacebar as you drag.

• To change the direction of a direction point, position the pointer on the direction point to move, and Alt-drag (Windows) or Option-drag (Mac OS) the anchor point.

• To change the direction of the curve sharply and create a noncontinuous curve, Alt-drag (Windows) or Option-drag (Mac OS) the direction point in the direction of the curve. Release the Alt or Option key, reposition the pointer where you want the segment to end, and drag in the opposite direction to complete the curve segment.

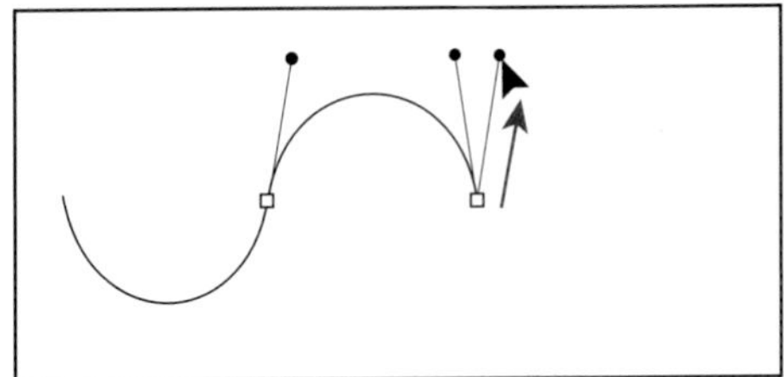

Alt-drag or Option-drag the direction point in the direction of the curve.

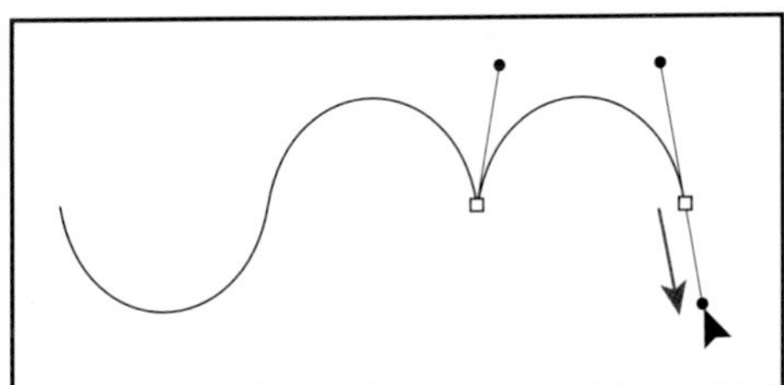

Then release the key and drag in the opposite direction.

7 Complete the path by doing one of the following (the path remains selected):

• To end an open path, click the pen tool. Or Ctrl-click (Windows) or Command-click (Mac OS) anywhere away from the path.

• To close the path, position the pointer over the first anchor point. A small loop appears next to the pointer when it is positioned correctly. Click or drag to close the path.

• Choose Edit > Deselect All.

• Select a different tool.

Tips for drawing curves

Keep the following guidelines in mind to help you draw any kind of curve quickly and easily:

• Always drag the first direction point in the direction of the bump of the curve, and drag the second direction point in the opposite direction to create a single curve. Dragging both direction points in the same direction creates an "S" curve.

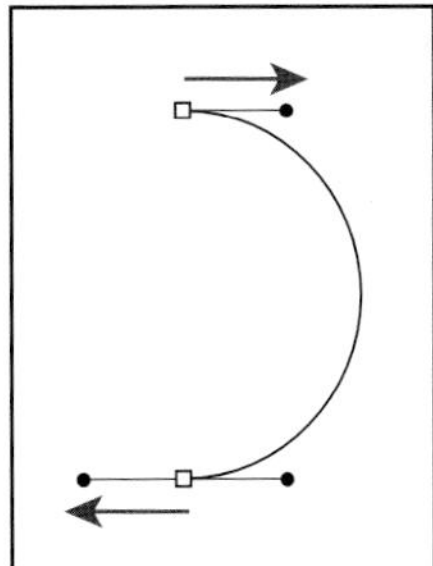

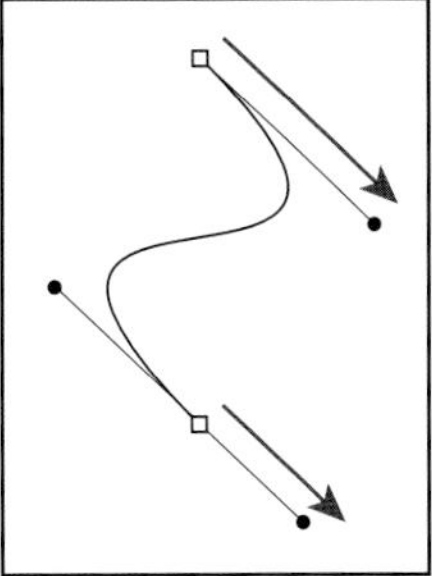

Drag in the opposite direction to create a smooth curve. Drag in the same direction to create an "S" curve.

• When drawing a series of continuous curves, draw one curve at a time, placing anchor points at the beginning and end of each curve, not at the tip of the curve. Use as few anchor points as possible, placing them as far apart as possible.

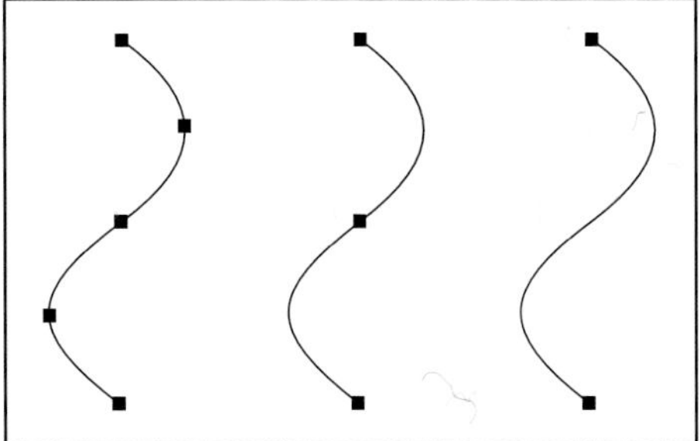

Less to more efficient curves

Adjusting path segments

You can modify the shape of a path by moving one or more of its segments or by moving the path's anchor points. To adjust a curved segment, you move the segment between the points anchoring it or you move one or more of its anchor or direction points. You can also adjust a path by converting smooth points to corner points and vice versa.

To adjust a path globally, keeping each point along the path in scale, use the reshape tool. (See "Using the reshape tool" on page 78.) This tool lets you pick points along a path and adjust all of the segments along the path by dragging a single point.

You can also adjust a portion of a path by using the pencil tool, smooth tool, or erase tool. (See "Drawing and editing freeform paths" on page 66.)

To adjust quickly a path you are drawing, hold down Ctrl (Windows) or Command (Mac OS) with the pen tool selected. Adjust the path, and then release the Ctrl or Command key to resume drawing with the pen tool.

Adding, deleting, and converting anchor points

You can add or delete anchor points on any path. Added anchor points can give you more control over the path shape. Similarly, you can delete anchor points to change the shape of a path or to simplify the path. If your path contains numerous anchor points, it's a good idea to delete any unnecessary points to reduce the complexity of the path.

When you want to add and delete individual anchor points at specific locations on a selected path segment, select the path and move the pen tool the over the path. When the pen tool is over a selected path segment, the tool changes to the add-anchor-point tool. When the pen tool is over an anchor point, the tool changes to the delete-anchor-point tool. You can also select the add-anchor-point tool or delete-anchor-point tool from the toolbox. In addition, you can temporarily override the automatic selection of the add-anchor-point or delete-anchor-point tools, or turn off the automatic selection of these tools in Preferences.

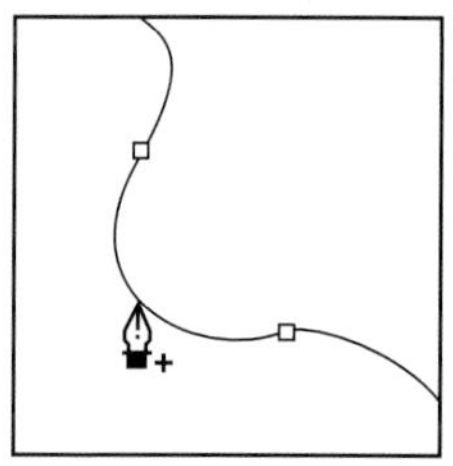
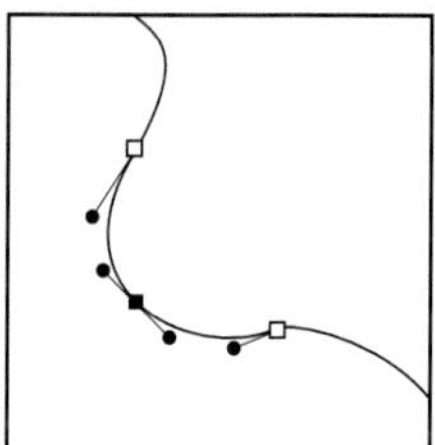

Adding anchor point

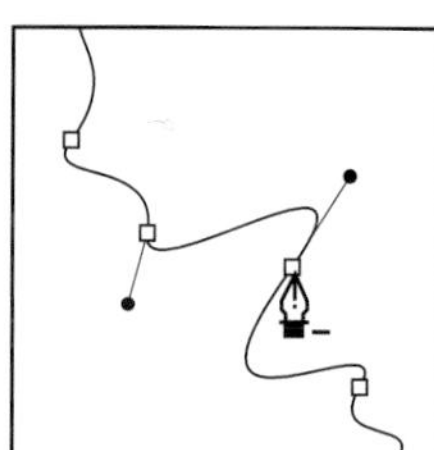
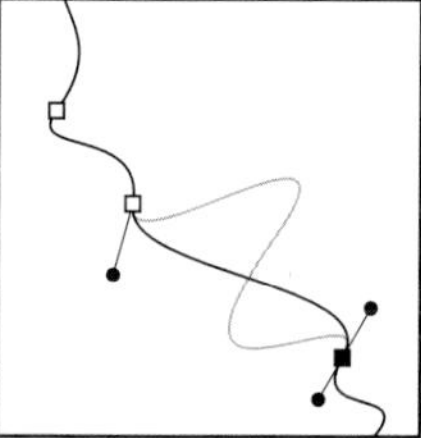

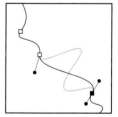

Deleting anchor point

When you want to add an anchor point between a pair of anchor points in a path, use the Add Anchor Points command in the Object menu. This command is especially useful when you intend to add effects to a path with the Punk, Bloat, and Twirl filters. Adding anchor points increases the intensity of these effects.

To add or delete an anchor point using the anchor-point tools:

1 Select the path or paths to which you want to add or delete anchor points. (See "Selecting objects" on page 113.)

2 Select the pen tool ( ), add-anchor-point tool ( ), or delete-anchor-point tool( ).

3 Do one of the following:

• To add an anchor point using either the pen tool or the add-anchor-point tool, position the pointer over a path segment and click.

• To delete an anchor point using either the pen tool or the delete-anchor-point tool, position the pointer over an anchor point and click.

To override adding or deleting anchor points:

To override the add-anchor-point or delete-anchor-point capabilities of the pen tool on-the-fly, hold down Shift as you move over the selected path or an anchor point.

To prevent Shift from constraining the path, release Shift before you release the mouse button.

To turn off automatic adding or deleting of anchor points:

1 Choose File > Preferences > General, or press Ctrl+K (Windows) or Command+K (Mac OS.)

2 Under General Options, click Disable Auto Add/Delete to turn off the option. Then click OK.

To add anchor points using the Add Anchor Points command:

With the selection tool ( ), select the object and choose Object > Path > Add Anchor Points.

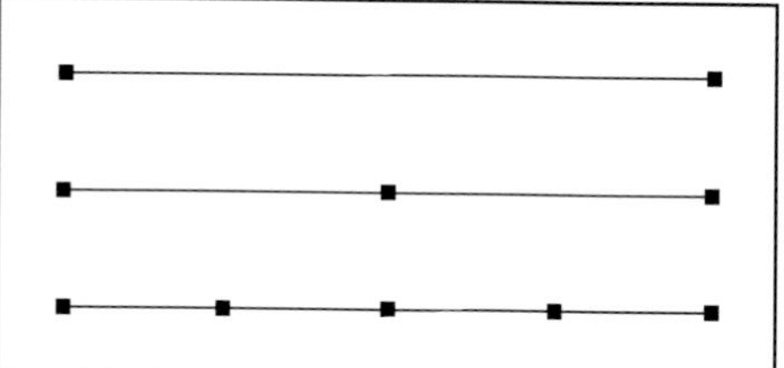

Original line, Add Anchor Points command applied once, and then twice

To convert a smooth point to a corner point, and vice versa, with the pen tool:

1 Select the pen tool ( ).

2 Position the pointer over the anchor point you want to convert and Alt-click (Windows) or Option-click (Mac OS). The pointer changes to the convert-direction-point tool ( ).

To convert a smooth point to a corner point, and vice versa, with the convert-direction-point tool:

1 Select the direct-selection tool (↖).

To switch to the convert-direction-point tool while the pen tool is selected, hold down Alt (Windows) or Option (Mac OS). With the convert-direction-point tool selected, press Ctrl (Windows) or Command (Mac OS) to use the previous selection tool.

2 Select the object and the anchor point you want to convert. (See "Selecting objects" on page 113.)

3 Select the convert-direction-point tool, or hold down Control+Alt (Windows) or Command+Option (Mac OS) while any selection tool is selected.

4 Do one of the following:

• Click a corner point and drag to create a smooth point.

• Click a smooth point, converting it into a corner point without direction lines.

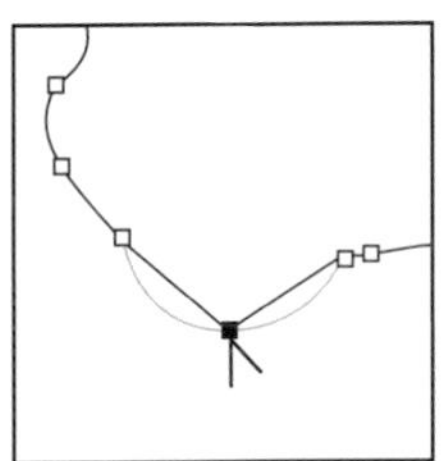
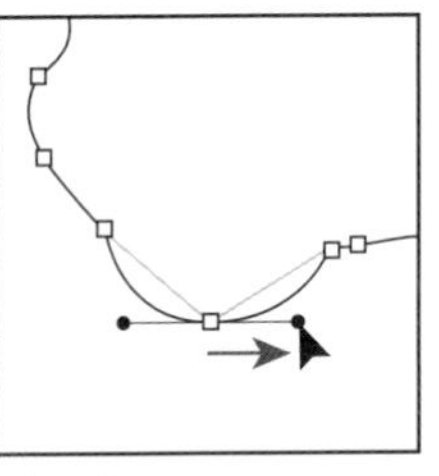

Click a point to create corner points. Drag to create a smooth point.

• Select a smooth point to display direction lines, and then Alt-drag (Windows) or Option-drag (Mac OS) a direction line to convert the segment into a corner point.

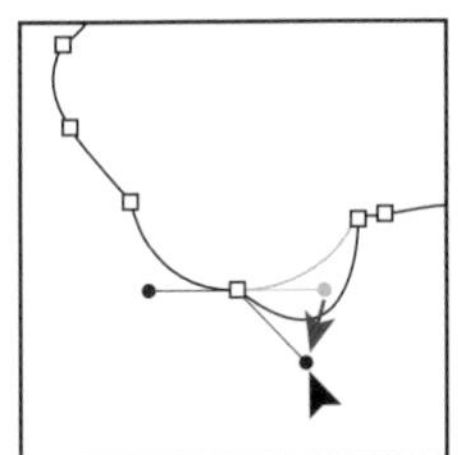

Alt/Option-drag the direction line to create a corner point.

Hiding the anchor points and edges of a selected object

When you select an object, Adobe Illustrator displays the object's anchor points and (if the object is in Preview view) outlines the path with a selection edge. When you are working with complex paths or moving selected objects, you might want to hide the anchor points and selection edges if they are obstructing your view.

The Hide Edges command makes all selection edges and anchor points invisible; however, the selected object can still be moved and manipulated.

To hide or display anchor points and selection edges:

Choose either View > Hide Edges or View > Show Edges.

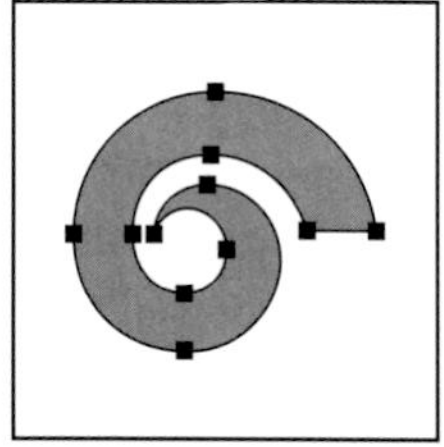

Show Edges on and Hide Edges on

Note: *You can also hide the bounding box. (See "Using the bounding box" on page 115.)*

Selecting and deleting stray points

Single, isolated anchor points make artwork unnecessarily complex and can even slow printing. Stray points can be created, for example, if you inadvertently click the pen tool in the artwork area and then choose another tool. The Stray Points command allows you to easily select unnecessary points. The Delete Stray Points option in the Cleanup Artwork dialog box finds and deletes all isolated single points in the artwork.

To select stray points:

Choose Edit > Select > Stray Points.

To delete all stray points:

1 Choose Object > Path > Cleanup.

2 Select the Delete Stray Points option, and click OK. (You can also delete any unpainted objects or any empty type paths by selecting the appropriate option in the dialog box.)

Moving and adjusting segments

Once you draw a path, you can move and adjust curved and straight segments, and adjust curves.

To move a curved segment without changing its slope:

1 Select the direct-selection tool (↖), and select the points or segments you want to move. (See "Selecting objects" on page 113.) Be sure to select both points anchoring the segment. To move a curved segment, Shift-click to select the points anchoring the curve.

2 Drag the selected anchor points or segments to their new positions. Shift-drag to constrain the tool to multiples of 45 degrees.

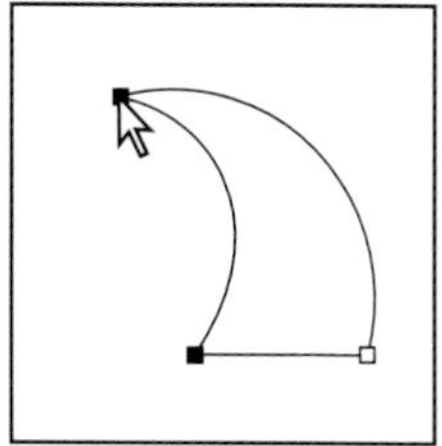

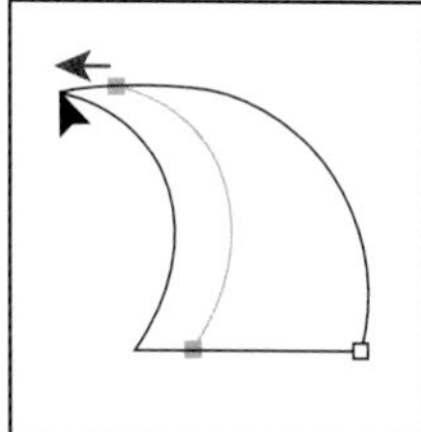

Select points anchoring curve. Then drag to move curve.

To adjust a straight segment:

1 Select the direct-selection tool, and click anywhere along the segment you want to adjust. To adjust the angle or length of the segment, select an anchor point. (See "Selecting objects" on page 113.)

2 Drag the selected segment to its new position.

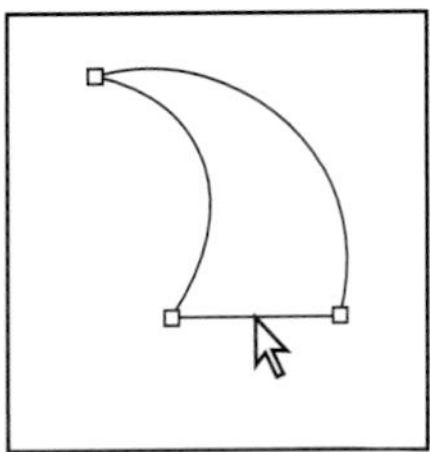
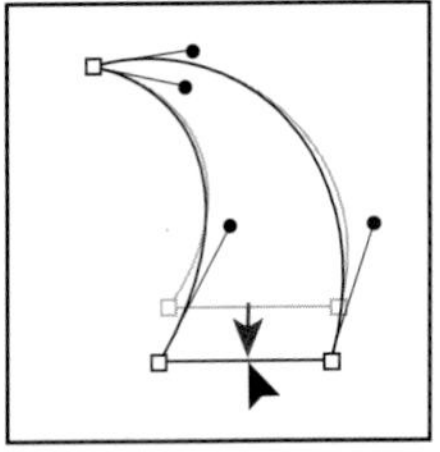

Click the straight segment. Then drag to adjust.

To adjust a curve:

1 Select the direct-selection tool, and select the curve you want to adjust. (See "Selecting objects" on page 113.) Direction lines appear for that segment.

2 Do one of the following:

• To adjust the location of the curve's anchor point, drag the anchor point.

• To adjust the position of the segment between two anchor points, drag the segment.

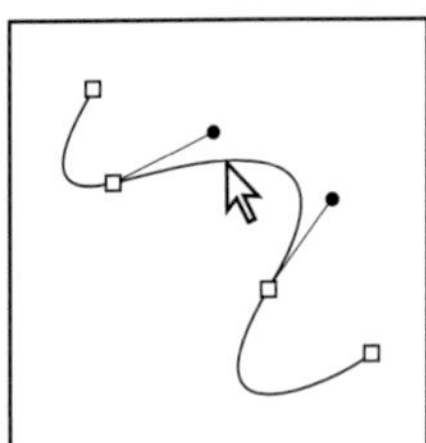
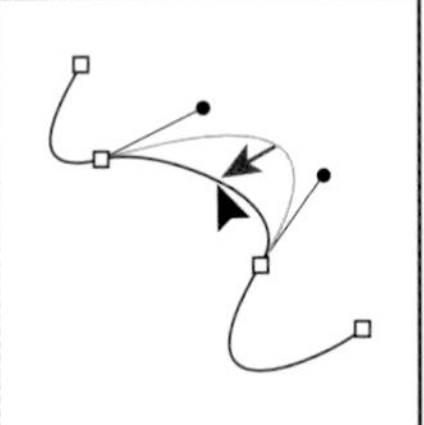

Click the curve. Then drag the segment.

• To adjust the shape of the curve on either side of the anchor point, drag the anchor point, or drag the direction point. Shift-drag to constrain the tool to multiples of 45 degrees.

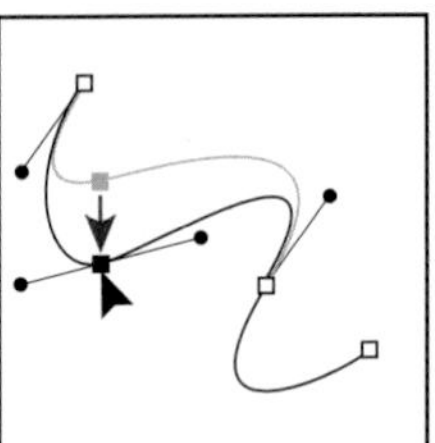
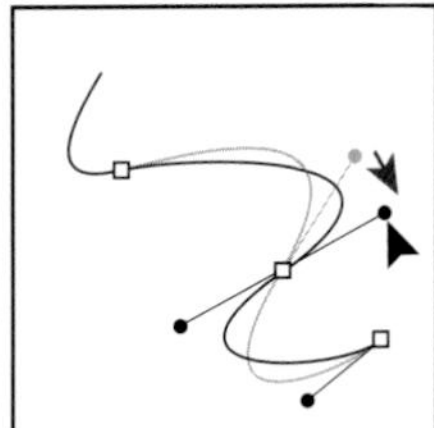

Drag the anchor point, or drag the direction point.

Using the reshape tool

The reshape tool lets you select one or more anchor points and sections of paths and then lets you adjust the selected points and paths globally. You can use the reshape tool to adjust paths containing many points while keeping the overall detail of the path intact. For example, if you have a drawing of a leaf with scallops along both edges, the reshape tool allows you to bend the leaf, keeping its overall smoothness, while retaining the scallops.

Points selected by the reshape tool are highlighted with small squares. When you drag anchor points, any paths containing regularly selected anchor points are smoothly distorted as if they were being pulled by the highlighted anchor points. Unselected anchor points remain in place.

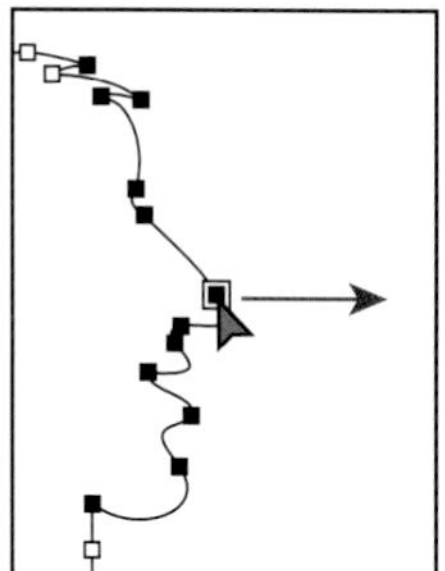
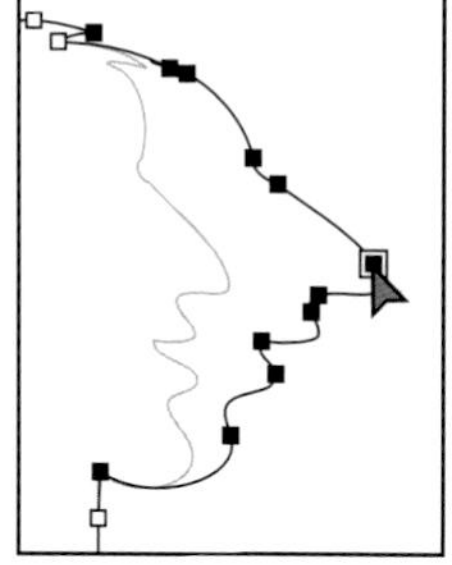

Select point with reshape tool and drag to adjust curve.

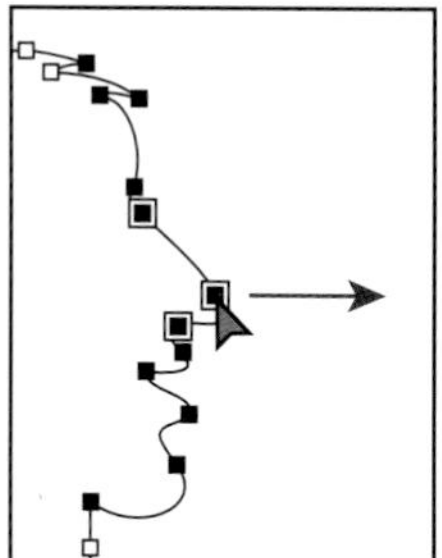
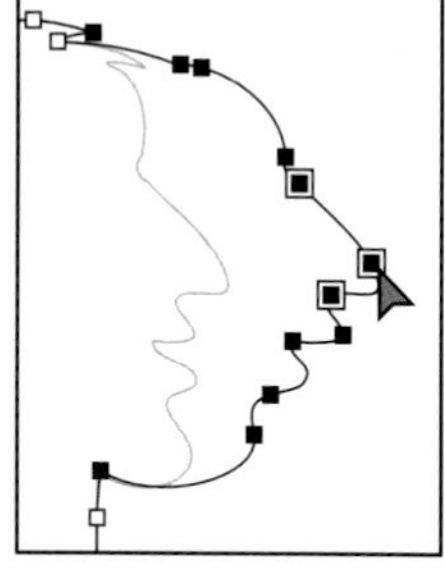

Select several points to retain shape, and drag to adjust regularly selected paths.

To adjust a path using the reshape tool:

1 Use any selection tool or drag a marquee to select the anchor points of the paths that you want to reshape. Deselect any points that you want to remain in place. (See "Selecting objects" on page 113.)

2 Select the reshape tool ( ).

3 Position the cursor over the anchor point or path segment that you want to act as a focal point (that is, a point that pulls selected path segments), and click the anchor point. If you click a path segment, a highlighted anchor point is added to the path.

4 Shift-click more anchor points or path segments to act as focal points. You can highlight an unlimited number of anchor points or path segments.

5 Drag the highlighted anchor points to adjust the path. The amount of movement of a given path segment is in proportion to its distance from a highlighted point:

- Selected points that act as the focal point move with the selection tool during dragging.
- Selected points that aren't the focal point move in proportion to the dragged focal point.
- Unselected anchor points are not affected by reshaping.

Splitting paths with the scissors tool

You may want to split paths that you have already created or that were created using the auto trace tool. Using the scissors tool, you can split an open path into two paths and split a closed path so that it becomes one or more open paths. You cannot split a type path.

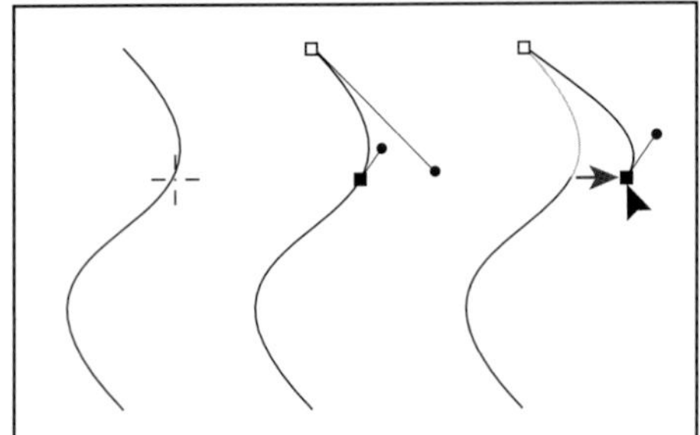

Path split with scissors tool and adjusted with direct-selection tool

To split a path and adjust it:

1 Select the path to see its current anchor points. (See "Selecting objects" on page 113.)

2 Select the scissors tool (✂).

3 Click the path where you want to split it.

When you split the path in the middle of a segment, two new endpoints are coincident (one on top of the other), and one endpoint is selected.

When you split the path at an anchor point, a new anchor point appears on top of the original anchor point, and one anchor point is selected.

4 Use the direct-selection tool (↖) to adjust the new anchor point or path segment.

Averaging anchor points

The Average command lets you move two or more anchor points to a position that is the average of their current locations.

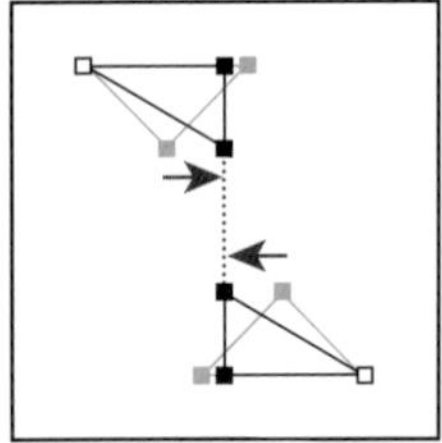

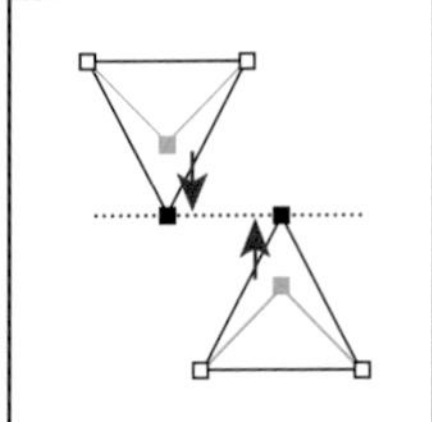

Average: Vertical applied, and Average: Horizontal applied

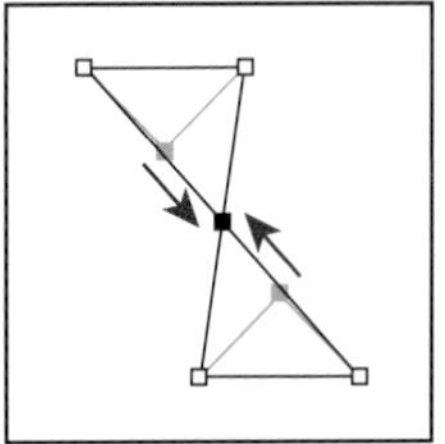

Average: Both Vertical and Horizontal applied

To average anchor points:

1 Use the direct-selection tool (↖) to select two or more anchor points. (See "Selecting objects" on page 113.)

2 Choose Object > Path > Average.

3 Choose to average along both axes, or the horizontal (x) axis only, or the vertical (y) axis only, and click OK.

To average two paths at the same time, select the two points and press Alt+Ctrl+J (Windows) or Option+Command+J (Mac OS). The selected endpoints of both paths are averaged at the midpoint of their original positions.

Joining endpoints

The Join command connects the endpoints of an open path to create a closed path or joins the endpoints of two open paths.

If you join two coincident endpoints (endpoints on top of each other), they are replaced with a single anchor point. If you join two noncoincident endpoints, a path is drawn between the two points.

To join two endpoints:

1 Use the direct-selection tool (↖) to select the endpoints. (See "Selecting objects" on page 113.) If the endpoints are coincident (on top of each other), drag a marquee through both endpoints to select them.

2 Choose Object > Path > Join. A line is drawn, joining the two endpoints.

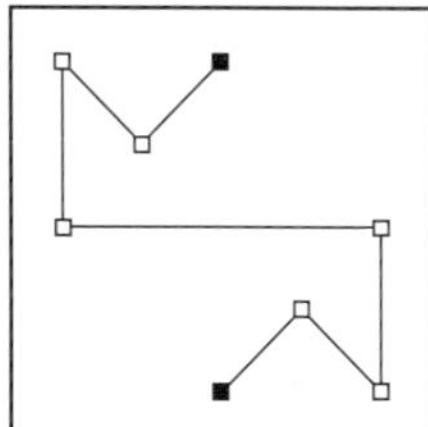
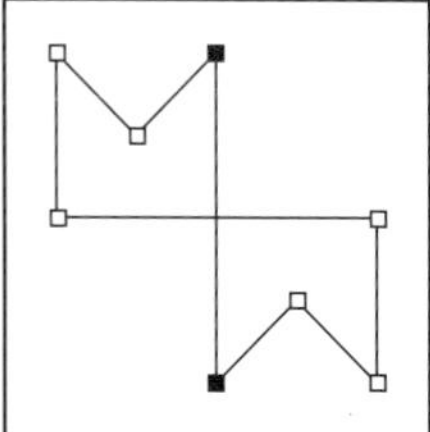

Select two noncoincident endpoints, and choose the Join command.

3 If the endpoints are coincident, select the Corner option (the default) or the Smooth option to specify the type of join you want.

4 Click OK.

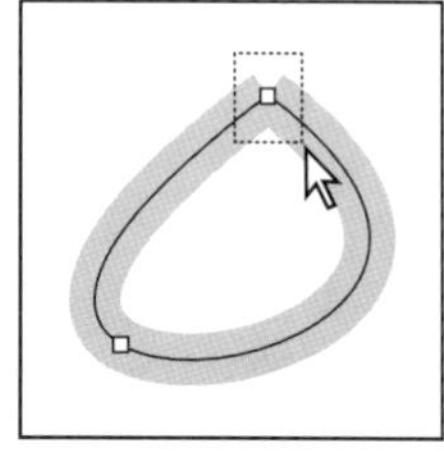
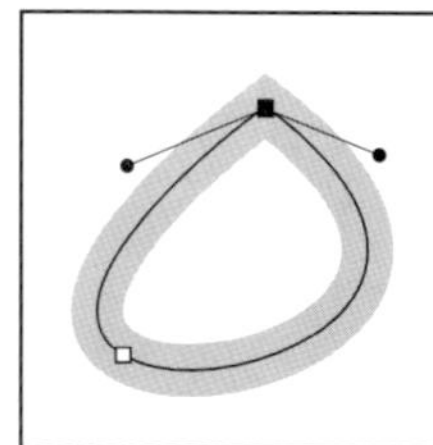

Drag a marquee through the coincident anchor points to select them, and choose the Join command.

Drawing shapes

You can create many objects in Adobe Illustrator by starting with basic shapes. The tools in Illustrator let you easily create rectangles, ellipses, polygons, spirals, and stars.

Drawing rectangles and ellipses

Adobe Illustrator provides two rectangle tools and one ellipse tool that let you quickly create these common graphic objects:

- The rectangle, rounded-rectangle, and ellipse tools let you draw rectangles (including squares) and ellipses (including circles) by dragging from one corner of the rectangle or edge of the ellipse to the opposite corner or edge.
- When a rectangle tool or the ellipse tool is selected, hold down Alt (Windows) or Option (Mac OS) to draw rectangles and ellipses by dragging from the center of the rectangle or ellipse outward.

When you create an object with a rectangle or the ellipse tool, a *center point* appears in the object. You can use this point to drag the object or to align the object with other elements in your artwork. The center point can be made visible or invisible, but it cannot be deleted.

To create a rectangle or ellipse by dragging from an edge:

1 Select the rectangle tool (□), the rounded-rectangle tool (▢), or the ellipse tool (○).

2 Position the pointer at one corner or edge of the shape you want to create, and drag diagonally until the shape is the desired size.

3 As you drag, you can do either of the following:

• To constrain the tool to multiples of 45 degrees, creating squares with the rectangle tool and circles with the ellipse tool, Shift-drag.

• To move a rectangle or ellipse as you draw it, hold down the spacebar.

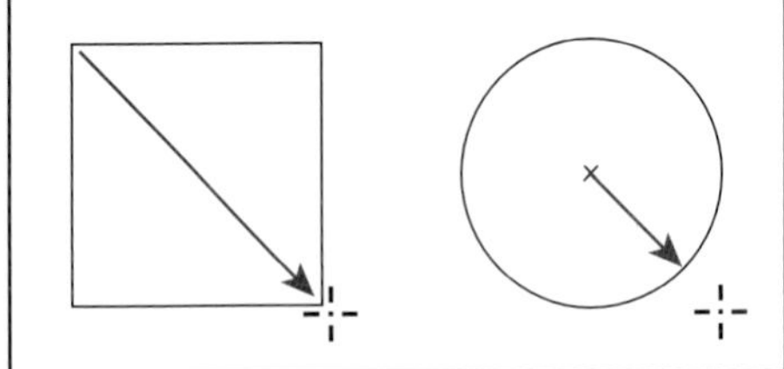

Drawing from corner and center

To adjust corners of a rounded rectangle as you draw:

1 Select the rounded-rectangle tool.

2 Position the pointer where you want the rectangle to begin, and start dragging diagonally.

3 As you drag, you can do any of the following:

• Press or hold down Up Arrow or Down Arrow to change the corner radius. When the corners are the desired roundness, release Up Arrow or Down Arrow.

• Press Left Arrow to change to the minimum radius (most angular corners).

• Press Right Arrow to change to the maximum radius (most rounded corners).

4 Continue dragging with the rectangle tool until the rectangle is the desired size.

To create a rectangle or ellipse by dragging from the center:

1 Press Alt (Windows) or Option (Mac OS) with the rectangle tool, rounded-rectangle tool, or ellipse tool selected.

2 Position the pointer where you want the center of the shape to be, and drag diagonally to any corner or edge until the shape is the desired size. Shift-drag to constrain the tool to multiples of 45 degrees.

To draw a rectangle or ellipse by specifying dimensions:

1 Select a rectangle tool or the ellipse tool.

2 Click in the artwork to set the origin from which you want to create the shape. To draw rectangles and ellipses from the center of the point of origin, Alt-click (Windows) or Option-click (Mac OS).

By default, the Rectangle and Ellipse dialog boxes display the dimensions of the last rectangle or ellipse drawn. The unit of measure is determined by the unit of measure set in the Document Setup or Units & Undo Preferences dialog box.

3 In the Width text box, enter the width you want the shape to be.

4 In the Height text box, enter the height you want the shape to be, and click OK.

To create a square or circle, enter a value in the Width text box and then click the word Height; this copies the width value to the Height text box.

If you are drawing a rounded rectangle, enter the corner radius value you want the rectangle to have. The corner radius value represents the radius of a hypothetical circle drawn in the corner of the rectangle or square. The default corner radius is 12 points. A corner radius of 0 creates square corners.

Note: *The corner style of the rectangle or square you draw is determined by the corner radius value you specify in either the Rectangle or General Preferences dialog box. Specifying a corner radius value in either dialog box updates the value in the other dialog box.*

To display or hide the center points:

1 Choose Window > Show Attributes.

2 Click either the Show Center button or Don't Show Center button.

Drawing polygons

The polygon tool draws an object with a specified number of sides of equal length, each side being the same distance from the center of the object.

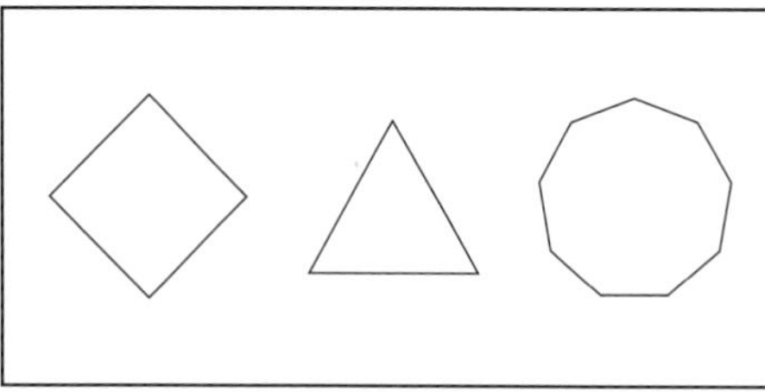

Polygons

To draw a polygon by dragging:

1 Select the polygon tool (⬡).

2 Position the pointer at the center of the polygon you want to create, and drag until the polygon is the desired size.

3 As you drag, do any of the following:

- Drag the pointer in an arc to rotate the polygon.
- Shift-drag to constrain the tool to multiples of 45 degrees or to the angle specified in the Constrain Angle text box in the General Preferences dialog box.
- Hold down the spacebar to move the polygon.
- Press or hold down Up Arrow or Down Arrow to add or delete sides to the polygon.

To draw a polygon by specifying dimensions:

1 Select the polygon tool.

2 Click where you want to place the center of the polygon.

By default, the Polygon dialog box displays the dimensions of the last polygon you drew. The unit of measure is determined by the unit of measure set in the Document Setup or Units & Undo Preferences dialog box.

3 In the Radius text box, enter the distance from the center point to each line's endpoint.

4 Click the arrows or enter the number of sides in the Sides text box, and click OK.

Drawing spirals

The spiral tool creates a spiral-shaped object of a given radius and number of winds; that is, the number of turns that the spiral completes from start to finish.

Spirals

To draw a spiral by dragging:

1 Select the spiral tool (◎).

2 Position the pointer at the center of the spiral you want to create, and drag until the spiral is the desired size.

3 As you drag, you can do any of the following:

- Drag the pointer in an arc to rotate the spiral.
- Shift-drag to constrain the tool to multiples of 45 degrees or to the angle specified in the Constrain Angle text box in the General Preferences dialog box.
- Hold down the spacebar to move the spiral.
- Press or hold down Up Arrow or Down Arrow to add or delete winds.

To draw a spiral by specifying dimensions:

1 Select the spiral tool, and click where you want to place the center of the spiral.

By default, the Spiral dialog box displays the dimensions of the last spiral you drew. The unit of measure is determined by the unit of measure set in the Document Setup or Units & Undo Preferences dialog box.

2 In the Radius text box, enter the distance from the center to the outermost point in the spiral.

3 In the Decay text box, enter the amount by which each wind of the spiral should decrease relative to the previous wind.

4 Click the arrows or enter the number of segments in the Segments text box. Each full wind of the spiral consists of four segments.

5 For Style, select the counterclockwise or clockwise option to specify the direction of the spiral, and click OK.

Drawing stars

The star tool creates a star-shaped object with a given number of points and size.

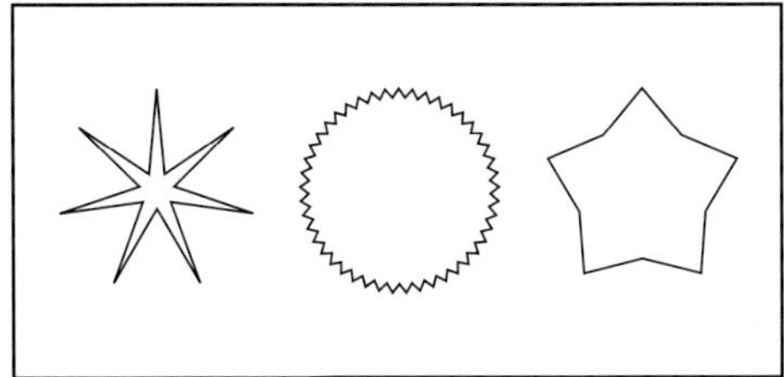

Stars

To draw a star by dragging:

1 Select the star tool (☆).

2 Position the pointer at the center of the star you want to create, and drag until the star is the desired size.

3 As you drag, you can do any of the following:

- Drag the pointer in an arc to rotate the star.
- Shift-drag to constrain the tool to multiples of 45 degrees.
- Hold down Ctrl (Windows) or Command (Mac OS) to hold the inner radius constant.
- Hold down Alt (Windows) or Option (Mac OS) to keep the sides of the star straight.
- Hold down the spacebar to move the star.
- Press or hold down Up Arrow or Down Arrow to add or delete sides to the star.

To draw a star by specifying dimensions:

1 Select the star tool.

2 Click where you want to place the center of the star. By default, the Star dialog box displays the dimensions of the last star you drew. The unit of measure is determined by the unit of measure set in the Document Setup or Units & Undo Preferences dialog box.

3 In the Radius 1 text box, enter the distance from the center to the innermost points.

4 In the Radius 2 text box, enter the distance from the center to the outermost points.

5 Click the arrows or enter the number of sides to the star in the Points text box, and click OK.

Drawing and editing brushed paths

The Brushes palette in Illustrator contains four brush types—Calligraphic, Scatter, Art, and Pattern brushes—to use in adding art to paths. You can choose from the brush effects that have been preloaded into the Brushes palette. You can also modify these brushes, create brushes, or import a brush from the Brush Libraries to the Brushes palette.

Brushes that you create and store in the Brushes palette are associated only with the current file. Each Illustrator file can have a different set of brushes in its Brushes palette.

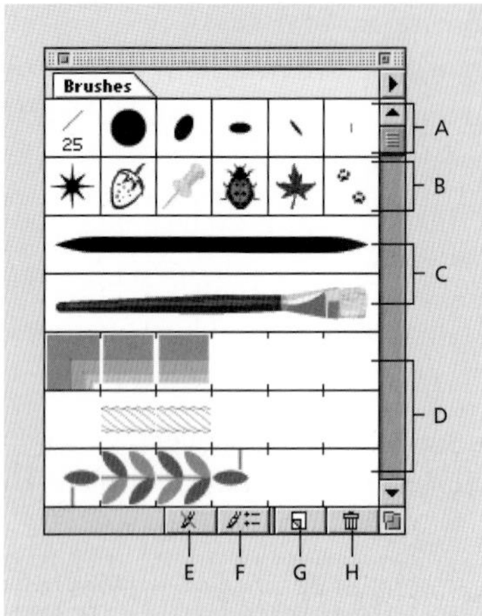

A. Calligraphic brushes ***B.*** *Scatter brushes*
C. Art brushes ***D.*** *Pattern brushes*
E. Remove Brush Stroke button
F. Options of Selected Object button
G. New Brush button ***H.*** *Delete Brush button*

You can achieve the following effects using the four brush types:

- Calligraphic brushes create strokes that resemble strokes drawn with the angled point of a calligraphic pen, drawn along the center of the path.
- Scatter brushes disperse copies of an object (such as a ladybug or a leaf) along the path.
- Art brushes stretch an object or artwork (such as an arrow or dog bone) evenly along the length of the path.
- Pattern brushes paint a pattern—made of individual *tiles*—that repeats along the path. Pattern brushes can include up to five tiles, for the sides, inner corner, outer corner, beginning, and end of the pattern.

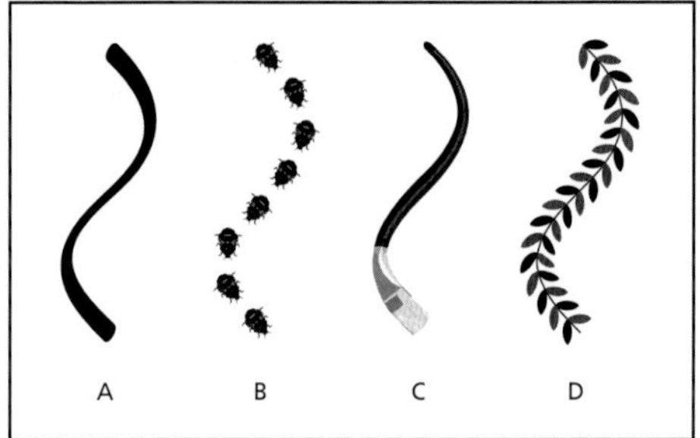

A. *Calligraphic brush* ***B.*** *Scatter brush* ***C.*** *Art brush*
D. *Pattern brush*

You draw brushed paths by selecting a brush in the Brushes palette and drawing a path with the paintbrush tool, or by creating a path using one of the Illustrator drawing tools (including the pen, pencil, or basic shapes tools) and then stroking the path with a brush from the Brushes palette.

You can edit a brushed path and retain the brush effect by using the paintbrush tool. You can also modify the path using any Illustrator path editing tool, including the pen, pencil, smooth, or erase tools. (See "Drawing and editing freeform paths" on page 66. Also see "Adjusting path segments" on page 73.)

Drawing a brushed path with the paintbrush tool

The paintbrush tool creates paths painted with a brush selected in the Brushes palette. You must select a brush in the Brushes palette to use the paintbrush tool.

You can set preferences for the paintbrush tool, which affect paths of any brush type that are drawn with the paintbrush tool. You can also draw closed paths with the paintbrush tool to apply further modifications to the brushed object, such as a fill color.

To draw a path with the paintbrush tool:

1 Choose Window > View Brushes to display the Brushes palette.

2 Select a brush from the Brushes palette.

3 Select the paintbrush tool ( ). The pointer changes to a paintbrush when you move it to the active window.

4 Position the tip of the paintbrush where you want the path to begin.

5 Drag the paintbrush to draw the path. By default, the path is selected when you release the mouse button.

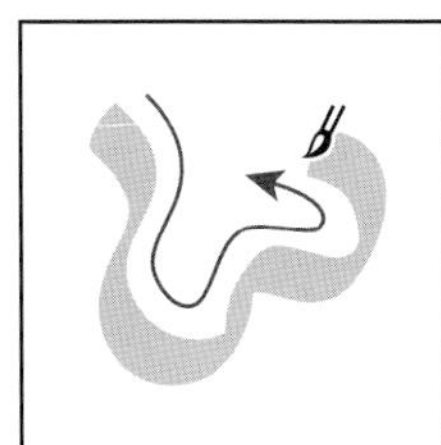
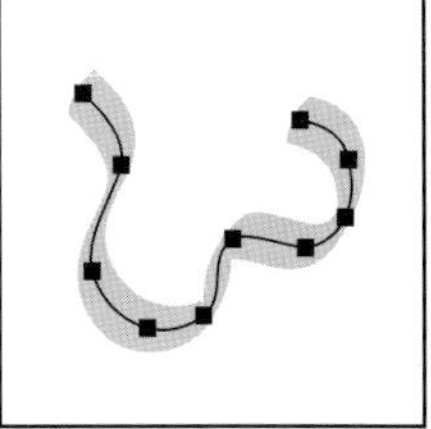

Dragging the paintbrush tool, with a Calligraphic brush

To set preferences for the paintbrush tool:

1 Double-click the paintbrush tool.

2 Set preferences for the paintbrush tool:

• In the Smoothness text box, enter a value (0% to 100%) for the percentage stroke and curve smoothness, or use the slider. The higher the value, the smoother the stroke or curve.

• In the Fidelity text box, enter the number of pixels (from 0.5 to 20) for the number of pixels the stroke can stray from the path to produce smooth curves, or use the slider. The higher the value, the smoother the stroke or curve.

• Select Fill New Brush Strokes to have paths drawn by the brush filled. When the option is unselected, paths are unfilled.

• Select Keep Selected to keep the path just drawn with the brush selected.

3 Click OK.

To draw a closed path with the paintbrush tool:

1 Select the paintbrush tool.

2 Position the pointer where you want the path to begin, and start dragging to draw a path.

3 As you drag, hold down Alt (Windows) or Option (Mac OS). The paintbrush tool displays a small loop to indicate drawing a closed path.

4 When the path is the size and shape you want, release the mouse button (but not the Alt or Option key). After the path closes, release the Alt or Option key.

To edit a brushed path with the paintbrush tool:

1 Select the path to edit with the selection tool (↖), or Ctrl-click (Windows) or Command-click (Mac OS) the path to select it.

2 Position the paintbrush tool on or near the path to redraw, and drag the tool until the path is the desired shape.

Creating a brushed path with a drawing tool

You can create a brushed path from any path created with an Illustrator drawing tool, including the pen or pencil tool or any of the basic shapes tools. You can then edit the brushed path as you would any path drawn with the tools.

To draw a brushed path with a drawing tool:

1 Draw a path using a drawing tool, including the pen or pencil tool or a basic shape tool.

2 Choose a method for applying a brush to the path:

• Select the path that is to be brushed. In the Brushes palette, select a brush with which to brush the path.

• Drag a brush from the Brushes palette onto a path.

Note: To preserve brush stroke options previously applied to the object when applying a new brush, Alt-click (Windows) or Option-click (Mac OS) the new brush.

Modifying brush attributes

You can change brush attributes by dragging a brush from the Brushes palette into your artwork, modifying the brush, and dragging the brush back to the palette. You can also change brush attributes for selected objects only and leave other objects painted with the brush unchanged.

In addition, you can modify brush options by using the Brush Options dialog box. See “Setting brush options” on page 91.

To modify brushes by dragging into your artwork:

1 Select a brush from the Brushes palette.

2 Drag the brush into your artwork.

3 Make the changes you want.

4 Drag the modified brush into the Brushes palette.

To change options of a selected object without changing the brush attributes for all objects:

1 Select a brush in the artwork.

2 Choose Options of Selected Object from the Brushes palette menu, or click the Options of Selected Object button.

3 Change the options, and click OK. Only the selected objects are changed with the new options. Any other objects in the artwork that were painted with the brush remain with the original brush attributes. Attributes of the brush are not affected; the next time you use the brush, it uses the current attributes.

***Note:** To reset changed objects to the original brush options, select the objects, apply a different brush to them, and then reapply the original brush.*

Modifying brushed paths

After you have applied a brush to a path, you can modify the attributes of the path in several ways. You can convert the brush to a set of masked objects, using the Expand command. You can also remove the brush from a path, to replace the brushed path with a stroked path.

To convert brushes in artwork to masked objects:

1 Select the object or objects to convert.

2 Choose Object > Expand.

3 Select Stroke, and click OK.

To remove a brush from a path:

1 Select the path to change.

2 Do one of the following:

• In the Brushes palette menu, choose Remove Brush Strokes, or click the Remove Brush Strokes button.

• In the toolbox or the Color palette, click the Stroke box and apply a stroke of None.

The brush is removed and the path remains.

Using the Brushes palette

You can use the Brushes palette to create and to organize your brushes.

Creating brushes

You can create each of the four types of brushes in the Brushes palette.

To create an Art or Scatter brush, you use artwork from an illustration to define the brush. To create a Pattern brush, you can use Pattern swatches in the Swatches palette or artwork from an illustration to define the tiles in the brush. When using swatches to define a Pattern brush, you can use preloaded Pattern swatches, or create your own Pattern swatches. See "Creating and working with patterns" on page 200 for information on creating artwork to use as pattern tiles.

All brushes must be made up of simple open and closed path vectors. Brushes cannot have patterns, gradients, blends, other brush strokes, gradient meshes, bitmap images, graphs, placed files, or masks.

Art brushes and Pattern brushes cannot include type. However, to achieve a brush stroke effect with type, create an outline of the type and then apply a brush stroke to the outline. (See "Modifying letterforms as graphic objects" on page 272.)

To create a Calligraphic brush:

1 Click the New Brush button in the Brushes palette, or choose New Brush from the palette menu.

2 Select New Calligraphic Brush and click OK.

3 Follow the instructions in "Setting Calligraphic brush options" on page 92 to set options for the brush.

To create an Art or Scatter brush:

1 Create or display the artwork that you want to use as an Art or Scatter brush.

2 Select the artwork to be used as a brush.

3 Click the New Brush button in the Brushes palette, or choose New Brush from the palette menu.

4 Select New Art Brush or New Scatter Brush and click OK.

5 Follow the instructions in "Setting Scatter brush options" on page 93 or "Setting Art brush options" on page 94 to set options for the brush.

To create a Pattern brush using Pattern swatches in the Swatches palette:

1 Click the New Brush button in the Brushes palette, or choose New Brush from the palette menu.

2 Select New Pattern Brush and click OK.

3 In the Name text box, enter a name for the brush (up to 30 characters).

4 Follow the instructions in "Setting Pattern brush options" on page 95 to set options for the brush.

To create a Pattern brush using artwork from an illustration:

1 Create or display the artwork that you want to use as a Pattern brush. (See "Creating and working with patterns" on page 200. Make sure to create artwork for each of the tiles in the Pattern brush, up to five tiles depending on the brush configuration desired.)

2 In the Brushes palette, make sure the brushes are displayed by icon. (If necessary, choose View By Name from the palette menu to deselect name view.)

3 Drag the artwork to be used as the Side tile onto the Brushes palette.

4 Select New Pattern Brush, then click OK.

5 Alt-drag (Windows) or Option-drag (Mac OS) artwork for additional tiles onto the appropriate tile buttons to define additional tiles as needed. For example, Alt/Option-drag artwork onto the Outer Corner tile button and Inner Corner tile button to define those tiles respectively.

6 Follow the instructions in steps 6–12 in "Setting Pattern brush options" on page 95 to set Size, Orientation, Fit, and Color options for the brush.

Managing brushes

You can use the Brushes palette to determine which brushes are displayed and how they are displayed. You can also move, duplicate, and delete brushes in the palette.

To display brushes by name:

1 Choose Window > Show Brushes.

2 Choose View By Name from the Brushes palette menu. A picture of the brush displays to the left of the name. The picture to the right of the name indicates the brush type.

To modify the type of brushes displayed:

1 Choose Window > Show Brushes.

2 From the Brushes palette menu, choose the type of brush to display in the palette. You can choose more than one brush.

To select all brushes not currently used in the file:

1 Choose Window > Show Brushes.

2 Choose Select All Unused from the Brushes palette menu. Only brushes that are not currently used in the active file are selected.

To move a brush in the Brushes palette:

Drag a brush to the new location in the Brushes palette. You can move brushes only within their type. (For example, you cannot move a Calligraphic brush to the Scatter brush area.)

To duplicate a brush in the Brushes palette:

1 Select a brush to duplicate. To select multiple brushes, Ctrl-click (Windows) or Command-click (Mac OS) each brush to duplicate. To select a range of brushes, Shift-click to define the range.

2 Do one of the following:

• Choose Duplicate Brush from the Brushes palette menu.

• Drag the selection to the New Brush button in the Brushes palette.

To delete a brush from the Brushes palette:

1 In the Brushes palette, select the brush to delete. To select multiple brushes, Ctrl-click (Windows) or Command-click (Mac OS) each brush to delete. To select a range of brushes, Shift-click to define the range.

2 Do one of the following:

• Choose Delete Brush from the Brushes palette menu.

• Click the Delete Brush button in the Brushes palette.

• Drag the selection to the Delete Brush button in the Brushes palette.

Setting brush options

You can choose brush options to modify existing brushes in the Brushes palette, or to define new brushes you create. (See "Creating brushes" on page 89.) Each type of brush has a different set of options.

When you change the options of a brush, you can apply the changes to brush strokes already drawn in the artwork with the brush, or apply the changes to new strokes only. You can also change the brush stroke options of a selected object without affecting other objects in the artwork and without changing the brush's attributes by choosing Options of Selected Object from the Brushes palette menu.

Setting Calligraphic brush options

You can change the angle, roundness, and diameter of strokes painted with Calligraphic brushes.

To set options for a Calligraphic brush:

1 Choose a method to display the Calligraphic Brush Options dialog box:

• To display the dialog box for an existing Calligraphic brush, double-click the brush in the Brushes palette or select the brush and choose Brush Options from the palette menu.

• To display the dialog box for a new brush, create the brush as described in "Creating brushes" on page 89.

2 In the Name text box, enter a name for the brush (up to 30 characters).

3 Specify values for the angle, roundness, and diameter of the brush (the preview in the dialog box reflects your settings):

• To set the ellipse angle of rotation, drag the arrowhead in the preview, or enter a value in the Angle text box.

• To set the roundness, drag a black dot in the preview away from or toward the center, or enter a value in the Roundness text box. The higher the value, the greater the roundness.

• To set the diameter, use the Diameter slider, or enter a value in the Diameter text box.

4 From each pop-up menu, choose the way in which you want to control variations in the angle, roundness, and diameter:

• Choose Fixed to use the value in the associated text box. For example, when the Diameter value is 20, Fixed always uses 20 for the brush diameter.

• Choose Random to use a random value within a specified range. When you choose Random, you also need to enter a value in the Variation text box, or use the Variation slider, to specify the range by which the brush characteristic can vary. For each stroke, Random uses any value between that in the text box for the brush characteristic plus or minus the Variation value. For example, when the Diameter value is 15 and the Variation value is 5, the diameter can be 10, or 20, or any value in between.

• Choose Pressure (if you will use the brush with a graphics tablet) to use a value determined by the pressure of your stylus. When you choose Pressure, you also need to enter a value in the Variation text box, or use the Variation slider. Pressure uses the value in the text box for the brush characteristic minus the Variation value for the lightest tablet pressure. It uses the value in the text box for the brush characteristic plus the Variation value for the heaviest pressure. For example, when the Roundness value is 75% and the Variation value is 25%, the lightest stroke is 50% and the heaviest stroke is 100%. The lighter the pressure, the more angular the brush stroke.

5 To preview the effect of your choices on artwork, select Preview.

6 Click OK.

7 If you are modifying a brush used previously in the artwork, choose an option for applying changes to the pre-existing strokes:

• Click Apply To Strokes to change pre-existing strokes. (The modified brush will be applied to new strokes as well.)

• Click Leave Strokes to leave pre-existing strokes unchanged, and apply the modified brush to new strokes only.

Setting Scatter brush options

You can change the size, spacing, scatter pattern, and rotation of objects painted on a path with Scatter brushes.

To set options for a Scatter brush:

1 Choose a method to display the Scatter Brush Options dialog box:

• To display the dialog box for an existing Scatter brush, double-click the brush in the Brushes palette or select the brush and choose Brush Options from the palette menu.

• To display the dialog box for a new brush, create the brush as described in "Creating brushes" on page 89.

2 In the Name text box, enter a name for the brush (up to 30 characters).

3 Drag each Minimum slider or enter a value in each leftmost text box for the brush's size, spacing, scattering, and angle of rotation:

• Size controls the size of the objects.

• Spacing controls the amount of space between objects.

• Scatter controls how closely objects follow the path independently on each side of the path. The higher the value, the farther the objects are from the path.

• Rotation controls the angle of rotation of the objects.

4 From each pop-up menu, choose the way in which you want to control variations in the size, spacing, scattering, and rotation:

• Choose Fixed to use the value in the associated text box. For example, when the Scatter value is 50%, Fixed always uses 50% to scatter objects along the path.

• Choose Random to use a random value. When you choose Random, you also need to enter a value in the rightmost text box, or use the Maximum slider, to specify the range by which the brush characteristic can vary. For each stroke, Random uses any value between the Minimum and the Maximum value. For example, when the Minimum value is 50% and the Maximum value is 100% for Size, the objects' sizes can be 50%, or 100%, or any size in between.

• Choose Pressure (if you will use the brush with a graphics tablet) to use a value determined by the pressure of your stylus. When you choose Pressure, you also need to enter a value in the rightmost text box, or use the Maximum slider. Pressure uses the Minimum value for the lightest tablet pressure and the Maximum value for the heaviest pressure. The heavier the stroke, the larger the objects.

Note: *To keep the same range of values between the two sliders, Shift-drag the sliders. To move the sliders an equal value apart or together, Alt-drag (Windows) or Option-drag (Mac OS) them.*

5 Choose a relative orientation from the Rotation Relative To pop-up menu:

• For Page, the angle of rotation of scattered objects is relative to the page (0 degrees points to the top).

• For Path, the angle of rotation of scattered objects is relative to the path (0 degrees is tangent to the path).

6 Choose a method of colorization from the Method pop-up menu. (See "Choosing a colorization method" on page 97.)

7 To preview the effect of your choices on artwork, select Preview.

8 Click OK.

9 If you are modifying a brush used previously in the artwork, choose an option for applying changes to the pre-existing strokes:

• Click Apply To Strokes to change pre-existing strokes. (The modified brush will be applied to new strokes as well.)

• Click Leave Strokes to leave pre-existing strokes unchanged, and apply the modified brush to new strokes only.

To reset Random options for Scatter brushes:

1 Select the Scatter brush in the artwork.

2 Choose Options of Selected Object from the Brushes palette menu, or click the Options of Selected Object button.

3 Make sure at least one brush characteristic is set to Random.

4 Click the Randomize button. (To see the effect of your changes on artwork, select Preview.) Click OK.

Setting Art brush options

You can change the direction and size of objects painted along a path with Art brushes, and also flip the objects along the path or across the path.

To set options for an Art brush:

1 Choose a method to display the Art Brush Options dialog box:

• To display the dialog box for an existing Art brush, double-click the brush in the Brushes palette or select the brush and choose Brush Options from the palette menu.

• To display the dialog box for a new brush, create the brush as described in "Creating brushes" on page 89.

2 In the Name text box, enter a name for the brush (up to 30 characters).

3 For Direction, click a button for the direction in which you want the art to be drawn as you drag the paintbrush. In each button, the arrowhead represents the end of the brush stroke.

When you drag the paintbrush in the artwork window, the art is drawn as follows:

- For (←), the left side of the art is the end of the stroke.
- For (→), the right side of the art is the end of the stroke.
- For (↑), the top of the art is the end of the stroke.
- For (↓), the bottom of the art is the end of the stroke.

4 For Size, enter a percentage by which to scale the art in the Width text box. To preserve the proportion, select Proportional.

5 To change the orientation of the art on the path, choose Flip Along or Flip Across.

6 Choose a method of colorization from the Method pop-up menu. (See "Choosing a colorization method" on page 97.)

7 To preview the effect of your choices on artwork, select Preview.

8 Click OK.

9 If you are modifying a brush used previously in the artwork, choose an option for applying changes to the pre-existing strokes:

- Click Apply To Strokes to change pre-existing strokes. (The modified brush will be applied to new strokes as well.)
- Click Leave Strokes to leave pre-existing strokes unchanged, and apply the modified brush to new strokes only.

Setting Pattern brush options

You can change the size, spacing, and orientation of pattern brushes. In addition, you can apply new artwork to any of the tiles in a pattern brush to redefine the brush.

To apply new art to tiles in existing pattern brushes, you select pattern swatches from the scroll list in the Pattern Brush Options dialog box. (The scroll list displays all the Pattern swatches available in the Swatches palette.)

If you want to apply new swatches to a Pattern brush, follow the instructions in "Creating brushes" on page 89. For information on creating new Pattern swatches in the Swatches palette, see "Creating and working with patterns" on page 200.

To set options for a Pattern brush:

1 Choose a method to display the Pattern Brush Options dialog box:

- To display the dialog box for an existing Pattern brush, double-click the brush in the Brushes palette or select the brush and choose Brush Options from the palette menu.
- To display the dialog box for a new brush, create the brush as described in "Creating brushes" on page 89.

2 In the Name text box, enter a name for the brush (up to 30 characters).

3 Click a tile button for the tile you want to define. For example, to define the side tile, click the Side tile button.

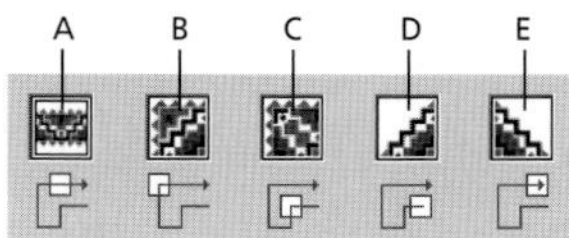

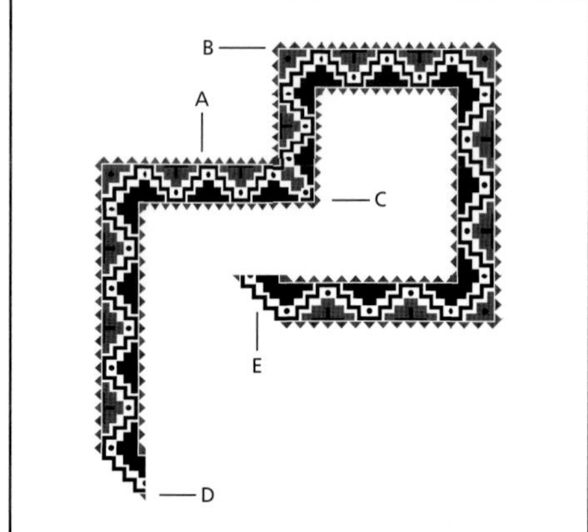

A. Side tile B. Outer Corner tile C. Inner Corner tile D. Start tile E. End tile

4 In the scroll list, select a Pattern swatch to apply to the selected tile.

The selected swatch appears in the selected tile button.

***Note:** To restore a pattern setting to its original value when modifying an existing Pattern brush, select Original from the scroll list.*

5 Repeat steps 3 and 4 to apply Pattern swatches to other tiles as needed.

6 For Size, enter values for the scale (which preserves the proportion) and the spacing between tiles.

Scaled pattern tiles

7 To change the orientation of the pattern on the path, choose Flip Along or Flip Across.

Tile position flipped along and flipped across the path

8 For Fit, choose how to fit the tiles on the path:

• Stretch to Fit lengthens or shortens the pattern tile to fit the object. This option can result in uneven tiling.

• Add Space to Fit adds blank space between each pattern tile to apply the pattern proportionally to the path.

• Approximate Path (for rectangular paths only) fits tiles to the closest approximate path without changing the tiles. This option applies the pattern slightly inside or outside the path, rather than centered on the path, to maintain even tiling.

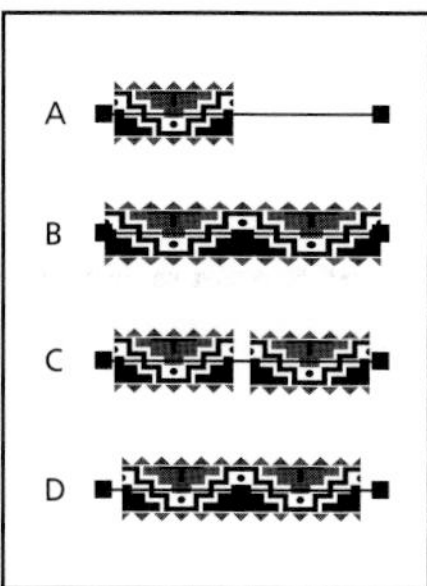

A. Default tile and Fit options
B. Stretch to Fit C. Add Space to Fit
D. Approximate Path

9 Choose a method of colorization from the Method pop-up menu. (See "Choosing a colorization method" on page 97.)

10 To preview the effect of your choices on artwork, select Preview.

11 Click OK.

12 If you are modifying a brush used previously in the artwork, choose an option for applying changes to the pre-existing strokes:

• Click Apply To Strokes to change pre-existing strokes. (The modified brush will be applied to new strokes as well.)

• Click Leave Strokes to leave pre-existing strokes unchanged, and apply the modified brush to new strokes only.

***Note:** After you define a Pattern brush with Pattern swatches, you can delete the Pattern swatches from the Swatches palette if you don't plan to use them for additional artwork.*

Choosing a colorization method

For Scatter, Art, and Pattern brushes, you can choose a method by which to colorize a brush.

For a color illustration showing colorization methods, see figure 4-1 on page 229

To choose a colorization method:

1 With the options dialog box for the selected brush type open, choose an option from the Method pop-up menu:

• None displays colors as they appear in the brush in the Brushes palette. Choose None to keep a brush the same colors as in the Brushes palette.

• Tints displays the brush stroke in tints of the stroke color. Portions of the art that are black become the stroke color, portions that aren't black become tints of the stroke color, and white remains white. If you use a spot color as the stroke, Tints generates tints of the spot color. Choose Tints for brushes that are in black and white, or when you want to paint a brush stroke with a spot color.

• Tints and Shades displays the brush stroke in tints and shades of the stroke color. Tints and Shades maintains black and white, and everything between becomes a blend from black to white through the stroke color. Because black is added you may not be able to print to a single plate when using Tints and Shades with a spot color. Choose Tints and Shades for brushes that are in grayscale.

• Hue Shift uses the key color in the brush artwork, as shown in the Key Color box. (By default, the key color is the most prominent color in the art.) Everything in the brush artwork that is the key color becomes the stroke color. Other colors in the brush artwork become colors related to the stroke color. Hue Shift maintains black, white, and gray. Choose Hue Shift for brushes that use multiple colors. You can change the key color.

For information and samples about each choice, click Tips.

Note: *You can experiment with different colorization methods to achieve the result you want.*

To change the key color:

1 With the options dialog box for the selected brush type open, click the Key Color eyedropper.

2 Move the eyedropper to the preview in the dialog box, and click the color you want to use as the key color. The color in the Key Color box changes.

3 Click the eyedropper again to deselect it.

Using the Brush Libraries

You can import brushes from other Adobe Illustrator files into a palette associated with the current file using the Brush Libraries command. These libraries are stored in the Brush Libraries folder, located in the Illustrator 8.0 folder. You cannot add, delete, or edit brushes in a library; however, once you import a brush, you can change its attributes.

You can also have the Brush Libraries menu display Brush Libraries that you use often, and you can create a Brush Library.

Be sure to explore the Illustrator Extras folder on the Illustrator 8 Application CD for libraries containing hundreds of brushes. Choose from professional-quality Scatter, Art, and Pattern brush designs.

To import a brush from a Brush Library to the current Brushes palette:

1 Make sure the Brushes palette into which you want to import a brush is open.

2 Choose Window > Brush Libraries > *Brush Library name.* To locate a Brush Library not stored in the Brush Libraries folder, choose Window > Brush Libraries > Other Library.

3 Select the brush you want, and then do one of the following:

• Use the selected brush in the current artwork (recommended for one or two brushes at a time). Once you use it in the artwork, the brush is copied from the Brush Library to the Brushes palette.

• Drag the selected brush to the current Brushes palette (recommended for multiple brushes at a time).

• Choose Add to Brushes from the Brushes palette menu.

To have a Brush Library appear in the Brush Libraries menu:

1 Drag the Brush Library file into the Brush Libraries folder.

2 Restart Adobe Illustrator.

To create a Brush Library:

1 Create an Adobe Illustrator file containing the brushes you want in the Brush Library.

2 Save the file in the Brush Libraries folder.

3 Restart Adobe Illustrator.

Tips for using brushes

When you work with brushes, keep the following points in mind:

• You can often use Scatter brushes and Pattern brushes to achieve the same effect. However, one way in which they differ is that Pattern brushes follow the path exactly, while Scatter brushes do not.

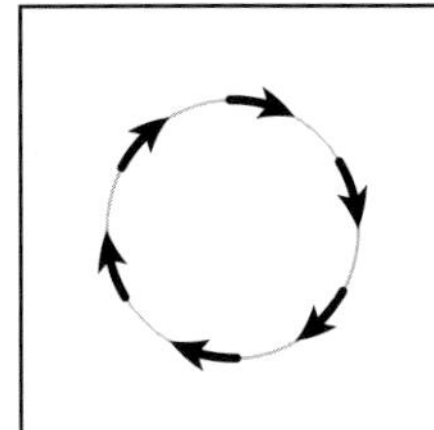
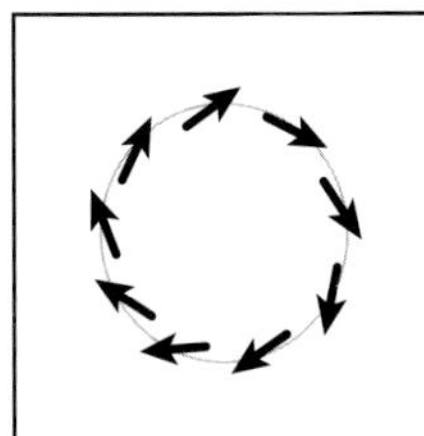

Arrows in a Pattern brush bend to follow the path; arrows remain straight in a Scatter brush.

• If you apply a brush to a closed path and want to control the placement of the end of the path, select the scissors tool and split the path. To change again, select the endpoints, choose Object > Path > Join, and use the scissors again. (See "Splitting paths with the scissors tool" on page 80.)

• To select all brush stroke paths in the current artwork, choose Edit > Select > Brush Strokes.

• For better performance when creating a brush from art that contains multiple overlapping paths filled with the same color and with no stroke, choose Unite from the Pathfinder palette before you create the brush.

Tracing artwork

There may be times when you want to base a new drawing on an existing piece of artwork. For example, you may want to create a graphic based on a pencil sketch drawn on paper or on an image saved in another graphics program. In either case, you can bring the image into Illustrator and trace over it.

Versions of Adobe Illustrator earlier than 7.0 supported the importing of 1-bit PICT and MacPaint images, to be used as template files over which you could trace an image. Adobe Illustrator no longer uses these template files. When you open a template file from a version of Illustrator earlier than 7.0, the file is converted to a bitmap image and placed onto the bottommost layer of the file. With version 8.0, you can create a layer to use especially as a template.

You can trace artwork in the following ways, depending on the source of the artwork to trace and how you want to trace it:

- Use the auto trace tool to trace automatically any image you bring into Illustrator.
- Place any EPS, PDF, or image file into an Illustrator file as a template layer and manually trace over it using the pen or pencil tool. (See "Creating template layers" on page 227.)

Tracing with the auto trace tool

The auto trace tool traces any image shape automatically. With this tool, you can click the edge of a shape you want to trace, and Illustrator draws the entire outline of the shape. You can use the auto trace tool to trace lines as well as shapes. When you use the auto trace tool to trace a line, it travels all the way around the line and comes back to where you clicked, forming a closed path.

The auto trace tool is especially suited to tracing simple shapes and lines. For the best results when tracing artwork, trace simpler shapes with the auto trace tool and draw more complex shapes with either the pencil tool or the pen tool. You can also use a dedicated tracing program such as Adobe Streamline™.

To trace a bitmap image shape:

1 Open the file that contains the bitmap image you want to trace.

2 Select the auto trace tool ( ).

3 Position the cross hair on the object you want to trace. You must position the cross hair within 6 pixels of the edge of a bitmap shape. The auto trace tool is guided by the boundary between differently shaded areas.

4 Do one of the following:

• To trace the entire object, click the object. Illustrator draws the path, beginning where you clicked, and follows the shape, keeping the shape on its right.

The path may be drawn clockwise or counter-clockwise, depending on where you click and on the shape of the path.

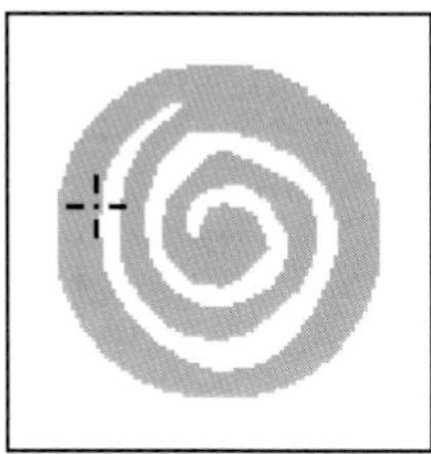
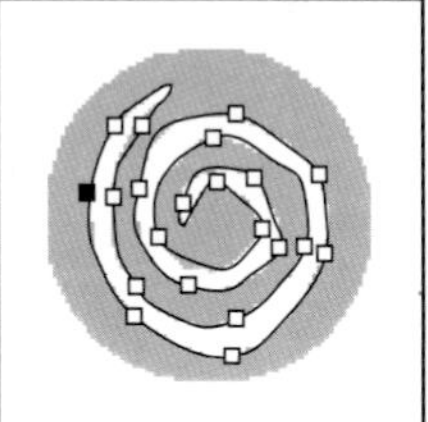

Click object to auto trace entire object.

• To trace part of the object, drag the pointer from the place on the bitmap shape where you want the path to start to the place where you want the path to end. When tracing only part of an image, you must start and stop dragging within 2 pixels of the edge of the shape.

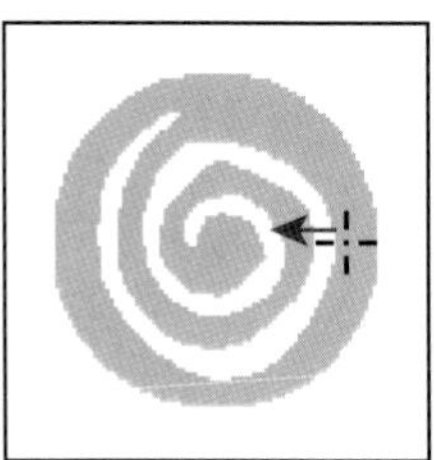
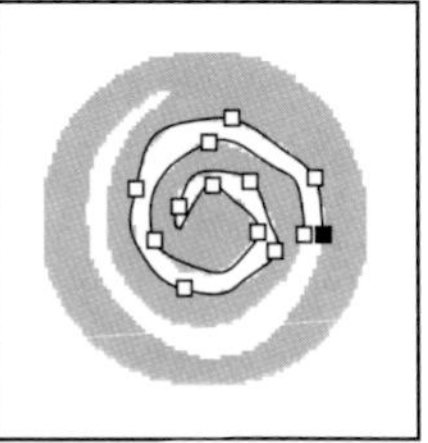

Drag the auto trace tool to auto trace part of object.

• To connect a new auto trace path to an existing auto trace path, start dragging at the anchor point where you want the paths to connect.

Setting the auto trace gap distance

The lines and shapes in bitmap images often contain gaps that become visible when you enlarge your view of the image. You can control the accuracy with which the auto trace tool traces these gaps using the Tracing Gap option in the Type & Auto Tracing Preferences dialog box.

The gap distance setting tells the auto trace tool to ignore gaps that are equal to or less than the number of pixels you specify. For example, setting the distance to 1 tells the auto trace tool to ignore gaps of 1 pixel or less.

To set the auto trace gap distance:

1 Choose File > Preferences > Type & Auto Tracing.

2 Enter 0 (the default), 1, or 2 in the Tracing Gap text box. The value is calculated in number of pixels. Click OK.

5

Chapter 5: Working with Objects

Editing your artwork is made easy in Adobe Illustrator with tools that allow you to select, move, and arrange objects precisely. Adobe Illustrator provides tools that let you measure and align objects, group objects so that they are treated as a single unit, and selectively lock and hide objects. There are also commands for correcting your mistakes and reverting to an earlier saved version of your file.

Correcting mistakes

You can use the Undo command to correct mistakes you make while using the Adobe Illustrator program. You can even undo an operation after you choose the Save command (but not if you closed and then reopened the file). If an operation cannot be undone, the Undo command is dimmed.

Depending on how much memory is available, you can undo an unlimited number of the last operations you performed, in reverse order, by repeatedly choosing the Undo command. The Illustrator performance is usually not affected by the number of undo levels you choose; however, if you are trying to display complex artwork, you may receive a message asking you to reduce the number of undo levels because of insufficient memory.

You can also revert a file to the version that was last saved (but not if you closed and then reopened the file).

To undo or redo an operation:

Choose Edit > Undo or Edit > Redo. (Depending on the memory available to your system, you can choose Undo an unlimited number of times.)

To change the minimum number of undo levels:

1 Choose File > Preferences > Units & Undo.

2 Enter a value for Minimum Undo Levels, and click OK. The default undo level is 5.

To revert a file to the last saved version:

Choose File > Revert. You cannot undo this action.

Using rulers

Illustrator can display rulers, one along the top and one along the left side of the illustration window.

When you open a new file, the rulers are not visible, but you can display them at any time. These rulers are a tool for accurately placing and measuring objects on the artboard. As you scroll and zoom around the file, the rulers adjust accordingly.

To show or hide rulers:

Choose View > Show Rulers, or View > Hide Rulers.

Defining ruler units

The large tick marks on the rulers indicate the unit of measure (such as inches), and the small tick marks indicate increments of the unit of measure (such as 1/8 inch). When you magnify or reduce your view, the increments of the unit of measure reflect the change in magnification.

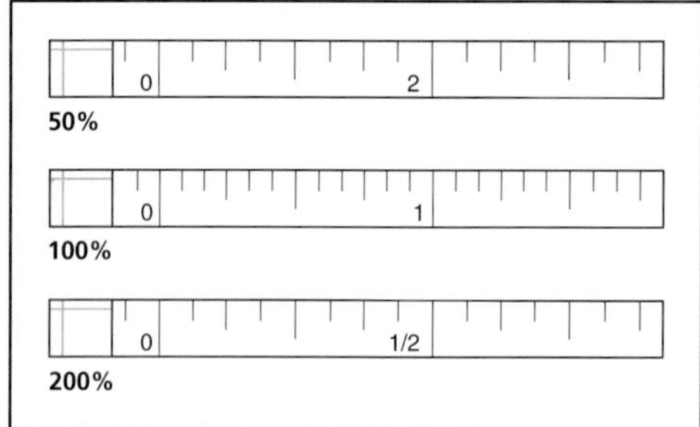

Art at different zoom levels and corresponding effect on rulers

The default units of measure for the rulers are *points* (a point equals .3528 millimeter). You can change the unit of measure to inches, millimeters, centimeters, or *picas* (a pica equals 12 points or 4.2333 millimeters) by using the Units & Undo Preferences dialog box or the Document Setup dialog box.

The unit of measure that you set for the rulers applies when you measure objects, move and transform objects, set grid and guides spacing, and create ellipses and rectangles. It does not affect the units in the Character and Paragraph palettes, which always display size, leading, vertical shift, line width, and line dash in the units set in the Type pop-up menu in the Units & Undo Preferences dialog box. (See "Setting type attributes" on page 259.)

To set the ruler unit of measure for all files:

1 Choose File > Preferences > Units & Undo.

2 From the General pop-up menu, choose the unit of measure you want to use, and click OK.

To set the ruler unit of measure for only the current file:

1 Choose File > Document Setup.

2 From the Units pop-up menu, choose the unit of measure you want to use, and click OK.

Automatically converting unit values in text boxes

If you use a unit other than the preset unit to enter values, Illustrator converts it to the set unit. For example, entering **3cm** in a text box set to inches converts the value to 1.1811 inches.

You can also add, subtract, multiply, divide, define percentages, and perform other mathematical operations in any Illustrator text box that accepts numeric values. For example, when specifying the size of a rectangle, you can type **72 pt + 2cm** for the height. Illustrator performs the calculation and uses the result.

The following rules apply when entering unit values:

• You can use the following units and abbreviations in text boxes: inch, inches, in, millimeters, millimetres, mm, Qs (one Q equals 0.25 millimeter), centimeters, centimetres, cm, points, p, pt, picas, and pc.

• Units are in points by default unless a different unit of measure was set in File > Preferences > Units & Undo.

• When mixing picas and points, you can enter values as *XpY*, where *X* and *Y* are the number of picas and points (for example, 12p6 for 12 picas, 6 points).

• A value without a specified unit uses the default unit for that text box, unless it follows a value with a specified unit. For example, in a text box that uses inches by default, typing **3 + 6** would equal 3 inches plus 6 inches, or 9 inches. Typing **3cm + 6** would equal 3 centimeters plus 6 centimeters, or 3.5433 inches.

• You can use percentages in combination with units. For example, typing **3cm*50%** would equal 3 centimeters multiplied by 50%, or 1.50 cm. Typing **50pt + 25%** would equal 50 points plus 25% of 50 points, or 62.5 points.

Changing the ruler origin

The point where 0 appears on each ruler is called the *ruler origin*. When you open a file, the position of the ruler origin depends on the View option selected in the Document Setup dialog box. Generally, if you selected either the Single Full Page or the Tile Full Pages option, the default ruler origin is located at the lower left corner of page 1.

When you change the ruler setting, the new setting becomes the default for the file whenever that file is opened. You can change the origin for the rulers at any time. For example, you may be working on a 3-inch-by-5-inch card that is centered on an 8.5-inch-by-11-inch page. Setting the ruler origin to line up with the 3-by-5-inch artwork rather than the 8.5-by-11-inch page can make precision editing easier for you.

Note: *The position of the ruler origin affects the tiling of patterns, as well as the bounding box information for the Separation Setup command.* *(See "Specifying the printing bounding box in the separation" on page 370.)*

To change the ruler origin:

1 Move the pointer to the upper left corner of the rulers where the rulers intersect.

2 Do one of the following:

• Drag the pointer to where you want the new ruler origin. As you drag, a cross hair in the window and in the rulers indicates the changing ruler origin.

• Double-click the upper-left corner where the rulers intersect to restore the default settings.

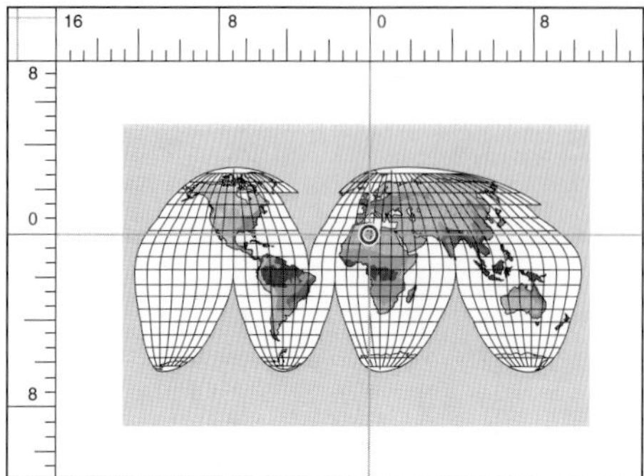

Original ruler origin

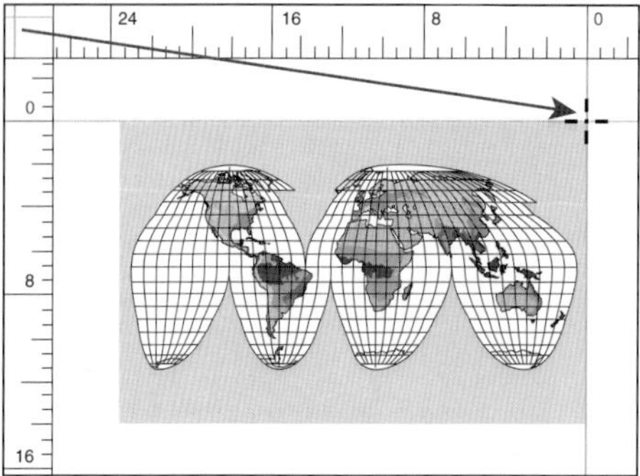

Setting a new ruler origin

Using the measure tool

The measure tool calculates the distance between any two points in the work area. When you measure from one point to another, the distance measured is displayed in the Info palette. The Info palette shows the horizontal and vertical distances from the *x* and *y* axes, the absolute horizontal and vertical distances, the total distances, and the angle measured.

All measurements except the angle are calculated in the unit of measure currently set in the Units & Undo Preferences dialog box or in the Document Setup dialog box. (See "Defining ruler units" on page 106.)

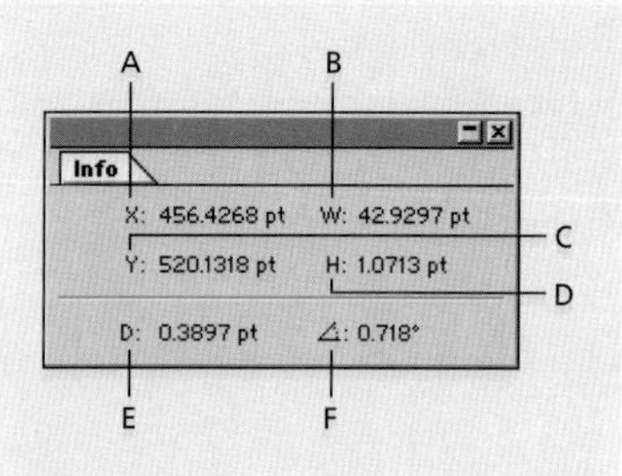

***A.** Horizontal distance from x axis*
***B.** Absolute horizontal distance measured*
***C.** Vertical distance from y axis*
***D.** Absolute vertical distance measured*
***E.** Total distance measured*
***F.** Angle diagonal distance measured*

To measure the distance between two points:

1 Select the measure tool (📏).

2 Do one of the following:

• Click the two points to measure the distance between them.

• Click the first point and drag to the second point. Shift-drag to constrain the tool to multiples of 45 degrees.

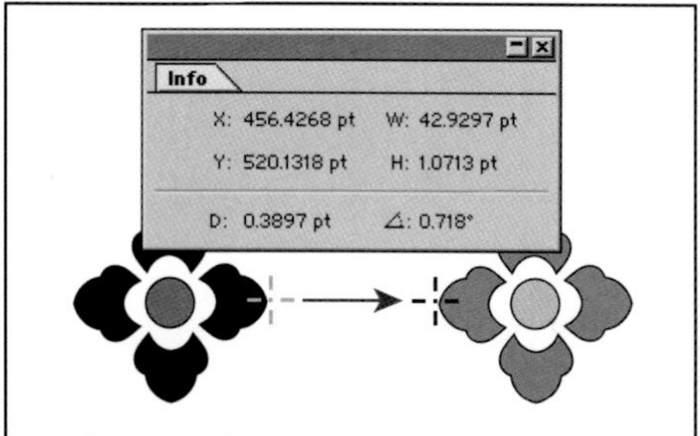

Using guides and grids

To help align text and graphic objects on the page, you can use background grids or you can create and display alignment outlines called *guides.*

Grids normally appear as lines or dots behind the artwork, and they do not print. You use grids to lay out objects or elements symmetrically. Selected artwork and tools snap to the grid if Snap To Grid is turned on. Grid spacing, color, and style can be different for each file.

Guides act as alignment tools. They also do not print. You can define any object as a guide to which you want to align artwork. Selected artwork and tools snap to guides when they are within tolerance of the guide. Guide color and style are the same for all files. (See “Setting guide and grid preferences” on page 111.)

Using guides

You can create two kinds of guides:

• *Ruler guides* are straight horizontal or vertical lines created with the ruler. These guides are the simplest to make and are useful for setting alignment lines across the length or width of the work area.

• *Guide objects* are objects (such as lines, rectangles, or any other artwork consisting of paths, except type) that are converted to guides. Using guide objects can help you plan and create your artwork around one or more objects. You can convert guide objects back into graphic objects at any point.

New guides are locked in place to orient your artwork. However, you can unlock a guide to select, move, delete, modify, or revert it to a graphic object.

By default, objects are aligned with guides whenever they are dragged within 2 pixels of the guide. (See “Moving, copying, and deleting objects” on page 117.)

To create a ruler guide:

1 If the rulers are not already displayed, choose View > Show Rulers.

2 Position the pointer on the left ruler for a vertical guide or on the top ruler for a horizontal guide. Press Alt (Windows) or Option (Mac OS) to switch the ruler guide from horizontal to vertical, and vice versa.

3 Drag the ruler guide into position.

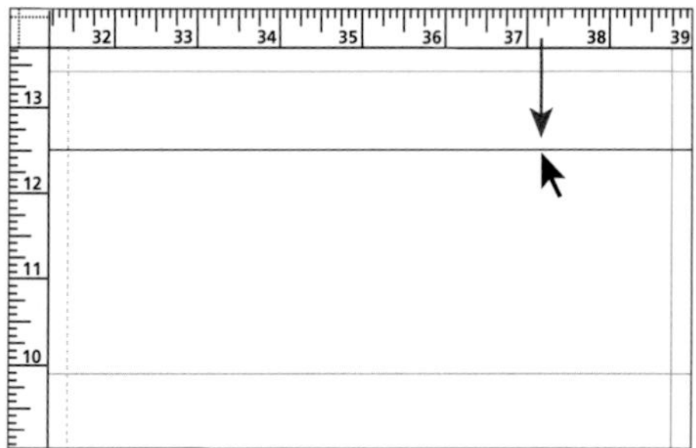

To make working with multiple guides easier, place all guides on a single layer. You can then choose the layer to select all guides for moving or adjusting. (See Chapter 9, "Using Layers.")

To convert an object into a guide object:

1 Select an object, a group of objects, or any combination of objects and groups.

2 Choose View > Make Guides.

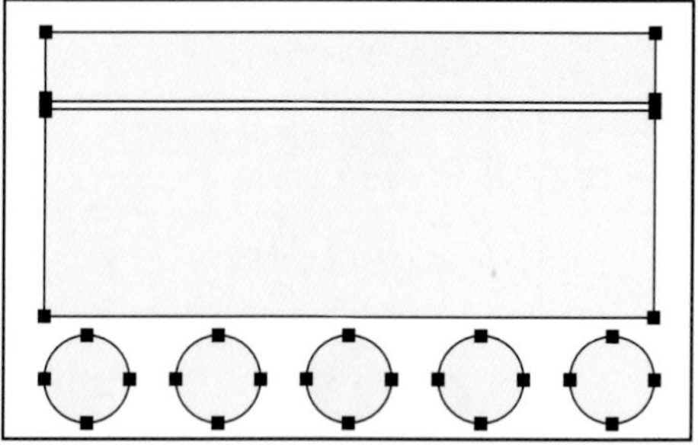

Objects selected

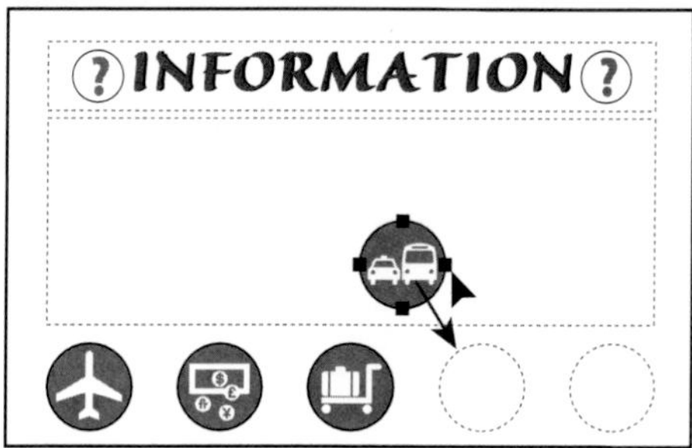

Object converted to guides, with artwork being aligned to guides

To move, delete, or release a guide:

1 Choose View > Lock Guides to lock or unlock the guide. When a guide is locked, a check mark appears next to the Lock Guides command.

2 Select the guide you want to move, delete, or release, and do one of the following:

- Move the guide by dragging or copying.
- Delete the guide by pressing Backspace or Del (Windows) or Delete (Mac OS), or by choosing Edit > Cut or Edit > Clear.

• Delete all guides at once by choosing View > Clear Guides.

• Release the guide object, turning it back into a regular graphic object, by choosing View > Release Guides.

To show or hide guides:

Choose View > Show Guides to show all guides or View > Hide Guides to hide them.

Using grids

You can choose between two grid styles—dots and lines—and you can change the color of the grid by using either predefined grid colors or colors you select using a color picker.

Spacing of grids is defined by two values: the distance between major lines, and the spacing between subdivisions. The visibility of the grid and snapping to the grid are controlled by the Show Grid command and the Snap to Grid command in the View menu.

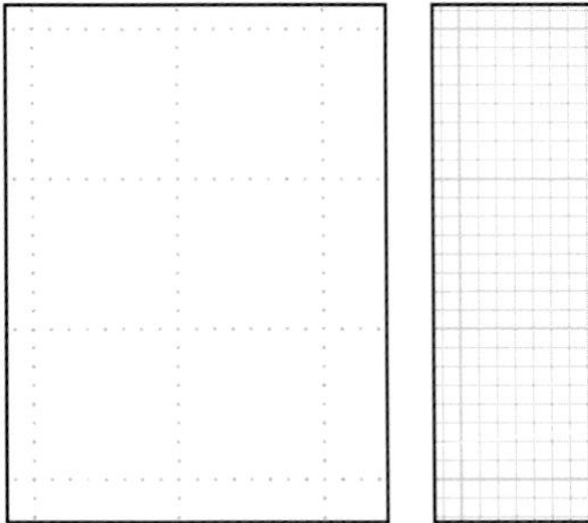

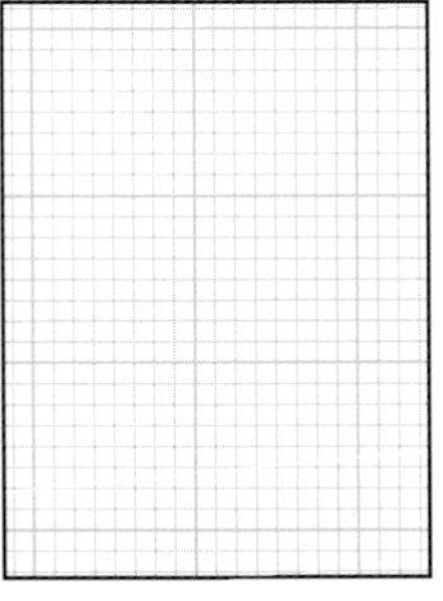

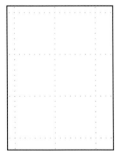

Setting guide and grid preferences

Use the Guides & Grid preferences to set the color and style of guides and the grid, and grid spacing.

To set guide and grid preferences:

1 Choose File > Preferences > Guides & Grid.

2 Set options for guides and the grid:

• For Color, choose a color for guides, or the grid, or both. If you choose Other, click the color box, choose a color from the color picker, and click OK.

• For Style, choose a display option for guides, or the grid, or both.

• For Gridline every, enter a new value (and unit of measure if necessary) for the spacing of primary gridlines.

• For Subdivisions, enter a value to subdivide the grid.

• For Grids in Back, select the option to display the grid behind all artwork; deselect the option to display the grid in front of all artwork.

3 Click OK.

Using Smart Guides

Smart Guides are temporary, "snap to" guides that help you create, align, edit, and transform objects relative to other objects. You can also use Smart Guides when rotating, scaling, and shearing objects. Objects can snap to locked objects and objects on locked layers.

You choose the point on the selected object at which you want to snap by selecting the object at that point. Illustrator determines additional points on artwork to create guides and snapping points. These points are determined by the last objects the cursor has passed over with the selected object.

You can create intersecting Smart Guides by passing over two Smart Guide lines, and then moving your selected object to the intersection point.

As you create, align, move, edit, and transform objects, Smart Guides appear from any anchor point on a nearby object over which the pointer recently passed. The direction, angle, tolerance, and appearance of Smart Guides are determined by settings in Preferences.

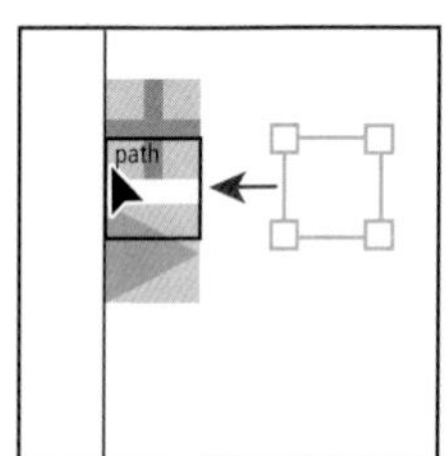

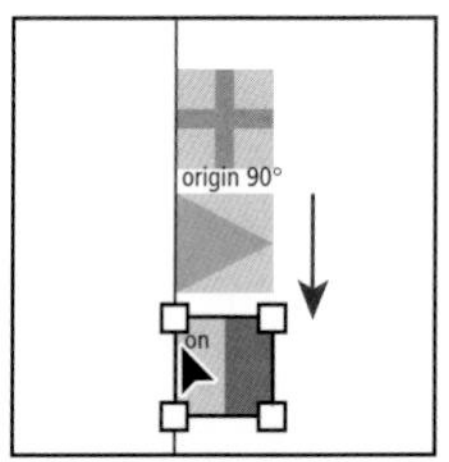

Click an object at the point that you want to align; drag over the path of the object that you want to align to. Drag the object until you see the Smart Guides, and align the objects.

To turn Smart Guides on or off:

To turn Smart Guides on or off, choose View > Smart Guides. A check mark appears next to the command when Smart Guides are turned on.

To change Smart Guide preferences:

1 Choose File > Preferences > Smart Guides.

2 Specify options for Smart Guides:

• Select Text Label Hints to display information about the position the cursor is currently snapped to (such as *center*) as you manipulate the cursor.

• Select Construction Guides to see guidelines in the file as you use Smart Guides.

• Select Transform Tools to have Smart Guides help when you scale, rotate, and shear objects.

• Select Object Highlighting to highlight the object below the pointer as you drag around it.

3 Click a text box and set an angle at which you want guide lines drawn from the anchor points of a nearby object (the preview reflects your settings). You can set up to six angles. Do one of the following:

• Enter an angle in the selected Angles text box.

• Choose a set of angles from the Angles pop-up menu.

• Choose a set of angles from the pop-up menu and change one of the values in the text box to customize a set of angles.

4 Type a value in the Snapping Tolerance text box to specify the number of points the pointer must be from another object for Smart Guides to take effect. Then click OK.

How Smart Guides work

When Smart Guides are turned on and you move the cursor over your artwork, the cursor looks for objects, page boundaries, and intersections of construction guides to snap to that are within the tolerance range set in Smart Guides Preferences.

You can use Smart Guides in the following ways when you create, move, and transform objects:

• When you create an object with the pen or shape tools, use the Smart Guides to position the new object's anchor points relative to the other object.

• When you move an object, use the Smart Guides to align to the point on the object that you have selected. You can align to the anchor point at the corner of a selected object near the bounding box. To do so, select the object just inside the bounding box handle. If the tolerance is 5 points or greater, you can snap to the corner point from 5 points away. (See "Using the bounding box" on page 115.)

• When the Transform Tools option is selected in Smart Guides Preferences and you transform an object, Smart Guides appear to assist the transformation.

***Note:** When Snap to Grid is turned on, you cannot use Smart Guides (even if the menu command is selected).*

Selecting objects

Before you can modify an object, you need to distinguish it from the objects around it. You do that by selecting the object with a selection tool. Once you've selected an object, or a part of an object, you can edit it by moving or copying, deleting, or adjusting paths.

Using the selection tools

You select objects with the following selection tools:

• The selection tool ( ) lets you select entire objects or an entire path by selecting any spot on the path. When the selection tool is over an unselected object or path, it changes to ( ). When it is over a selected object or path, it changes to ( ). When it is over an anchor point, you see a hollow square next to the arrow ( ).

• The direct-selection tool ( ) lets you select individual anchor points or segments on a path and displays all direction lines on a path for adjusting. When the direct-selection tool is over an unselected object or path, it changes to ( ). When it is over the anchor point of a selected object or path, it changes to ( ).

• The group-selection tool ( ) lets you select an object within a group, a single group within multiple groups, or a set of groups within the artwork. Each additional click adds the next object in the grouping hierarchy to the selection. (See "Grouping and ungrouping objects" on page 125.)

To use the last-used selection tool when using any other tool (except the selection tools), hold down Ctrl (Windows) or Command (Mac OS).

To select an entire object or line:

1 Choose the selection tool (![]) or the group-selection tool (![]).

2 Do one of the following:

• If the object is filled and you are in Preview view, click within the object.

Note: *Clicking a filled object in Preview view selects the object only if the Use Area Select option in the General Preferences dialog box is selected.* *(See "Selecting filled objects" on page 116.)*

• Click the path of the object.

• Click an anchor point of the object.

• Drag a dotted rectangle, called a *marquee,* around part or all of the object.

To select an object that is hidden behind another object:

1 Position the selection tool over the top object at a point directly above the object below. (Be sure that any objects you want to select are directly below the clicking point of the selection tool.)

2 Without moving the selection tool, right-click (Windows) or Control-click (Mac OS) to open the context-sensitive menu.

3 Choose an option from the Select submenu:

• Next Object Below selects the next object in the painting order that is below the selected object.

• Last Object Below selects the bottommost object in the stacking order that is below the selected object.

• Next Object Above selects the next object in the stacking order that is above the selected object.

• First Object Above selects the topmost object in the stacking order that is above the selected object.

You can also use the keyboard shortcuts listed in the Select submenu.

To select a segment:

Choose the direct-selection tool (![]), and then choose one of the following options:

• Click within 2 pixels of the segment.

• Drag a marquee over part of the segment.

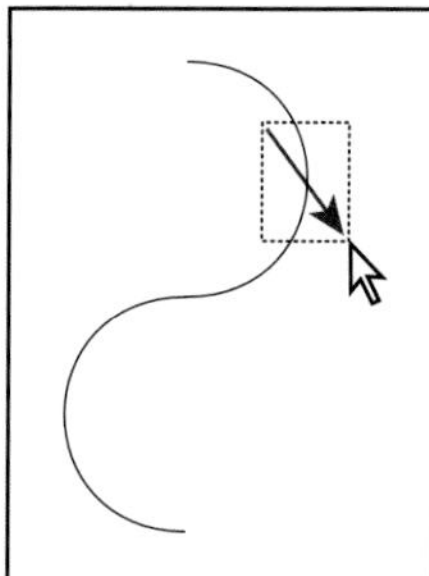

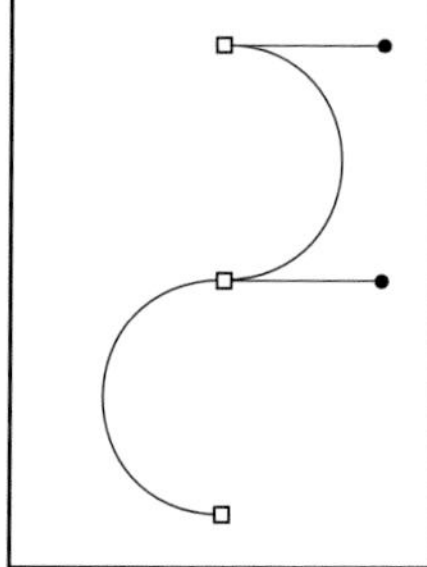

Drag the direct-selection tool to select the segment and display the direction lines.

When you select a segment, all of the anchor points on the path are displayed, including any direction lines and direction points if the selected segment is curved. Direction points appear as filled circles; selected anchor points appear as filled squares; unselected anchor points appear as hollow squares.

To add or remove selections:

Hold down Shift while selecting or deselecting additional objects or segments.

Using the bounding box

When you select one or more objects with the selection tool, you see a bounding box around them. With the bounding box, you can move, duplicate, and scale objects easily by dragging the selection or a handle (one of the hollow squares surrounding the selected objects).

The bounding box creates a temporary border around the selected object. You see an outline of the selection as you drag it. When you release the mouse button, the object snaps to the current border created by the bounding box, and you see the object's outline move.

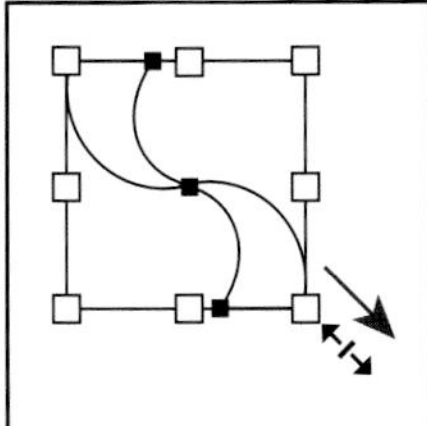
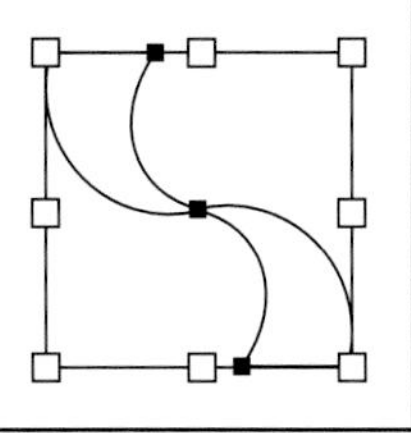

Selected objects during and after scaling using the bounding box.

To move, duplicate, or scale objects, use the selection tool (➤).

Note: *You can also move and scale selected objects, as well as perform other transformation actions, using the free transform tool, transformation tools, and the Transform palette. (See "Transforming selected objects" on page 131.)*

If you rotate an object with the free transform tool or the rotate tool, its bounding box is also rotated. To reorient the bounding box to the page, choose Object > Transform > Reset Bounding Box.

To turn the bounding box on or off:

1 Choose File > Preferences > General.

2 Select or deselect the Use Bounding Box option to show or hide the bounding box when objects are selected, and click OK.

To move objects with the bounding box:

1 Select one or more objects using the selection tool.

2 Drag any part of the selection (but not a handle).

To duplicate objects with the bounding box:

1 Select one or more objects using the selection tool.

2 Alt-drag (Windows) or Option-drag (Mac OS) the selection (but not a handle).

Selecting filled objects

The Use Area Select option in the General Preferences dialog box determines whether you can select a filled object in Preview view by clicking anywhere within the area or whether you must click a path segment or anchor point. By default, the Use Area Select option is on. In some cases, you may want to turn off the Use Area Select option—for example, when you work with overlapping filled objects.

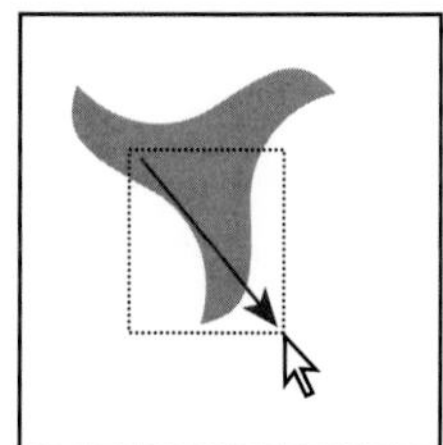
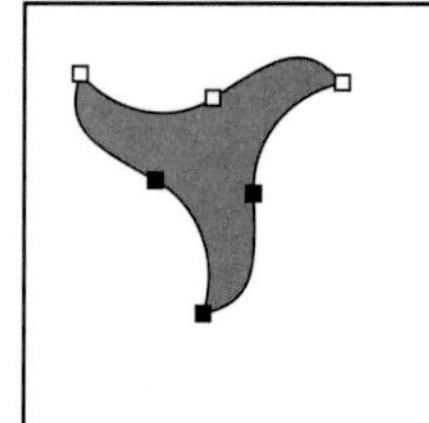

Use Area Select option off: Dragging selects points and segments within marquee.

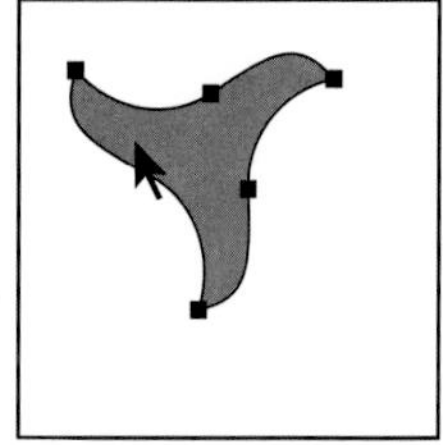
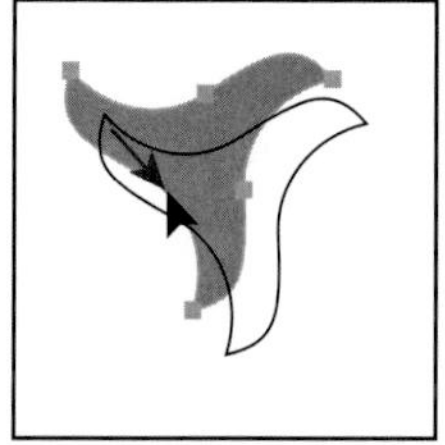

Use Area Select option on: Dragging selects object.

To turn the Use Area Select option on or off:

1 Choose File > Preferences > General.

2 Select or deselect the Use Area Select option, and click OK.

Selecting multiple objects

You can select several objects at a time and then move, paint, group, transform, or edit them using any editing tool.

To select or deselect multiple objects:

Do one of the following:

- With the selection tool, drag a marquee over all of the objects.
- With an object selected, Shift-drag a marquee over other objects to select.
- With the selection tool, select an object and then Shift-click to select additional objects.

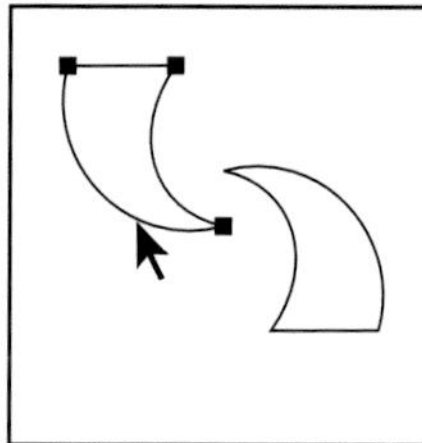
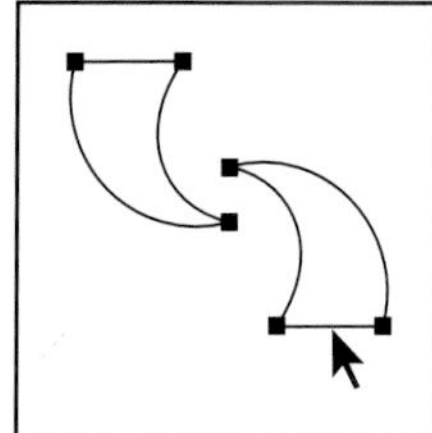

Click one object. Then Shift-click additional objects.

To select all objects in a file:

Choose Edit > Select All. This command selects all objects in a file except objects that have been locked or hidden. (See “Locking and hiding objects” on page 127.)

To select all unselected objects, and deselect all selected objects:

Choose Edit > Select > Inverse.

Deselecting objects

You deselect objects when you no longer want to edit them. You can deselect one object, several objects, or all objects in your artwork.

To deselect objects when you are using a selection tool:

Do one of the following:

- To deselect everything in the file, click or drag at least 2 pixels away from any object, or choose Edit > Deselect All.
- To deselect part of a selection, Shift-click or Shift-drag over the path or segment you want to deselect.

Moving, copying, and deleting objects

You can move objects in your artwork by cutting them from one spot and pasting them into another, by dragging them, and by using the arrow keys, the Move dialog box, and the Transform Each dialog box. Dragging also enables you to copy objects between open Illustrator and Photoshop files.

Note: *You can also move objects using the Transform palette. (See "Using the Transform palette" on page 140.)*

To set general preferences that affect how objects move:

1 Choose File > Preferences > General.

2 Choose options for Preferences:

- Enter an angle between 0 and 360 degrees in the Constrain Angle text box to rotate the *x* and *y* axes. The rotation of the axes determines how drawing and movement are constrained when you hold down Shift. (See "Rotating the x and y axes" on page 122.)
- Select Transform Pattern Tiles to specify whether you want to transform any patterns within objects when you apply a transformation such as scaling, rotating, or shearing. (See "Creating and working with patterns" on page 200.)
- Deselect Use Area Select to select objects by clicking an anchor point or path segment (in Preview view). (See "Selecting filled objects" on page 116.)

3 Click OK.

Note: *Smart Guides preferences also affect how objects move.*

To set keyboard preferences that affect how objects move:

1 Choose File > Preferences > General.

2 In the Cursor Key text box, enter the distance you want each press of an arrow key to move a selection, and then click OK.

To move or copy an object by pasting:

1 Select the object you want to cut or copy.

2 Choose Edit > Cut or Edit > Copy.

Note: *To copy a bitmap version of the selected object onto the Clipboard for pasting into Adobe Photoshop, choose Edit > Copy. (See "Using the Clipboard to copy artwork" on page 119.)*

3 To paste an object into another file, open the file and choose one of the following commands:

• Edit > Paste to paste the objects into the center of the active window.

• Edit > Paste in Front to paste the object directly in front of the selected object.

• Edit > Paste in Back to paste the object directly in back of the selected object.

Note: The Paste in Front and Paste in Back commands paste the object in the same position on the new file's artboard as in the original file.

To move an object or a copy of an object by dragging:

1 Select the object.

You can also select multiple objects.

2 Position the pointer on an anchor point or path segment of the selected object. In Preview view, you can click anywhere on the object when the Use Area Select option is selected in General Preferences.

3 Drag the object to its new location. Shift-drag to constrain the object to multiples of 45 degrees.

You can use the Snap to Point command in the View menu to have the cursor snap to an anchor point or guide when you drag an object within 2 pixels of the anchor point or guide. Snap to Point is turned on when a check mark appears by the menu command.

To drag a copy of the object, Alt-drag (Windows) or Option-drag (Mac OS) as you drag.

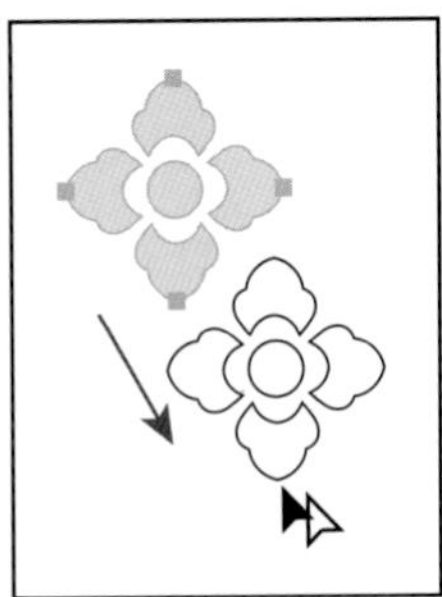

Press Alt/Option as you drag to copy.

***Note:** You can use this technique to drag copies of objects between Illustrator and Photoshop files. (See "Using the drag-and-drop feature to copy artwork" on page 119.)*

To move an object by using the arrow keys:

1 Select the object.

2 Press the arrow key for the direction in which you want to move the object.

The distance the object moves each time you press an arrow key is determined by the value specified in the Cursor Key text box in the General Preferences dialog box. The default distance is 1 point (1/72 of an inch, or .3528 millimeter).

To move a selection with the free transform tool:

1 With the selection tool (), select one or more objects to move.

2 Select the free transform tool ().

3 Drag any part of the selection (but not a handle).

To move or copy an object a specified distance and direction:

1 Select the object.

2 Choose Object > Transform > Move.

When an object is selected, you can also double-click the selection tool ( ) to open the Move dialog box.

The Move dialog box displays the results of the last move or measure operation using the unit of measure set in the Units & Undo Preferences dialog box.

3 Do one of the following:

• Enter the horizontal and vertical distances that you want the object to move. Positive values move the object up and to the right of the *x* axis; negative values move the object down and to the left.

• Enter the distance and angle for the move. The angle you enter is calculated in degrees from the *x* axis. Positive angles specify a counterclockwise move; negative angles specify a clockwise move. You can also enter values between 180 and 360 degrees; these values are converted to their corresponding negative values (for example, a value of 270 degrees is converted to –90 degrees).

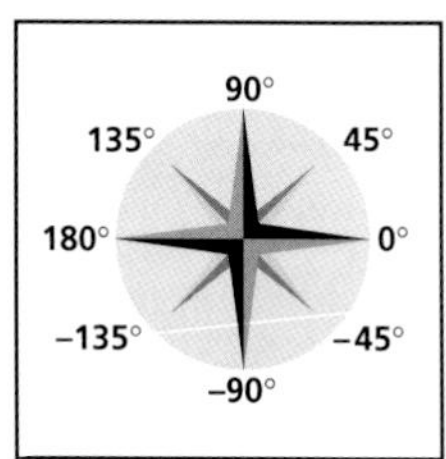

Directions relative to the x axis

Using the Clipboard to copy artwork

You can use the Clipboard to transfer selections between an Illustrator file and another application. The Clipboard is particularly useful for importing paths from Adobe products—such as Adobe Photoshop®, Adobe Streamline, Adobe Dimensions®, and Adobe Premiere®—since paths are copied to the Clipboard as PostScript language descriptions.

To copy using the Clipboard:

1 Select the object or objects you want to copy in a non-Illustrator file. Then choose Edit > Copy.

2 In the Illustrator file to which you want to paste the object, choose Edit > Paste.

Note: *Some file formats cannot be pasted into Illustrator, but they can be dropped into Illustrator by applications that support the drag-and-drop feature.*

Using the drag-and-drop feature to copy artwork

The drag-and-drop feature lets you copy and move artwork between Illustrator and other applications.

In Windows, the other application must be OLE-compliant. To copy an OLE object that contains .psd data, use the OLE Clipboard. (See your Windows documentation.) Dragging vector artwork from Adobe Illustrator or from other applications that use the Illustrator Clipboard converts the artwork to a bitmap image (also called *raster* format).

In Mac OS, the application must support Macintosh Drag Manager.

To drag and drop selections of artwork between Illustrator and the desktop (Mac OS only):

1 Select the artwork you want to copy.

2 Drag the selection onto the desktop. Selections are copied to the desktop as a picture clipping, which can be dragged and dropped into the desired document. Picture clippings are converted to PICT format when dragged to the desktop.

To drag and drop artwork into a Photoshop image window:

1 Select the artwork you want to copy.

2 Open the Photoshop image into which you want to copy the selection.

3 Drag the selection toward the Photoshop window, and when a black outline appears, release the mouse button. To position the selection in the center of the Photoshop image, hold down Shift before dragging the selection.

To drag and drop artwork into Photoshop as paths:

1 Select the artwork you want to copy.

2 Open the Photoshop image into which you want to copy the selection.

3 Hold down Ctrl (Windows) or Command (Mac OS), and drag the selection to the Photoshop document. When you release the mouse button, the selection becomes a Photoshop path. By default, selected objects are copied as bitmap images to the active layer.

To drag and drop artwork into Illustrator from Photoshop:

1 Open the Photoshop image from which you want to copy.

2 Select the artwork you want to copy.

3 Hold down Ctrl (Windows) or Command (Mac OS), and drag the selection from Photoshop into the Illustrator file. When you release the mouse button, the selection becomes an Illustrator path. Dragging a selection from Photoshop to Illustrator converts the selection to a 72-ppi RGB image.

Note: *If you're working with Adobe Photoshop 3.05 or earlier, you can drag from Photoshop into Illustrator, but you can't drag from Illustrator into Photoshop.*

Aligning and distributing objects vertically and horizontally

The Align palette enables you to align selected objects along the axis you specify. You can align objects along the vertical axis, using the rightmost, center, or leftmost anchor point of the selected objects. Or you can align objects along the horizontal axis, using the topmost, center, and bottommost anchor points of the selected objects.

***Note:** Paragraph alignment of point type overrides the Align Objects options. (See "Specifying alignment options" on page 280.)*

You can also distribute objects evenly along the horizontal axis or vertical axis.

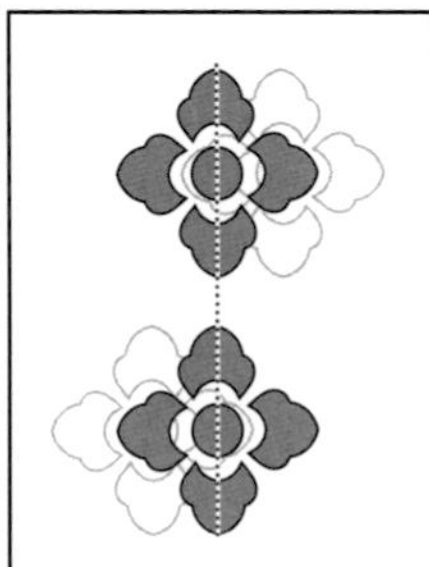

Align options: Vertical Center and Horizontal Center

In addition, you can distribute the space between objects evenly, both horizontally and vertically.

To align or distribute objects:

1 Select the objects to align or distribute.

2 Choose Window > Show Align.

In the Align palette, you see the Align Objects and Distribute Objects options. If you don't see the Distribute Spacing options, choose Show Options from the pop-up menu in the Align palette.

3 Click the button for the type of alignment or distribution you want.

Moving groups of objects

The Move option in the Transform Each dialog box moves objects in a selection in a specified or random direction. Use the Random option to give a slightly less rigid, more natural look to a group of items. For example, if you draw a brick wall and want the bricks to appear slightly offset from each other instead of perfectly aligned, you could select the Random option.

To move groups of objects:

1 Select the objects you want to move.

2 Choose Object > Transform > Transform Each.

3 In the Move Horizontal and Vertical text boxes, enter the distance you want to move the selected objects, or use the associated sliders. These numbers must be between –4000 and 4000 points and must not cause the objects to move beyond the edge of the artboard.

4 Do one of the following:

• To move the objects by the specified amounts, click OK.

• To move the objects randomly, but no more than the specified amounts, select the Random option. Then click OK.

Offsetting objects

You can create a replica of a path, set off from the selected path by a specified distance, by using the Offset Path command. This is useful when you want to create concentric shapes or make many replications of a path at a regular distance from the original path. You can create an offset path from a closed path or an open path; if created from a closed path, the new offset path appears at the specified distance outside or inside the original path.

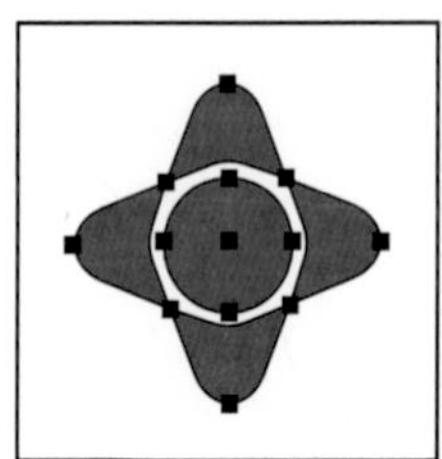
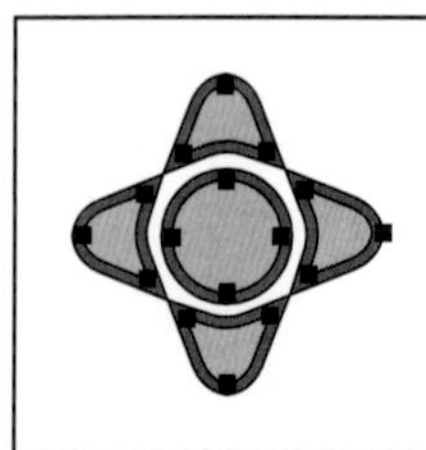

Original and Offset Paths –2 points

To create an offset path:

1 Select the paths you want to offset.

2 Select Object > Path > Offset Path.

3 Specify the offset distance, line join type, and miter limit. (For more information about line join type and miter limit, see "Creating line effects" on page 145.) Then click OK.

Deleting objects

Deleting an object removes it permanently.

To delete an object:

1 Select the object.

2 Press Backspace or Del (Windows) or Delete (Mac OS), or choose Edit > Clear or Edit > Cut.

Rotating the *x* and *y* axes

When you open a new file, the *x* and *y* axes are parallel to the horizontal and vertical sides of the window. You can rotate the axes by specifying an angle of constraint in the General Preferences dialog box.

Rotating the axes is useful if your artwork contains elements that are rotated to the same angle, such as a logo and text displayed on a 20-degree angle. Instead of rotating each element you add to the logo, you can simply rotate the axes by 20 degrees. Everything you draw is created along the new axes.

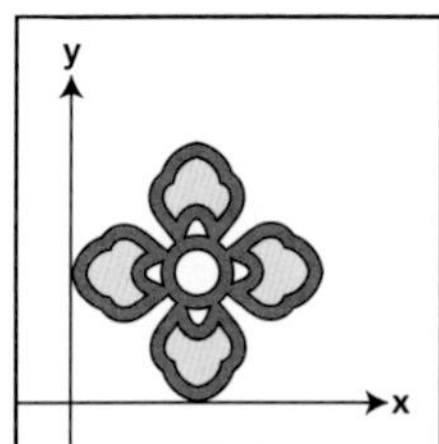

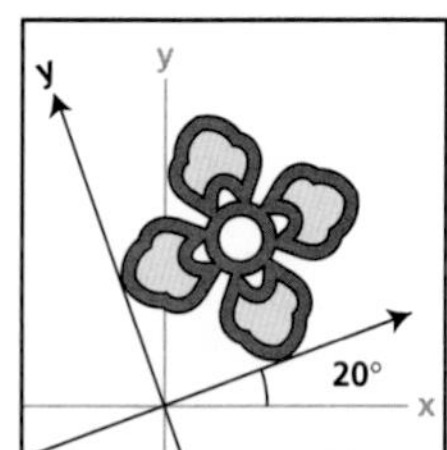

Object aligned with default axes and axes rotated 20°

You can then use the Shift key to constrain the movement of one or more objects so that they move in a precise horizontal, vertical, or diagonal direction relative to the current orientation of the *x* and *y* axes.

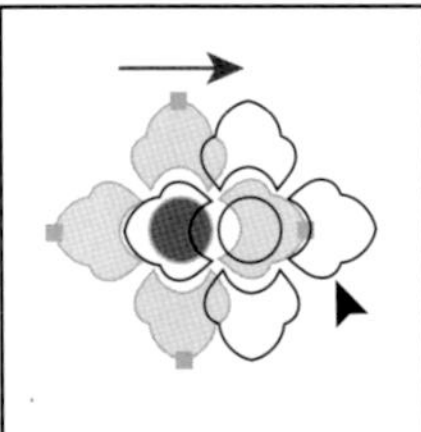
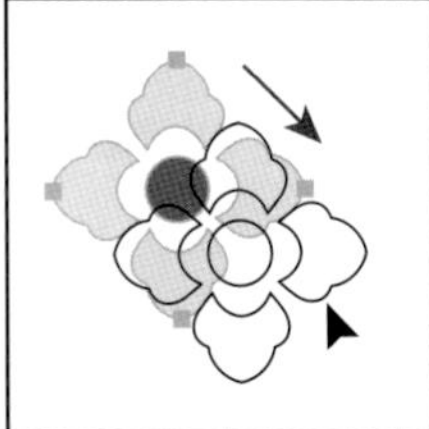

Hold down Shift while dragging or drawing to limit movement to the nearest 45° angle.

To rotate the axes:

1 Choose File > Preferences > General.

2 In the Constrain Angle text box, enter the angle at which you want the axes rotated. If you enter a positive number, the axes are rotated counter-clockwise. If you enter a negative number, the axes are rotated clockwise. Then click OK.

The rotation of the axes is saved in the Preferences file; it therefore affects new artwork in all files until you change its value or delete the Preferences file.

The following objects and actions are aligned along the new axes:

- Text and objects you draw with the graph tool.
- Scaling, reflecting, and shearing.
- Moving objects with the arrow keys.
- Any objects or operations to which you apply constraint (by holding down Shift while performing the action), limiting them to 45-degree multiples relative to the axes.
- The angle reported in the Info palette.
- Construction guides, which appear with Smart Guides.

The following objects and actions *are not* affected by the new axes:

- Objects that already exist.
- Rotating and blending.
- Drawing with the pencil or auto trace tool.

Stacking objects

The Adobe Illustrator program stacks successively drawn objects, beginning with the first object drawn. How objects are stacked determines how they are displayed when they overlap. In addition, stacking is important when you make masks. (See "Working with masks" on page 150.)

You can change the stacking order (also called the *painting order*) of objects in your artwork at any time. By creating multiple layers in your artwork, you can also control how overlapping objects are displayed. (See Chapter 9, "Using Layers.")

Note: *Grouping objects may affect the way the objects are stacked in relation to other, nongrouped objects in the artwork.* *(See "Grouping and ungrouping objects" on page 125.)*

Moving objects frontward or backward in a stack of objects

The Bring to Front and Send to Back commands let you move an object to the front or the back of the stack of objects on its layer. The Bring Forward and Send Backward commands let you move an object just one object forward or back in the stack of objects. (See Chapter 9, "Using Layers.")

If the object is part of any type of group—including masked artwork, compound paths, text, and word wraps—the object is moved to the front or back of the group rather than the front or back of the entire layer.

To make an object the frontmost or backmost object in its group or on its layer:

1 Select the object you want to move.

2 Choose either Object > Arrange > Bring to Front or Object > Arrange > Send to Back.

Selected object is at the bottom of the stack. Bring to Front command applied, and object repositioned to front of entire stack

To move an object one layer to the front or one layer to the back of a stack:

1 Select the object you want to move.

2 Choose either Object > Arrange > Bring Forward or Object > Arrange > Send Backward.

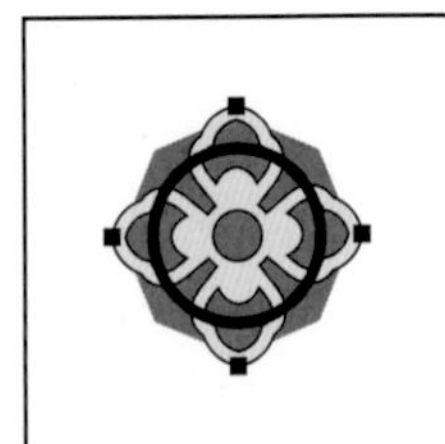

Bring Forward command applied, and object repositioned forward one layer in stack

Pasting objects in front or in back of other objects

The Paste in Front and Paste in Back commands let you paste copies of objects directly on top of and behind the objects you select. This is useful if you want to move the copy a specified distance from the original location. These commands also let you paste the artwork into the same position in a new file as it was in the old file, relative to the page origin.

To move an object in front or in back of other objects in the stacking order:

1 Select the object you want to move.

2 Choose Edit > Cut. The selected object is temporarily deleted and is placed onto the Clipboard.

3 Select the object or objects in front or in back of where you want the cut object to appear.

4 Choose Edit > Paste in Front or Edit > Paste in Back.

The cut object is pasted into position. If no object was selected in step 3, the object is pasted on top of or in back of the stack.

Square object selected and cut

Backmost object selected and square object pasted in front of it (beige petals are above the square, at the top of the stack)

If you paste more than one object, all pasted objects appear in front or in back of the selected artwork. However, the relative painting order among the individual pasted objects remains the same. If you are working with multiple layers in the file that you defined with the Layers palette, the layers may affect how objects are pasted. (See "Moving objects between layers" on page 222.)

Pasting objects in the current layer

Pasted objects (even if copied from different layers) are placed directly in front or in back of all selected objects on the current layer if the Paste Remembers Layers option is turned off in the General Preferences dialog box. However, the relative painting order among the individual pasted objects remains the same.

The Paste Remembers Layers option retains the layering order of objects you paste. (See "Moving objects between layers" on page 222.)

To paste objects into the current layer:

1 Choose File > Preferences > General.

2 Select Paste Remembers Layers, and click OK.

Grouping and ungrouping objects

You can combine several objects into a group so that the objects are treated as a single unit. You can then move or transform a number of objects without affecting their individual positions or attributes. For example, you might group the objects in a logo design so that you can move and scale the logo as one unit.

Groups can also be nested—that is, they can be grouped within other objects or groups to form larger groups.

To group or ungroup objects:

1 Select the objects to be grouped or ungrouped. Selecting part of an object and grouping it will group the entire object.

2 Choose either Object > Group or Object > Ungroup.

Selecting grouped objects

Once objects are grouped, selecting any part of the group with the selection tool selects the entire group. If you are unsure whether an object is part of a group, select it with the selection tool.

The direct-selection tool lets you select a single path or object that is part of one group or several groups. If you have groups of objects within other groups, you can select the next group in the grouping hierarchy by using the group-selection tool. Each successive click adds another subset of grouped objects to the selection.

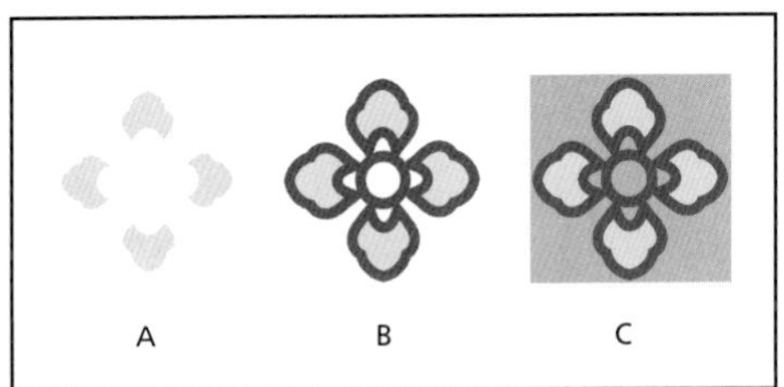

Three groups: Group A is part of group B, which in turn is part of group C.

To select grouped objects with the group-selection tool:

1 Select the group-selection tool (⇖⁺), and click the path you want to select.

2 Click the same place again to select successive groups until you have selected everything you want to include in your selection.

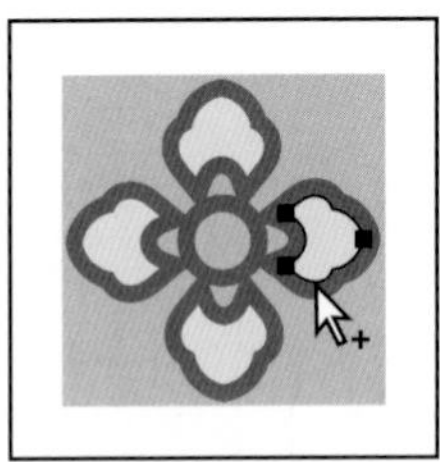

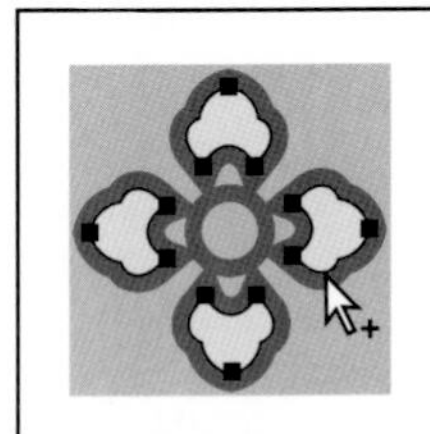

First click selects an object. Second click selects group A.

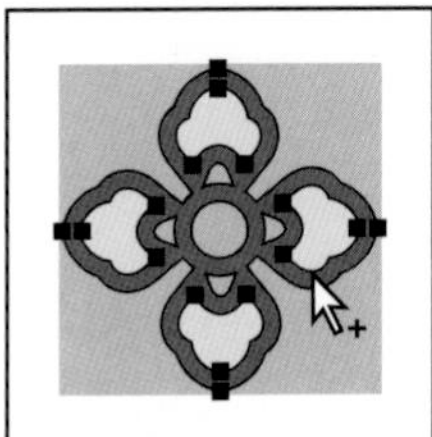

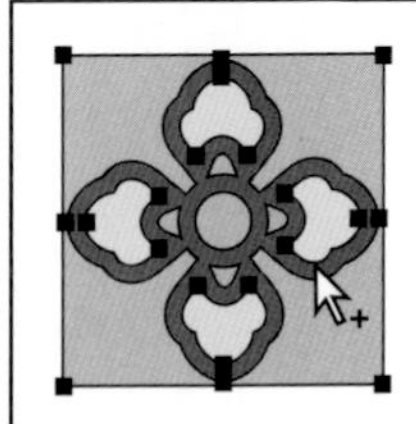

Third click selects next group (group B). Fourth click selects group C.

Grouping stacked objects

Grouped objects must be stacked in succession on the same layer of the artwork; therefore, grouping may change the layering of objects and their stacking order on a given layer. (See "Stacking objects" on page 123. Also see the introduction to Chapter 9, "Using Layers.")

Grouped objects are stacked together behind the frontmost object in the group. If you group two objects that are separated by a nongrouped object in the stacking order, the nongrouped object is moved behind the grouped objects.

 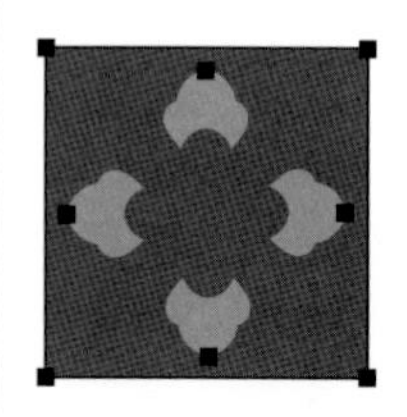

Three objects: front and back objects selected and then grouped

Locking and hiding objects

You can use the Lock and Hide commands to isolate parts of your artwork on which you do not want to work. Once an object is locked or hidden, it cannot be selected or modified in any way. These features are useful when you are working on objects that overlap. In addition, the Hide command makes objects temporarily invisible, and so may speed performance when you work on large or complex artwork.

Locked objects remain locked when files are closed and reopened. However, hidden objects reappear when files are reopened.

To lock or hide artwork:

Choose from the following options:

• To lock objects, select the objects and choose Object > Lock.

• To lock all unselected objects, press Alt (Windows) or Option (Mac OS) and choose Object > Lock.

• To hide a selected object, select the objects and choose Object > Hide Selection.

• To hide all unselected objects, press Shift+Alt (Windows) or Shift+Option (Mac OS) and choose Object > Hide Selection.

***Note:** You can lock or hide entire objects only. Selecting part of an object (anchor points or segments) and locking or hiding it affects the entire object.*

To unlock or show all objects:

Choose either Object > Unlock All or Object > Show All. All previously locked objects are unlocked and selected. Any previously selected objects are deselected.

To unlock or show all objects within a selected group:

1 Select an unlocked and visible element within a group.

2 Hold down Alt (Windows) or Option (Mac OS) and choose either Object > Unlock All or Object > Show All.

6

Chapter 6: Modifying Shapes

You can easily modify an object's size, orientation, or shape by using Adobe Illustrator tools and commands. You can also apply Adobe Illustrator filters to change an object's shape and path direction. And, by working with more than one object at a time, you can create complex designs using compound paths and masks.

Transforming selected objects

You can *transform* selected objects—that is, change their size, shape, and orientation by selecting one or more objects and then applying various transformation actions on them. For example, you can change the angle of an object by rotating it, or add perspective to an angle by shearing it.

To transform an object, you can use the free transform tool, individual transformation tools, or the Transform palette:

• Use the free transform tool to rotate, scale, reflect, shear, and distort objects quickly.

• Use the transformation tools to change the size, shape, and orientation of selected objects. The transformation tools are the rotate tool, scale tool, reflect tool, and shear tool. You can also use individual transform dialog boxes to specify numeric values, to preview the transformation before applying it, and to select other transformation options.

• Use the Transform palette to modify selected objects by changing information in the palette. (See "Using the Transform palette" on page 140.)

As you transform objects, keep the following in mind:

• Transformation dialog boxes and commands can be opened for selected objects by using context-sensitive menus. To display context-sensitive menus, hold down the right mouse button (Windows) or Control-click (Mac OS) when the pointer is over the object.

• You can move and duplicate selected objects by using the bounding box. (See "Using the bounding box" on page 115.)

Defining the point of origin

All transformation actions perform their functions in relation to some fixed point on or around the object. This fixed point is called the *point of origin*. The default point of origin is the object's center point.

You can drag anywhere on an object with the free transform tool or an individual transformation tool to transform the object around the object's center. For example, you can drag an object to rotate it around its center, or you can set a new point of origin by clicking and then dragging to rotate it. You can also click a point of origin that you have set, and then drag it to a new position.

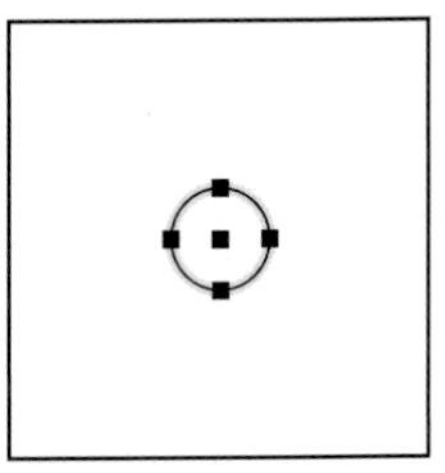
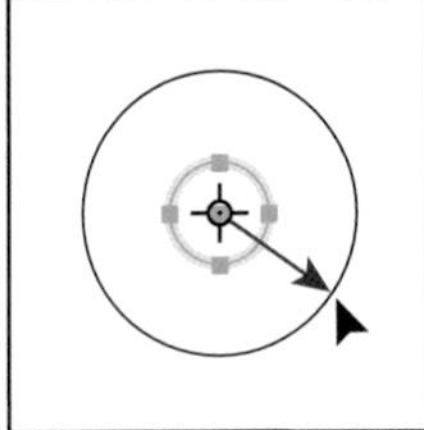

Original and scaled from center

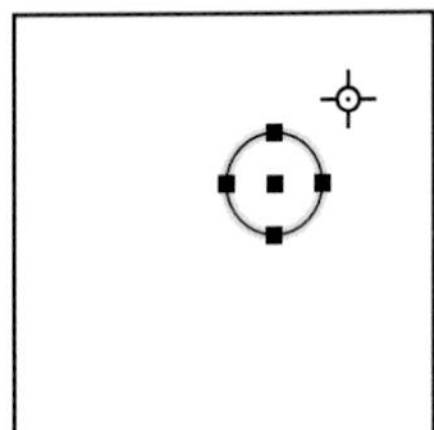
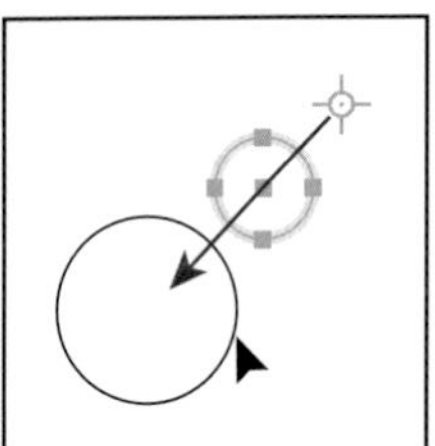

Original scaled from new point of origin

When you transform an object or objects, the changes take place horizontally (along the *x* axis), vertically (along the *y* axis), or along both axes.

Rotating

Rotating an object turns it around a fixed point that you designate. The default point of origin is the object's center point. Copying while rotating is a useful way to create radially symmetrical objects, such as the petals of a flower.

To rotate with the free transform tool:

1 With the selection tool (), select the object or objects to rotate.

2 Select the free transform tool ().

3 Position the pointer anywhere outside the bounding box. The pointer changes to ().

4 Drag until the selection is at the desired angle of rotation.

To rotate with the rotate tool:

1 With the selection tool, select the object or objects to rotate.

2 Select the rotate tool ().

3 Do one of the following:

- Drag to rotate around the object's center point.
- Click once to set the point of origin around which you want the object to rotate. Then move the arrowhead away from the point of origin and drag in a circular motion. Shift-drag to constrain the tool to multiples of 45 degrees.

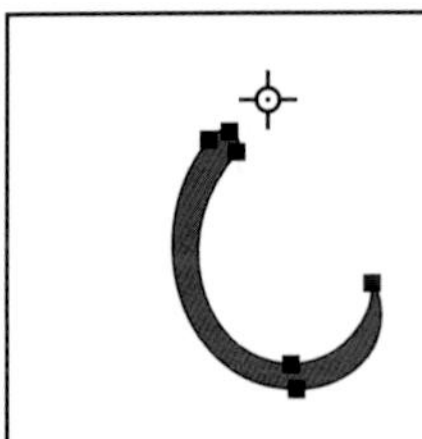
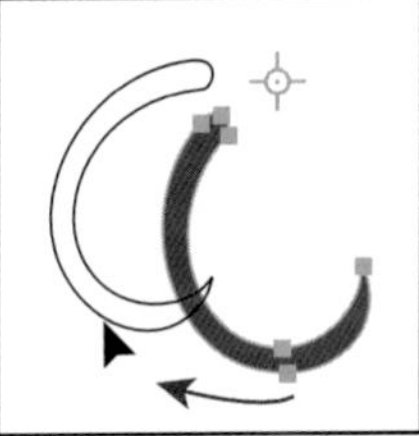

Click to set point of origin. Then drag to rotate.

• To rotate a copy of the object instead of the object itself, hold down Alt (Windows) or Option (Mac OS) after you start to drag.

• For finer control, drag farther from the object's point of origin.

To rotate by specifying an angle:

1 With the selection tool, select the object or objects to rotate.

2 Do one of the following:

• To set the center point as the point of origin, select the rotate tool ( ).

• To change the point of origin from which to rotate the object, select the rotate tool, and click where you want the new point of origin.

• To change the point of origin and specify the rotation angle in the Rotate dialog box, select the rotate tool, and Alt-click (Windows) or Option-click (Mac OS) the new point of origin.

• To specify the rotation angle in the Rotate dialog box, choose Object > Transform > Rotate, or double-click the rotate tool.

3 Enter the rotation angle, in degrees, in the Angle text box. Enter a negative angle to rotate the object clockwise; enter a positive angle to rotate the object counterclockwise.

4 Do one of the following:

• To rotate the object, click OK.

• To rotate a copy of the object, click Copy.

• To preview the effect before you apply it, select Preview.

• To place multiple copies of the object in a circular pattern around a point of origin, click Copy and then choose Object > Transform > Transform Again.

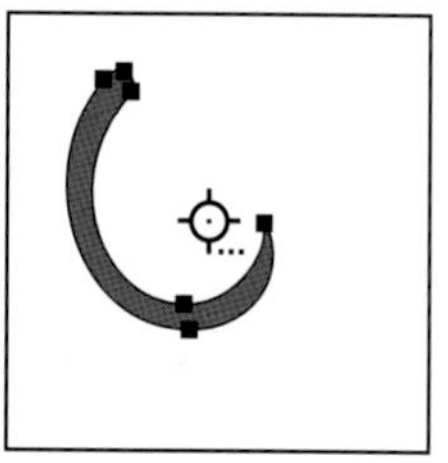
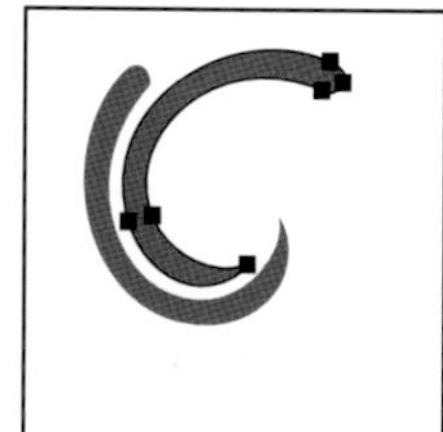

Set point of origin. Then use Rotate dialog box and Copy option to rotate.

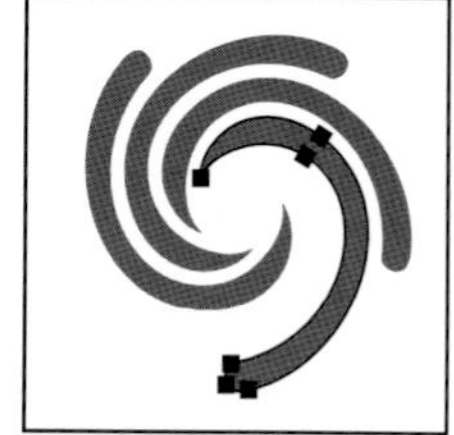

Choose Object > Transform >Transform Again. Result.

To rotate each object individually in a group:

1 With the selection tool, select the object or objects to rotate.

2 Choose Object > Transform > Transform Each.

3 In the Angle text box, enter the angle by which to rotate the selected objects, between –360 degrees and 360 degrees.

4 To preview the effect before you apply it, select Preview.

5 Do one of the following:

• To rotate the objects by the specified amount, click OK.

• To rotate the objects by a random amount, but by no more than the number of degrees specified in the Rotate text box, select Random, and click OK.

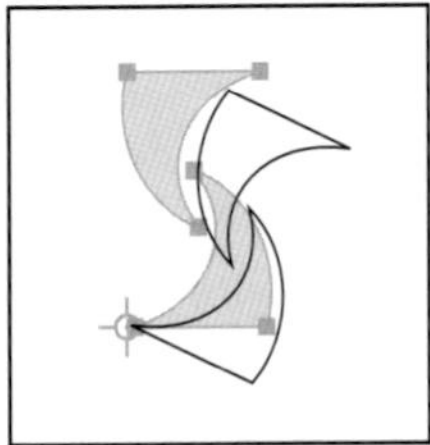
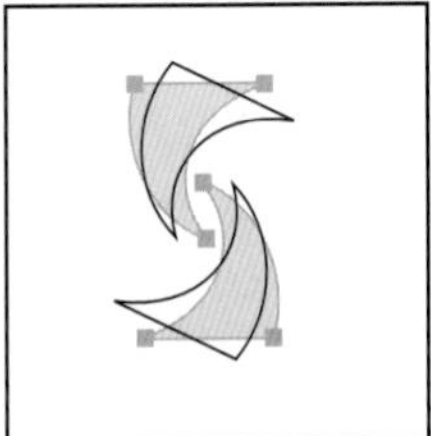

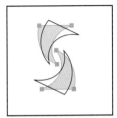

Rotate tool compared with the Transform Each command, Rotate option

Scaling

Scaling an object enlarges or reduces it horizontally (along the *x* axis), vertically (along the *y* axis), or both horizontally and vertically, relative to the point of origin you designate. The default point of origin is the object's center point.

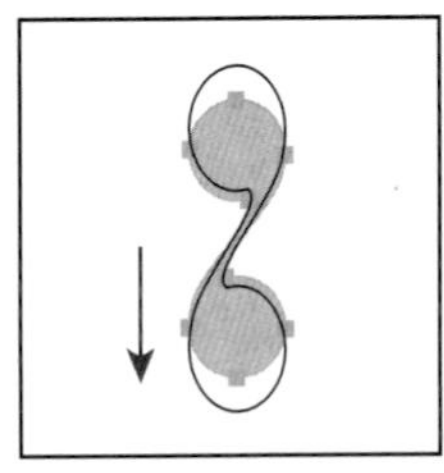
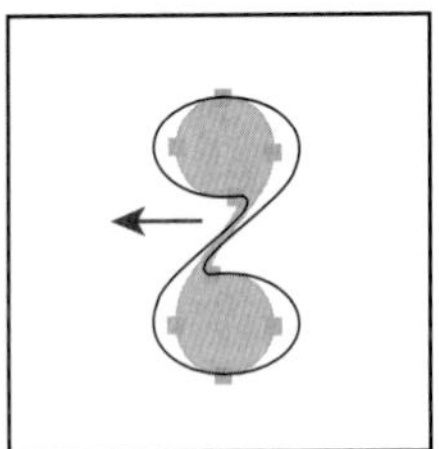

Scaling vertical and then horizontal

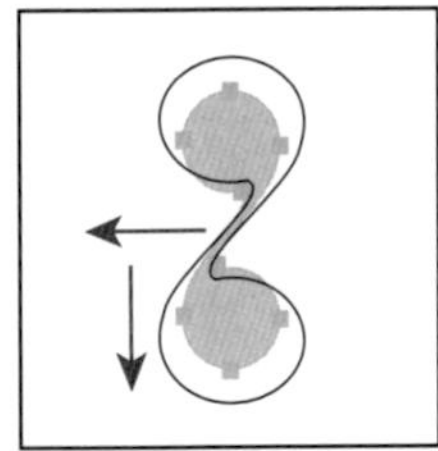

Scaling both vertical and horizontal

To scale with the bounding box:

1 With the selection tool, select the object or objects to scale.

2 Drag a handle until the selection is the desired size.

• Shift-drag the handle to preserve the proportion.

• Alt-drag (Windows) or Option-drag (Mac OS) to scale from the center of the bounding box (instead of the opposite handle).

To scale with the free transform tool:

1 With the selection tool, select the object or objects to scale.

2 Select the free transform tool ( ).

3 Drag a handle of the bounding box until the object is the desired size.

• Shift-drag the handle to preserve the proportion.

• Alt-drag (Windows) or Option-drag (Mac OS) to scale from the center of the bounding box (instead of the opposite handle).

To scale with the scale tool:

1 With the selection tool, select the object or objects to scale.

2 Select the scale tool ( ).

3 Do one of the following:

• Select the object, and drag to resize it around the center point.

• Click to set the point of origin from which you want the object to be resized, move the pointer away from the point of origin, and then drag to scale the object.

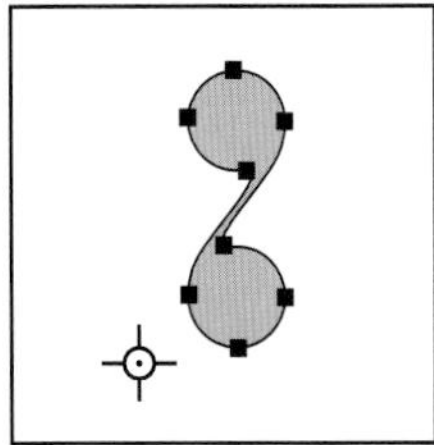

Click to set point of origin, and drag to scale.

• Shift-drag to scale the object uniformly.

• To scale a copy of the object instead of the object itself, start dragging and then hold down Alt (Windows) or Option (Mac OS).

• For finer control over scaling, start dragging farther from the point of origin.

To scale by specifying scale factors:

1 With the selection tool, select the object or objects to scale.

2 Do one of the following:

• To set the center point as the point of origin, select the scale tool.

• To change the point of origin from which to scale the object, select the scale tool, and click the new point of origin.

3 To specify the scale percentage in the Scale dialog box, choose Object > Transform > Scale, or double-click the scale tool.

4 In the Scale dialog box, do one of the following:

• Select Uniform, and enter a percentage in the Scale text box to preserve the relative height and width of the object. With uniform scaling, you can also choose to preserve stroke weights or to scale them. If you scale stroke weights, the line weights of all stroked paths (as specified in the Stroke palette) are scaled along with the objects.

You can also choose to scale stroke weights automatically, whether you scale objects by dragging or by using the Scale dialog box. To scale stroke weights automatically, select Scale Stroke Weight in the Scale dialog box or the General Preferences dialog box, or choose the command from the Transform palette menu.

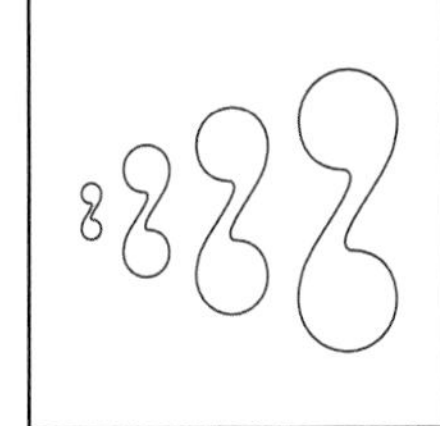

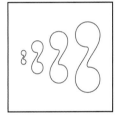

Scale Stroke Weight option on and off

• Select Non-Uniform, and enter the horizontal and vertical scale factors as percentages to scale the height and width separately. The scale factors are relative to the specified point of origin and can be negative numbers.

5 Do one of the following:

• To scale the object, click OK.

• To scale a copy of the object, click Copy.

• To preview the effect before you apply it, select Preview.

To scale objects individually in a group:

1 With the selection tool, select the objects to scale.

2 Choose Object > Transform > Transform Each.

3 In the Scale Horizontal and Vertical text boxes, enter the percentages by which to scale the selected objects.

4 Select Preview to preview the effect before you apply it.

5 Do one of the following:

• To scale the objects by the specified amounts, click OK.

• To scale the objects randomly, but by no more than the percentages specified in the Horizontal and Vertical text boxes, select Random, and click OK.

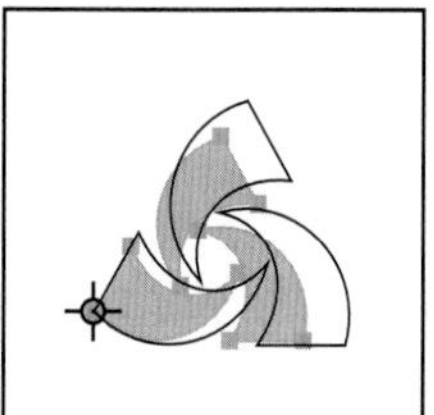
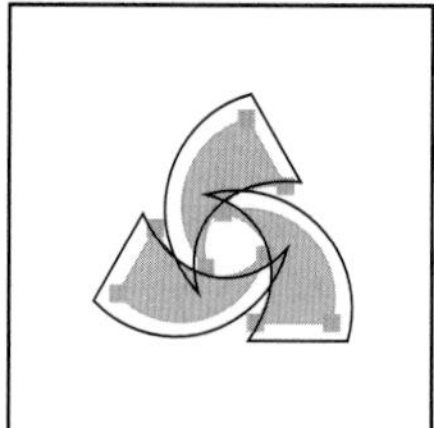

Scale tool compared with the Scale option in Transform Each dialog box

Reflecting

Reflecting an object flips the object across an invisible axis that you specify. Copying while reflecting lets you create a mirror image of an object.

To reflect with the free transform tool:

1 With the selection tool, select the object or objects to reflect.

2 Select the free transform tool ( ).

3 Drag a handle of the bounding box past the opposite edge or handle until the object is at the desired level of reflection.

To reflect with the reflect tool:

1 With the selection tool, select the object or objects to reflect.

2 Select the reflect tool ( ).

3 Position the pointer on one point along the invisible axis across which you want the reflection to occur, and click to set the point of origin. The pointer changes to an arrowhead.

4 Position the pointer at another point along the invisible axis, and do one of the following:

• Click to set a point across which to reflect the object. When you click, the selected object flips over the defined axis.

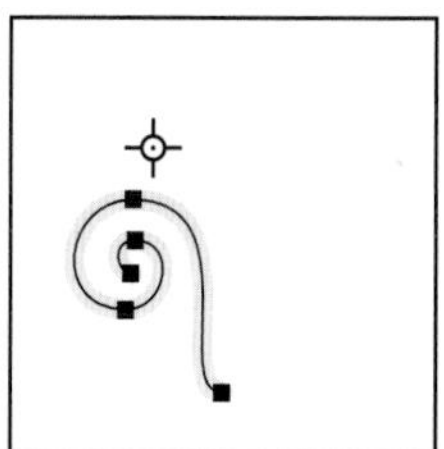

Click to set origin, then click again to reflect across axis.

• Adjust the axis of reflection by dragging instead of clicking. Shift-drag to constrain. As you drag, the invisible axis of reflection rotates around the point you clicked in step 3. When the image is in the desired position, release the mouse button.

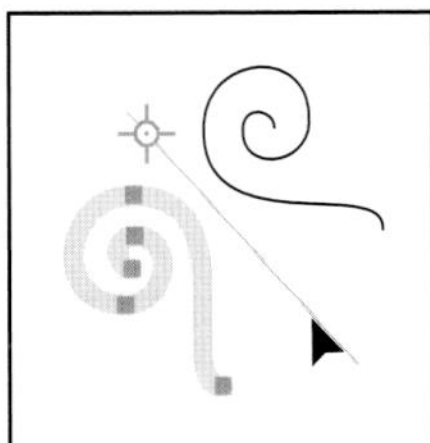

Drag reflect tool to rotate axis of reflection.

• For finer control over the reflection, drag farther from the object's point of origin.

To reflect by specifying an axis:

1 With the selection tool, select the object or objects to reflect.

2 Do one of the following:

• To set the center point as the point of origin, click the reflect tool.

• To change the point of origin from which to reflect the object, select the reflect tool and click where you want the new point of origin. To move the point of origin again, double-click where you want it to be.

3 To specify the reflect axis in the Reflect dialog box, choose Object > Transform > Reflect.

4 In the Reflect dialog box, select the axis across which you want the object to be reflected. You can reflect an object across a horizontal, a vertical, or an angled axis.

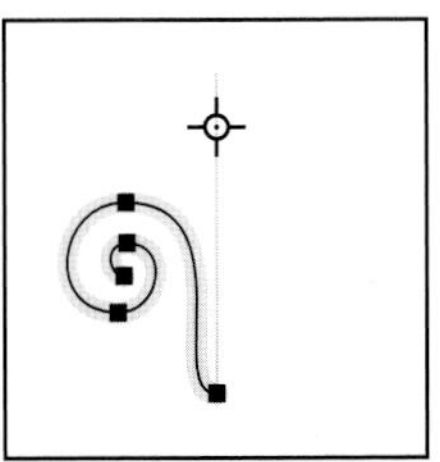
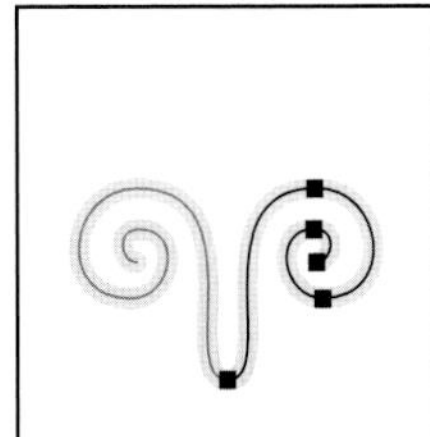

Set point of origin at top of object. Then reflect-copy across vertical axis.

If you choose an angled axis, enter the desired angle of reflection, in degrees, relative to the *x* axis. Positive angles reflect the axis counterclockwise; negative angles reflect it clockwise.

5 Do one of the following:

• To reflect the object, click OK.

• To reflect a copy of the object, click Copy.

• To preview the effect before you apply it, select Preview.

Shearing

Shearing an object slants, or *skews*, the object along the axis you specify. Copying while shearing is useful for creating cast shadows.

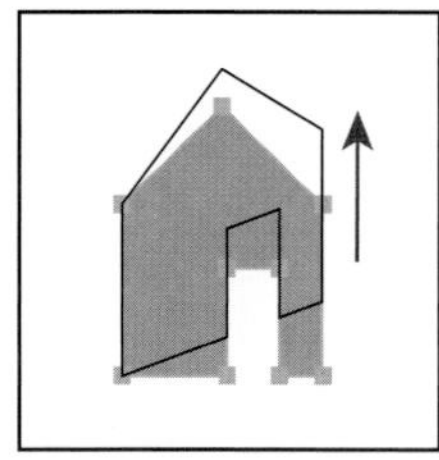
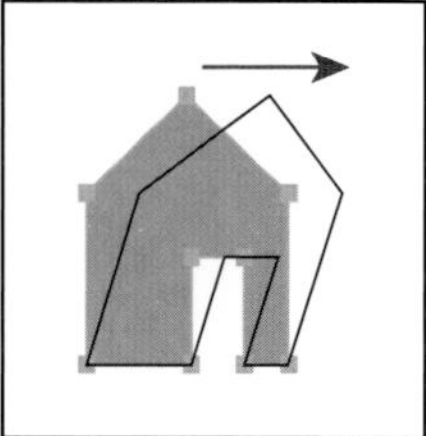

Shearing vertical and then horizontal

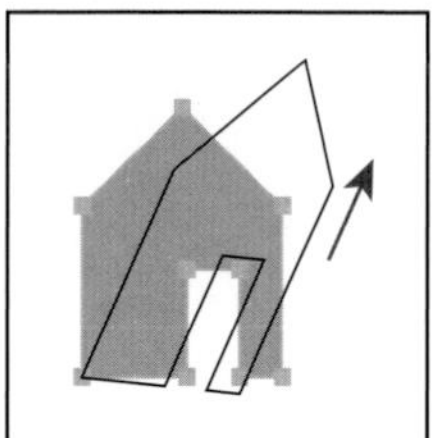

Shearing both vertical and horizontal

To shear with the free transform tool:

1 With the selection tool, select the object or objects to shear.

2 Select the free transform tool (⌗).

3 Start dragging a handle on the side of the bounding box (not a corner) and then hold down Ctrl+Alt (Windows) or Option+Command (Mac OS) as you drag until the object is at the desired perspective. Shift-drag to constrain the tool to multiples of 45 degrees.

To shear with the shear tool:

1 With the selection tool, select the object or objects to shear.

2 Select the shear tool ( ).

3 Do one of the following:

- Drag the object to shear by using the object's center point as the point of origin.
- Click to set the point of origin from which you want the object to be sheared. Then move the pointer away from the shear axis, and drag in the direction you want to shear the object.
- Shift-drag to constrain the tool.

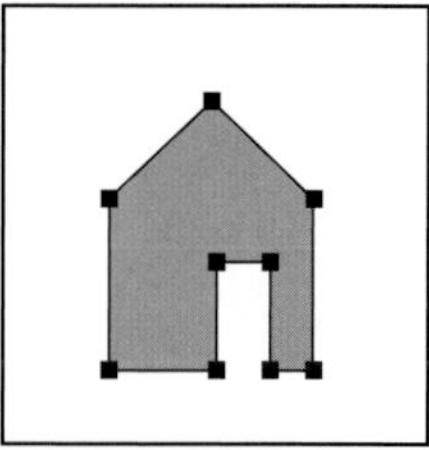
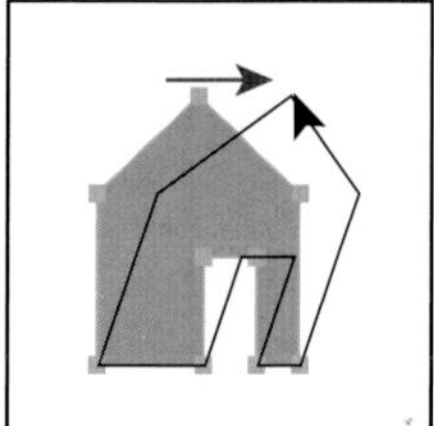

Select object. Then drag with the shear tool.

- To shear a copy of the object instead of the object itself, start dragging and then hold down Alt (Windows) or Option (Mac OS).
- For finer control over shearing, start dragging farther from the point of origin.

To shear by specifying an angle and an axis:

1 With the selection tool, select the object or objects to shear.

2 Do one of the following:

• To set the center point as the point of origin, click the shear tool.

• To change the point of origin from which to shear the object, select the shear tool and click where you want the point of origin.

3 To specify the shear angle and axis in the Shear dialog box, choose Object > Transform > Shear.

4 In the Shear dialog box, enter the new shear angle. The shear angle is the amount of slant to be applied to the object, relative to a line perpendicular to the shear axis. (Contrary to the way the program works with other transformation tools, the shear angle is calculated clockwise from the current axis.)

5 Specify the axis along which the object is to be sheared. You can shear an object along a horizontal, a vertical, or an angled axis.

If you choose an angled axis, enter the angle of the axis that you want, in degrees, relative to the *x* axis.

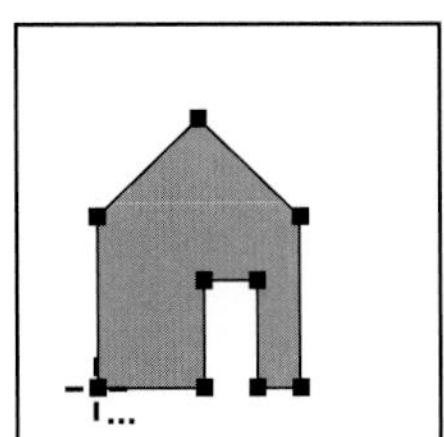

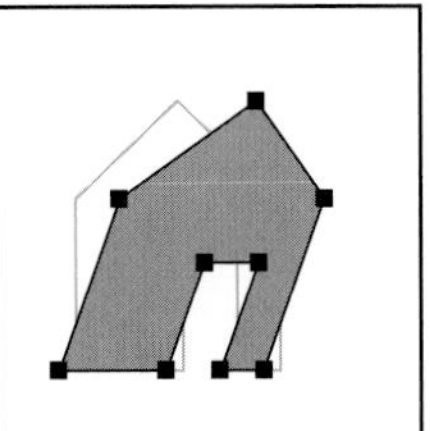

Point of origin placed at left corner, and shear angle entered into Shear dialog box

6 Do one of the following:

• To shear the object, click OK.

• To shear a copy of the object, click Copy.

• To preview the effect before you apply it, select Preview.

Distorting

Distorting an object varies the size and shape of an object by dragging the corner points of the free transform tool's bounding box. As you drag the corner handles of the bounding box, the object's shape is distorted accordingly.

To distort with the free transform tool:

1 With the selection tool, select the object or objects to distort.

2 Select the free transform tool ().

3 Start dragging a handle on the corner of the bounding box (not a side) and then do one of the following:

• Hold down Ctrl (Windows) or Command (Mac OS) until the selection is at the desired level of distortion.

• Hold down Shift+Alt+Ctrl (Windows) or Shift+Option+Command (Mac OS) to distort in perspective.

Original

Distorting in perspective

Resetting the bounding box angle

After you transform a selection, you can return the angle of the bounding box to its original orientation. You can do this after any transformation except shearing.

Choose Object > Transform > Reset Bounding Box.

Repeating transformations

Sometimes you may want to repeat the same transformation several times, especially when you are copying objects. The Transform Again command in the Object menu lets you repeat a move, scale, rotate, reflect, or shear operation as many times as you want. You must choose the command immediately after you perform the operation. The Transform Again command does not work with the blend tool.

To repeat a transformation:

Do the following immediately after performing a transformation:

1 Make sure the object on which you want to repeat the transformation is selected.

2 Do one of the following:

• Choose Object > Transform > Transform Again.

• Press the right mouse button (Windows), or Control-click (Mac OS), and choose Transform Again from the context-sensitive menu.

Using the Transform palette

The Transform palette displays information about the location, size, and orientation of one or more selected objects. By entering new values, you can modify the selected objects. All values in the palette refer to the bounding boxes of the objects. You can also use commands in the Transform palette menu for such actions as flipping an object across the path or scaling the stroke weight.

To use the Transform palette:

1 Choose Window > Show Transform.

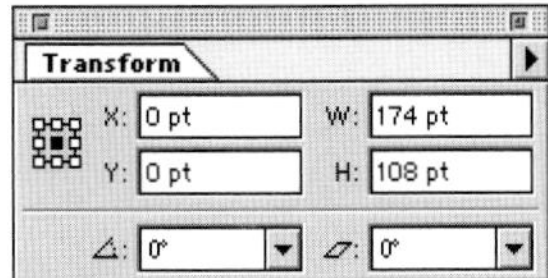

Transform palette

2 With the selection tool, select the object or objects to transform.

3 Enter options in the Transform palette:

• To select the reference point from which you are modifying the selection, click a handle on the square representing the object's bounding box.

• To change a selection to a horizontal orientation, enter a value in the X text box.

• To change a selection to a vertical orientation, enter a value in the Y text box.

• To change the width of a selection's bounding box, enter a value in the W text box.

• To change the height of a selection's bounding box, enter a value in the H text box.

• To rotate a selection, enter a new angle between 0 and 360 degrees in the Angle text box, or choose a value from the pop-up menu.

• To shear a selection, enter a value in the Shear text box, or choose a value from the pop-up menu.

4 Press Tab, or Enter (Windows), or Return (Mac OS) to apply the change.

To use commands in the Transform palette menu:

1 Choose Window > Show Transform.

2 With the selection tool, select the object or objects to transform.

3 Choose a command from the palette menu:

• To reflect a selection horizontally, choose Flip Horizontal.

• To reflect a selection vertically, choose Flip Vertical.

• To include the stroke when an object is transformed, choose Scale Stroke Weight.

• To transform only the object, choose Transform Object Only.

• To transform only the pattern, choose Transform Pattern Only.

• To transform both the object and pattern, choose Transform Both.

Note: *To ensure that values entered in the Info and Transform palettes include stroke weight, choose File > Preferences > General, select the Display Stroke Weight option, and click OK.*

Using filters to modify shapes

Illustrator provides a variety of filters for changing an object's shape and path direction. Using these filters results in special effects that alter the original object's shape.

Note: *All of the following filters work with vector graphics only; you cannot use these filters with raster images.*

Punking and bloating

The Punk & Bloat filter curves objects inward and outward from their anchor points.

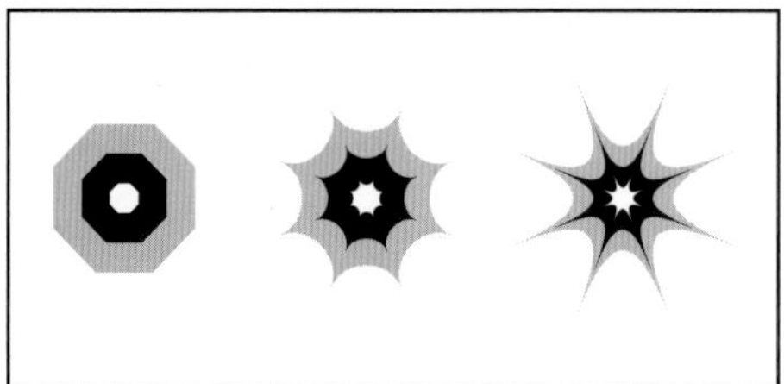

Original and Punk filter: -20% and -60%

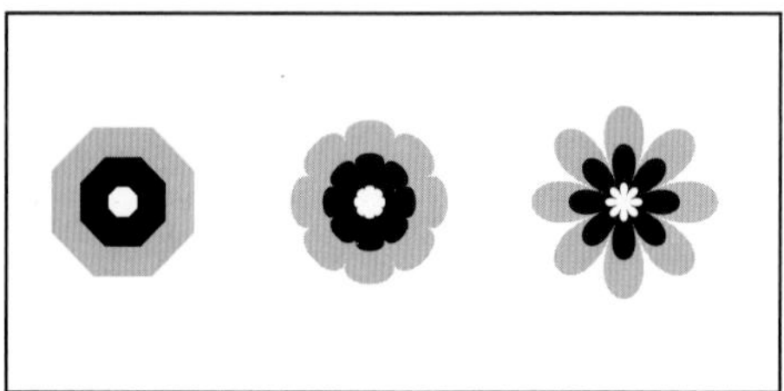

Original and Bloat filter: 20% and 60%

To bloat or punk an object:

1 With any selection tool, select the object to punk or bloat.

2 Choose Filter > Distort > Punk & Bloat.

3 Drag the slider toward Punk to curve the object inward from its anchor points and move the anchor points outward; drag the slider toward Bloat to curve the object outward from its anchor points and move the anchor points inward. You can also enter a value, from –200% to 200%, in the Percentage text box.

4 To preview the effect before you apply it, select Preview, and click OK.

Roughening

The Roughen filter moves anchor points in a jagged array from the original object, creating a rough edge on the object.

Original and Roughen filter: Smooth option and Corner option applied

To roughen an object:

1 With any selection tool, select the object to roughen.

2 Choose Filter > Distort > Roughen.

3 Set the size of the distortion by dragging the Size slider or entering a value between 0% and 100% in the Size text box.

4 Specify the details per inch by dragging the slider or entering a value between 0 and 100 in the Detail text box.

5 Select the type of distortion you want around each anchor point: Smooth (for soft edges) or Corner (for sharp edges).

6 To preview the effect before you apply it, select Preview, and click OK.

Scribbling and tweaking

The Scribble option randomly distorts objects by moving anchor points away from the original object. The Tweak option randomly distorts objects by moving anchor points on the selected object by an amount that you specify.

Original and Scribble and Tweak filters

To scribble or tweak an object:

1 With any selection tool, select the object to scribble or tweak.

2 Choose Filter > Distort > Scribble and Tweak.

3 Choose an option from the pop-up menu:

• Scribble moves anchor points randomly away from the original object. In the Horizontal and Vertical text boxes, enter the amount to move points, between 0% and 100%, or drag the sliders.

• Tweak moves anchor points on the selected object. In the Horizontal and Vertical text boxes, enter the amount to move points, between 0% and 100%, or drag the sliders.

4 Select options for the anchor points:

• Anchor Points moves anchor points. Deselecting this option keeps anchor points anchored while a filter is applied to the rest of the object.

• "In" Control Points moves control points that lead into anchor points on the path.

• "Out" Control Points moves control points that lead out of anchor points on the path.

5 Because results vary, select Preview to preview the effect before you apply it, and click OK.

Note: *Once you choose values, a different effect displays for both Scribble and Tweak when you select Preview.*

Twirling

The Twirl filter and the twirl tool rotate a selection more sharply in the center than at the edges.

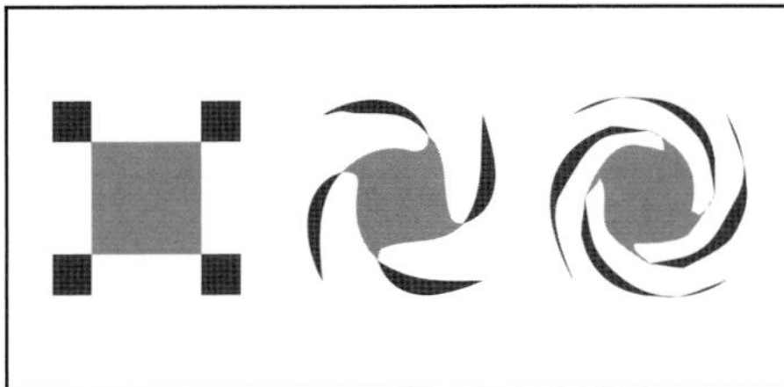

Original and Twirl filter: 160° and 320°

To twirl an object:

1 With any selection tool, select the object to twirl.

2 Do one of the following:

• Choose Filter > Distort > Twirl. Enter a value for the twirl angle, from –3600 to 3600 (a positive value twirls clockwise and a negative value twirls counterclockwise), and click OK.

• Select the twirl tool (), and drag the object clockwise or counterclockwise.

Adding drop shadows

The Drop Shadow filter creates a three-dimensional shadow effect on any selected object. You can offset the drop shadow any distance from the object along the *x* or *y* axis, as well as vary the darkness of the drop shadow.

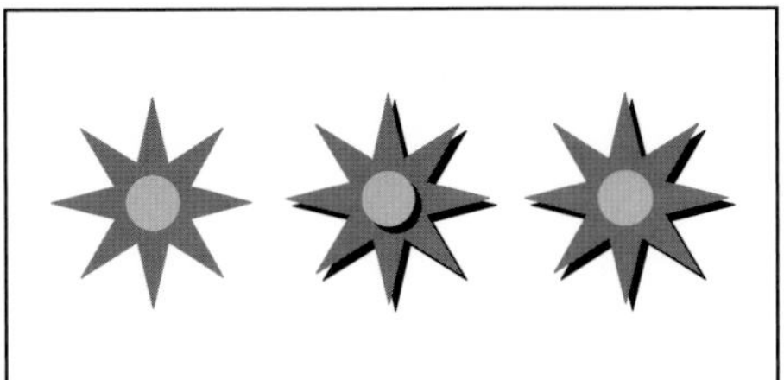

Original and Drop Shadow filter: grouped shadows and ungrouped shadows

To create a drop shadow:

1 With any selection tool, select the object that you want to give a drop shadow.

2 Choose Filter > Stylize > Drop Shadow.

3 Enter the distance you want the drop shadow to be offset from the object on the *x* axis or the *y* axis (in the unit of measure set in the General Preferences dialog box).

4 Enter the percentage darkness (percentage of black added) you want for the drop shadow. A value of 100% used with a selected object that contains a fill or stroke color other than black creates a multicolored black shadow. A value of 100% used with a selected object that contains only a black fill or stroke creates a 100% black shadow. A value of 0% creates a drop shadow the color of the selected object.

5 To make the shadow part of the object rather than a separate object in the background, select Group Shadows.

For example, if you have two objects currently selected and one overlaps the other, grouping the shadows makes the shadow of the top object appear on top of the bottom object. If you do not group the shadows, the shadows of both selected objects appear behind the bottom object.

6 Click OK.

Rounding corners

The Round Corners filter converts the corner points of an object to smooth curves.

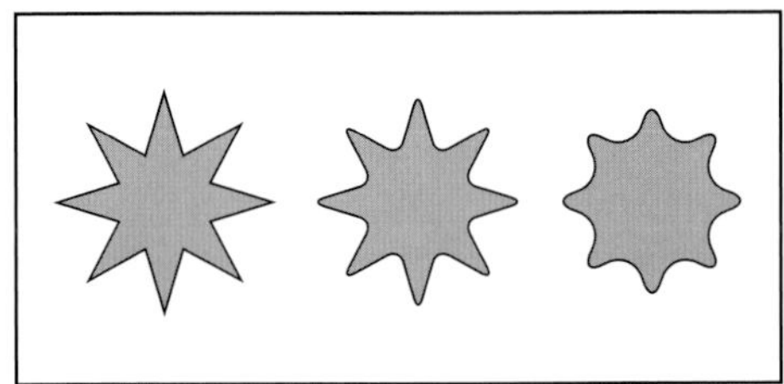

Original and Round Corners filter: 3 point and 18 point

To round corners on an object:

1 With any selection tool, select the object whose corners you want to round.

2 Choose Filter > Stylize > Round Corners.

3 Enter a value (in the unit of measure specified in the General Preferences dialog box) in the Radius text box to determine the curvature of the rounded curve, and click OK.

Creating line effects

Using the Zig Zag and Add Arrowheads filters, you can create wavy and Zig Zag effects and add various arrowhead styles to lines.

The Zig Zag filter adds anchor points to an existing line and then moves some of the points to the left of (or upward from) the line and some to the right of (or downward from) the line. You can specify the number of anchor points to create and the distance to move them. You can also choose whether to create smooth anchor points for a wavy line effect, or corner anchor points for a jagged line effect.

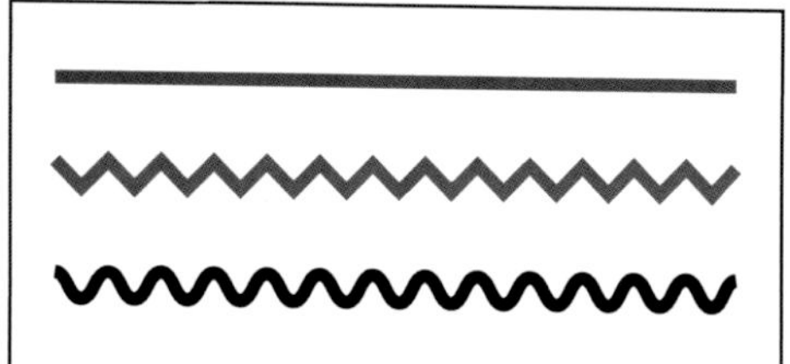

Original, Zig Zag, and wavy lines

The Add Arrowheads filter lets you add an arrowhead or arrow tail to any selected line. The resulting arrows can be edited like any other object.

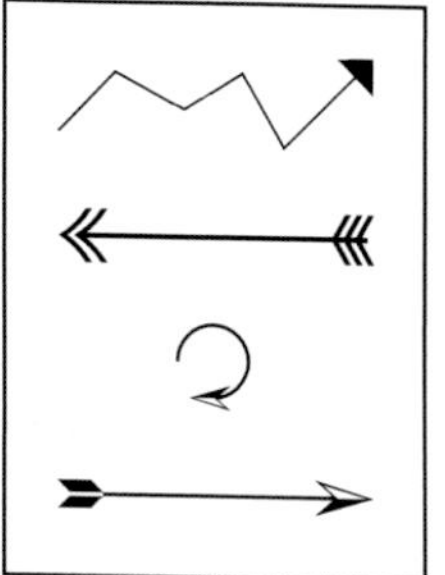

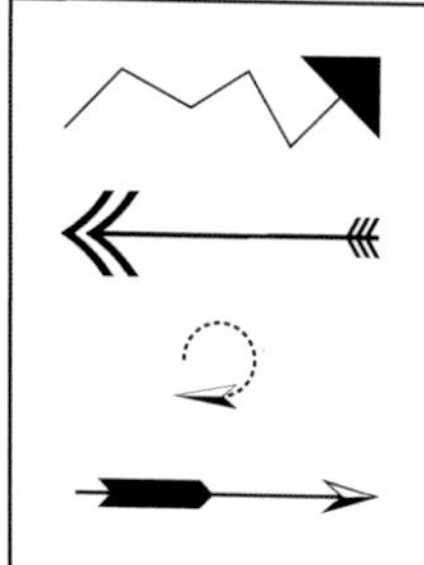

Arrowheads added and then edited

For information about creating stroked lines, see "Using the Stroke palette" on page 163.

To convert straight lines to Zig Zags:

1 With any selection tool, select the line you want to convert.

2 Choose Filter > Distort > Zig Zag.

3 In the Amount text box, enter the distance you want to move points on the line, or drag the slider.

4 In the Ridges text box, enter the number of ridges per inch you want, or drag the slider.

5 Select from the following options:

- Smooth to create smooth points, resulting in a wavy line.
- Corner to create corner points, resulting in a jagged line.
- Preview to preview the line.

6 Click OK.

To add arrowheads to a line:

1 With any selection tool, select a line to which you want to add arrowheads.

2 Choose Filter > Stylize > Add Arrowheads.

3 Choose from various arrowhead designs by clicking the forward or backward icons below the arrow box.

4 To rescale the size of an arrowhead, enter the percentage you want in the Scale text box. This scales the arrowhead relative to the stroke weight of the line.

5 Choose Start or End to place the arrowhead at the beginning or the end of the line; choose Both Ends to place the arrowhead at both ends of the line. The start and end of the line refer to the order in which the line was drawn.

6 Click OK.

Using the Pathfinder palette to modify shapes

The Pathfinder commands in the Pathfinder palette combine, isolate, and subdivide objects, and they build new objects formed by the intersections of objects.

For a color illustration of new objects formed by the intersections of objects, see the "Pathfinder Gallery" on page 235.

To use the Pathfinder palette, you click a button in the palette that corresponds to the action you want to do.

Most Pathfinder commands create compound paths. A *compound path* is a group of two or more paths that are painted so that overlapping paths can appear transparent. Except where noted, the objects created by all Pathfinder commands are assigned the same paint style as the top object in the current layer's stack. (See "Stacking objects" on page 123 and "Working with compound paths" on page 149.)

You can choose Show Options from the Pathfinder palette menu to mix colors that overlap or adjoin using the Hard Mix, Soft Mix, and Trap options. (See "Using the Hard Mix and Soft Mix commands" on page 172 and "Step 3: Create a trap to compensate for misregistration on press" on page 365.)

***Note:** Applying Pathfinder commands to complex selections, such as blends, may require large amounts of RAM. If you are unable to use a Pathfinder command with Mac OS successfully, try increasing the memory allotted to the Adobe Illustrator program.*

To use the Pathfinder commands:

***Note:** You cannot use Pathfinder commands with objects created using the gradient mesh tool.*

1 With the selection tool (↖), select the objects to modify.

2 Choose Window > Show Pathfinder.

3 Click a Pathfinder command:

Unite Traces the outline of all selected objects as if they were a single, merged object. The resulting shape takes on the paint attributes of the top object selected. Any objects inside the selected objects are deleted.

Intersect Traces the outline of all overlapping shapes in the selected objects, ignoring any nonoverlapping areas. This command works on two objects at a time.

Exclude Traces all nonoverlapping areas of the selected objects and makes overlapping areas transparent. Where an even number of objects overlap, the overlap becomes transparent. Where an odd number of objects overlap, the overlap becomes filled.

Minus Front Subtracts the frontmost selected objects from the backmost object. You can use this command to delete areas of an illustration by adjusting the stacking order. (See "Stacking objects" on page 123.)

Minus Back Subtracts the backmost selected objects from the frontmost object. You can use this command to delete areas of an illustration by adjusting the stacking order. (See "Stacking objects" on page 123.)

Divide Divides a piece of artwork into its component filled faces (a *face* is an area undivided by a line segment). The resulting faces can then be ungrouped and manipulated independently of each other.

You can choose to delete or preserve unfilled objects when applying the Divide command. See "Setting Pathfinder options" on page 147.

Trim Removes the part of a filled object that is hidden. It removes any strokes and does not merge objects of the same color.

Merge Removes the part of a filled object that is hidden. It removes any strokes and merges any adjoining or overlapping objects filled with the same color.

Crop Divides artwork into its component filled faces and then deletes all the parts of the artwork that fall outside the boundary of the topmost object. It also removes any strokes.

Outline Divides an object into its component line segments, or *edges*. Each edge can be ungrouped and independently manipulated. This command is useful for preparing artwork that needs a trap for overprinting objects. (See Chapter 15, "Producing Color Separations.")

You can choose to delete or preserve unfilled objects when applying the Outline command. See "Setting Pathfinder options" on page 147.

To repeat the most recent Pathfinder command:

In the Pathfinder palette menu, choose Repeat Command, where Command is the most recently used command. The command is applied with the most recently used settings.

Setting Pathfinder options

The Pathfinder Options dialog box lets you change the precision of Pathfinder commands and remove any redundant points created as a result of using Pathfinder commands. You can also control how the Divide and Outline commands affect unfilled objects.

Note: *Pathfinder works best with filled and closed objects without strokes. Using Pathfinder with open and stroked paths may give you unexpected results.*

To set Pathfinder options:

1 Choose Window > Show Pathfinder.

2 Choose Pathfinder Options from the Pathfinder palette menu.

3 Specify Pathfinder options:

• Enter a precision value in the Calculate Precision text box to affect the precision with which Pathfinder commands calculate when applied. The more precise the calculation, the more accurate the drawing and the more time is required to carry out a Pathfinder command. A more precise calculation may produce a more accurate drawing but carrying out a Pathfinder command will require more time.

• Select Remove Redundant Points to delete any points that are located directly on top of each other and that you created when using a Pathfinder command.

• Select Divide & Outline Will Remove Unpainted Artwork to delete any unfilled objects in the selected artwork that result from using the Divide or Outline command.

• To reset all options to their default settings, click Defaults.

4 Click OK.

Converting strokes to filled objects

The Outline Path command traces the outline of all stroked paths within the selected artwork and substitutes a filled object with the same width as the original stroked path. This commands lets you modify the outline of an object more than you could if it were only a stroke.

You can also use this command to create an overlay of your original artwork that strips out all stroked lines and replaces them with compound filled paths. The Outline Path command is useful when you prepare artwork for trapping color separations. (See Chapter 15, "Producing Color Separations.")

Selected path and Outline Path command applied

To create an outline of your artwork:

1 With the selection tool, select the artwork to outline. The artwork can contain filled and stroked paths; however, only stroked paths are outlined.

2 Choose Object > Path > Outline Path. The outline replaces the original artwork and is selected.

Cutting objects

The Slice command in the Object menu and the knife tool in the toolbox cut objects in a designated shape. When you use the Slice command, the object you cut must be ungrouped. The knife tool slices grouped and ungrouped objects.

The Slice command lets you use a selected object as a cookie cutter or stencil to cut through other objects. The Slice command slices overlapping objects into discrete shapes according to the selection's boundaries, and it discards the original selection.

The knife tool slices objects along a freehand path you draw with the tool, dividing objects into their component filled faces (a *face* is an area undivided by a line segment).

To cut objects by using the Slice command:

1 With the selection tool, select the object to use as a cutter, and position it so that it touches the object to cut. (To retain the original selection, save a copy elsewhere in your file.) The object cuts any filled object or objects that it's touching.

2 To cut the object, choose Object > Path > Slice. The shapes that result are ungrouped and selected.

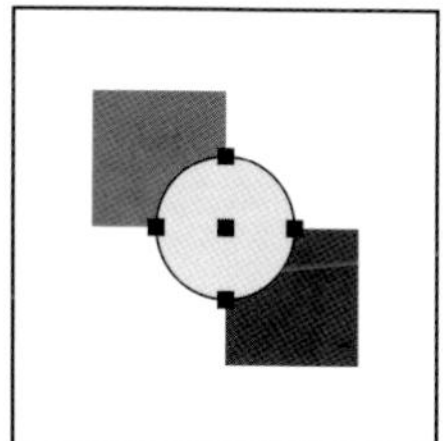

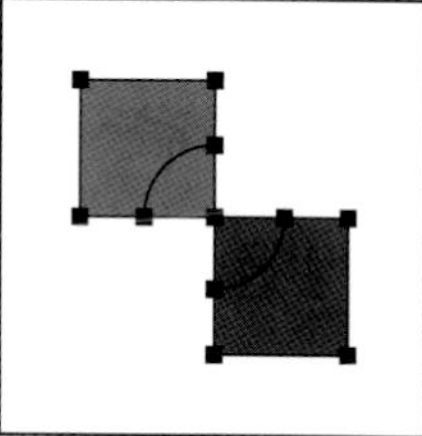

Object selected and with Slice command applied

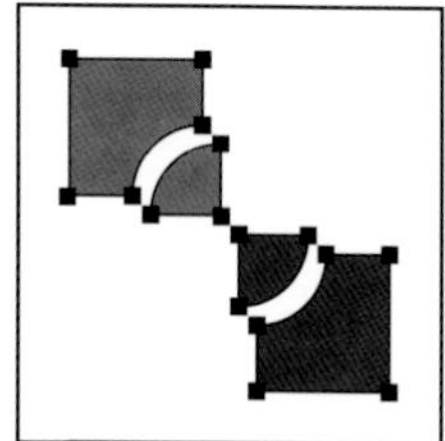

Resulting objects pulled apart

To cut objects by using the knife tool:

1 Select the knife tool ( ).

2 Drag the pointer over the object. The knife cuts in a curved path.

To cut in a straight path, Alt-drag (Windows) or Option-drag (Mac OS) the knife tool.

Working with compound paths

Using the Compound Paths command enables you to create paths that have transparent interior spaces where the original objects overlapped (such as the interiors of the letters *o* and *g*). This method lets you create objects more complex than you could easily create using the drawing tools or Pathfinder commands.

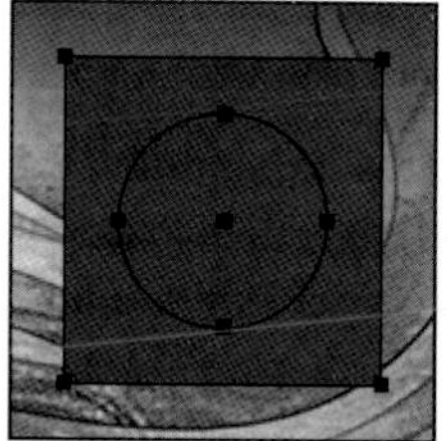

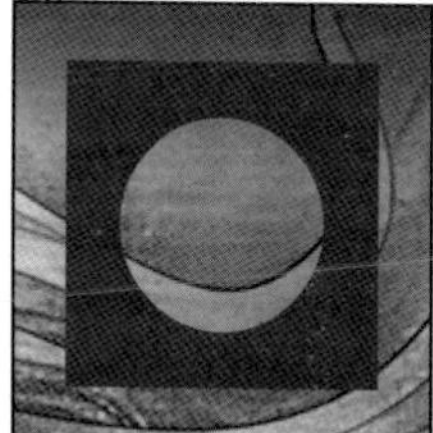

Original: Object on top of textured background. Result: Object converted to compound path, revealing background.

Compound paths act as grouped objects. To select part of a compound path, you must use the direct-selection tool.

Important: *If you use complex shapes as compound paths, or if you use several compound paths in a file, you may have problems printing the file. If you experience printing problems, simplify or eliminate the compound paths.*

Creating and adjusting compound paths

When you are learning to create compound paths, you may find it helpful to work in Preview view or to open two windows so that you can preview your artwork in one window as you work in Artwork view in the other window. Viewing both windows helps you understand how compound paths work.

Once you define objects as a compound path, all objects in the compound path take on the paint attributes of the backmost object in the stacking order. Releasing the compound path does not reapply the objects' previous paint attributes.

To create a compound path:

1 Make sure the objects you want to see through are in front of the background object in the painting order.

2 Use the selection tool, or drag a marquee to select all of the objects to include in the compound path.

3 Choose Object > Compound Paths > Make. You create a hole in the overlapping objects.

When you create a compound path, you can specify whether overlapping paths appear transparent or filled by clicking a Reverse Path Direction button in the Attributes palette.

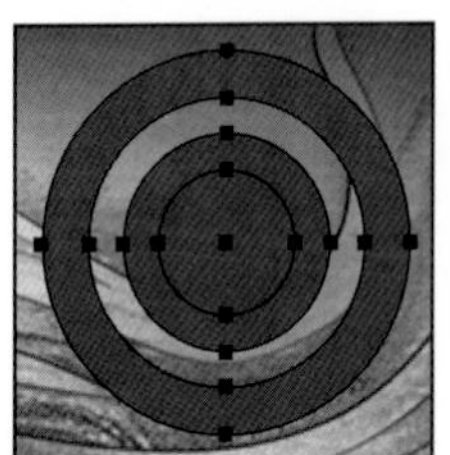
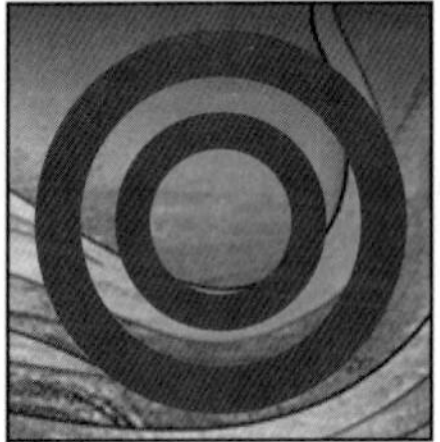

Compound path: Inner circle selected and Reversed option changed on inner circle

To release compound paths:

1 With the selection tool, select the compound path to release.

2 Choose Object > Compound Paths > Release.

To reverse paths within compound paths:

1 With the selection tool (↖), select the part of the compound path to reverse. Do not select the entire compound path.

2 Choose Window > Show Attributes.

3 Click the Reverse Path Direction Off button or the Reverse Path Direction On button.

Working with masks

Masks crop part of the artwork so that only a portion of the artwork appears through the shape or shapes you create. In Adobe Illustrator, you mask objects by using the Make Mask command.

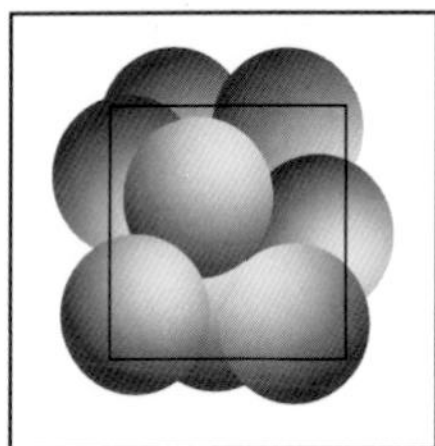

Masking object placed on top of artwork and Mask command applied

Important: *If you use complex shapes as masks, or if you use several masks in a file, you may have problems printing the file. If you experience printing problems, simplify or eliminate the masks.*

To see whether an object is a mask:

1 With the selection tool, select the object.

2 Choose File > Selection Info. The Selection Info dialog box lists the masking status of the selected object.

You can also select all masks in your artwork by using the Select Masks command. (See "Modifying and selecting masks" on page 151.)

Creating masks

A masking object can consist of a single path or a compound path.

To mask objects:

1 Draw or use the selection tool to select the object to use as a mask.

2 Make sure that the object is on top of the objects you want to mask.

When you mask objects on different layers, keep in mind that objects on intermediate layers become part of the masked artwork. (See "About painting in Adobe Illustrator" on page 159.)

3 Select the mask and the objects you want masked.

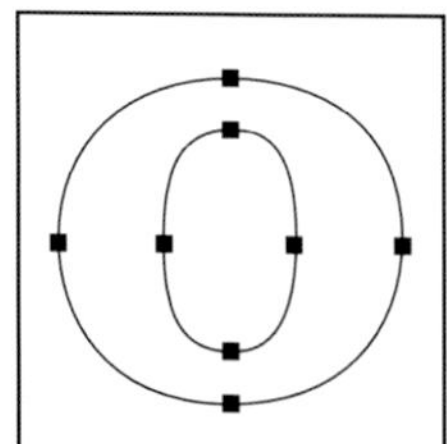

Mask and objects to be masked

4 Choose Object > Masks > Make. The mask loses its paint attributes and is assigned a fill and stroke value of None.

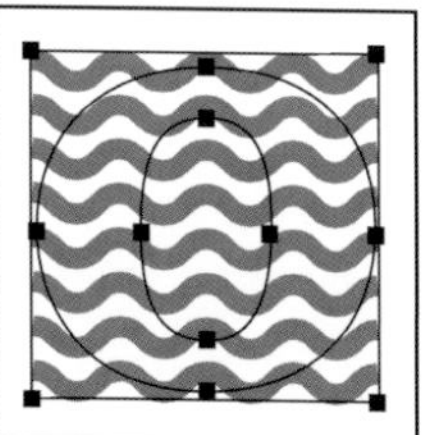

Mask and objects selected and Make Mask command applied

To undo the effects of a mask:

1 Use the selection tool or drag a marquee to select the objects you no longer want to use as a mask.

2 Choose Object > Masks > Release.

Because the mask was assigned a fill and stroke value of None, it is not visible unless you select it or assign it new paint attributes.

Modifying and selecting masks

Once you create a mask, the mask and the masked objects can be selected and modified as any other object. Masked objects are unlocked by default. You can lock the mask so that mask objects are secured together. By locking the mask, individual objects cannot be unintentionally moved with the direct-selection tool.

The Select Masks command finds and selects masks in the file. If there are no objects selected, the command selects all of the masks in your file. If objects are selected, the command deselects any objects that are not masks.

When you rasterize a mask, the full stroke value of the mask is displayed. (See Chapter 10, "Working with Bitmap Images.")

To select all masks in a file:

Choose Edit > Select > Masks.

To find out which objects are affected by a mask:

1 Select the group-selection tool.

2 Click the mask once to select it, and then continue clicking until all masked objects are selected.

To add an object to masked artwork:

1 Use the selection tool to select the object to add to the masked artwork, and drag it in front of the mask.

2 Choose Edit > Cut.

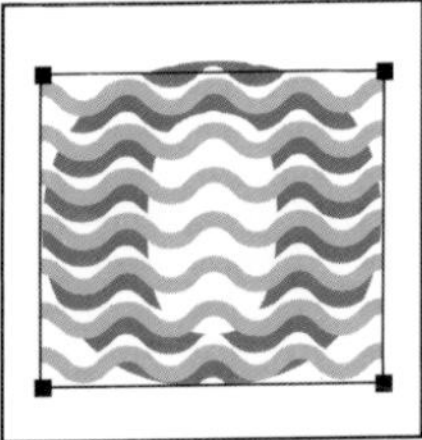

Selection in front of mask and cut

3 With the direct-selection tool, select an object within the masked artwork.

4 Choose either Edit > Paste in Front or Edit > Paste in Back. The object is pasted in front of or behind the selected object and becomes part of the masked artwork.

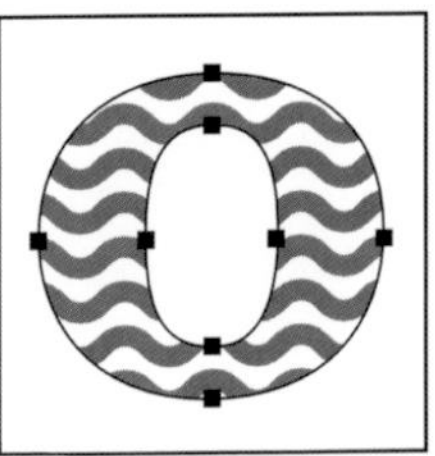

Object in Mask selected and new object pasted in front

To remove an object from masked artwork:

1 With the direct-selection tool, select the object you want to remove.

2 Choose Edit > Cut.

To lock or unlock a mask:

1 With the direct-selection tool, select the mask to lock or unlock.

2 Choose either Object > Masks > Lock or Object > Masks > Unlock.

Filling and stroking masks

You can add a fill and stroke to a mask by setting these attributes using either the toolbox or the Color palette. (See "Painting using the toolbox" on page 161 and "Using the Color palette" on page 162.)

To apply a fill and stroke to a mask:

1 With the direct-selection tool, select the mask you want to fill or stroke.

2 Use the Fill selection box or the Stroke selection box in the toolbox or Color palette to choose the mask's fill or stroke. If the Color palette is not visible, choose Window > Show Color.

3 Choose a fill color or stroke color for the mask.

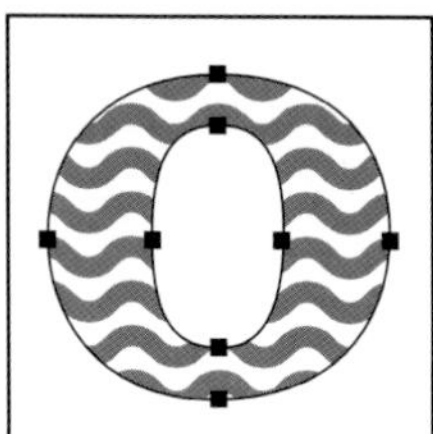

Mask selected and fill and stroke applied

7

Chapter 7: Working with Color

Applying colors, gradients, and patterns to artwork is a common Adobe Illustrator task, and one that requires some knowledge of color management for print media and for publishing on the Web. When applying color to artwork, keep in mind the final medium in which the artwork will be published, so as to use the correct color model and color definitions. Also, to ensure that colors are reproduced accurately in print and on-screen, verify that your monitor has been color-calibrated.

Adding color to artwork requires a combination of tools in Illustrator, including the Color palette, the Swatches palette, the Stroke palette, and the paint icons in the toolbox.

Color modes and models

A color mode in Illustrator determines the color model used to display and print Illustrator files. Illustrator bases its color modes on established models for describing and reproducing color. Common models include HSB (for hue, saturation, brightness); RGB (for red, green, blue); and CMYK (for cyan, magenta, yellow, black).

HSB model

Based on the human perception of color, the HSB model describes three fundamental characteristics of color:

• *Hue* is the color reflected from or transmitted through an object. It is measured as a location on the standard color wheel, expressed as a degree between 0° and 360°. In common use, hue is identified by the name of the color such as red, orange, or green.

• *Saturation*, sometimes called *chroma*, is the strength or purity of the color. Saturation represents the amount of gray in proportion to the hue, measured as a percentage from 0% (gray) to 100% (fully saturated). On the standard color wheel, saturation increases from the center to the edge.

• *Brightness* is the relative lightness or darkness of the color, usually measured as a percentage from 0% (black) to 100% (white).

For a color illustration of the HSB model, see figure 7-1 on page 229.

RGB model

A large percentage of the visible spectrum can be represented by mixing red, green, and blue (RGB) colored light in various proportions and intensities. Where the colors overlap, they create cyan, magenta, and yellow.

Because the RGB colors combine to create white, they are also called *additive colors*. Adding all colors together creates white—that is, all light is reflected back to the eye. Additive colors are used for lighting, video, and monitors. Your monitor, for example, creates color by emitting light through red, green, and blue phosphors. (See "About exporting artwork" on page 325.)

For a color illustration of additive colors, see figure 7-2 on page 229.

How Illustrator uses the RGB model

For each of the RGB components in a color object, Illustrator assigns an intensity value ranging from 0 (black) to 255 (white). For example, a bright red color might have an R value of 246, a G value of 20, and a B value of 50. When the values of all three components are equal, the result is a shade of gray. When the value of all components is 255, the result is pure white; when all components have values of 0, the result is pure black. To assign RGB colors to artwork in Adobe Illustrator, see "Using the Color palette" on page 162.

CMYK model

Whereas the RGB model depends on a light source to create color, the CMYK model is based on the light-absorbing quality of ink printed on paper. As white light strikes translucent inks, a portion of the spectrum is absorbed. Color that is not absorbed is reflected back to your eye.

In theory, pure cyan (C), magenta (M), and yellow (Y) pigments should combine to absorb all color and produce black; for this reason they are also called *subtractive* colors. Because all printing inks contain some impurities, these three inks actually produce a muddy brown and must be combined with black (K) ink to produce a true black. (The letter *K* is used to avoid confusion, because *B* also stands for blue.) Combining these inks to reproduce color is called *four-color process printing*. (See "About separations" on page 361.)

For a color illustration of subtractive colors, see figure 7-3 on page 229.

How Illustrator uses the CMYK model

For each CMYK object, Illustrator assigns a percentage value for each of the process inks. The lightest (highlight) colors are assigned small percentages of process ink colors; darker (shadow) colors have higher percentage values. For example, a bright red might contain 2% cyan, 93% magenta, 90% yellow, and 0% black. In CMYK objects, pure white is generated when all four components have values of 0%.

CMYK is the model to use when preparing artwork to be printed using process colors. The process of converting RGB artwork into CMYK for this purpose creates a *color separation*. (See Chapter 15, "Producing Color Separations.")

Grayscale model

Grayscale uses shades of gray to represent an object. In Adobe Illustrator, every grayscale object has a brightness value ranging from 0% (white) to 100% (black). Images produced using black-and-white or grayscale scanners are typically displayed in grayscale.

Grayscale also lets you convert color artwork to high-quality black-and-white artwork. In this case, Adobe Illustrator discards all color information in the original artwork; the gray levels (shades) of the converted objects represent the luminosity of the original objects.

When you convert grayscale objects to RGB, the color values for each object are assigned that object's previous gray value. You can also convert a grayscale object to a CMYK object.

Color gamuts

The *gamut* of a color system is the range of colors that can be displayed or printed. The spectrum of colors that can be viewed by the human eye is wider than any method of reproducing color.

Among the color models used in Adobe Illustrator, RGB has the largest gamut. The RGB gamut contains the subset of colors that can be viewed on a computer or television monitor (which emits red, green, and blue light). Some colors, such as pure cyan or pure yellow, can't be displayed accurately on a monitor. The smallest gamut is that of the CMYK model, which consists of colors that can be printed using process-color inks. When colors that cannot be printed are displayed on the screen, they are referred to as *out-of-gamut* colors (that is, they are outside the CMYK gamut).

For a color illustration of color gamuts, see figure 7-4 on page 229.

About painting in Adobe Illustrator

Painting with colors in Illustrator is accomplished using four steps:

1 Select the object.

2 Select the fill or stroke using the Fill and Stroke boxes in the Color palette and in the toolbox.

3 Mix and edit colors using the Color palette and gradients using the Gradient palette.

4 Add predefined colors (or store colors that you've created) using the Swatches palette. You can also apply colors that are stored in color libraries such as PANTONE, using the Color Libraries.

When you paint paths and objects in Adobe Illustrator, the current paint attributes are shown in the Fill and Stroke boxes in the toolbox and the Color palette. *Filling* an object paints the area enclosed by the path. *Stroking* an object outlines the path. Paths can be filled or stroked, or filled *and* stroked.

Filling and stroking affect closed and open paths differently. Open paths are filled as if the endpoints were connected by a straight line.

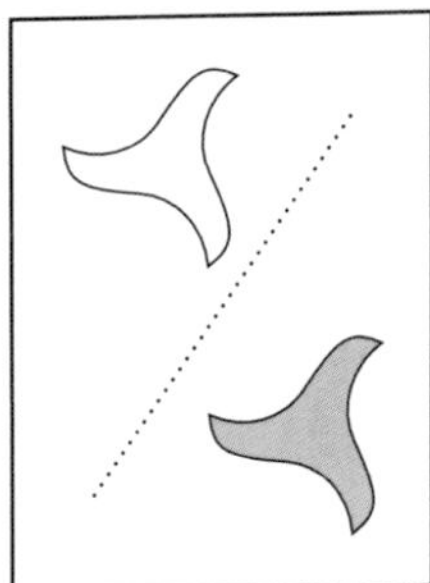
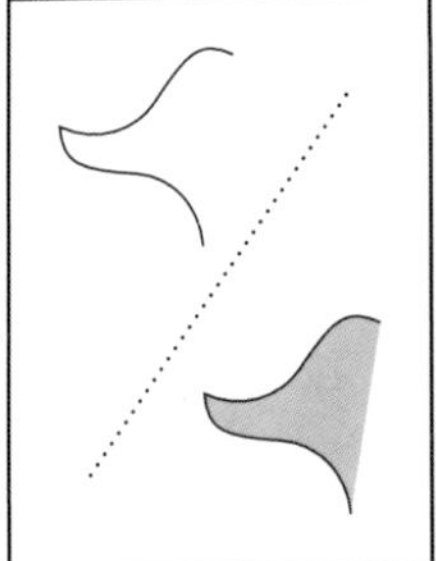

Closed paths and open paths

Working with process colors, spot colors, and registration color

It is important to understand the different types of color used in Adobe Illustrator—global process color, non-global process color, spot color, and registration color—since the color type determines how colors are updated throughout the document, and how they are separated and printed.

Global process color Process colors are the four inks used in traditional color separations: cyan, magenta, yellow, and black. In Illustrator, all four color models that result in color separations when printed—that is, CMYK, RGB, HSB, and Grayscale—are referred to as *process colors*. Global process colors are those that automatically update throughout the document when the swatch is edited, that is, every object containing the color changes when the swatch is modified.

Non-global process color Non-global process colors also can be assigned any of the four color models (CMYK, RGB, HSB, and Grayscale), but do not automatically update throughout the document when the color is edited. Process colors are non-global by default; a non-global process color can be changed to a global process color using the Swatch Options dialog box. (See "Editing swatches" on page 168.)

Spot colors Spot colors are special premixed colors that are used instead of, or in addition to, CMYK inks, and that require their own separations and their own plates on a printing press. When a spot color swatch is edited, the color is updated globally throughout the document.

You can assign any of the four color models to a spot color. Spot colors may or may not fall within the CMYK gamut; for example, a spot color may be a neon or metallic ink that is not within the CMYK gamut, or it may be a shade of green that falls within the gamut.

Registration color A registration color is applied to objects that you want to print on all plates in the printing process, including any spot color plates. Registration color is typically used for crop marks and trim marks. (See "Outputting registration colors" on page 362 and "Setting crop marks and trim marks" on page 345.)

Applying colors to artwork

When you create an object or when you want to change the paint attributes of an existing object in Illustrator, you use a combination of the Fill and Stroke boxes in the toolbox, the Color palette, the Gradient palette, and the Swatches palette.

To apply colors to artwork:

1 Select an object's fill or stroke using one of the following:

- Select the object and then click the Fill or Stroke box in the toolbox. (See "Painting using the toolbox" on page 161.)
- Click the Color button in the toolbox or choose Window > Show Color. Select the object and click the Fill or Stroke box in the Color palette.

2 Apply a color to the selected fill or stroke, or a gradient to a fill, using one of the following:

- In the Color palette, mix a color using the Grayscale, RGB, HSB, or CMYK sliders, or select a color from the color bar. (See"Using the Color palette" on page 162.)
- Choose Window > Show Swatches and select a predefined color or gradient. (See"Using the Swatches palette" on page 166.)
- Choose Window > Swatch Libraries, and select a predefined color library. (See "Using the Swatch Libraries command" on page 173.)
- Drag a color or gradient to the artwork. (See "Painting by dragging and dropping" on page 163.)
- Use the paint bucket or eyedropper tool to copy paint attributes between objects. (See "Copying paint attributes between objects" on page 171.)
- If you are stroking the object or path, choose line attributes. (See "Using the Stroke palette" on page 163.)

Painting using the toolbox

Use the Fill and Stroke boxes in the toolbox to select an object's fill and stroke, to swap the fill color with the stroke color, and to return the fill and stroke to their default colors.

To switch between fill and stroke as the active selection, press x *on the keyboard. To swap the fill and stroke colors of a selected object, press Shift+x.*

Below the Fill and Stroke boxes are the Color, Gradient, and None buttons. You use these buttons to change the selected fill or stroke to a color, to change a fill to a gradient, or to remove the fill or stroke from the selected object.

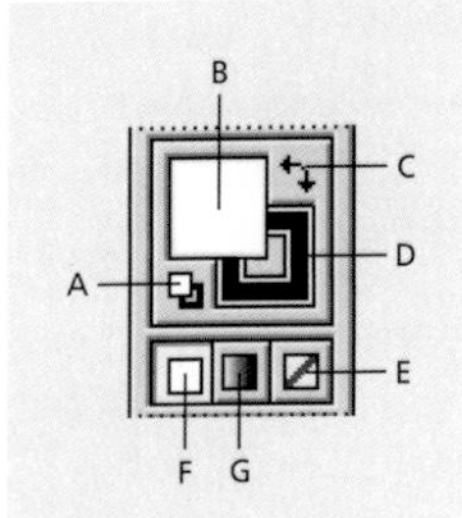

A. Default fill and stroke B. Fill box C. Swap fill and stroke D. Stroke box E. None F. Color G. Gradient

To change fill or stroke attributes using the toolbox:

1 Select an object using any selection tool.

2 Do one of the following:

• Click the Swap Fill and Stroke button (or press Shift+x) to swap colors between the fill and the stroke.

• Click the Default Fill and Stroke button to return to the default color settings (white fill and black stroke).

• Click the Color button to change the currently selected stroke or fill to the last-selected solid color in the Color palette.

• Click the Gradient button to change the currently selected fill to the last-selected gradient in the Gradient palette.

• Click the None button to remove the object's fill or stroke.

Use keyboard shortcuts to switch to Color, Gradient, or None: Press < to change the selection to a solid color; > to change the selection to a gradient; and / to change to None.

Using the Color palette

You use the Color palette to apply color to an object's fill and stroke, and also to edit and mix colors—either colors that you create or colors that you selected from the Swatches palette, from an object, or from a color library.

To edit the fill or stroke color using the Color palette:

1 Select an object using any selection tool.

2 Choose Window > Show Color.

3 Select the Fill box or Stroke box in the Color palette or in the toolbox.

4 Do one of the following:

• Position the pointer over the color bar (the pointer turns into the eyedropper), and click.

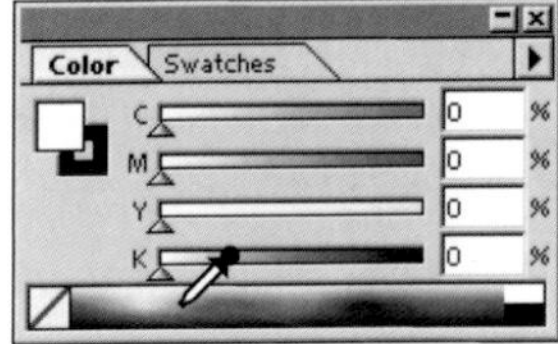

• Choose an RGB, HSB, CMYK, or Grayscale color model from the pop-up menu, and use the sliders to change the color values. You can also enter numeric values in the text boxes next to the color sliders. (See "Color modes and models" on page 157.)

***Note:** An exclamation point inside a yellow triangle in the Color palette when using HSB or RGB color indicates that you have chosen an* out-of-gamut color*—that is, a color that cannot be printed using CMYK inks. The closest CMYK equivalent appears next to the triangle. Click the CMYK equivalent to substitute it for the out-of-gamut color.*

• Adjust the Tint slider if using a global color from the Swatches palette. (See "Creating global colors and tints" on page 169.)

Painting by dragging and dropping

An easy way to paint an object is to drag a color directly from the Fill box or Stroke box in the toolbox, the Color palette, or the Gradient palette and drop the color onto the object, or to drag a swatch from the Swatches palette and drop it on an object. Dragging and dropping lets you paint objects without first selecting them. You can also drag and drop colors from the Swatches palette to the Fill box or Stroke box in the toolbox, the Color palette, or the Gradient palette.

When you drag, the color is applied to either the object's fill or stroke, depending on whether the Fill box or Stroke box is currently selected. (For example, if you drag a red color to an unselected object when the stroke box in the toolbox is selected, the object's stroke is painted red.)

Using the Stroke palette

Stroke attributes are available only when you stroke a path. These attributes, available in the Stroke palette, control whether a line is solid or dashed, the dash sequence if it is dashed, the stroke weight, the miter limit, and the styles of line joins and line caps.

Use the Stroke palette to select stroke attributes, including the thickness (weight) of the stroke, how the stroke is capped and joined, and whether a stroke is solid or dashed.

To set stroke attributes using the Stroke palette:

1 With any selection tool, select the object with the stroke attributes you want to change.

2 Click the Stroke box in the toolbox to select the object's stroke.

3 Choose Window > Show Stroke.

4 To specify a stroke weight, enter the desired weight in the Weight text box or choose a value from the pop-up menu. You can enter a value in inches (in), millimeters (mm), centimeters (cm), or picas (pi), and Illustrator converts it to an equal value in points.

The stroke weight determines the thickness of the stroke, in points. Illustrator strokes a path by centering the stroke on the path; half of the stroke appears on one side of the path, and the other half of the stroke appears on the other side of the path.

If you enter a weight of 0, the stroke is changed to None.

5 Select from the following options:

• Butt Cap for stroked lines with squared ends.

• Round Cap for stroked lines with semicircular ends.

• Projecting Cap for stroked lines with squared ends that extend half the line width beyond the end of the line. This option makes the weight of the line extend equally in all directions around the line.

6 Select one of the following options:

• Miter Join for stroked lines with pointed corners. Enter a miter limit between 1 and 500. The miter limit controls when the program switches from a mitered (pointed) join to a beveled (squared-off) join. The default miter limit is 4, which means that when the length of the point reaches four times the stroke weight, the program switches from a miter join to a bevel join. A miter limit of 1 results in a bevel join.

• Round Join for stroked lines with rounded corners.

• Bevel Join for stroked lines with squared corners.

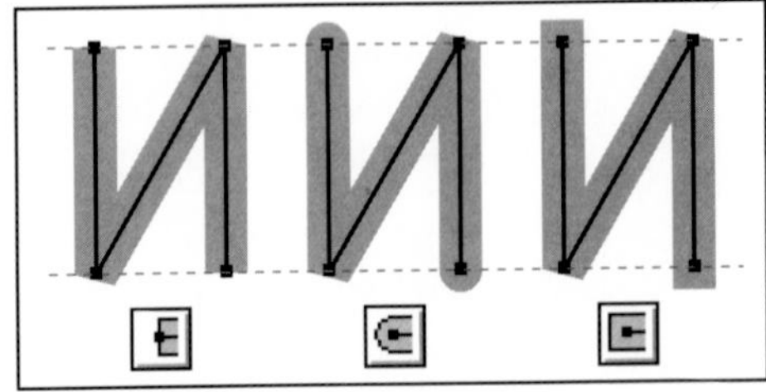

Butt, round, and projecting caps (with default miter joins)

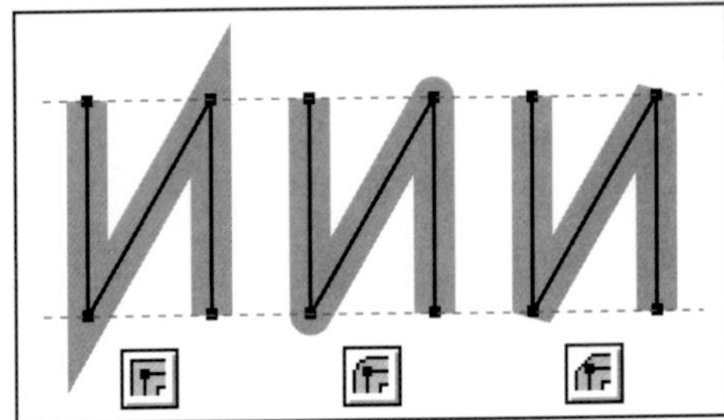

Miter, rounded, and bevel joins (with default butt caps)

• Dashed Line for a dashed line; then specify a dash sequence by entering the lengths of dashes and the gaps between them in the Dash Pattern text boxes. As with the stroke weight, you can enter a value in inches (in), millimeters (mm), centimeters (cm), or picas and Illustrator converts it to an equal value in points.

The numbers entered are repeated in sequence so that once you have established the pattern, you don't need to fill in all the text boxes. Dash patterns are specified in points.

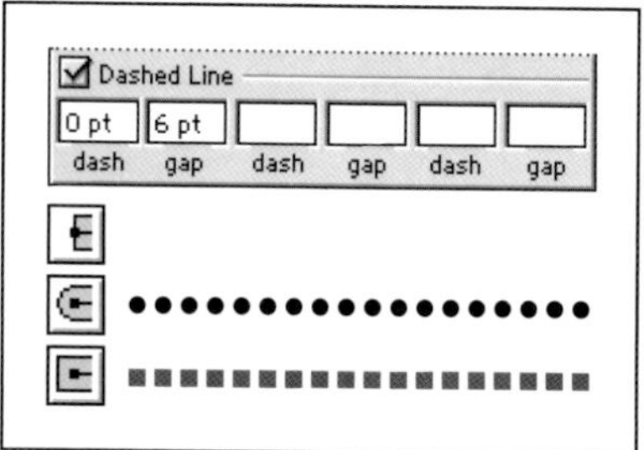

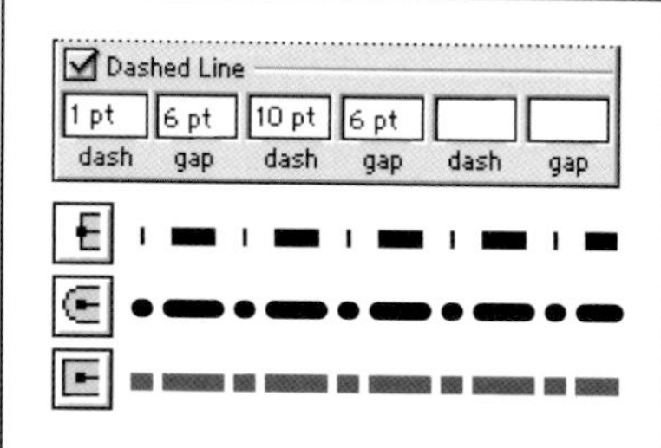

Effects of line cap styles on dashed lines

DASHED-LINE EFFECTS You can create a variety of borders and lines by layering copies of dashed lines and painting them differently.

Artwork/ Preview	Line order/ Stroke color	End Cap/ Weight	Dash; Gap
	1 - Color	2 pts	D, 0; G, 4
	1 - Color 2 - White	3 pts 2 pts	D, 0; G, 4 D, 0; G, 4
	1 - Color 2 - White	3 pts 2 pts	D, 0; G, 4 D, 0; G, 4 *Offset amount: Move second line 1.5 pts down and right*
	1 - Color 2 - White	5 pts 5 pts	D, 0; G, 4.5 D, 0; G, 4.5 *Offset amount: Move second line 1.5 pts right*
	1 - Color 2 - Color	2 pts 2.5 pts	D, 3; G, 8 D, 0; G, 11 *Offset amount: Move second line 7 pts up*
	1 - Color 2 - Color	3 pts 1.5 pts	D, 0; G, 7; D, 0; G, 4.5 D, 7; G, 4.5
	1 - Color 2 - White	4.5 pts 3 pts	Solid line Solid line
	1 - Color 2 - Color 3 - Color	8.5 pts 6.5 pts 2 pts	D, 0; G, 6 D, 0; G, 6 D, 0; G, 6
	1 - Color 2 - Color 3 - Color	12 pts 8 pts 4 pts	Solid line Solid line D, 0; G, 6

Using the Swatches palette

The Swatches palette contains the colors, gradients, and patterns that are preloaded into Adobe Illustrator as well as those you create and save for reuse. When a selected object contains a color that has been applied from the Swatches palette, the relevant swatch is highlighted in the Swatches palette.

Working with the Swatches palette

You can add colors and gradients to the Swatches palette by dragging them from the Color palette, from the Gradient palette, or from the toolbox Fill and Stroke boxes to the Swatches palette. You can add a pattern to the Swatches palette by dragging it from the artwork or by selecting it and choosing Edit > Define Pattern. (See "Creating and working with patterns" on page 200.)

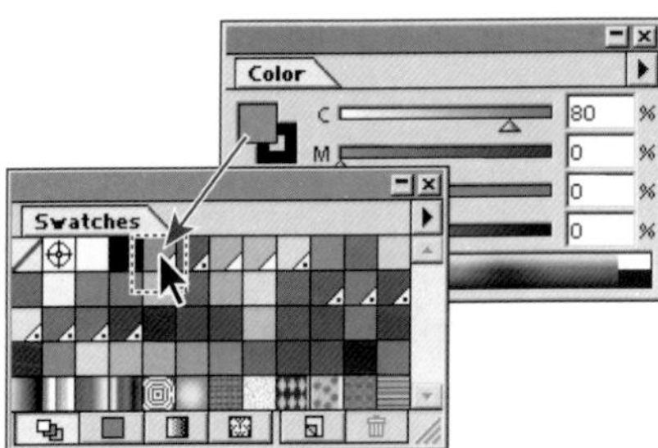

Drag to add a color or gradient.

New colors, gradients, or patterns that you create and store in the Swatches palette are associated only with the current file. Each new Adobe Illustrator file can have a different set of swatches stored in its Swatches palette. Swatches stored in the Startup file are loaded into all new Illustrator documents. (See "Creating a custom startup file" on page 176.)

To choose a color, gradient, or pattern from the Swatches palette:

1 Choose Window > Show Swatches.

2 Click a color, gradient, or pattern swatch in the Swatches palette. The selected color, gradient, or pattern appears in the Color palette and in the Fill box or Stroke box in the toolbox, and it is applied to any selected object.

To modify the swatch display:

1 Choose Window > Show Swatches.

2 Choose one of the following display options from the pop-up menu:

• Name displays a small swatch next to the name of the swatch. The icons to the right of the name show the color model (CMYK, RGB, and so on), and whether the color is a spot color, global process color, non-global process color, registration color, or none.

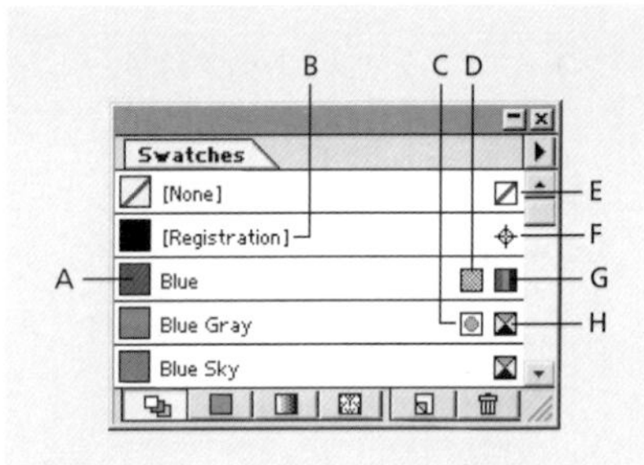

A. Color swatch B. Color name C. Spot color D. Global process color E. None F. Registration color G. RGB color H. CMYK color

• Small Swatch or Large Swatch displays only the swatch. A triangle with a dot in the corner of the swatch indicates that the color is a spot color. A triangle without a dot indicates a global process color.

To modify the type of swatches displayed:

1 Choose Window > Show Swatches.

2 Click one of the following buttons at the bottom of the Swatches palette:

• Show All Swatches displays all color, gradient, and pattern swatches.

• Show Color Swatches displays only process color and spot color swatches.

• Show Gradient Swatches displays only gradient swatches.

• Show Pattern Swatches displays only pattern swatches.

To select all swatches not currently used in the file:

1 Choose Window > Show Swatches.

2 Choose Select All Unused from the pop-up menu. Only swatches that are not currently used in the active file are selected.

To sort swatches by swatch type or by name:

1 Choose Window > Show Swatches.

2 Choose from the sorting options in the pop-up menu:

• Sort by Name sorts all swatches alphabetically by name.

• Sort by Kind sorts all swatches in ascending order by swatch type: colors, gradients, and patterns.

Adding, duplicating, and deleting swatches

You can add color swatches to the Swatches palette by dragging and dropping colors on the palette or by using commands in the Swatches palette. To duplicate swatches, use the commands in the Swatches palette or drag the swatch onto the New Swatch button.

To add a color to the Swatches palette:

1 In the Color palette, Gradient palette, or the Fill box and Stroke box in the toolbox, select the color or gradient you want to add to the Swatches palette.

2 Do one of the following:

• Click the New Swatch button at the bottom of the Swatches palette.

• Choose New Swatch from the pop-up menu in the Swatches palette. Enter a name in the Swatch Name text box, choose Process Color or Spot Color from the Color Type pop-up menu, and click OK.

• Drag the color or gradient to the Swatches palette, positioning the pointer where you want the new swatch to appear.

• Ctrl-drag (Windows) or Command-drag (Mac OS) a color to the Swatches palette to create a spot color. You can also press Ctrl (Windows) or Command (Mac OS) while clicking the New Swatch button to create a spot color.

To duplicate a swatch in the Swatches palette:

1 Select the swatch you want to duplicate. To select multiple swatches, hold down Ctrl (Windows) or Command (Mac OS) and click each swatch. To select a range of swatches, hold down Shift and click to define the range.

2 Do one of the following:

- Choose Duplicate Swatch from the pop-up menu.
- Drag the swatches to the New Swatch button on the bottom of the palette.

To replace a swatch in the Swatches palette:

Hold down Alt (Windows) or Option (Mac OS) and drag the color or gradient from the Color palette, Gradient palette, or the Fill box and Stroke box in the toolbox to the Swatches palette, highlighting the swatch you want to replace.

Important: *Replacing an existing color, gradient, or pattern in the Swatches palette globally changes artwork in the file containing that swatch color with the new color, gradient, or pattern. The only exception is for a process color that has the Non-Global option selected in the Swatch Options dialog box.*

To delete a swatch from the Swatches palette:

1 Select the swatch you want to delete. To select multiple swatches, hold down Ctrl (Windows) or Command (Mac OS) and click each swatch. To select adjacent swatches, hold down Shift and click to define the range.

2 Delete the selected swatches in one of the following ways:

- Choose Delete Swatch from the pop-up menu.
- Click the Delete Swatch button at the bottom of the palette.
- Drag the selected swatches to the Delete Swatch button.

Note: *When a spot color or global process color swatch is deleted, all objects painted with those colors will be converted to the non-global process color equivalent.*

Editing swatches

You can change individual attributes of a swatch—such as its name, color mode, color definition, whether it is process or spot, or whether a process color can be changed globally—using the Swatch Options dialog box.

Any swatch can be named in Adobe Illustrator; for example, you can change the name of a CMYK process color, and it still prints and separates with each of its CMYK values intact.

To edit a swatch:

1 Choose Window > Show Swatches.

2 Select a swatch, and do one of the following:

- Double-click the swatch.
- Choose Swatch Options from the pop-up menu in the Swatches palette.

3 Enter the relevant information in the Swatch Options dialog box:

• Enter a name in the Swatch Name text box.

• Choose Spot Color or Process Color from the Color Type pop-up menu. Both spot colors and process colors can be changed globally.

• Click Non-Global if you do not want changes to the selected process color to be applied globally throughout the document. (For more information, see "Working with process colors, spot colors, and registration color" on page 160.)

• Choose CMYK, RGB, HSB, or Grayscale from the Color Mode pop-up menu and change the color definition (if desired) using the color sliders or text boxes at the bottom of the palette.

4 Click OK.

Note: *When separated, each spot color is converted to a process color by default, unless you deselect the Convert to Process option in the Separation Setup dialog box. (See "Separating spot colors as process colors" on page 373.)*

Creating global colors and tints

You can make global changes in an individual file either by selecting all objects with the characteristics you want to change, or by editing or replacing global process color or spot color swatches in the Swatches palette.

The Tint slider in the Color palette is used to modify a global color's intensity. The tint range is from 0% to 100%; the lower the number, the lighter the tint will be.

To modify the tint of a global process color or spot color:

1 Do one of the following to select a global color:

• Click an object and select the appropriate fill or stroke.

• Click a color swatch in the Swatches palette.

Important: *To ensure that a process color is global, make sure the Non-Global option is deselected in the Swatch Options dialog box. (See "Editing swatches" on page 168.)*

2 In the Color palette, drag the Tint slider or enter a tint value in the Tint Percentage text box.

For a color illustration of a color tint adjustment, see figure 7-5 on page 230.

To save a tint in the Swatches palette:

1 Create a tint by modifying the swatch.

2 Save the tint in the Swatches palette using one of the following:

• Drag the Fill or Stroke box in the toolbox to the Swatches palette.

• Click the New button in the Swatches palette.

The tint is saved with the same name as the base color, but with the tint percentage added to the name. For example, if you saved a color named "Sky Blue" at 51 percent, the swatch name would be "Sky Blue 51%."

Important: *Tints of the same color are linked together, so that if you edit a tint swatch, all associated tint swatches (and the objects painted with those swatches) are also changed.*

To select all objects with the same properties:

1 Do one of the following:

• To select all objects with the same fill, stroke, and stroke weight, select an object with these attributes or choose the fill, stroke, and stroke weight attributes from the Color palette, Swatches palette, or Stroke palette. Then choose Edit > Select > Same Paint Style.

• To select all objects with the same fill or stroke color, select an object with that fill color or choose the fill color from the Color palette or Swatches palette. Then choose Edit > Select > Same Fill Color or Edit > Select > Same Stroke Color.

• To select all objects with the same stroke weight, select an object with that stroke weight or choose the stroke weight from the Stroke palette. Then choose Edit > Select > Same Stroke Weight.

For a color illustration of Select filters, see figure 7-6 on page 230.

2 To apply the same selection options using a different object (for example, if you have already selected all red objects using the Same Fill Color command and now you want to search for all green objects), select a new object and then choose Edit > Select > Select Again.

To change a color throughout a file:

Replace a color swatch in the Swatches palette using one of the following options:

• Alt-drag (Windows) or Option-drag (Mac OS) a swatch from the Swatches palette over the swatch you want to replace.

• Alt-drag (Windows) or Option-drag (Mac OS) a color from the Color palette over the swatch you want to replace in the Swatches palette.

• Alt-drag (Windows) or Option-drag (Mac OS) a color from the Fill box or the Stroke box over the swatch you want to replace in the Swatches palette.

• Double-click the swatch and edit the color in the Swatch Options dialog box.

Adding colors from other documents and merging swatch names

When you copy objects from one document to another, any swatches (global process colors, spot colors, patterns, or gradients) contained in the object are added to the destination document's Swatches palette. If swatches in the two documents have the same name, but different color values, a warning dialog appears and you can choose to either add the duplicate swatch or merge the swatches together and use only one set of color values.

You can also merge swatches together using the Merge Swatches command. When you merge swatches together, all objects painted with either of the swatch colors will be updated with the merged swatch color.

To add color, gradient, or pattern swatches from one document to another:

1 Copy an object into the current document using drag-and-drop, copy-and-paste, or the Place command. You can also use the Swatch Libraries command to add new swatch palettes. (See "Using the Swatch Libraries command" on page 173.)

2 If one or more swatches have the same name (but with different color values), select from the following options in the Swatch Conflict dialog box:

• Add Swatches adds the new swatch to the Swatches palette, appending the word *copy* to the name of the new swatch.

• Merge Swatches combines the two swatches into a single swatch, using the color value of the destination document's swatch.

3 If there are multiple naming conflicts, select the Apply to All check box to automatically apply the selected method (either adding swatches or merging swatches) to all naming conflicts in the document. This prevents the Swatch Conflict dialog box from appearing for each naming conflict in the document.

To merge multiple colors in the Swatches palette:

1 In the Swatches palette select two or more swatches to merge. Press Shift and click to select a range of swatches; press Ctrl (Windows) or Command (Mac OS) and click to select non-contiguous swatches.

2 Choose Merge Swatches from the Swatches palette menu. The first selected swatch name and color value replaces all other selected swatches.

Modifying colors

Illustrator provides a wide variety of tools to modify and edit colors in your file. You can use the paint bucket and eyedropper tools to copy paint attributes from one object to another.

Copying paint attributes between objects

You can use the eyedropper tool to copy colors from any object in an Illustrator file—from a paint swatch or from anywhere on the desktop, including from another application. You can then use the paint bucket tool to apply the current paint attributes to an object. Together these tools let you copy the paint attributes from anywhere on-screen to other objects.

By default, the eyedropper and paint bucket tools affect all paint attributes of an object. You can use the tool's options dialog box to change the object's attributes. You can also use the eyedropper tool and paint bucket tool to copy and paste type attributes. (See "Copying type attributes between objects" on page 268.)

To copy paint attributes using the eyedropper tool:

1 Select the object with the paint attributes you want to change.

2 Select the eyedropper tool (🖉).

3 Click the object that has the attributes you want to sample with the eyedropper tool. The selected object is automatically updated with the paint attributes of the sampled object.

To copy paint attributes from the desktop to Illustrator using the eyedropper tool:

1 Select the object whose paint attributes you want to change.

2 Select the eyedropper tool.

3 Click anywhere on the document and continue to hold down the mouse button.

4 Without releasing the mouse button, move the pointer over the object on your computer's desktop whose paint attributes you want to copy. When directly over the object, release the mouse button.

Important: *When you copy an object's paint characteristics from the desktop, the eyedropper tool only copies the RGB color from the screen, even if the object in another application is colored in the CMYK color mode. To convert back to CMYK, use the Convert to CMYK filter, or use the Color palette to change the color back to the CMYK mode.*

To apply paint attributes using the paint bucket tool:

1 Select the paint bucket tool ( ).

2 Click any object to paint it with the attributes currently in the Color palette.

If you are working in Artwork view or if the object is stroked and not filled, be sure to click the object's outline.

To toggle between the eyedropper tool and the paint bucket tool, press Alt (Windows) or Option (Mac OS) while either tool is selected.

To change the paint attributes affected by the paint bucket or eyedropper tool:

1 Double-click the paint bucket or eyedropper tool.

2 Select the attributes you want to copy with the eyedropper tool and apply with the paint bucket tool and click OK.

Using the Hard Mix and Soft Mix commands

The Hard Mix and Soft Mix Pathfinder commands let you control the mix of overlapping fill colors. (See "Step 2: Select overprint options for colors that you want to appear transparent" on page 364.)

- The Hard Mix command combines colors by choosing the highest value of each of the color components. For example, if Color 1 is 20% cyan, 66% magenta, 40% yellow, and 0% black; and Color 2 is 40% cyan, 20% magenta, 30% yellow, and 10% black; the resulting hard color is 40% cyan, 66% magenta, 40% yellow, and 10% black.
- The Soft Mix command makes the top color of overlapping colors semitransparent and then divides the image into its component faces. You specify the amount of transparency you want in the overlapping colors.

Note: *Applying either the Hard Mix or Soft Mix command to objects removes their strokes and groups the objects.*

In most cases, applying the Hard Mix or Soft Mix command to objects painted using a mix of process and spot colors, or a mix of color models, converts the color to CMYK. In the case of mixing a non-global process RGB color with a spot RGB color, all spot colors are converted to a non-global process RGB color.

If you overlap multiple objects, each overlapping object is given the level of transparency you select.

For a color illustration of Hard Mix and Soft Mix commands, see figure 7-7 on page 230.

To mix colors by selecting each highest CMYK component value:

1 Select the objects whose fill colors you want to mix.

2 Choose Window > Show Pathfinder.

3 Choose Show Options from the pop-up menu in the Pathfinder palette.

4 Click the Hard Mix button at the bottom of the palette.

To mix colors by specifying transparency:

1 Select the objects whose fill colors you want to mix.

2 Choose Window > Show Pathfinder.

3 Choose Show Options from the pop-up menu in the Pathfinder palette.

4 Click the Soft Mix button at the bottom of the palette.

5 Enter a value between 1% and 100% in the Mixing Rate text box to determine the percentage of transparency you want in the overlapping colors and click OK.

Using the Swatch Libraries command

The Swatch Libraries command lets you import colors, gradients, and patterns from other Adobe Illustrator files into a palette. It also lets you import entire color libraries from other color systems, such as the PANTONE Process Color System®.

When you import color libraries into Adobe Illustrator, the colors in the library are permanent. You must copy a color in a color library to the Swatches palette to modify it.

Loading colors from other files

Use the Swatch Libraries > Other Library command to import colors, gradients, and patterns from other Adobe Illustrator files. When you select a file using the Swatch Libraries > Other Library command, all of the source file's spot and process colors, gradients, and patterns are added to a new palette.

To import colors, gradients, or patterns from other files:

1 Choose Window > Swatch Libraries > Other Library.

2 Select the file from which you want to import swatches, and click Select.

To add colors from the other file's library into the Swatches palette:

1 Select one or more swatches in the library:

- Click to select a single swatch.
- Shift-click to select a range of swatches.
- Ctrl-click (Windows) or Command-click (Mac OS) to select noncontiguous swatches.

2 Do one of the following:

- Drag and drop the selected swatches from the library to the Swatches palette.
- Choose Add to Swatches from the library palette's pop-up menu.

Loading colors from other color systems

The Swatch Libraries command lets you select from a range of color libraries—including the PANTONE Process Color System, Toyo™ Ink Electronic Color Finder™ 1050, the Focoltone® color system, the Trumatch™ color swatching system, the DIC Process Color Note, and libraries created especially for Web use. Each color system that you select appears in its own Swatch Library palette.

Spot colors from color libraries, as are all spot colors, are converted to process colors when separated unless you deselect the Convert to Process option in the Separation Setup dialog box. (See Chapter 15, "Producing Color Separations.")

To load predefined custom color libraries into Illustrator:

1 Choose Window > Swatch Libraries.

2 Select the color system you want from the submenu. The color system that you select appears as a tabbed palette.

To make a custom color library appear each time Illustrator is started:

1 Select a custom color swatch library.

2 Choose Persistent from the swatch library palette's pop-up menu. The library will now automatically open in the same position each time the Illustrator application is started.

To select a swatch by its name or number:

1 Select the Swatches palette or a swatch library of a particular color system (for example, the PANTONE color system).

2 Press Ctrl+Alt (Windows) or Command+Option (Mac OS) and click in the swatch library palette window.

3 Type the name or the number of a swatch to select it. (For example, in the PANTONE Process library palette you can type **11-7 CVS** to select PANTONE swatch 11-7.)

PANTONE Used for printing inks. Each PANTONE color has a specified CMYK equivalent. To select a PANTONE color, first determine the ink color you want, using either the *PANTONE Color Formula Guide 747XR* or an ink chart obtained from your printer. PANTONE books are available from printers and graphic arts supply stores.

You can select from PANTONE Coated, PANTONE Uncoated, and PANTONE Process colors. For more information, contact PANTONE, Inc., in Carlstadt, New Jersey, U.S.A.

Trumatch Provides predictable CMYK color matching with over 2000 achievable, computer-generated colors. Trumatch colors cover the visible spectrum of the CMYK gamut in even steps. The Trumatch Color Finder displays up to 40 tints and shades of each hue, each originally created in four-color process and each reproducible in four colors on electronic imagesetters. In addition, four-color grays using different hues are included. For more information, contact Trumatch Inc. in New York, New York, U.S.A.

Focoltone Consists of 763 CMYK colors. You can use Focoltone colors to help avoid prepress trapping and registration problems by viewing the Focoltone charts that show the overprints that make up the colors.

A swatch book with specifications for process and spot colors, overprint charts, and a chip book for marking up layouts are available from Focoltone. For more information, contact Focoltone International, Ltd. in Stafford, United Kingdom.

Toyo Color Finder 1050 Consists of over 1000 colors based on the most common printing inks used in Japan. The *TOYO Color Finder 1050 Book* contains printed samples of Toyo colors and is available from printers and graphic arts supply stores. For more information, contact Toyo Ink Manufacturing Co., Ltd. in Tokyo, Japan.

DIC Color Provides 1280 CMYK spot colors from the DIC Process Color Note. Colors may be matched against the *DIC Color Guide*, published by Dainippon Ink & Chemicals, Inc. For more information, contact Dainippon Ink & Chemicals, Inc., in Tokyo, Japan.

Web Includes the 216 RGB Web-safe colors most often used by Web browsers to display 8-bit images. This library allows you to create artwork for the Web using colors that display consistently across Windows and Macintosh systems.

System (Windows) Includes 256 colors of the Windows default 8-bit palette, which is based on a uniform sampling of RGB colors.

System (Mac OS) Includes 256 colors of the Mac OS default 8-bit palette, which is based on a uniform sampling of RGB colors.

Creating a custom startup file

You can create a custom startup file that defines the contents of the Swatches palette by default, including any custom color libraries that you want to appear in the Swatches palette. In this way, you can have easy access to the patterns, gradients, brushes, graph designs, colors, and color libraries that you use most frequently. By adding these elements to the startup file, you make them available in every new Adobe Illustrator file you create.

In addition, any files you create have the same Document Setup and Page Setup settings as those found in the startup file, and they use the same zoom level, window size, viewing preferences, and scroll position as that of the startup file when it was last saved.

To create a custom startup file:

1 Make a backup copy of the current default startup file, Startup.ai (Windows) or Adobe Illustrator Startup (Mac OS), and then save the backup file outside of the Plug-ins folder. This action saves the original startup file in case you need it again. The startup file is located in the Plug-ins folder in the Adobe Illustrator application folder.

2 Open the default startup file to use as a template for the custom startup file. This file contains labeled squares filled with the default colors, patterns, and gradients available in the Swatches palette.

3 Delete any existing colors, patterns, and gradients you don't want to retain. Note that you must delete them from their respective palettes as well as from the artwork in the startup file.

4 Add new paint style attributes to the startup file as follows:

• Create any colors, patterns, and gradients you want. You can also import swatches using the Swatch Libraries command and then move the swatches you want in the startup file into the default Swatches palette. (See "Loading colors from other files" on page 173.)

• Save any graph designs that you want available in your files using the Graph Design dialog box. (See Chapter 12, "Using Graphs.") As with the new paint style attributes, add the graphs to the artwork in the startup file so you can see and refer to the graphs later if necessary.

5 Select the options you want as default settings in the Page Setup and Document Setup dialog boxes, as well as the view preferences, the ruler origins, and the page origins.

Save the new file as Startup.ai (Windows) or Adobe Illustrator Startup (Mac OS) and place it inside the Plug-ins folder.

Important: *You must quit the Illustrator application and restart it before the new startup settings are applied to a new document.*

Using filters to modify colors

Illustrator filters provide shortcuts for changing color attributes or blending colors between objects.

Using the Adjust Colors and Convert filters

The Adjust Colors filter lets you change the grayscale, RGB, or CMYK values in objects, as well as the tint of global colors. You can also use the Convert filters to convert objects between color models. (See "Color modes and models" on page 157.)

To adjust colors using the Adjust Colors filter:

1 Select the objects whose colors you want to adjust.

2 Choose Filter > Colors > Adjust Colors.

3 Do one of the following:

• Select Convert and then a color model if you want to convert the artwork to one model.

• Deselect Convert if you want the Adjust Color filter to display the sliders for the first color mode it encounters in the following order of priority: CMYK, RGB, grayscale. Using the sliders then adjusts only the colors in that particular color mode.

4 Select Fill or Stroke (or both) to adjust the fill or stroke or both.

5 Drag the sliders or enter values in the color value text boxes.

6 Click Preview to preview the effect and click OK.

For a color illustration describing the Adjust Colors filter, see figure 7-8 on page 230.

To convert an object to a different color model using the Convert filters:

1 Select the object you want to convert.

2 Choose Filter > Colors, and choose Convert to CMYK, Convert to Grayscale, or Convert to RGB.

Saturating and desaturating colors

The Saturate filter darkens or lightens the colors of selected objects by increasing or decreasing the percentages of color values or the percentage tint of spot colors. You set the desired percentage using the Saturate dialog box.

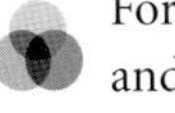

For a color illustration showing saturating and desaturating colors, see figure 7-9 on page 230.

To saturate or desaturate colors:

1 Select the objects whose colors you want to saturate or desaturate.

2 Choose Filter > Colors > Saturate.

3 Drag the slider or enter a value from –100% to 100% to specify the percentage by which to decrease or increase the color or the spot color tint.

4 Click Preview to preview the effect and click OK.

Inverting colors

The Invert Colors filter creates a color negative (or inverse) of the selected object. When you invert an object, it is converted to RGB (if it is not already an RGB object), its color values are converted to the inverse of the color values of the original, and it is reconverted back to the original color model using the new values.

For a color illustration showing inverted colors, see figure 7-10 on page 230.

To invert colors:

1 Select the objects whose colors you want to invert.

2 Choose Filter > Colors > Invert Colors.

Ensuring accurate color

One of the methods Illustrator can use to manage color is based on the use of ICC profiles. An ICC profile is a color space description. The ICC profile format was defined by the International Color Consortium (ICC) as a cross-application standard. ICC profiles help you reproduce colors accurately across different platforms, devices, and ICC-compliant applications (such as Adobe Photoshop and Adobe PageMaker®).

Adobe Illustrator uses a Color Management Module (CMM) to interpret the ICC profiles that describe the RGB and CMYK color spaces you are using in your system. You can select from existing ICC profiles or create your own. These profiles can then become part of your image files. The CMM interprets the ICC profiles to automatically manage color issues among different color models as well as color issues between your monitor, other monitors, and the final print image. Although you do not have to use ICC profiles, it can greatly simplify managing color.

Important: *To ensure that color management works correctly on your system, change the color management settings every time you change printing devices.*

Choosing a Color Management System

To work with ICC profiles in Adobe Illustrator, you can choose which Color Management System (CMS) to use for converting images. These are typical CMS modules:

• The Adobe CMS. In most cases, this CMS will give you the best results. If you have trouble matching colors between applications, you can try setting Illustrator's CMS to match the other application's.

• The Kodak Digital Science Color Management System®, which is installed on your system by default during a standard Windows installation.

• Any other CMS on your system supported by Adobe Systems.

Important: *For best color management results, you can purchase third-party calibration software for monitors, scanners, printers, and other output devices. These programs create customized ICC profiles for your specific devices.*

Verifying that a Color Management System is installed

Color management in Adobe Illustrator requires a CMS application in the Adobe Illustrator folder (Windows/Mac OS) or your System Folder (Mac OS). By default, the Adobe CMS is installed in the Adobe Illustrator folder under the filename *RB2Connection.win* (Windows) or *RB2Connection.mac* (Mac OS). The Color Conversion and Color Conversion Utilities plug-ins must also be installed in the Adobe Illustrator > Plug-ins > Extensions folder.

The Color Conversion and Color Conversion Utilities plug-ins are automatically installed on your system by the Adobe Illustrator installer program.

Important: *If a Color Management System application, the Color Conversion plug-in, or the Color Conversion Utilities plug-in are not installed, you can still calibrate color settings for your monitor by using the Color Settings dialog box.*

Changing color management settings

You can use the File > Color Settings command to change parameters for color management.

To set color management device settings:

1 Make sure that you have the Adobe CMS installed on your system and that the Color Conversion and Color Conversion Utilities plug-ins are installed in the Adobe Illustrator > Plug-ins folder.

2 If necessary, start Adobe Illustrator.

3 Choose File > Color Settings.

4 Select the monitor, printer, CMS engine, and rendering intent specifications for your computer system from the pop-up menu. Rendering intent includes the following options:

• Perceptual (Images) to maintain the relative color values as they are mapped to the printer gamut. This method preserves the relationship between colors, although the color values themselves may change.

• Saturation (Graphics) to maintain the relative saturation values. Out-of-gamut colors are converted to colors that have the same saturation but fall just inside the gamut.

• Relative Colorimetric to leave colors that fall inside the gamut unchanged. This method usually converts out-of-gamut colors to colors that have the same lightness but fall just inside the gamut.

• Absolute Colorimetric to disable white point matching when converting colors. This option is not generally recommended.

5 Click the Use Embedded ICC Profiles option to have Illustrator save the file with an ICC color management profile (for color management between applications). This setting *only* saves ICC profile information when the file is saved in PDF, TIFF, JPEG, or Photoshop 5.0 formats.

The Use Embedded ICC Profiles option also enables color management for PDF, TIFF, JPEG, or Photoshop 5.0 format files that are opened in Illustrator, if these files have previously had ICC profiles saved with them. If the Use Embedded ICC Profiles option is *not* selected, color management of an opened file does not take place, even if the opened file includes color management profile information.

For example, if a Photoshop image has been imported into Illustrator with specific ICC profiles attached (using the Embed ICC Profiles option in the Photoshop application), the embedded profiles would automatically color-manage the file when opened in Illustrator.

Important: *Encapsulated Postscript Format (EPS) files cannot have ICC Profile information saved with them, even if the Use Embedded ICC Profiles option is selected.*

6 Click the Simulate Print Colors on Display option if you want your monitor to display a simulation of the CMYK colors that will be seen in the printed output.

To color-manage artwork between applications:

1 Make sure that you have the Adobe Color Management System installed on your system, and the Color Conversion Utilities plug-in installed in the Adobe Illustrator > Plug-ins > Extensions folder.

2 Open the software application in which you intend to export the Adobe Illustrator artwork.

3 Set the application's color management settings to the same values as those set in the Adobe Illustrator Color Settings dialog box. (For information on how to adjust color management settings in third-party software applications, refer to the software's user documentation.)

4 Export the artwork to the new software application as described in Chapter 13, "Saving and Exporting Artwork."

To uninstall color management on your system:

Remove the Color Conversion and Color Conversion Utilities files from the Adobe Illustrator > Plug-ins > Extensions folder.

Calibrating your monitor

Whether preparing artwork for print or online use, you should begin by calibrating your monitor. This will ensure the closest possible match between your colors on-screen and those produced by a printer, a video display, or a different computer monitor, and also between your colors in Adobe Illustrator and in other software programs. If your monitor isn't calibrated, the resulting colors may not even be close to what you originally saw on it.

About calibration

Calibration is the process of adjusting your monitor and Illustrator's color conversion settings to compensate for factors that affect how colors in the image appear on-screen and in print. Calibration helps you do the following:

- Display printed colors accurately on the screen. With a well-calibrated system, the color corrections you make to the image are an accurate reflection of what will come out of the printer.
- Display RGB colors accurately on the screen.
- Display CMYK colors accurately on the screen.

Using the Adobe Gamma utility

The Adobe Gamma utility lets you calibrate the contrast and brightness, gamma (midtones), color balance, and white point of monitors. This helps you eliminate any color cast in your monitor display, make your monitor grays as neutral as possible, and standardize your display of images on different monitors (whatever the combinations of monitor and video card). The utility then saves these settings as an ICC profile for your monitor.

The following guidelines can help you in calibrating your monitor:

- You can use a third-party calibration utility that is supported by Adobe Systems. (See the utility's documentation for details.)
- You don't need to recalibrate your monitor if you have already done so with an ICC-aware calibration tool and you have not changed your monitor settings.
- You only need to set calibration and save it as an ICC profile once on your system, for all applications, unless you change any of the factors affecting calibration. For example, if you change the room lighting or readjust the monitor brightness and contrast controls, you must recalibrate the system. If you haven't done so already, after calibrating the monitor consider taping down your monitor's brightness and contrast controls and your room's lighting controls.

To calibrate a monitor:

1 Make sure your monitor has been turned on for at least half an hour, to stabilize the monitor display.

2 Set the room lighting at the level you plan to maintain.

3 Turn off any desktop patterns and change the background color on your monitor to a light gray. This prevents the background color from interfering with your color perception and helps you adjust the display to a neutral gray. (For more on how to do this, refer to the manual for your operating system.)

4 To start the Adobe Gamma utility, move the Adobe Gamma file from Program Files > Common Files > Adobe > Calibration into the System Folder (Windows 95/98) or the System32 folder (Windows NT). Then launch from the Control Panel folder (Windows), or from System Folder > Control Panels (Mac OS).

5 Select which version of the utility you want:

• Step by Step (Assistant) and click Next for a version of the utility that will guide you through each step of the process. If you choose this option, follow the instructions described in the utility.

• Control Panel and click Next for a version of the utility that is contained in a single dialog box. If you choose this option, follow the instructions in the rest of this section.

6 If desired, click Load and select the monitor ICC profile that most closely matches your monitor. Use this as a starting point from which to calibrate your monitor.

Note: *In Windows, the folder Windows/System/Color is displayed by default, and contains .icm files in 8.3 format. Select a file to display the type of monitor ICC profile at the bottom of the Open Monitor Profile dialog box.*

7 Turn up the contrast and brightness controls on your monitor to their maximum settings. Leave the contrast control at maximum.

8 For Brightness and Contrast, adjust the brightness control on your monitor to make the alternating gray squares in the top bar as dark as possible (but not black), while keeping the bottom bar a bright white.

9 For Phosphors, choose a monitor type. If the correct type is not listed, choose Custom, and enter the red, green, and blue chromaticity coordinates as specified by the monitor manufacturer. This option accounts for the different red, green, and blue phosphors used by monitors to display color.

10 For Gamma, choose one of the following options to establish your current gamma settings:

• View Single Gamma Only to adjust the gamma based on a single combined grayscale reading. Drag the slider under the gamma preview until the center box fades into the patterned frame.

• Deselect View Single Gamma Only to adjust the gamma based on Red, Blue, and Green reading. Drag the slider under each box, until the center box matches the patterned frame.

The gamma setting of your monitor defines how bright the midtones are.

11 For Desired, choose the target gamma you want. For example, the default target gamma in Windows is 2.2 and in Mac OS is 1.8.

Note: *This option is not available on Windows systems that cannot control the monitor.*

12 For White Point, enter the following settings:

• Choose the hardware white point of your monitor as described by your monitor's manufacturer. This setting determines whether you are using a warm or cool white. To measure the hardware white point, click Measure and follow the instructions on-screen.

• If you know the color temperature at which the finished image will be viewed, choose it from the Adjusted pop-up menu. Otherwise, choose Same As Hardware. Only choose a different setting to work at a different white point than your monitor's factory-specified hardware setting.

Note: *This option is not available on Windows systems that cannot control the monitor.*

13 Click the close button on the window.

14 Save the settings.

To calibrate multiple monitors:

1 Drag the Adobe Gamma control panel onto the secondary monitor.

2 Repeat the calibration steps for that monitor.

3 Deselect Use As Default Monitor Profile in the Adobe Gamma control panel unless you want the secondary monitor's profile to be used as the default monitor profile for all of your monitors.

8

Chapter 8: Using Gradients, Blends, and Patterns

Filling artwork with patterns, gradients, multiple colors, and textures is easily accomplished with Illustrator. You can fill an object or type with a pattern, or objects with a gradient, much the way you apply a color. You can also smoothly flow multiple colors in multiple directions within an object, using the gradient mesh tool. Mesh objects can be manipulated for very detailed shifts in color. You can also blend shapes, and modify the blends using standard Illustrator editing techniques. Special effects, such as simulated ink pen hatching effects, can also be applied to artwork using the Pen and Ink filters.

Illustrator provides a variety of ways to create and apply patterns to artwork. You can create pattern tiles and save them in the Swatches palette. Patterns can also be applied to a path using the brush tools.

About gradients, gradient meshes, and blends

Depending on the effect you want, you can choose different ways to apply blends or color gradients to objects.

To apply a graduated blend of colors as you would apply any other color, you can create a gradient fill. You use the Gradient palette or the gradient tool to apply a gradient; applying a gradient in this way does not transform the object. Creating a gradient fill is a good way to create a smooth color gradation across one or more objects.

In contrast, the gradient mesh tool transforms a path object (or a bitmap image) into a single, multicolored object. When an object is transformed into a gradient mesh object, you create smooth shifts in color that can be precisely adjusted and manipulated—the color is controlled by a mesh that can be moved and adjusted to vary the color shift from one part of the object to another. The gradient mesh tool provides the most precise method for shifting colors within a single object.

You can create blends of colors and shapes between objects using the Blend command or the blend tool. Blending shapes and colors allows you to select the beginning and ending shapes and colors, and have Illustrator create the intermediate steps to create the final blend. You can also make changes to elements between the blending steps and Illustrator will adjust the blends instantly.

Creating and working with gradient fills

A *gradient fill* is a graduated blend between two or more colors or tints of the same color. You use the Gradient palette to create your own gradients and —in combination with the Color palette and Swatches palette—to modify existing gradients. You can also add intermediate colors to a gradient to create a fill defined by multiple blends among colors. For details on using the Color palette and the Swatches palette when working with gradients, see Chapter 7, "Working with Color."

Gradient colors can be assigned as CMYK process color, RGB process color, or a spot color. When a gradient is printed or separated, mixed-mode gradient colors are all converted to CMYK process color. (See "Printing gradients, gradient mesh objects, and color blends" on page 347.)

To create a gradient:

1 Select an object with a selection tool, and click the Fill box in the toolbox to select the object's fill.

2 To apply a gradient, do one of the following:

• Choose Window > Show Gradient, and click the Gradient Fill box at the upper left of the Gradient palette. (If the Gradient Fill box is not displayed, choose Show Options from the pop-up menu in the Gradient palette.)

• Click the Gradient button in the toolbox.

• Click a gradient swatch in the Swatches palette.

3 To define the starting color of a gradient, click the left square below the gradient bar and then do one of the following:

• Alt-click (Windows) or Option-click (Mac OS) a color swatch in the Swatches palette.

• Create a color using the sliders or the color bar in the Color palette.

• Drag a color from the Color palette or the Swatches palette to the square below the gradient bar.

Note: *If you create a gradient between spot colors, you must deselect Convert to Process in the Separation Setup dialog box to print the gradient in individual spot color separations. (See "Printing gradients as separations" on page 363.)*

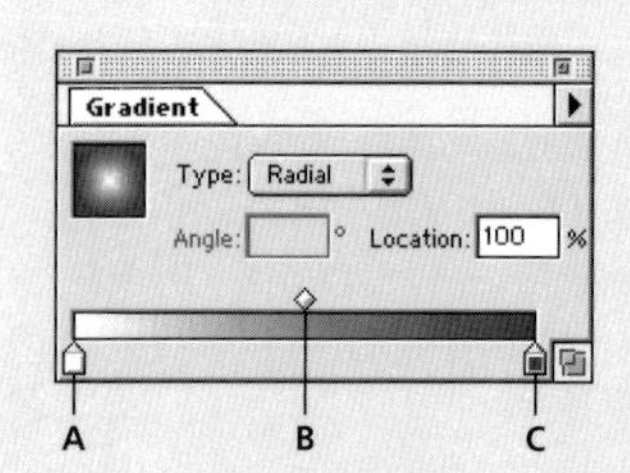

A. *Starting color* ***B.*** *Midpoint* ***C.*** *Ending color*

4 To define the ending color of the gradient, click the right square below the gradient bar. Then choose the color you want as described in step 3.

5 Choose Linear or Radial from the pop-up menu to indicate the type of gradient you want. With a radial gradient, the beginning point of the gradient defines the center point of the fill, which radiates outward to the endpoint.

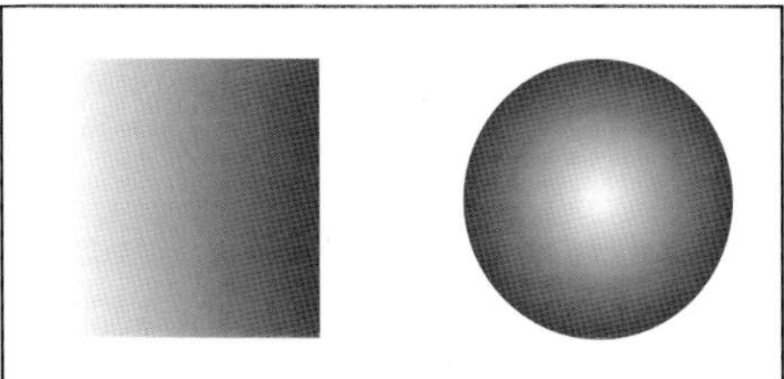

Linear and radial gradients

6 To adjust the beginning point or endpoint of the gradient, drag the squares located below the bar. To adjust the midpoint of the gradient (the point at which the colors are at 50%), drag the diamond icon located above the bar.

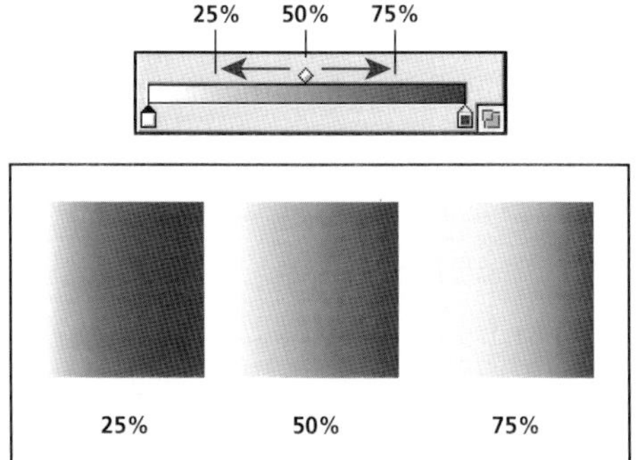

Gradient fills with midpoint at different percentages

7 Enter the angle of direction for the gradient in the Angle text box. The angle can range from -180 to 180 degrees. (The angle option is not available when a radial gradient is chosen.)

8 To save the gradient, do one of the following:

- Drag the completed gradient from the Gradient palette to the Swatches palette.
- Drag the gradient from the Fill box in the toolbox to the Swatches palette.
- Click the New Swatch button in the Swatches palette.

Modifying gradients

You can modify gradients by adding colors to make blends from multiple colors or by adjusting the endpoints and midpoints of the gradients.

Gradient colors are defined by a series of stops in the gradient bar. A *stop* is the point at which a gradient changes from one color to the next and is identified by a square below the gradient bar. The squares in the Gradient palette display the color currently assigned to each gradient stop.

It's a good idea to fill an object with the gradient you plan to adjust so that you can preview the effect on the artwork as you adjust the gradient.

To add intermediate colors to a gradient:

Do one of the following:

- Drag and drop a color from the Swatches palette or the Color palette onto the gradient bar in the Gradient palette.

• Click anywhere below the gradient bar to define another color square. You can then select a color and adjust the square as you would any other starting or ending color. To delete an intermediate color, drag the square off the gradient bar.

For a color illustration of linear and multi-color gradients, see figure 8-1 on page 231.

Adjusting gradients with the gradient tool

Once you have filled an object with a gradient, the gradient tool lets you modify the gradient by "repainting" the fill along an imaginary line you drag. This tool lets you change the direction of a gradient, change the beginning point and endpoint of a gradient, and apply a gradient across multiple objects.

To use the gradient tool:

1 Select an object whose gradient you want to modify.

2 Select the gradient tool (▦).

3 Position the pointer where you want to define the beginning point of the gradient, and drag across the object in the direction you want the gradient to be painted. Hold down Shift to constrain the tool to multiples of 45 degrees.

4 Release the mouse button where you want to define the endpoint of the gradient.

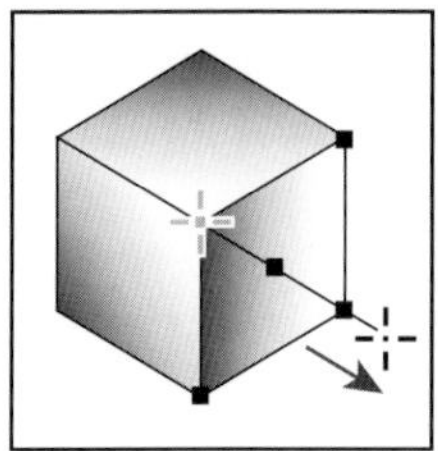

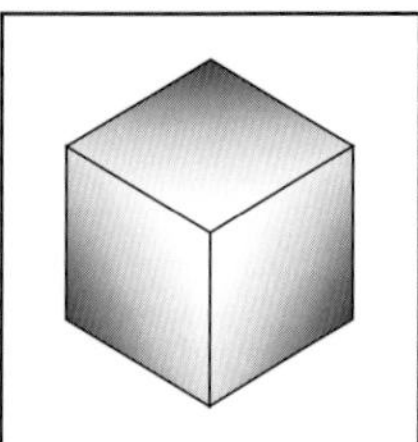

Drag to set direction and length of gradient.

To apply a gradient across multiple objects:

1 Fill each object with a gradient using the Gradient palette, the Swatches palette, or the paint bucket tool.

2 Select all of the objects.

3 Select the gradient tool (▦).

4 Position the pointer where you want to define the beginning point of the gradient, and drag across the objects in the direction you want the gradient to be painted.

5 Release the mouse button where you want to define the endpoint of the gradient.

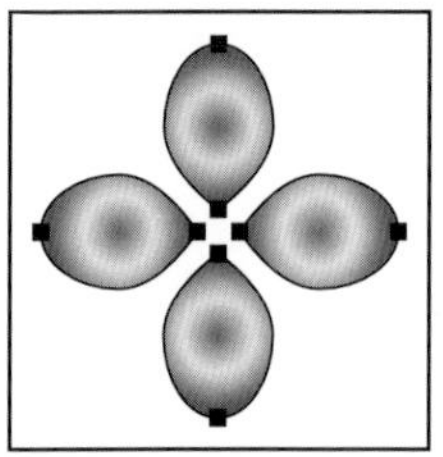

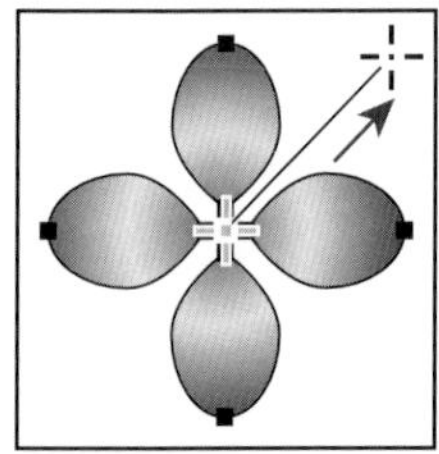

Default gradient fill and gradient applied across objects

Creating multicolored objects with the gradient mesh tool

The gradient mesh tool, the Create Gradient Mesh command, and the Expand command can all be used to transform an object into a *mesh object*. A mesh object is a single, multicolored object on which colors can flow in different directions, and transition smoothly from one point to another.

By creating a fine mesh on an object and manipulating the color characteristics at each point in the mesh, you can precisely manipulate the coloring of the mesh object. You can also apply color to four mesh points at the same time by clicking the patch between them, to create broad color changes on part of the object.

Gradient mesh tool applied; highlights and colors added

About gradient meshes

When you create a mesh object, multiple lines called *mesh lines* crisscross the object and provide a way to easily manipulate color transitions on the object. By moving and editing points on the mesh lines, you can change the intensity of a color shift, or change the extent of a colored area on the object.

At the intersection of two mesh lines is a special kind of anchor point called a *mesh point*. Mesh points appear as diamonds and have all of the same properties as anchor points but with the added capability of accepting color. You can add and delete mesh points, edit the mesh points, or change the color associated with each mesh point.

Anchor points also appear in the mesh (differentiated by their square rather than diamond shape), and can be added, deleted, edited, and moved as with any anchor points in Illustrator. Anchor points can be placed on any mesh line; you can click an anchor point and drag its direction lines to modify it. (See "About direction lines and direction points" on page 70.)

The area between any four mesh points is called the *mesh patch*. You can also change the color of the mesh patch using the same techniques as changing colors on a mesh point.

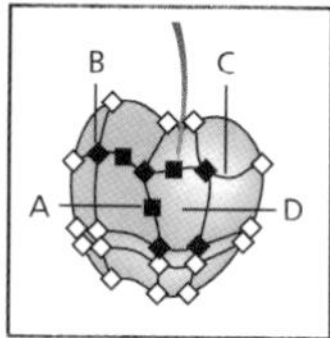

A. *Anchor point*
B. *Mesh point*
C. *Mesh line*
D. *Mesh patch*

Tips for creating mesh objects

You can create a mesh object out of any path object, or any bitmap image (such as a photographic image imported from Adobe Photoshop). There are a few important guidelines to keep in mind when creating mesh objects:

• You cannot create mesh objects from compound paths, text objects, or placed EPS files.

• Once a mesh object has been created, it cannot be converted back to a path object.

• When converting complex objects, use the Create Gradient Mesh command for the best results.

• When converting simple objects, use either the gradient mesh tool or the Create Gradient Mesh command. However, if you want to add a highlight to a particular spot, use the gradient mesh tool and click at the point you want the highlight to appear.

• To create a mesh object with a regular pattern of mesh points and mesh lines, use the Create Gradient Mesh command.

• When converting complex objects, Illustrator can add hidden anchor points to maintain the shape of a line. If you want to edit, add, or delete one or more of these anchor points, use the add-anchor-point tool or the delete-anchor-point tool.

• To improve performance and speed of redrawing, keep the size of mesh objects to a minimum. Complex mesh objects can greatly reduce performance. Therefore, it is better to create a few small, simple mesh objects than to create a single, complex mesh object.

Creating a mesh object

Use the gradient mesh tool or the Create Gradient Mesh command to convert objects to mesh objects. You can also use the Expand command to convert radial or linear gradient path objects into mesh objects.

To create a gradient mesh object with the gradient mesh tool:

Choose the gradient mesh tool (▧) and click a filled object. The object is converted to a gradient mesh object with the minimum number of mesh lines.

To create a gradient mesh object with the Create Gradient Mesh command:

1 Select a filled object.

2 Choose Object > Create Gradient Mesh.

3 Enter the number of horizontal rows of mesh lines to create on the object in the Rows text box.

4 Enter the number of vertical columns of mesh lines to create on the object in the Columns text box.

5 Select the direction of the highlight from the Appearance pop-up menu:

• To Center creates a highlight in the center of the object.

• To Edge creates a highlight on the edges of the object.

• Flat applies the object's original color evenly across the surface, resulting in no highlight.

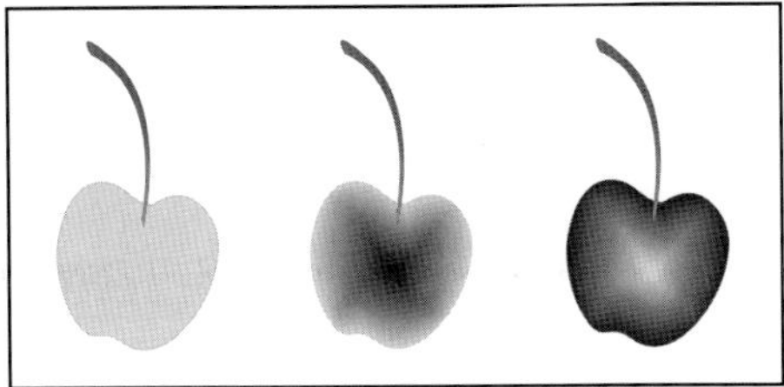

Mesh object with the highlight appearance set to Flat, To Edge, and To Center.

6 Enter a percentage of white highlight to apply to the mesh object. A value of 100% applies maximum white highlight to the object; a value of 0% applies no white highlight to the object.

Creating a mesh object using the Expand command:

1 Select an object containing a radial or linear gradient fill.

2 Choose Object > Expand.

3 Select the Gradient Mesh option in the Expand dialog box and click OK. The selected object is converted to a mesh object that takes the shape of the gradient, either circular (radial) or rectangular (linear).

Editing mesh objects

Once you have created a mesh object, you can adjust or edit its mesh points, anchor points, and mesh lines. Anchor points can be added with the add-anchor-point tool or deleted with the delete-anchor-point tool on any mesh line.

To add or delete mesh points and mesh lines:

1 Select the gradient mesh tool ( ).

2 Do one of the following:

• To add a mesh point colored with the current fill color, click anywhere in the mesh object. The corresponding mesh lines extend from the new mesh point to the edges of the object. Clicking on an existing mesh line adds a single intersecting mesh line.

• To add a mesh point without changing to the current fill color, press Shift and click.

• To delete a mesh point and the corresponding mesh lines, Alt-click (Windows) or Option-click (Mac OS) directly on the mesh point.

To edit a mesh point:

1 Select the gradient mesh tool and click directly on a mesh point. Direction lines appear on the mesh point.

2 Do one of the following:

• Drag the direction lines to edit the mesh point as you would any anchor point. For more information about editing anchor points, see "About direction lines and direction points" on page 70.

• Shift-drag a direction line to move all direction lines from the mesh point at once.

• Use the direct-selection tool, the convert-selection-point tool, or the transformation tools to edit mesh points.

To move a mesh point:

1 Select the gradient mesh tool.

2 Do one of the following:

• Click a mesh point and drag to freely move the point and the connecting mesh lines.

• Press Shift and drag the mesh point to constrain the movement to follow a mesh line. This is a convenient way to move a mesh point along a curved mesh line without distorting the mesh line.

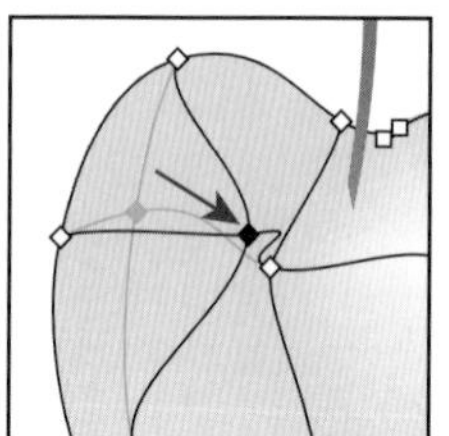
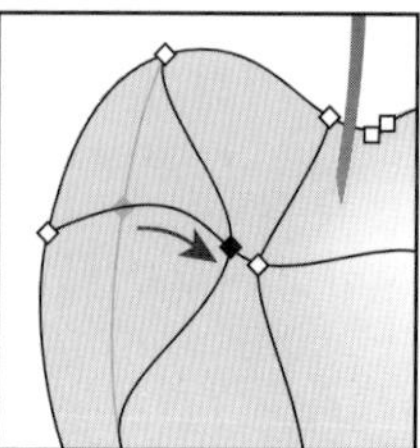

Dragging to move mesh point and Shift-dragging with the gradient mesh tool to constrain to mesh line

Adjusting colors on gradient mesh objects

Colors are added to gradient mesh objects using the Color palette, by dragging and dropping colors, or by using the paint bucket tool. When you select and color a mesh point, the mesh point and surrounding area are colored with the current fill color. When you click over a mesh patch, all four mesh points surrounding the patch are colored. You can also use color filters to change the color of mesh points. (See “Using filters to modify colors” on page 176.)

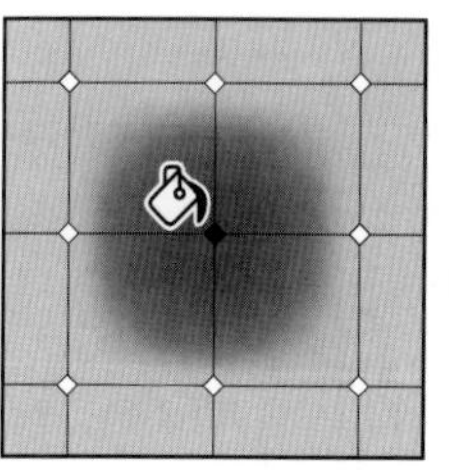
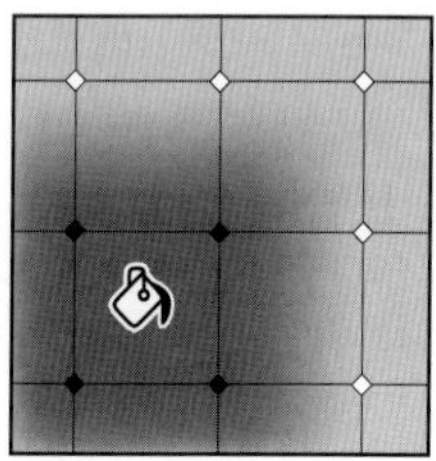

Adding color to a mesh point and to a mesh patch

Once color is applied to parts of a mesh object, you can change the shape and extent of the colored areas by editing the mesh points, anchor points, and mesh lines. (See “Editing mesh objects” on page 193.)

To add color to a mesh point or mesh patch with the Color palette:

1 Select a mesh point or mesh patch with the gradient mesh tool ( ) or the direct-selection tool ( ).

2 Do one of the following:

• In the Color palette, select a color using the sliders or the color bar.

• In the Swatches palette, select a swatch.

To add color to a mesh point or mesh patch by dragging and dropping:

Do one of the following:

• Drag a color from the Color palette directly over a mesh point or mesh patch and release the mouse button.

• Drag a swatch color from the Swatches palette directly over a mesh point or mesh patch and release the mouse button.

To add color to a mesh point or mesh patch with the paint bucket:

1 Select the paint bucket tool.

2 Click directly on a mesh point or a mesh patch. The point or patch is colored with the current fill color.

Blending shapes

The Adobe Illustrator blend tool and the Make Blend command let you create a series of intermediate objects and colors between two or more selected objects. You can blend between two open paths (such as two different lines), between two closed paths (such as a circle and a square), between gradients, or between other blends. Depending on the way you paint the objects you are blending, you can produce airbrush effects such as complex shading, highlighting, and contouring. The Blend filters can also be used to blend colors between filled objects.

You can edit blends that you created by moving, resizing, deleting, or adding objects. After you make editing changes, the artwork is automatically reblended.

About blending

One of the simplest uses for blending is to create and distribute shapes evenly between two objects. For example, you can create a series of evenly spaced bars using the blend tool or the Make Blend command.

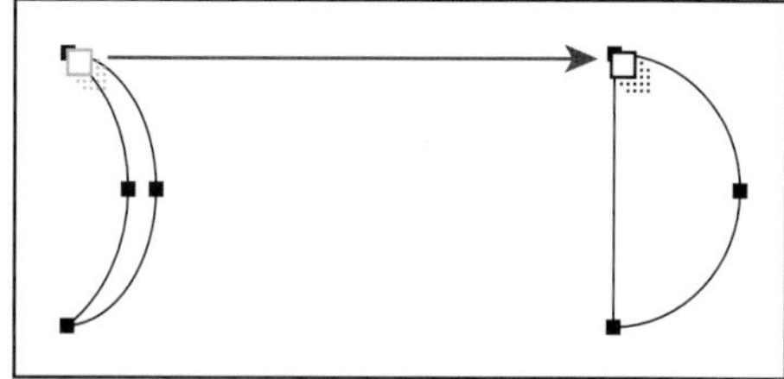

Two objects selected

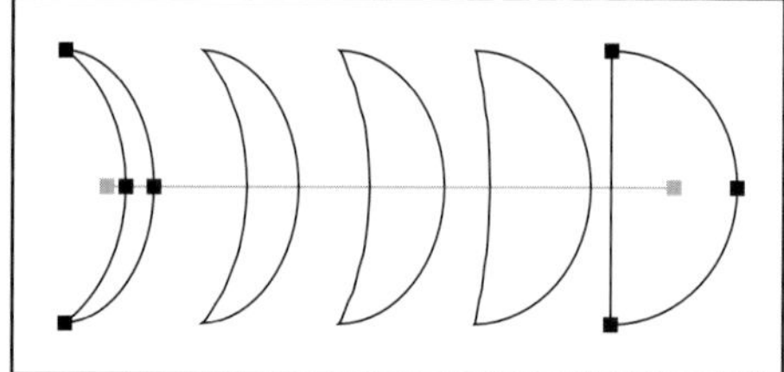

Blending distributes shapes evenly

You can also blend between two open paths to create a smooth transition between objects, or you can combine blends of colors and objects to create color transitions in the shape of a particular object.

The following rules apply to blending shapes and their associated colors:

• You can blend between an unlimited number of objects, colors, or gradients.

• Blends can be directly edited with tools such as the selection tools, the rotate tool, or the scale tool.

• A straight path is created between blended objects when the blend is first applied. You can edit the blend path by dragging anchor points and path segments. (See “Adjusting path segments” on page 73.)

• You cannot blend between gradient mesh objects.

• If you blend between one object painted with a process color and another object painted with a spot color, the blended shapes are painted with a blended process color. If you blend between two different spot colors, process colors are used to paint the intermediate steps. If, however, you blend between tints of the same spot color, the steps are all painted with percentages of the spot color.

• If you blend between two patterned objects, the blended steps will only use the fill of the object on the topmost layer.

• The Adobe Illustrator program automatically calculates the number of steps in a blend, unless you select Specify Steps in the Blend Options dialog box.

Creating blends

You create blends in Illustrator by clicking objects with the blend tool, or by selecting objects with a selection tool and using the Blend commands.

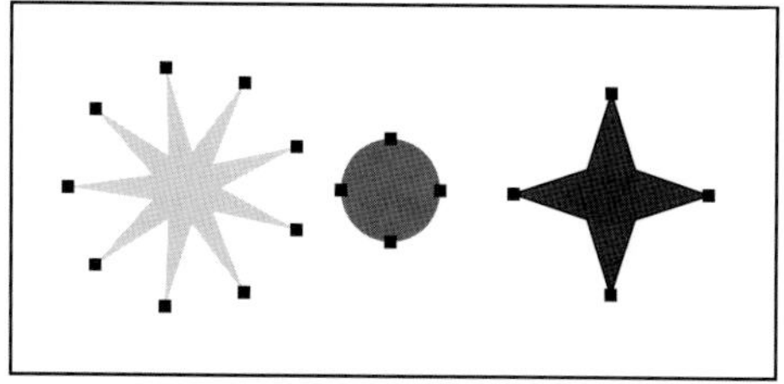

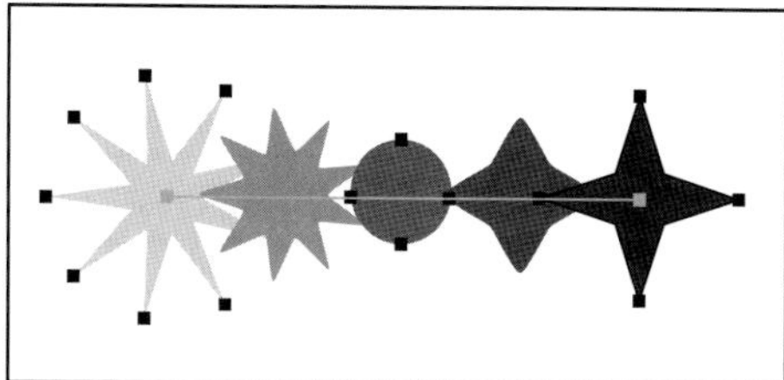

Multiple objects are clicked sequentially with the blend tool

Objects are blended relative to selected anchor points on each blended object. If the objects are unselected, or if you have only one anchor point selected, Illustrator automatically selects the two points from which the blend commences and finishes. You can also select two or more anchor points from which to blend by clicking anchor points with the blend tool. By selecting different anchor points on the objects, you can create the effect of rotating the blend from one point in an object to a selected point in the next object.

To create a blend with the blend tool:

1 Select the blend tool ( ).

2 Click objects to blend in sequential order. If you want to blend to a specific anchor point on an object, click the anchor point with the blend tool. If you are blending open paths, select an endpoint on each path.

3 When you are finished adding objects to the blend, you can click the blend tool again to start a new blend.

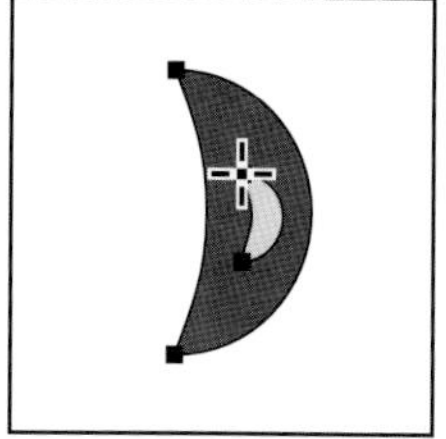

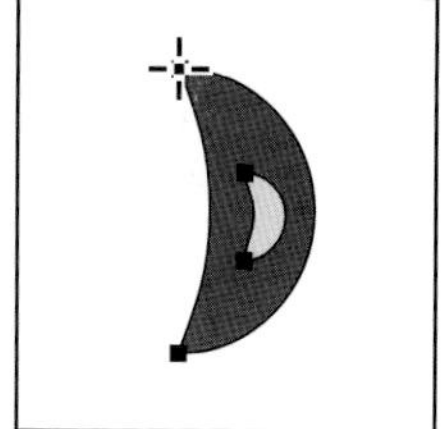

Click anchor point on first object with blend tool. Then click anchor point on second object.

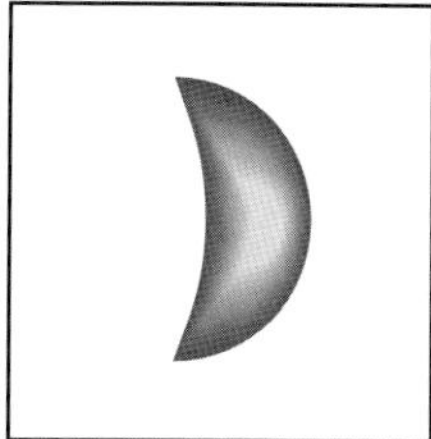

Result

To create a blend with the Make Blend command:

1 Select the objects to blend with any selection tool.

2 Choose Object > Blends > Make.

To unmake a blend:

1 Select the blend with any selection tool.

2 Choose Object > Blends > Release.

To change the number of steps between blends:

1 Choose Object > Blends > Blend Options.

2 Select from the following options in the Spacing pop-up menu:

- Specified Steps. Enter a value to specify the number of steps between the start and end of the blend.

- Specified Distance. Enter a value to specify the distance between the steps in the blend. The distance specified is measured from the edge of one object to the corresponding edge on the next object (for example, from the rightmost edge of one object to the rightmost edge of the next object).

- Smooth Color has the Adobe Illustrator program autocalculate the number of steps for the blends. If objects are filled or stroked with different colors, the steps are calculated to provide the optimum number of steps for a smooth color transition. If the objects contain identical colors, or if they contain gradients or patterns, the number of steps is based on the longest distance between the bounding box edges of the two objects.

To change the orientation of the blend to the path:

1 Choose Objects > Blends > Blend Options.

2 Select from the following options:

- Click the Align to Page button to orient the blend perpendicular to the *x* axis of the page.

- Click the Align to Path button to orient the blend perpendicular to the path.

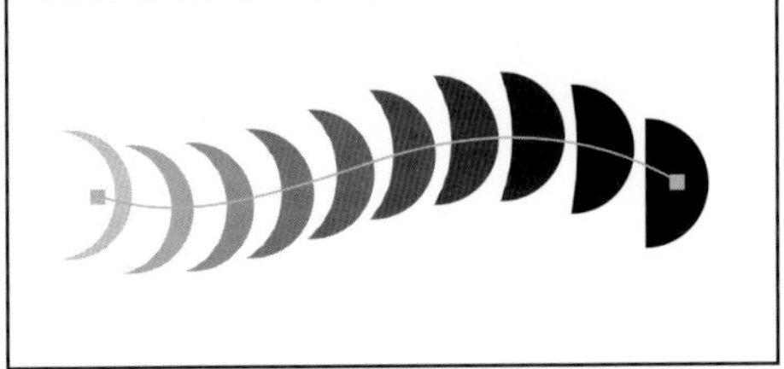

Align to Page option applied

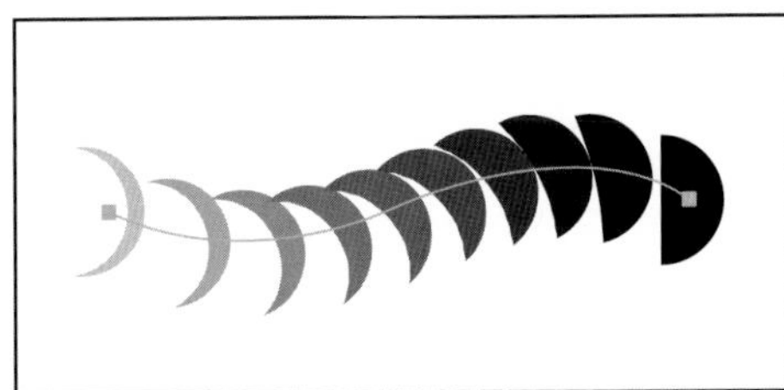

Align to Path option applied

Creating blends on paths

Once you create a blend, you can then apply the blend to a path. Applying a blend to a path is an easy way to wrap a blend around an object or create special effects in your artwork.

The blend follows the contours of the path in the orientation specified in the Blend Options dialog box. If Align to Path is selected, the alignment of the blend follows the contours of the path. If Align to Page (the default setting) is selected, the blend is aligned with the *x* axis of the page.

To apply a blend to a path:

1 Select a blend and hold down Shift to select a path.

2 Choose Object > Blends > Replace Spine.

To reverse the order of a blend on a path:

1 Select the blend.

2 Choose Object > Blends > Reverse Spine. The objects are ordered in reverse on the path.

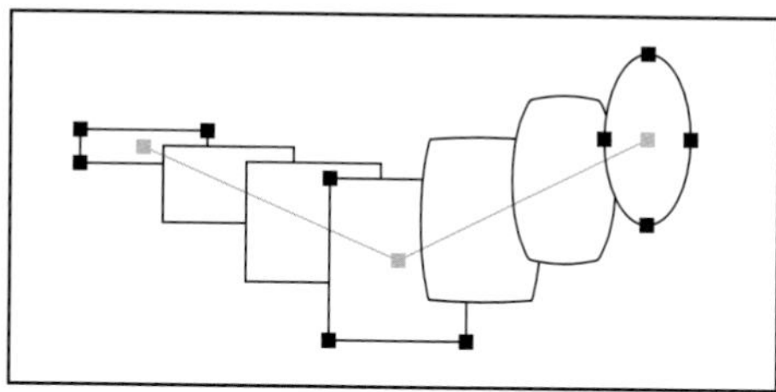

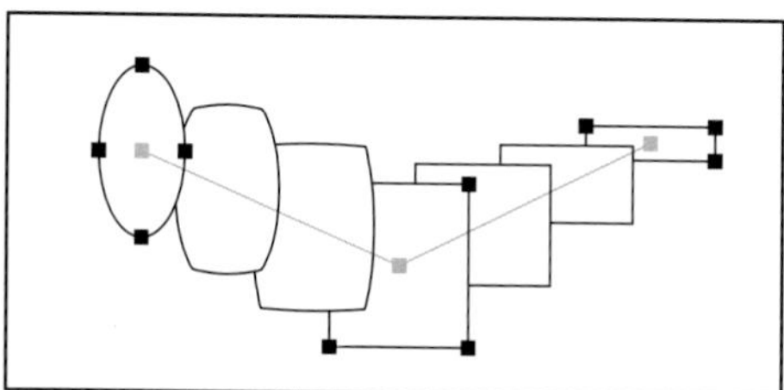

Original and with Reverse Spine command applied

To reverse the stacking order of a blend on a path:

1 Select the blend.

2 Choose Object > Blends > Reverse Front to Back. The objects are reversed in the stacking order on the path, so that those objects on the frontmost stacking order are moved to the back of the stacking order, and vice-versa. (See "Stacking objects" on page 123.)

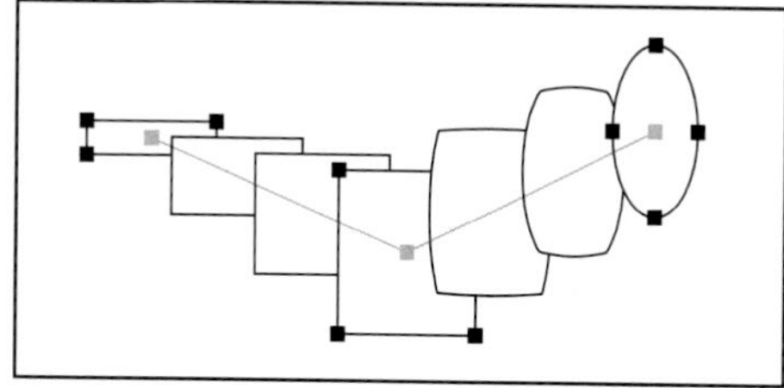

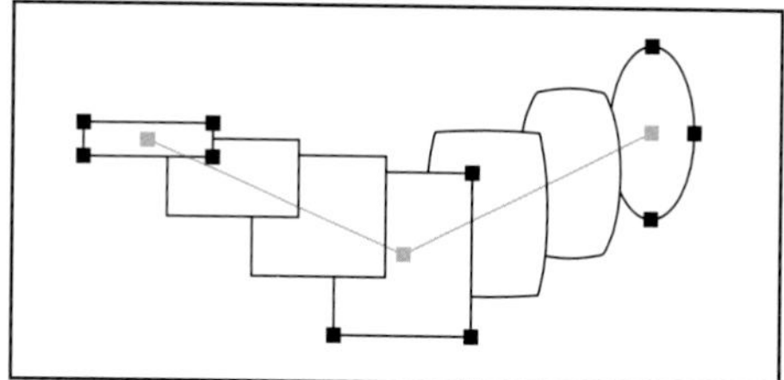

Original and with Reverse Front to Back command applied

Editing blends

You can move, delete, transform, edit anchor points and Bezier curves, or change colors on blends, using any of the editing tools available in the Adobe Illustrator program. When you edit a blend path, the changes take place interactively while you work.

Blending colors between filled objects

The Blend filters create a series of intermediate colors from a group of three or more filled objects, based on the objects' vertical or horizontal orientation, or on their stacking order. The filters do not affect strokes or unpainted objects. (See "Stacking objects" on page 123.)

Applying a Blend filter to objects painted using a mix of process and spot color, or a mix of color models, converts the color to CMYK.

Original and with Blend Front to Back filter applied

To blend colors between filled objects:

1 Select three or more filled objects to blend.

2 Do one of the following:

• To fill the intermediate objects with gradated blends between the frontmost and backmost filled objects, choose Filter > Colors > Blend Front to Back.

• To fill the intermediate objects with gradated blends between the leftmost and rightmost filled objects, choose Filter > Colors > Blend Horizontally.

• To fill the intermediate objects with gradated blends between the topmost and bottommost filled objects, choose Filter > Colors > Blend Vertically.

Creating and working with patterns

To create a pattern, you create artwork you want to use as a pattern and then drag the artwork to the Swatches palette or use the Edit > Define Pattern command. You can use paths, compound paths, or text with solid fills (or no fill) for a pattern, or you can design a pattern from scratch with any of the tools in the Adobe Illustrator program. (However, you cannot use patterns, gradients, blends, brushstrokes, gradient meshes, bitmap images, graphs, placed files, or masks in a pattern.) You can customize any pattern by resizing the pattern, moving or transforming it, or coloring its objects.

***Note:** The Illustrator Extras folder on the Adobe Illustrator CD includes pattern and texture libraries. In addition, the Adobe Illustrator Startup file and the Adobe Illustrator 8.0 > Libraries folder contain a smaller collection of these patterns.*

Patterns intended for filling objects (*fill patterns*) differ in design and tiling from patterns intended to be applied to a path with the Brushes palette (*brush patterns*). For best results, use fill patterns to fill objects and brush patterns to outline objects. (See "Using the Brush Libraries" on page 98 and "Creating corner tiles for brush patterns" on page 206.)

How patterns tile

When designing patterns, it helps to understand how Adobe Illustrator tiles patterns:

• Patterns tile from left to right from the ruler origin (by default, the bottom of the artwork) to the top of the artwork. Typically, only one tile makes up a fill pattern. Brush patterns can consist of up to five tiles—for the sides, outer corners, inner corners, and the beginning and end of the path. The additional corner tiles enable brush patterns to flow smoothly at corners.

• Fill patterns tile perpendicular to the *x* axis. In contrast, brush patterns tile perpendicular to the path (with the top of the pattern tile always facing outward). Also, corner tiles rotate 90 degrees clockwise each time the path changes direction.

• Fill and brush patterns also tile differently in relation to the *pattern bounding box*—an unfilled and unstroked rectangle backmost in the artwork. For fill patterns, the bounding box acts as a mask; fill patterns tile only the artwork within the pattern's bounding box. In contrast, brush patterns tile artwork within the bounding box and protruding from or grouped with it.

Constructing simple patterns and defining patterns

To create a pattern, you create artwork that you want to use as a pattern tile and then drag it to the Swatches palette.

To create a pattern:

1 Create artwork for the pattern following "Guidelines for constructing patterns" on page 202.

2 To make the pattern less complex so that it prints more rapidly, remove any unnecessary detail from the pattern artwork, and group objects that are painted with the same color so that they are adjacent in the stacking order.

3 Optionally, to control the spacing between pattern elements or to clip out portions of the pattern, draw a pattern bounding box (an unfilled rectangle) around the artwork you want to use as a pattern. Choose Object > Arrange > Send to Back to make the rectangle the backmost object. To use the rectangle as a bounding box for a brush or fill pattern, fill and stroke it with None.

4 Use the selection tool to select the artwork and bounding box (if any) that will make up the pattern tile.

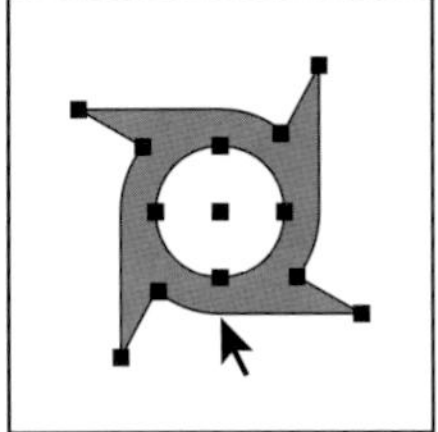

5 Do one of the following:

• Choose Edit > Define Pattern, and enter a name in the New Swatch dialog box.

• Choose Window > Show Swatches, and then drag the artwork to the Swatches palette.

To name a pattern in the Swatches palette:

1 Double-click a pattern swatch.

2 Enter the new pattern name in the Swatch Name text box, and click OK.

Guidelines for constructing patterns

Follow these general guidelines for constructing pattern tiles:

• As you create your pattern tile, zoom in on the artwork to align elements more accurately, and then zoom out from the artwork for the final selection.

• For greatest efficiency in previewing and printing, a fill pattern tile should be about 1/2 inch to 1 inch square. Side tiles for brush patterns should be no larger than 1/2 inch to 1 inch high by 1 inch to 2 inches wide; the corner tiles must be the same height as the side tiles and should be square.

• The more complex the pattern, the smaller the selection used to create it should be; however, the smaller the selection (and the pattern tile it creates), the more copies are needed to create the pattern. Thus, a 1-inch-square tile is more efficient than a 1/4-inch-square tile. If you are creating a simple pattern, you can include multiple copies of the object within the selection intended for the pattern tile.

• To create simple line patterns, layer stroked lines of varying widths and colors and place an unfilled and unstroked bounding box behind the lines to create a pattern tile.

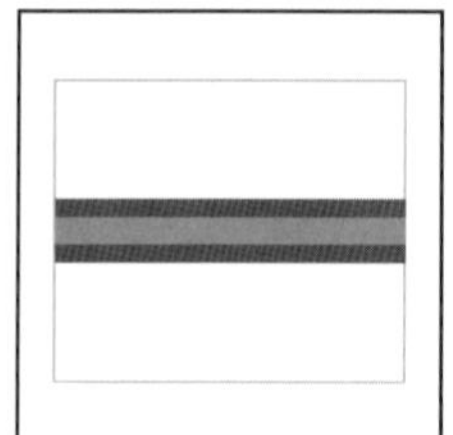

Corner tile and side tile

• To make an organic or textural pattern appear irregular, vary the tile artwork subtly, not dramatically, for a more realistic effect. You can use the Roughen filter in the Distort menu to control variations.

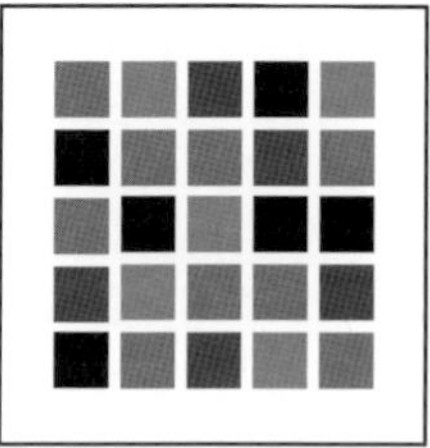
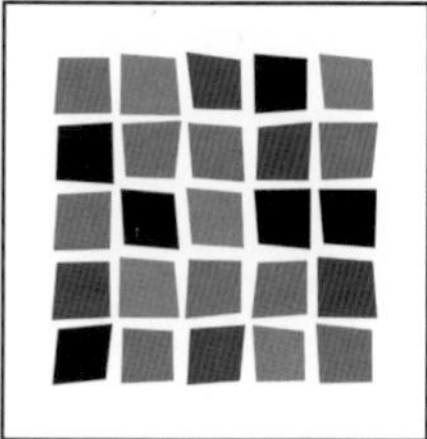

Original and Roughen filter applied

• To ensure smooth tiling, close paths before defining the pattern.

• Enlarge your artwork view, and check for flaws before defining a pattern.

• If you draw a bounding box around the artwork, make sure that the box is a rectangle, that it is the backmost object of the tile, and that it is unfilled and unstroked. To have Illustrator use this bounding box for a brush pattern, do not fill or stroke the box and make sure that nothing protrudes from it.

Follow these additional guidelines when creating brush patterns:

• When possible, confine artwork to an unpainted bounding box so that you can control how the pattern tiles. (See "How patterns tile" on page 201.)

• Corner tiles must be square and have the same height as side tiles to align properly on the path. If you plan to use corner tiles with your brush pattern, align objects in the corner tiles horizontally with objects in the side tiles so that the patterns tile correctly.

Side tile

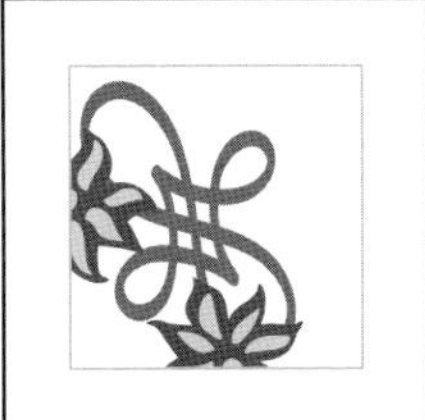

Incorrect corner tile and correct corner tile

• Create special corner effects for brush patterns using corner tiles. (See "Creating corner tiles for brush patterns" on page 206.)

Constructing geometric patterns

To construct a geometric pattern that tiles uniformly, first construct a geometric object with a center point and paint the object. Then arrange copies of the object in the pattern you want, select the artwork, and define it as a pattern tile by dragging it to the Swatches palette.

To construct a geometric pattern:

1 Make sure that Smart Guides are turned on and that the View > Snap to Point command has been selected.

2 Select the geometric object. For precise positioning, use the selection tool positioned on one of the object's points.

3 Begin dragging the object vertically from one of its anchor points; then press Alt+Shift (Windows) or Option+Shift (Mac OS) to copy the object and constrain its movement.

4 When the copy of the object has snapped into place, release the mouse button and then release Alt+Shift (Windows) or Option+Shift (Mac OS).

5 Shift-click to select both objects, and begin dragging the objects horizontally by one of their anchor points; then press Alt+Shift (Windows) or Option+Shift (Mac OS) to create a copy and constrain the move.

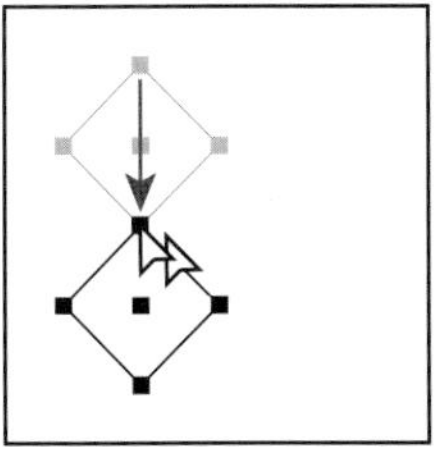

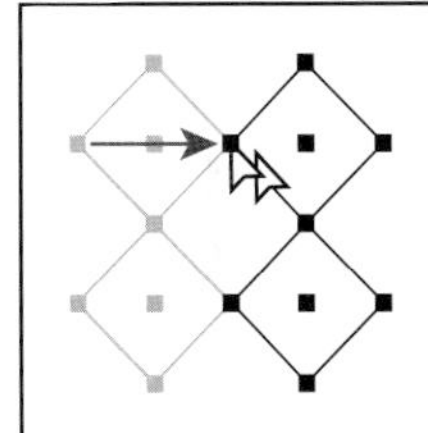

6 When the copy of the object has snapped into place, release the mouse button, and then release Alt+Shift (Windows) or Option+Shift (Mac OS).

7 Repeat steps 2 through 6 until you've built the pattern you want.

8 Using the rectangle tool (□), follow one of two methods:

• For a fill pattern, draw a bounding box from the center point of the upper left object to the center point of the lower right object.

• For a brush pattern, draw a bounding box that surrounds the objects and coincides with their outer boundaries. If the pattern is to be a corner tile, hold down Shift as you drag to constrain the bounding box to a square. The bounding box should surround the objects and coincide with their outer boundaries.

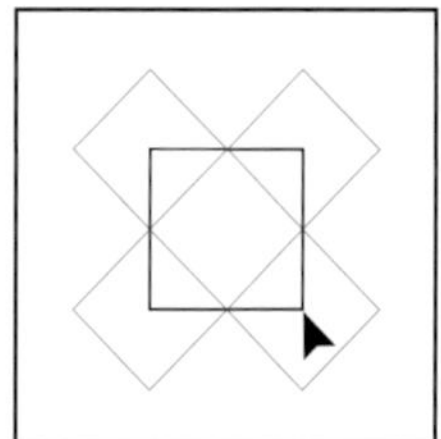

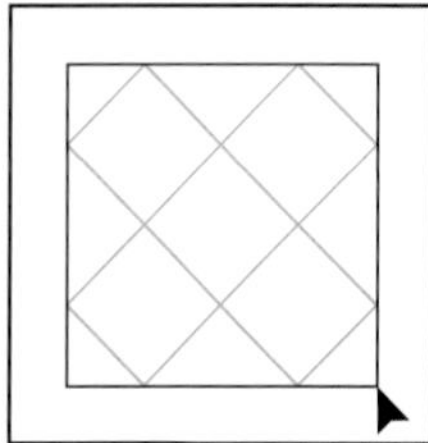

Bounding box for a fill pattern and for a brush pattern

9 Paint the geometric objects the desired color.

10 Define the geometric objects as a pattern, following the procedure in "Constructing simple patterns and defining patterns" on page 201.

Constructing patterns with irregular textures

You can create an irregularly textured fill pattern that tiles seamlessly. Remember that fill patterns clip any artwork outside the bounding box, whereas brush patterns do not. To create an irregularly textured brush pattern, you should select and define as a pattern only the textured artwork within the bounding box.

To create an irregular texture:

1 Make sure that View > Snap to Point has been selected.

2 Draw a bounding box. If you are creating a brush pattern, skip to step 13.

3 Draw the texture with the objects or lines that intersect only the left side of the bounding rectangle.

4 Select the texture and the rectangle, and place the pointer on the lower left corner of the rectangle.

5 Drag the rectangle to the right; then press Alt+Shift (Windows) or Option+Shift (Mac OS) to create a copy and to constrain the move.

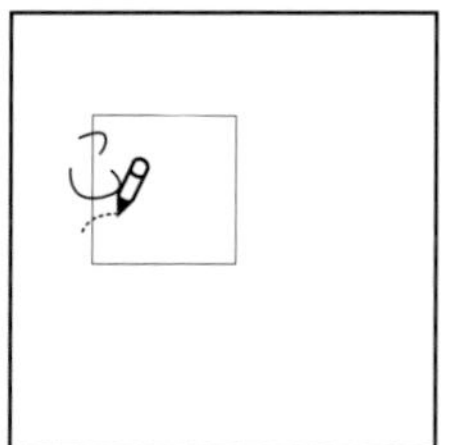

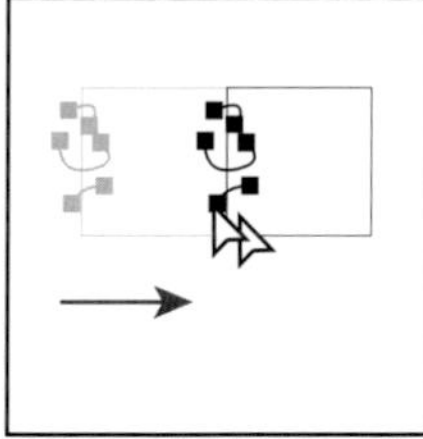

Draw texture on left side of bounding box. Then copy texture and rectangle.

When the upper left corner point of the copy snaps to the upper right corner point of the bounding box, release the mouse button, and then release Alt+Shift (Windows) or Option+Shift (Mac OS).

If you know the exact dimensions of the bounding box, you can select only the textures and use the Move command to specify a horizontal move the width of the rectangle. Be sure to click Copy instead of OK in the Move dialog box.

6 Click outside the rectangle to deselect it.

7 Select the right rectangle, and delete it.

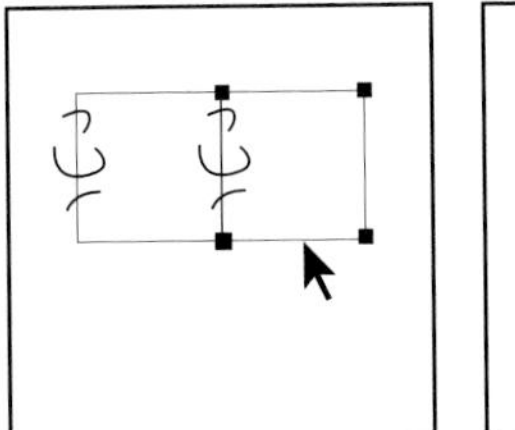

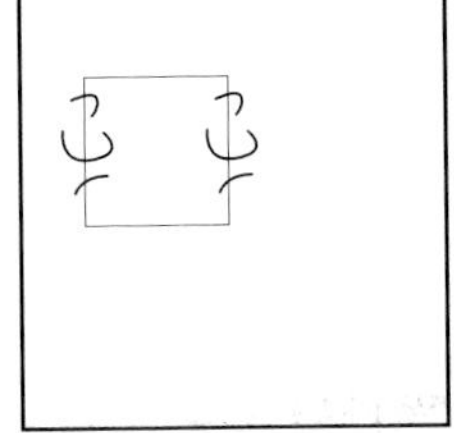

Select the right rectangle and delete it to create identical texture on right and left.

8 Using the pencil tool (✎), continue drawing your texture with only the objects or lines that intersect the top side of the rectangle. When you finish with the top side only, select all of the lines or objects crossing the top side and the bounding box.

9 Edit the corner tile so that its artwork lines up vertically and horizontally with the tiles next to it. Select and delete any portions of the tile that you do not want in the corner and edit the remaining art to create the final outer corner tile.

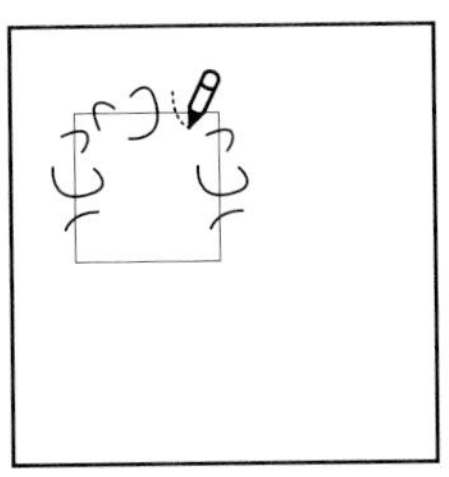

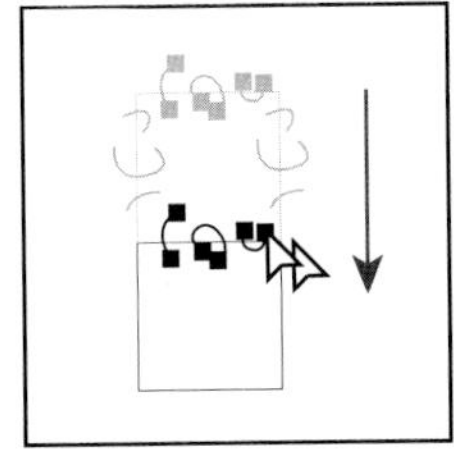

Draw texture on top side of bounding box. Then copy texture and rectangle.

10 When the upper left corner point of the copy snaps to the lower left corner point of the rectangle, release the mouse button and then Alt+Shift (Windows) or Option+Shift (Mac OS).

11 Deselect everything.

12 Select the lower rectangle and any objects that don't cross the top rectangle, and delete them.

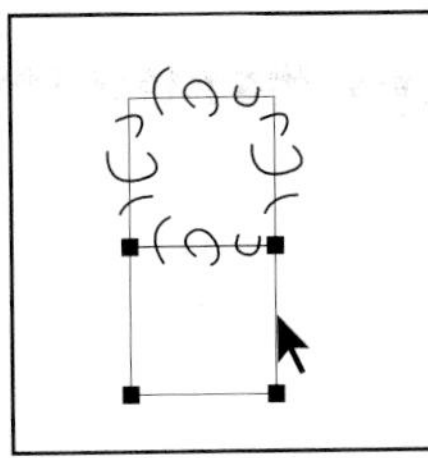

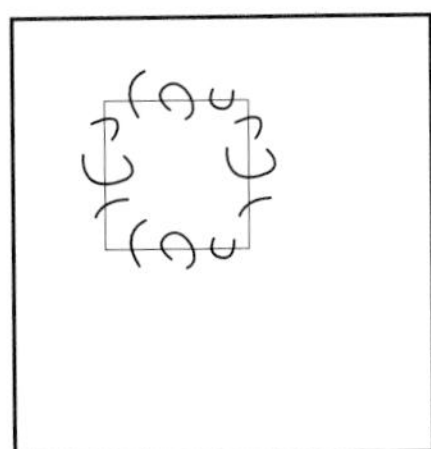

Select the lower rectangle and delete it to create an identical texture on top and bottom.

13 Using the pencil tool, fill the middle of the rectangle with your texture. Be careful not to intersect any of the rectangle edges. Paint the texture.

14 Define the artwork and rectangle as a pattern, following the procedure in "Constructing simple patterns and defining patterns" on page 201.

Creating corner tiles for brush patterns

Corner tiles lend special border effects when applying brush patterns. You can create corner tiles from scratch, or you can use a brush pattern's side tile as the basis for designing complementary outer and inner (reflected –135 degrees) corner tiles.

To create symmetrical corner tiles from a side tile:

1 Open a brush pattern file, supplied with Adobe Illustrator, that you want to use.

2 Choose Window > Show Swatches. Select the tile you want to use, and drag it to the center of your artwork.

3 If the tile does not have a square bounding box, create a box that completely encompasses the artwork, the same height as the side tile. (Side tiles can be rectangular.) Fill and stroke the box with None, and choose Object > Arrange > Send to Back to make the box backmost in your artwork. (The bounding box helps you align the new tile.)

4 Select the tile and the bounding box.

5 Use the rotate tool (⟲) to rotate the tile and its bounding box 180 degrees.

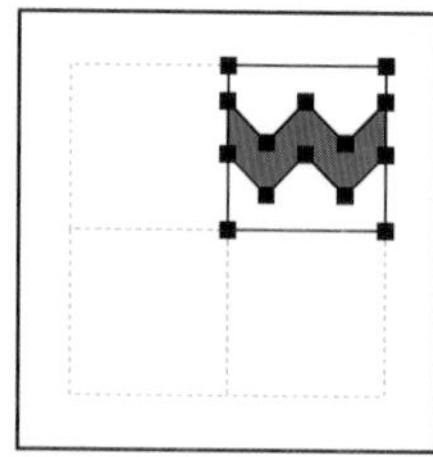
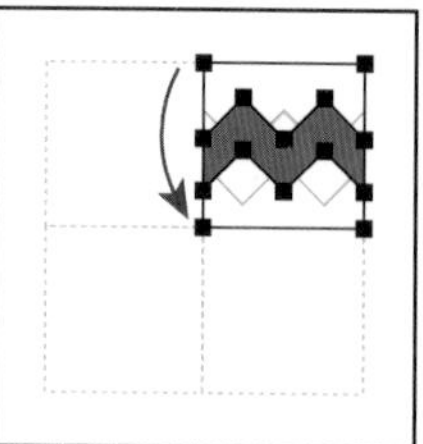

Pasted tile and tile rotated 180°

6 Using the rotate tool, Alt+Shift (Windows) or Option+Shift (Mac OS) the lower left corner of the bounding box. Enter a value of 90 degrees, and click Copy to create a copy flush left of the first tile. This tile becomes the corner tile.

7 Using the selection tool, drag the left tile down by the top right anchor point, pressing Alt+Shift (Windows) or Option+Shift (Mac OS) to make a copy and constrain the move so that you create a third tile beneath the second. When the copy's upper right anchor point snaps to the corner tile's lower right anchor point, release the mouse button and Alt+Shift (Windows) or Option+Shift (Mac OS).

You use the third copy for alignment.

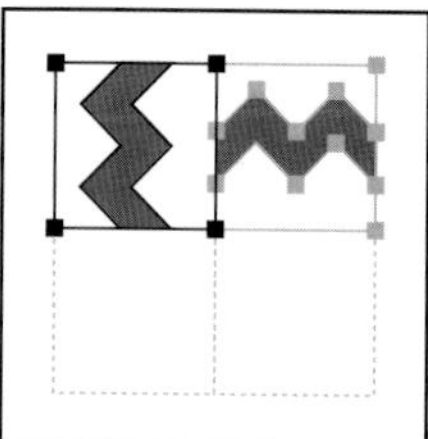
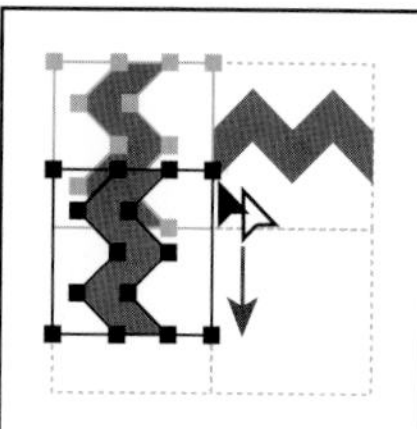

Rotate 90° and copy left tile. Then Alt-drag/Option-drag corner tile to make copy beneath it.

8 Select the artwork in the right tile. Drag it to the left, pressing Alt+Shift (Windows) or Option+Shift (Mac OS) so that the artwork overlaps that in the corner tile.

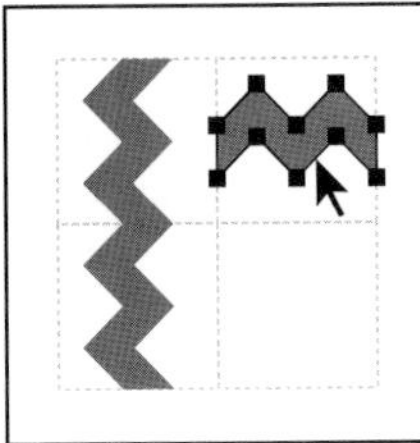
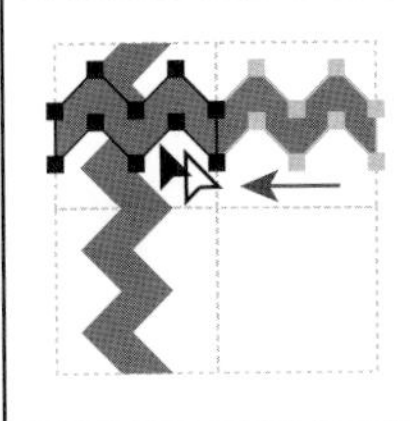

Copy and move upper right tile over corner tile.

9 Edit the corner tile so that its artwork lines up vertically and horizontally with the tiles next to it. Select and delete any portions of the tile that you do not want in the corner and edit the remaining art to create the final outer corner tile.

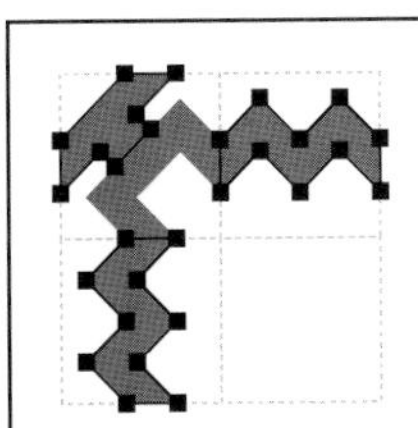
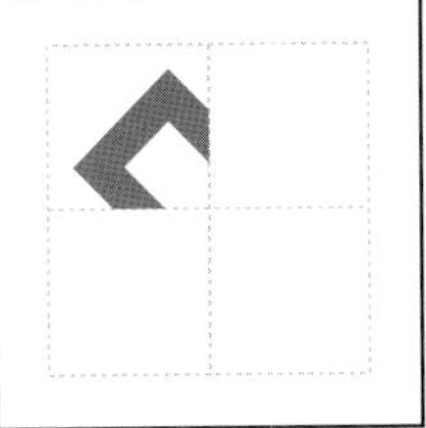

Unneeded elements selected and deleted; Final outer corner tile

10 Select all of the tile including the bounding box.

11 Save the new pattern following the procedure in "Constructing simple patterns and defining patterns" on page 201.

12 Double-click the new pattern swatch to bring up the Swatch Options dialog box, name the tile as a variation of the original (for example, use the suffix *.outer*), and click OK.

To create an inner corner tile:

Do one of the following:

- If the side tile for the brush pattern is horizontally symmetric (that is, if it looks the same when flipped top to bottom), you can use the same tile for the inner corner tile as for the outer corner tile.
- If the side tile for the brush pattern is not horizontally symmetric, follow the same steps as to create symmetrical corner tiles from a side tile, but skip step 5 (rotating the tile by 180 degrees).

Modifying patterns

You can modify a pattern by editing the artwork and then replacing the old pattern in the Swatches palette with the new artwork. If you replace an old pattern with a new pattern, any new and existing objects painted with that pattern are painted with the new definition rather than with the old definition.

To modify an existing pattern:

1 Make sure that nothing is selected in your artwork.

2 Choose Windows > Show Swatches, and select the pattern swatch you want to modify.

3 Drag the pattern swatch onto your artwork.

4 Select artwork in the pattern tile, and edit the tile. (To do this, use the direct-selection tool or group-selection tool, or ungroup the pattern.)

5 Select the pattern tile.

6 Alt-drag (Windows) or Option-drag (Mac OS) the modified pattern on top of the old pattern swatch in the Swatches palette. The pattern is replaced in the Swatches palette and is updated in the current file.

Moving patterns

Patterns begin tiling from the ruler origin and continue to tile in a left-to-right sequence, from bottom to top, until the object is filled. To adjust where all patterns in your artwork begin tiling, you can change the file's ruler origin.

To move all of the patterns within a file:

1 Choose View > Show Rulers.

2 Move the selection pointer to the box in the upper left corner where the rulers intersect.

3 As you drag into the window, two intersecting lines, indicating the ruler origin, follow the pointer. When the ruler origins are positioned as desired, release the mouse button. (See "Changing the ruler origin" on page 107.)

Transforming pattern-filled objects

If an object that you want to transform is filled with a pattern, you can choose to transform only the pattern, transform only the object, or transform the pattern and the object simultaneously.

Once you have transformed a fill pattern, all patterns that you subsequently apply are transformed the same way. To return fill patterns to their original states, select another paint style and then reselect the desired pattern.

You can transform fill patterns using the dialog box associated with a transformation tool. Regardless of the method you choose, turning this option on or off in any dialog box updates the option in all dialog boxes. (See "Moving, copying, and deleting objects" on page 117.)

To transform a pattern and object using a transformation tool:

1 Use the selection tool to select the pattern-filled object.

2 Double-click the transformation tool you want to use.

3 Select one or both of the following options:

- Patterns to transform the pattern tiles.
- Objects to transform the object.

4 Enter the desired transformation values in the text boxes and click OK.

To transform patterns using the mouse:

1 Select the pattern-filled object.

2 Hold down the tilde key (~) and drag.

3 Release the mouse button when the transformation is as desired.

Important: *The borders of the object appear to be transformed while dragging with the mouse, but when the mouse button is released the borders snap back to their original configuration, leaving only the pattern transformed.*

To select the Transform Pattern Tiles preferences option:

1 Choose File > Preferences > General.

2 Select Transform Pattern Tiles to select Pattern Tiles automatically in the transformation dialog boxes, and click OK.

Changing gradients, blends, and patterns into filled objects

The Expand command can convert gradients, blends, or patterns into filled objects. This command can be particularly useful if you are having difficulty printing objects that contain gradients, blends, or patterns. The Expand command can also convert fills and strokes into individual objects, and can convert gradients into mesh objects. (See "Creating a mesh object" on page 192.)

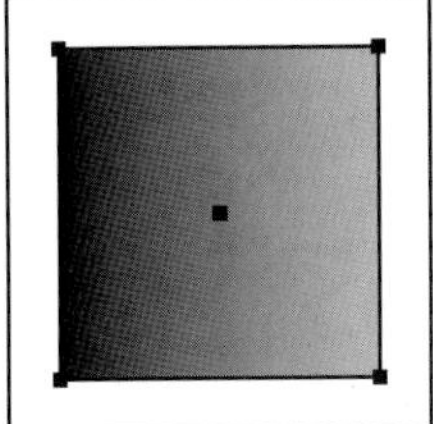
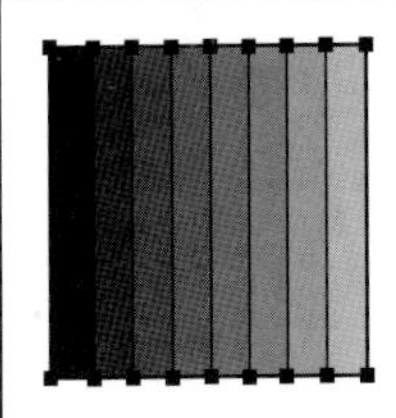

Original gradient and Expand command applied

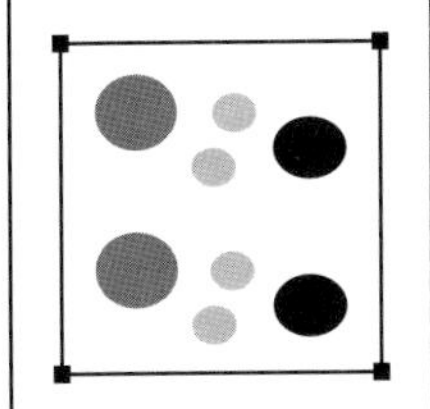
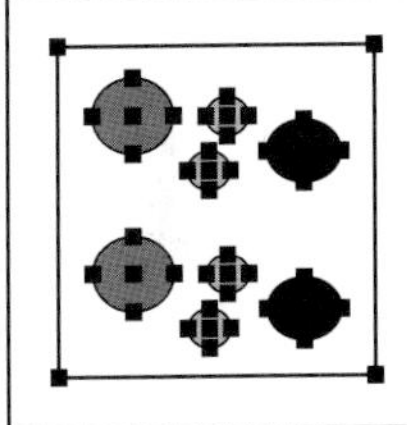

Original pattern and Expand command applied

To convert fills or strokes into objects:

1 Select a filled or stroked object, or an object that has been both filled and stroked.

2 Choose Object > Expand.

3 Do one of the following:

• To expand only the fill, select the Fill check box.

• To expand only the Stroke, select the Stroke check box.

• To expand both the fill and the stroke, select both check boxes.

4 Click OK.

To convert gradients, blends, and patterns into objects:

1 Select objects that have been blends, or objects that have been filled or stroked with a gradient or pattern.

2 Choose Object > Expand.

3 Do one of the following:

• If you are expanding a complex object, select the Object check box and click OK.

• If you are expanding a gradient, select the Specify Objects option, enter the number of steps to which you want to convert the gradient, and click OK.

Hold down Alt (Windows) or Option (Mac OS) as you choose Object > Expand to expand a gradient using the last number of steps entered in the Expand dialog box.

Using the Pen and Ink filters

The Pen and Ink > Hatch Effects filter creates textured gradations, such as cross-hatching, and irregular random textures, such as wood grains, that you can apply to artwork to simulate the look of an ink pen drawing. A similar tool, called the Photo Crosshatch filter, can convert a bitmap photographic image into a series of hatched layers, so that it appears to be sketched by an ink pen. (See "Using the Photo Crosshatch filter" on page 245.)

The Hatch Effects filter converts a selected object into a mask and then draws lines or shapes behind it. The shapes created by the Hatch Effects filter are objects and can require significant program memory. Thus, consider applying Pen and Ink effects as the last step in creating your artwork: Make the entire drawing and paint it as desired. Then apply the hatch effects.

The *hatch* (or *hatch style*) is the design element of the Hatch Effects filter. The particular options associated with a hatch are called *hatch settings*. You can select from hatch settings supplied with the Adobe Illustrator program by using the Hatch Effects dialog box. You can also create your own hatched designs by drawing or selecting an object, naming it as a hatch in the New Hatch dialog box, and then applying it to artwork by using the Hatch Effects dialog box. Try experimenting with applying different hatches to your artwork before creating your own.

Applying a hatch effect

To apply a hatch effect to a selected object, you choose a hatch setting and its associated hatch style, modify the settings if desired, and apply them through the Hatch Effects dialog box. The Hatch Effects dialog box lets you adjust the hatch.

To fill an object with an existing ink pen hatch:

1 Select the object you want to fill with a hatch.

2 Choose Filter > Pen and Ink > Hatch Effects.

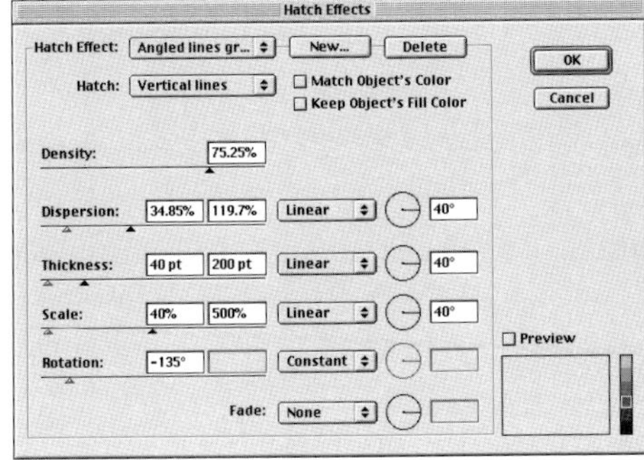

3 Choose a hatch from the Hatch pop-up menu and an effect from the Hatch Effect pop-up menu.

4 To improve the program's performance by turning off the hatch preview, deselect the Preview option at the lower right of the dialog box.

5 To adjust the number of hatch elements applied to the selection, drag the Density slider or enter values in the text box. To intensify the effect, click a gradation within the density adjustment bar.

Hatch concentration and direction

6 To specify hatch uniformity or design characteristics, adjust sliders or enter values for Dispersion, Thickness, Scale, or Rotation.

Enter an angle along which to apply the effect by entering a value from -360 to 360 in the text boxes. Then drag the slider or enter values in the text boxes to specify a range, as follows:

- Dispersion, which controls the spacing of hatch elements, ranges from 0% to 300%.
- Thickness, or stroke weight, of the hatch elements ranges from 10 pts to 1000 pts. (This option is dimmed if the selection is unstroked.)
- Scale, which sets the size of the hatch elements, ranges from 10% to 1000%.
- Rotation, which sets the angle at which the hatch elements are applied, ranges from –180 degrees to 180 degrees.

7 Use the dial or text boxes to enter a value between -360 and 360 for effect variables as follows:

- Linear increases the effect progressively.
- Reflect varies the effect from the center of the object outward.
- Constant creates the same effect evenly across the shape.
- Symmetric varies the effect proportionately and evenly, for example, if applying hatches to round or cylindrical shapes.
- Random applies the effect irregularly.
- Fade specifies whether the hatch fades across the object. Choose the fade properties from the Fade pop-up menu: None for no fade, To White to fade the hatch to white, To Black to fade the hatch to black, or Use Gradient if the object is filled with a gradient and you want that gradient to define the fade's direction and colors.

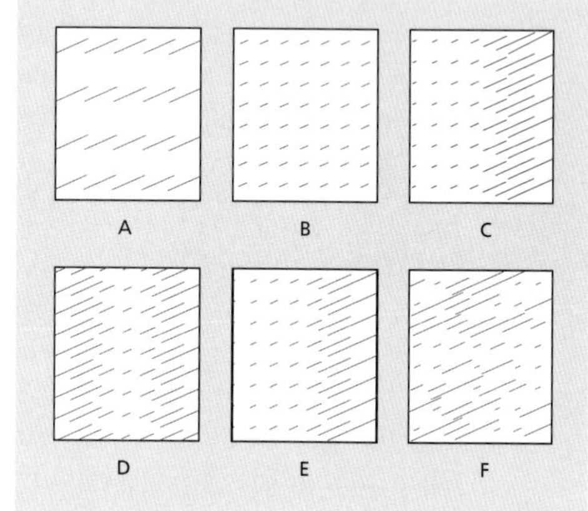

***A.** Original hatch **B.** Constant **C.** Linear **D.** Reflect*
***E.** Symmetric **F.** Random*

8 Select from the following color options for the hatch:

- Match Object's Color changes the hatch fill to the selection's fill.
- Keep Object's Fill Color applies the hatch in its original color on top of the object's fill color.

9 When you finish adjusting the hatch options, click OK.

Creating and saving hatches

You can create and save your own hatches or modify existing hatches and save them for reuse. To save hatches, you use either the New Hatch or the Hatch Effects dialog box.

To create a hatch:

1 Draw the objects you want to convert to a hatch design for the ink pen effect.

2 Select the artwork.

3 Choose Filter > Pen and Ink > New Hatch.

4 Click New. Enter a name for the new hatch and click OK.

5 To improve the program's performance, deselect Preview to turn off the preview of the hatch and click OK.

To modify an existing hatch:

1 Make sure that nothing is selected in the artwork.

2 Choose Filter > Pen and Ink > New Hatch.

3 Choose a hatch from the Hatch pop-up menu.

4 Click Paste and then click OK.

5 Edit the hatch as desired, and then select it.

6 Choose Filter > Pen and Ink > New Hatch.

7 Click New. Name the new hatch and click OK.

To save hatch settings:

1 Choose Filter > Pen and Ink > Hatch Effects.

2 Specify the hatch settings and any style options you want to save.

3 To save the settings in the file, click New. Enter a new name for the settings, and click OK.

To delete hatch settings:

1 Choose Filter > Pen and Ink > Hatch Effects.

2 Select the hatch settings and any style options you want to delete.

3 Click Delete, and then click OK.

To delete an existing hatch:

1 Choose Filter > Pen and Ink > New Hatch.

2 Choose a hatch from the Hatch pop-up menu.

3 Click Delete, and then click OK.

Using Pen and Ink hatch libraries

When using the Hatch Effects filter you may want to import hatches that you previously created in Illustrator, or save the current set of hatches you made into a hatch library. Hatch libraries are stored in the Illustrator 8.0 \ Plug-Ins \ Illustrator Filters \ Ink Pen folder.

Once you have opened a hatch library, all the hatches in the library are loaded into the Hatch Effects dialog and can be viewed in the Hatch Effect pop-up menu at the upper left corner of the dialog.

To load a pen and ink hatch library into Illustrator:

1 Choose Filter > Pen and Ink > Library Open.

2 In the dialog box, locate the hatch library you want to open and click OK. The hatch libraries are located in the Illustrator 8.0 \ Plug-Ins \ Illustrator Filters \ Ink Pen folder.

Once the new library has been loaded, use the Pen and Ink filter as described in "Applying a hatch effect" on page 211.

To save new hatches in an ink pen library:

1 Create new hatches as described in "Creating and saving hatches" on page 213.

2 Choose Filter > Pen and Ink > Library Save As.

3 In the dialog box, name the new file, save it in the Illustrator 8.0 \ Plug-Ins \ Illustrator Filters \ Ink Pen folder, and click OK.

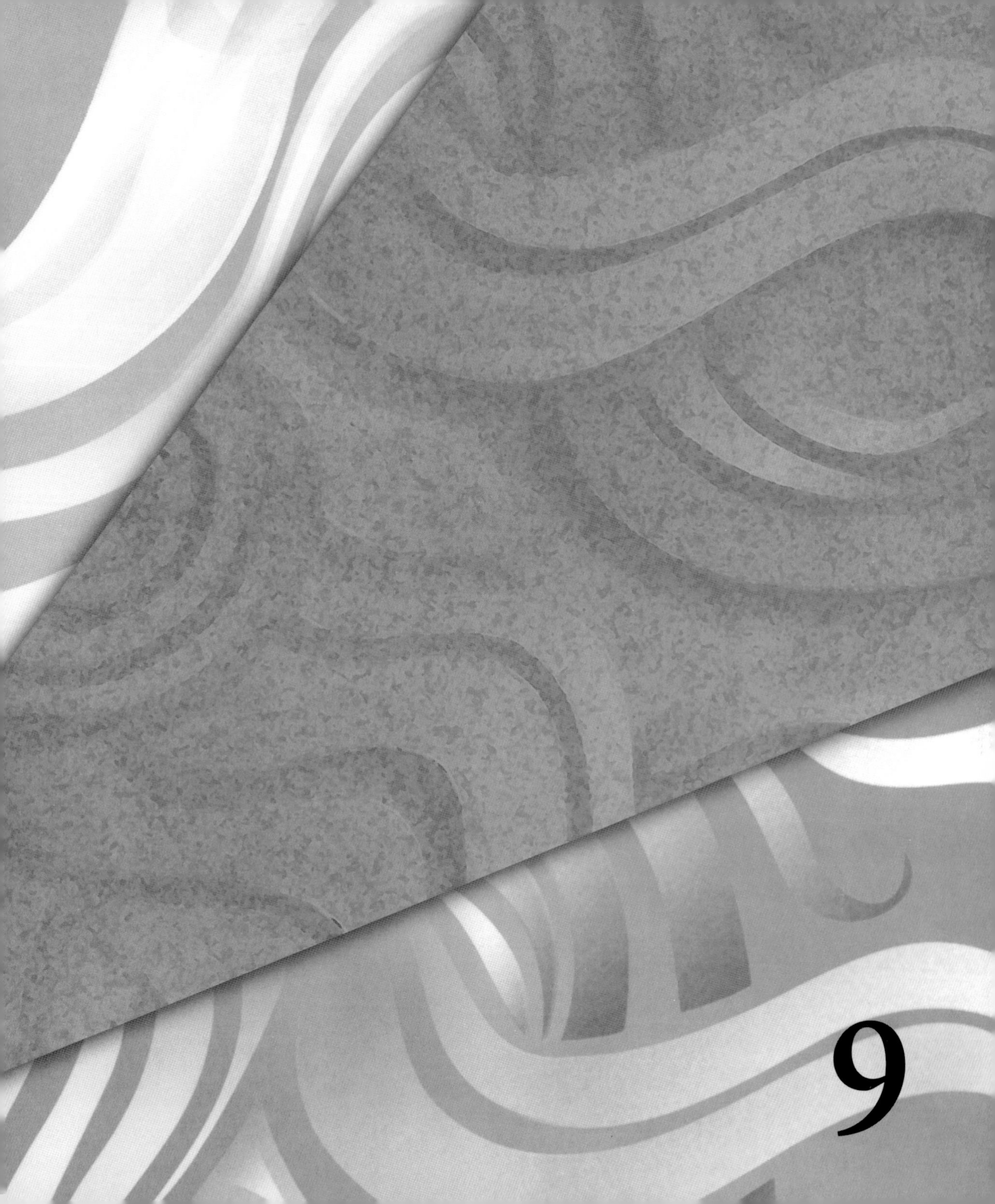

9

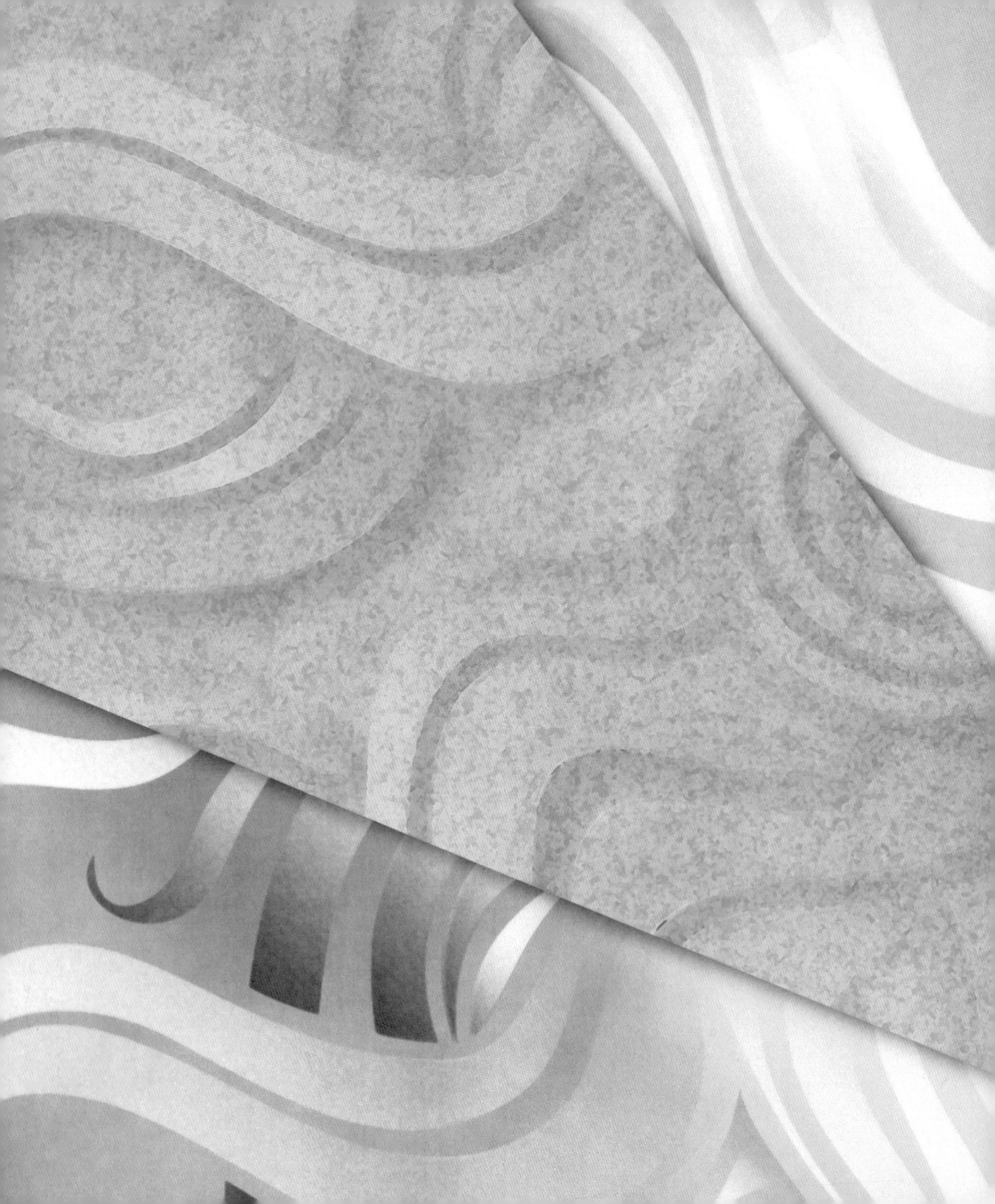

Chapter 9: Using Layers

Layers are useful for organizing your work into distinct levels, which you can edit and view as individual units.

About layers

Every Adobe Illustrator file contains at least one layer. Creating multiple layers in your artwork lets you easily control how artwork is printed, organized, displayed, and edited.

Once you create your layers, you can work with them in various ways, such as duplicating, reordering, merging, flattening them, and adding objects to them. You can even create template layers, which you can use to trace artwork. In addition, you can import layers from Photoshop.

The following rules affect how objects appear in layers:

- Within each layer, objects are stacked according to their stacking order. (See "Stacking objects" on page 123.)
- Grouped objects are on the same layer; if you group objects from different layers, all objects are placed on the frontmost layer of the group, directly behind the frontmost object in the group.
- When you mask objects on different layers, objects on intermediate layers become part of the masked artwork. (See "Creating masks" on page 151.)

USING LAYERS By using the Layers palette, you can create multiple levels of artwork that reside on separate, overlapping layers in the same file. Layers act like individual, clear sheets containing one or more objects. Where there are no overlapping filled objects, you can see through any layer to the layer below.

You can create and modify objects on any layer without affecting the artwork on any other layer. You can also display, print, lock, and reorder layers as distinct units.

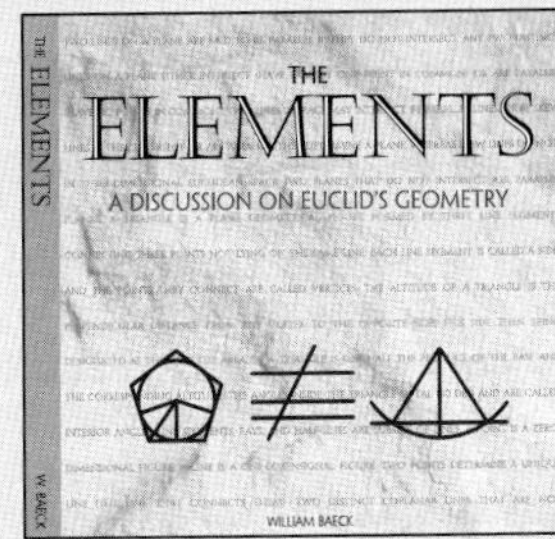

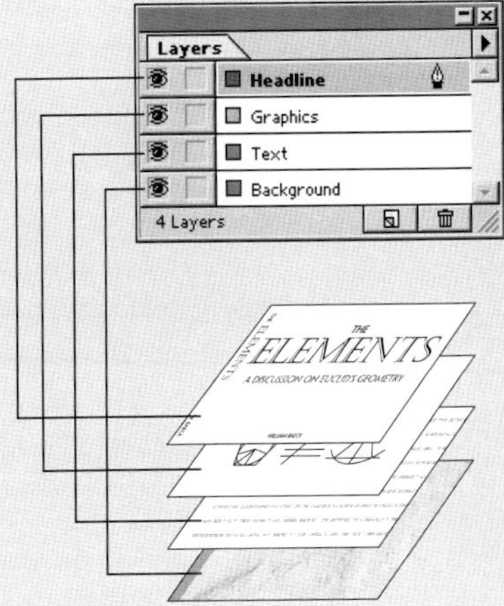

Example of Composite art and how layers break out individually.

Using the Layers palette

You can use the Layers palette to create and delete layers, hide and lock them, and merge and flatten them, and to choose options for determining how layers are displayed and printed. The active layer (the layer that displays the pen icon (✎) in the Layers palette) is the layer onto which all new artwork is placed.

To display the Layers palette:

Choose Window > Show Layers.

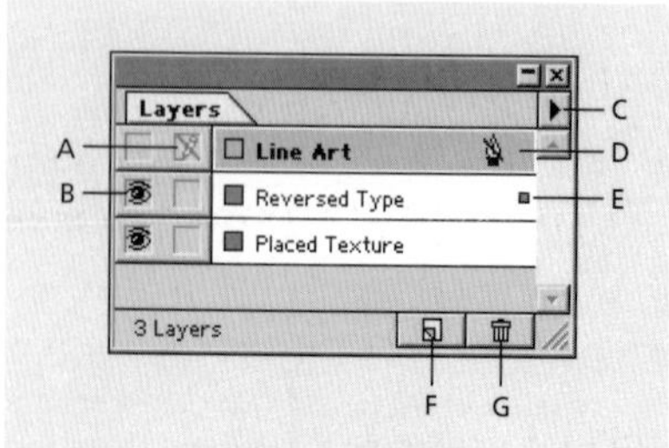

A. Lock/Unlock B. Show/Hide C. Displays Layers palette menu D. Active layer E. Current selection in artwork F. New layer/Duplicate layer G. Delete layer

The Layers palette lists the layers in a file, starting with the frontmost layer. The current layer is indicated by a pen icon to the right of the layer name. If any object on a layer is selected in the artwork, a colored dot appears at the right edge of the layer row.

Any object created in a file using a drawing or object tool is placed onto the active layer. (Objects created by other means, such as a filter, are placed with the objects they are based on.)

To select a layer on which to work:

Click the name of the layer you want on the Layers palette.

If you have many layers that aren't visible in the palette, you can go directly to a specific layer. To do so, Ctrl+Alt-click (Windows) or Option+Command-click (Mac OS) anywhere in the layer list. When you see a heavy black border around the list, type the name or number of the layer you want to select. You can omit prefixes. For example, you can type **30** to go to "Layer 30."

To select all objects on one or more layers:

Alt-click (Windows) or Option-click (Mac OS) a layer name in the Layers palette, or Alt-drag (Windows) or Option-drag (Mac OS) through the layer names to select all objects on the selected layers.

To select multiple layers:

Do one of the following:

- Shift-click the layer name to select contiguous layers.
- Ctrl-click (Windows) or Command-click (Mac OS) the layer name to select or deselect noncontiguous layers.

To view smaller layers:

Choose Small Palette Rows from the Layers palette menu. A check mark appears next to the command. To see the palette in its original view, choose the command again.

Viewing layers

By selecting options in the Layers palette and Layer Options dialog box, you can control the ways in which selected layers are displayed in the artwork.

Hiding or displaying layers

Hidden layers cannot be viewed or edited.

To hide or display a layer:

Click the eye icon to the left of the layer name. This turns off the Show option in the Layer Options dialog box. Click again to turn the option back on and redisplay the layer.

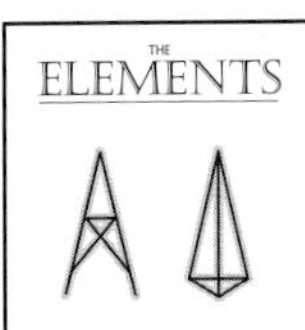

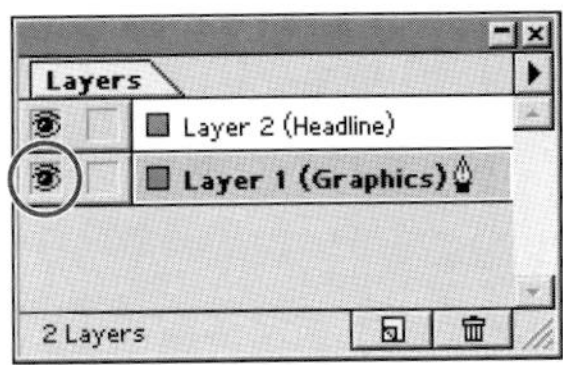

Solid eye icon: Layer art is visible.

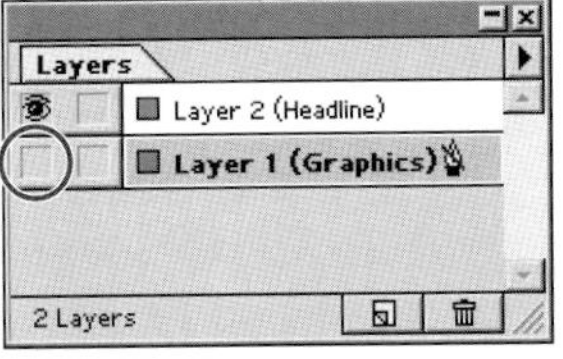

No eye icon: Layer art is hidden.

To hide all inactive layers:

1 Do one of the following:

• If no other layer is currently hidden, select the layer you want to view and choose Hide Others from the Layers palette menu.

• Alt-click (Windows) or Option-click (Mac OS) the eye icon.

To display all layers:

Choose Show All Layers from the Layers palette menu.

Choosing a layer color

Selecting a different color for each layer makes it easy to distinguish layers in your artwork as you work. By default, the first layer is highlighted in light blue, the second layer in red, the third layer in green, and each subsequent layer in a different color. By changing the color, you can more easily contrast the layer color with the artwork color on the layer. For example, if your artwork is primarily a blue color, you can set the layer color to red so that layer selection marks can be more easily seen as you work on the layer.

To specify a selection color for a layer:

1 In the Layers palette, choose the layer for which you want to specify a selection color.

2 Choose Options for <*layer name*> from the Layers palette menu, or double-click a layer name.

3 Select a color from the Color pop-up menu to indicate selections on that layer, and click OK. Or, double-click the color sample to open the Color dialog box.

Displaying layers in Artwork view

Displaying a layer in Artwork view is similar to choosing the Artwork command from the View menu—all artwork on the layer is displayed as outlines. (See Chapter 2, "Looking at the Work Area.")

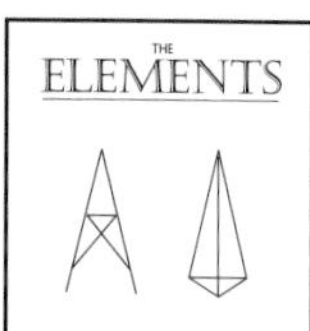

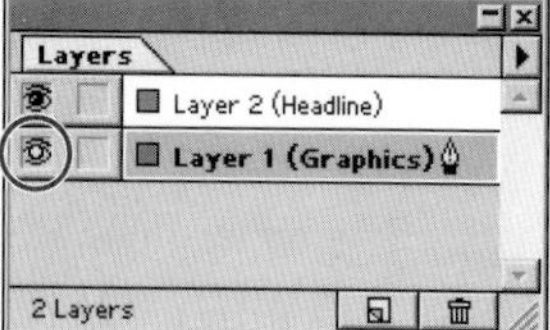

Hollow eye icon: Layer 1 art is in Artwork view.

To display a layer in Artwork view:

Do one of the following:

• Ctrl-click (Windows) or Command-click (Mac OS) the eye icon to the left of the layer name.

• Deselect the Preview option in the Layer Options dialog box.

To display all inactive layers in Artwork view:

1 Do one of the following:

• Select the layer or layers you want to display in Preview view. Then choose Artwork Others from the Layers palette menu.

• Alt+Ctrl-click (Windows) or Option+Command-click (Mac OS) the eye icon.

Dimming and showing raster images on layers

The Dim Images To option in the Layer Options dialog box makes raster images on a given layer appear dimmed on-screen. This option dims raster images to make it easier to edit objects on top of the image. You can use this option as a design guide with raster images, for laying out artwork on top of them, or using them as a template you can trace over.

You can show all raster images on all layers, including template layers. Raster images on template layers appear the same in both Artwork and Preview views. Raster images on regular layers appear as frames in Artwork view.

To dim a raster image on the screen:

1 In the Layers palette, choose the layer that contains the raster image, or images, you want to dim.

2 Choose Options for <*layer name*> from the Layers palette menu, or double-click the layer's name.

3 Select Dim Images To and enter a value for the percentage (0% to 100%) by which you want images dimmed, and click OK.

Images are dimmed on the screen, but not when they are printed or exported to another format.

To show raster images on template layers:

1 Choose File > Document Setup.

2 Select the Show Images In Artwork option, and click OK.

Creating layered artwork

Every new Adobe Illustrator file contains one layer named by default "Layer 1." You can create any number of layers in your file. The number of layers a file can have is limited only by your computer's memory.

Once a layer is created, you can then set options, such as whether the layer displays or prints. By default, layers are named according to the order in which they were created.

After you create layers, you can duplicate, merge, flatten, and hide them, make them nonprintable, and move objects between them.

To create a layer and set layer options:

1 Choose Window > Show Layers.

2 Do one of the following:

• Click the New Layer button on the bottom of the Layers palette to create a layer, with the default options, above the active layer.

• Ctrl-click (Windows) or Command-click (Mac OS) the New Layer button to create a layer on top of the layer list.

• Alt+Ctrl-click (Windows) or Command+Option-click (Mac OS) the New Layer button to create a layer below the selected layer.

• Choose New Layer from the Layers palette menu. The Layer Options dialog box appears.

• Alt-click (Windows) or Option-click (Mac OS) the New Layer button. The Layer Options dialog box appears.

3 If the Layer Options dialog box is not displayed, choose Options for <*layer name*> from the Layers palette menu.

4 If you want to rename the default, type a name in the Name text box.

5 Select a color from the Color pop-up menu to indicate selected objects in that layer. (See "Choosing a layer color" on page 219.)

6 Select other options for the layer:

• Template makes the layer a template layer. (See "Creating template layers" on page 227.) When the option is selected, the template layer icon replaces the eyeball icon, and the layer becomes locked.

• Show displays or hides the layer. (See "Hiding or displaying layers" on page 219.)

• Preview displays the layer in Preview or Artwork view. When the option is unselected, the eyeball changes to a hollow eyeball to indicate that layer is in Artwork view.

• Lock prevents a layer from being edited. When the option is selected, the lock icon appears to the left of the layer name. (See "Locking layers" on page 226.)

• Print makes the layer printable or nonprintable. When the option is unselected (and the layer is nonprintable), the layer name is displayed in italics. (See "Making selected layers nonprintable" on page 224.)

• Dim Images To dims placed or rasterized images according to the value (0% to 100%) you enter in the text box. (See "Dimming and showing raster images on layers" on page 220.)

7 Click OK.

Moving objects between layers

You can move objects from one layer to another (including to hidden layers) by cutting objects from one layer and pasting them into another or by using the Layers palette. You can also reorder the layers in your artwork.

The Paste commands can be used to move objects between layers. With the Paste commands, objects cut or copied from different layers are pasted together onto the selected layer by default.

With the Paste Remembers Layers option on, objects are always pasted onto the layer from which they originated. If no layer exists with the original name, a layer is created and the objects are pasted onto the new layer.

To ensure that objects are pasted onto the layer from which they originated:

1 Choose File > Preferences > General.

2 Select Paste Remembers Layers, and click OK.

To move an object to a different layer using the Paste commands:

1 Make sure that Paste Remember Layers in the General Preferences dialog box is unselected, or deselect Paste Remembers Layers in the Layers palette menu.

2 Select the object that you want to move, and choose Edit > Cut.

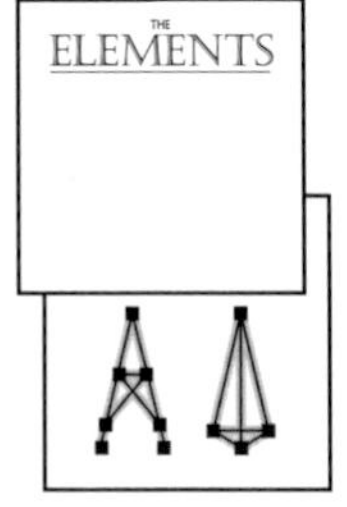

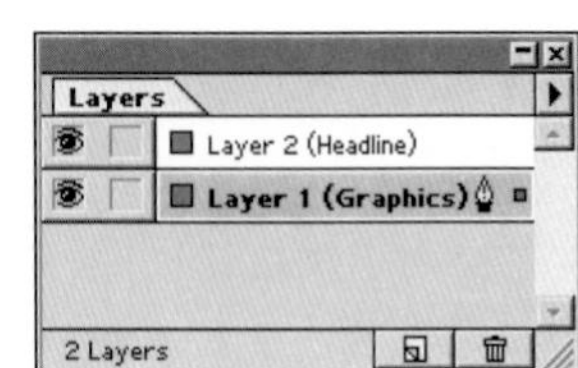

Layer 1 objects selected

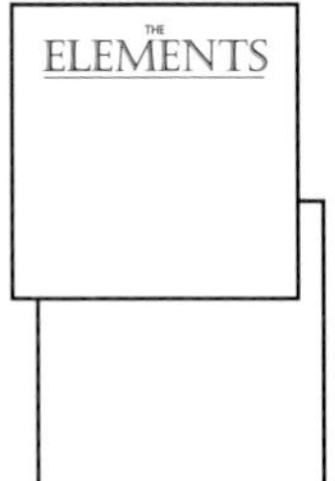

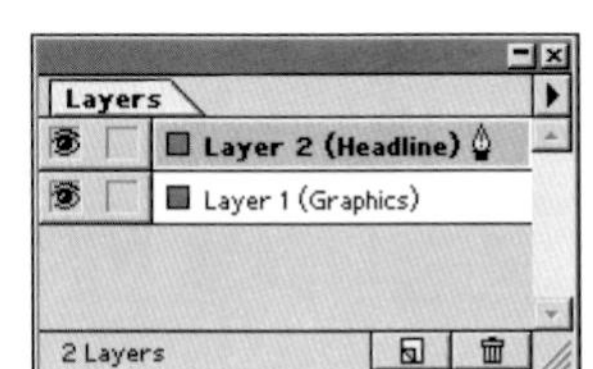

Objects cut; Layer 2 selected

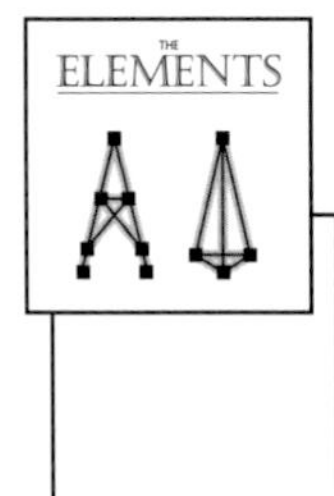

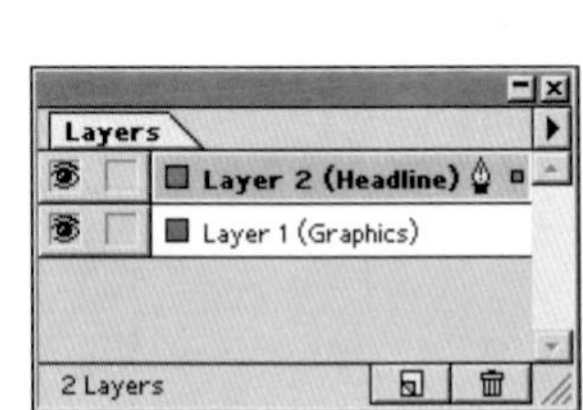

Objects pasted in front on Layer 2

3 Select any object on the layer to which you want to move the cut object, or select the layer name in the Layers palette.

4 Choose one of the following commands:

- Edit > Paste pastes the object into the center of the artwork as the frontmost object on the selected layer.
- Edit > Paste in Front pastes the object into its original position in the artwork, in front of the topmost selected object. If the selected object is in a group, the pasted selection becomes part of the group.
- Edit > Paste in Back pastes the object into its original position in the artwork, behind the backmost selected object. If the selected object is in a group, the pasted selection becomes part of the group. If Paste Remember Layers is selected, the object is pasted onto the layer from which it originated.

Once the object is pasted, you can move it and use the commands in the Object menu to change the stacking order of the object on its new layer.

To move an object to a different layer using the Layers palette:

1 Select the object you want to move. A colored dot appears to the right of that layer in the Layers palette, to indicate the current selection.

2 Drag the colored dot to the layer to which you want to move the object. The layer can be visible or hidden. To copy the selected objects to the new layer, Alt-drag (Windows) or Option-drag (Mac OS) the colored dot. To move the object to a locked layer, hold down Ctrl (Windows) or Command (Mac OS) after starting to drag.

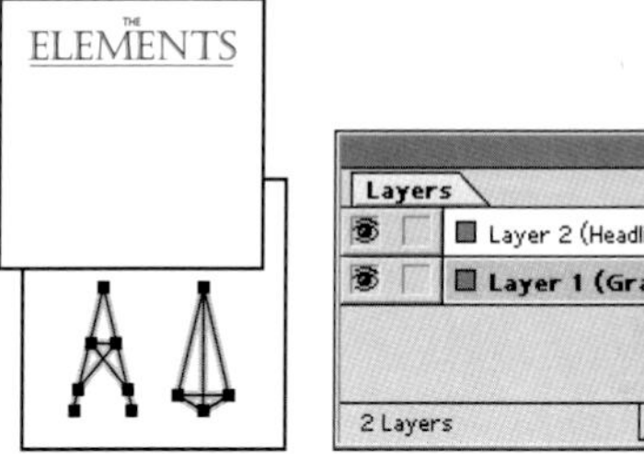

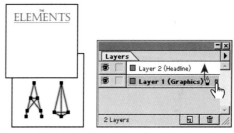

Layer 1 objects selected, and then colored dot dragged in palette

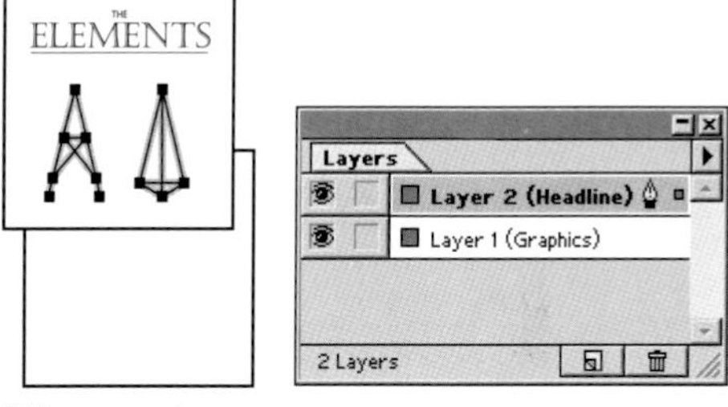

Objects moved

Duplicating and merging layers

Duplicating a layer places a new layer above the currently selected layer and duplicates all the layer options of the original. The duplicate layer contains copies of all the artwork on the original layer.

When layers are merged, the contents of all selected layers are merged into the active layer. (If the active layer is locked or hidden, the layers are merged into the top selected layer that isn't locked or hidden.) The objects on the merged layers retain their original stacking order.

To duplicate a layer:

1 In the Layers palette, select any layers you want to duplicate.

2 Do one of the following:

• Choose Duplicate Layer from the Layers palette menu.

• Drag the selected layers to the New Layer button at the bottom of the palette.

To merge layers:

1 Select the layers that you want to merge into a single layer.

2 Choose Merge Layers from the Layers palette menu.

Making selected layers nonprintable

Illustrator provides several ways to make layers nonprintable. You can deselect the eye icon to hide a layer, or you can deselect the Print option in the Layer Options dialog box for the layer.

Hiding a layer is useful for printing only the segments of your artwork that you want to proof. For example, you could put all type in a document on a single layer and then print only that layer for proofing. Hidden layers do not print or export.

For layers that you don't normally print, such as annotations, you can make layers nonprintable using the Print option in the Layer Options dialog box. Layers with the Print option unselected do not print even when they are visible, but they do export.

For layers that you do not want to print or export, you can create a template layer by selecting the Template option in the Layer Options dialog box. Template Layers do not print or export, even when visible.

To make a layer nonprintable from any application by hiding it:

In the Layers palette, select the layer and click the eye icon (to the left of the layer name) to hide the layer.

To make layers nonprintable from Illustrator using the Layer Options dialog box:

1 Do one of the following:

• In the Layers palette, select the layer that you don't want to print, and choose Options for *<layer name>* from the palette menu.

• Double-click the name of the layer in the palette.

2 Deselect the Print option, and click OK. The layer name is displayed in italics.

Deleting layers

You can remove a layer from a file by removing it from the Layers palette. Deleting a layer deletes from the file all objects on that layer.

Before deleting a layer, hide all the other layers so that you can check what's on the remaining layer and verify that there are no objects on the layer you don't want deleted.

To delete a layer:

1 Select the layer name in the Layers palette.

2 Do one of the following:

- Choose Delete <*layer name*> from the Layers palette menu.
- Click the Trash button at the bottom of the Layer palette.
- Drag the layer onto the Trash button at the bottom of the Layers palette.

Flattening artwork

In flattened artwork, all visible layers are merged into the selected layer, and hidden layers are deleted. If you flatten a hidden layer that contains artwork, you can choose to delete the artwork along with the hidden layer, or make all artwork visible and flatten it into one layer. In most cases, you won't want to flatten a file until you finish editing individual layers.

To flatten specific layers without deleting hidden layers, select the layers you want to flatten, and then choose Merge Layers from the Layers palette menu. *(See "Duplicating and merging layers" on page 223.)*

To flatten artwork:

1 Make sure all the layers you want to flatten are visible.

2 Select the layer that you want to flatten the artwork into. You cannot flatten artwork into layers that are hidden, locked, or templates. Doing this results in the topmost layer that is not hidden, locked, or a template being chosen instead.

***Note:** Regardless of the layer you select, the options for the layer and the stacking order of the artwork don't change.*

3 Choose Flatten Artwork from the Layers palette menu.

If artwork is present on a hidden layer, a dialog box appears to allow you to choose whether to make all artwork visible and flatten it into one layer, or delete the artwork along with the layer.

Changing the order of layers

By rearranging the layers on the Layers palette, you can change the order of layers in your file.

To change the order of layers:

In the Layers palette, drag the layer you want to move to its new location.

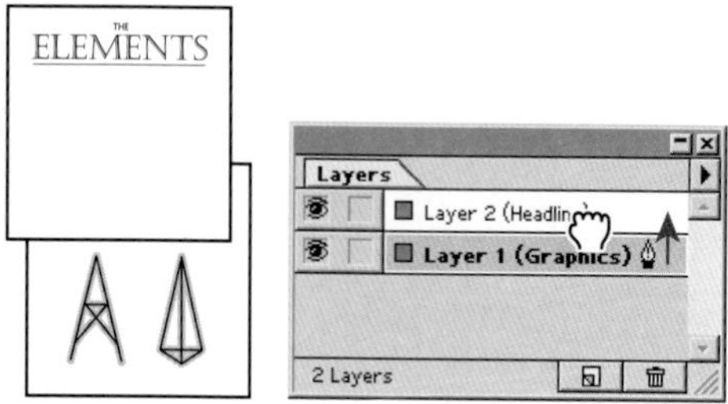

Layer 1 moved to top of Layers palette

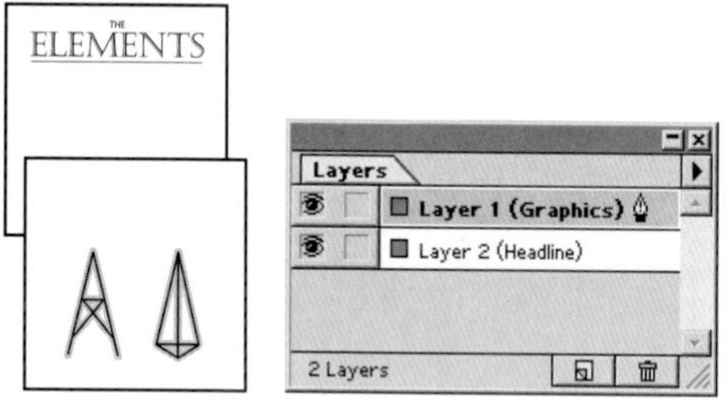

Result

Note: *Rearranging layers may release multilayer masks, if the movement causes the mask to change its paint order relative to other masks or to the layer containing the bottom object that it masks.*

Locking layers

Locking a layer has an effect similar to that of choosing the Lock command from the Object menu—artwork on locked layers cannot be selected or edited in any way. When a layer is locked, the cursor becomes a crossed-out pencil when it's over the page, and a crossed-out pencil appears in the edit column. When a layer is unlocked, the edit column appears empty.

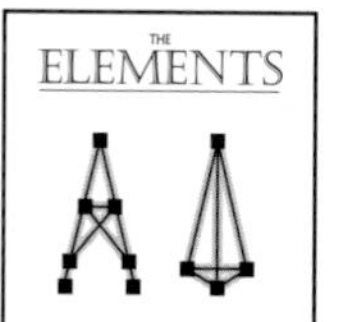

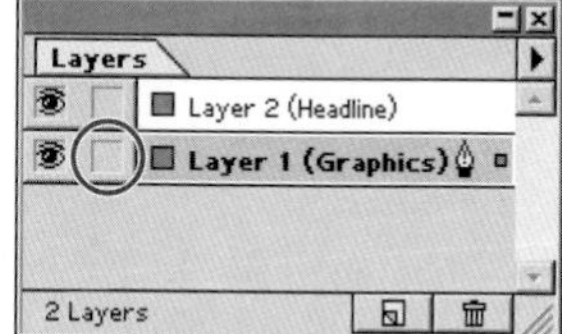

No icon in edit column indicates art can be edited.

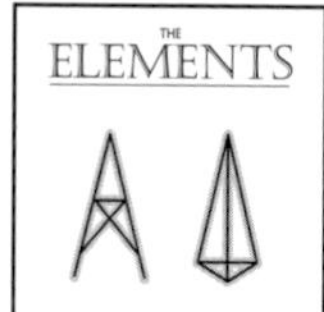

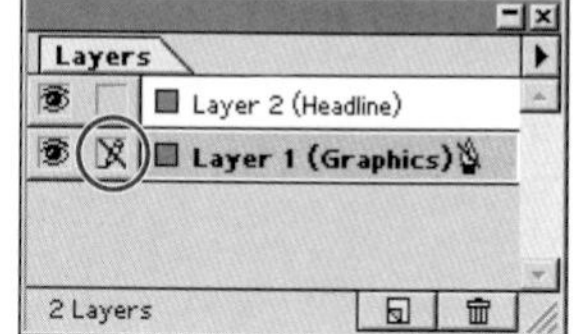

Crossed-out pencil icon indicates art cannot be edited.

To lock or unlock a layer:

Click the edit column button to the left of the layer name. This turns on the Lock option in the Layer Options dialog box. Click again to turn the option back off and unlock the layer.

To lock all inactive layers:

1 Do one of the following:

• Select the layer or layers you want to edit. Then choose Lock Others from the Layers palette menu.

2 Alt-click (Windows) or Option-click (Mac OS) the edit column to the left of the layer you want to change.

To unlock all layers:

Do one of the following:

• Choose Unlock All Layers from the Layers palette menu.

• Hold down Alt (Windows) or Option (Mac OS) and click twice on the crossed-out pencil icon or the empty edit column for any layer.

Creating template layers

Create a template layer whenever you want to base a new illustration on an existing piece of artwork and, for example, trace over it or build an illustration from it. (See "Tracing artwork" on page 100.)

A template layer is locked, dimmed, and previewed. Template layers remain visible in Artwork view. When a template layer is in Artwork view, all raster images display as dimmed and in normal color. Images in PICT format display in color. Template layers neither print nor export.

You can create a template from an existing layer or as a new layer.

To create a template layer:

1 Do one of the following:

• Choose New Layer from the Layers palette menu; or double-click the name of the layer to be a template; or Alt-click (Windows) or Option-click (Mac OS) the New Layer button (◲) in the palette. Click Template in the Layer Options dialog box, then click OK. The Preview, Lock, and Print options are then dimmed.

• Select a layer to be a template and choose Template from the palette menu.

• Choose File > Place, and click Template. A new template layer, with the default name "Template *filename*," appears below the currently active layer in the palette. Link the placed image if you want. (See "Placing files" on page 56.)

The eye icon is replaced by the template icon, and the layer becomes locked.

Importing and exporting Adobe Photoshop layers

When you import a Photoshop file that has multiple layers, the layers are flattened and appear as one layer in the Illustrator file. You can import Adobe Photoshop files using the Place command. (See "Placing files" on page 56.)

When you export layers, you can flatten them into one layer or preserve the individual layers so you can work with them in the Photoshop file. You can export Illustrator layers to Photoshop using the Export command. (See "About exporting artwork" on page 325.) Hidden layers and template layers aren't exported.

To import Adobe Photoshop layers as a flattened Illustrator layer:

1 If the Layers palette is not displayed, choose Window > Show Layers, and then create or select the layer where you want the image to appear.

2 Choose File > Place.

3 Locate and select the Photoshop file you want to import.

4 Click Open (Windows) or Place (Mac OS).

If the Photoshop file had multiple layers, the layers are flattened in Illustrator. The Photoshop image appears as a selected object on the layer you specified.

To export Adobe Illustrator layers to Adobe Photoshop:

1 If the Layers palette is not displayed, choose Window > Show Layers, and then create or show the layers you want to export.

2 Choose File > Export.

3 Select the folder where you want to save the file, and rename the file. Changing the filename ensures that your original artwork is preserved on disk.

4 Choose Photoshop 5 from the Save as Type (Windows) or Format (Mac OS) pop-up menu.

5 Click Save, and choose from the following options:

- To change the color format, select a format from the Color Model pop-up menu.
- To set the resolution for the bitmap image, choose a resolution or type a number in the Other text box. (See "About resolution in bitmap images" on page 45.)
- To smooth jagged edges around the bitmap image, select Anti-Alias. (Anti-aliasing may cause small type or thin lines to look blurry.)
- To preserve Illustrator layers when the file is exported to Photoshop, select Write Layers. (To flatten the layers so they appear as one layer in Photoshop, deselect Write Layers.)

6 Click OK.

The Illustrator layers appear as raster objects in the Photoshop file, and you can work with them in the Photoshop Layers dialog box.

4-1 Colorization Methods

Colorization method: None and Tints

Colorization method: Tints and Shades, and Hue Shift

7-1 HSB Model

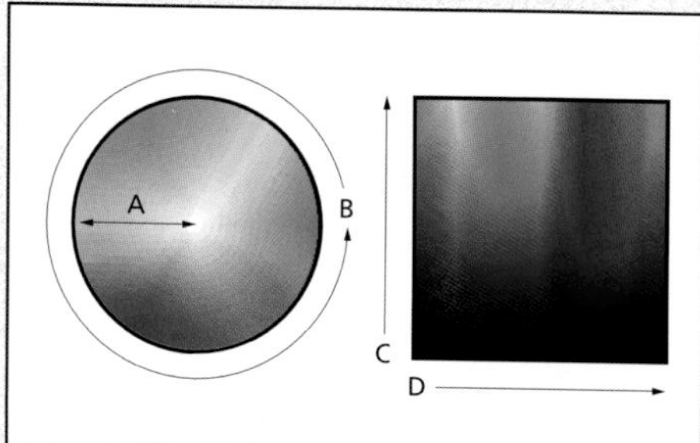

***A.** Saturation **B.** Hue **C.** Brightness **D.** All hues*

7-2 Additive Color

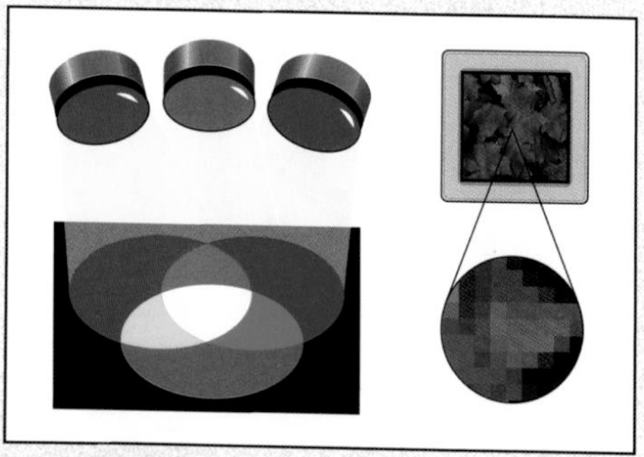

Additive colors (RGB)

7-3 Subtractive Color

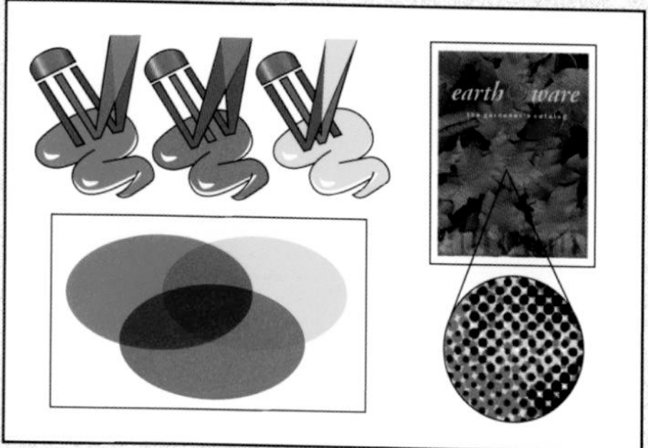

Subtractive colors (CMYK)

7-4 Color Gamuts

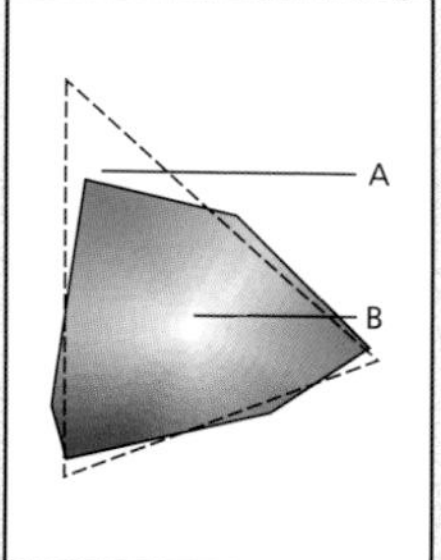

***A.** RGB color gamut **B.** CMYK color gamut*
The extent of the RGB color gamut exceeds that of the CMYK color gamut.

7-5 Global Colors and Tints

Color and Tint adjusted downward

7-6 Select Filters

Selected object and other objects in file

Select filters: Same Fill Color; Same Paint Style; Same Stroke Style; Same Stroke Weight

7-7 Pathfinder Commands

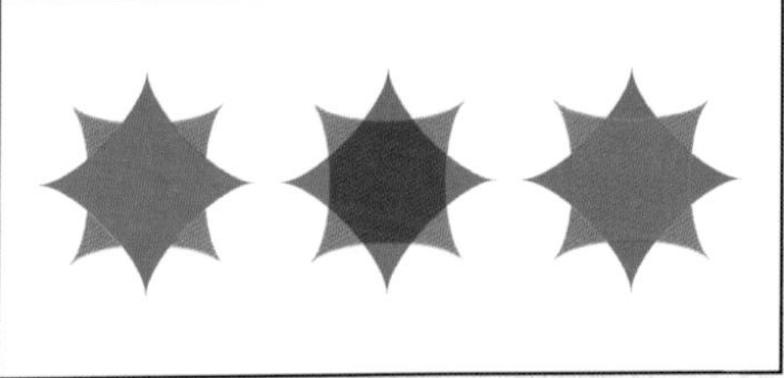

Original, and Hard Mix and Soft Mix Pathfinder commands

7-8 Adjust Colors Filter

Original, Adjusting colors: Decrease and Increase

7-9 Saturate and Desaturate Filter

Original, and saturating and desaturating objects

7-10 Invert Colors Filter

Original and Invert Colors filter

8-1 Adding Intermediate Colors to Gradients

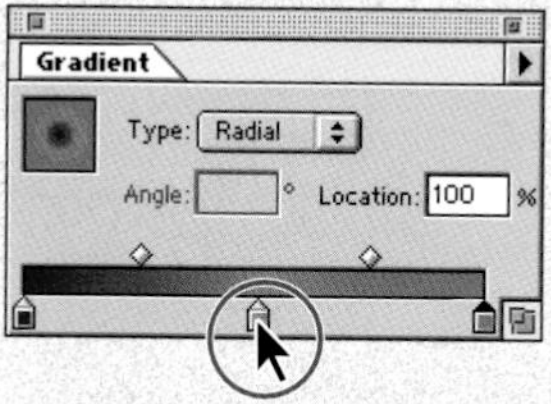

Click below the bar to define a new color square.

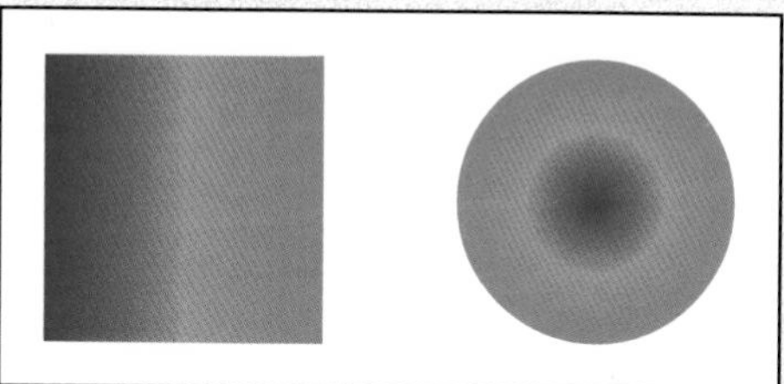

Linear and radial multicolor gradients

10-1 Colorizing 1-bit images

Original 1-bit image and colorized

14-1 Four-Color Separation Process

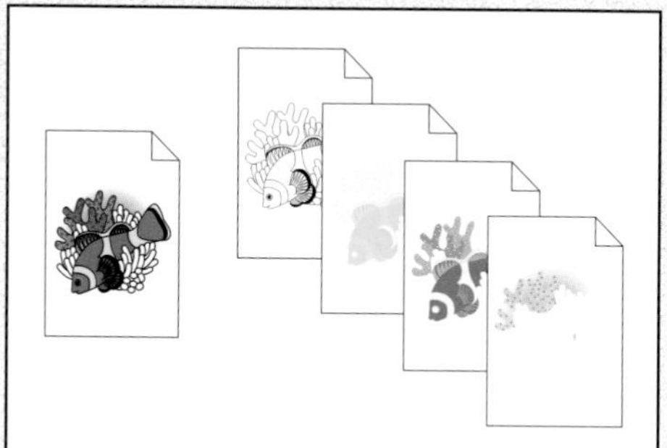

Image printed as composite on color laser printer and as four-color separation on imagesetter

15-1 Overprint Option

Colors knocked out by default and Overprint option selected

15-2 Printing Colors Transparently by Overprinting

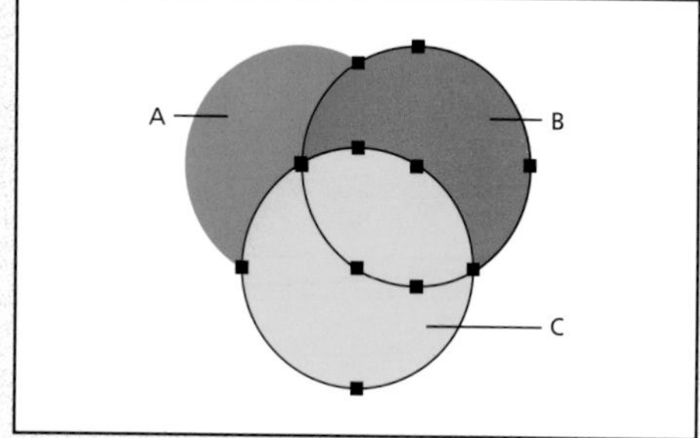

A. *Cyan (bottom)* **B.** *Magenta (middle)* **C.** *Yellow (top)*

15-3 On-screen and Printed Artwork

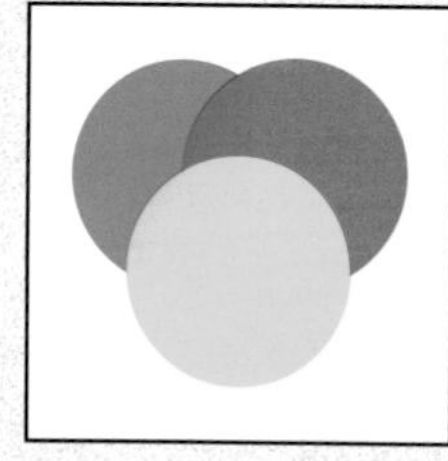

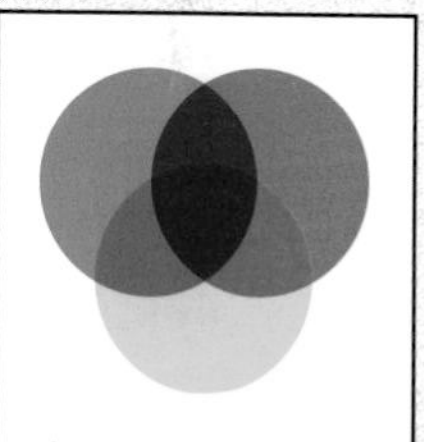

Appearance of artwork on the screen and in printed artwork

15-4 Creating a Trap

Artwork without trap and with trap

Appropriate and inappropriate artwork for Trap filter

15-5 Spread and Choke

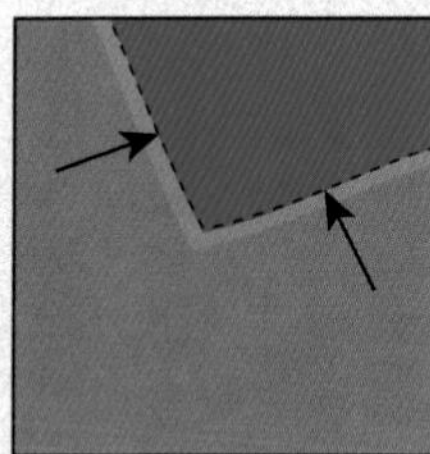

Spread: Object overlaps background. Choke: Background overlaps object.

15-6 Using the Trap Command

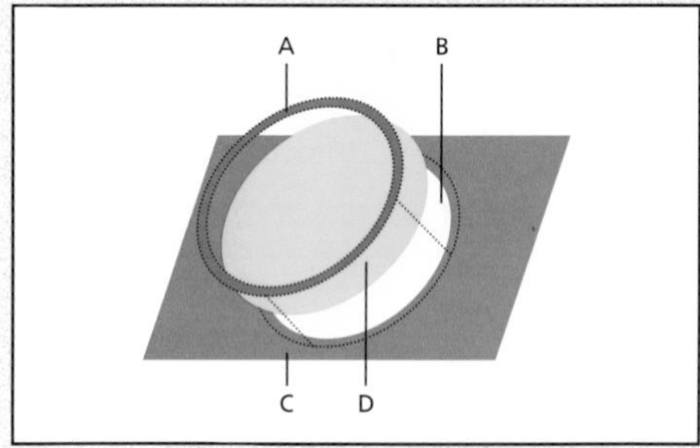

Function of Trap command: **A.** *Area of overprint* **B.** *Area of knockout* **C.** *Background color* **D.** *Foreground color*

15-7 Using the Trap Command to Create Spreads and Chokes

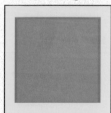

Light object and dark background: Trap command creates spread. Dark object and light background: Trap command creates choke.

15-8 Decreasing and Increasing Trap Thickness

Height/Width set to 50% and 200%

15-9 Tint Reduction Values

With tint reduction value of 100%, trap contains 100% of lighter color. With tint reduction value of 50%, trap contains 50% of lighter color.

15-10 Overprint Stroked with Fill Color

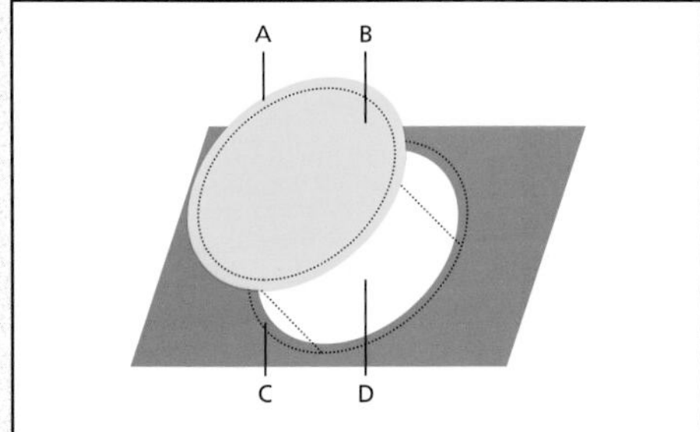

Object stroked with 1-point stroke of fill color:
***A.** Stroke creates spread trap* ***B.** Fill creates knockout*
***C.** Area of trap* ***D.** Area of knockout*

15-11 Overprint Stroked with Background Color

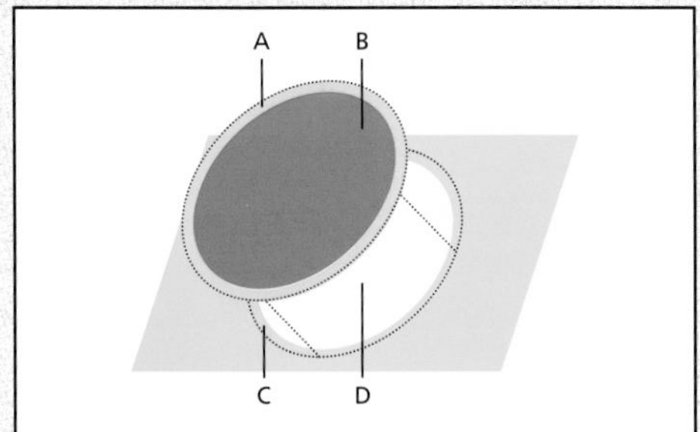

Object stroked with 1-point stroke of background color:
***A.** Stroke creates choke trap* ***B.** Fill creates knockout*
***C.** Area of trap* ***D.** Area of knockout*

15-12 Creating a Spread Trap Using Strokes

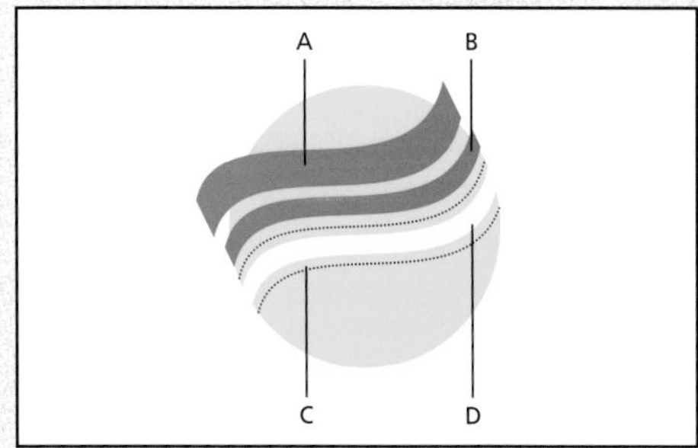

Copy of stroke used for spread trap: ***A.** Top stroke creates spread trap* ***B.** Bottom stroke creates knockout* ***C.** Area of knockout* ***D.** Area of trap*

15-13 Printer's Marks

***A.** Star target* ***B.** Label* ***C.** Registration marks*
***D.** Black overprint color bar* ***E.** Crop mark*
***F.** Gradient tint bar* ***G.** Progressive color bar*

SEPARATING COLORS Artwork can consist of spot colors, process colors, registration colors, or a combination. When you separate artwork containing spot colors, a separate plate is created for each spot color. The plate contains only objects of that specific color.

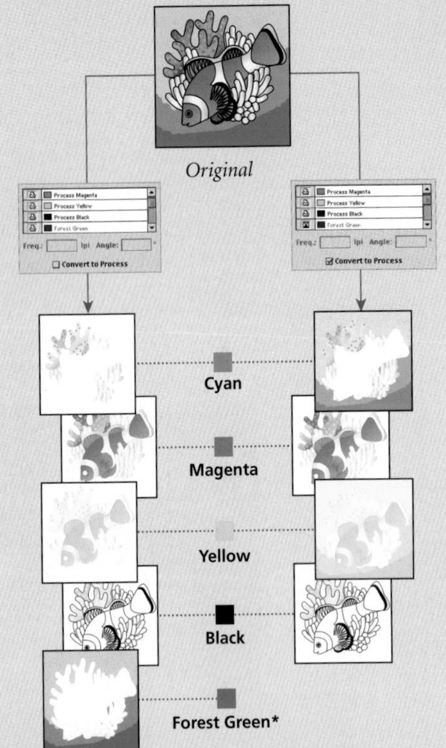

Process plus spot color: *Spot color is printed on separate plate. Options are set in Color Separation dialog box.*

Process colors: *Spot color is converted to process color equivalent and printed as part of process color plates. Options are set in Color Separation dialog box.*

** Forest Green is actually a process color mix printed as a fifth plate for this example.*

PATHFINDER GALLERY You can use Pathfinder commands to combine, isolate, and subdivide objects, building new objects formed by the intersection.

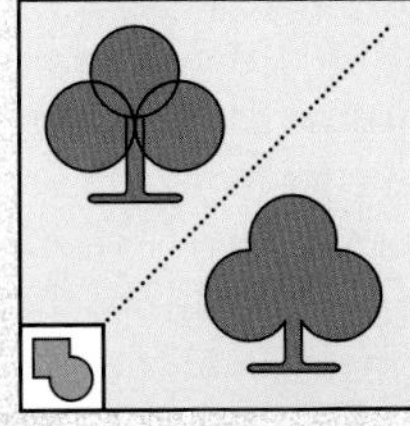

Unite *creates one shape from overlapping shapes.*

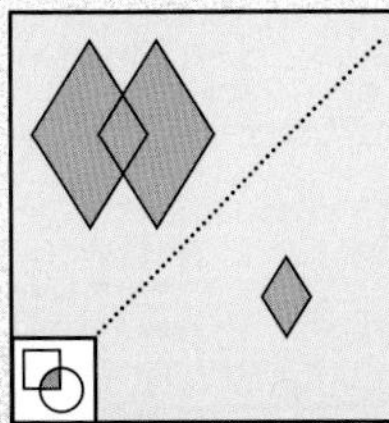

Intersect *creates a new object from shared space.*

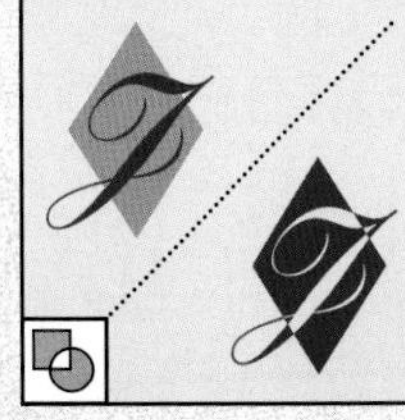

Exclude *removes an overlapping area.*

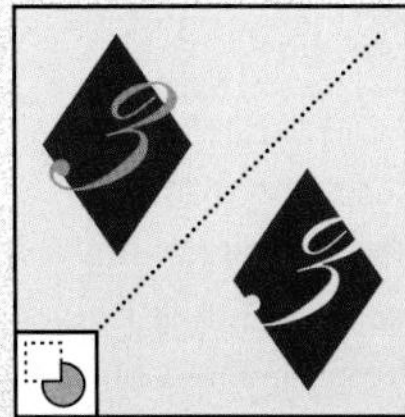

Minus Front *subtracts front object from back.*

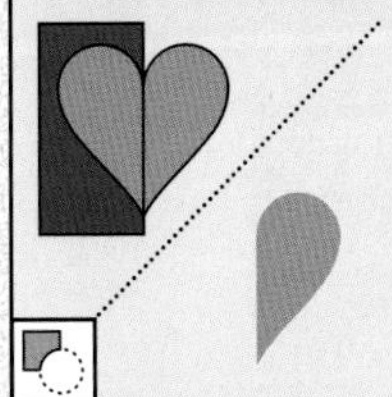

Minus Back *subtracts back object from front.*

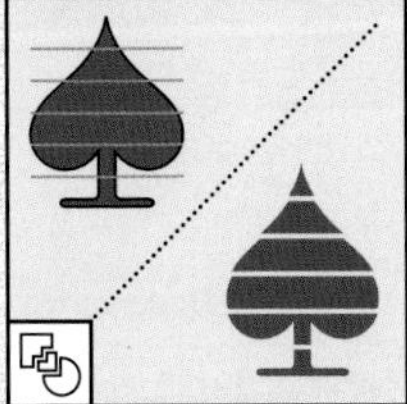

Divide *creates independent objects from component faces.*

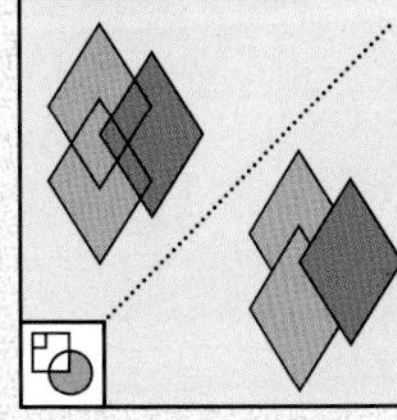

Trim *removes hidden part of filled paths*

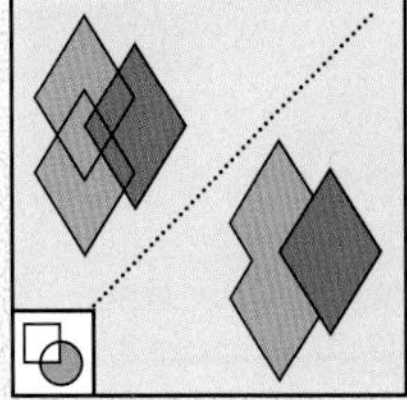

Merge *removes hidden part of filled paths and merges overlapping objects.*

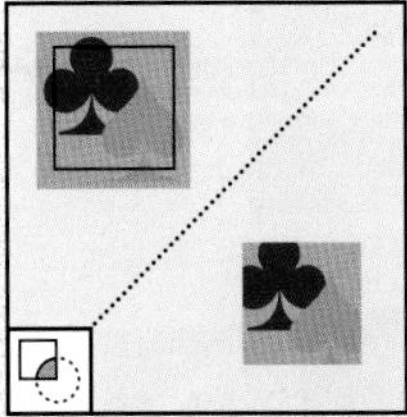

Crop *divides shapes and crops images.*

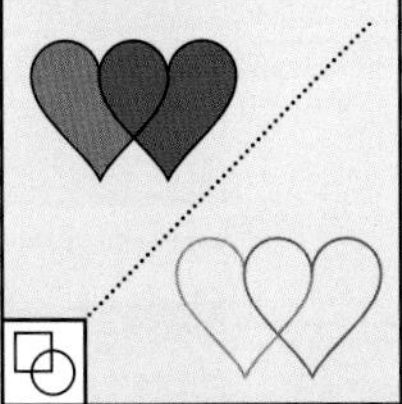

Outline *creates independent lines divided at each intersection.*

JPEG OR GIF? When preparing images for the Web, keep in mind that the smaller the image, the faster the download time. However, it's also a good idea to consider image quality. For artwork that is photo realistic or that contains gradients, use JPEG format. For artwork that contains flat colors, requires transparency, or requires a specific palette, export to GIF89a. If you're exporting artwork to GIF89a format for a target audience whose monitors display more than 256 colors, use the Adaptive palette to achieve the best representation of the colors in your artwork; use the System or Web palettes for a target audience whose monitors are limited to 256 colors. Also, remember that the effects of JPEG and GIF compression are more noticeable on the Web than in print. The samples below represent original artwork of 4.5 x 4.5 inches. All insets appear at 250% of actual size. The original artwork was created in Illustrator.

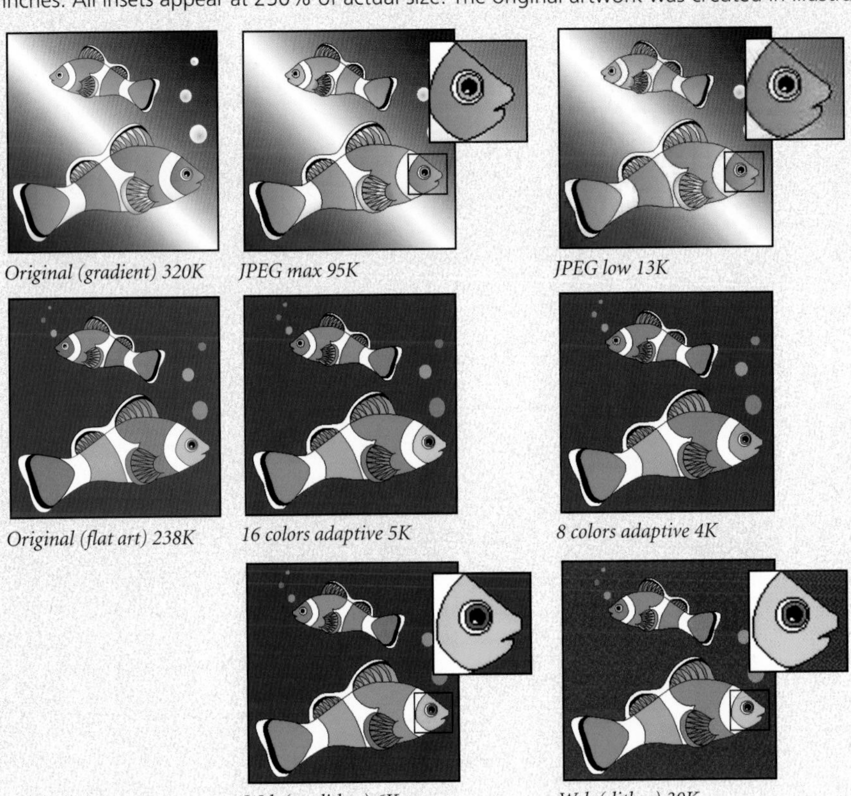

10

Chapter 10: Working with Bitmap Images

Much of the work you do with the Adobe Illustrator program may involve using bitmap images. Illustrator provides many features that allow you great flexibility in working with bitmap images.

Using bitmap images

You can do the following with bitmap images:

- Place an image into a file. (See "Placing files" on page 56.)
- Use the Links palette to see information about the image. (See "Managing linked and embedded images" on page 58.)
- Trace images using the auto trace tool. (See "Tracing artwork" on page 100.)
- Create a mask when you rasterize an object. Doing so masks away transparent portions of the original objects to keep them transparent. (See "Working with masks" on page 150.)
- Use the Rasterize dialog box to convert vector objects (including paths and text objects) into an image, and choose other options for the image. You can also change the color model for the image by reselecting Rasterize and changing the color. (See "Changing vector graphics into bitmap images" on page 239.)
- Colorize 1-bit images. (See "Colorizing 1-bit images" on page 240.)
- Use bitmap filters. (See "Choosing a filter effect" on page 243.)
- Use the Object Mosaic filter to convert the pixels to a collection of colored squares. Then you can use Illustrator tools. (See "Using the Object Mosaic filter" on page 244.)
- Apply the Photo Crosshatch filter, which gives a photographic image the appearance of a pen drawing. (See "Using the Photo Crosshatch filter" on page 245.)

Changing vector graphics into bitmap images

The Rasterize command converts vector objects into bitmap images.

Once objects are converted, you can apply plug-in filters, such as those designed for Adobe Photoshop, to the image as you would with any placed image. However, you cannot apply vector tools and commands (such as the type tools and the Pathfinder commands) to modify the bitmap image.

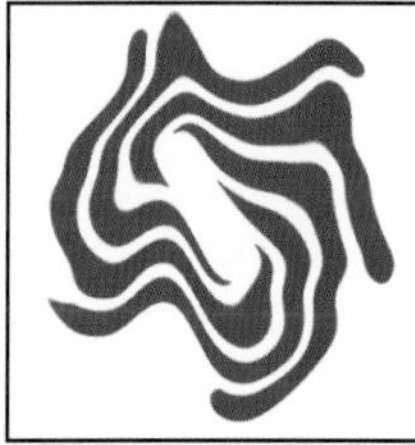

Original vector graphic and bitmap conversion with Wave filter applied

To create a bitmap version of artwork:

1 Select the object you want to convert.

2 Choose Object > Rasterize.

3 Choose an image format for the conversion from the Color Model pop-up menu. You can generate an RGB or CMYK color image, a grayscale image, or a 1-bit (black-and-white) bitmap image.

4 Choose a resolution from the Resolution area: Screen for monitor output, Medium for laser printer output, High for imagesetter output. Or type a value in the Other text box.

In the Rasterize dialog box, resolution is measured in ppi (pixels per inch). For more information about units of measure, see "About resolution in bitmap images" on page 45.

5 To smooth the jagged edges around the bitmap image when it's converted, select the Anti-Alias option.

6 To create a bitmap image mask that makes its background appear transparent, select the Create Mask option. (See "Working with masks" on page 150.) Then click OK.

Note: *The Anti-Alias option can take longer to rasterize. Also, text and thin lines may look blurry.*

Colorizing 1-bit images

You can add color to 1-bit images using the Color palette.

For a color illustration of colorizing 1-bit images, see figure 10-1 on page 231.

To colorize a 1-bit image:

1 Select the image. Make sure the Fill button is selected, and no stroke is applied.

2 Use the Color palette to paint the image with black, white, a process color, or a spot color.

For more information about color and painting, see Chapter 7, "Working with Color."

Using filters on bitmap images

Some filters in Adobe Illustrator let you apply special effects to bitmap images. For example, you can apply an impressionistic or mosaic effect, apply lighting effects, distort images, and produce many other interesting visual effects.

Filters don't work on linked bitmap images. If you apply a filter to a linked bitmap image, Illustrator applies the filter to an embedded copy of the image instead of to the original.

To place a bitmap image in Illustrator, see "Opening and placing artwork" on page 55.

About plug-in filters

Adobe Illustrator supports plug-in filters from Adobe products such as Adobe Photoshop and from non-Adobe software developers. Once installed, most plug-in filters appear in the Filter menu and work the same as built-in filters. (For information on installing and developing these plug-in modules, see "Using plug-in modules" on page 39.)

Previewing and applying filters

To use a filter, choose the appropriate submenu command from the Filter menu. The last filter chosen appears at the top of the menu.

The filters in the top part of the menu can be applied to vector images, with the exception of Pen and Ink > Photo Crosshatch. The filters in the bottom part of the menu can be applied to bitmap images, but not to 1-bit (black and white) images. All the bitmap filters work on RGB and Grayscale images. The following filters do not work with CMYK images: Artistic, Brush Strokes, Distort, Sketch, Stylize, Texture, and Video.

Some Illustrator filters let you preview a filter effect before applying the filter. Because applying a filter—especially to large bitmap images—can be time-consuming, use the Preview box to save time and prevent unintended results.

***Note:** Some bitmap images take more memory to process. Make sure Illustrator has enough RAM allocated for performing tasks and for the scratch disk—temporary disk space used to work with bitmap images. (See Appendix A, "Improving Performance.")*

To preview and apply a filter:

1 Select a bitmap image on which to apply the filter.

2 Choose a filter from the submenu in the Filter menu. If a filter name has an ellipsis, a dialog box appears.

3 If a dialog box appears, enter values or select options.

4 To preview the effect with the filter's preview box, do either of the following:

- Drag in the image window to center a specific area of the bitmap image in the preview box.
- Move the cursor inside the preview box to activate the hand tool to see part of the image that is not visible. Drag to see the bitmap image. Use the + or – button under the preview box to zoom in or zoom out of the preview. A flashing line beneath the preview size indicates that Illustrator is still rendering the preview.

5 Click OK to apply the filter.

When a filter takes some time to be applied, you see a progress dialog box that indicates the time remaining until the filter is applied.

Using filter shortcuts

Use the following techniques to help save time when you work with filters:

- To cancel a filter as it is being applied, press Esc (Windows) or Command+period (Mac OS).
- To undo a filter, press Ctrl+Z (Windows) or Command+Z (Mac OS).
- To reapply the most recently used filter with its last values, press Ctrl+E (Windows) or Command+E (Mac OS).
- To display the dialog box for the last filter you applied, press Ctrl+Alt+E (Windows) or Command+Option+E (Mac OS).

Loading bitmap images and textures

Some filters let you load other bitmap images, such as textures and displacement maps, to use with a filter. These filters include Glass and Rough Pastels.

To load bitmap images and textures:

1 Choose Filter > Artistic > Rough Pastels, or Filter> Distort > Glass, and then choose Load Texture from the Texture pop-up menu.

2 Open the texture bitmap image.

3 Click OK in the filter dialog box to apply the settings.

Using texture and glass surface controls

Some filters included in Illustrator have texturizing options, such as the Glass, Rough Pastels, Grain, and Fresco filters. The texturizing options can make a bitmap image appear as though painted onto various textures, such as canvas and brick, or viewed through glass blocks.

To use texture and glass surface controls:

1 From the Filter menu, choose Artistic > Rough Pastels; Artistic > Fresco, Distort > Glass; or Texture > Grain.

2 Choose a texture type from the Texture pop-up menu (if available), or choose Load Texture from the Texture pop-up menu to specify a file.

3 Drag the Scaling slider (if available) to enlarge or reduce the effect on the bitmap image's surface.

4 Choose other available options:

- Drag the Relief slider (if available) to adjust the depth of the texture's surface.
- From the Light Direction pop-up menu (if available), choose the direction from which you want the light to appear.
- Select Invert (if available) to reverse the surface's light and dark colors.

5 Click OK to apply the settings.

Improving performance with filters

Some filter effects can be memory intensive, especially when applied to a high-resolution bitmap image. Use the following techniques to improve performance when applying filters:

- Change the settings. Some filters, such as the Glass filter, are extremely memory-intensive. Try different settings to increase the speed of the filter.
- If you plan to print to a grayscale printer, convert a copy of the bitmap image to grayscale before applying filters. Note, however, that in some cases, applying a filter to a color bitmap image and then converting it to grayscale may not have the same effect as applying the same filter to a grayscale version of the image.

Choosing a filter effect

The Illustrator filters fall into the following general categories. In addition, third-party filters appear at the bottom of the Filter menu.

For detailed information on individual filters and a gallery of examples, see online Help.

Artistic filters Give a bitmap image the appearance of different media for a more organic (and less computer-generated) look. (See “Using texture and glass surface controls” on page 242.)

Blur filters Soften a bitmap image and are useful for retouching images. Blur filters smooth transitions by averaging the pixels next to the hard edges of defined lines and shaded areas where significant color transitions occur in a bitmap image.

Brush Strokes filters Give a bitmap image a fine-arts look by using different brush and ink stroke effects.

Distort filters Geometrically distort a bitmap image and can be used to create 3-D or other plastic effects.

Pixelate filters Sharply define a selection by clumping pixels of similar color values in cells. (See “Using the Color Halftone filter” on page 244.)

Sharpen filter Focus a blurry image by increasing the contrast of adjacent pixels.

Sketch filters Add fine-arts and hand-drawn effects to a bitmap image.

Stylize filters Produce a painted or impressionistic effect on a selection by displacing pixels and by finding and heightening contrast in an image.

Texture filters Apply texturing effects to an image, including effects that add grain, paint, glass, or texture to a bitmap image. (See “Using texture and glass surface controls” on page 242.)

Video filters Include the National Television Standards Committee (NTSC) Colors and De-Interlace filters. The NTSC Colors filter restricts the gamut of colors to those acceptable for television reproduction, to prevent oversaturated colors from bleeding across television scan lines. The De-Interlace filter smooths moving bitmap images captured on video by removing either the odd or even interlaced lines in a video image. The filter gives you the option of replacing the discarded lines by duplication or interpolation.

Using the Color Halftone filter

The Color Halftone filter simulates the effect of using an enlarged halftone screen on each channel of the bitmap image. (Color information channels are created automatically when you open a new image. The image's color mode determines the number of color channels created.) For each channel, the filter divides the image into rectangles and replaces each rectangle with a circle. The circle size is proportional to the brightness of the rectangle. To use the Color Halftone filter, you specify a screen-angle value for each channel of the image.

To use the Color Halftone filter:

1 Choose Filter > Pixelate > Color Halftone.

2 Enter a value in pixels, from 4 to 127, for the maximum radius of a halftone dot.

3 Enter a screen-angle value (the angle of the dot from the true horizontal) for each channel, as follows:

- Grayscale bitmap images use only Channels 1.
- In RGB bitmap images, Channel 1, 2, and 3 correspond to the red, green, and blue channels.
- In CMYK bitmap images, the four channels correspond to the cyan, magenta, yellow, and black channels, respectively.
- Click Defaults to return all the screen angles to their default values.

4 Click OK.

Using the Object Mosaic filter

The Object Mosaic filter creates sharp definition in an image by clustering pixels of similar color values together into individual tiles. You can control the tile size, the spacing between tiles, and the total number of tiles, and you can preserve the proportions of the original image when creating the mosaic copy.

The Object Mosaic filter works with any bitmap image format that Illustrator can place, and with bitmap images created with the Rasterize command. The Object Mosaic filter creates a tiled vector version of the bitmap image. You can choose to keep the original image or delete it.

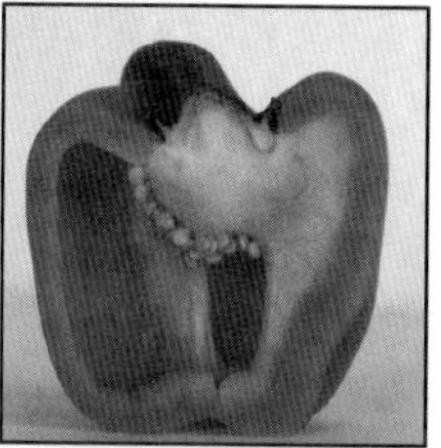
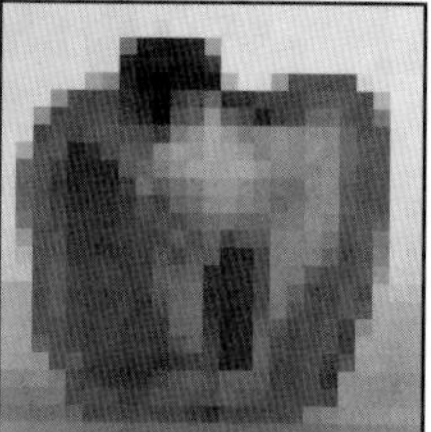

Original bitmap image, and vector version with the Object Mosaic filter applied

To create a tiled effect on a copy of a bitmap image:

1 Select a bitmap image.

2 Choose Filter > Create > Object Mosaic.

The dimensions of the bitmap image are displayed at the top left of the Object Mosaic dialog box.

3 Choose from the following options:

• To set the width and height of the mosaic in points, enter values for New Size.

• To set the distance in points between each tile in the mosaic, enter values for Tile Spacing.

• To set the number of tiles horizontally and vertically in the mosaic, enter values for Number of Tiles.

• To lock the width or height dimensions to those of the original bitmap image, choose Width or Height for the Constrain Ratio option. Choosing Width calculates the appropriate number of tiles to use for the width of the mosaic, based on the original number of tiles for the width. Choosing Height calculates the appropriate number of tiles to use for the height of the mosaic, based on the original number of tiles for the height.

• To have the result appear as a color or grayscale image, select Color or Gray.

• To change the size of the image by percentages of width and height, select Resize Using Percentages and enter new percentages in the Width and Height text boxes.

• To delete the original bitmap image, select Delete Raster.

• To make tiles square, using the number of tiles specified in Number of Tiles, click Use Ratio.

4 Click OK.

Using the Photo Crosshatch filter

The Photo Crosshatch filter can convert a photographic image, or any rasterized image, into a hatched ink pen image. The filter converts the photo into a series of overlapping hatch layers, each hatch layer representing different lightness areas of the original photo. Since there are many hatch layers overlapping where the image is darkest, and few where the image is lightest, the result is a simulated crosshatched drawing of the original photographic image.

Photographic image and Photo Crosshatch filter applied

Note: *You can apply various hatch filters to images, to give the image the appearance of a pen drawing.* *(See "Using the Pen and Ink filters" on page 210.)*

To convert a rasterized image into a crosshatched drawing:

1 Select a rasterized image.

2 Choose Filter > Pen and Ink > Photo Crosshatch.

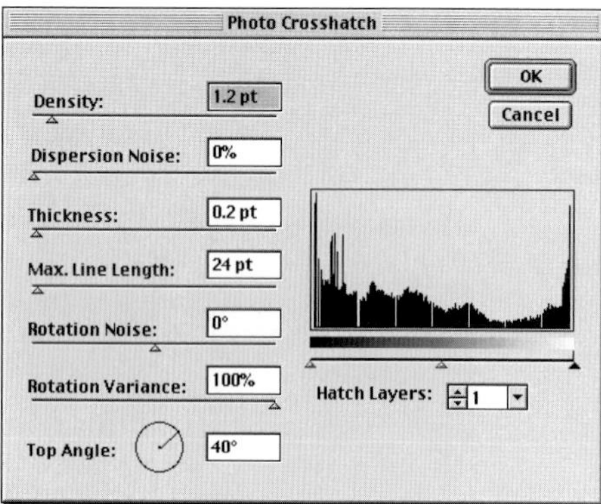

3 Enter the number of hatch layers to create in the Hatch Layers text box. The maximum number of layers is 8. Each hatch layer receives a distribution of the lightness values between 0 and 255. For example, if you enter a Hatch Layer of 4, the first layer contains lightness values of 0 to 64, the second values of 0 to 128, the third values of 0 to 192, and the fourth values of 0 to 255.

Original image

Image with Hatch layer set at 2 and 4

4 Use the slider under the histogram to adjust the weighting of the threshold levels toward light or dark. The histogram shows how many pixels of the hatched image fall into each value of lightness between 0 and 255. Use the middle slider to skew the threshold levels on each level toward light (by moving the slider to the right) or dark (by moving the slider to the left). Adjust the end sliders to moderate the highest levels of light (the rightmost slider) and dark (the leftmost slider).

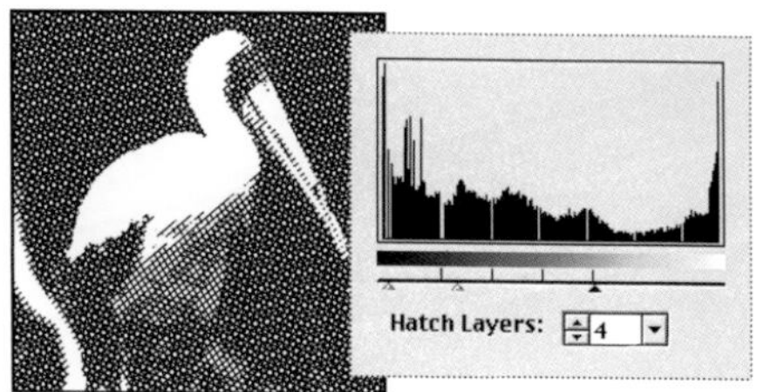

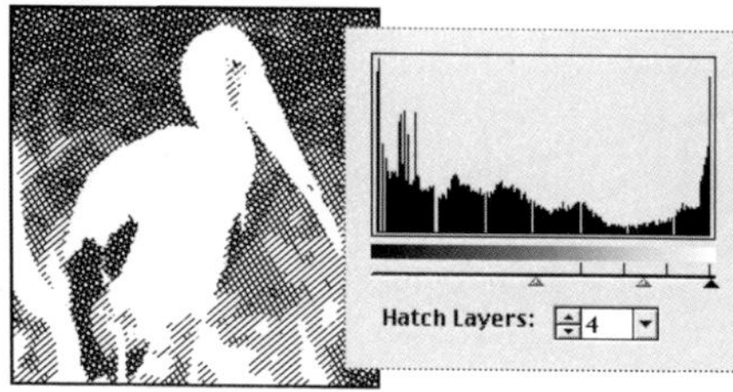

Image with Hatch layer set at 4 and the sliders adjusted

5 Use the sliders on the left side of the dialog box to adjust options as follows:

• Density adjusts the number of hatch elements applied to the selection, from .5 pt to 10 pts.

• Dispersion Noise controls the spacing of hatch elements, from 0 to 300%.

• Thickness controls the stroke weight of the hatch elements, from .1 pt to 10 pts. (This option is dimmed if the selection is unstroked.)

• Max. Line Length sets the length of the hatch elements, from 5 pts to 999 pts.

• Rotation Noise sets the amount of random rotation of objects within the hatch layers, from –360 degrees to 360 degrees.

• Rotation Variance sets the amount that each layer is rotated from the previous layer, from 0 to 100%.

• Top Angle sets the angle of rotation for the top-most hatch layer, from –360 degrees to 360 degrees.

6 Click OK.

11

Chapter 11: Using Type

Among the most powerful aspects of Adobe Illustrator are the type features. You can quickly change type size, shape, and scale; you can flow type precisely into virtually any shape of object; and you can flow type horizontally or vertically along differently shaped pathways. The range of type tools in Illustrator make it easy to place type along a path in your artwork, such as along a circle or irregular path that you create. To enhance your designs, you can also paint type with colors and patterns, or transform type into entirely new shapes.

No matter which language version you are using, Adobe Illustrator provides a wide range of multinational language features—from spell-checking and hyphenation support for numerous European languages to advanced typography features for Chinese, Japanese, and Korean (CJK) text.

Note: *Your operating system must support the languages in which you wish to work. Consult your system software manufacturer for more information.*

TYPE EFFECTS IN ILLUSTRATOR In Illustrator, you can customize type for use as display type, manipulate type as a graphic object, align type vertically, flow type along and within a path, and wrap type in columns for body text.

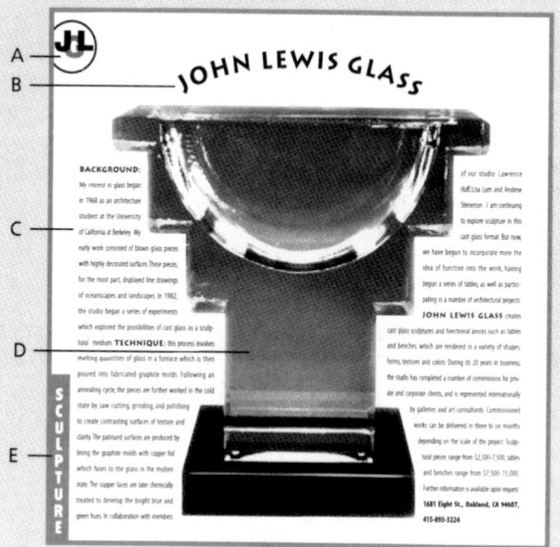

A. Type as graphic objects You can convert type to graphic objects. The resulting type can be modified the same as other graphic objects in Illustrator.
B. Type on a path You can enter type that flows along a path.
C. Area type You can enter type in a graphic object. For example, by entering type in a rectangle, you create a column of text.
D. Wrapped type You can make area type wrap around another object.
E. Vertical type You can enter vertical type in objects or along paths.

Creating type

Using the type tools, you can create horizontal or vertical type anywhere in a file. In addition, you can flow text into shapes or onto paths in a variety of ways: You can enter type in a containing column or rectangle, inside an irregularly shaped object, and inside or along a path. You can also place (or import) type into your artwork from another application.

Adobe Illustrator imports and exports vertical text files, such as MS Word or RTF, as horizontal. Vertical text is imported into Illustrator horizontally, and vertical text is exported from Illustrator horizontally.

Entering type at a point

The horizontal and vertical type tools are used to enter type anywhere in the Illustrator work area, without needing to define a bounding area for the type. Entering type this way, for example, is useful for adding a caption to an illustration.

To enter horizontal or vertical type at a specific point:

1 Select the type tool (T) or the vertical type tool (IT). The pointer changes to an I-beam within a dotted box.

The small horizontal line near the bottom of the I-beam marks the position of the type *baseline.* The baseline is the line on which the type rests.

2 Click where you want the type to begin.

Important: *Be sure not to click an existing object, because doing so converts the object into a container or path for the type. If an existing object is located where you want to enter type, lock or hide the object or enter the type away from the object and reposition the type over the object afterward.*

3 Enter the type you want. Press Enter (Windows) or Return (Mac OS) to begin a new line of type.

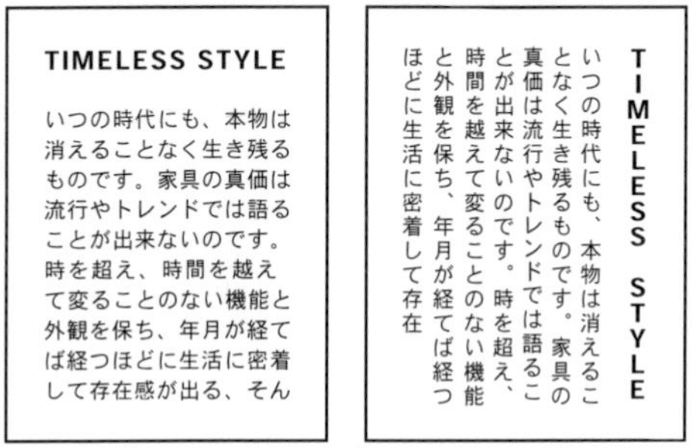

Horizontal type and vertical type

Selecting type

The type or vertical type tool's I-beam pointer lets you select individual characters, words, and paragraphs, and lets you change the type's attributes. To select all of the type on a path or in a type container, use the selection tool on the path or type container. (See "Selecting objects" on page 113.)

By default, Type Area Select is selected in the Type & Auto Tracing Preferences dialog box. You can reset your preferences to select type from the baseline.

To select characters and words:

1 Select any type tool.

2 Do one of the following:

• Drag to select the type you want to change. (Shift-drag to extend or reduce the selection.)

• Position the pointer in a word, and double-click to select that word.

• Position the pointer at the beginning of a paragraph, and press Shift+Ctrl+Up Arrow (Windows) or Shift+Command+Up Arrow (Mac OS) to select the previous paragraph. With the pointer at the end of a paragraph, press Shift+Ctrl+Down Arrow (Windows) or Shift+Command+Down Arrow (Mac OS) to select the next paragraph.

• Press Shift+Ctrl+Right Arrow (Windows) or Shift+Command+Right Arrow (Mac OS) to select one word to the right. Press Shift+Ctrl+Left Arrow (Windows) or Shift+Command+Left Arrow (Mac OS) to select one word to the left.

To select blocks of type:

1 Select any type tool.

2 Do one of the following:

• Drag to select the type you want to change. (Shift-drag to extend or reduce the selection.)

• Position the I-beam pointer in a paragraph, and triple-click to select the entire paragraph.

• Click the type with a type tool, and then choose Edit > Select All to select all the type on the type path or in the type container.

To set the preference for selecting type from the baseline:

1 Choose File > Preferences > Type & Auto Tracing.

2 Deselect the Type Area Select option, and click OK.

To select type from the baseline:

1 Use the selection tool ( ) or direct-selection tool ( ) to select the type path. You see the text baseline.

2 Click the baseline to select it.

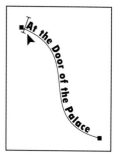

Type selected at baseline

Entering horizontal or vertical type in a rectangle

You can use the type or vertical type tool to define a text rectangle into which you enter type. This method is useful when you want to create one or more columns of text, such as for a brochure. You can also create a rectangle with the rectangle tool and then use any type tool to convert it to a text rectangle.

Once you've entered type, you can change the shape and size of the text rectangle.

To create a text rectangle using a type tool:

1 Select the type tool (T) or the vertical type tool (IT). The pointer changes to an I-beam within a dotted box.

2 Drag diagonally to define the text rectangle. The text rectangle you create is unpainted (not filled or stroked). Text rectangles are not visible in Preview view or when printing, unless filled or stroked with color. (See "Using the Color palette" on page 162.)

When you release the mouse button, the pointer reverts to an I-beam. (In Artwork view, a rectangle appears with an insertion point at the top left corner of the text rectangle.)

3 Enter the type. The type wraps to fit inside the defined area.

4 Press Enter (Windows) or Return (Mac OS) to begin a new paragraph.

If you enter more type than can fit within the rectangle, a small box containing a plus symbol (+) appears near the bottom of the rectangle when in Artwork view or when the text rectangle or type is selected. The plus symbol is positioned at the end of the baseline of the last visible line of type.

Horizontal type that fits within its container and that overflows its container

You can adjust the size of the rectangle to accommodate the type using either the bounding box or the direct-selection tool. When you adjust the size or shape of the rectangle, the text reflows within the adjusted shape.

Note: *If you select objects, point text, or path text in addition to a text rectangle, scaling with the bounding box will cause all objects, including the area text, to be rescaled.*

You can also create a linked copy of the rectangle to force extra type to flow into another text rectangle or object. (See "Linking type containers" on page 275.)

To change the size or shape of a text rectangle using the bounding box:

1 Select the selection tool (➧).

2 Select the text rectangle to adjust.

3 Drag a handle of the selection until the text rectangle is the desired size or shape. Shift-drag to maintain the proportion.

To change the size or shape of a text rectangle using the direct-selection tool:

1 Select the direct-selection tool (⇖).

2 If the type is selected, click outside the rectangle to deselect it.

3 Position the pointer on the edge of the text container you want to adjust. Do not select any type baselines.

4 Click to select an edge or corner of the text rectangle, and drag to adjust the rectangle's shape. Shift-drag to constrain the tool to multiples of 45 degrees (constraining makes it easier to retain the shape of a rectangle).

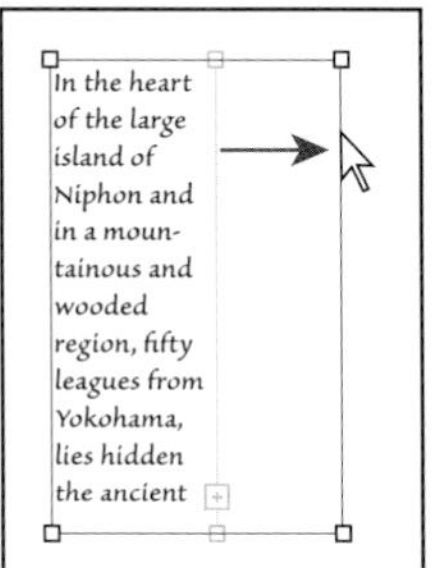

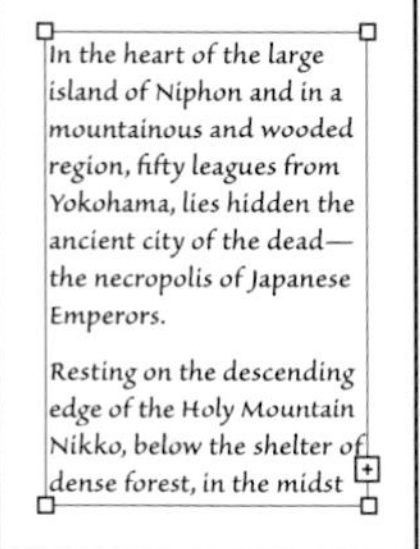

Changing shape of text rectangle and result

Adjusting the text rectangle using the direct-selection tool is easiest when you're in Artwork view.

Entering horizontal or vertical type in an object

You can use any object as an area within which to enter type. If the object is an open path, the program draws an imaginary line between the endpoints of the path to define the object for the type, just as it does to paint open paths.

To create only area type or to create area type on an open path, you can use the type or vertical area-type tools exclusively. If, however, you want to create several kinds of type, you should use the type tool or the vertical type tool. When you move a type tool over different kinds of objects, the type tool appropriate to the specific object (for example, an area-type tool or a path-type tool) appears.

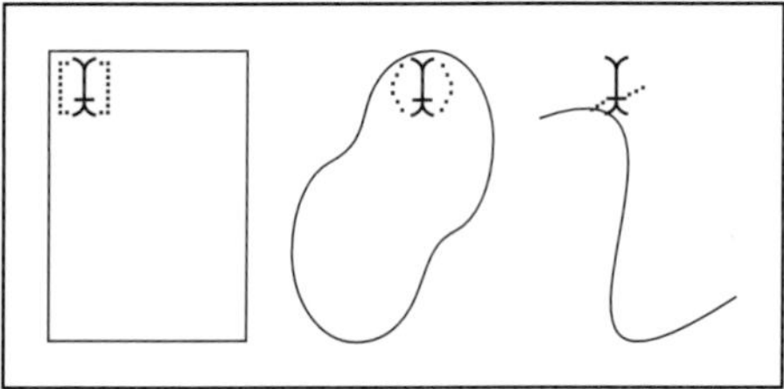

Type cursors: type tool, area-type tool, and path-type tool

To enter type in an object:

1 Select the type tool (T) or the area-type tool (T) if the object is a filled open path.

2 Position the pointer on the path, and click. An insertion point appears.

When you turn an object into a type path, the path becomes unstroked and unfilled, even if the path was originally stroked or filled. When the entire text object is selected, any changes to the paint settings affect only the type, not the path.

3 Enter some type.

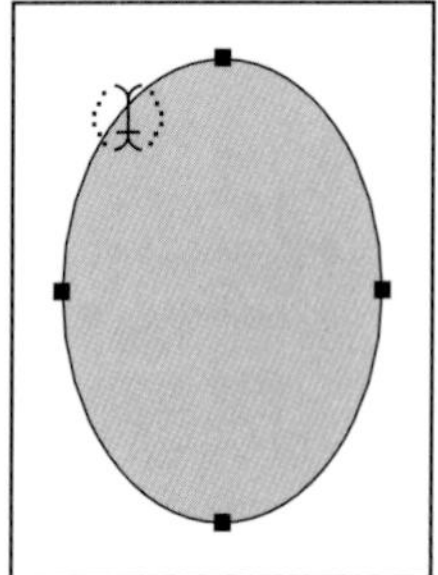

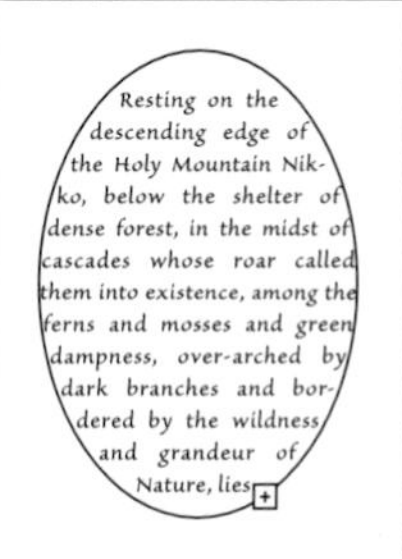

Clicking filled object with area-type tool changes object into text container so that you can enter text.

As with text rectangles, if you enter more type than can fit within the area, in Artwork view and in Preview view (only when text is selected), a small box with a plus symbol (+) appears near the bottom of the area.

You can paint the path after you enter type by selecting the path with the direct-selection tool and using the Color palette or Swatches palette. (See Chapter 7, "Working with Color.")

Entering horizontal or vertical type along a path

You can enter type that flows along the edge of an open or a closed path. The path can be regularly or irregularly shaped. When you enter type along a path, the path is no longer stroked or filled. You can paint it later if you want, without affecting the paint attributes of the type.

Entering horizontal type on a path results in letters that are perpendicular to the baseline. Entering vertical type on a path results in text orientation parallel to the baseline.

To toggle between the type tool and the vertical type tool when another type tool is currently selected, Shift-click.

To enter horizontal type along a path:

1 Select the type tool (T) or the path-type tool ( ).

2 Position the pointer on the path, and click. An insertion point appears on the path.

3 Enter the type you want. Type appears along the path, perpendicular to the baseline.

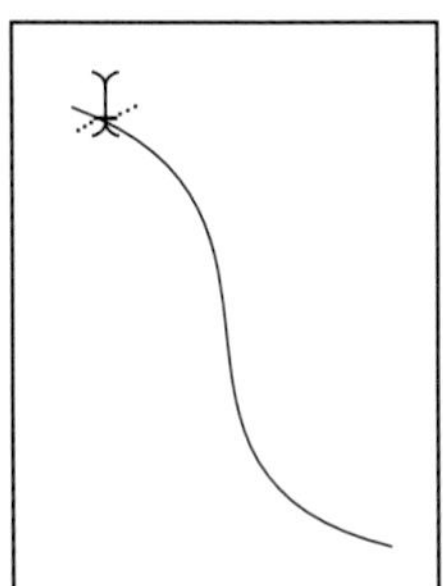

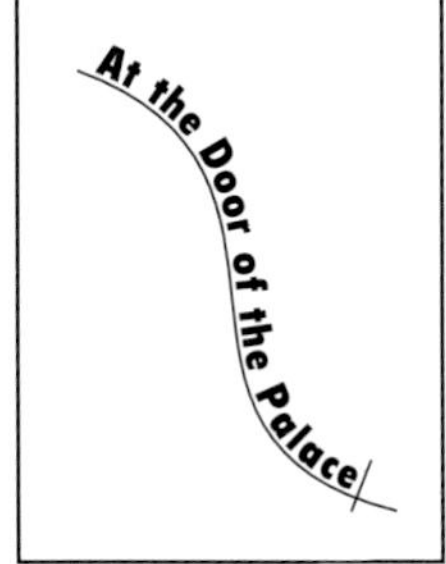

Set the insertion point. Then enter type.

To enter vertical type along a path:

1 Select the vertical type tool (IT) or the vertical-path-type tool ( ).

2 Choose Standard from the Direction pop-up menu in the Character palette.

3 Position the pointer on the path, and click. An insertion point appears on the path.

4 Enter the type you want. Type appears along the path, parallel to the baseline.

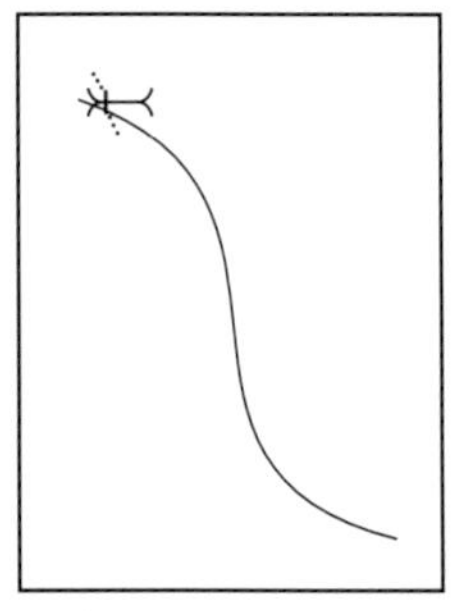

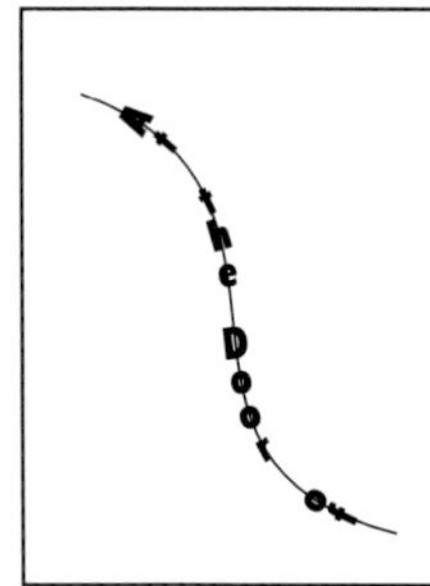

Set the insertion point. Then enter vertical type.

***Note:** For 1-byte vertical CJK text, Roman characters rotate by default.*

To move type along a path:

1 Use the selection tool ( ) or the direct-selection tool ( ) to select the type path if it is not already selected.

2 Position the pointer on the I-beam in the type.

3 Use the selection tool to move the selected type along the path. Be careful not to drag across the path.

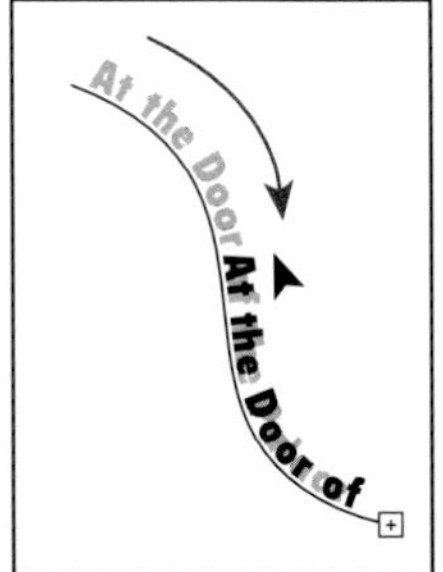

Position pointer on I-beam. Then drag to move type.

To align horizontal type evenly along a path, enter a negative baseline shift value in the Character palette so that the type runs along the center of the path. This method creates an even flow of type along the curve. *(See “Specifying baseline shift” on page 266.)*

To flip the direction of the type along a path:

1 Select the selection tool (↖).

2 Position the pointer precisely on the I-beam.

3 Do one of the following:

- Drag the I-beam across the path.
- Double-click the I-beam.

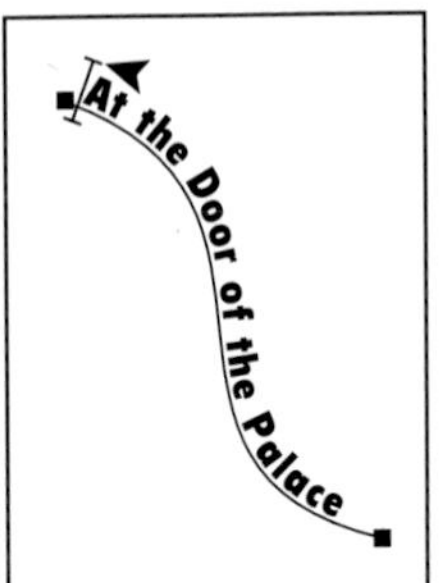

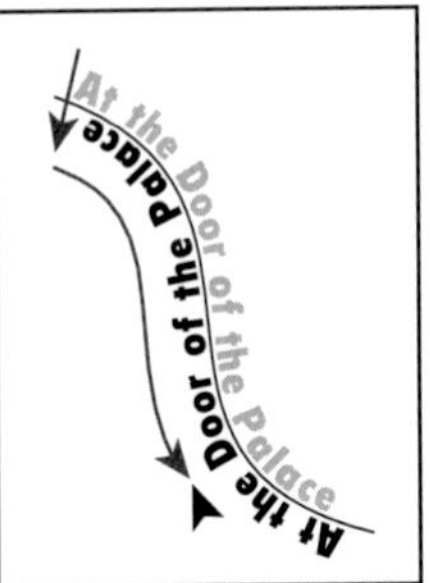

Position pointer on I-beam. Then drag across path to flip type.

The initial direction of type flows in the order that points were added to the path. If you want your text to flow from left-to-right without having to flip the I-beam, construct your paths in that order.

To move type across a path without changing the direction of the type, use the Baseline Shift option in the Character palette. (See “Specifying baseline shift” on page 266.) For example, if you created type that runs from left to right across the top of a circle, you can enter a negative number in the Baseline Shift text box to drop the type so that it flows inside the top of the circle.

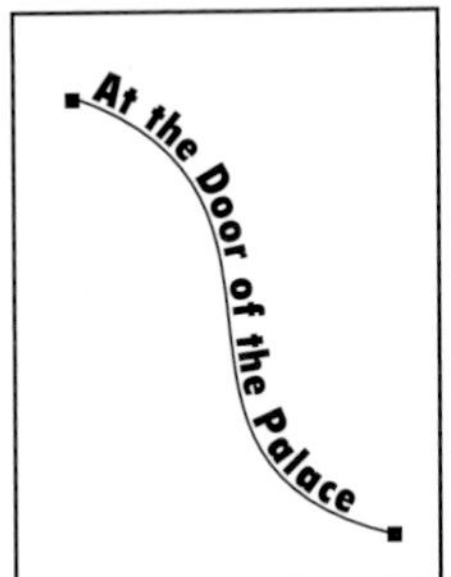

Type on a path and with baseline shift adjusted down

Deleting empty type paths from artwork

The Delete Empty Text Paths option in the Cleanup dialog box lets you delete unused type paths and containers from your artwork. Doing so makes your artwork more efficient and easier to print. You can create empty type paths, for example, by inadvertently clicking the type tool in the artwork area and then choosing another tool.

To delete an empty type path from your artwork:

1 Choose Object > Path > Cleanup.

2 Select Delete Empty Text Paths, and click OK.

Using or modifying multiple master fonts

Illustrator supports the Adobe multiple master font technology and provides special options for working with those fonts.

Multiple master fonts are customizable Type 1 fonts whose typeface characteristics are described in terms of linear design axes such as weight, width, style, and optical size. Multiple master fonts include a number of primary instances. For example, MyriadMM® includes 15 primary instances, ranging from 215LT 300CN (Light condensed) to 830BL 700SE (Black SemiExtended). Standard Type 1 fonts are single master fonts, which means they are adjustable in style only (for example, Roman, bold, italic).

When you create a multiple master font, the font is available only when the file for which it was created is open. To have a multiple master font instance always available for Illustrator and other applications, you must first create it in Adobe Type Manager®.

To modify a multiple master font from within Illustrator:

1 Using the type tool (T), select the text that uses a multiple master font.

2 Display the Multiple Master design palette using one of the following methods:

- Choose Type > MM Design.
- Click the MM Design tab in the Character palette.

3 Edit the font as described in the documentation included with your multiple master font.

Showing hidden characters

As you work with type, nonprinting characters are embedded into the file to indicate keyboard actions or states, such as spaces, returns (line breaks), and tabs. These characters include hard returns (line breaks), soft returns (line breaks), tabs, spaces, nonbreaking spaces, double-byte characters (including spaces), discretionary hyphens, other nonprinting characters, and end of text.

These characters are by default hidden. To help you format and edit type, you can make the characters visible.

To show hidden characters:

Choose Type > Show Hidden Characters. A check mark appears next to the menu command. To hide visible characters, choose the command to remove the check mark.

Setting type attributes

The Adobe Illustrator program gives you precise control over type attributes, including font, type size, leading, kerning, tracking, baseline shift, horizontal and vertical scale, spacing, and letter orientation. You can either set type attributes before you enter new type or reset them to change the appearance of existing, selected type. You can also set attributes for several type paths and type containers at once, if they are all selected.

You change the type attributes using the Character and Paragraph palettes. Some of the type attributes also have separate submenus or palettes so that you do not have to open the Character or Paragraph palette to change only one attribute. In addition, some attributes can be changed using keyboard shortcuts. For a complete list of shortcuts, see the *Adobe Illustrator Quick Reference Card.*

To apply a value in the Character or Paragraph palette to the selected type without moving to the next text box in the palette, press Enter (Windows) or Return (Mac OS). To apply a value and then highlight the value just edited, press Shift+Enter (Windows) or Shift+Return (Mac OS). To apply a value and move to the next text box in the palette, press Tab.

To open the Character or Paragraph palette:

Choose either Type > Character or Type > Paragraph.

To show character options in the Character palette:

Choose Type > Character, and then choose Show Options from the Character palette menu.

To show multilingual and orientation options in the Character palette:

Choose Type > Character, and then choose Show Multilingual from the Character palette menu.

Choosing a font family

A *font family* is a complete set of characters, letters, and symbols of a particular typeface design. For example, the font used in this paragraph is Minion®.

You can choose a font from the Character palette, or you can choose Type > Font and choose from the submenu.

You do not see fonts in their respective faces, even when you have a utility that shows typefaces installed (such as Adobe Type Reunion®).

To choose a font from the Character palette:

1 Do one of the following:

• Select any type container or type path using a selection tool.

• Select a block of type using a type tool.

2 Choose Type > Character.

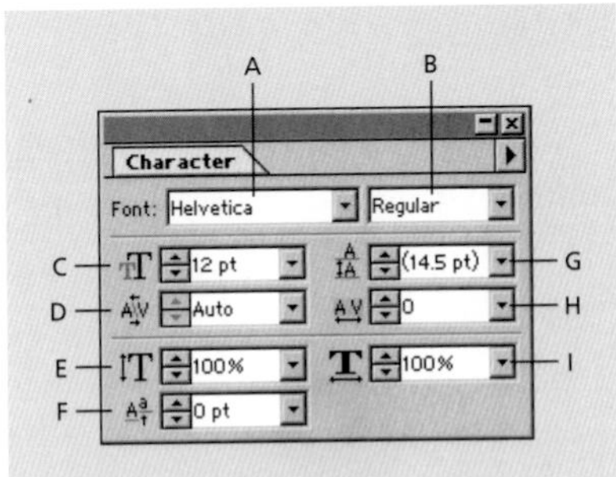

A. Family B. Style C. Font size D. Kerning E. Vertical scale F. Baseline shift G. Leading H. Tracking I. Horizontal scale

3 Do one of the following:

• In the Font text box, type the name of the font family you want to use. In the Style text box, enter the type style (for example, Bold, Condensed, Italic). As you type, the name of the first font or style beginning with that letter appears. Continue typing the name until the correct font or style name appears.

• Choose a font and style from the pop-up menu in which you see styles (to the right of the Font text box).

4 Press Enter (Windows) or Return (Mac OS) or Tab to apply the new font.

To choose a font from the Type menu:

1 Do one of the following:

• Select any type container or type path using a selection tool.

• Set an insertion point or select a range of text using the type tool (T) or the vertical-type tool (IT).

2 Choose Type > Font. A check mark appears next to the selected font.

3 Drag to choose the font family you want. If more than one style of the font is installed, you see a submenu, which contains a list of styles available for the font family you choose.

4 Select the style you want. The font you choose becomes the active font.

Note: *When using 2-byte fonts, you can switch between showing a font's name in a 2-byte script or showing the font in its English name by selecting or deselecting the Show Font Names in English option in the Type & Auto Tracing Preferences dialog box.*

Choosing a type size

You can choose the type size in the Character palette, or from the Size submenu in the Type menu, or by using keyboard commands. The default type size is 12 points. Type size units can be set to points, inches, millimeters, or Q in the Units & Undo Preferences dialog box.

To choose a type size in the Character palette:

1 Do one of the following:

• Select any type container or type path using a selection tool.

• Set an insertion point or select a range of text using the type tools.

2 Choose Type > Character. The Character palette opens, displaying the currently selected type size in the Font Size text box.

If the selection contains fonts of more than one size, the text box is blank.

3 Choose a new type size from the Size pop-up menu. You can also press Up Arrow or Down Arrow to change the size, or enter the size in the Font Size text box and press Enter (Windows) or Return (Mac OS), or Tab.

To choose a type size from the Type menu:

1 Do one of the following:

• Select any type container or type path using a selection tool.

• Set an insertion point or select a block of type using a type tool.

2 Choose Type > Size. A check mark appears next to the current type size in the Size submenu.

3 Do one of the following:

• Select a new type size from the Size submenu.

• If the desired type size does not appear in the Size submenu, choose Other to display the Character palette. Enter a value in the Size text box, and press Enter (Windows) or Return (Mac OS) or Tab.

To change the point size from the keyboard:

Do one of the following:

• To increase the point size, press Shift+Ctrl+> (Windows) or Shift+Command+> (Mac OS).

• To decrease the point size, press Shift+Ctrl+< (Windows) or Shift+Command+< (Mac OS). The point size changes by the increment set in the Size/Leading text box in the Type & Auto Tracing Preferences dialog box. The default is 2 points.

To change type size units:

1 Choose File > Preferences > Units & Undo.

2 In the Type pop-up menu, choose the type units you want to use, and click OK.

At the door of the palace
8

At the door of the palace
16

At the door
32

Point sizes

Finding and replacing fonts

The Find Font command creates a list of all the fonts in your file and allows you to search for and replace them (including the font's type style) by name. This command also lets you save the list of fonts as a separate file, which can be useful for a service bureau that is printing the file.

To find and replace fonts in your file:

1 Choose Type > Find Font.

2 Do one of the following:

• Select the Multiple Master, Standard (Chicago, Geneva, Monaco, New York, Courier, Souvenir, Symbol, Hobo, Helvetica*, and Times*), Roman, Type 1, TrueType™, or CID option to display these fonts. To display multiple master fonts, you must click the Multiple Master *and* Type 1 options (multiple master fonts are Type 1 fonts).

• Choose System from the Replace Font From pop-up menu to make all fonts currently installed on your system (as filtered through the previous options you chose) available as replacements.

• Choose Document from the Replace Font From pop-up menu to limit the fonts you can use as replacements to those already in your file.

3 Select a font name from the Fonts in Document list. Illustrator selects the next instance of that font in your file.

4 Click Find Next to find the next instance of the font.

5 Select the font you want to use as a replacement from the Replace Font From list, and do one of the following:

• Click Change to change just that instance of the selected font.

• Click Change All to change all instances of the selected font.

When there are no more instances of a font in your file, that font name is removed from the list of fonts to find.

6 To save a list of all fonts found in the file, click Save List, enter a filename and location in the Save Font List As text box, and click Save.

7 Click Done.

Specifying leading

Leading determines the amount of vertical space between baselines. Leading is always measured in units specified in the Type pop-up menu in the Units & Undo Preferences dialog box; the default units are points. If a line of type contains characters with different leading values, the line's leading is set to the greater of the two values.

In the heart of the large island of Niphon and in a mountainous and wooded region, fifty leagues from Yokohama, lies hidden the ancient city of the dead—the necropolis of Japanese Emperors.

Resting on the descending edge of the Holy Mountain Nikko, below the shelter of dense forest, in the midst

In the heart of the large island of Niphon and in a mountainous and wooded region, fifty leagues from Yokohama, lies hidden the ancient city of the dead—the necropolis of Japanese

6-point type with default leading and with 12-point leading

You can adjust leading in the Character palette or directly from the keyboard. The default Auto-Leading option sets the leading at 120% of the type size. For example, 10-point type would have a leading value of 12 points (120% of 10 points).

To change the leading value using the Character palette:

1 Do one of the following:

• Select any type container or type path using a selection tool.

• Select a block of type using the type tools.

2 Choose Type > Character.

3 Enter a value in the Leading text box, or choose a value from the pop-up menu.

4 Press Enter (Windows) or Return (Mac OS).

Note: *To set the leading to the same value as the font size, double-click the Leading icon. To reset a setting to its default value, Ctrl-click (Windows) or Command-click (Mac OS) the associated icon in the palette.*

To change the leading value from the keyboard:

1 Do one of the following:

- Select any type container or type path using a selection tool.
- Select a block of type using the type tools.

2 Do one of the following:

- Press Alt+Up Arrow (Windows) or Option+Up Arrow (Mac OS) to decrease the leading.
- Press Alt+Down Arrow (Windows) or Option+Down Arrow (Mac OS) to increase the leading.

The leading changes by the increment set in the Size/Leading text box in the Type & Auto Tracing Preferences dialog box. The default is 2 points.

To specify leading before a paragraph:

1 Do one of the following:

- To apply leading to a single paragraph in text, use the type tool to click anywhere in the paragraph.
- To apply leading to all paragraphs in a type container, use the selection tool to select the entire type container.

2 Choose Type > Paragraph.

3 Do one of the following:

- Click the Space Before Paragraph button and enter a value in the text box.
- Press Up Arrow or Down Arrow to increase or decrease the leading value.

4 Press Enter (Windows) or Return (Mac OS) or Tab.

In the heart of the large island of Niphon and in a mountainous and wooded region, fifty leagues from Yokohama, lies hidden the ancient city of the dead—the necropolis of Japanese Emperors.

Resting on the descending edge of the Holy Mountain Nikko, below the shelter of dense forest, in the midst a

In the heart of the large island of Niphon and in a mountainous and wooded region, fifty leagues from Yokohama, lies hidden the ancient city of the dead—the necropolis of Japanese Emperors.

Resting on the descending edge of the Holy Mountain Nikko, below the shelter of

6 points leading before paragraph and with 14 points

Note: *You can specify leading before a paragraph with Area Type only.*

Specifying kerning and tracking

Kerning controls the spacing between two characters. You can control kerning manually, or you can turn on the kerning built into a font by the font designer. (See "Spacing characters with auto-kerning" on page 266.) *Tracking* inserts uniform spacing between more than two characters in selected type. Use tracking to adjust the spacing of a word or an entire block of type.

Positive kerning or tracking values move characters apart; negative kerning or tracking values move characters closer together. Kerning and tracking values are measured in units that are 1/1000 of an *em space*. The width of an em space is relative to the current type size. In a 1-point font, 1 em corresponds to 1 point; in a 10-point font, 1 em corresponds to 10 points. Because kerning units are 1/1000 em, 100 kerning units in a 10-point font are equivalent to 1 point.

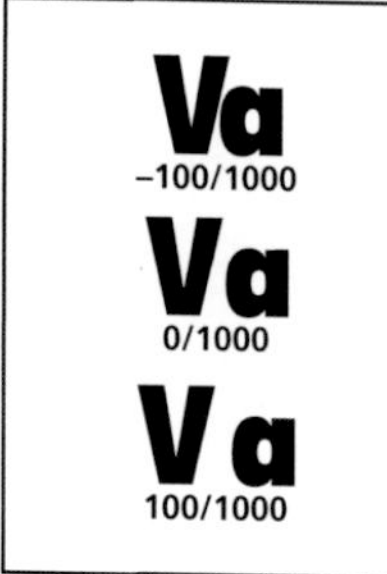

Kerning values, and tracking values ("The Emperor's")

To change the kerning or tracking value using the Character palette:

1 Set an insertion point between two characters for kerning or select type for tracking using the type tools.

2 Choose Type > Character.

3 Do one of the following:

• Click the Kerning button and enter a value in the Kerning text box.

• Click the Tracking button and enter a value in the Tracking text box.

4 Press Enter (Windows) or Return (Mac OS) or Tab.

To change the kerning or tracking value from the keyboard:

1 Set an insertion point between two characters for kerning or select type for tracking using the type tools.

2 Do one of the following:

• Press Alt+Left Arrow (Windows) or Option+Left Arrow (Mac OS) to move characters closer together. Press Alt+Right Arrow (Windows) or Option+Right Arrow (Mac OS) to move characters farther apart. The distance moved is equal to the Tracking value set in the Type & Auto Tracing Preferences dialog box (the default is 20/1000 of an em space).

• Press Alt+Ctrl+Left Arrow (Windows) or Option+Command+Left Arrow (Mac OS) to move characters closer together by five times the Tracking value set in the Type & Auto Tracing Preferences dialog box. Press Alt+Ctrl+Right Arrow (Windows) or Option+Command+Right Arrow (Mac OS) to move characters farther apart by five times the Tracking value set in the Type & Auto Tracing Preferences dialog box.

To view the kerning value between two characters:

1 Set an insertion point between two characters whose kerning value you want to view, using the type tools.

2 Choose Window > Show Info.

The Info palette displays the total spacing value for the two characters. For example, if the Info palette displays *109 = 100 + 9/1000 em*, the characters have 9/1000 em kerning and the word has 100/1000 em tracking.

Spacing characters with auto-kerning

To use a font's kerning information to space characters, you can select the Auto-Kerning option in the Character palette. Many Roman fonts contain information about the spacing of character pairs. For example, the spacing between an *A* and a *W* often is less than the spacing between an *A* and an *F*.

You can also choose a specific kerning value, rather than Auto-Kerning, in the Character palette until you finish creating your type. Then select the type and apply auto-kerning to it.

To apply auto-kerning to existing type in a file:

1 Choose Edit > Select All.

2 Choose Type > Character, and choose Auto from the Kerning pop-up menu or type **Auto** in the text box.

To turn auto-kerning off:

Choose Type > Character, and enter **0** in the Kerning text box.

Specifying baseline shift

Baseline shift controls the distance that type appears from its baseline, either raising or lowering the selected type. The Baseline Shift option lets you create subscripts or superscripts or move path type above or below a path without changing the direction of the type flow. For example, using the path-type tool on a circle positions type above the circle. Using the Baseline Shift option, you can move the type inside the circle without changing the type's orientation.

A positive value moves type above the baseline; a negative value moves it below the baseline. Baseline shift is measured by points unless you change the option set in the Type pop-up menu in the Units & Undo Preferences dialog box.

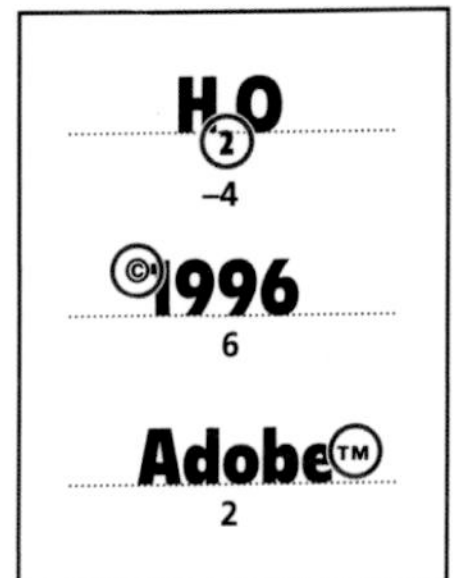

Baseline shifts

To specify baseline shift using the Character palette:

1 Select a type container or type path using a selection tool, or select a block of type using the type tools.

2 Choose Type > Character. If the Baseline Shift button is not visible, choose Show Options from the Character palette menu.

3 Enter a value in the Baseline Shift text box, or press Up Arrow or Down Arrow to increase or decrease baseline shift.

4 Press Enter (Windows) or Return (Mac OS).

To specify baseline shift from the keyboard:

1 Do one of the following:

• Select a type container or type path using a selection tool.

• Select a block of type using type tools.

2 Do one of the following:

• Press Shift+Alt+Up Arrow (Windows) or Shift+Option+Up Arrow (Mac OS) to increase the baseline shift equal to the value set in the Type & Auto Tracing Preferences dialog box (2 points, by default).

• Press Shift+Alt+Down Arrow (Windows) or Shift+Option+Down Arrow (Mac OS) to decrease the baseline shift equal to the value set in the Type & Auto Tracing Preferences dialog box.

Adjusting horizontal or vertical scale

Horizontal scale and *vertical scale* specify the proportion between the height and width of the type relative to the baseline. Unscaled characters have a value of 100%. You can adjust scale to compress or expand selected characters in both width and height.

Scaling type using a transformation tool affects the type's horizontal scale as well as the type size, leading, indentation, and baseline shift. You can return type scaled using a transformation tool to its original horizontal scale by setting the horizontal scale to 100%.

AT THE DOOR OF THE PALACE
50%

AT THE DOOR OF THE PALACE
100%

AT THE DOOR O
200%

Horizontal scale values with 9-point font

Note: *Depending on the value you enter when you use vertical type, the horizontal scale may make the text appear narrower, because it functions relative to the baseline. The opposite is true for vertical scale.*

To adjust the horizontal or vertical scale of type:

1 Select any type container or type path using a selection tool, or select a range of text using the type tools.

2 Choose Type > Character. If the Horizontal Scale or Vertical Scale pop-up menus are not visible, choose Show Options from the Character palette menu.

3 Enter a percentage in the Horizontal Scale or the Vertical Scale text box.

4 Press Enter (Windows) or Return (Mac OS).

Adjusting spacing using the keyboard

You can set the increments in which baseline shift and kerning/tracking values increase or decrease when you use keyboard shortcuts. The default key increment values are 2 points for size/leading, 2 points for baseline shift, and 20/1000 of an em space for kerning/tracking.

Settings in the Type & Auto Tracing Preferences and General Preferences dialog boxes control the keyboard shortcuts.

The type units preference determines the units for font size, leading, and baseline shift.

To change keyboard increments:

1 Choose File > Preferences > Type & Auto Tracing.

2 Enter the values you want in the Size/Leading, Baseline Shift, and Tracking text boxes, and click OK.

To change the cursor key increment value:

1 Choose File > Preferences > General.

2 Enter the value you want in the Cursor Key text box, and click OK.

To change type units:

1 Choose File > Preferences > Units & Undo.

2 Choose a type unit from the Type pop-up menu, and click OK.

The default type unit is *points* (a point equals 1/72 of an inch). You can choose inches, millimeters, or Q (a Q equals 0.25 millimeter).

Painting type

You can paint type, the type container, or the type path. You may want to paint the container to create a background for your type, or paint the type path as a visual base for the type. (See Chapter 7, "Working with Color.")

To paint type, a type container, or a type path:

1 Do one of the following:

• To paint the type, use the selection tool (↖) to select the type.

• To paint a type container or type path, use the direct-selection tool (↖) or the group-selection tool (↖⁺) and click the path or object.

Do not select the baselines.

• Use a type tool to select characters, words, or paragraphs.

2 Choose either Window > Show Color or Window > Show Swatches.

3 Paint the type or type path as desired, except for gradient swatches. (See "Using the Color palette" on page 162. Also see "Using the Swatches palette" on page 166.)

Copying type attributes between objects

You can use the eyedropper tool to copy—or *sample*—the character, paragraph, fill, and stroke attributes from type in an Illustrator file. You can then use the paint bucket tool to apply the copied attributes to other type.

By default, the eyedropper and paint bucket tools affect all attributes of a type selection. To customize the attributes you want affected by these tools, use the Paint bucket/Eyedropper dialog box.

Note: *When you select an entire type path or container, the fill, stroke, character, and paragraph attributes of that object are copied and applied to the new text. When you select a portion of text, only the fill, stroke, and character attributes are copied.*

To copy type attributes to selected text objects:

1 With the selection tool or any type tool, select the type container, type path, or a portion of text to which you want attributes copied.

2 Select the eyedropper tool.

3 Click the text from which you want attributes copied. The text can be unselected, locked, or in an inactive artwork file. The attributes are applied to the selected type, and that type remains selected.

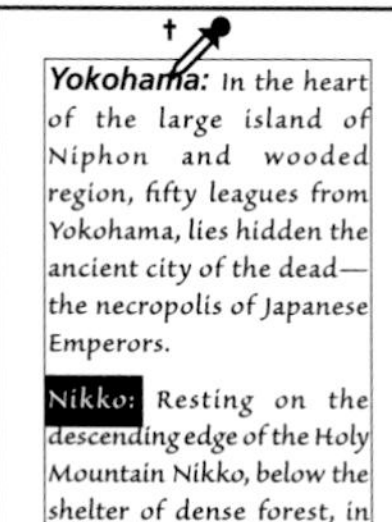

Type attributes copied to selected text

To copy type attributes using the paint bucket tool:

1 Select the paint bucket tool.

2 Click the type path or type container, or drag to select a portion of text, to which you want attributes applied. The paint bucket displays a small *t* next to it, to indicate you are copying type attributes.

The attributes are applied to the selected type.

To toggle between the eyedropper tool and the paint bucket tool, press Alt (Windows) or Option (Mac OS) when either tool is selected.

To change type attributes:

1 Double-click the paint bucket or the eyedropper tool.

2 Select or deselect the attributes for the eyedropper to copy and the paint bucket to apply.

- To expand or collapse the list of attributes for each characteristic (for example, Paragraph), click the triangle to the left of the list.
- To select or deselect all the attributes for each characteristic, click the group option.
- To select or deselect individual attributes for a characteristic, click the attribute.

3 Click OK.

For a description of each attribute, see the appropriate sections in this guide.

Transforming type

The selection tool lets you select an entire type path or type container so that you can transform the type along with the path or container. You can also transform individual type containers within linked type containers.

To transform type including its path:

1 Do one of the following:

- To transform all of the type, use the selection tool ( ) to select the type path or type container, or click its baseline.
- To transform individual type containers in a series of linked type containers, use the direct-selection tool ( ) to select the linked type containers you want to transform. Make sure the baselines appear, indicating that the type is selected within the containers.

Note: *To transform the type path or type container without transforming the type, use the direct-selection tool to select just the path. Make sure that the baselines do not appear, indicating type is deselected.*

2 Select the rotate ( ), scale ( ), or shear ( ) tool to transform the type container and its path. (See Chapter 6, "Modifying Shapes.")

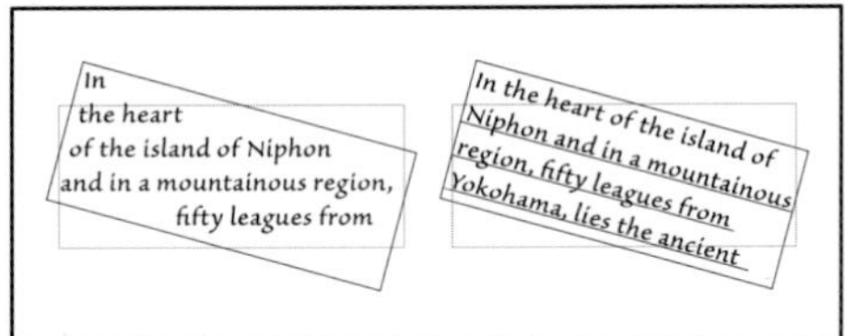

Rotated type container only compared to rotated type container and type

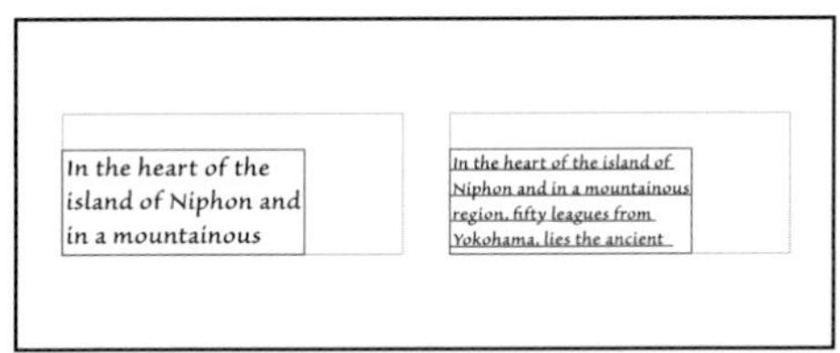

Scaled type container only compared to scaled type container and type

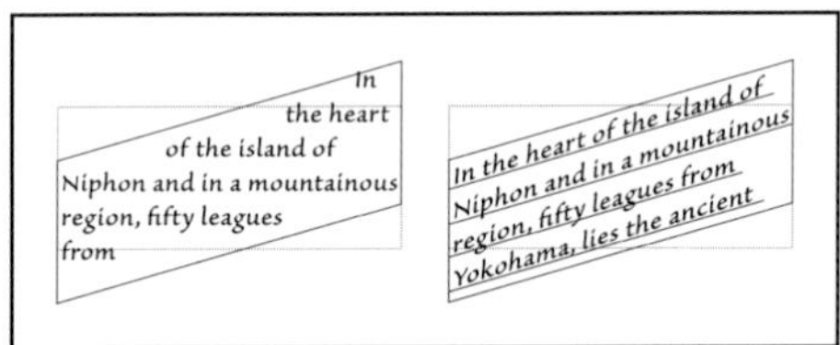

Sheared type container only compared to sheared type container and type

Changing text orientation

You can change the direction of individual characters as well as the flow of an entire block of text, using type tools, the Character palette, or the Text Orientation command.

Enter vertical type along a path or in an object by using vertical-type tools in the toolbox. (See “Creating type” on page 252.)

Change the direction of individual characters or change the entire orientation of a block of text using the Character palette or the Text Orientation command.

Changing character direction using the Character palette

You can change the direction of individual characters or portions of a vertical text block using the Direction pop-up menu in the Character palette.

Changing character direction maintains the original orientation of the text (for example, vertical text remains in a vertical orientation), but the direction of the individual character or portions of text are rotated 90 degrees.

To change the direction of type:

1 Select the text whose direction you want to change.

2 Choose Type > Character. If the multilingual options aren’t visible, choose Show Multilingual from the Character palette menu.

3 Choose a direction from the Direction pop-up menu.

• Standard orients text characters in line with the axis of the page.

• Rotate rotates Roman fonts and other one-byte characters 90 degrees from standard.

• Tate Chu Yoko rotates the selected block of text (1- or 2-byte characters) in the plane opposite from the rest of the text.

TIMELESS STYLE
いつの時代にも、本物は消えるこ
となく生き残るものです。家具の
真価は流行やトレンドでは語るこ
とが出来ないのです。時を超え、
時間を越えても変ることのない機
能と外観を保ち、年月が経てば経
つほどに生活に密着して存在感が

Vertical text in Standard direction and with Rotate option applied

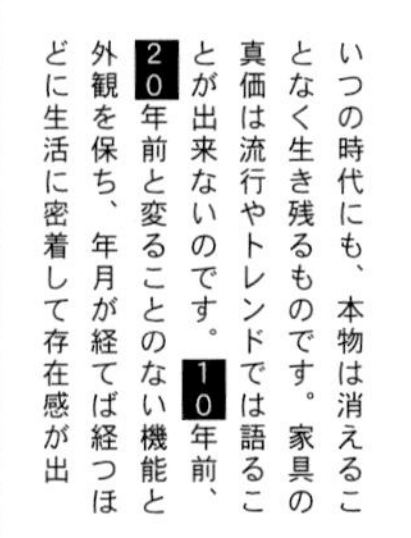

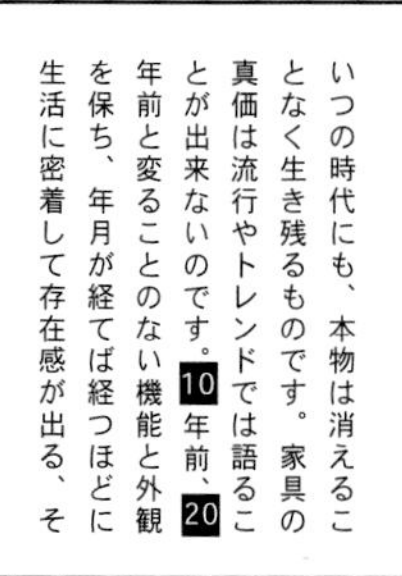

Vertical text in Standard direction and with Tate Chu Yoko option applied

Changing text orientation using the Text Orientation command

The Text Orientation command lets you change text from a horizontal orientation to a vertical orientation, and vice versa.

To change a text block orientation from horizontal to vertical, and vice versa:

1 Select a text block with any selection tool.

2 Choose either Type > Type Orientation > Horizontal or Type > Type Orientation > Vertical.

Horizontal text and vertical text

Using the Wari-Chu (divided note) option

The Wari-Chu option in the Character palette decreases the type size of selected text to a percentage of the original and stacks the type—horizontally or vertically, according to the orientation—on two lines.

Regardless of the point size of wari-chu text, the number of wari-chu lines is always two.

Selected text without and with Wari-Chu option applied

Note: *The Wari-Chu option does not work with path type and does not affect type entered on open or closed paths.*

To create a divided note with the Wari-Chu option:

1 Using any type tool, select the type to be divided.

2 Choose Type > Character. If the multilingual options are not visible, choose Show Multilingual from the Character palette menu.

3 Select the Wari-Chu option.

4 To change the wari-chu type size (as a percentage of the original point size), enter a percentage in the Scale text box (below the Wari-Chu option). The default is 50%.

Modifying letterforms as graphic objects

The Create Outlines command lets you turn type into a set of compound paths that you can edit and manipulate as you would any other graphic object. To use the Create Outlines command with a given typeface, you must have the Type 1 or TrueType font outlines for that typeface installed on your system.

The Create Outlines command retains all formatting of the selected type. It also retains the paint attributes of the type; for example, if the type is stroked, the outlines are also stroked.

You must convert all the type to outlines; you cannot convert a single letter within a string of type. To convert a single letter into an outline, create a separate piece of type containing only that letter.

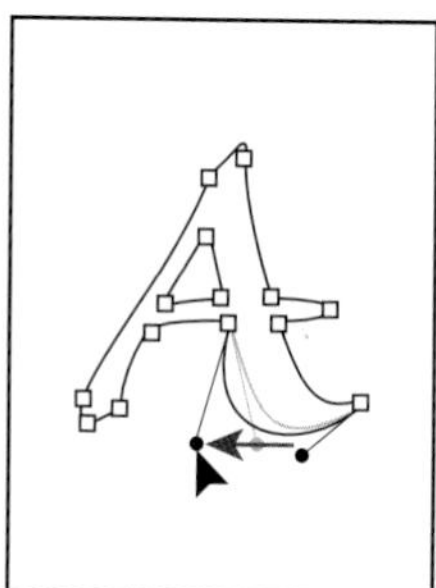

Editing type outlines

When you convert type to outlines, the type loses *hints*. Hints are instructions built into fonts that allow character shapes, especially subtle curves printed at small point sizes and low resolutions, to print as close to the designed character shape as possible. Type 1 and TrueType fonts contain hinting information. When you convert type to outlines, any hinting information in the font is lost and the objects may look jagged, chunky, or bolder.

Note: *Outline protected fonts cannot be converted to outlines.*

To convert type to path outlines:

1 Using any selection tool, select the type you want to convert.

2 Choose Type > Create Outlines.

If you select type outlines and choose Object > Compound Paths > Release, you can use the outlines as type containers.

To use several outlined letters as a mask:

1 Select all of the letters.

2 Choose Object > Compound Paths > Make.

3 Mask the letters. (See "Working with masks" on page 150.)

Working with columns of text

Adobe Illustrator provides several commands that make creating and working with columns or blocks of type easy. The various features enable you to import and export text from non-Illustrator files, link text so that it flows from one column to another, create sets of columns for text, wrap text so that it flows around a piece of artwork, and speed up the display of type when you don't need to read the text in your artwork.

Importing text files

You can import text files into the Adobe Illustrator program from other applications. Use the File > Open command to import text into a new file, or use the Place command to import type into the current file. (See Chapter 3, "Setting Up Artwork in Illustrator.")

Note: *You can paste text cut from another application that is now on the Clipboard. However, the styles and fonts are not retained.*

To import text using the Place command:

1 Select any type tool and define the point or area in which you want the imported text to appear. If no point is defined, Illustrator places the imported text into a box in the center of the window.

2 Choose File > Place.

3 Select the text file you want to open, and click Place. The text from the file you select flows into the type container.

Most of the styles you used in typing the original file are retained. If the original text is word wrapped and you import it as a point-type object, each paragraph appears on a single line.

Exporting text files

The Export command exports text from point type, type paths, and type containers to a new text file in one of many file formats supported by Illustrator (for example, Microsoft Word or Rich Text Format). (See Chapter 13, "Saving and Exporting Artwork.")

To export text:

1 Using a type tool, select the text to export.

2 Choose File > Export.

3 Select the desired file format in the Export File pop-up menu.

4 Enter the name of the new text file in the name box, and click Save.

Displaying overflow text

If a type container is too small, you cannot see all of the text within it. You can adjust the type container so that all of the text is visible.

To display all text:

Do one of the following:

- Adjust the size of the type container.
- Link the type container to another type container so that the overflow text flows into the second type container. Create one or more copies of the type container, if necessary.

Linking type containers

You can link type containers created with the type tool or the area-type tool. When you link type containers, the text flows from one type container to another to fill in blank areas in one type container. Thus, the text can fill several different objects, such as several columns or several irregular shapes.

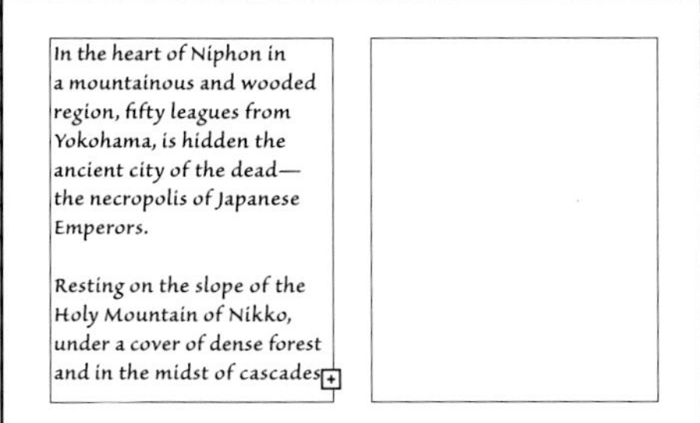

Unlinked type containers

In the heart of Niphon in a mountainous and wooded region, fifty leagues from Yokohama, is hidden the ancient city of the dead—the necropolis of Japanese Emperors.

Resting on the slope of the Holy Mountain of Nikko, under a cover of dense forest and in the midst of cascades

whose roar called them into existence, among the ferns and mosses and green dampness, over-arched by dark branches and bordered by the wildness and grandeur of Nature, lies this ancient structure. Here are both the living and the dead—an unforgettable setting of wilderness that serves as the final resting place for some

Linked type containers

Type flows from one object to another based on the type container's stacking order. Type flows first into the backmost object in the stacking order and continues to the next object in the stacking order. The most recently created object is frontmost. (See "Stacking objects" on page 123.)

The following options are available when working with linked type containers:

- You can change the order in which type flows by changing the stacking order of type containers using the Send to Front and Send to Back commands. You can adjust the stacking order before or after linking type.
- If you are working with type containers and you run out of room in a container, you can create a copy of the container for overflow type.
- You can also unlink type containers to change their stacking order without affecting the flow of type. Unlinking does not return the type to its original object and does not reflow the text. To return it to its original object, you must cut and paste the type. If you want to delete a single or unlinked type container without deleting the type within it, copy and paste the text elsewhere, and then delete the container.

To create a linked copy of a type container:

1 If you are not already in Artwork view, choose View > Artwork.

2 Select the group-selection tool (↖+) and position the pointer on the type container. Make sure the baselines aren't selected.

3 Alt-drag (Windows) or Option-drag (Mac OS) the copy of the container to its new position. Shift-drag to constrain the tool to multiples of 45 degrees.

4 When the new type container is in position, release the mouse button, and then Shift+Alt (Windows) or Shift+Option (Mac OS). You must release the mouse button *before* you release the keys.

The type flows from the first type container to the second, and the two type containers are linked.

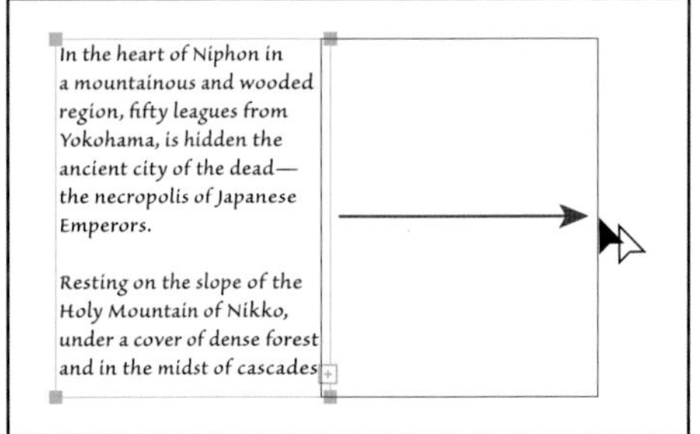

Alt-drag/Option-drag to create linked copy.

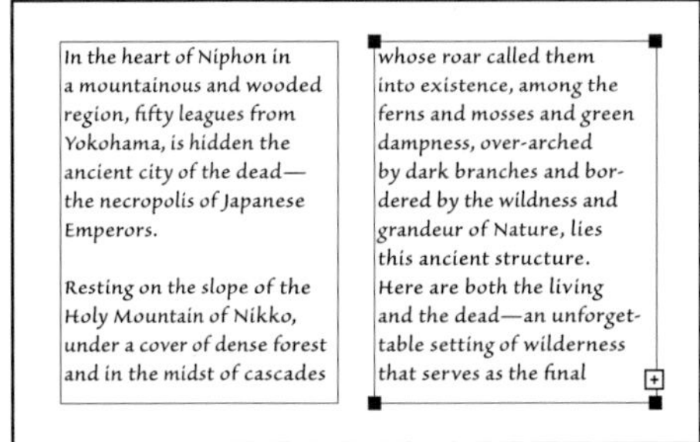

Type linked automatically

You can choose Object > Transform > Transform Again to create additional columns.

To link or unlink type containers:

1 Select the selection tool ( ).

2 Drag a marquee through the type containers to be linked, or Shift-click with the selection tool. The baselines should be selected.

3 Choose either Type > Blocks > Link or Type > Blocks > Unlink.

To remove or replace a linked type container without deleting the type:

1 Select the group-selection tool ( ).

2 Click the edge of the type container you want to remove.

3 Click Delete. The type container you selected disappears, and the type that it contained flows into the next grouped or linked object in the stacking order.

4 To add a new type container, create or select a type container, select the group-selection tool, and Shift-click the type container to which you want to link the new type container. Then choose Type > Blocks > Link. The type flows into the new type container.

Creating rows and columns

By using the Rows & Columns dialog box, you can divide rectangles and text blocks into blocks of rows and columns and precisely change the height, width, and gutter size between rows and columns. The Rows & Columns dialog box can also be used to change the way in which text flows (from left-to-right or right-to-left for both vertical and horizontal text) by clicking the Text Flow buttons.

It is also possible to create rows and columns of linked type containers. (See "Linking type containers" on page 275.)

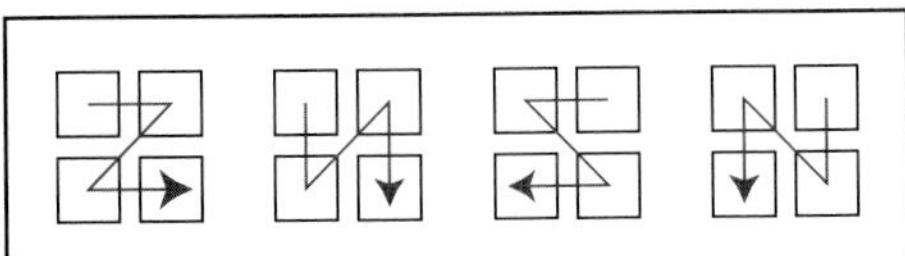

Horizontal text left to right; vertical text left to right; horizontal text right to left; vertical text right to left

Because the rows and columns created are simply graphic objects unless they contain type, you can also use the Rows & Columns dialog box to create rectangles. Select an existing rectangle and divide it into multiple rectangles using the dialog box.

In addition, using the Rows & Columns dialog box is a fast way to create guides for laying out artwork. (See "Using guides" on page 109.)

To divide a rectangular graphic object or type container into rows and columns:

1 Using the selection tool ( ), select a rectangle or type container. If the selected object is not rectangular, it is converted into rows and columns based on the object's rectangular bounding box.

2 Choose Type > Rows & Columns.

3 Enter the number of columns you want in the Number (Columns) text box, and the number of rows you want in the Number (Rows) text box. You can either enter the number in the text boxes or use the buttons on the sides of the text boxes to increase or decrease the values. The dialog box adjusts the column-width and row-height values to fill the selected text box.

4 Change the dimensions of the column width, row height, column gutter, row gutter, or overall width and height by entering a new value in the corresponding text box or by using the buttons to increase or decrease the values.

5 Do any of the following:

- To change the direction of vertical or horizontal text flow from left-to-right or right-to-left, click the Text Flow buttons.
- To preview the effect, select Preview.
- To add path guides along the row and column edges, select Add Guides.

6 Click OK.

Wrapping type around a graphic object

You can make type wrap around a graphic object (except a brush object), including type paths and compound paths, by using the Make Wrap command. You must use area type when wrapping type around a path; point type and path type do not wrap around an object. You can make one or several type containers wrap around any number of objects.

To wrap type around a graphic object:

1 Make sure that the object or objects around which you want to wrap type are in front of the type. If necessary, use either the Bring to Front or Paste in Front command to position the objects in front.

2 If desired, use any of the drawing tools to outline a graphic boundary for the area around which the type wraps. (This is necessary if you want to wrap text around a placed EPS file or bitmap image.) If the boundary is stroked or filled, it must be behind the graphic element but in front of the type.

You can use an unpainted graphic boundary to control how closely type wraps around an object. A boundary is useful to wrap type around a large type container consisting of a single piece of type, such as a large initial capital letter. You can then adjust and resize the unpainted boundary using a selection tool to achieve the exact kind of text wrap you want.

3 Using the selection tool (➤), select the type containers that you want to wrap and the graphic object around which to wrap them.

4 Choose Type > Wrap > Make. The type wraps around the graphic object.

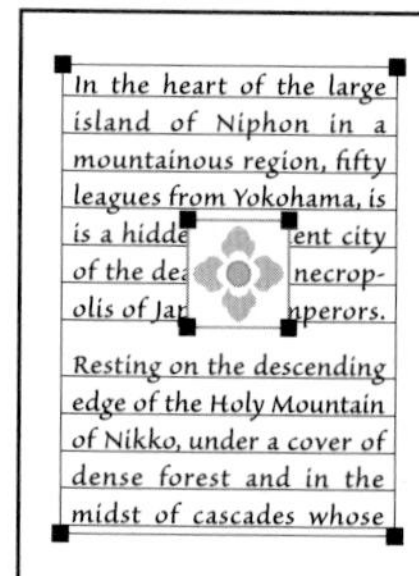

In the heart of the large island of Niphon in a mountainous region, fifty leagues from Yokohama, is a hidden ancient city of the dead—the necropolis of Japanese Emperors.

Resting on the descending edge of the Holy Mountain of Nikko, under a cover of of dense forest, in the midst

Type containers and graphic boundary selected and with Make Wrap command applied

To separate a wrapped type container from a graphic object:

1 Select the type container or graphic object.

2 Choose Type > Wrap > Release.

Greeking type below a specified font size

Adobe Illustrator *greeks*—displays as a dimmed bar—type below a specified type size, as set in the Greeking Limit text box in the Type & Auto Tracing Preferences dialog box. Any type at or below the specified type size is replaced on-screen with non-letterforms that act as placeholders in the artwork. Greeking type affects only artwork displayed on-screen, not the printed image.

In the heart of the large island of Niphon and in a mountainous and wooded region, fifty leagues from Yokohama, lies hidden the ancient city of the dead—the necropolis of Japanese Emperors.

Resting on the descending ing edge of the Holy Mountain Nikko, below the shelter of dense forest, in

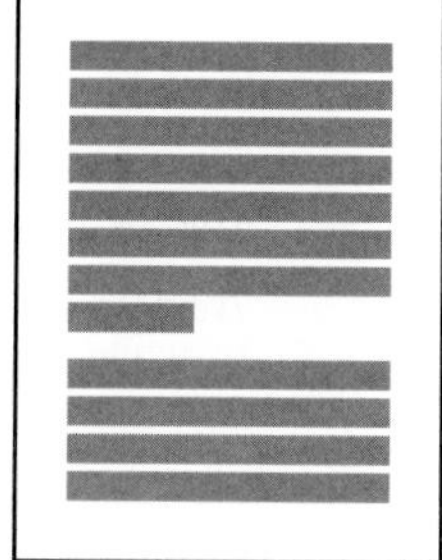

Type above greek type limit and below

In addition, if you reduce the document view so that type on-screen falls below the greek type limit, the type appears greeked. For example, if the greek type limit is set at 6 points, 12-point type viewed at a 50% zoom level appears greeked.

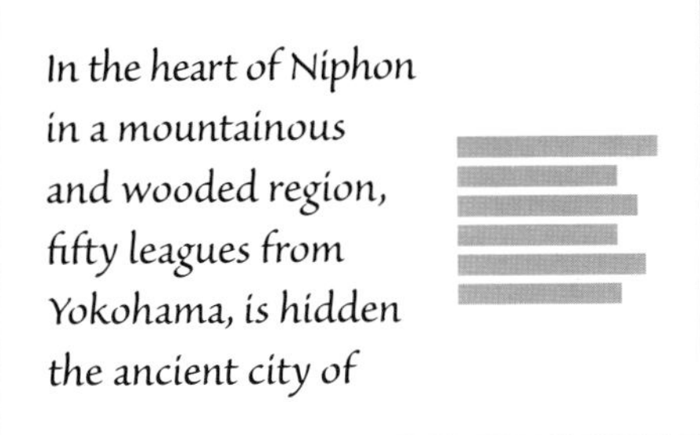

12-point type at actual size and at 50% zoom level

To set the greek type limit:

1 Choose File > Preferences > Type & Auto Tracing.

2 Enter a value in points in the Greeking text box, and click OK.

Formatting columns and paragraphs

The Paragraph palette includes a number of features especially useful for working with larger groups of type, such as type laid out within columns. These functions enable you to set the paragraph indentation and text alignment, change the amount of space between paragraphs, set tab marks, and fit type to fill a set width. You can even specify where words break in paragraphs, using the hyphenation feature.

To open the Paragraph palette:

Choose Type > Paragraph. If the paragraph options are not visible, choose Show Options from the Paragraph palette menu.

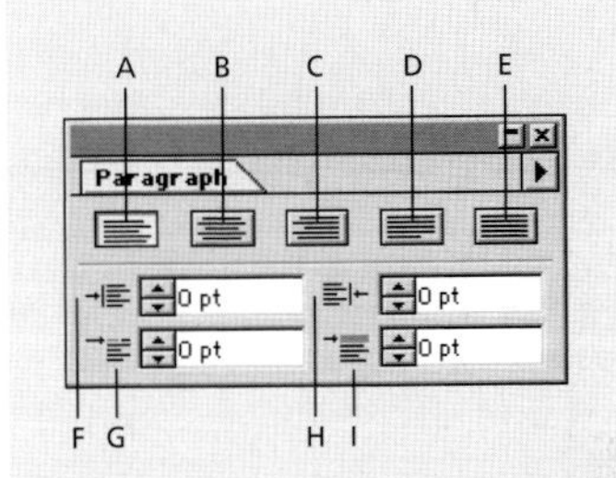

***A.** Align left **B.** Align center **C.** Align right **D.** Justify full lines **E.** Justify all lines **F.** Left indent **G.** First line left indent **H.** Right indent **I.** Space before paragraph*

Specifying paragraph indentation

Indentation specifies the amount of space between the ends of each line of type and the path that contains that type. You can indent from the left or the right side of the path, and you can choose additional indentation for the first line of a paragraph. Negative indentation moves the type outside the margin.

***Note:** The First line left indent and the Left indent on the Paragraph palette also appear on the Tab Ruler palette as small triangles. (See "Using the Tab Ruler palette" on page 288.)*

Indentation is measured in the units specified in the Type pop-up menu in the Units & Undo Preferences dialog box and is selected using the Paragraph palette.

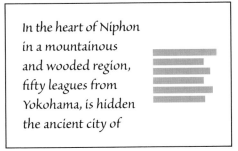

Indentation affects only the selected paragraph or paragraphs, so you can easily set different indentations for paragraphs.

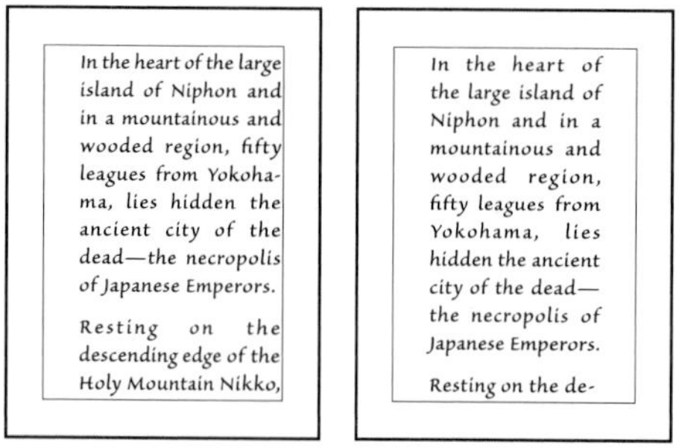

In the heart of the large island of Niphon and in a mountainous and wooded region, fifty leagues from Yokohama, lies hidden the ancient city of the dead—the necropolis of Japanese Emperors.

Resting on the descending edge of the Holy Mountain Nikko,

In the heart of the large island of Niphon and in a mountainous and wooded region, fifty leagues from Yokohama, lies hidden the ancient city of the dead—the necropolis of Japanese Emperors.

Resting on the de-

Left indentation and left-and-right indentation

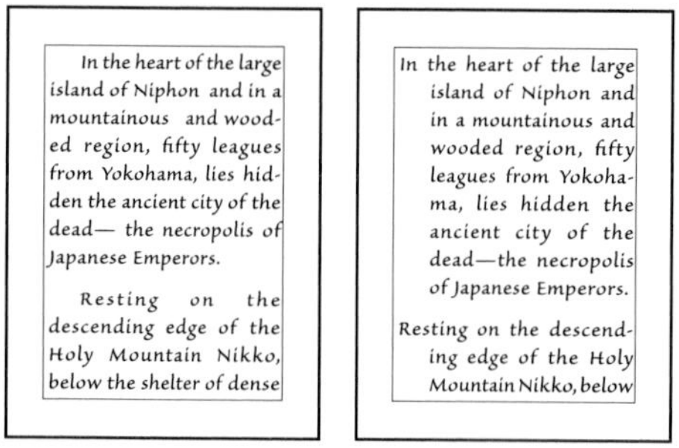

In the heart of the large island of Niphon and in a mountainous and wooded region, fifty leagues from Yokohama, lies hidden the ancient city of the dead— the necropolis of Japanese Emperors.

Resting on the descending edge of the Holy Mountain Nikko, below the shelter of dense

In the heart of the large island of Niphon and in a mountainous and wooded region, fifty leagues from Yokohama, lies hidden the ancient city of the dead—the necropolis of Japanese Emperors.

Resting on the descending edge of the Holy Mountain Nikko, below

First line indentation and hanging indentation

To specify paragraph indentation:

1 Select any type container or type path using a selection tool, or set an insertion point, or select a block of type using the type tools.

2 Choose Type > Paragraph.

3 Select the indentation text box you want to change: Left indent, Right indent, or First line left indent.

4 Enter an indentation value.

To create a first line hanging indentation, type a negative value in the First line left indent text box.

5 Press Enter (Windows) or Return (Mac OS) or Tab.

Specifying alignment options

Alignment controls how lines of type are arranged in paragraphs. Each paragraph (or line in point type) can be aligned left, right, centered, or justified.

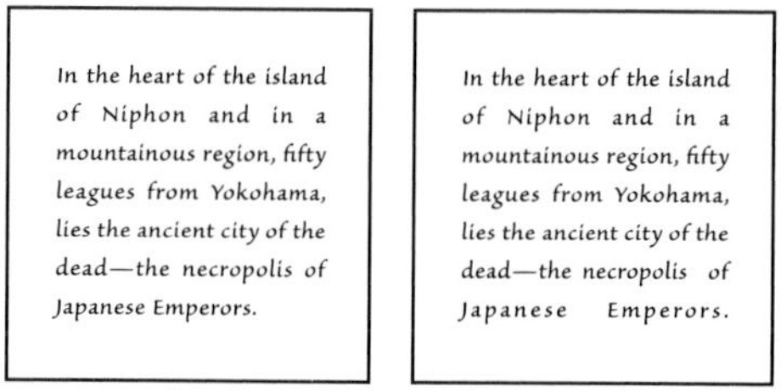

In the heart of the island of Niphon and in a mountainous region, fifty leagues from Yokohama, lies the ancient city of the dead—the necropolis of Japanese Emperors.

In the heart of the island of Niphon and in a mountainous region, fifty leagues from Yokohama, lies the ancient city of the dead—the necropolis of Japanese Emperors.

Justify full lines and Justify all lines

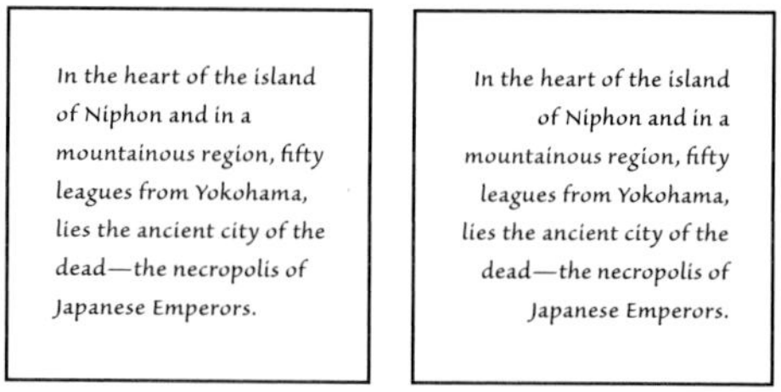

In the heart of the island of Niphon and in a mountainous region, fifty leagues from Yokohama, lies the ancient city of the dead—the necropolis of Japanese Emperors.

In the heart of the island of Niphon and in a mountainous region, fifty leagues from Yokohama, lies the ancient city of the dead—the necropolis of Japanese Emperors.

Align left and Align right

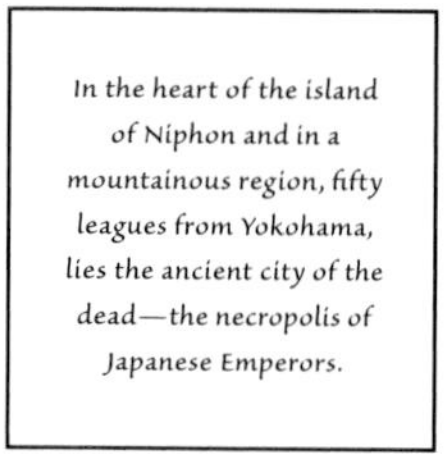

In the heart of the island of Niphon and in a mountainous region, fifty leagues from Yokohama, lies the ancient city of the dead—the necropolis of Japanese Emperors.

Align center

Justify All Lines justifies all the type and forces the last line in a paragraph to be justified to both margins. By default, the last line of a justified paragraph is left aligned with a ragged right margin.

To change alignment options from the Paragraph palette:

1 Do one of the following:

• Select any type container or type path using a selection tool.

• Set an insertion point or select a block of type using the type tools.

2 Choose Type > Paragraph.

3 Click the alignment style you want.

Specifying hanging punctuation

Hanging punctuation controls whether punctuation marks fall inside or outside the margins. Hanging punctuation is controlled by the Hang Punctuation option in the Paragraph palette. If hanging punctuation is turned on, the following characters appear outside the margins: periods, commas, single-quotation marks, double-quotation marks, apostrophes, hyphens, em dashes, en dashes, colons, and semicolons.

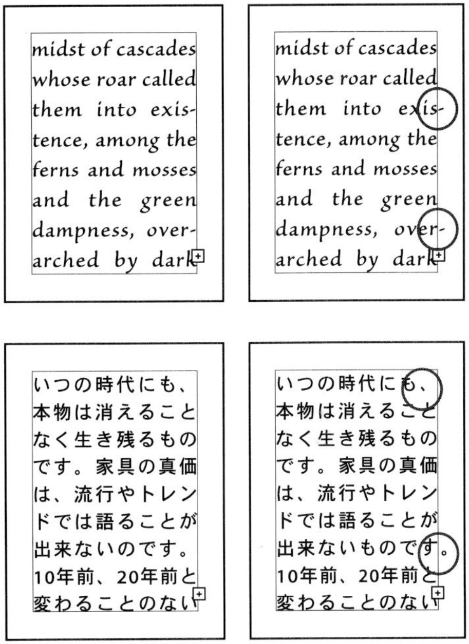

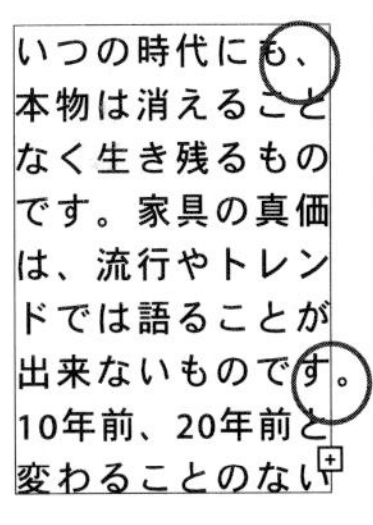

Paragraphs without (left) and with (right) hanging punctuation

Punctuation hangs when text is aligned right, aligned left, centered, or justified. When a punctuation character is followed by an end quotation mark, both characters hang.

If you select Hang Punctuation on 2-byte text, punctuation hangs only when there is no room to adjust spacing and prevent hanging; otherwise, punctuation does not hang. You can ensure that punctuation always hangs by also deselecting the Punctuation Hangs Only If Space Unavailable option in the Paragraph palette menu. (See "Using the Kinsoku Shori (line breaking) option" on page 285.)

To select hanging punctuation:

1 Select any type container or type path using a selection tool, or set an insertion point, or select a block of type using the type tools.

2 Choose Type > Paragraph. If the paragraph options are not visible, choose Show Options from the Paragraph palette menu.

3 Select the Hang Punctuation option.

Specifying spacing options

Spacing options control the word spacing and letterspacing in lines of justified or unjustified type. In unjustified type, you can adjust the word spacing without affecting the letterspacing. The Word Spacing and Letter Spacing options apply primarily to justified type, although you can also apply spacing to unjustified type.

Spacing options are always applied to an entire paragraph. To adjust the spacing in a few characters but not an entire paragraph, use the Tracking option.

To change spacing in type:

1 Select any type container or type path using a selection tool, or set an insertion point.

2 Choose Type > Paragraph. If the Word Spacing and the Letter Spacing options are not visible, choose Show Options from the Paragraph palette menu.

3 Do one of the following:

- To change the amount of space between words in a line of type, enter minimum, desired, and maximum values in the Word Spacing text boxes. (If the text is not justified, only the Desired text box is available.) For justified type, the default values for word spacing are 100% minimum, 100% desired, and 200% maximum. At 100%, no additional space is added between words.

- To change the amount of space between letters in a line of type, enter minimum, desired, and maximum values in the Letter Spacing text boxes. (If the text is not justified, only the Desired text box is available.) The default values for letter-spacing are 0% minimum, 0% desired, and 5% maximum. At 0%, no space is added between letters.

Word spacing and letterspacing are both measured as percentages of the width of a space in the selected type size.

In the heart of the large island of Niphon and in a mountainous and wooded region, fifty leagues from Yokohama, lies hidden the ancient city of the dead—the necropolis of Japanese Emperors.	In the heart of the large island of Niphon and in a mountainous and wooded region, fifty leagues from Yokohama, lies hidden the the ancient city of the dead—the necropo-

Default word spacing and word spacing increased

In the heart of the large island of Niphon and in a mountainous and wooded region, fifty leagues from Yokohama, lies hidden the ancient city of the dead—the necropolis of Japanese Emperors.	In the heart of the large island of Niphon and in a mountain-ous and wooded region, fifty leagues from Yokohama, lies hid-den the ancient city ofthedead—thenecropolis

Default letterspacing and letterspacing increased

Using the Tsume (proportional spacing) option

Most CJK characters are traditionally monospaced; that is, each character is the same horizontal width (and height when using vertical text) as all other characters. Some fonts, however, use built-in proportional spacing to account for differing widths among characters.

You can change the default monospacing to proportional width (and height) spacing for text by using the Tsume option in the Character palette.

本物は消えることなく生き残るものです。家具の真価は流行やtrendでは語ることが出来ないのです。時を超え、時代を越えても変わることのない機能と概観を保ち、年月が経てば経つほど益々、生活に密着して存在感	本物は消えることなく生き残るものです。家具の真価は流行やtrendでは語ることが出来ないのです。時を超え、時代を越えても変わることのない機能と概観を保ち、年月が経てば経つほど益々、生活に密着して存在感が出る、そん

Default monospacing of CJK font and Tsume option applied

You can change monospaced text into proportionally spaced text with the following fonts:

- Type 1 CID fonts (Mac OS), which contain the proportional width data.
- Type 1 OCF fonts (Mac OS) with associated files containing proportional width tables. These files, with the suffix .SBX, provide proportional width functionality with some applications, such as Illustrator.
- Japanese TrueType fonts shipped with KanjiTalk 7.5 and later (Mac OS).

To use proportional spacing between CJK characters:

1 Select the text to which you want to apply proportional spacing.

2 Choose Type > Character. If the multilingual options are not visible, choose Show Multilingual from the Character palette menu.

3 Select the Tsume option.

Using the Moji Gumi (Japanese layout rules) option

The Moji Gumi option in the Character palette lets you specify the amount of spacing placed between CJK characters and punctuation, or between Roman characters and CJK characters. By changing the percentage of space between different types of characters, the Moji Gumi option eliminates spacing problems that can arise when using a mixture of these characters in a single file.

When the Moji Gumi option is used with the Tsume option, proportional spacing is applied first, followed by the Japanese layout rules.

To specify Japanese layout rules:

1 Select the text to which you want to apply layout rules.

2 Choose Type > Character. If the multilingual options aren't visible, choose Show Multilingual from the Character palette menu.

3 Select the Moji Gumi option.

4 To change the spacing between CJK characters and punctuation marks (such as parentheses) in the text, enter a spacing percentage, from 0% to 200%, in the CJK/CJK text box.

A value of 100% is standard spacing, a value of 0% eliminates the extra space between characters, and a value of 200% doubles the standard spacing.

私たちは、「本当に
機能的な家具には
空間や時間のメリッ
トはない。」という
信念を持っていま
す。流行やトレンド
に流されることな
く、常に変わること
のない機能と外観

私たちは、「本当
に機能的な家具に
は空間や時間のメ
リットはない。」
という信念を持っ
ています。流行や
トレンドに流され
ることなく、常に
変わることのない

CJK/CJK text setting of 0% and 200%

5 To change the spacing between CJK characters and Roman characters, enter a spacing percentage, from 0% to 200%, in the CJK/Roman text box.

私たちは、「本当に
機能的な家具には
空間や時間のメリッ
トはない。」という
信念を持っていま
す。流行やTrendに
流されることなく、
常に変わることの
ない機能と外観を

私たちは、「本当に
機能的な家具には
空間や時間のメリッ
トはない。」という
信念を持っていま
す。流行や Trend
に流されることな
く、常に変わること
のない機能と外観

CJK/Roman value of 0% and 200%

Using the Kinsoku Shori (line breaking) option

Where a line breaks in CJK text is generally determined by the boundaries of the text bounding box, the size of the characters, and the amount of spacing between the characters. In general, a line breaks when there is no more room for the next character.

Illustrator allows for control of characters that must not end a line, begin a line, or be divided over two lines. Selecting the Kinsoku Shori option and by using the options in the Kinsoku Shori dialog box, you can control how these characters are handled during line breaking, and you can choose which sets of characters to include. For example, you can have a line of text compressed to accommodate a punctuation mark (such as an end quotation mark), which must remain on the same line as the text it encloses.

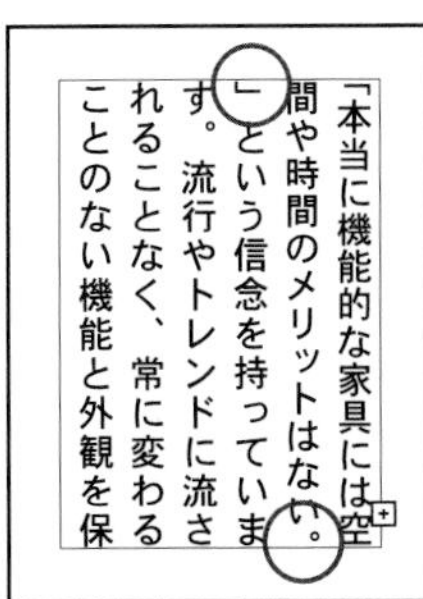

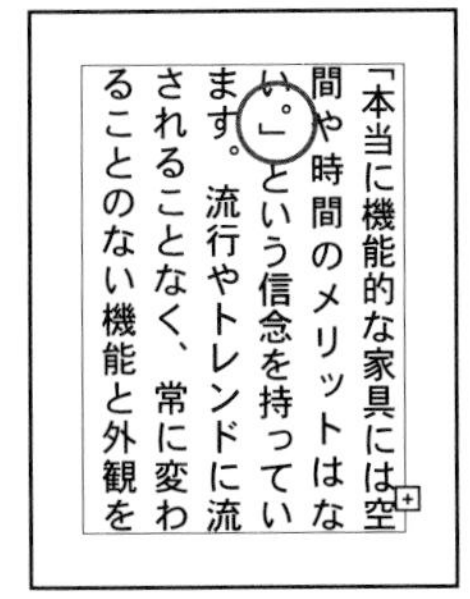

Kinsoku Shori option unselected and selected

To specify a character set for breaking lines:

1 Choose Type > Paragraph. If the paragraph options aren't visible, choose Show Options from the Paragraph palette menu.

2 Select the Kinsoku Shori option.

3 In the Kinsoku Shori pop-up menu, choose a character set to which to apply line breaking rules.

• Hard includes all characters that should not begin or end a line.

• Soft includes a subset of the hard characters. This option is selected by default.

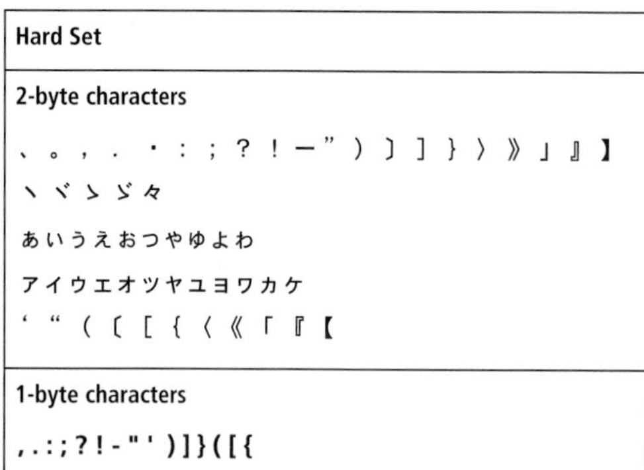

Hard Set
2-byte characters
、。，．・：；？！ー”）〕］｝〉》」』】
ヽヾゝゞ々
ぁぃぅぇぉっゃゅょゎ
ァィゥェォッャュョヮヵヶ
‘“（〔［｛〈《「『【
1-byte characters
,.:;?!-"')]}([{

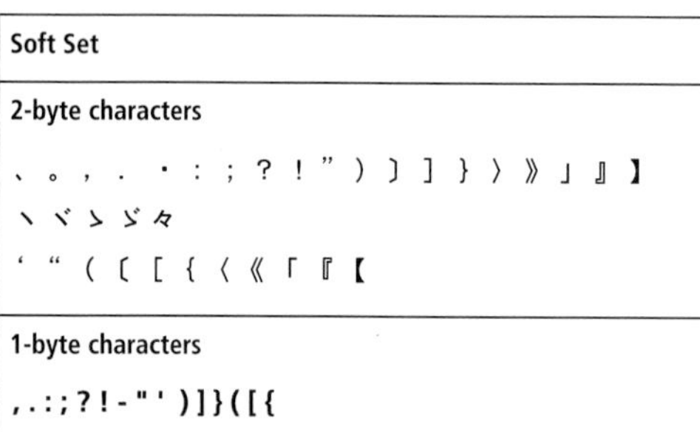

Soft Set
2-byte characters
、。，．・：；？！”）〕］｝〉》」』】
ヽヾゝゞ々
‘“（〔［｛〈《「『【
1-byte characters
,.:;?!-"')]}([{

Characters included in Hard set and Soft set

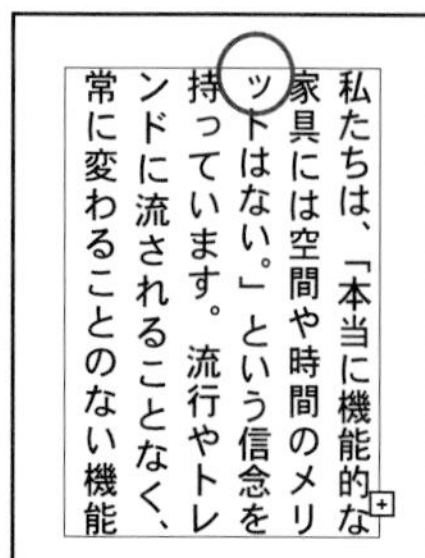

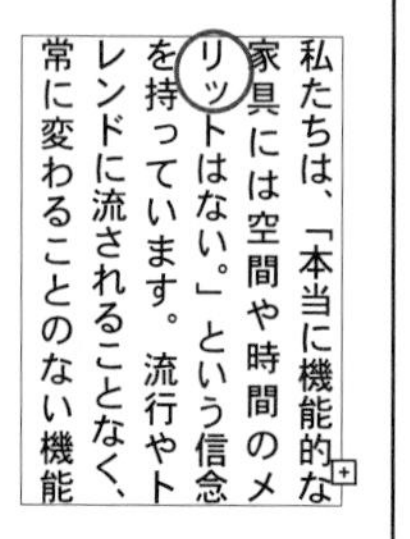

Soft option selected and Hard option selected

***Note:** With the addition of single-byte characters, the Soft set is consistent with the set included in the Kinsoku Shori option of Adobe Illustrator 5.5J; the Hard set is consistent with the set of Adobe Illustrator 7.x.*

To set line breaking options:

1 Choose Type > Paragraph. If the paragraph options aren't visible, choose Show Options from the Paragraph palette menu.

2 Choose Kinsoku Shori from the Paragraph palette menu.

3 Select options to apply to the character set selected in the Kinsoku Shori option in the Paragraph palette:

• Oikomi Maximum Spacing includes the character on the same line and condenses all characters evenly to fit on the line (when text is justified). In the text box, enter a maximum value by which to condense text. When the option is unselected, the character is moved to the next line and characters on the original line are evenly spaced to fill the width (or height) of the line. This option is selected by default.

• Don't Condense Space After Punctuation keeps spacing after a two-byte period uncondensed. This option is unselected by default.

• Bunri Kinshi Moji Shori includes the .. , ... , and — characters in the set of characters (Soft or Hard) to which line breaking rules are applied. This option is unselected by default.

• Delete Space Between Bunri Kinshi Moji closes up space between the .. , ... , and -- characters. This option is unselected by default.

• Hang Punctuation Only If Space Unavailable ensures that text always hangs. This option is selected by default.

4 Click OK.

About the Punctuation Hangs Only If Space Unavailable option

When the Hang Punctuation option is selected in the Paragraph palette, the Punctuation Hangs Only If Space Unavailable option is available and selected in the Kinsoku Shori dialog box. When this option is unselected, text hangs under any circumstance. If you want punctuation to hang only when there is no room to adjust spacing and prevent hanging, select the Hang Punctuation Only If Space Unavailable option.

***Note:** When you open a file created or saved in Illustrator 7.0 and the Punctuation Hangs Only If Space Unavailable option is unselected, text in the file is reformatted.*

Working with repeated characters

You can control how repeated characters in Japanese text are handled using the Kurikaeshi Moji Shori option in the Paragraph palette. By default, a repeat character mark is substituted for the second character when two identical characters follow one after the other in a body of text. When this option is selected, both characters are displayed if they are separated by a line break.

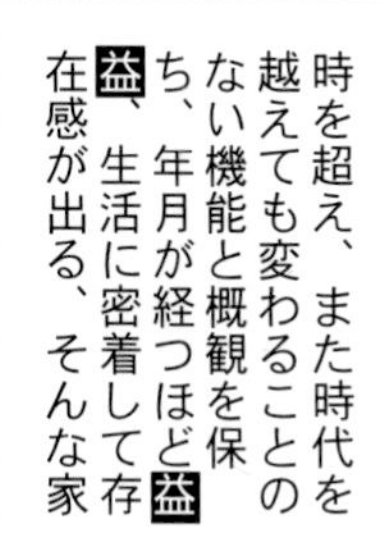

Kurikaeshi Moji Shori option turned off and on

To use repeated character processing:

1 Using any type tool, select a paragraph of text to which you want to apply repeated character processing. If no text exists, the setting applies to new text typed.

2 Choose Type > Paragraph. If the paragraph options aren't visible, choose Show Options from the Paragraph palette menu.

3 Select the Kurikaeshi Moji Shori option.

Using the Tab Ruler palette

The Tab Ruler palette lets you quickly set left, right, center, and decimal-point tabs in horizontal type, and top, bottom, center, and decimal-point tabs in vertical type (up to 15 tab stops). When you set tabs, a visual tab guide appears in the selected type to help you set them, even when the type path is rotated or wrapped. The units of measure for the tab ruler are defined by the General units specified in the Units & Undo Preferences dialog box (for all files) or by the units specified in the Document Setup dialog box (for the current file).

When using the Tab Ruler for vertical type, the Tab Ruler appears in a vertical format. When used for horizontal type, the Tab Ruler appears in a horizontal format.

To set tabs in text:

1 Do one of the following:

• Select any type container or type path using a selection tool.

• Set an insertion point or select a range of text using type tools.

2 Choose Type > Tab Ruler.

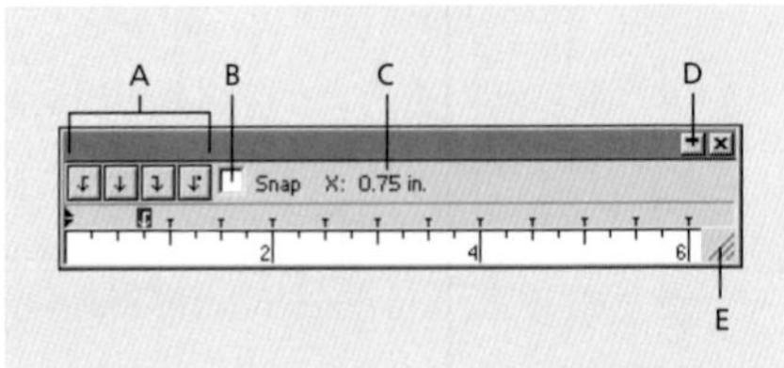

A. Tab style buttons ***B.*** *Snap option* ***C.*** *Tab position* ***D.*** *Alignment box (Windows only)* ***E.*** *Extend Tab Ruler button*

3 Do one of the following:

• Click the Alignment box (Windows only) at the upper right of the palette to align the Tab Ruler with the left margin of the selected text for horizontal type, or with the top margin for vertical type.

• Drag the Extend Tab Ruler button at the lower right of the palette to extend the ruler.

• Select Snap to snap tabs to ruler units as you drag them. You can also Ctrl-drag (Windows) or Command-drag (Mac OS) tabs to turn Snap on or off temporarily.

4 Click the Tab Ruler where you want the tab to appear. The tab position (relative to the left margin of the selected horizontal text or the top margin of the vertical text) appears in the top center of the palette.

5 Select a type tool, and click to set an insertion point in the text. Then press Tab to move the text to the next tab.

To change an existing tab setting:

1 With the Tab Ruler palette open, click a tab mark to highlight it. Click a Tab Style button to change the tab style:

• Left-Justified Tab aligns horizontal text to the left, keeping the right margin ragged.

• Center-Justified Tab centers text on the tab mark.

• Right-Justified Tab aligns horizontal text to the right, keeping the left margin ragged.

• Bottom-Justified Tab aligns vertical text to the bottom margin, keeping the top margin ragged.

• Decimal-Justified Tab places text in alignment with a decimal point (useful for creating columns of numbers).

2 Do any of the following:

• To move a tab, drag it to a new position. As you drag, a line indicates where the tab is moving in the text.

• To remove default tabs, drag to the right (horizontal text) or toward the bottom (vertical text).

• To replace default tabs, drag to the left (horizontal text) or to the top (vertical text).

• To move all tab stops simultaneously to the right/bottom of the selected tab, Shift-drag the tab stop.

• To remove a tab, drag it off the top right or left side of the ruler.

Fitting headline type

Illustrator lets you fit type across the full width of a type path in an object by using the Fit Headline command. The Fit Headline command was designed to work with Adobe Multiple Master fonts by adjusting the weight of the font and the tracking value when distributing type along a path. However, the Fit Headline command also works with other fonts by adjusting only the tracking value. (See "Specifying kerning and tracking" on page 264.)

If you change the tracking value or the type, be sure to reapply the Fit Headline command.

THE JADE PALACE In the heart of the large island of Niphon and in a mountainous and wooded region, fifty leagues from Yokohama, lies hidden the ancient city of the dead—the necropolis of Japanese Emperors. Resting on the descending edge of the Holy Mountain Nikko, below the shelter of	**THE JADE PALACE** In the heart of the large island of Niphon and in a mountainous and wooded region, fifty leagues from Yokohama, lies hidden the ancient city of the dead—the necropolis of Japanese Emperors. Resting on the descending edge of the Holy Mountain Nikko, below the shelter of

Multiple Master headline font and Fit Headline command applied

To fit headline type across a specified area:

1 Enter type in a type container using a type tool (T) or an area-type tool (T).

2 Select the type using any type tool.

3 Choose Type > Fit Headline.

Hyphenating words

The autohyphenation feature automatically hyphenates words where appropriate at the ends of lines. You can set the hyphenation parameters in the Paragraph palette. When you select the autohyphenation option, you can specify the minimum number of letters allowed at the beginning or end of a hyphenated word. You can also limit the number of consecutive hyphenated lines.

You can enter a *discretionary hyphen* to hyphenate a word manually. Illustrator always breaks a word at a discretionary hyphen, regardless of the autohyphenation setting.

You can also specify the hyphenation for a specific word or exclude a word from being hyphenated by using the Hyphenation Options command.

In addition, you can select the language in which the hyphenation exception takes place.

To enter a discretionary hyphen:

1 Select a type tool, and click where you want to enter the hyphen.

2 Press Shift+Ctrl+hyphen (Windows) or Shift+Command+hyphen (Mac OS).

To set the autohyphenation feature:

1 Choose Type > Paragraph.

2 Click Auto Hyphenate. If the option is not visible, choose Show Options from the Paragraph palette menu.

3 Choose Hyphenation from the Paragraph palette menu.

4 In the Hyphenate text boxes, enter the minimum number of letters allowed from the beginning and end of a hyphenated word.

5 If desired, enter the maximum number of consecutive hyphenated lines in the Limit Consecutive Hyphens To text box.

6 Click OK.

To specify how a word is hyphenated in Illustrator:

1 Choose File > Preferences > Hyphenation Options.

2 If desired, choose the language in which the hyphenation rules apply (to new text typed) from the Languages pop-up menu. When you select a different language, the rules for hyphenating words change to match that language's rules.

You can also change the hyphenation language for just the selected text by using the Languages pop-up menu in the Character palette. (If the pop-up menu isn't visible, choose Show Multilingual from the Character palette menu.) Doing so is useful for hyphenating multilingual projects easily, such as a brochure with instructions in several languages.

3 Enter the word for which you want to specify hyphenation characteristics. If you enter the word with no hyphens inserted, Illustrator never hyphenates the word. If you enter the word with one or more hyphens inserted, Illustrator hyphenates the word only at those places.

4 Click Add.

5 To remove a word from the hyphenation list, click the word to select it, and press Backspace or Del (Windows) or Delete (Mac OS).

Note: *Hyphenation information is saved with the application, and not with the file. For example, if you use the file on a different computer that has different hyphenation exceptions, your text may hyphenate differently.*

Editing text

Once you have selected type, you can use any standard word-processing method to edit the text.

You can use the Cut, Copy, Paste, Clear, and Select All commands in the Edit menu to copy type from Illustrator to other applications, to bring type from another application into an Illustrator file, or to edit type within an Illustrator file. When you use the Copy command to copy type to and from other applications, you copy only the characters, not the styles.

Illustrator also includes commands designed specifically for editing blocks of type. These tools enable you to check your spelling, find and replace text, modify capitalization, and add typographically correct punctuation marks in your text.

Checking spelling

The Check Spelling command compiles a list of misspelled words in a file and offers a list of alternative spellings. If Illustrator has incorrectly identified a word as misspelled, you can either skip the word without changing it in the file or add the word to the dictionary list. These new words are then added to the custom file AI User Dictionary in the Text Filters folder in the Plug-ins folder. You can edit this list of words as well.

Note: *The Check Spelling command can be used only with Roman fonts; CJK fonts cannot be spell checked with the Check Spelling command.*

To check the spelling in a file:

1 Choose Type > Check Spelling.

The Check Spelling dialog box displays a list of words not found in the current Adobe Illustrator dictionary.

2 To list separately words that are misspelled in the same way but that are in different cases (such as *Mispell* and *mispell*), select the Case Sensitive option.

3 To see a list of alternative spellings for a misspelled word, click the word in the Misspelled Words list. The first instance of that word is highlighted in your file, and any alternative spellings appear in the Suggested Corrections list.

4 Do one of the following:

• To enter a new spelling for a misspelled word, either click the correct spelling in the Suggested Corrections text box or type the corrected spelling in the text box. To change the first instance of the misspelled word in the file, click Change or double-click the correct word. To change every instance of the selected misspelled word in the file, select the correct word, and click Change All.

• To skip a word without changing it, click Skip. To skip every instance of the word in the file, click Skip All. This option removes the word from the Misspelled Words list, but the word reappears the next time the file is checked.

• To add the word to your dictionary, click Add to List. To add several words at once, hold down Ctrl (Windows) or Shift+Command (Mac OS) while clicking or dragging the mouse to select the words.

5 To edit your current dictionary list, click Edit List and do one of the following:

• To change a word in the dictionary list, select a word in the list, retype it in the text box, and click Change.

• To add a new word, type it in the text box, and click Add.

• To remove a word, select the word, and click Remove.

6 Click Done.

To change language dictionaries in the Spell Checking filter:

1 Choose Type > Check Spelling.

2 Click Language. Locate the language dictionary in the Text Filters folder in the Plug-ins folder inside the Adobe Illustrator folder.

3 Select the language dictionary you want to use, and click Open.

Finding and replacing text

The Find command finds and replaces text strings on paths and within type containers while retaining the type style, color, kerning, and other type attributes of the text.

To find and replace text:

1 Choose Type > Find/Change.

2 Enter the text string you want to find and, if desired, the text string with which to replace it.

3 Select one of the following options:

• Whole Word searches only for entire words that match the text in the Find text box.

• Case Sensitive searches only for text strings that exactly match the uppercase and lowercase text in the Find text box.

• Search Backward searches the file in reverse order from the insertion point to the beginning of the file.

• Wrap Around searches the entire file, starting from the text selection point to the end of the file and then from the beginning of the file to the text selection point.

4 Select one of the following options:

• Find Next searches for the next instance of the text string, without replacing it.

• Change/Find replaces the text string and then searches for the next instance of it.

• Change replaces just the currently found instance of the text string in the file.

• Change All replaces all occurrences of the text string in the file.

5 Click Done.

Changing capitalization

The Change Case command enables you to change text from the current case setting to all uppercase, all lowercase, or mixed case (that is, each word beginning with an uppercase letter).

Note: *The Change Case command only works with 1-byte Roman text. CJK Roman (2-byte) text is not affected.*

To change the capitalization of selected text:

1 Select a type tool, and select the text to be changed.

2 Choose Type > Change Case.

3 Select Uppercase, Lowercase, or Mixed Case, and click OK.

Using smart punctuation

The Smart Punctuation dialog box searches for keyboard text symbols and replaces them with publishing text symbols. It can also report the number of symbols replaced.

To replace standard keyboard characters with publishing characters:

1 Choose Type > Smart Punctuation.

2 Select one or more of the following options:

• V, W, Y Ligatures changes any occurrence of the ff, fi, or letter combinations into *ligatures* (that is, a text symbol that combines two or more letters into a single, special character). To change to the V and Y ligatures, you must have the appropriate Adobe Expert font installed on your system.

• V, X, Z Ligatures changes any occurrence of the ff, fl, or ffl letter combinations into ligatures. To change to the V and Z ligatures, you must have the appropriate Adobe Expert font installed on your system.

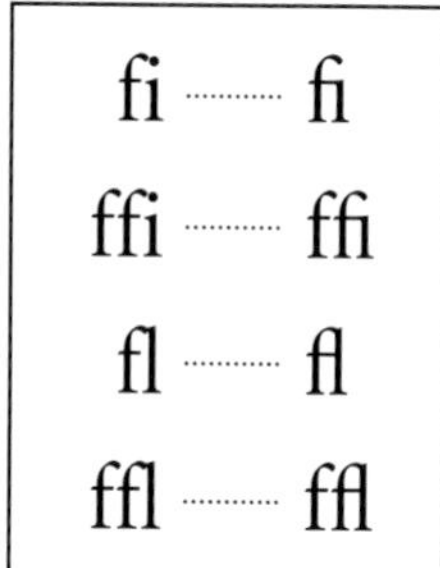

Regular type (left) and ligatures (right)

• Smart Quotes (“ ”) changes straight keyboard quotation marks (" " and ' ') into printer’s quotation marks (“ ” and ‘ ’).

• Smart Spaces (.) replaces multiple spaces after a period with a single space.

• En, Em Dashes (--) replaces a double keyboard dash (--) with an en dash (–) and to replace a triple keyboard dash (---) with an em dash (—).

• Ellipses (. . .) replaces three keyboard periods (...) with ellipsis points (. . .).

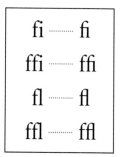

• Expert Fractions replaces separate characters used to represent fractions with their single-character equivalents. To change to expert fractions, you must have the appropriate Adobe Expert font installed on your system.

1/2 .... 1/2

3/4 .... 3/4

5/8 .... 5/8

7/16 .... 7/16

Regular type (left) and expert fractions (right)

3 Select one of the following options:

• Entire Document searches and replaces text symbols in the entire file.

• Selected Text Only replaces symbols only in selected text.

4 Select Report Results to see a list of the number of symbols replaced.

5 Click OK to search for and replace selected characters.

Using the Glyph Options command (Mac OS only)

Some Japanese fonts contain information on alternative or historical variants for certain characters. You can specify an alternative glyph for an existing kanji using the Glyph Options command. When you use Type 1 CID fonts (Mac OS), you can substitute a standard character with a variant character belonging to the JIS 78, Expert, and Traditional character sets.

To print files containing alternative characters, the corresponding CID font containing the glyphs must be installed on the printer.

Note: *Alternative glyphs revert to standard characters when an Illustrator file is imported to Adobe Photoshop, Adobe Premiere, or Adobe After Effects®. To save alternative glyph information, save the Illustrator file in EPS format (be sure to select Include Document Fonts in the EPS Format dialog box), and then import it.*

To specify an alternative glyph for the current character set:

1 Using any type tool, select the character to be replaced. To select more than one character, Option-click the characters.

2 Choose Type > Glyph Options.

3 Select the character set from the scrolling menu in the Glyph Options dialog box, and click OK.

12

Chapter 12: Using Graphs

The graph tools and commands enable you to display and compare data visually in Illustrator files. Once you have created your graphs, you can easily customize and add special effects to them.

About graphs

Adobe Illustrator's graph tools let you create nine different graph types:

Column The default graph type. It compares one or more sets of values by using rectangles whose lengths are proportional to the values.

Stacked column Similar to a column graph, but stacks the columns on top of one another, instead of side by side. This graph type is useful for showing the relationship of parts to the total.

Bar Similar to a column graph, but positions the rectangles horizontally instead of vertically.

Stacked bar Similar to a stacked column graph, but stacks the bars horizontally instead of vertically.

Line Uses points to represent one or more sets of values, with a different line joining the points in each set. This type of graph is often used to show the trend of one or more subjects over a period of time.

Area Similar to a line graph, but emphasizes totals as well as changes in values.

Scatter Plots data points as paired sets of coordinates along the *x* and *y* axes. Scatter graphs are useful for identifying patterns or trends in data. They also can indicate whether variables affect one another.

Pie A circular graph whose wedges represent the relative percentages of the values compared.

Radar Compares sets of values at given points in time or in particular categories, and is displayed in a circular format. This type of graph is also called a *web graph.*

For a gallery of graph tools, see the toolbox overview in online Help.

Working with graphs

Once you create a graph, you can customize it by using colors and designs, and you can select options for the type. Each time you change the graph data, the graph is updated. However, certain graph options—such as font size and column markers—revert to their defaults if you change the graph data.

Graphs are created as grouped objects. You can select elements of a graph with the direct-selection and group-selection tools, and you can change the elements. However, if you ungroup a graph, you cannot change the graph's type or modify the graph's data. (See "Selecting parts of a graph" on page 313.)

To create a graph:

1 Do one of the following:

- Select a graph tool from the toolbox.
- Double-click a graph tool (icon).
- Choose Object > Graphs > Type.

2 Select the type of graph you want.

3 Select options for the selected graph type, as described in “Selecting graph options” on page 304.

4 Click OK.

5 Select the graph tool. The pointer changes to a cross hair when you move it to the active window.

6 Do one of the following to create a graph:

• Drag diagonally from the corner where you want the graph to begin to the opposite corner. Hold down Alt (Windows) or Option (Mac OS) to drag from the center of the graph.

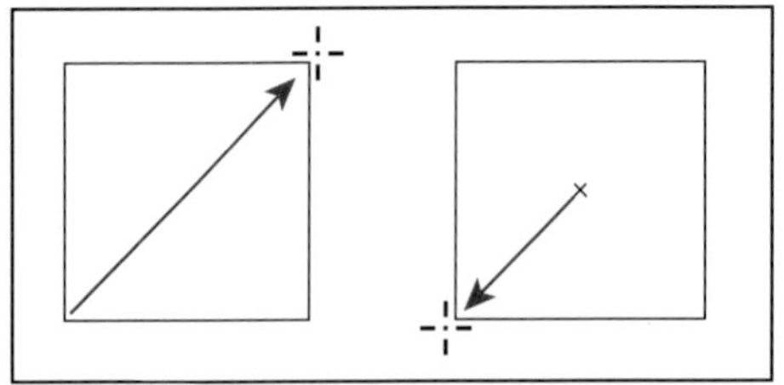

Dragging from corner to corner or from center to corner

• Click the graph tool in the artwork where you want to create the graph, and then specify the dimensions for the graph in the Graph dialog box. Hold down Alt (Windows) or Option (Mac OS) to specify a point as the center of the graph. By default, the Graph dialog box displays the dimensions of the most recently drawn graph. Dimensions are displayed in the units of measure specified in the Preferences > Units & Undo dialog box.

You see a graph of the shape and dimensions you designated, as well as the Graph Data palette. The anchor points on the graph indicate that it is selected.

7 Enter the graph data.

Entering and editing graph data

You can enter data in a graph in three ways: by typing it into the Graph Data palette, by importing data from another file, or by pasting data from another program or from another graph. Regardless of the method you use, you can edit the data once it has been entered.

Entering graph data

Note the following about graph data:

• You must select an entire graph before you can change its data.

• You can enter data in up to 32,767 rows by 32,767 columns, as memory permits.

• Graph data cannot contain nonnumerical characters other than decimal points (.) or decimal commas; if it does, the data is not plotted. For example, you would enter **245000**, not **245,000**. However, you can enter nonnumerical characters in labels, as described later in this section.

To enter data manually:

1 Create a graph using the procedure described in "Working with graphs" on page 297. Make sure that the graph is selected.

2 If the Graph Data palette is not already open, choose Object > Graphs > Data.

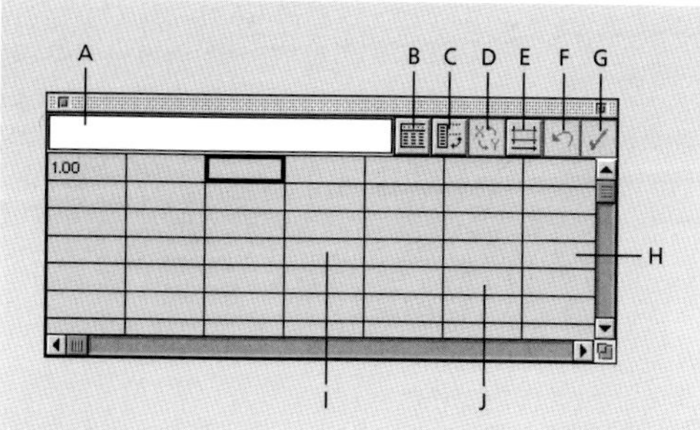

A. Entry line B. Import data C. Transpose row/column D. Switch x/y E. Cell style F. Revert G. Apply H. Row I. Column J. Cell

At the top of a work sheet is the entry line for entering data. You enter labels and then data that correspond to the labels. Each label or value you enter is placed into a separate cell. A *cell* is the intersection of a row and a column.

Labels are words or numbers that describe two things: *categories*, whose data is entered in rows; and *legends*, whose data is entered in columns. In the final graph, legends appear as boxes that you can place above or to the right of a graph.

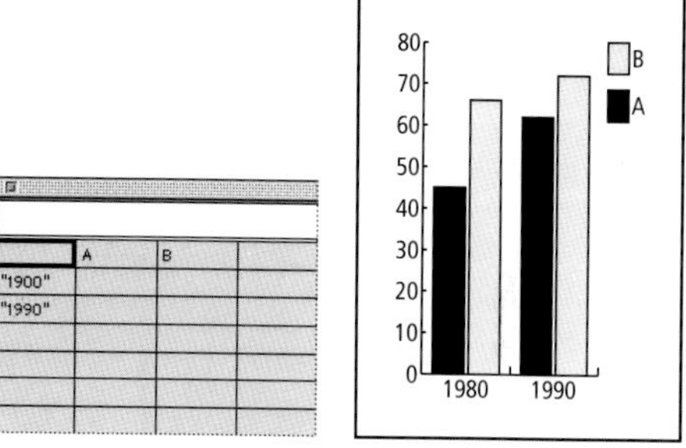

Categories (1900 and 1990) and legends (A and B)

3 Enter labels and data for the particular graph type, according to the guidelines in "Entering labels and data for particular graph types" on page 300. Also see "Selecting graph options" on page 304.

Usually, you enter a label in at least the first row and the first column of the work sheet. Follow these guidelines:

- To create category labels for the horizontal (*x*) axis, enter the labels in the first column. (Do not enter a label in the first cell if you are also creating legend names for the vertical (*y*) axis.)
- To create legend labels for the vertical (*y*) axis, enter the labels in the first row. (Do not enter a legend label in the first cell of the row if you are also creating labels for the horizontal (*x*) axis.)

• To create labels consisting only of numbers, enclose the numbers in straight quotation marks (that is, not "curly" quotation marks). For example, to use the year 1996 as a label, enter **"1996"**; to use quotation marks around a number label, use text quotation marks within another set of straight quotation marks—for example **"“1996”"**. If a label includes both text and numbers, you do not need to use quotation marks.

• To create line breaks in legends or labels, use the vertical bar key to separate lines. For example, enter **Total|subscriptions|1996** to produce the following graph label:

Total
subscriptions
1996

4 Continue entering data in the work sheet, choosing one of the following methods to move to another cell:

• Press Tab to enter the data and select the next cell in the same row.

• Press Enter (Windows) or Return (Mac OS) to enter the data and select the next cell in the same column.

• Use the arrow keys to move from cell to cell.

• Click any cell.

5 To correct a mistake or to change how data is entered in the Graph Data palette, do one of the following:

• If you accidentally enter graph data backward (that is, in rows instead of columns, or vice versa), click the Transpose button () to switch the columns and rows of data. (See "Adjusting graphs" on page 303.)

• To switch the *x* and *y* axes of a scatter graph, click the Switch X/Y button ().

6 To adjust the cell column width to display more or fewer digits, click the Cell Style button () and enter a new value in the Cell Style dialog box.

7 When you finish entering data in the work sheet, do one of the following:

• Click the Apply button (✓) to keep the Graph Data palette open and apply the data to the graph.

• Click the close box to close the Graph Data palette and apply the data to the graph.

• Click the Revert button () to return data to its state when you last applied it to the graph.

Entering labels and data for particular graph types

Labels can be words that describe columns of data, or they can be years, months, or days for comparing data over time.

Follow these additional guidelines for entering data for the selected graph type:

Column and stacked column graphs Enter numbers along the vertical (*y*) axis; enter labels for the data along the horizontal (*x*) axis.

Bar and stacked bar graphs Enter numbers along the horizontal (*x*) axis; enter labels for the data along the vertical (*y*) axis.

Column, stacked column, bar, and stacked bar graphs The height of the column or the length of the bar corresponds to the amount being compared. For column or bar graphs, you can combine positive and negative values; negative values appear as columns extending below the horizontal axis. For stacked column graphs, numbers must be all positive or all negative.

Line graphs Enter numbers representing quantities along the *y* axis; enter numbers representing time along the *x* axis. Each column of data corresponds to one line in the line graph. You can combine positive and negative values in a line graph.

Area graphs Plot at least two rows of data; values must be all positive or all negative. Each row of data entered corresponds to a filled area on the area graph. Area graphs add each column's values to the previous column's totals. Therefore, even if area graphs and line graphs contain the same data, they appear substantially different.

Scatter graphs Enter *y* axis data in the first column and *x* axis in the second column. A scatter graph differs from the other kinds of graphs, because both axes measure values; there are no categories. If the first column contains labels, it is ignored, and the second column produces values for the *y* coordinates.

Pie graphs Plot only one row of data, either all positive or all negative values. If you plot additional rows of data, a separate pie graph is created for each additional row. You cannot combine positive and negative values. The size of the individual pie graphs is proportional to the total of each graph's data.

Radar graphs Enter labels for the axes in the first column and a set of numbers in each successive column. Each label results in a separate axis; unlike other graphs, a radar graph can have more than two axes per graph. Each number is plotted on an axis and connected to the others in the same axis to create a "web." (See "Selecting graph options" on page 304.)

Importing data from another application

If you first save data files as text in other applications, you can import the data files into Adobe Illustrator. In the text files, each cell must be separated by a tab, and each row must be separated by a carriage return.

You can cut and paste data from a spreadsheet application such as Lotus® 1-2-3 or Microsoft Excel using your computer's cut and paste procedures.

The data can only contain decimal points or decimal commas; otherwise, the data is not plotted. For example, enter **732000**, not **732,000**.

Also, Mac OS users can subscribe to data that is updated interactively from the original source using the Publish and Subscribe feature. See "Using the Publish and Subscribe commands (for Mac OS only)" on page 330.

To import data from another application:

1 Create a graph. Make sure that the graph is selected.

2 If the Graph Data palette is not already open, choose Object > Graphs > Data.

3 Click the cell that will be the top left cell of the data that you import.

4 Click the Import Data button (▦).

5 Open the file that you want to import. The data is imported and entered into the work sheet in the Graph Data palette.

6 Click the Apply button (✓). The graph is updated with the imported data.

To copy and paste data from another application:

1 Open the application and file containing the data you want to copy, select the data, and choose Edit > Copy to copy the data to the Clipboard.

2 Open the Adobe Illustrator program.

3 Create a graph. Make sure that the graph is selected.

4 If the Graph Data palette is not already open, choose Object > Graphs > Data.

5 Click the cell that will be the top left cell of the data you paste.

6 Choose Edit > Paste. The data is pasted into the cells in the Graph Data palette.

7 Click the Apply button (✓). The graph is updated with the pasted data.

Editing existing data

You can edit data you entered in the Graph Data palette. The Cut and Copy commands move data to the Clipboard; the Paste command moves data from the Clipboard into a work sheet. The Clear command erases the entire selection, either within the text or as a set of cells. The Delete key functions as both a Delete key and a Backspace key for a single cell.

To edit existing data:

1 Click the cell you want to edit. The cell is highlighted, and the cell's data is shown in the entry line.

2 Do one of the following for editing data:

- Enter a value in the selected text box.
- Click in the entry line. Type new information.
- Press Delete to delete an entire cell entry.
- Use the Cut, Copy, Paste, or Clear command in the Edit menu to edit the data. You can cut and paste any cell or group of cells to another selected cell or group of cells.

3 Click the Apply button (✓).

Adjusting graphs

You can transpose data, switch the *x* and *y* axes in scatter graphs, and adjust the cell column width and decimal precision. To adjust data, use the Graph Data palette.

To transpose rows and columns of data:

1 Choose Object > Graphs > Data.

2 Click the Transpose button (). Labels and data that were listed across the top row are now listed along the left column. When the categories and legends are reversed, all the data is transposed accordingly.

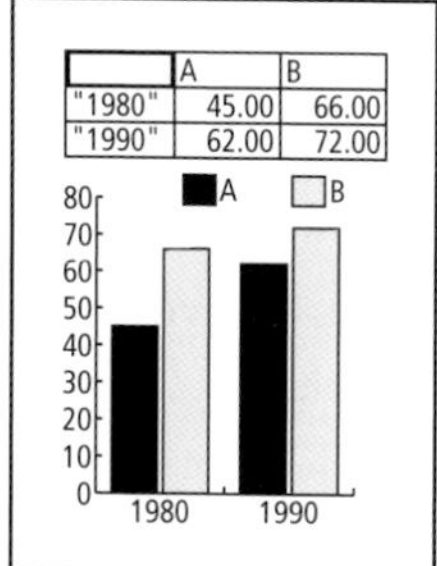

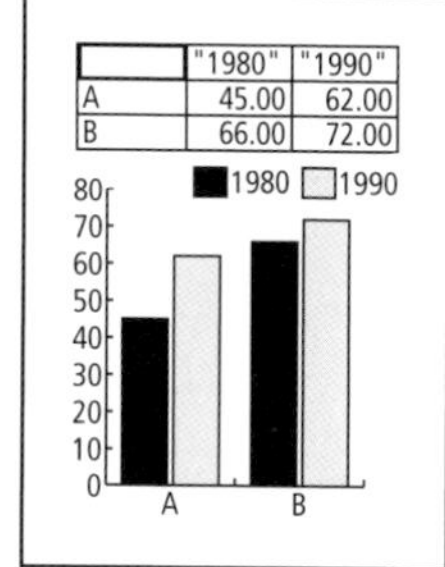

Default column graph and with data transposed

To switch the *x* and *y* axes in a scatter graph:

1 Choose Object > Graphs > Data.

2 Click the Switch X/Y button () to reverse the data columns.

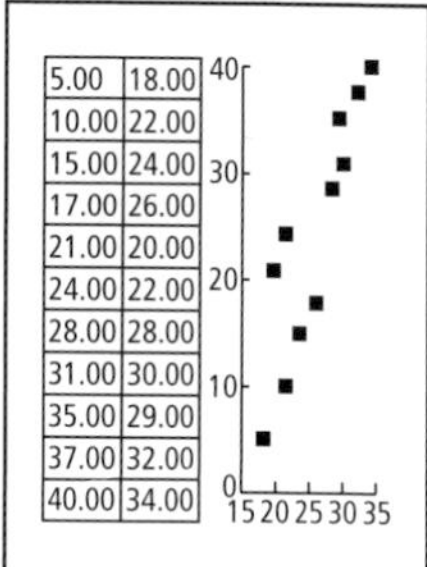

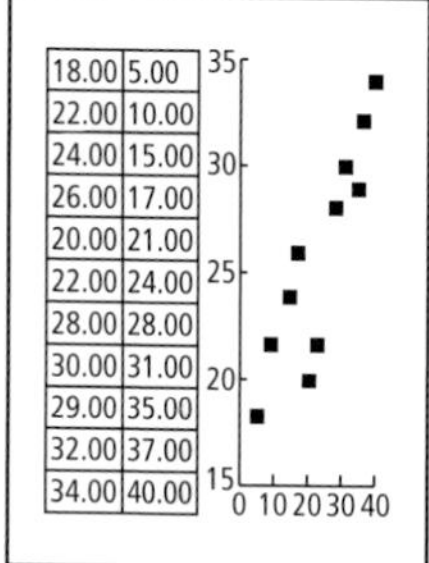

Default x and y axes, and with x and y axes transposed

To adjust a column width manually:

1 In the Graph Data palette, position the pointer at the edge of the column you want to adjust. The pointer changes to a double arrow.

2 Drag the handle to the desired position.

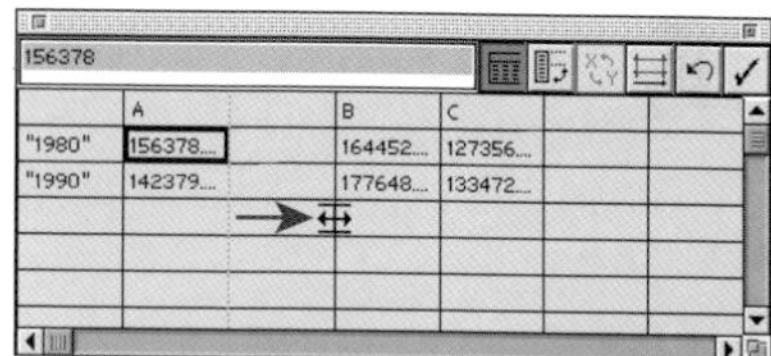

To reset the column width, you must drag the column width again; you cannot use the Cell Style dialog box. If you drag the column width to zero, the column reverts to the column width set in the Cell Style dialog box.

To change the width of columns you have not previously changed manually:

1 Click the Cell Style button (⌸) in the Graph Data palette.

2 Enter a value between 0 and 20 in the Column Width text box. Click OK.

Changing the value in the Column Width text box changes the width of the columns in the Graph Data palette only; it has no effect on the width of columns in the graph.

To adjust decimal precision:

1 Click the Cell Style button in the Graph Data palette.

2 Enter a value between 0 and 10 in the Number of Decimals text box. The default is 2. This means that if you enter the number 4, it appears in the Graph Data palette as 4.00; if you enter the number 1.55823 with the Number of Decimals text box set to 2, the cell displays 1.56. Click OK.

Selecting graph options

Here are additional options that are available, depending on the graph type selected.

Note: *Area graphs have no unique options.*

To select graph type options:

1 If you want to change an existing graph, select the entire graph.

2 Choose Object > Graphs > Type, or double-click the graph tool.

3 Choose Graph Options from the pop-up menu at the top left of the Graph Type dialog box.

4 Select options for the selected graph type, as described in the following sections.

Selecting column and stacked column options

Column Width and Cluster Width values can range from 1% to 1000%. These values allow space between columns and between clusters. A value of 100% moves both columns and clusters flush against each other. A value above 100% causes the columns and clusters to overlap one another.

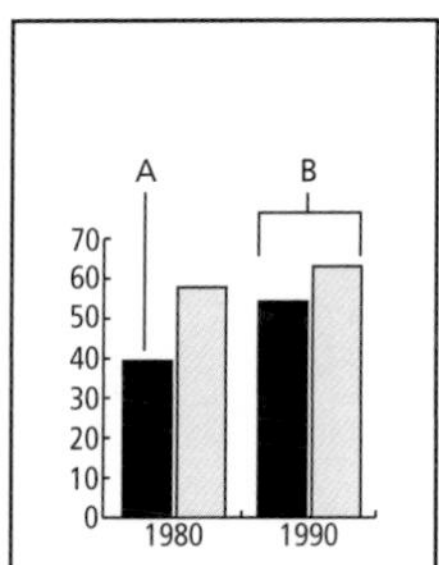

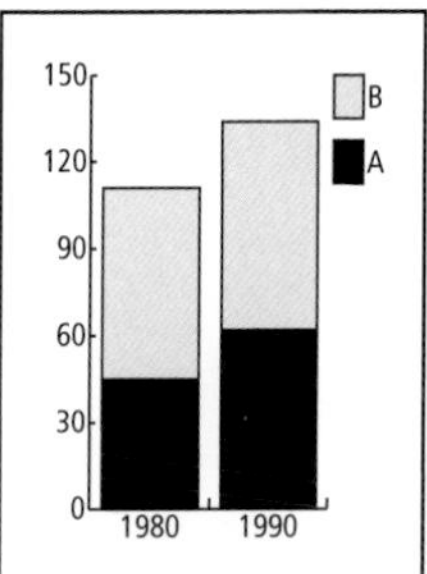

A. *Column Width* ***B.*** *Cluster Width, and stacked column graph*

Column and stacked column graph options are the same. They include the following:

• Column Width, by default, is 90%.

• Cluster Width is the total width of all columns in a cluster. A *cluster* is a group of columns corresponding to a row of data in the work sheet. The default cluster width is 80%. If you are using stacked column graphs exclusively, it is recommended that you set the cluster width to 100% and use only the Column Width option to adjust the width.

Selecting bar and stacked bar options

Bar Width and Cluster Width values can range from 1% to 1000%. These values allow space between bars and between clusters. A value of 100% moves both bars and clusters flush against each other. A value above 100% causes the bars and clusters to overlap one another.

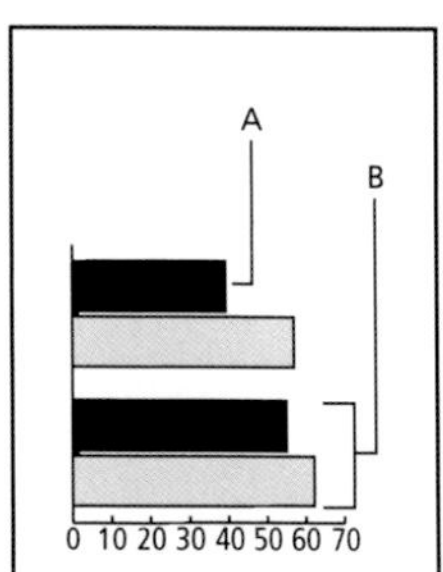

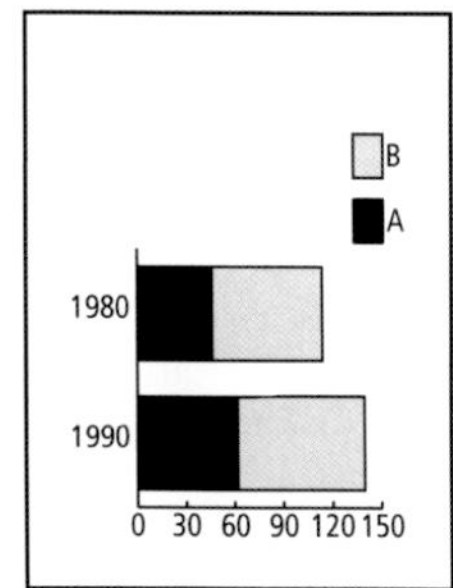

A. Bar Width B. Cluster Width, bar graph, and stacked bar graph

Bar and stacked bar graph options are the same. They include the following:

• Bar Width, by default, is 90%.

• Cluster Width is the total width of all bars in a cluster. A *cluster* is a group of bars that correspond to a row of data in the work sheet. The default cluster width is 80%. If you are using stacked bar graphs exclusively, it is recommended that you set the cluster width to 100% and use only the Bar Width option to adjust the width.

Selecting line graph options

The following graph type options let you choose how to display line graphs:

• Mark Data Points places square markers at each data point.

• Connect Data Points draws lines that connect the data points and makes it easier to see relationships between data.

• Edge-to-Edge Lines draws lines that extend across the graph, from left to right along the horizontal (x) axis.

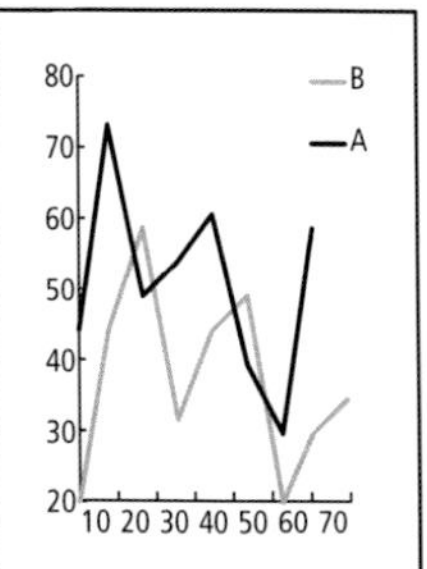

Line graph

• Draw Filled Lines becomes available when you select Connect Data Points. Draw Filled Lines creates a wider line according to the value you enter in the Line Width text box, and it fills the line with paint according to the specifications for that series of data. When you select Draw Filled Lines, a check mark appears in its check box; if you then deselect Connect Data Points, Draw Filled Lines is dimmed. The check mark indicates that you can recall the line width value without having to specify it again in the Connect Data Points option.

Selecting scatter graph options

The graph type options for scatter graphs are the same as those for line graphs, except that the Edge-to-Edge Lines option is not available. The default options for scatter graphs are Mark Data Points and Connect Data Points.

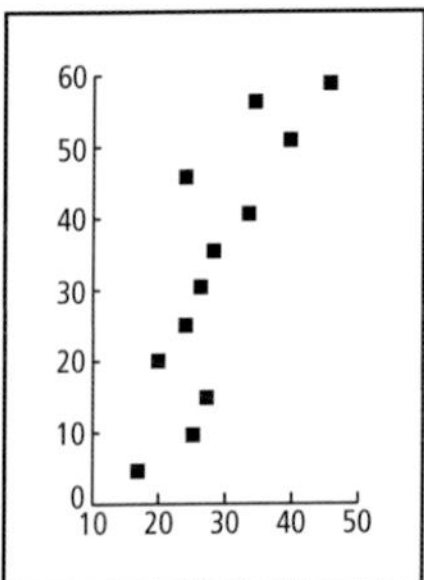

Scatter graph

Selecting pie graph options

The following legend options let you choose how to display legends with pie graphs:

• Standard Legend places column labels outside the graph; this is the default. Use this option when you combine pie graphs with other kinds of graphs.

• Legends in Wedges inserts labels into the corresponding wedges.

• No Legend omits legends entirely.

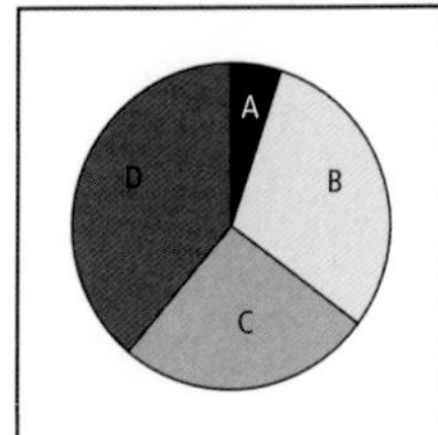

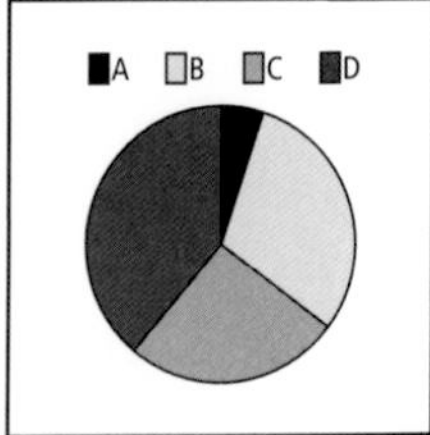

Pie graph with legends in wedges and with legends across top

Percentages and legends are painted black by default. If a pie wedge with a dark background obscures a legend, repaint the dark background. Use the group-selection tool to select the dark pie wedges, and paint the wedges using the Color palette or Swatches palette.

The following position options let you choose how to display multiple pie graphs:

• Ratio sizes the graphs proportionally.

• Even makes all the pie graphs the same diameter.

• Stacked stacks each pie graph on top of the other, and each graph is sized proportionally.

The following sort options let you choose which element is displayed first, proceeding clockwise from the top of the pie graph:

• All sorts the wedges of the selected pie graph from largest to smallest value.

- First sorts the wedges of the selected pie graphs so that the largest value in the first graph will be placed in the first wedge, and the rest will sort from largest to smallest. All other graphs will follow the order of the wedges in the first graph.
- None sorts the wedges of the selected pie graphs in the order in which you entered values.

Selecting radar graph options

The graph type options for radar graphs are the same as those for line graphs. The default options for radar graphs are Mark Data Points and Connect Data Points.

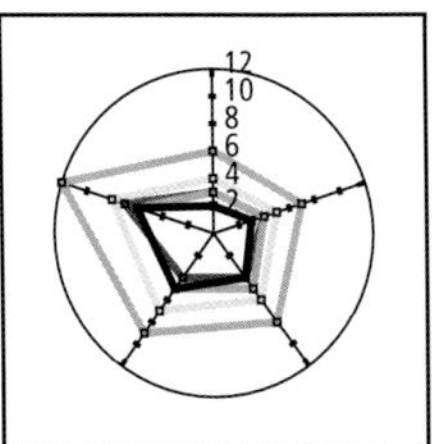

Radar graph

Specifying the value axis position

You can specify whether to have the value axis (typically the *y* axis) displayed on the left side, the right side, or both sides of the graph. You can have the same axis displayed on both sides, or, if you want different scales to appear on either side, you can select specific data to apply to one side or another. It is important to keep the following in mind when specifying value axes to the right or left side of the graph:

- If you select the entire graph and then select the On Both Sides option, both sides will show the same axis scale.
- If you want to have different scales on the right side versus the left side, you must assign data columns to the appropriate side of the graph. For example, if you want the left side of a graph to show Meters and the right side Feet, you need to select the data to show in Feet and specifically assign it to On Right Side to have the right side of the graph show the desired scale in Feet.
- There are no value axis options for pie graphs.

(See "Combining different graph types" on page 312.)

To specify the axis position:

1 In the Graph Type dialog box, choose one of the following options from the Value Axis pop-up menu:

- For column, stacked column, line, or area graphs, choose On Left Side, On Right Side, or On Both Sides.
- For scatter graphs, choose On Left Side or On Both Sides.
- For bar and stacked bar graphs, choose On Bottom Side, On Top Side, or On Both Sides.

Note: *If you select On Both Sides without assigning data to a specific side, the scales on the axes will be identical on both sides of the graph.*

- For Radar graphs, choose On All Sides.

2 Click OK.

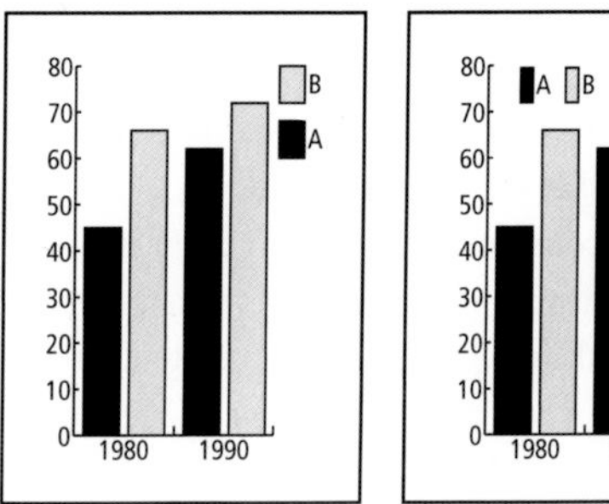

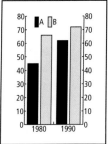

Graph with left axis and with same axis on both sides

To specify different scales for axes on both sides:

1 Use the group-selection tool (↖+) to select a set of data and its legend box or legend line.

2 In the Graph Type dialog box, choose one of the following options from the Value Axis pop-up menu:

• For column, stacked column, line, area, or scatter graphs, choose On Left Side or On Right Side.

• For bar and stacked bar graphs, choose On Bottom Side or On Top Side.

3 You can manually set the tick marks for the axis you have selected by choosing Value Axis from the pop-up menu and then selecting the Override Calculated Values option, as described in "Setting axis tick mark and label options" on page 309. Click OK.

4 Repeat steps 1 through 3 to assign data values to the other axis.

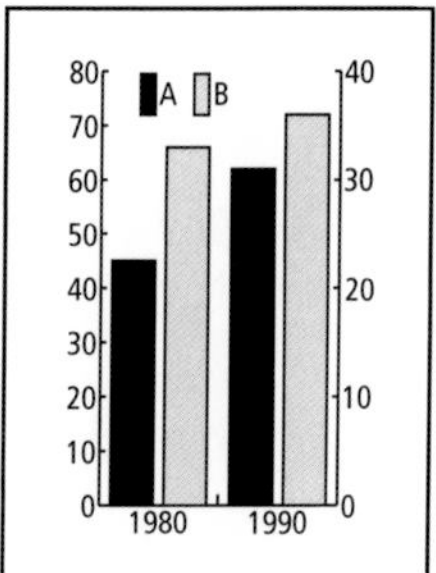

Selecting data and assigning to right axis. Scales are assigned different values using the Override Calculated Values option.

To set the graph so that all data can be read on two different scales:

1 Assign some data columns to one scale and the rest of the data columns to the other scale, as described in "Specifying the value axis position" on page 307.

2 Set the minimum and maximum on the two axes to be equivalent as described in "Setting axis tick mark and label options" on page 309. For example, for a graph in which one axis displays a Celsius scale and the other a Fahrenheit scale, you can set the Celsius scale to 0 (minimum) and 32 (maximum), and set the Fahrenheit scale to 32 (minimum) and 122 (maximum). All the data in the graph can then be read accurately on either scale.

Setting axis tick mark and label options

You can add tick marks to show units of measurement in a graph, and you can add information to labels including units of measurement such as "$."

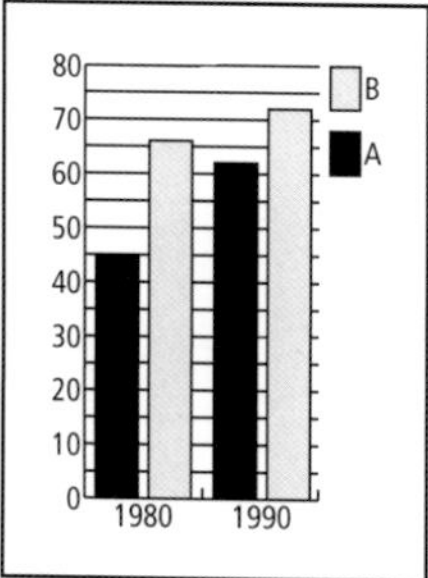

Full-length tick marks with labels

Tick marks are the lines placed perpendicular to the axes to show the units of measurement. They can be used either horizontally or vertically or both to set categories apart in a line graph, for example, or to separate categories in a column or scatter graph.

You may need to change axis attributes such as tick marks or labels when a single graph contains more than one graph type. (See "Combining different graph types" on page 312.)

To set horizontal tick mark and label options for either the left or right *y* axis:

1 Choose Graph Options from the pop-up menu in the top left of the Graph Type dialog box.

2 Depending on the type of Graph you selected, choose On Left Side, On Right Side, on Top Side, On Bottom Side, On Both Sides, or On All Sides from the Value Axis pop-up menu to apply changes to one or both axes.

3 Choose Value Axis from the pop-up menu in the top left of the dialog box.

4 Select Override Calculated Values to manually calculate the placement of the horizontal tick marks along the left or right *y* axis.

You can use this option, for example, to display very large numbers for the tick marks. Changing the *y* axes individually also lets you specify different options for the *x* and *y* axes or for the right and left *y* axes when you combine different graph types.

5 Either accept the values set when you created the graph or enter a minimum value, a maximum value, and the number of divisions between labels. To prevent numbers from appearing on an axis, enter 0 in the Tick Marks per Division text box.

6 Specify one or more of the following options:

• Enter characters in the Prefix or Suffix text box to add more information before (Prefix) or after (Suffix) the *y*-axis values, such as a dollar sign before a number, or the word *units*, or a percent sign after the values.

• Choose Short or Full Width from the Length menu to extend horizontal tick lines across the graph.

• Enter a value in the Draw Tick Marks Per Division text box to specify how many tick lines to draw.

7 Click OK.

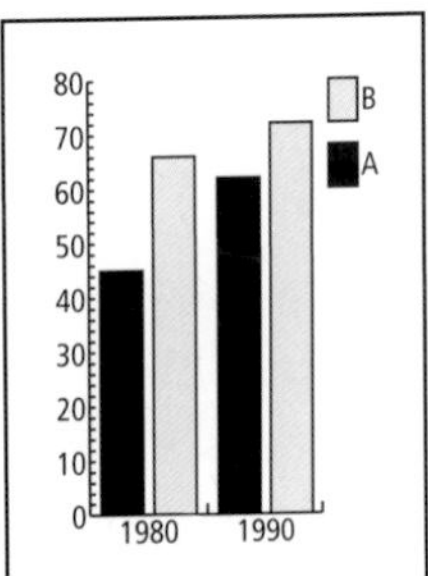

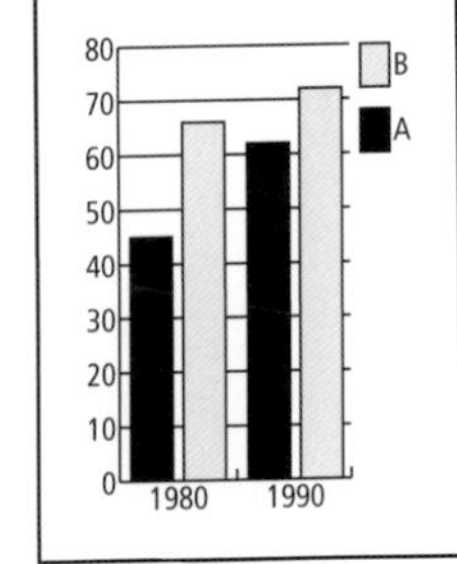

Short tick lines and full-width tick lines

To place vertical tick marks on the *x* axis:

1 From the pop-up menu in the top left of the Graph Type dialog box, choose Bottom Axis if you selected a scatter graph; otherwise, choose Category Axis.

2 Do any of the following:

• Choose Short or Full Width from the Length menu to extend vertical tick lines across the graph.

• Select Draw Tick Marks Between Labels to draw tick lines on either side of the labels or columns, or deselect the option to center tick lines over the labels or columns.

• Enter a value in the Draw Tick Marks Per Division text box to specify how many tick lines to draw.

3 Click OK.

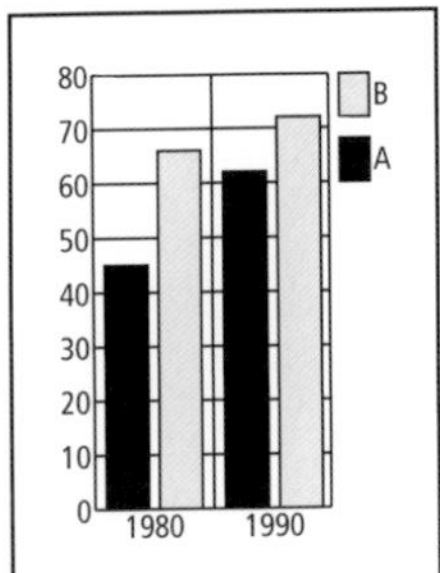

Vertical tick lines added to graph

Adding visual emphasis to graphs

You can refine the look of a graph using visual aids, including drop shadows, adding legends at the top of the graph, or overlapping the columns in a bar graph.

To add a drop shadow:

In the Graph Type dialog box, select Add Drop Shadow and click OK.

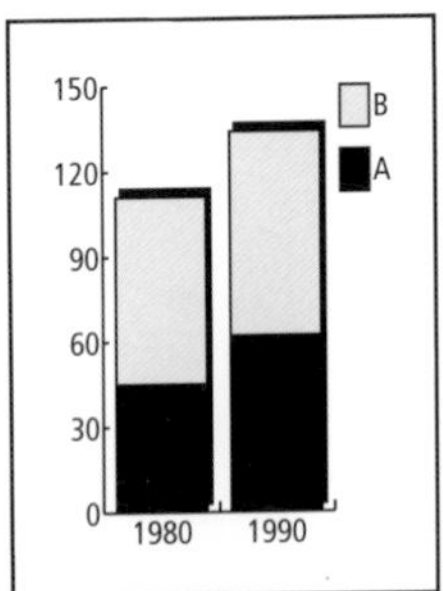

Drop shadows

To display legends across the top of a graph:

1 In the Graph Type dialog box, select Add Legend Across Top.

2 Click OK. By default, legends are displayed to the right of the graph. You can choose to display them horizontally across the top of the graph.

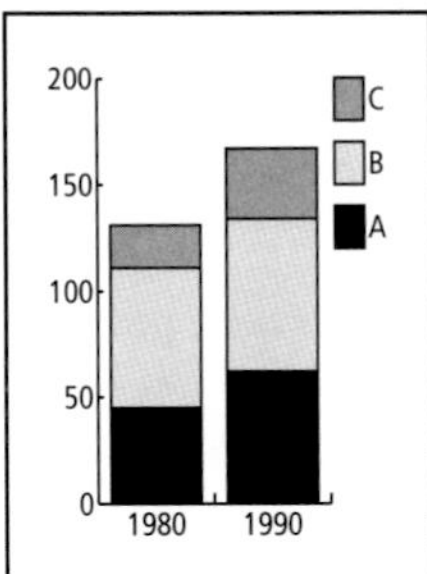

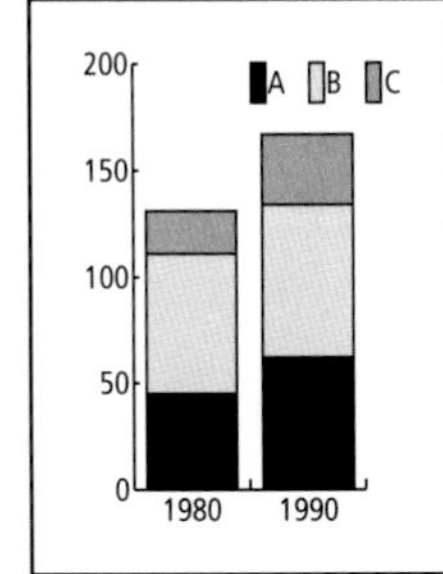

Default legends and legends across top

To make columns or bars of data overlap:

1 When creating a Stacked Column or Stacked Bar graph, in the Graph Type dialog box enter a value in the Column Width or Bar Width text box greater than 100%.

2 Select First Column in Front, and click OK.

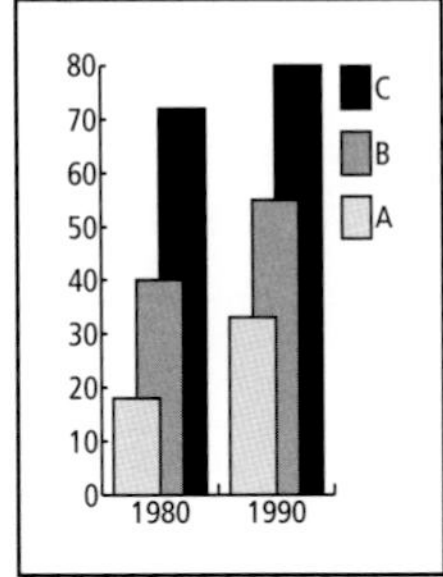

First Column in Front option selected

To specify the order in which columns overlap:

1 In the Graph Type dialog box, to place the first row or column of data in the work sheet frontmost in the graph, select First Row in Front or First Column in Front (the default). You must always select this option for an area graph; if you do not, some areas may not appear.

2 Click OK.

Changing graph types

Once you create a graph, you can change to another graph type to illustrate the data more effectively by using the Graph Type dialog box.

To change the graph type of an individual series of data, use the group-selection tool to select the data series. Be sure to include the legend in the selection. (See “Combining different graph types” on page 312.)

***Note:** Once graph objects are painted with gradients, changing graph types can cause unexpected results. To prevent undesirable results, either do not apply gradients until the graph is finished, or use the direct-selection tool to select gradient-painted objects and paint those objects with a process color; then reapply the original gradients.*

To change graph types:

1 Select the graph.

2 Choose Object > Graphs > Type, or double-click the graph tool.

3 Choose Graph Options from the pop-up menu at the top left of the Graph Type dialog box.

4 Click the desired graph type. The options for the particular type of graph you selected appear in the bottom half of the dialog box.

5 Click the desired graph options and click OK.

Combining different graph types

You can combine different graph types in one graph. For example, you may want one set of data to appear as a column graph and other sets of data to appear as a line graph. You can combine any type of graph with any other, with the exception of scatter graphs. Scatter graphs cannot be combined with any other graph type.

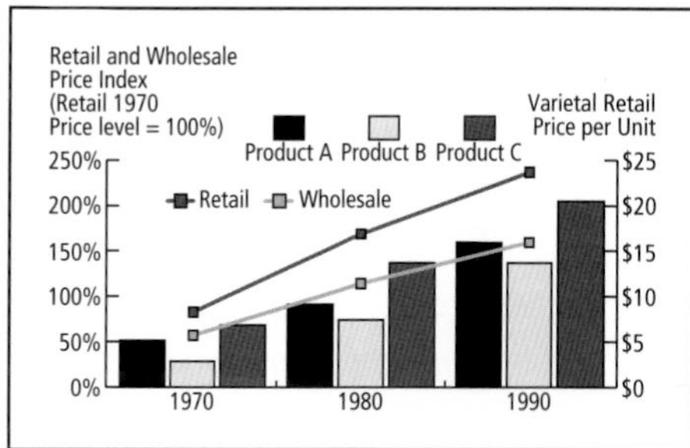

Column and line graph types combined

If a graph uses more than one graph type, you may want one set of data along the right axis and the other set of data along the left axis. In this way, each axis measures different data. For information on assigning data to different sides of the graph, see "Specifying the value axis position" on page 307 and "Setting axis tick mark and label options" on page 309.

Note: *To create two axes for a graph with different scales, you need to assign data to the left side (or the bottom side) and different data to the right side (or the top side) using the Value Axis menu in the Graph Type dialog box. If you select the entire graph and the On Both Sides option, both axes will display identical scale values.*

If you use stacked column graphs with other graph types, be sure to use the same axis for all sets of data that are represented by stacked column graphs. If some sets of data use the right axis while other sets of data use the left axis, the column heights may be misleading or may overlap.

To combine different graph types:

1 Use the group-selection tool (⁺) to select a set of data and its legend box or legend line. (See "Selecting parts of a graph" on page 313.) Once you select the series, you can then change the graph type in the Graph Type dialog box.

2 Choose Object > Graphs > Type, or double-click the graph tool.

3 Select the graph type and options you want. (See "Selecting graph options" on page 304.)

4 Apply the selected data to an axis by selecting On Right Side, On Left Side, On Top Side, or on Bottom Side from the Value Axis pop-up menu and click OK.

5 Use the group-selection tool (↖⁺) again to select a different set of data on which to apply a different graph type, and which will be assigned to a different axis.

6 Perform steps 2 through 4 again on the new data, creating a different graph type and assigning the data to the opposite axis, and then click OK.

Exporting graph designs to other files

You can create a custom startup file that contains the graph designs you use most frequently. The graph designs contained in the startup file then appear in the graph design list in the Graph Design dialog box and are available in every new Adobe Illustrator file you create. (See "Creating a custom startup file" on page 176.)

Customizing a graph

You can customize a graph in numerous ways. You can change the colors of shading; change the typeface and type style; and move, reflect, shear, rotate, or scale any or all of the graph. You can use customized column and marker designs. (See "Combining different graph types" on page 312.)

About graph elements

It is essential to keep in mind when you customize a graph that a graph is a grouped object that is related to its data. Never ungroup the graph; if you do, you cannot change the graph. To edit a graph, you select the parts you want to edit without ungrouping the graph, using either the direct-selection tool or the group-selection tool.

It is also important to understand how elements of a graph are related. The entire graph with its legends is one group. All the sets of data are a subgroup of the graph; in turn, each set of data with its legend box is a subgroup of all the sets of data. Each value is a subgroup of its set of data, and so on. Never ungroup or regroup objects that are within the group.

You can see the hierarchy of grouping within a graph by creating a column graph with two or more columns of data. The first column in the first cluster of columns is grouped with the first column in the next cluster of columns. In addition, the group of the first columns is grouped with the first legend.

Selecting parts of a graph

If you want to select some objects in a graph and send them to the back or front of other objects, it's important that you send only objects that represent an entire set of data or individual numbers. You can select individual columns, lines, pie wedges, or series and move them to the front or back. Do not, however, select and move individual category labels, individual legend labels, individual axis tick lines, individual axis tick labels, or vertical or horizontal axis lines.

If you want to move a set of data in a line graph in front or in back of another set of data, you must select the entire set of data, including the legend. Selecting just the data points is not sufficient.

To select an entire data set in a graph:

1 Select the group-selection tool (↖⁺).

2 Click the legend of the columns you want (for example, Group A).

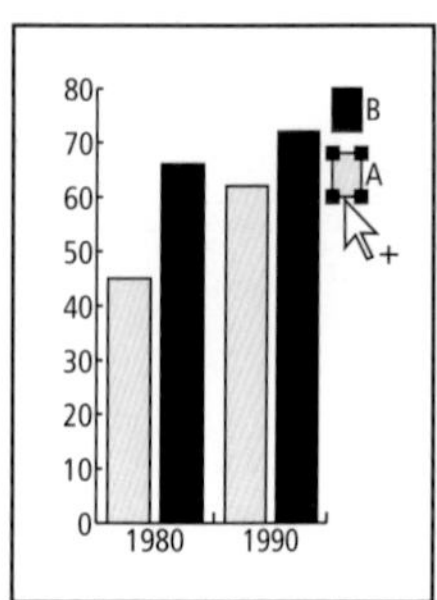

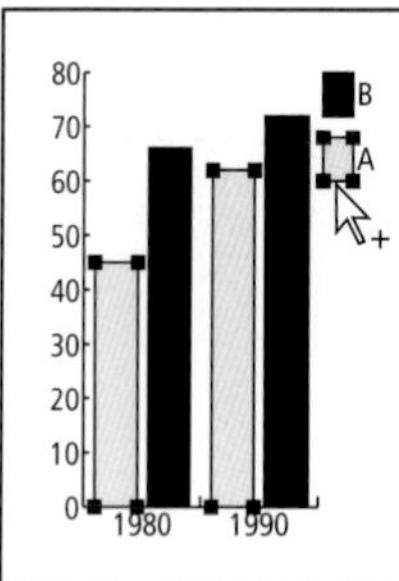

First click selects a legend. Second click adds columns to selection.

3 Without moving the group-selection tool pointer from the legend, click again. All of the columns grouped with the legend are selected.

You can also select a group by clicking one of its parts, clicking again to select columns grouped with it, and clicking a third time to select the legend.

Each click adds another layer of grouped objects to the selection, beginning with the next group up in the hierarchy. You can click as many times as the number of groups to add to a selection.

To deselect part of a selected group:

1 Select either the direct-selection tool (↖) or the group-selection tool (↖⁺), and position the tool on the object you want to deselect.

2 Hold down Shift, and click to deselect the object.

To change part of the type in a graph:

1 Select the group-selection tool (↖⁺).

2 Click once to select the baseline of the type you want to change; click twice to select all of the type.

3 Choose Type > Character or Type > Paragraph.

4 Set the type attributes you want to change. Changes you make apply only to the selected type.

About graph designs

You can create and apply custom markers or columns to represent data in graphs. You can also use the designs located in the Adobe Illustrator 8.0 > Goodies > Graphs & Graphs Designs directory. Graph designs can be a simple drawing, logo, or other symbol representing values in a graph, such as a bicycle; they can also be complex objects that contain patterns, guide objects, and type. You can reuse graph designs and edit them to make a new design.

Using a graph design is different from painting a column with a pattern. Graph designs are scaled so that the design fits within the column. Once the design is used in the graph, the design can be selected and modified.

You can apply a graph design in a column or stacked column graph, or in a bar or stacked bar graph. You can also use a graph design to replace markers in a line or scatter graph.

You can create the following types of graph designs:

- A *vertically scaled* design is stretched or compressed vertically. Its width does not change.
- A *uniformly scaled* design is scaled both vertically and horizontally. The horizontal spacing of the designs is not adjusted for the different widths.

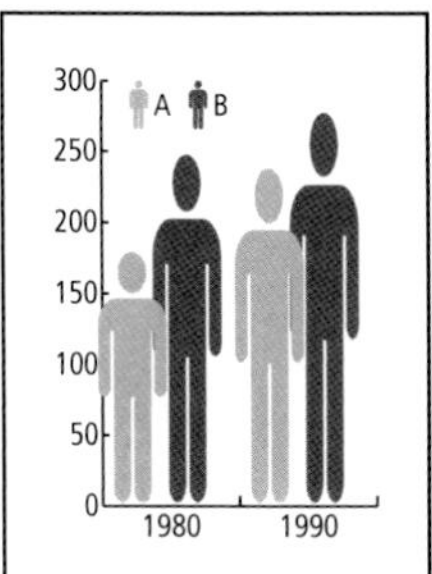

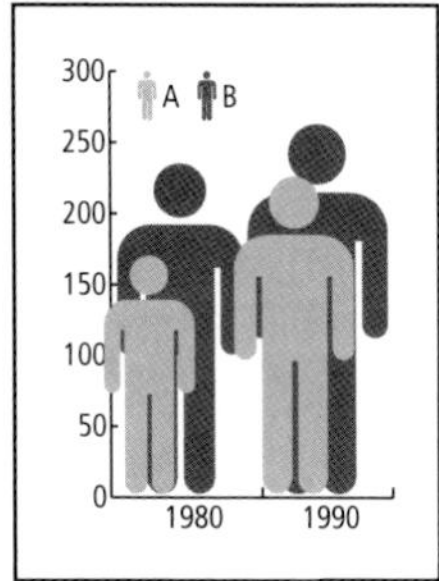

Vertically scaled design and uniformly scaled design

- A *repeating* design stacks a design to fill the columns. You can specify the value that each design represents, as well as whether you want to chop or scale designs that represent fractions.

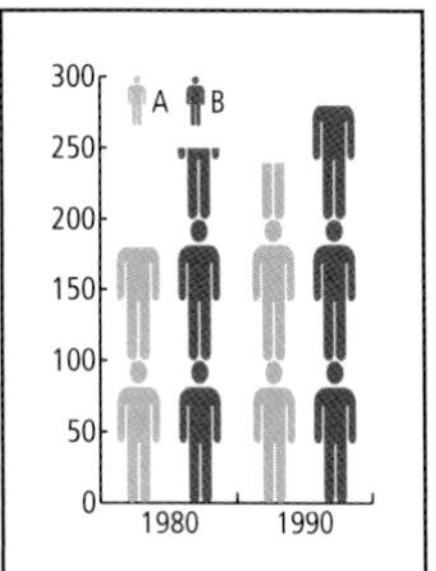

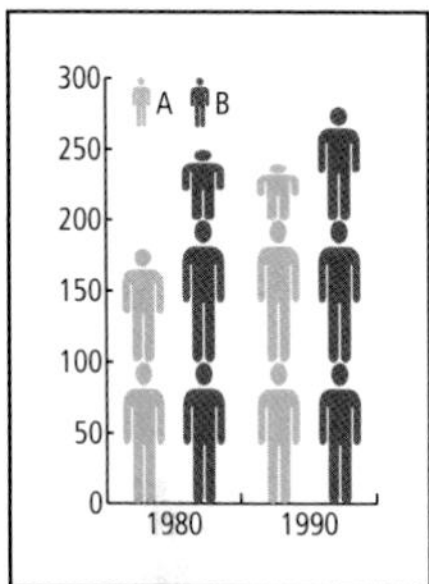

Repeating graph design with Chop Design option and with Scale Design option

- A *sliding* design is similar to a vertically scaled design, except that you can specify where in the design to stretch or compress it. For example, if you were using a person to represent data, you might stretch or compress only the body, but not the person's head. Using the Vertically Scaled option would scale the entire person.

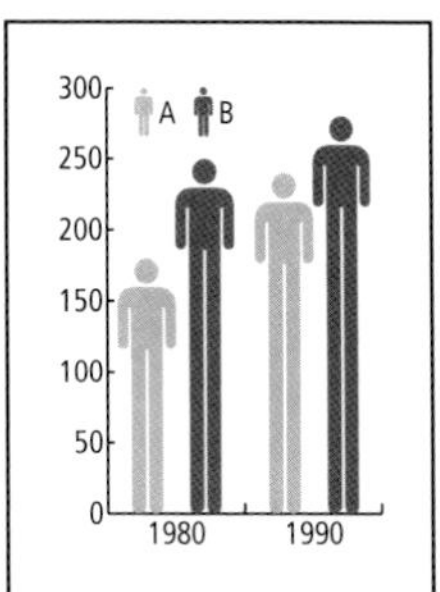

Sliding graph design

When you use a graph design with a column or bar graph, you scale the design vertically or horizontally, repeat the design, or slide the design with the columns or bars.

You can also rotate the design in the Graph Column dialog legend box. By default, the design is rotated to appear horizontal in the legend box. You can turn this option off so that the design appears vertically in the legend box.

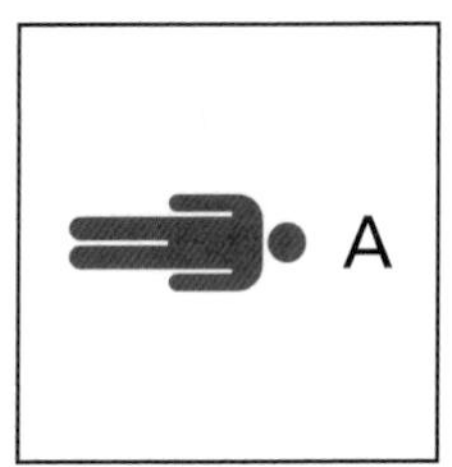

Rotation on and off

Creating a graph design

Creating a graph design is similar to creating a pattern. (For design ideas that you might use when creating graphs, see "Creating and working with patterns" on page 200.)

When you create a design or use a design in a file, the design is saved. To use that design in another file, either open the file in which you created the design or use the Window > Swatch Libraries > Other Library command and choose the file whose designs you want to import. (When the designs are imported, you will see the colors, gradients, and patterns in the new file, but the actual graph designs will only be visible in the Graph Design dialog box.)

To create a graph design:

1 Create a rectangle as the backmost object in the design. The rectangle represents the boundary of the graph design.

2 Paint the rectangle as desired, or fill and stroke it with None so that it is invisible.

Copy and paste the smallest column in your graph to use it as the bounding rectangle for your design.

3 Create the design using any of the drawing tools, or position an existing design in front of the rectangle.

4 To display column totals with the graph design, skip to that procedure later in this section.

5 Using the selection tool ( ), select the entire design, including the rectangle.

6 Choose Object > Group to group the design.

7 Choose Object > Graphs > Design.

8 Click New Design. A preview of the selected design appears.

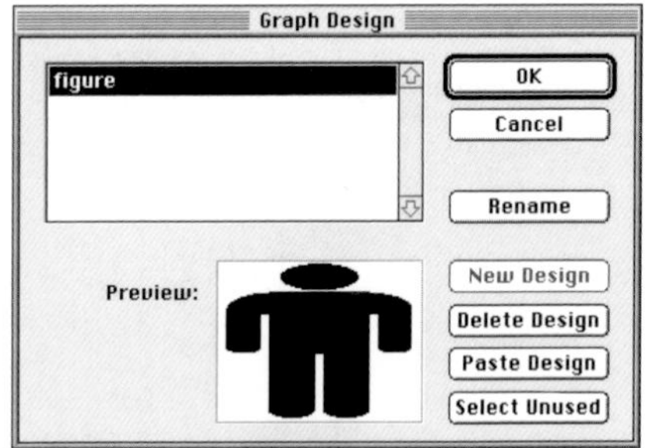

Only the portion of the design that fits inside the backmost rectangle appears, but the whole design appears when used in the graph.

9 Click Rename. Name the design, and click OK. Then click OK again.

10 To apply the design to a graph, see "Applying graph designs to a graph" on page 318.

To create a sliding graph design:

1 Create a rectangle as the backmost object in the design. This rectangle is the boundary for the graph design.

2 Create the design using one of the drawing tools, or place an existing design in front of the rectangle.

3 Use the pen tool ( ) to draw a horizontal line to define where the design is stretched or compressed.

4 Select all parts of the design, including the horizontal line.

5 Choose Object > Group.

6 Use the direct-selection tool ( ) or group-selection tool ( ) to select the horizontal line. Be sure to select only the horizontal line.

7 Choose View > Make Guides.

8 Choose View > Lock Guides to remove the check mark next to Lock so you can unlock the guides. Move the design around to make sure that the guide moves with the design.

9 Use the selection tool ( ) to select the whole design.

10 Choose Object > Graphs > Design.

11 Click New Design. You see a small preview of the selected design.

12 Click Rename. Name the design, and click OK. Then click OK again.

To display column totals with the graph design:

1 Create the graph design.

2 Select the type tool (T). Position the pointer at a point where you want the value to appear, near or in the rectangle that defines the design.

For example, you can place the value in, above, below, to the left, or to the right of the design.

3 Click and type a percent sign (%) followed by two digits from 0 to 9. The digits control how the data is displayed.

The first digit determines how many places appear before the decimal point. For example, if your total was 122, a digit of 3 would display 122. If you enter 0 for the first digit, the program adds the number of places necessary for the value.

The second digit determines how many places appear after the decimal point. Zeros are added as necessary, and values are rounded up or down as necessary. You can vary these numbers, depending on how many digits you need.

	0124.369
%30	124
%31	124.4
%32	124.37

Column total designs

4 To change the type attributes, choose Type > Character, specify the attributes you want, and close the palette.

5 To align the decimal points, choose Type > Paragraph and select Right Alignment.

6 Using the selection tool (), select the entire design, including the rectangle and any type.

7 Choose Object > Group to group the design.

8 Choose Object > Graphs > Design.

9 Click New Design. You see a preview of the selected design.

10 Click Rename. Name the design, and click OK. Then click OK again.

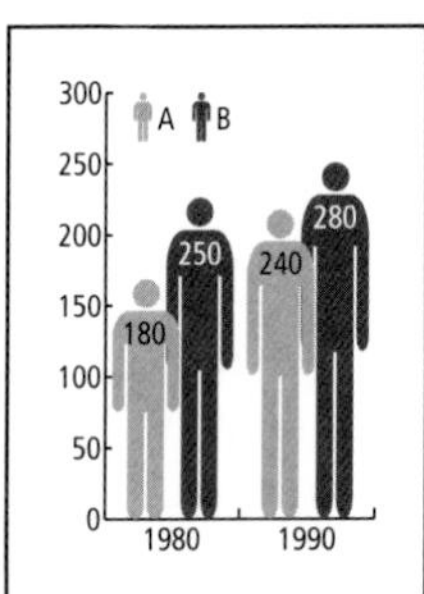

Sliding graph design with data totals

Applying graph designs to a graph

Once you have created a graph design, you can apply it either as a column in a column graph, as a bar in a bar graph, or as a marker in a line or scatter graph.

To use a graph design in a column graph or bar graph:

1 Use the group-selection tool () to select the columns or bars you want to fill with the design, or select the entire graph.

2 Choose Object > Graphs > Column.

3 Select a column design type, as described in "About graph designs" on page 314.

If you choose the Repeating Column Type, enter a value in the Each Design Represents text box for what each design represents. Also select whether to chop or scale any fractions of the design in the For Fractions pop-up menu. Chop Design cuts off a fraction of the top design as necessary; Scale Design scales the last design to fit in the column.

4 Select the design you want to use; you see a preview of the selected design. Click OK.

To create a marker design:

1 Start by copying a marker rectangle from the graph, and using the rectangle as the backmost object, to set the marker size.

2 Make the marker artwork the size you want it to be in the graph, even if it's larger than the marker rectangle you copied.

3 Once you've got the marker design the way you want it, select the design, then choose Object > Graphs > Design, and click New Design.

4 Click the Rename button, enter a new name for the design, and click OK.

To use a marker design in a line or scatter graph:.

1 Use the direct-selection tool (↖) to select the markers and the legends in the graph that you want to replace with a design. Do not select any lines.

2 Choose Object > Graphs > Marker. Then click OK.

The design is scaled so that the backmost rectangle in the design is the same size as the default square marker on the line or scatter graph.

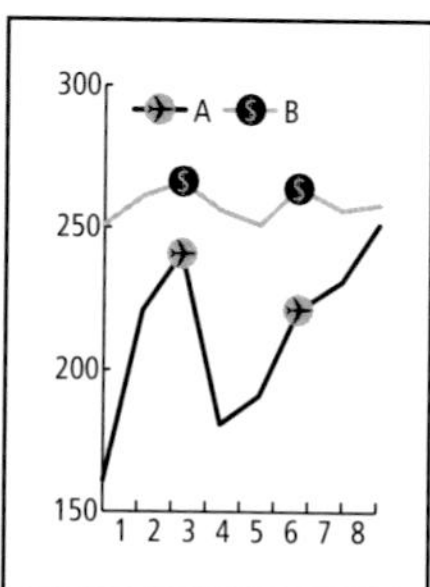

Line graph with marker designs

Reusing a graph design

You can reuse a graph design that you created and edit it to make a new design. If you have the original artwork, you can alter it and then rename the design using the Graph Design dialog box. (See "Creating a graph design" on page 316.)

If you don't have the original artwork defined as a graph design, you can retrieve the original by pasting the graph design into your artwork.

To paste an existing graph design into your artwork:

1 Choose Edit > Deselect All to deselect all of the artwork.

2 Choose Object > Graphs > Design.

3 Select the graph design that you want to paste into your artwork, and click Paste Design.

4 Click OK. The graph design is pasted into your artwork. You can now edit it and define it as a new graph design.

13

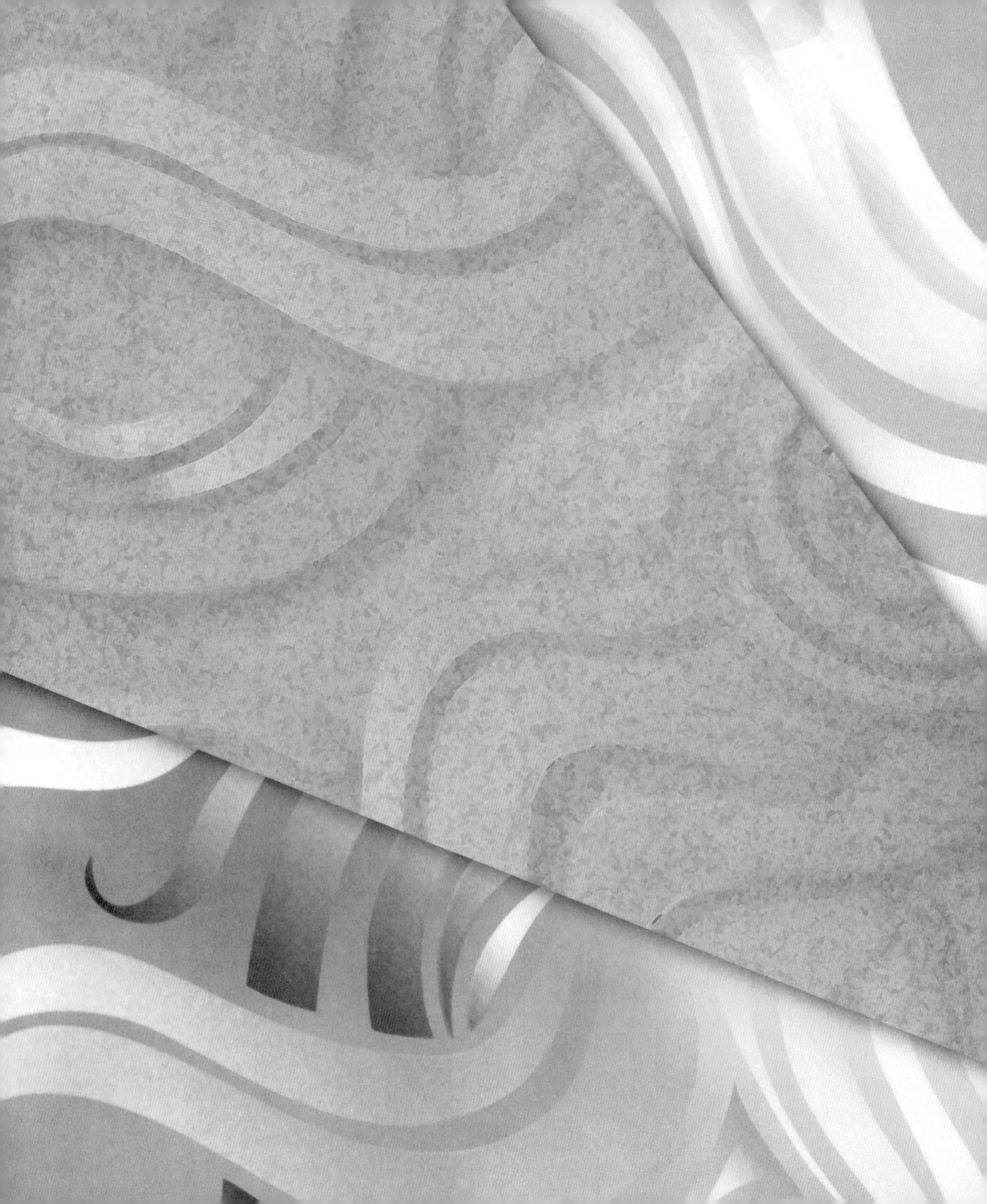

Chapter 13: Saving and Exporting Artwork

Saving artwork in Adobe Illustrator and exporting artwork created in Adobe Illustrator to other file formats is easily performed using various Adobe Illustrator commands.

Illustrator can export in many common graphic file formats, including EPS, GIF, JPEG, PICT, Photoshop 5.0, PostScript™, RTF, TIFF, Microsoft Word, WordPerfect™, and others. In addition, Illustrator can save in earlier versions of Adobe Illustrator, Illustrator EPS, and Acrobat PDF formats.

Saving files

Adobe Illustrator provides several ways to save files:

• The Save command saves the file with its current name, location, and file format.

• The Save As command lets you save an alternative version of the file with a different name, location, or file format.

• The Save a Copy command saves an identical copy of the file, with the word *Copy* added to the filename. This command leaves the original file as the active file.

Saving a file as a previous version of Adobe Illustrator

Some applications can import Illustrator files directly without requiring that the files first be saved in a different format. However, some applications may not be able to import the current version of the Illustrator file format.

Note that many features new to a given version of Illustrator are not preserved when you export the file in a previous version. For example, when saving an Illustrator 8 file as an Illustrator 4 format, gradient fills and layers are not preserved. Also, text features such as hanging punctuation may not be preserved, causing text breaks and text flows to change.

To save a file in an earlier version of Illustrator:

1 Choose File > Save As.

2 Select Illustrator in the Save as Type (Windows) or Format (Mac OS) pop-up menu.

3 In the Illustrator Format dialog box, select the desired version; then click OK.

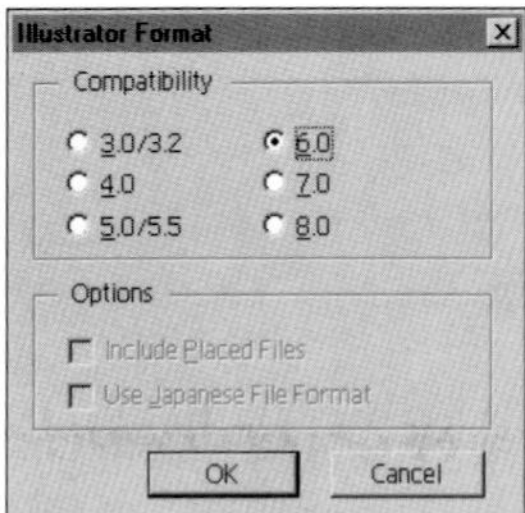

A warning appears, indicating that some features may be disabled when the file is opened.

Important: *When saving a Japanese format file to an earlier version than Illustrator 7.0, you must select the Use Japanese File Format option to preserve formats in the file.*

Saving files in EPS format

The most common way of sharing Illustrator artwork is to save the artwork as an EPS file. Saving an Illustrator file in EPS format has the following advantages:

• Virtually all page layout, word-processing, and graphic applications accept imported or placed EPS files.

• Unlike many other graphic file formats, EPS files preserve all the graphic elements you can create with Adobe Illustrator.

• RGB and CMYK objects remain in their respective color models.

• Illustrator files saved as EPS files remain Illustrator files.

• Most applications cannot display EPS artwork directly, but they can display a preview image saved as part of the EPS file. When working with other applications, you can use the preview image to locate and size the EPS artwork. See "Encapsulated PostScript (EPS) file format" on page 336 for a description of the preview options.

To save a file as an EPS file:

1 Choose File > Save As.

2 Select the folder where you want to save the EPS file, and enter a name for the file.

Note: *When you save a file in Windows format, the extension* .eps *is automatically added to the filename.*

3 Choose Illustrator EPS from the Save as Type (Windows) or Format (Mac OS) pop-up menu, and then click Save.

4 If desired, select the Adobe Illustrator file format with which you want your file to be compatible. Keep in mind that certain features, such as gradients and layers, are not supported by earlier versions of the Illustrator file format.

5 Choose from the following:

• Include Placed Files if the Illustrator document contains placed files and you want the files included in the document.

• Include Document Thumbnails to display a thumbnail image of the EPS artwork in the Illustrator Open dialog box.

• Use Japanese File Format to save the file as a Japanese language file compatible with Illustrator versions 3, 4, or 5. It is not necessary to use this option for Illustrator versions 7 or 8.

• Include Document Fonts forces any fonts used in the file to be saved with the file. Protected Japanese fonts cannot be embedded in the file.

• CMYK PostScript to enable vector objects containing RGB colors to print from applications that do not support RGB output. When the EPS file is reopened in Illustrator, the RGB colors are preserved.

• Select a PostScript format for the file. You can select between PostScript Level 1, PostScript Level 2, or PostScript 3. If gradient mesh objects are included in the file, and you expect to print the file to a PostScript 3 printer, you should select PostScript 3 to eliminate slow print times or error messages.

***Note:** When placing an EPS image containing a gradient mesh object as an embedded file (that is, the Link option is deselected in the Place dialog box), the file should be saved as an EPS Level 1 PostScript file.*

• Select an EPS preview format for the file. You can select from IBM® PC (TIFF format) or Macintosh (PICT format) previews and 1-bit or 8-bit preview formats.

6 Click OK.

Saving files in Acrobat PDF format

You can save an Illustrator file as a PDF file, and also link to and embed Portable Document Format (PDF) files within the Illustrator file. (See "Importing EPS and PDF files into Illustrator" on page 57.) In addition, after saving an Illustrator file as a PDF file, you can later open the file as an Illustrator file, without losing many file features such as fonts, color characteristics, patterns, or vertical type blocks.

To save in PDF format:

1 Choose File > Save As or File > Save a Copy.

2 Select Acrobat PDF from the Save as Type (Windows) or Format (Mac OS) pop-up menu.

3 Select options in the PDF Format dialog and then click Save.

About exporting artwork

To use an Adobe Illustrator file in another application, you must save or export the file in a graphics file format that the other application can use.

To save files in Illustrator, Illustrator EPS, or Acrobat PDF formats, use the Save As or Save a Copy command. All other file formats are saved using the File > Export command. If a file format does not appear, install the format's plug-in module following the instructions in "Using plug-in modules" on page 39.

In addition to being able to save complete Illustrator files in various graphic formats, you can also export selected portions of Illustrator files using the Clipboard and the drag-and-drop feature. (See "Using the Clipboard to copy artwork" on page 119, and "Using the drag-and-drop feature to copy artwork" on page 119 for more information on these features.)

File Format	Export Methods	Considerations
AI	Save, Save As, Save a copy	Files may be saved as Illustrator version 3.0 and later.
EPS	Save, Save As, Save a copy	When saving as EPS, selecting the "CMYK PostScript" option prints all RGB colors as their CMYK equivalents.
PDF	Save, Save As, Save a copy	
Photoshop	Export	Layers are preserved when exporting in Photoshop format. Drag and drop artwork directly into Photoshop (flattens layers).
PICT	Export	Macintosh only.
Enhanced Meta-File (EMF)	Export	Windows only. Drag and drop artwork directly into Microsoft Office.
All raster formats supported by Photoshop-compatible filters	Export	Supports the following formats: Amiga IFF, BMP, GIF89a, JPEG, PCX, Pixar, PNG, TIFF, and Targa.
Text Formats	Export	Supports the following formats: plain text, MS RTF (Roman only), MS Word (Roman only), Corel WordPerfect (Roman only).

To export an Illustrator file in another format:

1 Choose File > Export.

2 Select the folder where you want to save the file, and rename the file or change the file extension to reflect the new file format. Changing the filename ensures that your original artwork is preserved on disk.

3 Choose a file format from the Save as Type (Windows) or Format (Mac OS) pop-up menu.

4 Click Save. If you are exporting the file to a bitmap format, you may be asked to choose a resolution and bit depth for the bitmap. (See "About resolution in bitmap images" on page 45 for more information.)

Exporting artwork in JPEG and GIF formats

JPEG is the appropriate file format to use for full-color artwork, for artwork containing gradients, and for artwork containing smooth transitions of color common with photographic images. GIF89a is the appropriate file format to use for artwork with flat color, a limited number of colors, and sharp detail (such as type). For gradients, JPEG format produces smaller files than GIF format. When exporting in JPEG format, you can specify an image quality and compression level for the file, in addition to other formatting options.

The GIF89a Export module lets you convert images to indexed-color or grayscale GIF files. Adobe Illustrator can open and save CompuServe® GIF files as 8-bit indexed color.

To export artwork to JPEG format:

1 Choose File > Export.

2 Select JPEG from the Save as Type (Windows) or Format (Mac OS) pop-up menu.

3 To specify the desired image quality, use one of the following methods:

• Enter a value between 0 and 10 in the text box.

• Choose Low, Medium, High, or Maximum from the Quality menu.

• Drag the slider to the desired value; the Quality menu reflects the quality of the value you select.

An image compressed using Maximum quality is less compressed (and thus takes up more disk space) than an image compressed using the Low quality option.

4 Select a format option for the JPEG file. Choose one of the following methods:

• Baseline (Standard)

• Baseline Optimized, to optimize the color quality of the image.

• Progressive, to save the file as a progressive JPEG file; then select a scan rate from the Scan menu. The Progressive option displays the image as a series of overlays, enabling viewers to see a low-resolution version of the image before it downloads completely. When you specify progressive, you can also specify the number of progressive scans. However, keep in mind that progressive JPEG images require more RAM for viewing and are not supported by all Web browsers.

5 Select a resolution level:

• Screen to export as a 72-dpi image.

• Medium to export as a 150-dpi image.

• High to export as a 300-dpi image.

• Custom to enter another resolution level in units of dots per inch (dpi).

6 Select from the other export options:

• Anti-alias to smooth the edges of the artwork.

• Imagemap to save Illustrator artwork as an imagemap if you have linked objects in the artwork to URLs in the Attributes palette.

Select one of the following options for the imagemap type:

• Client-side (.html) prepares the image for use in a Web page creation application. Choosing the Client-side option saves two files: a .jpg file containing the artwork and an .html file containing the HTML link information. These two files must be saved or placed in the same location to be interpreted correctly by the Web page creation application or Web browser.

• Server-side (.map) prepares the artwork to be loaded on a Web server. To use the Server-side option, you need to know the parameters of the Web server being used. Consult your service provider or your Web server documentation for information about .map files.

To export artwork to GIF89a format:

1 Choose File > Export.

2 Select GIF89a from the Save as Type (Windows) or Format (Mac OS) pop-up menu.

3 For Palette, choose one of the following options:

• The Exact palette uses the same colors for the palettes as those that appear in the image. No dithering option is available. (Dithering mixes color to approximate colors used in the image that are not present in the palette.) The Exact option is available only if 256 or fewer colors are used in the image.

• The System (Macintosh or Windows) option builds a color table by using the color table of the system you select. It is an 8-bit palette, capable of displaying 256 colors. Note that the System option may produce unexpected results when the image is displayed on an 8-bit monitor using a different built-in palette.

• The Web palette is a cross-platform 8-bit color palette. Use this palette option to ensure that the image will appear the same on different systems.

• The Adaptive palette uses a representative sample of colors in the image. Use this option for the best results if the Exact option is unavailable. If you choose the Adaptive palette option, select or type the smallest number of colors that retain the necessary detail in your image.

• The Custom palette lets you select a custom palette.

4 Select Halftone Dithering to simulate colors not in the palette, and minimize clashing between adjacent blocks of color.

5 To determine how the image displays, select any of the following options:

• Interlace to display the image gradually increasing in detail as it is downloaded.

• Transparent to make the unpainted areas of the artwork transparent in the Web browser. You cannot specify which areas you want to make transparent; Illustrator defines the transparent areas based on the area of the artwork that is unpainted.

• Anti-alias to smooth the edges of the artwork.

• Imagemap to save Illustrator artwork as an imagemap if you have linked objects in the artwork to URLs in the Attributes palette.

Select one of the following options for the imagemap type:

• Client-side (.html) prepares the image for use in a Web page creation application. Choosing the Client-side option saves two files: a .gif file containing the artwork and an .html file containing the HTML link information. These two files must be saved or placed in the same location to be interpreted correctly by the Web page creation application or Web browser.

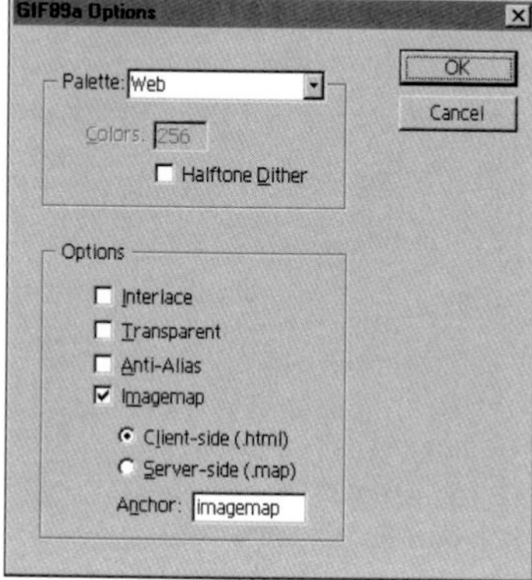

• Server-side (.map) prepares the artwork to be loaded on a Web server. To use the Server-side option, you need to know the parameters of the Web server being used. Consult your service provider or your Web server documentation for information about .map files.

• The Anchor option is used only when creating GIFs with client-side imagemaps to be used in HTML documents. If more than one imagemap is to be used in an HTML document, you must specify a discrete name for each imagemap in the HTML file. You can use any name for the imagemap; it is used only by the HTML file and is transparent to the user.

Exporting files in Photoshop 5.0 format

You can export Illustrator files in Photoshop 5.0 format, retaining many of the features of the Illustrator artwork.

To export a file in Photoshop 5.0 format:

1 Choose File > Export and select Photoshop 5.0 from the Save as Type (Windows) or Format (Mac OS) pop-up menu.

2 Select from the following options:

• Color Model to choose between RGB, CMYK, or Grayscale color models in which to export the file.

• Resolution to choose a resolution level in units of dots per inch.

• Anti-alias to smooth the edges of the artwork.

• Write Layers to maintain the artwork on layers when exported into Photoshop format.

Using the Publish and Subscribe commands (for Mac OS only)

On the Macintosh, you can use Adobe Illustrator Publish and Subscribe commands to share and update material among documents. Publish and Subscribe lets you copy and update material from one file to other files. Once you've subscribed to a published edition, the material can be updated automatically whenever the original file is modified. (For a detailed description of Publish and Subscribe, see your Macintosh documentation.)

To use Publish and Subscribe, you first define the material that you want to be made available to other files; this material is called a *publisher.* The material in the publisher is then saved as a separate file called an *edition.*

You can then open the file in which you want to insert the edition; this file is called a *subscriber.* Each time you make changes to the published selection and save the changes, the artwork in the subscribing files is updated. If you do not want updates to be sent automatically, you can send them manually using the options in the Publisher Options dialog box.

To publish artwork:

1 Using a selection tool, select the objects to be published.

2 Choose Edit > Publishing > Create Publisher.

3 If necessary, select the file folder or disk drive on which you want to save the published file.

4 Select the file format in which you want to save your artwork, either PICT only or PICT and EPS. You can publish your artwork as a PICT file containing a PostScript language resource for printing or as a combination PICT and EPS file. If the file is being subscribed to by an application that is compatible with the EPS format, such as Adobe Illustrator, save the file as PICT and EPS. If the subscribing application is not EPS compatible, save the file as PICT only.

5 Type in a name for your artwork in the Name of new edition text box. Click Publish.

To update published artwork:

1 Choose Edit > Publishing > Publisher Options.

2 Choose the edition you want to update from the Publisher pop-up menu.

3 Choose one of two update options:

• On Save, the default option, to update the published artwork every time a change is saved using the Save or Save As command.

• Manually to update the edition only when you click the Update Edition Now button.

4 Select the file format in which to update the edition, either PICT only or PICT and EPS, and click OK.

To subscribe to published artwork:

1 Choose Edit > Publishing > Subscribe To.

2 Select the edition to which you want to subscribe. A preview of the artwork is shown in the preview box.

3 Click Subscribe. The subscribed artwork appears in your file as if it were placed with the Place EPS command.

Sending artwork as electronic mail using the Send command (Windows only)

If you have Microsoft Mail installed on your system, you can send the current file as electronic mail, using the Send command. The Send command is only active when Microsoft Mail is installed on your Windows system.

To send artwork as electronic mail:

1 Choose File > Send.

2 In the Send dialog box, address the mail message and click OK.

Object linking and embedding (OLE) (Windows only)

Object linking and embedding are two ways to import an Adobe Illustrator image into another application and update that image when it is modified. Illustrator is an OLE 2.0 server, which means it supports embedding or linking an image in an OLE container application (usually a word-processor or page-layout program). For example, you can insert Adobe Illustrator files and selections into other OLE applications, such as Adobe PageMaker 6.5® and Microsoft Word® 7.0, by using copy and paste, drag and drop, or other methods.

Once an image is in the container application, you can double-click it to open and edit it in Illustrator. When you close the file in Illustrator, the image is updated in the container application.

To link or embed a selection or image in an OLE application:

Do one of the following:

- With the selection tool, select the object and drag the selection to the OLE container application (if it supports this feature).
- Copy a selection in Illustrator and insert it into your OLE container application using its Paste Special command. Refer to your word-processing or page-layout application documentation for more instructions. Pasted selections can only be embedded, not linked.
- Use your OLE container application's Insert Object command to insert new Illustrator artwork or an existing Illustrator file as an OLE-embedded or OLE-linked object. Refer to your word-processing or page-layout application documentation for instructions.

To insert an unlinked screen-resolution bitmap into an OLE application:

With the selection tool, use the left-mouse button to drag a selection to the OLE container application. When you drop the object, the file format or resolution of the object is determined by the source application.

To modify and update a linked or embedded image in an OLE application:

1 Double-click the linked or embedded object in your word-processor or page-layout application to launch Adobe Illustrator (if it is not already running), and open the object for editing.

2 Modify the image as desired.

3 Do one of the following:

• For embedded images, close the file, or choose File > Update or File > Close & Return to <*application name*>.

• For linked objects, save and close the file.

Note: *You can also modify linked files without first opening the container document; the linked image will be updated the next time you open the document in its OLE container application.*

Linking objects to URLs for Internet Web pages

Any object you create in Adobe Illustrator can be linked to a Uniform Resource Locator (URL) string, transforming the object into a button that links the user to an Internet Web site. This feature is useful when creating artwork for Web pages, allowing you to preattach Web links to individual objects before importing the artwork into a Web page design application.

After assigning a URL to an object in an illustration, you can verify that the URL is valid by using the Launch Browser button in the Attributes palette. If your computer has an Internet browser (such as Netscape™ Navigator™ or Microsoft Explorer), clicking the Launch Browser button automatically connects to the URL you have defined as the object's link.

To activate URL links to objects, you must export the artwork either to a JPEG or GIF89a format (with the Imagemap option selected) and then import the HTML artwork into a Web page design program, such as Adobe PageMill®.

***Important:** The prefix* http:// *must precede the URL address to ensure that the link works correctly, once the file is exported in GIF or JPEG format.*

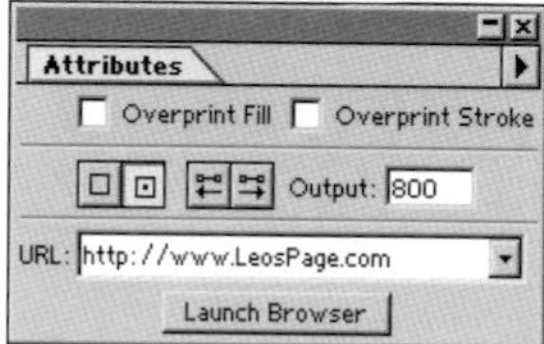

Select an object, and enter the corresponding URL address in the Attributes palette.

Use a Web page design application to verify the URL link.

To link an object to a URL:

1 Select the object to which you want to link a URL.

2 Choose Window > Show Attributes.

3 Enter a URL in the URL text box, or choose one from the list of available URLs.

4 If you have a Web browser on your system, you can verify the URL location by clicking Launch Browser in the Attributes palette.

To prepare artwork containing URL links for use in a Web page application:

1 Attach URL links to the object or objects in your illustration.

2 Choose File > Export. Choose JPEG or GIF89a from the Format menu in the Export dialog box.

3 Enter a name for the file, including a *.jpg* or *.gif* extension; then click Save.

4 Choose Web from the Palette menu to ensure Web-safe colors across platforms. (You can choose another palette, but colors may appear differently on different platforms.)

5 Choose Imagemap from the Options section of the dialog box; then choose one of the following options for the type of imagemap:

- Click Client-side (*.html*) to prepare the image for use in a Web page creation application. Choosing the Client-side option saves two files: the .jpg or .gif file containing the artwork and an HTML file containing the link information. These two files must be saved in the same location to be interpreted by the Web page creation application.

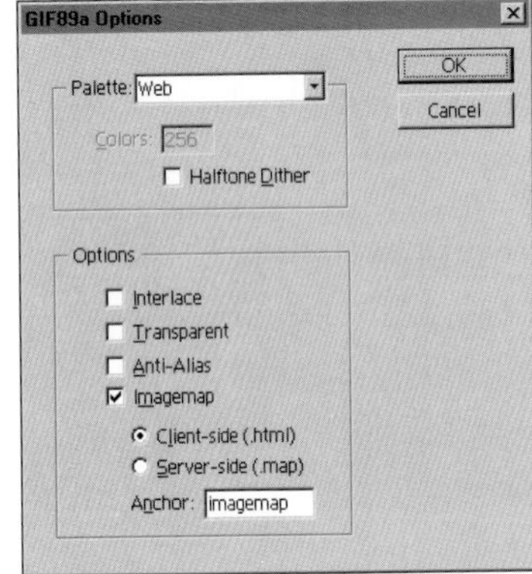

If more than one imagemap is to be used in an HTML document, you must specify a discrete name for each imagemap in the HTML file. You can use any name for the imagemap; it is used only by the HTML file and is transparent to the user.

- Server-side (.map) to prepare the artwork to be loaded on a Web server. To use the Server-side option, you need to know the parameters of the Web server being used. Consult your service provider or your Web server documentation for information about .map files.

6 Click OK to save the file. Two files are written: an HTML file and the file containing the artwork. Make sure that both files are saved in the same location.

7 Quit the Adobe Illustrator program.

8 Open a Web page creation application, for example, Adobe PageMill, or open a Web browser.

9 Choose File > Open, and open the file with the *.html* extension.

The artwork is displayed in the window.

Position the pointer over the artwork where you linked a URL to the object or objects to check the URL addresses.

10 Follow the instructions in your Web creation application or Web browser to activate the link.

Note: *If the URL string does not appear when you position the pointer over the object, the .jpg or .gif file and the html file are not in the same location. Move the two files into the same location.*

To increase the number of visible entries in the URL menu:

1 Choose Window > Show Attributes.

2 Choose Palette Options from the Attributes palette.

3 Enter a value from 1 to 30 to define how many URL entries you want displayed in the URL list.

4 Click OK.

File size and image compression

The storage required for bitmap images is the product of the image size, resolution, and bit depth. A 2-by-4-inch, 1200-ppi, 24-bit color image, for example, requires more than 34 MB (megabytes) of storage; the same image at 300 ppi requires about 2 MB.

Because bitmap images can require so much storage, many techniques have been developed for compressing image data to reduce storage.

Compression techniques are distinguished by whether they remove detail from the image. *Lossless* techniques compress image data without removing detail; *lossy* techniques compress images by removing detail.

The following techniques are commonly used to compress bitmap image data:

• Run Length Encoding (RLE) is a lossless compression technique supported by the TIFF file format and some common Windows file formats.

• Lemple-Zif-Welch (LZW) is a lossless compression technique supported by TIFF, PDF, GIF89a, and PostScript language file formats.

• Joint Photographic Experts Group (JPEG) is a lossy compression technique supported by the PDF and PostScript language file formats.

• CCITT encoding is a family of lossless compression techniques for black-and-white images that is supported by the PDF and PostScript language file formats.

Enhancing the quality of online output

Several factors affect the quality and speed of your online output, including the image size and resolution, and the file format you use for the final image. The suggestions below will help you determine the best way to prepare your images for online distribution.

PREPARING IMAGES FOR DISTRIBUTION ON THE WEB

1. Create the artwork in Adobe Illustrator.

2. Select the object you want to use in the Web page, and then link the URL address to the object using the Attributes palette.

3. If the image consists of flat-colored areas, requires transparency, or requires a specific palette, or if you want to link a URL to your artwork, export to GIF89a or JPEG format.

4. Open your artwork in a Web browser or Web page creation application, and position the pointer over the object to verify the link.

5. If the artwork contains gradients, or placed images or is photo realistic, export to JPEG.

About graphic file formats

There are several common file formats you can use to get images into and out of Adobe Illustrator. Graphic file formats are distinguished by the way they represent graphic information. Graphic information can be represented as either vector drawings or bitmap images. Some graphic file formats contain only vector drawings or only bitmap images, but many can include both in the same file.

BMP BMP is the standard Windows bitmap image format on DOS and Windows-compatible computers. When saving an image in this format, you can specify either Microsoft Windows or OS/2® format, but you are limited to 24-bit depth for the image.

Encapsulated PostScript (EPS) file format The Encapsulated PostScript (EPS) language file format is used to transfer PostScript language artwork between applications, and it is supported by most illustration and page-layout programs. Typically, EPS files represent single illustrations or tables that are placed onto a host page, but an EPS file can also represent a complete page.

Because they are based on the PostScript language, EPS files can contain both vector and bitmap graphics. Like PostScript language files, early versions of EPS files contain only grayscale vector bitmap graphics, whereas later versions support color graphics and compressed bitmap images.

In addition to the PostScript language representation of the graphics to be placed, many EPS files contain an application-specific preview bitmap representation of the graphic that an application can display. EPS files intended to be used by Macintosh applications, for example, can contain PICT or TIFF images for screen preview; those intended for use by Windows applications contain either TIFF or Windows Metafile bitmap images.

Not all applications that create EPS files create preview images, however. When you place an EPS file without a preview image, Illustrator displays a box with an "*X*" to represent the EPS artwork. When you place an EPS file with a TIFF preview image, Illustrator also displays a box with an "*X*" for the EPS artwork. For more information on importing and exporting EPS files in Illustrator, see "Opening and placing artwork" on page 55 and "Managing linked and embedded images" on page 58.

GIF89a GIF89a (Graphics Interchange Format) is commonly used to display indexed-color graphics and images in hypertext markup language (HTML) files over the World Wide Web and other online services. GIF is a compressed format that is designed to minimize file transfer time over phone lines.

Adobe Illustrator can save 8-bit indexed RGB color images in GIF89a.

For color images showing quality considerations for the Web, see "JPEG or GIF?" on page 236.

Amiga IFF The Amiga™ Interchange File Format (IFF) is used for working with Video Toaster and transferring files to and from the Commodore Amiga system. In addition, this format is supported by a number of paint programs on IBM-compatible computers, including Deluxe-Paint from Electronic Arts; IFF is the best export format to use with that program.

JPEG The Joint Photographic Experts Group (JPEG) format is commonly used to display photographs and other continuous-tone images in hypertext markup language (HTML) files over the World Wide Web and other online services. Unlike GIF, JPEG retains all the color information in an RGB image. JPEG also uses a compression scheme that effectively reduces file size by identifying and discarding extra data not essential to the display of the image. Opening a JPEG image automatically decompresses it.

Because it discards data, the JPEG compression scheme is referred to as *lossy.* This means that once an image has been compressed and then decompressed, it will not be identical to the original image. A higher level of compression results in lower image quality; a lower level of compression results in better image quality. In most cases, compressing an image using the Maximum quality option produces a result that is indistinguishable from the original. For information on choosing JPEG options, see "Exporting artwork in JPEG and GIF formats" on page 326.

PCX PCX format, established by Z-Soft® for its PC Paintbrush® software, is commonly used by IBM PC-compatible computers. Most PC software supports version 5 of the PCX format. Version 3 files do not support a custom color palette. For this reason, when you open a version 3 PCX file, the palette is ignored and a standard VGA color palette is used instead.

PDF The PDF format is used by Adobe Acrobat®, Adobe's electronic publishing software for Macintosh, Windows, UNIX®, and DOS. You can view PDF files using the Acrobat Reader® software included on your Adobe Illustrator CD.

Based on the PostScript Level 2 language, PDF can represent both vector and bitmap graphics. PDF pages are identical to PostScript pages, but PDF files can also contain electronic document search and navigation features. PDF files, for example, can contain hypertext links and an electronic table of contents.

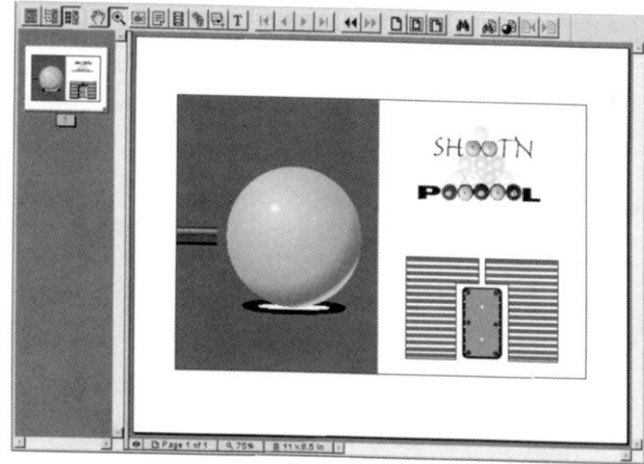

PDF file as displayed by Acrobat Exchange® viewer

Because Illustrator can open a PDF file, you can use the vector artwork or bitmap images from any PDF file in an Illustrator file.

You can also use Illustrator to make changes to individual PDF pages. To modify a page within a PDF file, open the PDF file, select the page to modify, make changes, and save the modified PDF file. The modified page is restored to its original position in the PDF file.

Macintosh PICT The PICT format is widely used among Macintosh graphics and page-layout applications as an intermediary file format for transferring files between applications. The PICT format is especially effective at compressing images that contain large areas of solid color.

PIXAR The PIXAR format is designed specifically for exchanging files with PIXAR image computers. PIXAR workstations are designed for high-end graphics applications, such as those used for three-dimensional images and animation.

PNG The PNG format was developed as an alternative to the GIF format and, like GIF, it is used for displaying images on the World Wide Web and other online services. PNG preserves all the color information in an image and uses a lossless compression scheme to reduce file size.

When saving an image in PNG format, you can choose to display the image in gradually increasing detail as it is downloaded. To do this, select Adam7 for Interlace. You can also select a filtering algorithm, which is used to prepare the image data for compression.

PostScript language file format PostScript is a page description language that is built into many desktop printers and virtually all high-end printing systems. Because it is built into so many printers, most Macintosh, Windows, and UNIX® applications can create PostScript files for printing.

The first version of the PostScript file format, PostScript Level 1, represents both grayscale vector graphics and grayscale bitmap images. The second version, PostScript Level 2, represents color as well as grayscale vector and bitmap images, and supports RGB, CYMK, and CIE-based color models for both vector and bitmap graphics. (Some PostScript Level 1 files also represent color with extensions to the PostScript language that were generalized in PostScript Level 2.) PostScript 3 provides additional functionality to Level 2, including the ability to print gradient mesh objects when printing to a PostScript 3 printer. Since printing to PostScript Level 1 and Level 2 devices converts gradient mesh objects to bitmap images, it is preferable to print artwork that contains gradient mesh objects to a PostScript 3 printer.

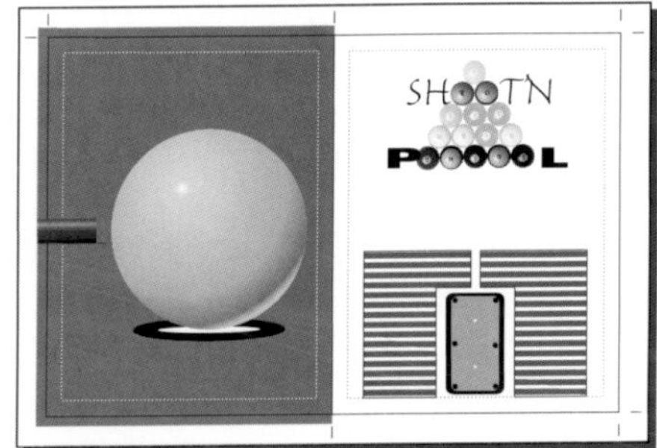

The PostScript file format describes both vector and bitmap graphics.

PostScript Level 2 also supports a number of compression techniques for bitmap images, including the LZW, CCITT, and JPEG methods.

Illustrator does not save PostScript files directly (but it does open PostScript files), but if you are using a PostScript printer, you can use the Print-to-File option in the Print dialog box to create a PostScript file.

***Note:** For best results, Adobe recommends that you create PostScript files with the Apple LaserWriter 8 or Adobe PostScript printer driver.*

Targa The TGA (Targa) format is designed for use on systems that use the Truevision® video board and is commonly supported by MS-DOS color applications. If you are saving artwork in this format, you can choose the resolution and color depth you want.

TIFF The Tagged-Image File Format (TIFF) is used to exchange files between applications and computer platforms. TIFF is a flexible bitmap image format that is supported by virtually all paint, image-editing, and page-layout applications. Also, virtually all desktop scanners can produce TIFF images.

TIFF supports RGB, CMYK, and grayscale color models. It also supports LZW compression, a lossless compression method that does not discard detail from the image.

When you export Illustrator artwork in TIFF, you can choose to save in a format that can be read either by Macintosh or by IBM PC-compatible computers. You can also choose an RGB, CMYK, or grayscale color model and define the image resolution. To compress the file to a smaller size automatically, click the LZW Compression option.

14

Chapter 14: Printing

You will probably want to print intermediate copies of your artwork as you design it, before you print the final version. To make optimum decisions about printing, you should understand basic printing principles, including how the resolution of your printer or the calibration and resolution of your monitor can affect the way your artwork appears when printed.

About printing

Whether you are providing multicolored artwork to an outside service bureau or just sending a quick draft of a drawing to an inkjet or laser printer, knowing a few basics about printing will make the print job go more smoothly and help ensure that the finished artwork appears as intended.

Types of printing When you print a file, the Adobe Illustrator program sends it to a printing device, either to be printed directly onto paper, to a digital printing press, or to be converted to a positive or negative image on film. In the latter case, the film can then be used to create a master plate for printing by a mechanical press.

Types of images The simplest types of images, such as a page of text, use only one color in one level of gray. A more complex image is one whose color tones vary within the image. This type of image is known as a *continuous-tone image*. A scanned photograph is an example of a continuous-tone image.

Halftoning To create the illusion of continuous tone when printed, images are broken down into a series of dots. This process is called *halftoning*. Varying the sizes and densities of the dots in a halftone screen creates the optical illusion of variations of gray or continuous color in the image.

Color separation Artwork that will be commercially reproduced and that contains more than a single color must be printed on separate master plates, one for each color. This process is called *color separation*. (See Chapter 15, "Producing Color Separations.")

For a comparison of a color composite versus a four-color separation printing process, see figure 14-1 on page 231.

Getting detail The detail in a printed image results from a combination of resolution and screen frequency. The higher an output device's resolution, the finer (higher) a screen ruling you can use. (See "Specifying the halftone screen ruling" on page 374.)

Printing artwork and composites

You can choose from a set of standard printing options in Adobe Illustrator for any type of artwork you print. These printing options appear in the Print Setup > Properties dialog box (Windows) or Page Setup (Mac OS) dialog box. You can then print the artwork using the Print dialog box.

If you are making color separations, you can print a color or grayscale composite proof to check your work. A composite image can help you to design and proof your artwork before printing final (and costly) separations.

When Illustrator prints a composite, it prints all of the colors used in the file on one plate, regardless of whether any individual colors are selected.

Keep in mind that any overprinting specified in the artwork won't appear on the composite from most printers. Also, as with color monitors, color printers vary greatly in color reproduction quality; thus, composites from a color printer never substitute for proofs made by the print shop.

To select printing options:

1 Choose File > Print Setup (Windows) or File > Page Setup (Mac OS).

2 Do one of the following:

- In Windows, click Properties.
- In Mac OS, select Page Attributes or PostScript Options from the pop-up menu.

3 Do one of the following:

- In Windows, select the options you want in the Properties dialog box, and click OK.
- In Mac OS, select the options you want from the selected pop-up menu, and click OK.

To print a file:

1 Choose File > Print.

The number of pages that Illustrator prints is determined by the View options selected in the Document Setup dialog box. If the Single Full Page option in the Document Setup dialog box is selected, a single page prints. If any other View option is selected, for example, the Tile Full Pages option, you can specify a page or a range of pages to print by entering beginning and ending page numbers in the From and To text boxes.

2 Indicate which pages you want printed.

3 Choose from the following options in the Print dialog box (Windows) or choose Adobe Illustrator 8.0 from the pop-up menu (Mac OS) and set the advanced printing options:

- PostScript. If your printer driver and printer support PostScript Level 1, 2, or 3, you can select one of these options. These options enable you to optimize printing of gradient mesh objects or other complex artwork. (See "Printing with gradient mesh objects" on page 350 and "Additional tips for efficient printing" on page 353.)
- Output. Select Composite to print a single composite color image or Separate to print a four-color separation. The Separate option only becomes available after you have set the separation options in the File > Separation Setup dialog box.
- Data. This option for printing bitmap images is only available on Mac OS systems. Select Binary to decrease the amount of data and therefore to speed up the printing of bitmap images, or ASCII to provide all bitmap data.

• Bitmap Printing (Windows only). Select Bitmap Printing when printing to a low-resolution, non-PostScript printer. The image is sent to the printer as a bitmap image; although the print speed may be diminished, the possibility of error messages is reduced.

4 Click OK (Windows) or Print (Mac OS).

By default, Adobe Illustrator prints all visible layers. To print an individual layer, see "Making selected layers nonprintable" on page 224.

Important: *Adobe Illustrator does not support PDF Writer format; if you attempt to print to PDF Writer you may experience delays or errors in printing.*

Setting crop marks and trim marks

Crop marks define where the artwork is trimmed after it is printed. You can place crop marks directly into your artwork using the Object > Crop Marks > Make command. If you select Japanese Crop Marks in the General Preferences dialog box, any crop marks you create in your file will appear as Japanese-style crop marks.

Like crop marks, *trim marks* also define where a printed image should be trimmed; however, you use trim marks to create multiple marks inside your artwork. The Trim Marks filter creates trim marks based on an imaginary rectangle drawn around the imageable area of the object.

Illustrator does not recognize trim marks created with the Trim Marks filter as special objects when creating color separations. As a result, trim marks do not affect the printing bounding box around the artwork. Trim marks are useful, therefore, when you want to create several sets of marks around objects on a page—for example, when you are creating a sheet of business cards to be printed.

To set crop marks directly in the artwork:

1 Draw a rectangle to define the boundaries of where you want the crop marks to appear. (It doesn't matter if the rectangle is filled or stroked.)

2 Select the rectangle.

3 Choose Object > Crop Marks > Make. If you have selected a rectangle as the border, the crop marks replace the selected rectangle. If no rectangle has been selected, crop marks are placed at the corners of the artboard.

Once you've set crop marks, you cannot directly select or edit them. To indirectly edit crop marks, you can choose Object > Crop Marks > Release, edit the rectangle that defines the crop marks boundary, and then remake them using the Object > Crop Marks > Make command. If you want to delete the existing crop marks, you can use the Object > Crop Marks > Release command.

If you selected Single Full Page in the Document Setup dialog box, you can use the Make Cropmarks command without first creating and selecting a rectangle to define the boundaries of the crop marks. The crop marks are set at the outer corners of the document.

Image with crop marks and image with Japanese crop marks

If you plan to separate a color Illustrator file, you should first set crop marks in the artwork. If you don't set crop marks, by default Illustrator sets them around the bounding box of all objects in the artwork.

For more information on setting crop marks in color separations, see "Step 4: Set the printing bounding box and place crop marks around the image to be separated" on page 369.

To eliminate crop marks:

Choose Object > Crop marks > Release. The original rectangle reappears to define the bounding area of your artwork. The rectangle may then be deleted or moved.

To specify Japanese crop marks:

1 Choose File > Preferences > General.

2 Select Japanese Crop Marks, and then click OK.

To create trim marks around an object:

Select the object, and choose Filter > Create > Trim Marks.

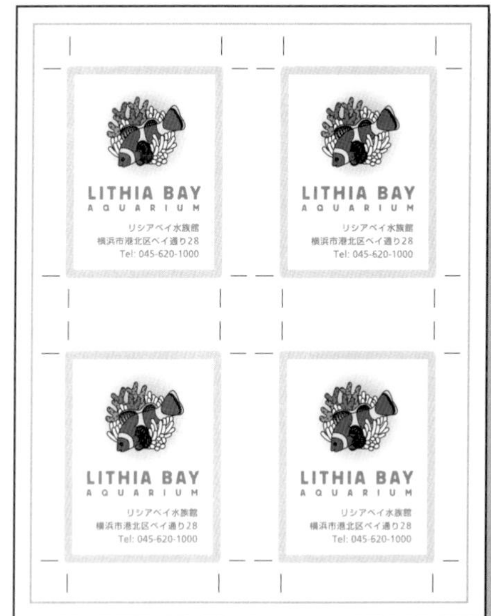

Image with multiple trim marks

Trim marks created with the Trim Marks filter do not replace crop marks created with the Color Separation Setup dialog box or with the Object > Crop Marks > Make command.

Printing gradients, gradient mesh objects, and color blends

Files with gradients, gradient mesh objects, or color blends can be difficult for some printers to print smoothly (without discrete bands of color) or at all. There are ways to improve the printed results of gradients, gradient meshes, and color blends on such printers.

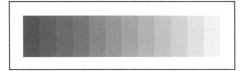

Banding in a blend

Follow these general guidelines to help avoid banding:

• Use a blend that changes at least 50% between two or more process color components.

• Use shorter blends. The optimum length depends on the colors in your blend, but try to keep blends shorter than 7.5 inches. (See “Calculating the maximum blend length based on the color change” on page 348.)

• Use lighter colors or make dark blends short. Banding is most likely to occur between very dark colors and white.

• Use an appropriate line screen that retains 256 levels of gray.

Ensuring your resolution/line screen produces 256 grays

In printing your file, you may find that the resolution of your printer, when combined with the chosen line screen, allows fewer than 256 levels of gray. A higher screen frequency decreases the levels of gray available to the printer. (For example, if you are printing at a resolution of 2400 dpi, using a line screen higher than 150 results in fewer than 256 levels of gray.)

The following table lists the maximum line screens you can use with printers to maintain all 256 levels of gray.

Final Imagesetter Resolution	Maximum Line Screen to Use
300	19
400	25
600	38
900	56
1000	63
1270	79
1446	90
1524	95
1693	106
2000	125
2400	150
2540	159
3000	188
3252	203
3600	225
4000	250

Calculating the maximum blend length based on the color change

Adobe Illustrator calculates the number of steps in a gradient based on the percentage of change between the colors in the gradient. The number of steps, in turn, determines the maximum length of the blend before banding occurs.

The gradient's number of steps and maximum length assume that you are printing the file with a line screen and resolution that produce 256 levels of gray.

To determine the maximum blend length based on the color change:

1 Select the measure tool (), and click the beginning point and the endpoint of the gradient.

2 Note the distance displayed in the Info palette on a piece of paper. This distance represents the length of the gradient or color blend.

3 Calculate the number of steps in the blend using this formula:

Number of steps = 256 (number of grays) X *Percentage change in color*

To figure out the percentage change in color, subtract the lower color value from the higher color value. For example, a blend between 20% black and 100% black is an 80%—or 0.8—change in color.

When blending process colors, use the largest change between the colors. For instance, a blend from 20% cyan, 30% magenta, 80% yellow, and 60% black to 20% cyan, 90% magenta, 70% yellow, and 40% black indicates a 60% change, because the greatest change occurs in magenta, from 30% to 90%.

4 Using the number of steps calculated in step 3, see if the length of the gradient is larger than that indicated in the chart. If it is, reduce the length of the gradient or change the colors.

Number of Steps Adobe Illustrator Recommends	Maximum Blend Length		
	Points	Inches	Cms
10	21.6	.3	.762
20	43.2	.6	1.524
30	64.8	.9	2.286
40	86.4	1.2	3.048
50	108.0	1.5	3.810
60	129.6	1.8	4.572
70	151.2	2.1	5.334
80	172.8	2.4	6.096
90	194.4	2.7	6.858
100	216.0	3.0	7.620
110	237.6	3.3	8.382
120	259.2	3.6	9.144
130	280.8	3.9	9.906
140	302.4	4.2	10.668
150	324.0	4.5	11.430
160	345.6	4.8	12.192

Number of Steps Adobe Illustrator Recommends	Maximum Blend Length		
	Points	Inches	Cms
170	367.2	5.1	12.954
180	388.8	5.4	13.716
190	410.4	5.7	14.478
200	432.0	6.0	15.240
210	453.6	6.3	16.002
220	475.2	6.6	16.764
230	496.8	6.9	17.526
240	518.4	7.2	18.288
250	540.0	7.5	19.050
256	553.0	7.7	19.507

Using the Compatible Gradient and Gradient Mesh Printing option

Some printer have difficulty printing gradients and gradient mesh objects. For example, gradients may take excessively long to print on older Level 1 printers or may print with a banding effect on Level 2 devices. In addition, gradient mesh objects may print incorrectly to some PostScript 3 devices. The Compatible Gradient Printing and Gradient Mesh Printing option enables such printers to print your files.

Important: *Use this option only with files that contain gradients and gradient mesh objects that will be printed on devices that have difficulty printing such files. This option can slow printing on printers that don't have problems with gradients.*

To improve gradient printing:

1 Choose File > Document Setup.

2 Select the Compatible Gradient and Gradient Mesh Printing option. Click OK.

Printing with gradient mesh objects

Adobe Illustrator 7.0 and earlier cannot read gradient mesh objects created with later versions of Adobe Illustrator. If you want to use files with gradient mesh objects in Adobe Illustrator 6.0 or 7.0, save the file in the earlier format.

When printing files with gradient mesh objects, you can optimize your printing results by printing to a PostScript Level 3 printer. When printing to a Level 1 printer, the mesh object is converted to a bitmap image; when printing to a Level 2 printer, the mesh object is converted to a JPEG image at 150 dpi.

Note: Even if you are printing to a Level 3 printer, printing may be delayed if the PostScript field in the Print dialog box is set to Level 1 or Level 2. Therefore, when printing to a Level 3 printer only, you can optimize the speed by setting the PostScript field to Level 3.

Improving gradient printing on low-resolution printers

When a gradient fill is applied to an object, Illustrator uses the printer's default screens. If you turn off the printer's default screen in the Document Setup dialog box, Illustrator uses Adobe screens to enhance the output of gradients when printing to low-resolution printers (600 dpi and less) that support fewer than 256 gray levels. On some low-resolution printers, turning off the Use Printer's Default Screen option may improve the output quality of gradients, gradient meshes, and raster images.

To turn off the printer's default screens, with low-resolution printers:

1 Choose File > Document Setup.

2 Deselect Use Printer's Default Screens and click OK.

Improving printer performance

Objects that contain overly complex paths are a main cause of printing problems. A path's complexity is determined by the number of line segments and anchor points it contains. The more complex the path, the longer it takes to print. Before printing, make sure that paths contain only the necessary anchor points.

Here are some suggestions for simplifying paths:

- Use the pen tool instead of the pencil tool, when possible. Drawings made with the pen tool typically contain fewer points than those created with the pencil tool.
- Remove unnecessary points. (See "Adding, deleting, and converting anchor points" on page 74.)
- Delete stray points. (See "Selecting and deleting stray points" on page 77.)
- Change the output resolution. (See "Changing the output resolution" on page 352.)
- Increase the flatness of curves. (See "Creating a printer override (EPSF Riders) file" on page 355.)
- Split overly complex paths.

Splitting paths to print large, complex shapes

If you are printing Adobe Illustrator files containing overly long or complicated paths, the file may not print and you may receive limit-check error messages from your printer. To simplify paths, you can split long, complex paths into two or more separate paths using Split Long Paths in the Document Setup dialog box.

When Split Long Paths is selected, the Adobe Illustrator program checks whether a closed path is too long to print whenever you save or print an image. If the path length exceeds what the printer's memory can handle, Illustrator breaks the closed path into pieces represented on-screen by lines through the path. These lines appear only in Artwork view; they do not preview or print. The image previews and prints as if the paths were joined.

Complex object, and Split Long Paths option applied

Keep the following in mind when using Split Long Paths:

- It's a good idea to save a copy of your original artwork before splitting paths. That way, you still have the original, unsplit file to work with if needed.
- Illustrator treats split paths in the artwork as separate objects. To change your artwork once paths are split, you must either work with the separate shapes or rejoin the paths to work with the image as a single shape.
- Split Long Paths has no effect on stroked paths or compound paths. When you use Split Long Paths on an object that is both filled and stroked, the object is split into two objects.

To split long paths:

1 Choose File > Document Setup.

2 Select Split Long Paths, and click OK. Illustrator splits paths as needed when you print or save the file.

To split a stroked path:

Split the path with the scissors tool.

To split a compound path:

1 Choose Object > Compound Paths > Release to remove the compound path.

2 Break the path into pieces using the scissors tool.

3 Redefine the pieces as compound paths.

To split a mask:

1 Choose Object > Mask > Release to remove the mask.

2 Break the path into pieces using the scissors tool.

3 Redefine the pieces as masks.

To rejoin a split path:

1 Delete any extra lines created with Split Long Paths by selecting the lines and pressing Delete.

2 Select all of the split paths that made up the original object.

3 Choose Window > Pathfinder and click the Unite button in the Pathfinder palette. The path is rejoined, with an anchor point placed at each intersection where a split path was reconnected.

Changing the output resolution

Curves in artwork are defined by the PostScript interpreter as small line segments; and the smaller the line segments, the more accurate the curve. However, when small line segments are used to draw a curve, the total number of line segments increases, thereby increasing the complexity of the curve. If a curve is too complex for a PostScript interpreter to rasterize, a PostScript error can result, and the curve won't print.

The output resolution determines the flatness of the curve: A lower output resolution results in greater flatness, and thus longer and fewer line segments. Using a lower output resolution creates a less accurate curve, but improves printing performance.

Adobe Illustrator prints fastest and best by using a default output resolution setting of 800 dots per inch (dpi). However, in some cases, you might want to decrease the output resolution—for example, if you draw a very long curved path that won't print due to a limit-check error, if printing is slow, or if objects are not being printed at an adequate resolution.

To avoid or correct the limit-check error, you can split long paths, as described in "Splitting paths to print large, complex shapes" on page 351, or you can set the output resolution for that object to a lower value. If objects are not being printed at an adequate resolution, you can increase the output resolution for the object.

Output resolution for all new objects is set at the value in the Output Resolution text box in the Document Setup dialog box.

***Note:** You can also change the output resolution of future objects you create with the Document Setup dialog box. Changing the Output Resolution value in the Document Setup dialog box does not affect existing objects.*

To change the output resolution of an existing object, use the Output text box in the Attributes palette. When you change output resolution for the object, you set *flatness* for that object. Flatness determines the number of straight-line segments that are used to define a given curve and is based on the resolution of the printing device and the output resolution set for the object in Adobe Illustrator. (See "Creating a printer override (EPSF Riders) file" on page 355.)

$$\text{Flatness} = \frac{\text{Printing device resolution}}{\text{Output resolution setting}}$$

The flatness value is greater than 1 if the printer resolution is greater than the output resolution set for the artwork. For example, if the printer resolution is 2400 dpi and the output resolution for an object is set at 800 dpi, the flatness value equals 3. If the calculated flatness value is smaller than 1.0, a flatness value of 1.0 is used.

To change the output resolution for an object:

1 Select the object for which you want to adjust the output resolution.

2 Choose Window > Show Attributes.

3 Enter the output resolution for the object. (Recommended values are between 100 dpi and 300 dpi for printing at 300 dpi, and between 800 and 2400 dpi for printing at 2400 dpi. The limits are 100 and 9600 dpi.)

4 Press Enter (Windows) or Return (Mac OS).

Additional tips for efficient printing

You may not be able to print your artwork, your artwork may take a long time to print, or your printer may simply quit with or without issuing an error message. Error messages include a range-check error and VM error (virtual memory error). Many of these errors are caused by overly complex paths in your artwork.

If your artwork takes a long time to print, consider simplifying its shape. Other tips to help you print more efficiently include the following:

• Limit the complexity of patterns, masks, and compound paths you use in the artwork file. Delete unused patterns from the Swatches palette.

When painting objects with patterns, note that patterns can significantly slow performance. Painting compound paths with patterns or using several patterns in your artwork may slow printing or cause your file not to print at all.

In addition, anything stroked with patterns using the Swatches palette other than very simple paths do not print well unless you set the file for PostScript Level 2 or PostScript 3 printing, as described in "Printing artwork and composites" on page 343.

- If the artwork contains ink pen effects, gradients, or patterns that are too complex to print on the current printer, you can print it on a PostScript Level 2 or PostScript 3 imagesetter instead. You can also copy the file and rasterize the nonprinting artwork as described in "Changing vector graphics into bitmap images" on page 239.

- The same version of Adobe Illustrator that was used to create the files must be used to print them.

Illustrator 8.0 contains various printing enhancements and new text features. Using version 7.01 or earlier to open or print an Illustrator file strips many of these enhancements from the file and reflows any tabbed text. Make sure that you or your service bureau uses Adobe Illustrator 8.0 to print 8.0 files.

To retain 8.0 printing and text enhancements when your service bureau does not have version 8.0, use Adobe Illustrator 8.0 to save a copy of the 8.0 file in EPS format so that it can be placed into an earlier version of Adobe Illustrator or into another desktop publishing program. When you save a file in EPS format, you do not lose any of the printing enhancements or tabs in the file. (See "Using the Tab Ruler palette" on page 288.)

- Limit the number of downloadable typefaces you use in the artwork file.

About the EPSF Riders file

The EPSF Riders file sets the screen frequency, angle, spot function, and flatness for all files, or adds an annotation or an error handler message to all files. The settings you specify in the EPSF Riders file override any settings you specified using the Separation Setup dialog box. Before you can create an EPSF Riders file, you must move it into the Plug-ins folder.

To use the EPSF Riders plug-in:

1 Move the Riders plug-in into the Plug-ins folder. The Riders plug-in is located in the Riders Folder, within the Utilities folder.

2 Once you have moved the Riders plug-in to the Plug-ins folder, quit Illustrator and then restart the program. Restarting the program acknowledges the presence of the Riders plug-in in the Plug-ins folder.

Once the Riders plug-in is in your directory or Plug-ins folder and you have created an EPSF Riders file, all files saved or printed from Illustrator are affected. To remove the EPSF Riders information from your files, you can either delete the Adobe Illustrator EPSF Riders file or move it out of the Plug-ins folder, and then resave all the files that contain the embedded Riders information.

Creating a printer override (EPSF Riders) file

The Make Riders filter creates an Adobe Illustrator EPSF Riders file. The EPSF Riders file contains PostScript code that, when added to an Adobe Illustrator file, overrides how a file prints. The Delete Riders filter removes the EPSF Riders file from your system. Only one file, named *EPSF Riders*, is created when you choose the Make Riders filter. You cannot create multiple Riders' files, and you must not change the name of the EPSF Riders file.

To create an EPSF Riders file:

1 Choose Filter > Other > Make Riders.

Note: *If you haven't moved the Riders plug-in into the Plug-ins folder, the Other category does not appear in the Filter menu. If necessary, follow the steps in the previous section to move the Riders plug-in into the correct location.*

2 Do any of the following:

• Choose a screen frequency, or *line screen,* to designate the number of rows of halftone dots per inch when printing. The screen frequency value must be between 1 and 999.

• Choose a screen angle to determine the angle at which the rows of halftone dots print. (The default setting for black-and-white printing, 45 degrees, is intended to make the dot rows less conspicuous to the eye.) The screen angle value must be between 0 and 360.

• Choose a spot function to determine the halftone dot's shape. Choose Import from the Spot Function pop-up menu to select and import a spot function.

Important: *An imported spot function must be in PostScript language, correctly formatted. Importing an incorrectly formatted spot function can corrupt a file or make it unprintable. See the Spot Function Template file, located in the Utilities/Riders folder or directory.*

• Choose a flatness setting to simplify complex paths. The Riders flatness setting must be between 0.2 and 200 and is applied to all curves in an Illustrator file.

Note: *The Riders flatness setting overrides the output resolution setting and is not recommended in most cases. (See "Changing the output resolution" on page 352.)*

• Choose Setup from the Annotation pop-up menu, and enter an annotation of up to 254 characters. The annotation appears at the bottom left corner of the printed page.

• Choose Error Handler to print error information on the page if a PostScript error occurs. If you are using the Adobe PSPrinter™ or the LaserWriter 8.0 or later printer driver, turn on the printer driver's error handling instead of the Riders' error handler.

3 When you have selected the options you want, click Make.

Important: *Do not rename the EPSF Riders file. (The name* Adobe Illustrator EPSF Riders *is selected by default.) If you change the name, Illustrator ignores the file.*

4 Save the EPSF Riders file in the Plug-ins directory (Windows) or Plug-ins folder (Mac OS).

To delete the Riders file:

1 Choose Filter > Other > Delete Rider.

2 Select the *Adobe Illustrator EPSF Riders* file.

3 Click Delete.

To move a Riders file:

1 Locate the EPSF Riders file in the Plug-ins directory or Plug-ins folder.

2 Move the EPSF Riders file out of the Plug-ins folder. You can move it anywhere, but you may want to move it into the Illustrator folder or directory.

3 Quit Adobe Illustrator, then restart the program, and resave all the files that contain embedded Riders information.

File data and annotating objects

The Document Info command lists general file information and object characteristics, as well as the number and names of custom colors, patterns, gradients, fonts, and placed art. The Selection Info command lists specific object information for a selected object.

You can use the Note text box in the Attributes dialog box to annotate an object so that it can easily be located in the PostScript file with a text editor. This feature can help service bureaus or other professionals trying to troubleshoot printing problems.

To view file information using the Document Info or Selection Info command:

1 Select an object with a selection tool, or if you want information on all objects in the file, deselect all objects by choosing Edit > Deselect All.

If you have selected one or more objects, the Selection Info command is listed in the File menu; if no object is selected, the Document Info command appears in the File menu.

2 Choose File > Document Info or File > Selection Info.

3 Choose from the information screens listed in the Info pop-up menu: Document, Objects, Brush Objects, Spot Color Objects, Pattern Objects, Gradient Objects, Fonts, Linked Images, Embedded Images, and Font Details.

4 To save a copy of the file information as a text file, click Save.

To annotate an object:

1 Select the object you want to annotate.

2 Choose Window > Show Attributes.

3 Choose Show Note from the Attributes menu; then type the annotation.

You can enter up to 240 characters in the Note text box. For example, you can enter a short description of the object, the creation date, and the name of the creator of the artwork.

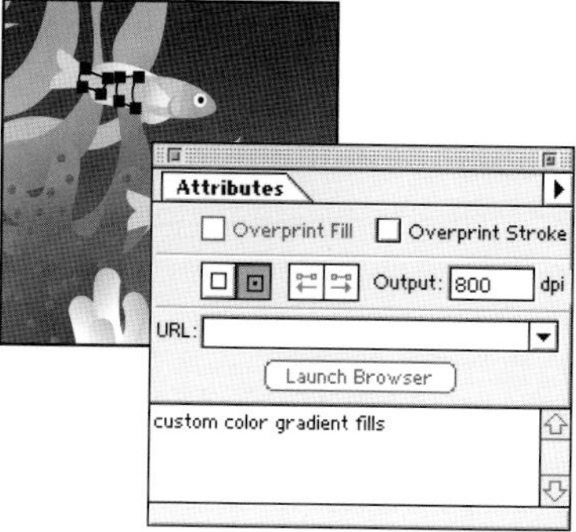

When you save the artwork, the object is annotated in the PostScript language program with your annotation preceded by the text string *%AI3_Note*.

15

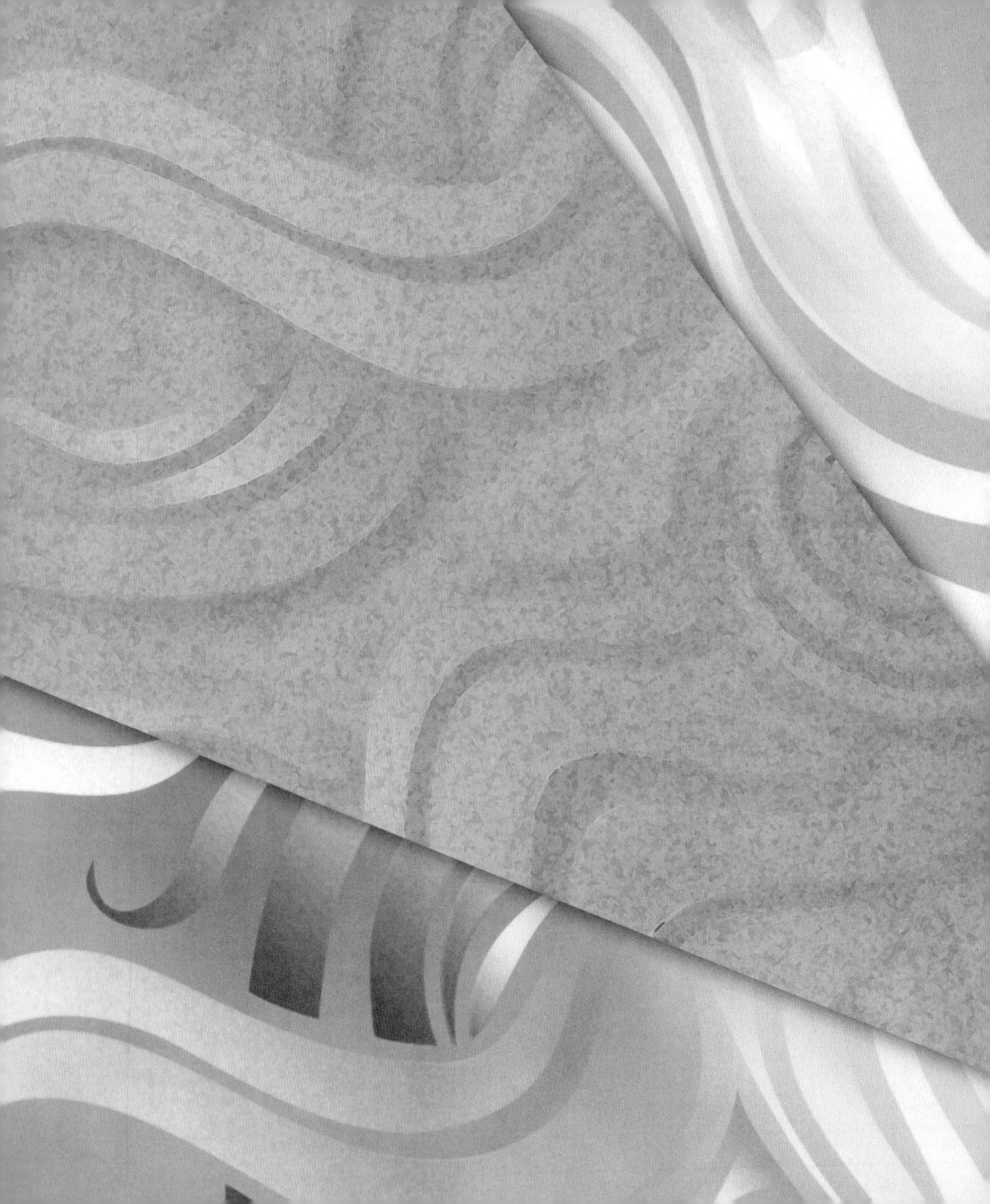

Chapter 15: Producing Color Separations

The most common way to print color artwork is to produce a positive or negative image of the artwork on paper or film and then transfer the image to a printing plate to be run on a press. To prepare artwork for this process, called *color separation*, you first separate the composite art into its component colors used in the printing process—cyan, magenta, yellow, black, and any spot colors needed to print the artwork.

About separations

To produce high-quality separations, it helps to be familiar with the basics of printing, including line screens, resolution, process colors, and spot colors.

It is also recommended that you work closely with the print shop that will produce your separations, consulting its experts before beginning each job and during the process.

To reproduce color and continuous-tone images, printers usually separate artwork into four plates—one plate for each of the cyan, magenta, yellow, and black portions of the image. When inked with the appropriate color and printed in register with one another, these colors combine to reproduce the original artwork. The process of dividing the image into two or more colors is called *color separating,* and the films from which the plates are created are called the *separations.*

PRODUCING A COLOR SEPARATION

1. Calibrate your color monitor.
2. Compare colors in your artwork before and after calibration.
3. Optional: Select overprint options for colors you want to appear transparent.
4. Optional: Create a trap to compensate for misregistration on press.
5. Set a printing bounding box and create crop marks.
6. Set separation options.
7. Print separations.

Outputting to CMYK

Artwork is separated into CMYK output when you're preparing an image to be printed using the process colors cyan (C), magenta (M), yellow (Y), and black (K). (The letter *K* is used for black to avoid confusion, because *B* might also stand for blue.)

Outputting spot colors

You can use custom inks, called *spot colors*, in addition to or in place of process colors. Because a spot color is printed on its own plate, spot colors can often reduce the complexity and cost of printing artwork.

For example, instead of using the four process colors to reproduce artwork consisting of black text and bluish-green line drawings, you could use two spot colors—one of black and one representing that exact shade of green. In addition, you can use spot color inks to produce colors not reproducible by CMYK inks, such as fluorescent and metallic colors.

You can use the Color palette to display the CMYK equivalent of a spot color.

To view the process color equivalent of a spot color:

1 In the Swatches palette, double-click the spot color whose process color equivalent you want to view.

2 In the Swatch Options dialog box, choose Process Color from the Color Type menu and click OK.

The CMYK equivalent values for the spot color are displayed in the Color palette.

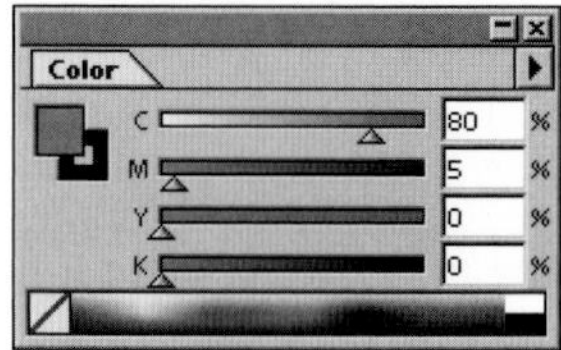

Outputting registration colors

If you want to print a color on all plates in the printing process, including spot color plates, you can convert it into a *registration color*. Registration color is typically used for crop marks and trim marks. (See “Setting crop marks and trim marks” on page 345.)

To output registration color:

1 Select the object on which you want to apply registration color.

2 Choose Window > Show Swatches.

3 In the Swatches palette, click the Registration color swatch (⊕), located in the first row of swatches. The selected objects are converted into registration color objects.

4 To change the color from the default black registration color, use the Color palette:

- To change the registration color to a tint of black, use the Tint slider in the Color palette.
- To change the registration color to a CMYK or Grayscale color, select the color option from the pop-up menu in the Color palette and use the sliders to adjust the color.

For a color illustration showing process versus spot colors when creating separations, see "Separating Colors" on page 234.

Step 1: Calibrate your monitor and check colors in your artwork

Printed colors may not match the colors that were displayed on your monitor. For example, an object that looked red on-screen before may now look orange. At this point, you need to correct any color problems in your artwork. You also should verify that your monitor has been color-calibrated, as described in "Calibrating your monitor" on page 180.

Types of colors you can use, and how they are separated

You can paint artwork with process colors, spot colors, or a combination of both. For information on your color choices, see "Adding, duplicating, and deleting swatches" on page 167 and "Loading colors from other color systems" on page 174.

When printing separations, you can convert spot colors to their process color equivalents so that they will be printed on the CMYK plates. (See "Separating spot colors as process colors" on page 373.)

For instructions on assigning colors to your artwork, see Chapter 7, "Working with Color."

Printing gradients as separations

A gradient that contains process colors will be separated onto the process plates. A gradient that contains two tints of the same spot color will be separated on a single spot color plate. To create a gradient that separates on one piece of film between a spot color and white, create a gradient fill between the spot color and a 0% tint of the color.

Note: *If you create a gradient between two spot colors, you should assign different screen angles to those spot colors in the Separation Setup dialog box. This is because if two spot colors have the same screen angle, they will overprint each other. If you're not sure what the angles should be, consult your print shop. (See "Specifying the halftone screen ruling" on page 374.)*

You cannot separate gradients as a combination of custom (spot) and process color plates, because the spot color is automatically converted to its process color equivalents. To print a gradient with both spot and process colors from a separation program, convert all spot colors to process equivalents.

Printing gradient mesh objects as separations

Gradient mesh objects that are composed of different tints of the same spot color will print on a single spot color plate. However, if the mesh object contains different colors, it will be separated on the process color plates.

Step 2: Select overprint options for colors that you want to appear transparent

By default, both fills and strokes in the Adobe Illustrator program appear opaque because the top color *knocks out,* or cuts out, the area underneath. You can prevent knockout by using the Overprint option in the Attributes palette to make overlapping printing inks appear transparent.

Note: *The degree of transparency depends on the ink, paper, and printing method used. Consult your print shop to determine how these variables will affect your final artwork.*

You cannot preview the effects of overprinting. On-screen, you can approximate the colors on overprinted objects with the Hard command, as described in "Using the Hard Mix and Soft Mix commands" on page 172.

However, it is important that you carefully check overprinted colors on separated artwork using integral or overlay proofs.

For a color illustration of the Overprint option, see figure 15-1 on page 231.

The Filter > Color > Overprint Black command allows you to set black fill or black stroked lines to overprint (or, alternatively, to remove overprinting commands from black fill or black stroked lines).

You may want to overprint in the following situations:

- Overprint 100% black lines against a color background when the illustration style allows.
- Overprint when the artwork does not share common ink colors and you want to create a trap or overlaid ink effects. When overprinting process color mixes or custom colors that do not share common ink colors, the overprint color is added to the background color. For example, if you print a fill of 100% magenta over a fill of 100% cyan, the overlapping fills appear violet, not magenta.

To print colors transparently by overprinting:

1 Select the object or objects that you want to overprint.

For a color illustration of transparent color printing using overprinting techniques, see figure 15-2 on page 231.

2 Choose Window > Attributes.

3 Select Overprint Fill.

If you use the Overprint option on a 100% black stroke or fill, the black ink may not be opaque enough to prevent the underlying ink colors from showing through. To eliminate the show-through problem, use a four-color (rich) black instead of a 100% black. Consult with your print shop about the exact percentages of color to add to the black.

The preview on-screen appears the same as before, but the selected colors overprint when printed as a separation.

For a color illustration comparing artwork on a monitor versus printed artwork, see figure 15-3 on page 231.

To set or remove overprinting from black lines:

1 Select the objects to have overprinting added or removed. You can set overprinting for custom colors whose process equivalents contain specific percentages of black or for process colors that include black.

2 Choose Filter > Colors > Overprint Black.

3 In the dialog box, choose Add Black to add overprinting or Remove Black to remove overprinting commands.

4 Enter the percentage of black to indicate which objects have overprinting added or removed. For example, enter 80% to select only objects containing at least 80% black.

5 Choose any of the following options:

• Fill, Stroke, or both options to apply overprinting to filled paths, stroked paths, or both types of paths.

• Include Blacks with CMY to apply overprinting to paths painted with cyan, magenta, or yellow if the path also contains black at the specified percentage.

• Include Spot Blacks to apply overprinting to custom colors whose process equivalents include black at the specified percentage.

Note: *If you are overprinting a spot color that also contains black at the specified percentage, it is necessary to choose* both *the Include Blacks with CMY option and the Include Spot Blacks option.*

6 Click OK.

Step 3: Create a trap to compensate for misregistration on press

Misregistration can cause gaps between colors on the final output when colors printed from separate plates overlap or adjoin one another. To compensate for potential gaps between colors in artwork, print shops use a technique called *trapping* to create a small area of overlap (called a *trap*) between two adjoining colors.

You can use a separate, dedicated trapping program, such as TrapWise®, to create a trap.

For a color illustration of different types of traps, see figure 15-4 on page 232.

About traps

When overlapping painted objects share a common color, trapping may be unnecessary if the color that is common to both objects creates an automatic trap. For example, if two overlapping objects contain cyan as part of their CMYK values, any gap between them is covered by the cyan content of the object underneath.

Note: *When artwork does contain common ink colors, overprinting does not occur on the shared plate.*

There are two types of trap: a *spread,* in which a lighter object overlaps a darker background and seems to expand into the background; and a *choke,* in which a lighter background overlaps a darker object that falls within the background and seems to squeeze or reduce the object.

For a color illustration of spreads and chokes, see figure 15-5 on page 232.

You can create both spreads and chokes in the Adobe Illustrator program.

It is generally best to scale your graphic to its final size before adding a trap. Once you create a trap for an object, the amount of trapping increases or decreases if you scale the object (unless you deselect the Scale line weight option in the Scale dialog box). For example, if you create a graphic that has a 0.5-point trap and scale it to five times its original size, the result is a 2.5-point trap for the enlarged graphic.

Trapping with tints

When trapping two light-colored objects, the trap line may show through the darker of the two colors, resulting in an unsightly dark border. For example, if you trap a light yellow object into a light blue object, a bright green border is visible where the trap is created.

To prevent the trap line from showing through, you can specify a tint of the trapping color (in this example, the yellow color) to create a more pleasing effect. Check with your print shop to find out what percentage of tint is most appropriate given the type of press, inks, paper stock, and so on being used.

Trapping type

Trapping type can present special problems. Avoid applying mixed process colors or tints of process colors to type at small point sizes, because any misregistration can make the text difficult to read. Likewise, trapping type at small point sizes can result in hard-to-read type. As with tint reduction, check with your print shop before trapping such type. For example, if you are printing black type on a colored background, simply overprinting the type onto the background may be enough.

To trap type, you can put a copy of the text behind the original and create the trap line as a stroke set to overprint.

You can also trap type by first converting it to outlines with the Create Outline filter. You can then create a trap for it as you would with any other graphic object. However, when you convert type to outlines, *hinting* is lost. Hinting optimizes how type prints at small point sizes on printers with a resolution of 600 dots per inch (dpi) or lower. Also, you cannot edit text with the text tools after you convert it to outlines, because it is no longer type.

Using the Trap command

The Trap command creates traps for simple objects by identifying the lighter artwork—whether it's the object or the background—and overprinting (trapping) it into the darker artwork.

For a color illustration of how to use the Trap command, see figure 15-6 on page 232.

For instructions on using the Stroke palette to create a trap with strokes on individual objects, see "Trapping by overprinting" on page 368.

In some cases, the top and bottom objects may have similar color densities so that one color is not obviously darker than the other. In this case, the Trap command determines the trap based on slight differences in color; if the trap specified by the Trap dialog box is not satisfactory, you can use the Reverse Trap option to switch the way in which the Trap command traps the two objects.

For a color illustration describing how the Trap command creates spreads and chokes, see figure 15-7 on page 232.

To create a trap using the Trap command:

1 Select two or more objects.

2 Choose Window > Show Pathfinder.

3 In the Pathfinder palette, if the Trap icon is not displayed, choose Show Options from the pop-up menu.

4 Click the Trap button at the lower right of the Pathfinder dialog box.

5 In the Thickness text box, enter a stroke width of between 0.01 and 5000 points. Check with your print shop to determine what value to use.

6 Enter a value in the Height/Width% text box to specify the trap on horizontal lines as a percentage of the trap on vertical lines.

Specifying different horizontal and vertical trap values lets you compensate for on-press irregularities, such as paper stretch. Contact your print shop for help in determining this value. The default value of 100% results in the same trap width on horizontal lines and on vertical lines.

To increase the trap thickness on horizontal lines without changing the vertical trap, set the Height/Width value to greater than 100%. To decrease the trap thickness on horizontal lines without changing the vertical trap, set the Height/Width value to less than 100%.

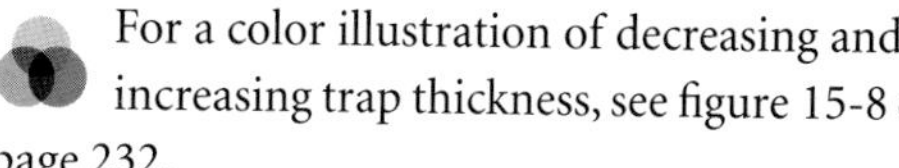

For a color illustration of decreasing and increasing trap thickness, see figure 15-8 on page 232.

7 Enter a Tint Reduction value to change the tint of the trap. The default value is 40%.

The Tint Reduction value reduces the values of the lighter color being trapped; the darker color values remain at 100%. The Tint Reduction value also affects the values of custom colors.

For a color illustration of overprint options, see figure 15-9 on page 233.

8 Select additional trapping options as required:

• Traps with Process Color if you want to convert spot color traps to equivalent process colors. This option creates an object of the lighter of the spot colors and overprints it.

• Reverse Traps to trap darker colors into lighter colors. This option does not work with rich black—that is, black that contains additional CMY colors.

9 Click OK to create a trap on the selected objects. Click Defaults to return to the default trapping values.

Trapping by overprinting

For more precise control of trapping and for trapping complex objects, you can create the effect of a trap by stroking an object and setting the stroke to overprint.

To create a spread or choke by overprinting:

1 Select the topmost object of the two objects that must trap into each other.

2 In the Stroke box in the toolbox or the Color palette, do one of the following:

• Create a spread by entering the same color values for the Stroke as appear in the Fill option. You can change the stroke's color values by selecting the stroke and then adjusting its color values in the Color palette. This method enlarges the object by stroking its boundaries with the same color as the object's fill.

For a color illustration of overprint stroked with fill color, see figure 15-10 on page 233.

• Create a choke by entering the same color values for the Stroke as appear in the lighter background (again, using the Color palette); the Stroke and Fill values will differ. This method reduces the darker object by stroking its boundaries with the lighter background color.

For a color illustration of overprint stroked with background color, see figure 15-11 on page 233.

3 Choose Window > Show Stroke.

4 In the Stroke palette, in the Weight text box enter a stroke width of between 0.6 and 2.0 points.

A stroke weight of 0.6 point creates a trap of 0.3 point. A stroke weight of 2.0 points creates a trap of 1.0 point. Check with your print shop to determine what value to use.

5 Choose Window > Show Attributes.

6 Select Overprint Stroke.

In a spread, the lighter object traps into (overprints) the darker background. In a choke, overprinting the stroke causes the lighter background to trap into the darker object.

To trap a line:

1 Select the line to be trapped.

2 In the Stroke box in the toolbox or the Color palette, assign the stroke a color of white.

3 In the Stroke palette, select the desired line weight.

4 Copy the line, and choose Edit > Paste in Front. The copy is used to create a trap.

5 In the Stroke box in the toolbox or the Color palette, stroke the copy with the desired color.

6 In the Stroke palette, choose a line weight that is wider than the bottom line.

7 Choose Window > Show Attributes.

8 Select Overprint Stroke for the top line.

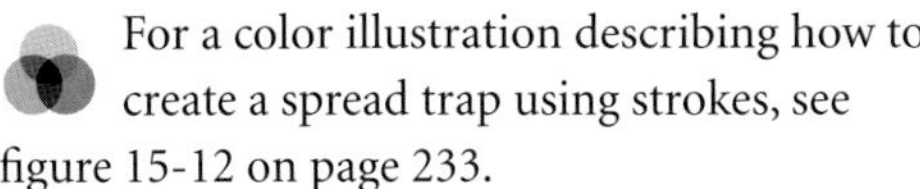

For a color illustration describing how to create a spread trap using strokes, see figure 15-12 on page 233.

To trap a portion of an object:

1 Draw a line along the edge or edges that you want to trap. If the object is complex, use the direct-selection tool (↖) to select the edges, copy it, and choose Edit > Paste in Front to paste the copy directly on top of the original.

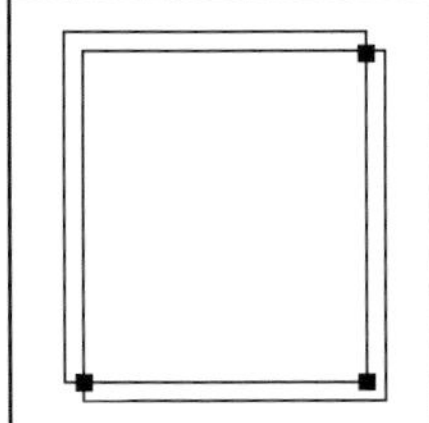

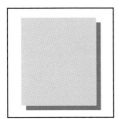

Drop shadow with a trap. The line drawn at the intersection of two shapes creates a trap.

2 In the Stroke box in the toolbox or the Color palette, select a color value for the Stroke to create either a spread or a choke.

If you are uncertain about what type of trap is appropriate, see “About traps” on page 365.

3 Choose Window > Show Attributes.

4 Select Overprint Stroke.

Step 4: Set the printing bounding box and place crop marks around the image to be separated

You can place crop marks around the image to be separated, either directly on the artwork or in the separations. Crop marks indicate the image area.

Keep these points in mind when creating crop marks for color separations:

• If you are setting crop marks in the original artwork and want the artwork to contain a *bleed* (a margin added to the image so that it can be trimmed after printing), make sure that you extend the artwork past the crop marks to accommodate the bleed. (See “Specifying the bleed area” on page 378.)

• If you plan to separate several small pieces of artwork in the same file, you can create a set of trim marks for each piece of artwork. You might want more than one set, for example, if the file contains several business cards that you plan to separate. To create more than one set of crop marks, draw them in the artwork or use the Trim Marks filter. See “Setting crop marks and trim marks” on page 345.

Specifying the printing bounding box in the separation

The printing bounding box is represented as a gray rectangle surrounding the artwork in the Separation Setup preview window. The bounding box sets the position of the crop marks on your separations and defines the printable boundaries of the artwork, as well as nonprintable boundaries such as direction lines.

You can define the printing bounding box either by using the Object > Crop Marks > Make command, or by using the Separations Setup dialog box to set the bounding box at the artwork boundaries. You can also modify the current bounding box dimensions in the Separations Setup dialog box.

The numbers in the Margins text boxes show where the image lies within the page. These numbers measure the distance from the 0,0 point in the imageable area to the edges of the bounding box. The 0,0 point is in its default position at the bottom left corner of the page boundary.

If you select a different page size, the margin numbers change as Illustrator calculates the distance of the bounding box from the edge of a new page size.

Note: *The Margins numbers for a given page size (such as Letter) may vary by PPD file. This is because printers and imagesetters may differ in how they define the size of an imageable area.*

To specify the printing bounding box using crop marks:

1 Do one of the following:

• Draw a rectangle to define a customized printing bounding box, and then select the rectangle.

• Choose Edit > Deselect All to set the printing bounding box around the artboard.

2 Choose Object > Crop Marks > Make.

To define the printing bounding box boundary using the Separation Setup dialog box:

1 Do not set any crop marks in the document, or remove existing crop marks by choosing Objects > Crop Marks > Release.

2 Choose File > Separation Setup. The printing bounding box is placed by default as tightly as possible around all the artwork.

To modify the existing printing bounding box:

1 In the Separation Setup dialog box, do one of the following:

• Enter values in the Left, Right, Top, and Bottom margin text boxes. Press Tab to go to the next text box.

• Drag any of the size handles in the preview.

• Select Revert to cancel any changes and revert to the previous bounding box settings.

2 Specify another separation option, or click OK.

Specifying printer's marks

When you prepare artwork for printing, a number of marks are needed for the printer to register the artwork elements precisely and verify correct color. These marks include elements such as crop marks, registration marks, star targets, calibration bars, and labels. The Separation Setup dialog box enables you to add these marks to your separations.

For a color illustration describing printer's marks, see figure 15-13 on page 233.

In Illustrator, the printer's marks are either turned on or turned off. You cannot choose individual marks to be placed around the artwork. The Use Printer's Marks option adds the following marks to the separations:

Registration marks and star targets Illustrator places around your artwork two types of marks that the print shop uses to align the separations: *registration marks* and *star targets*. Registration marks are the most commonly used marks in printing, because they are easy to line up accurately. Star targets are harder than registration marks to align, but they are extremely accurate.

Labels Illustrator labels the film with the name of the file, the line screen used, the screen angle for the separation, and the color of each particular plate. These labels appear at the tops of the images.

Crop marks Illustrator places crop marks at the edges of the printing bounding box. If the Japanese Crop Marks option is selected in the Edit\Preferences\General dialog box, a double set of crop marks is displayed.

To include printer's marks on the separations:

1 In the Separation Setup dialog box, select Use Printer's Marks.

2 Specify another separation option, or click OK.

Step 5: Set separation options

Setting up a separation involves choosing the separation options and then printing or saving the file.

Preparing a file for separation includes specifying which printer settings and halftone screen ruling to use and whether the separation should be a positive or negative image. In addition, you can specify a bleed around the artwork.

The separation settings you choose for a file are saved with the separated file. If you open a file that has never been separated in Illustrator, the program returns to the default settings.

To choose separation options:

1 Choose one of the following options:

• File > Separation Setup.

• File > Print, and then click Separation Setup in the Print dialog box.

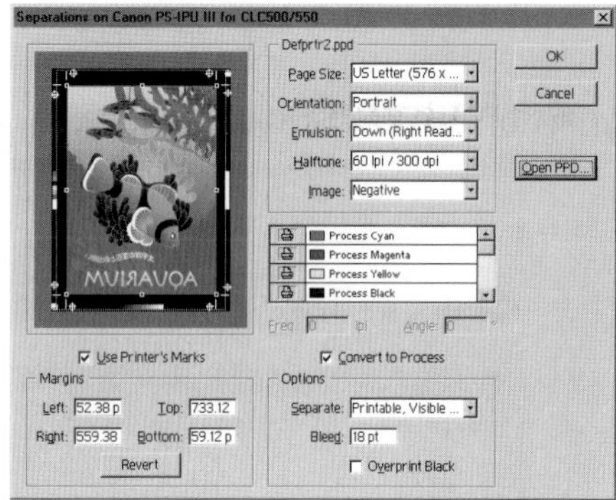

2 Select the PPD file that corresponds to your printer or imagesetter, as described in "Selecting a PPD file." Choose options as described in the rest of that section.

3 Click OK or Print.

Selecting a PPD file

To define the output device for the separation, you select the PostScript Printer Descriptions (PPD) file that corresponds to your PostScript printer or imagesetter. (You cannot separate to a non-PostScript device.) To obtain PPD files not included with the program, see the Read Me file in the Utilities/PPDs folder in the Adobe Illustrator folder.

A PPD file contains information about your output device, including its resolution, available page sizes, line screen rulings, and screen angles. Loading the file displays the different settings for the output device, in the Separation Setup dialog box.

To select a PPD file:

1 Choose File > Separation Setup. In the Separation Setup dialog box, click Open PPD.

2 Locate the Windows subdirectory (Windows) or the Printer Descriptions folder (Mac OS).

3 Select a PPD file that corresponds to the output device you use to print your separations. The filenames correspond to the printer or imagesetter name and model and have a *.ppd* file extension (Windows).

4 Click Open. The name of the PPD file you selected appears in the dialog box. The name of the currently selected printer appears in the title of the dialog box.

5 Choose other separation options as described in the following sections, or click OK.

Specifying which layers to separate

The Layer pop-up menu lets you specify which layers to include in the separation. (See Chapter 9, "Using Layers.")

To specify which layers to separate:

1 In the Separation Setup dialog box under Options, choose one of the following options from the Separate menu:

• Printable, Visible Layers to separate only layers that are both printable and visible. These correspond to the layers that print when creating a composite proof.

• Visible Layers to separate only the visible layers.

• All Layers to separate all layers.

2 Specify another separation option, or click OK.

Specifying which colors to create separations for

In the Separation Setup dialog box, each separation is labeled with the color name that Illustrator assigned it. If an icon of a printer appears next to the color name, Illustrator creates a separation for the color.

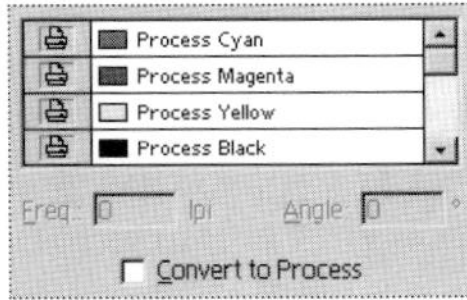

To specify whether to create a separation for a color:

1 Do one of the following:

• By default, Illustrator creates a separation for each CMYK color in the art. To create a separation, make sure the printer icon is displayed next to the color name in the Separation Setup dialog box.

• To choose not to create a separation, click the printer icon next to the color's name. The printer icon disappears, and no separation is created.

Separating spot colors as process colors

You can separate spot colors or named colors as equivalent CMYK process colors in the Separation Setup dialog box. When spot colors or named CMYK colors are converted to their process color equivalents, they are printed as separations rather than on a single plate.

To separate all spot colors as process colors:

In the Separation Setup dialog box, click Convert to Process. (This option is on by default.)

A four-color process icon appears next to all the spot colors in the artwork.

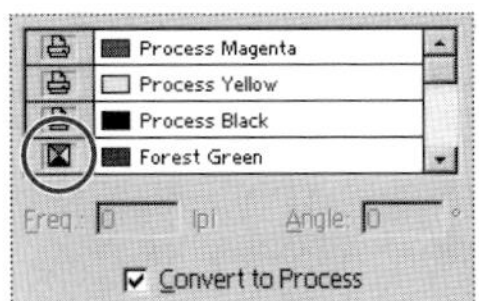

To separate individual spot colors as process colors:

1 In the Separation Setup dialog box, deselect Convert to Process.

2 Click the printer icon next to the spot color in the list of colors. A four-color process icon appears.

3 For each spot color you want to convert to a process color, click the printer icon next to its name in the list of colors.

4 Specify another separation option, or click OK.

Specifying the halftone screen ruling

The Halftone menu displays one or more sets of line screens (lines per inch, or *lpi*) and resolutions (dots per inch, or *dpi*) available on the printer or imagesetter that prints the color separations.

A high line-screen ruling (for example, 150 lpi) spaces the dots used to create an image closely together to create a finely rendered image on the press; a low screen ruling (60 lpi to 85 lpi) spaces the dots farther apart to create a coarser image. The size of the dots is also determined by the line screen. A high line-screen ruling uses small dots; a low screen ruling uses large dots. The most important factor in choosing a line-screen ruling is the type of printing press your job uses. Ask your print shop how fine a line screen its press can hold, and make your choices accordingly.

The PPD files for high-resolution imagesetters offer a wide range of possible line-screen rulings paired with various imagesetter resolutions. The PPD files for lower-resolution printers typically have only a few choices for line screens, and they are coarser screens of between 53 lpi and 85 lpi. The coarser screens, however, give optimum results on lower-resolution printers. Using a finer screen of 100 lpi, for example, actually decreases the quality of your image when a low-resolution printer is used for final output.

To specify a halftone screen ruling and resolution:

1 In the Separation Setup dialog box, choose one of the following options:

- To select one of the preset halftone screen ruling and printer resolution combinations, choose an option from the Halftone pop-up menu.
- To specify a custom halftone screen ruling, select the plate to be customized and then enter the lpi value in the Frequency text box and a screen angle value in the Angle text box.

Note: *The default angles and frequencies are determined by the selected PPD file. Be sure to check with your print shop for the preferred frequency and angle before creating your own halftone screens.*

2 Specify another separation option, or click OK.

Specifying the page size and orientation

Adobe Illustrator normally uses the page size default in the PPD file for the selected printer. However, you can change the page size to any of the sizes listed in the PPD file as well as specify portrait (vertical) or landscape (horizontal) orientation. Page sizes are listed by familiar names (such as *Letter*) and by dimensions in points. The dimensions shown in parentheses after the page size are the limits of the *imageable area*. The imageable area is the total page size less any unprintable border used by the printer or imagesetter. Most laser printers cannot print to the exact edge of a page.

SCREEN FREQUENCY The line screen arranges the image in each separation into rows of halftone dots for printing. The frequency of these rows of dots is described in lines per inch, or lpi. A low lpi setting creates a coarse screen that produces large, well-separated dots. This is useful for printing newspapers, for example. A high lpi setting creates many small dots for printing detailed images, such as those found in art books. The appropriate line screen setting depends on the resolution of the printer and on the types of paper, press, and inks used to print the artwork.

65 lpi: Coarse screen for printing newsletters and grocery coupons

85 lpi: Average screen for printing newspapers

133 lpi: High-quality screen for printing four-color magazines

177 lpi: Very fine screen for printing annual reports and images in art books

If you select a different page size (for example, change from letter to legal), the artwork is rescaled in the preview window. This is because the preview window displays the entire imageable area of the selected page; when the page size is changed, the preview window automatically rescales to include the imageable area.

***Note:** The imageable area may vary by PPD file, even for the same page size (for example, Letter), because different printers and imagesetters define the sizes of their imageable areas differently.*

Make sure that your page size is large enough to contain your artwork as well as crop marks, registration marks, and other necessary printing information. To conserve imagesetter film or paper, however, select the smallest page size that accommodates your artwork and necessary printing information.

Page size: Letter and Legal

To specify a page size:

1 In the Separation Setup dialog box, choose an option from the Page Size pop-up menu.

2 Specify another separation option, or click OK.

To specify the orientation of the page:

1 In the Separation Setup dialog box, choose Portrait or Landscape from the Orientation pop-up menu.

2 Specify another separation option, or click OK.

Specifying a custom page size

You can specify a custom page size using the Custom Page Size option in the Page Size pop-up menu. This option is available only if you are using a printer that accommodates various page sizes, such as a high-resolution imagesetter. The PPD file for a laser printer, for example, does not provide this option.

The largest custom page size you can specify depends on the maximum imageable area of your imagesetter. Consult the documentation on your specific printer for more information.

To specify a custom page size:

1 In the Separation Setup dialog box, choose Custom from the Page Size pop-up menu.

2 Do one of the following:

• To specify the smallest page size needed for your artwork and printer's marks, click OK to accept the default values.

• To specify a page size larger than the default, enter a new width and height in the Width and Height fields. Be sure to increase the values; decreasing the default values may clip your artwork.

• If desired, change the placement of the page by entering a value in the Offset field.

In the first illustration, the page placement is off; in the second illustration, Offset shifts the pages to the left.

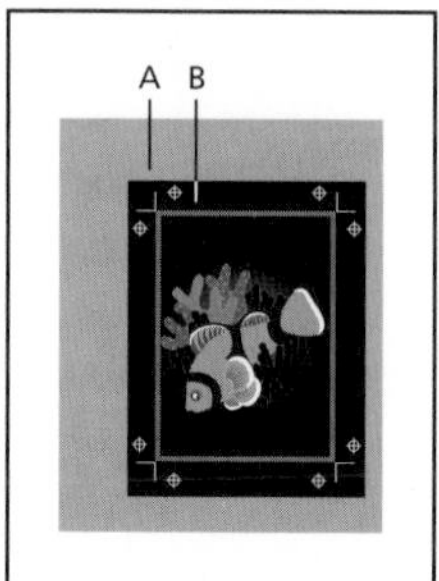

A. Film B. Page C. Offset

The Offset value specifies the amount of space along the right side of the imageable area. For example, entering a value of 30 points in the Offset option moves your page 30 points to the left.

• To rotate your page 90 degrees, select Transverse and click OK.

Transverse off and page rotated 90 degrees with Transverse on

If your imagesetter can accommodate the longest side of your imageable area, you can conserve a considerable amount of film or paper by using Transverse in conjunction with Offset. Compare the following examples of an image printed by Adobe Illustrator with Transverse on and off.

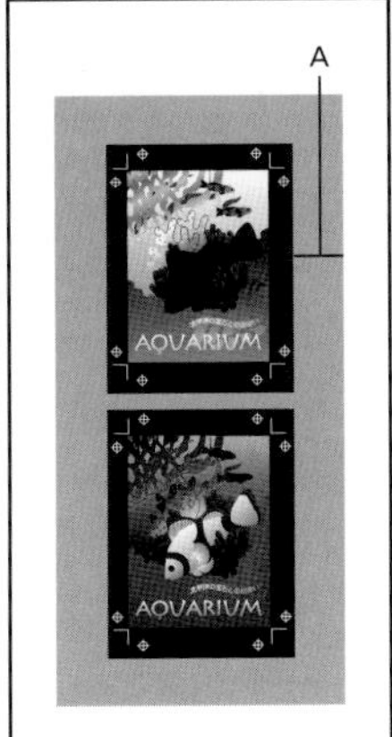

Transverse off and film saved with Transverse on:
A. *Offset value* **B.** *Film saved*

When both Offset and Transverse are selected, Offset controls the amount of space between the separations.

Specifying the emulsion

Emulsion refers to the photosensitive layer on a piece of film or paper. *Up (Right Reading)* means that type in the image is readable (that is, "right reading") when the photosensitive layer is facing you. *Down (Right Reading)* means that type is readable when the photosensitive layer is facing away from you. Normally, images printed on paper are printed Up (Right Reading), whereas images printed on film are often printed Down (Right Reading). Check with your print shop to determine which emulsion direction it prefers.

To tell whether you are looking at the emulsion side or the nonemulsion side (also referred to as the *base*), examine the final film under bright light. One side appears shinier than the other. The dull side is the emulsion side; the shiny side is the base.

To specify the emulsion:

1 In the Separation Setup dialog box, choose Up (Right Reading) or Down (Right Reading) from the Emulsion pop-up menu. The image flips.

2 Specify another separation option, or click OK.

Specifying the image type

The image options determine the image exposure: negative or positive. Typically, print shops require negative film in the United States and positive film in Europe and Japan. If you are unsure about which image type to use, consult your print shop.

To specify the image type:

1 In the Separation Setup dialog box, choose Positive or Negative from the Image pop-up menu.

2 Specify another separation option, or click OK.

Overprinting black in the separation

It can be cheaper and easier to have the print shop overprint black on the press. You can choose whether to overprint black when printing or saving selected separations.

See "Step 2: Select overprint options for colors that you want to appear transparent" on page 364.

To overprint black in the separation:

1 Under Options in the Separation Setup dialog box, select Overprint Black.

2 Specify another separation option, or click OK.

Specifying the bleed area

Bleed is the amount of artwork that falls outside of the printing bounding box, or outside the crop marks and trim marks. You can include bleed in your artwork as a margin of error—to ensure that the ink is still printed to the edge of the page after the page is trimmed or to ensure that an image can be stripped into a keyline in a document. Once you create the artwork that extends into the bleed, you can use Illustrator to specify the extent of the bleed.

Changing the bleed moves the crop marks farther from or closer to the image; the crop marks still define the same size printing bounding box, however.

Small bleed and large bleed

To specify bleed:

1 Under Options in the Separation Setup dialog box, enter an amount in the Bleed text box.

By default, Illustrator applies a bleed of 18 points. This means that the artwork extends 18 points beyond the crop marks on your film. The maximum bleed you can set is 72 points; the minimum bleed is 0 points.

The size of the bleed you use depends on its purpose. A *press bleed* (that is, an image that bleeds off the edge of the printed sheet) should be at least 18 points. If the bleed is to ensure that an image fits a keyline, it needs to be no more than 2 or 3 points. Your print shop can advise you on the size of the bleed necessary for your particular job.

2 Specify another separation option, or click OK.

Step 6: Print and save separations

When you have completed setting up the separations, you are ready to print or save your separations.

Note: The printer or imagesetter you plan to use to print separations must match the PPD file you specified when setting up the separations. If the output device and PPD file don't match, you will receive a warning message.

Saving the file saves the separation setup, the PPD information, and any color conversions you have specified in the Separation Setup dialog box.

To print the separations you selected:

1 Select the separations you want to print, as described in "Specifying which layers to separate" on page 372. (For information about placing crop marks with the Separation Setup dialog box, see "Setting crop marks and trim marks" on page 345 and "Specifying printer's marks" on page 371.)

2 Choose File > Print, or return to the Print dialog box if it is still open.

3 Choose any print options, as described in Chapter 14, "Printing."

4 Choose a method for selecting the Separate output option:

• On Windows, choose Separate from the Output pop-up menu.

• On Mac OS, choose Adobe Illustrator 8.0 from the Options pop-up menu. Then choose Separate from the Output pop-up menu.

5 Deselect the Print to File option and click OK (Windows) or select Printer from the Destination pop-up menu and click Print (Mac OS).

To save the separations you selected as a PostScript file:

1 Select the separations you want to save, as described in "Specifying which layers to separate" on page 372.

2 Choose File > Print, or return to the Print dialog box if it is still open.

3 Choose any print options, as described in Chapter 14, "Printing."

4 Choose a method for selecting the Separate output option:

• Choose Separate from the Output pop-up menu (Windows).

• Choose Adobe Illustrator 8.0 from the Options pop-up menu. Then choose Separate from the Output pop-up menu (Mac OS).

5 Select the Print to File option (Windows) or choose File from the Destination pop-up menu (Mac OS).

6 Do one of the following:

• Click OK and enter a filename in the Print to File dialog box. Then click OK again (Windows).

• Accept the default filename or enter another name for the separation and click Print (Mac OS).

16

Chapter 16: Automating Tasks

Adobe Illustrator lets you automate tasks by grouping a series of commands into a single *action*. For example, you can create an action that applies a series of commands to reproduce a favorite effect or combine commands to prepare artwork for online publishing. Actions can be grouped into sets to help you better organize your actions.

Illustrator also provides prerecorded actions to create special effects on graphic objects and type. These prerecorded actions are installed as a default set in the Actions palette when you install the Illustrator application. More action sets can also be found in the Illustrator Extras folder on the Adobe Illustrator CD.

Using the Actions palette

You use the Actions palette to record, play, edit, and delete actions. It also lets you save, load, and replace action sets.

To display the Actions palette:

Choose Window > Show Actions.

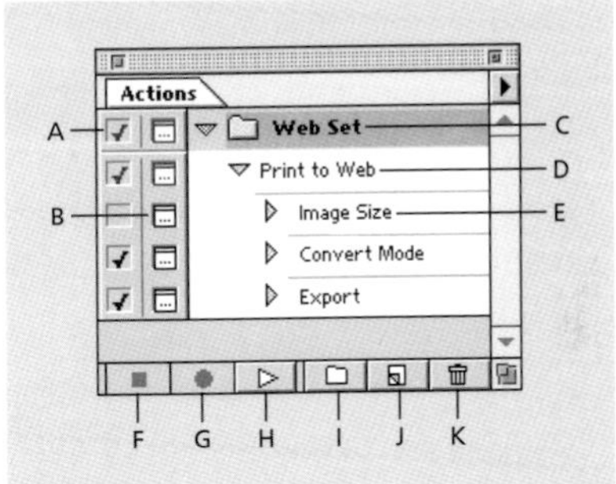

***A.** Toggles item on or off **B.** Toggles modal control on or off **C.** Set **D.** Action **E.** Recorded command **F.** Stop playing/recording **G.** Begin recording **H.** Play current selection **I.** Create new set **J.** Create new action **K.** Delete selection*

You can display actions in the Actions palette in either list view or button view. In list view, sets can be expanded to display actions, which in turn can be expanded to display individual commands. Commands can then be expanded to display recorded values.

To display actions as buttons:

Choose Button Mode from the Actions palette menu. Choose Button Mode again to return to list view.

To expand and collapse sets and commands:

Click the triangle to the left of the set or command in the Actions palette.

Creating and recording actions

When you create an action, Illustrator records the commands (including any specified values), palettes, and tools you use, in the order you use them.

The following guidelines can help you in designing actions:

• Most, but not all, commands can be recorded. However, you can allow for commands that cannot be recorded. (See "Inserting nonrecordable commands" on page 386.)

• Unrecordable commands include those that change your view of the screen (including most commands in the View menu), commands that display or hide palettes, and gradient mesh commands. Also, tools such as the gradient and gradient mesh tools, eyedropper, paint bucket, and scissors are not recordable.

• When recording an action, keep in mind that playback results depend on such variables as the current fill and stroke colors, and on file and program settings.

Because Illustrator executes the commands as you record them, it's a good idea to record a complicated action using a copy of a file, and then play the action on the original.

• Until you specifically save a set of actions with the Save Actions command, actions are automatically saved in the preferences file located in the Adobe Illustrator application folder (Windows) or in the Preferences folder in the System Folder (Mac OS).

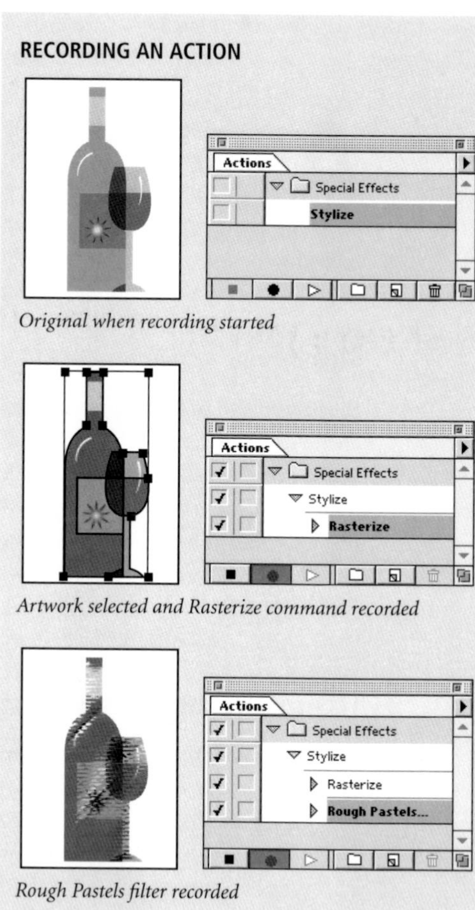

Original when recording started

Artwork selected and Rasterize command recorded

Rough Pastels filter recorded

To create and record an action:

1 Open a file.

2 In the Actions palette, click the Create New Set button to create a new actions set if desired, or click on an existing set to add the new action to that set.

3 In the Actions palette, click the Create New Action button (▫) or choose New Action from the pop-up menu on the palette.

4 Name the action, assign it to any combination of the Ctrl key (Windows) or Command key (Mac OS), the Shift key, and the Function keys (for example, Ctrl+Shift+F3), and choose a color for its display in the Actions palette.

5 Click Record. The Begin Recording button in the Actions palette turns red.

6 To guard against mistakes, record the File > Save a Copy command at the beginning of the action.

7 Choose commands as you want them recorded.

If the command you choose opens a dialog box, clicking OK records the command and clicking Cancel does not record it. If a chosen command is not recorded, it must be inserted in the action. See "Inserting nonrecordable commands" on page 386.

Tip: *Pressing Alt (Windows) or Option (Mac OS) and clicking the Create New Action button automatically creates an action.*

8 Stop recording by clicking the Stop Playing/Recording button.

9 If you want to keep the action for use in future work sessions, save the action (see "Organizing sets of actions" on page 392).

Recording paths

The Insert Selected Path command lets you record a path as part of an action. When played back, the entire path is reproduced as part of the action.

To record a path:

1 Start recording an action.

2 Select a path.

3 Choose Insert Select Path from the Actions palette menu.

Selecting an object during an action

The Select Object command lets you select a particular object during the course of an action. You identify the object to be selected using the Note text box in the Attributes palette. The Select Object function is useful for choosing a particular object during an action on which to perform commands, use palettes, or make selections in dialog boxes. For example, you could pick a specific ellipse in the artwork on which to perform transformation effects such as scale or rotate, change stroke characteristics using the Stroke palette, or apply colors with the Color palette.

To name an object for use during an action:

1 Select the object to be used in the action.

2 Choose Window > Show Attributes.

3 Choose Show Note from the pop-up menu in the Attributes palette.

4 Type a unique name for the object in the Note text box. The object now can be used in an action sequence.

To select an object during an action:

1 Record an action as described in "Creating and recording actions" on page 384 up to the point where the object is to be selected.

2 Choose Select Object from the pop-up menu in the Actions palette.

3 Enter the object name in the Set Selection dialog box. (The name should match the object name entered in the Note text box of the Attributes dialog box.)

4 Set the following options in the Set Selection dialog box:

- Select Case Sensitive to select only objects that exactly match the uppercase or lowercase words in their Note text.
- Select Whole Word to select only objects whose names match every word listed in the Note text box associated with the object.

5 Click OK and continue recording the actions.

Inserting nonrecordable commands

The painting tools, tool options, view commands, and preferences cannot be recorded. However, many commands that cannot be recorded can be inserted into an action using the Insert Menu Item command.

An inserted command is not executed until the action is played. No values for the command are recorded in the action, so the file remains unchanged when the command is inserted. If the command has a dialog box, the dialog box appears during playback, and the action pauses until you click OK or Cancel. You can insert a command when recording an action or after it has been recorded.

To insert a menu item in an action:

1 Choose where to insert the menu item in the Actions palette:

- Select an action's name to insert the item at the end of the action.
- Select a command to insert the item after the command.

2 Choose Insert Menu Item from the Actions palette menu.

3 Do one of the following:

- Choose a command from its menu.
- Enter a command in the Insert Menu Item dialog box. If you don't know the full name of the command, enter part of it and click Find. You can also use the Tab key to find the command.

4 Click OK.

Inserting stops

You may want to include a stop in your action so that you can perform a task that cannot be recorded. Once you've performed the task, you can then continue by clicking the Play Current Selection button in the Actions palette.

You can also display a short message when the action reaches the stop. For example, you can remind yourself what you need to do before continuing with the action. A Continue button can be included in the message box. This way you can check for a certain condition in the file (for example, a selection) and continue if nothing needs to be done. You can insert a stop when recording an action or after it has been recorded.

To insert a stop:

1 Choose where to insert the stop in the Actions palette:

• Select an action's name to insert the stop at the end of the action.

• Select a command to insert the stop after the command.

2 Choose Insert Stop from the Actions palette menu.

3 Type the message you want to appear.

4 If you want the option to continue the action without stopping, select Allow Continue.

5 Click OK.

Setting modal controls and excluding commands

After recording an action, you can insert a *modal control.* This lets you pause a command to display its dialog box and specify different values, and to manipulate a modal tool to apply new settings. (A modal tool requires pressing Enter or Return to apply its effect.)

If you do not use a modal control, Illustrator runs the command using the values specified when you first recorded the action (and the dialog box does not appear).

You can also exclude commands that you don't want to include as part of a recorded action or that you don't want to play when running the action.

To set a modal control:

1 Make sure that the Actions palette is in list view. (If necessary, deselect Button Mode in the Actions palette menu.)

2 Do one of the following:

• Click the column to the left of the command name to display the dialog box icon. Click again to remove the modal control.

• To turn on or disable modal controls for all commands in an action or set, click the column to the left of the action or set name.

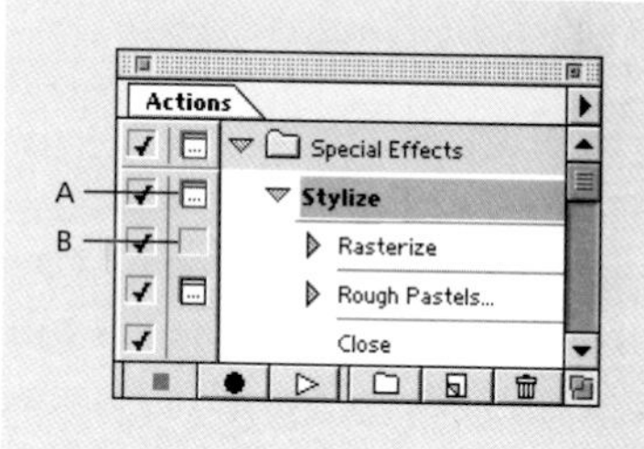

A. *Action with a modal control*
B. *Modal control off*

To exclude or include a command:

Do one of the following:

• Click to clear the check mark to the left of the command name. Click again to include the command.

• To exclude or include all commands in an action or set, click the check box to the left of the action or set name.

• To exclude or include all commands *except* the selected command, Alt-click (Windows) or Option-click (Mac OS) the command.

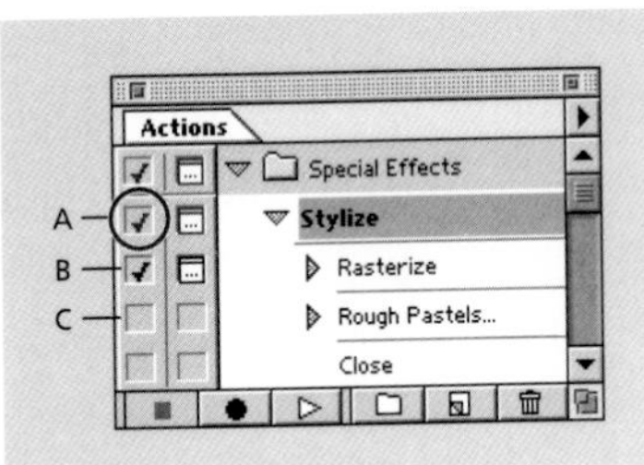

A. Action with excluded commands
B. Included command C. Excluded command

Playing actions

When you play an action, Illustrator executes the series of commands as you recorded them. But you can begin with any command, exclude commands, or play a single command in an action. If you have inserted a modal control in your action, you can specify values in a dialog box or reapply a modal tool (any tool that requires you to press Enter or Return to apply it) when the action pauses. (See "Setting modal controls and excluding commands" on page 387.)

In button view, clicking a button executes the entire action—though commands previously excluded are not executed.

To play an action or set on a single file:

1 Open the file.

2 Specify what to play:

• To play a set of actions, select the set name.

• To play a single action, select the action name.

• To play only part of an action, select the command from which you want the action to start.

3 To exclude or include a command within an action from playing, click the check box to the left of the action name.

4 Click the Play Current Selection button in the Actions palette or choose Play from the pop-up menu.

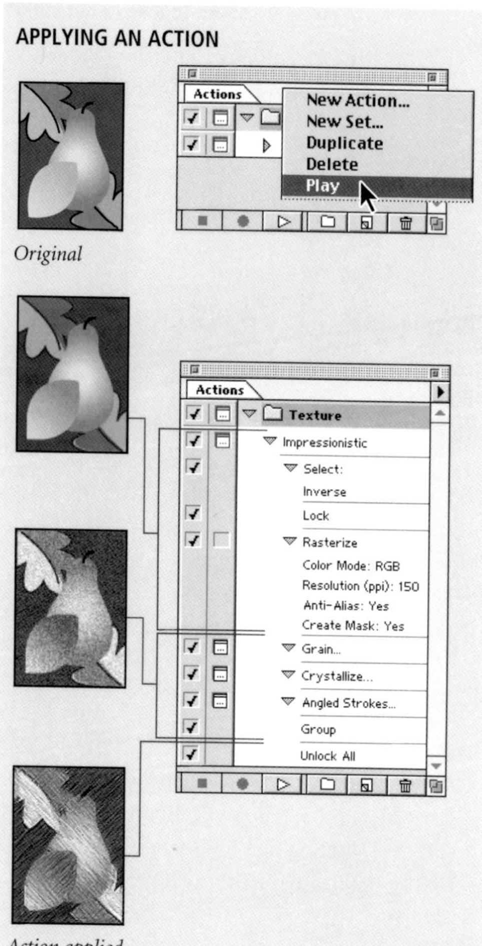

Original

Action applied

To play a single command in an action:

1 Select the command you want to play.

2 Do one of the following:

• Ctrl-click (Windows) or Command-click (Mac OS) the Play Current Selection button in the Actions palette.

• Hold down Ctrl (Windows) or Command (Mac OS), and double-click the command.

Slowing actions during playback

Sometimes a long, complicated action does not play properly, but it is difficult to tell where the problem occurs. The Playback Options command gives you three speeds at which to play actions, so that you can watch each command as it is carried out.

To specify how fast actions should play:

1 Choose Playback Options from the Actions palette pop-up menu.

2 Specify a speed:

• Accelerated to play the action at normal speed (the default).

• Step by Step to complete each command and redraw the image before going on to the next command in the action.

• Pause and enter the amount of time Illustrator should pause between carrying out each command in the action.

3 Click OK.

Editing actions

You can edit actions in the following ways:

- Rearrange actions, or rearrange commands within an action and their order of execution.
- Add commands to an action.
- Record new commands or new values for actions with dialog boxes.
- Change action options such as the action name, button color, and shortcut key.
- Duplicate actions and commands. This helps you experiment with changing an action without losing the original version, and for creating an action based on an existing one.
- Delete actions and commands.
- Reset the actions to the default list.

To move an action to a different set:

In the Actions palette, drag the action to a different set. When the highlighted line appears in the desired position, release the mouse button.

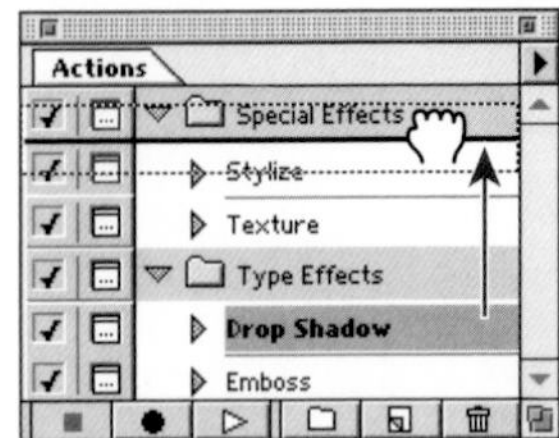

Dragging Drop Shadow action into different set

To rearrange commands within an action:

In the Actions palette, drag the command to its new location within the same action. When the highlighted line appears in the desired position, release the mouse button.

To record additional commands:

1 Do one of the following:

• Select the action name to insert the new command at the end of the action.

• Select a command in the action to insert the command after it.

2 Click the Begin Recording button on the Actions palette.

3 Record the additional commands.

4 Click the Stop Playing/Recording button to stop recording.

Note: *You can also insert nonrecordable commands (see "Inserting nonrecordable commands" on page 386), or drag commands from other actions.*

To record an action again:

1 Select an action and choose Record Again from the Actions palette menu.

2 If a modal tool appears, do one of the following:

• Use the tool differently and press Enter (Windows) or Return (Mac OS) to change the tool's effect.

• Press Enter (Windows) or Return (Mac OS) to retain the same settings.

3 If a dialog box appears, do one of the following:

• Change the values and click OK to record them.

• Click Cancel to retain the same values.

To record a single command again:

1 Select an object of the same type for which you want to re-record the action. For example, if a command is only available for vector objects, then you must have a vector object selected when you re-record.

2 In the Actions palette, double-click the command.

3 Enter the new values, and click OK.

To change action options:

1 Do one of the following:

• Double-click the action name.

• Select the action, and choose Action Options from the Actions palette menu.

2 If desired, type a new name for the action, choose a color for the action button, assign a Function key and select the Shift or Ctrl key (Windows) or the Command key (Mac OS) to combine with the function key for an action shortcut.

3 Click OK.

To duplicate a set, action, or command:

Do one of the following:

• Select a single set, action, or command. You can Shift-click or Ctrl-click (Windows) or Command-click (Mac OS) to select multiple items. Then choose Duplicate from the Actions palette menu. The copied sets appear at the bottom of the Actions palette. The copied commands or actions appear after the original command or action.

• Drag an action or command to the Create New Action button at the bottom of the Actions palette, or drag a set to the Create New Set button at the bottom of the Actions palette. The copied action appears at the bottom of the Actions palette. The copied command appears after the original command. The copied set appears after the original set.

To delete a set, action, or command:

1 In the Actions palette, select the set, action, or command you want to delete. You can Shift-click, or Ctrl-click (Windows) or Command-click (Mac OS) to select multiple commands within an action.

2 Do one of the following:

• Click the Delete Selection button on the Actions palette. Click OK to delete the action or command.

• Drag the selection to the Delete Selection button on the Actions palette.

• Choose Delete from the Actions palette menu.

To delete all actions:

Choose Clear Actions from the Actions palette menu. Click OK to delete all the actions.

To delete a selected action or command automatically, Alt-click (Windows) or Option-click (Mac OS) the Delete Selection button.

To reset actions to the default set:

1 Choose Reset Actions from the Actions palette menu.

2 Click Append to add the set of default actions to the current actions in the Actions palette, or OK to replace the current actions in the Actions palette with the default set.

Organizing sets of actions

To help you organize your actions, you can create sets in which to place them and save the sets to disk. You can organize sets of actions for different types of work—for example, print publishing and online publishing—and transfer sets to other computers. You can save only the entire contents of the selected set in the Actions palette, not individual actions.

Note: *Unsaved actions are automatically saved to the preferences file. If this preferences file is lost or removed, any unsaved actions you may have created will be lost. Be sure to use the Save Actions command in the Actions palette to save your actions to a separate actions file so you can load them later, and to keep them safe.*

Replacing a saved set of actions replaces all existing actions. Loading a saved set adds to existing actions, with new ones appearing at the bottom of the Actions palette.

To create a new set for actions:

1 In the Actions palette, do one of the following:

- Choose New Set from the pop-up menu.
- Click the Create New Set button at the bottom of the Actions palette.

2 Enter the name of the set and click OK.

To rename a set of actions:

1 In the Actions palette, do one of the following:

- Double-click the name of the set in the Actions palette.
- Select the name of the set and choose Set Options from the pop-up menu.

2 Enter the name of the set, and click OK.

To save a set of actions:

1 Select a set.

2 Choose Save Actions from the Actions palette menu.

3 Type a name for the set, choose a location, and click Save. The default actions set is saved in the Actions Sets folder within the Adobe Illustrator application folder.

To replace all actions in the Actions palette with a new set of actions:

1 Choose Replace Actions from the Actions palette menu.

2 Locate and select an actions file.

3 Click Open.

Important: *Using the Replace Actions command will replace all sets of actions in the current document. Before using the Replace Actions command, you should make sure that you have already saved a copy of your current set of actions using the Save Actions command.*

To load a set of actions:

1 Choose Load Actions from the Actions palette menu.

2 Locate and select the actions file.

3 Click Open (Windows) or Select (Mac OS).

Appendix A: Improving Performance

A program's *performance* is the amount of time it takes the program to complete certain operations, such as opening a file, sending a file to a printer, or redrawing the screen after you edit artwork.

To a great extent, your computer processor speed and the amount of RAM you have affect the performance of Adobe Illustrator. Other factors that can dramatically affect the application's performance are how you set up your software, how you use virtual memory, and the size and complexity of your files.

Using the scratch disk when working with bitmap images

When you are working with bitmap images and your system does not have enough RAM to perform an operation, Adobe Illustrator uses temporary disk space, called the *scratch disk.* By default, Illustrator uses the hard drive on which the operating system is installed as its primary scratch disk. You can change the primary scratch disk or designate a secondary scratch disk to be used when the primary disk is full. Your primary scratch disk should be your fastest hard disk and should have plenty of defragmented space available. It is recommended that the scratch disk not be a network drive and also that it not be a removable disk, because removable media are more susceptible to damage and are often slower than dedicated hard disk media.

To change the scratch disk assignment:

1 Choose File > Preferences > Plug-ins & Scratch Disk.

2 Select the desired disk from the menu. Then restart Adobe Illustrator for the change to take effect.

Important: *Adobe recommends that you use a disk tool utility, such as Defrag or Norton Utilities, to optimize and defragment your hard drive on a regular basis. See your Windows or Mac OS documentation.*

Increasing the application memory size in the Mac OS

If your computer has more RAM than Illustrator's default RAM allocation, you may significantly improve Illustrator's performance by increasing the application memory size.

To change the application memory size:

1 Start all applications—except Adobe Illustrator—that you must use at the same time as Adobe Illustrator. Keep in mind, however, that running other applications uses RAM that could be allocated to Illustrator.

2 Return to the Finder. Choose About This Computer from the Apple menu.

3 Note the Largest Unused Block value. (You use this result in step 5.) This value shows the amount of memory currently available.

4 In the Finder, select the Adobe Illustrator program icon (not the folder or the alias icon), and choose File > Get Info.

You cannot increase the application memory size while Illustrator is running.

5 In the Adobe Illustrator Info window, set Preferred Size to no more than 90% of the Largest Unused Block value you noted in step 3.

6 Close the Adobe Illustrator Info window.

Note: *Adobe recommends that you reduce the size of the disk cache, turn off the RAM disk, and on Mac OS computers turn off System 7 Virtual Memory when working with Adobe Illustrator or Adobe Photoshop. For instructions on using the Memory control panel, see your Mac OS documentation.*

Restoring default preferences

The preferences file controls how palettes and command settings appear on your screen when you open the Adobe Illustrator program. Each time you quit Adobe Illustrator, the position of the palettes and certain command settings are recorded in the preferences file. If you want to restore the tools and palettes to their original default settings, you can delete the current Adobe Illustrator 8.0 preferences file. (Adobe Illustrator creates a preferences file if one doesn't already exist the next time you start the program and save a file.)

Important: *If you want to save the current settings, rename the preferences file rather than throwing it away. When you are ready to restore the settings, change the name back and make sure that the file is located in the Illustrator 8.0 folder (Windows) or the Preferences folder (Mac OS).*

To restore the default preferences:

1 Locate the AIPrefs file in the Illustrator 8.0 folder(Windows) or the *Adobe Illustrator 8.0 Prefs* file in the Preferences folder in the System folder (Mac OS).

If you can't find the file, choose Find from the Start menu and then choose Files or Folders (Windows) or choose Find from the desktop File menu (Mac OS). Type **AIPrefs** or **Adobe Illustrator 8.0 Prefs** in the text box, and click Find Now (Windows) or Find (Mac OS).

Note: *If you still can't find the file, you probably haven't started Adobe Illustrator for the first time yet. The preferences file is created after you quit the program the first time and it's updated thereafter.*

2 Delete or rename the AIPrefs file (Windows) or the Adobe Illustrator 8.0 Prefs file (Mac OS).

3 Start Adobe Illustrator.

To locate and delete the Adobe Illustrator preferences file quickly each time you begin a new project, create a shortcut (Windows) or an alias (Mac OS) for the Illustrator 8.0 or Preferences folder.

Tips for working efficiently

Because the results of most Adobe Illustrator operations are displayed only in Preview mode, most performance issues for Illustrator are directly related to previewing artwork. Once you have set up your system for maximum efficiency, you can minimize the time it takes to preview and print by simplifying your files and by working around complex paths and artwork whenever possible.

Reduce fonts and plug-ins to speed launch time

To speed the application's launch time, reduce the number of active fonts and plug-ins that it must load. For example, you can use a font management utility such as Adobe ATM to keep active fonts to a minimum. Also, remove unnecessary third-party plug-ins you're not using. If you use the Adobe Photoshop application, remove the Photoshop plug-ins from the Illustrator plug-ins folder.

Preview selectively

If your file is large or complex, you can dramatically speed up previewing by using the Preview Selection command to preview selected objects only. You can also use the Layers palette to preview objects on selected layers.

Work with two windows open

You can avoid having to switch back and forth between two views of an illustration by working with two windows open. For example, if you've magnified art for detail work, choose Window > New Window and display the art at full size in the second window to monitor the effects of your changes. You can also use a second window to display artwork in Preview mode while you work in the first window in Artwork mode.

Link placed images

Because bitmap images can dramatically increase the size of a file, place images using the Link option in the Place dialog box so that the image remains outside the Illustrator file. If you need to include the image with the file, replace the image without the Link option as a last step before final output. (See "Opening and placing artwork" on page 55.)

Also, transform or crop bitmap images in their source application, such as Photoshop, before placing them in Illustrator.

Minimize file size of included images

If you plan to include placed bitmap images in the file, make sure that the print resolution and dimensions are no greater than the size you need for your final output. In general, the recommended image resolution is 1.5 to 2 times the screen frequency you use to print the image; for online images, the resolution should be no higher than the monitor resolution (usually 72 dots per inch, or 640 by 480 pixels for a 13-inch monitor).

Use shortcuts

Learn to use the command shortcuts that appear to the right of the commands in the menus. These are especially useful for operations that you perform frequently, such as displaying a specific command's dialog box.

For complete information on shortcuts, see the *Adobe Illustrator Quick Reference Card*; or choose Adobe Illustrator Help from Contents from the Help menu, and then click Quick Reference.

Create custom views

Use the New View command in the View menu to create custom views of your file. This feature is especially useful when you're working on several parts of a large file. Once you have created your custom views, use shortcut keys to switch quickly from view to view.

Delete unused swatches

It's good practice to delete any swatches you are no longer using before you save or print the file. To delete swatches, open the Swatches palette, choose Select All Unused from the Swatches palette menu, and click Delete.

Simplify paths

Complex paths—including masks, compound paths, and paths with many anchor points—can slow processing and cause printing problems. You can simplify paths by deleting anchor points. You can also simplify how paths of individual Illustrator objects are printed by decreasing the Output Resolution value for the objects in the Attributes palette. See "Changing the output resolution" on page 352.

It's also a good idea to remove any unnecessary points and paths from your file with the Cleanup command. See "Selecting and deleting stray points" on page 77.

Split paths

Another way to simplify paths is to split them when printing (after you have saved a copy of your artwork). You can split paths by selecting Split Long Paths in the Document Setup dialog box. Split Long Paths does not work, however, on stroked paths or compound paths; to simplify one of these paths, select the path and split it manually using the scissors tool.

Because Split Long Paths can alter artwork, make a copy of your original file before printing or saving with the option selected. Also, be sure to turn off Split Long Paths immediately after printing. If you do not deselect this option, Illustrator continues to split paths each time a file is saved or printed.

Store frequently used colors, gradients, and patterns

The Adobe Illustrator Startup file in the Plug-ins folder enables you to customize your Swatches and Brushes palettes. Each time the program is started, Illustrator loads the information in the Startup file. Be sure, however, to keep the Startup file clear of unused items, because a large Startup file may slow opening of the program.

Avoid overusing complex elements

Using a lot of complex elements, such as compound paths, pattern fills, gradient fills, and bitmap files, can make your Illustrator file memory-intensive. Other elements that can add complexity to your file are gradient mesh objects, brush strokes, vector EPS files, EPS files containing clipping paths, masks, transformations, stroked text, text with horizontal scaling, tracking, or kerning applied, and large page sizes.

Appendix B: Troubleshooting

This appendix contains common solutions to problems you may encounter when using the Adobe Illustrator program. Also see the Read Me file installed with the program for last-minute information not included in this user guide.

Before you call Adobe technical support

There are several steps you can take before calling technical support to receive assistance. Performing these steps can solve many problems and often eliminates the need for telephone assistance.

Deactivate the preferences file To check whether your problem is caused by a corrupted preferences file, quit Adobe Illustrator, deactivate the preferences file, and restart Illustrator. (However, when you delete the preferences file, you will lose certain preferences such as palette positions, window sizes and positions, and so on.)

To deactivate the preferences file in Windows, rename the AIPrefs file (located in your Illustrator directory). To deactivate the preferences file in Mac OS, drag the Adobe Illustrator Prefs file (located in the Preferences folder in your System Folder) to the Trash. If the problem disappears, delete the preferences. If the problem persists, restore the preferences file to its original name (Windows) or location (Mac OS) to preserve your preferences settings.

Reinstall Adobe Illustrator If you are experiencing installation problems, delete all of your Illustrator applications files, including the preferences file (located in the Illustrator folder in Windows or in the System Folder \ Preferences folder in Mac OS). Windows users should use the Uninstall utility on their systems to uninstall Illustrator. Then try the following:

- To do a clean installation of the program, install the program in Safe Mode (Windows) or with Extensions off (Mac OS). You should first copy the install folder from the Illustrator CD to your hard drive before you restart in Safe Mode or with Extensions off.

- You can also restart in Safe mode with CD Support (Windows) or with a CD extension set using the Extensions Manager (Mac OS).

Check for new software or setting conflicts Very often, problems with Adobe Illustrator can be traced to a recent installation of new software or utilities that are running at the same time as Illustrator. If you have recently installed new software or changed other system configuration settings, such as your monitor setting, try deinstalling the software or restoring your original settings. (If you deinstall software, you must also reinstall Illustrator, following the instructions in the previous section. This ensures that any Illustrator files that might have been damaged by your new software installation are restored.) If the problem disappears, try reinstalling the problem software or system utility, or contact the manufacturer for a new version and for compatibility information.

If you are experiencing redraw problems If your system is redrawing the screen slowly, or if the screen is not redrawing correctly, there are a few common steps to take to correct the problem. First, reduce the resolution of your monitor (see your monitor documentation for more information). You can also switch your monitor display options to Standard VGA. Finally, you can contact your system's manufacturer to request an updated video driver.

If you are having problems launching the application You should reduce the number of active fonts on your system—use only the fonts you need. Use a font management program such as ATM to reduce the number of active fonts. You can also check the default printer by reinstalling or updating the printer driver. Install the AdobePS driver (found on the Illustrator installation CD) and set this driver as the default printer driver.

You can also increase the available system resources by doing one of the following:

• Close other applications that are currently running.

• On Windows systems, you can set Windows to automatically manage virtual memory settings.

• Remove items from the Startup group.

Check for a utility conflict In Windows, remove all items from the startup group and remark out the load/run lines in the win.ini file. In Mac OS, hold down Shift and restart the computer to restart with Extensions off. In Windows 95, restart the system in Safe Mode. (See your Windows or Mac OS documentation for more information on deactivating startup software.) If the problem disappears after restarting Illustrator, try restarting your computer with selected startup items reactivated until you have identified the problem software. You can then try reinstalling the software, or you can remove the software and contact the software manufacturer for a new version and for compatibility information.

Check SCSI device connections Make sure that the devices you are using are securely and fully connected to your computer and that device cords are not damaged. The cause of the problem could be a bad connection. You should also update your SCSI drivers. To test to see if you have a problem with the SCSI drive, physically disconnect the device and then recheck for a conflict.

Important: *Be sure to turn off your computer and SCSI devices before checking cord connections. Failure to do so can damage your hardware.*

Defragment and optimize your hard disk Make sure that you have at least 10 percent of the hard disk free, and use a disk tool utility, such as Scandisk or Norton Utilities, to check whether your hard disk contains bad sectors that may be causing the crashes. You can then use the Defrag utility or Norton Speed Disk to defragment and optimize the hard drive. (Defragmenting cleans up any leftover file fragments and orders data contiguously so that it can be accessed quickly.) For instructions, see the utility's documentation. On Mac OS systems, you should also rebuild the desktop by holding down the Command+Option keys when rebooting the system.

Additional technical support resources

Adobe Systems provides several forms of automated technical support free of charge:

- See the Read Me file installed with the program for last-minute information not included in this user guide.
- Explore the extensive customer support information on the Adobe Web site. Choose File \ Adobe Online or enter http://www.adobe.com into a Web browser.
- Browse through the technical notes on the application CD for additional technical and troubleshooting information.

Problems with artwork appearance

Printed color appears different from color on-screen.

For accurate color printing, it is essential that you have your system's Color Management System software installed and that you calibrate your monitor and the Adobe Illustrator program for the various factors that affect the printed output. If you are working with artwork from another program, such as Adobe Photoshop, the color management settings must be the same in Adobe Illustrator and in the other program. (See "Loading colors from other color systems" on page 174, and "Calibrating your monitor" on page 180.)

Banding or shade stepping occurs on printed blends or gradient fills.

The blends or gradient fills are too long, or there are too many steps in the blend.

The maximum number of gray levels that can be printed by an imagesetter is 256. If the blend is too long or the number of steps too many, the artwork may exhibit bands when printed. To prevent banding, shorten the length of the blend to less than 7.5 inches, use lighter colors, shorten the length of dark blends, or increase the percentage of change in the blend. Less than a 50% change can result in banding.

(See "Printing gradients, gradient mesh objects, and color blends" on page 347.)

A rotated, reflected, or sheared object disappears.

You have rotated, reflected, or sheared the object off the screen.

To redisplay the object, scroll or zoom out to display the object in its new location, or choose Edit > Undo.

Stroked shapes do not line up when previewed or printed, or sharp spikes show in stroked letters, such as *M* and *W*, in printed output.

The miter line join style is causing the corner points to extend beyond the actual anchor points. When you specify this style of line join, the outer edges of two lines that form a corner are extended until they meet. If the lines form a sharp angle or are stroked with a heavy line weight, the outer corner can extend farther than you had anticipated.

To line up corners properly, select the path that has the jutting corners, and change the line join style in the Stroke palette by selecting either Bevel (Flat) Join or Round Join.

Another solution is to specify a lower miter limit for mitered corners. A lower miter limit causes the program to use a shorter path (and smaller angle) when determining at what point to switch from a bevel join to a miter join.

A streak appears in a filled object when you preview or print it.

The path is not closed.

To close the path, find the anchor points that are not connected (zoom in to magnify the artwork if necessary), and use the Average and Join commands, or the Unite command, to close the path.

Printing problems

Unexpected blank pages appear in printed output.

You are drawing too close to the Adobe Illustrator program's page border. A direction point in one of your curves may extend to another page.

When you are ready to print, choose File > Print. Then click the From button, and specify the pages you want to print.

Another option is to use the page tool to adjust the page grid so that the artwork is farther away from the edge of the page.

If you want to print just one page, select the Single Full Page option in the Document Setup dialog box.

File does not print, or an error message appears when trying to print.

Objects in the artwork may be too complex to print. The inability to print generally occurs with very complex objects such as blends, masks, compound paths, patterns, multiple groupings, and so on. You can either increase the memory on your printer or simplify the artwork. Reset the printer's memory by turning the printer or the RIP off, waiting approximately 30 seconds, then turning it back on.

You can also do the following:

• When the document includes downloadable fonts, download the outline (printer) fonts to the printer's RAM or hard disk, or decrease the number of downloadable fonts used in the document. Instructions for manually downloading fonts can be found in the documentation for the download utility such as Adobe Downloader.

• When printing to a desktop printer, print with a smaller paper size selected in the Page Setup dialog box (such as Letter instead of Legal).

• Create a Riders file to increase the flatness of Illustrator objects. When printing to a 300-dpi printer increase flatness to 3, when printing to a 1270-dpi printer increase flatness to 6, and when printing to a 2450-dpi printer increase flatness to 8.

• Convert gradient fills into masked blends.

• Reduce the number of steps used in blended objects.

• Simplify the patterns used in the document (for example, avoid using blends, gradient fills, or fonts in a pattern).

See also "Improving printer performance" on page 350.

Unexpected output when printing separations.

When printing separations from Illustrator on Mac OS systems, you will get an extra blank page for each plate you print if you are using LaserWriter 7.x.

Make sure the PPD you have selected in Separation Setup is the same one you specified with the driver. Otherwise, your output may be clipped or printed unexpectedly.

Make sure the Page Size you have selected in Separation Setup matches the Paper Size you have selected in Print Setup. Otherwise, your output may be clipped or printed unexpectedly.

Unexpected color output when file contains linked RGB EPS.

The color in an RGB EPS image differs from the same image, only embedded. Embedded images are part of a file, and so are color-managed when sent to a printing device. Linked images, however, are not color-managed, even if color management is turned on for the rest of the file. This does not affect CMYK EPS files or other formats. (See "Managing linked and embedded images" on page 58.)

CVC color converts to CV when imported.

When PANTONE colors in Illustrator files are imported into some applications, separate CV and CVC plates may be created. The issue of duplicate plates results from inconsistent use of the PANTONE standards. Illustrator 8.0 uses the nomenclature provided by PANTONE, which is CVC (computer video coated) or CVU (computer video uncoated). In some applications, these suffixes have been incorrectly shortened to CV or CU for either convenience or space considerations.

When choosing PANTONE colors in other applications and experiencing this problem, Adobe recommends using the POCE™ (PANTONE® Open Color Environment™) color picker, supplied by PANTONE to display and append correctly the color names with CVC/CVU.

Difficulty printing files containing a gradient mesh object.

Try one or more of the following:

- Print to a PostScript Level 2 or PostScript Level 3 output device.
- Save the file as a Level 2 or Level 1 EPS file.
- Check the Compatible Gradient and Gradient Mesh Printing option in the Document Setup.

Other problems

Commands don't appear in menus; Filter (or Import or Export) menu and submenus are gray or missing.

Often, missing commands and menu items are caused by low system resources or by installing too many fonts.

Sometimes this problem can be fixed by deactivating the preferences file because it forces Illustrator to relocate the plug-ins folder.

Try choosing File > Preferences > Plug-ins & Scratch Disks, and verify that you have selected the plug-ins folder containing the modules that you want to use. Make sure that all the plug-ins you want to use are within a single umbrella folder. Although you can nest plug-ins in folders within folders, you can select only one umbrella plug-in folder at a time. See "Using plug-in modules" on page 39 for information on choosing the plug-ins folder.

The Make Wrap command in the Type menu doesn't work.

There are several possible causes and solutions to this problem:

• The type container is in front of the wrapping object; it must be behind the wrapping object.

To place the type container in back of the wrapping object, select the wrapping object and choose Arrange > Bring to Front.

• The type container is grouped with another object.

To ungroup the type container, use the selection tool to select the type container; if other objects are selected, the type container is clearly grouped. Choose Arrange > Ungroup.

• You did not select both the type container and the graphic object.

Select both the type container and the graphic object, and choose Type > Make Wrap.

An unexpected behavior occurs; can't open a file that was opened or saved over a network.

An error or unexpected behavior, such as a crash when performing a routine task or objects failing to preview, may be caused by a damaged Illustrator file. Try repeating the same tasks that caused the problem in a new file. If the new file behaves as expected, then the initial file may be damaged. Do the following:

1 Create a backup copy and save it to your local hard drive.

2 Choose Object > Path > Cleanup to remove stray points from your artwork.

3 With the direct-selection tool or by Shift-dragging a marquee, select your artwork.

4 Copy and paste the artwork to a new file.

Note: *Do not use the Select All command before copying and pasting. (See "Selecting objects" on page 113.)*

If an application or system error occurs when you try to open a file saved over a network, then do one or more of the following:

- Copy the file to your hard drive, and then try to open it.
- Open a backup copy of the file.
- Recreate the file, saving it often and making incremental backup copies. Save all copies to your hard drive.

To prevent this problem from happening again, save and open files on your hard drive. If you need to store the file on a network server or removable media, copy the closed file after you've first saved it on your hard drive.

Note: *These suggestions assume that files created on your hard drive (and not opened from or saved to a network server or removable media) open without error.*

Problems opening or placing EPS files containing a gradient mesh object.

Try one or more of the following:

- Save the file containing the gradient mesh object as an EPS Level 1 Postscript file.
- Save the file in an older file format. (Note that some features may not be supported in earlier versions of Illustrator.)

Appendix C: Upgrading from Illustrator 6.0 to 8.0 for Mac OS

This Mac OS upgrade appendix is designed to help Adobe Illustrator 6.0 users make a seamless transition to Illustrator 8.0. It contains information that has changed from Illustrator 6.0 to 8.0, including a table of shortcut changes, moved or changed menu commands and tools, and a view of the basic color workflow. Mastering these changes will make it easier to use other Adobe products—the streamlined Illustrator 8.0 interface closely matches that in Adobe Photoshop and Adobe PageMaker in design, features, and keyboard shortcuts.

Shortcut changes

⇧ Shift key

⌥ Option key

⌘ Command key

	ILLUSTRATOR 8.0	Illustrator 6.0
Selection tools		
⌃ (convert-direction-point tool)	↖ ⇖ + ⌥ + ⌘	↖ ⇖ + Control
⌃ (convert-direction-point tool)	✒ + ⌥ *	✒ + Control + ⌥
Changing the view		
Artwork and Preview	**⌘ + Y**	⌘ + E, ⌘ + Y
Previews selection	**⇧ + ⌘ + Y**	⌥ + ⌘ + Y
Hides selected objects	**⌘ + 3**	No change
Shows all	**⌥ + ⌘ + 3**	⌘ + 4
Hides deselected objects	**⇧ + ⌥ + ⌘ + 3**	⌥ + ⌘ + 3
Zooms in	⌘ + **plus sign***	⌘ +]
Zooms out	⌘ + **minus sign***	⌘ + [
Fits in window	⌘ + **0***	⌘ + M
Sets to actual size	⌘ + **1***	⌘ + H
Hides/shows selection edges	⌘ + **H***	⇧ + ⌘ + H
Hides all palettes + toolbox	**Tab***	No change
Hides all palettes but toolbox	**⇧ + Tab***	—

**Same as Photoshop 5.0*

⇧ *Shift key*

⌥ *Option key*

⌘ *Command key*

	ILLUSTRATOR 8.0	Illustrator 6.0
Managing files		
Saves As	**⇧ ⌘ + S***	—
Saves a Copy	**⌥ + ⌘ + S***	—
Document Setup	**⌥ + ⌘ + P**	⇧ + ⌘ + D
Page Setup	**⇧ + ⌘ + P***	—
General palette shortcuts		
Applies palette value but keeps value active	**⇧ + Return***	—
Highlights value in last palette used	**⌘ + ~**	—
Editing objects		
Brings to front	**⇧ + ⌘ +]***	⌘ + =
Sends to back	**⇧ + ⌘ + [***	⌘ + –
Brings forward	**⌘ +]***	—
Sends backward	**⌘ + [***	—
Groups	**⌘ + G***	No change
Ungroups	**⇧ + ⌘ + G***	⌘ + U
Locks	**⌘ + 2***	⌘ + 1
Unlocks all	**⌥ + ⌘ + 2**	⌘ + 2
Locks deselected artwork	**⌥ + ⌘ + L**	⌥ + ⌘ + 1
Averages points	**⌥ + ⌘ + J**	⌘ + L
Joins points	**⌘ + J**	No change
Averages and Joins points	**⇧ + ⌥ + ⌘ + J**	⌥ + ⌘ + J
Masks > Make	**⌘ + 7**	—
Masks > Release	**⌥ + ⌘ + 7**	—
Compound Paths > Make	**⌘ + 8**	No change
Compound Paths > Release	**⌥ + ⌘ + 8**	⌘ + 9
Repeats Pathfinder	**⌘ + 4**	⇧ + ⌘ + E
Displays Move dialog box	**Double-click** ↖	⌥ - click ↖
Transforms pattern fill only	**Tool + ~ –drag**	Tool + P –drag

**Same as Photoshop 5.0*

⇧ *Shift key*

⌥ *Option key*

⌘ *Command key*

	ILLUSTRATOR 8.0	Illustrator 6.0
Working with color		
See Chapter 7, "Working with Color" or online Help.		
Switches between fill/stroke	**X***	—
Fills/strokes to none	**/**	—
Resets to default colors	**D***	—
Displays Color palette	**<**	—
Displays Gradient palette	**>**	—
Samples color from gradient	+ ⇧	—
Switches color models	⇧ **– click Color palette ramp***	—
Applying filters		
Applies last filter	⌘ **+ E**	⇧ + ⌘ + E
Last Filter (opens dialog box)	⌥ **+** ⌘ **+ E**	—
Adding type		
Paragraph palette	⌘ **+ M**	⇧ + ⌘ + P
Character palette	⌘ **+ T**	No change
Creates outlines	⇧ **+** ⌘ **+ O**	—
Highlight point size field		⇧ + ⌘ + S
Changes point size by 1 unit**	⇧ **+** ⌘ **+ > or <**	No change
Using guides		
Hides/shows guides	⌘ **+ ; ***	—
Locks/unlocks guides	⌥ **+** ⌘ **+ ; ***	⌘ + 7
Makes guides	⌘ **+ 5**	No change
Releases guides	⌥ **+** ⌘ **+ 5**	⌘ + 6

* *Same as Photoshop 5.0*
***Amount is set in File > Preferences > General > Type.*

Moved and changed menu commands

These menus highlight commands and groups of commands that have moved or changed in Version 8.0. The illustrations don't highlight all new features.

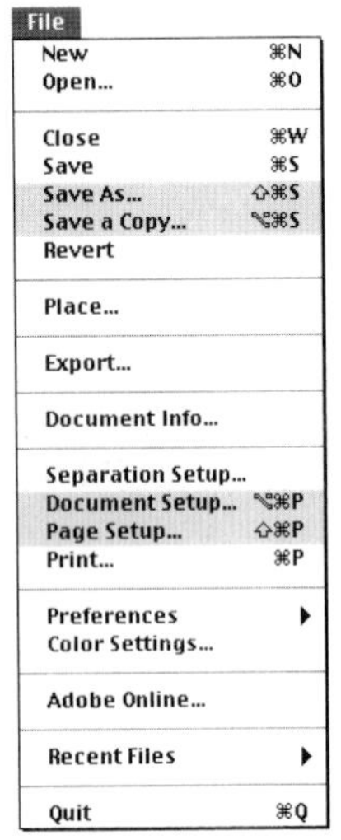

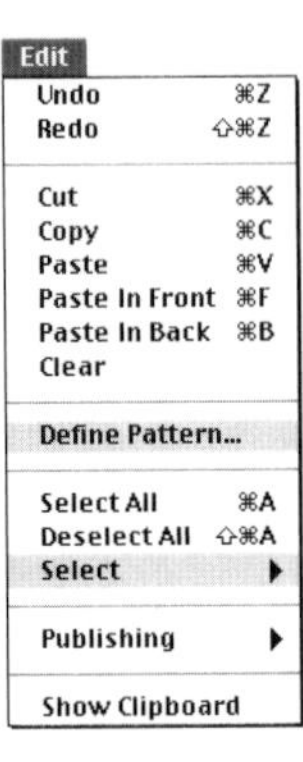

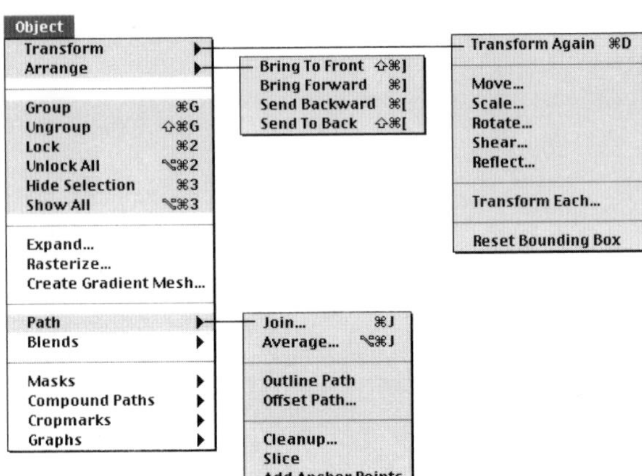

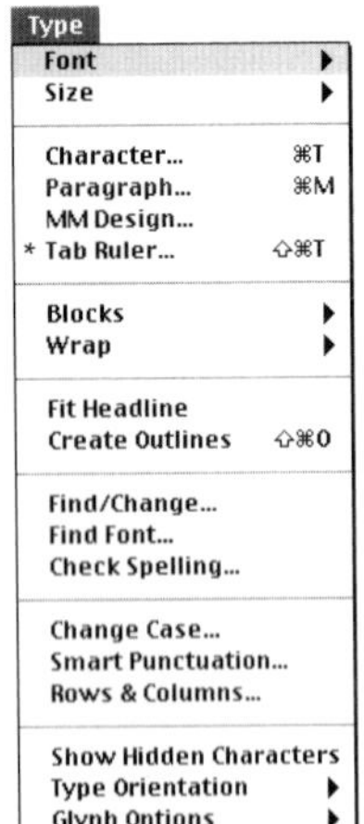

* Look in the Character and Paragraph palettes for Alignment, Tracking, and Spacing options.

Filter
Apply Last Filter ⌘E
Last Filter ⌥⌘E
Colors
Create
Distort
Pen and Ink
Stylize
Artistic
Blur
Brush Strokes
Distort
Pixelate
Sharpen
Sketch
Stylize
Texture
Video

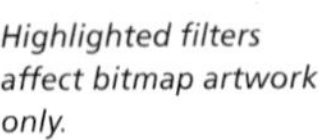

Highlighted filters affect bitmap artwork only.

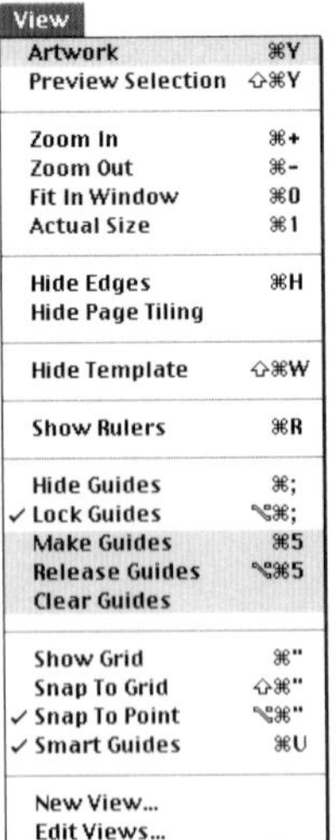

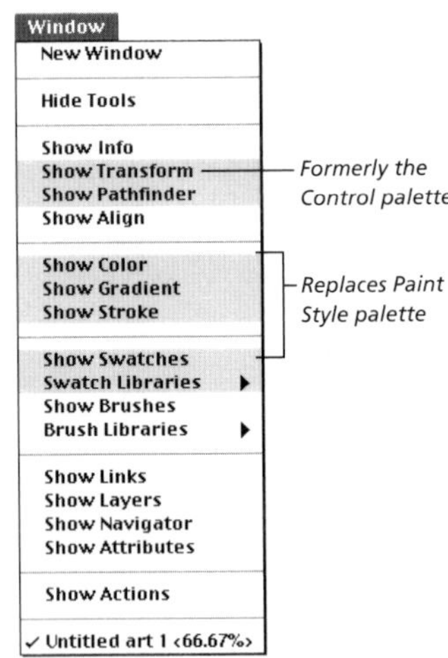

Color and gradient workflow

Version 8.0 features four new palettes that reorganize the Paint Style and Gradient palettes and the Custom Color dialog box in Version 6.0—to eliminate overlapping features and improve consistency across products. For complete information on using these features, see the Adobe Illustrator Help system or Chapter 7, "Working with Color" and Chapter 8, "Using Gradients, Blends, and Patterns."

All palettes Can be docked together for easy access to common options or pulled apart to suit your workflow.

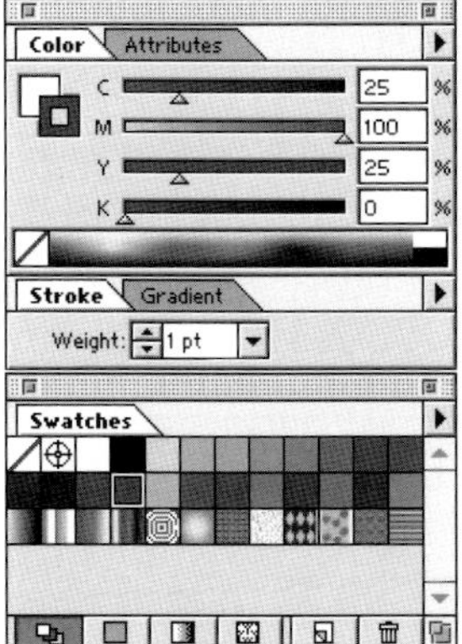

Fill and stroke options Are set using either the toolbox or the Color palette.

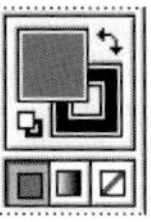

The Color palette Lets you mix RGB, CMYK, and HSB colors and adjust the tint of grayscale and spot colors (formerly called custom colors). You can also use the Color palette to mix colors for gradients.

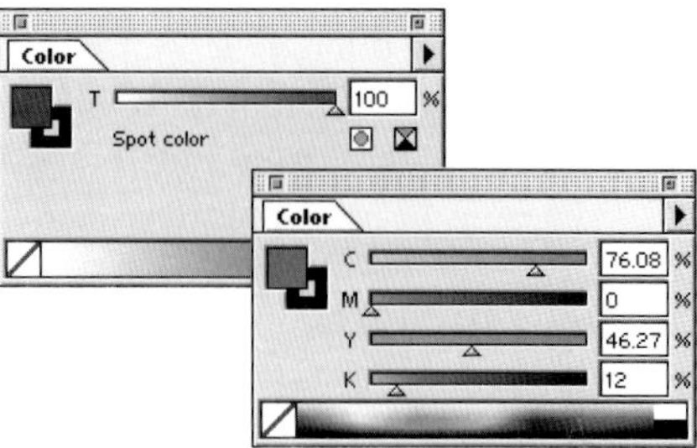

The Stroke palette Lets you set the thickness (or weight) of the stroke, whether a stroke is solid or dashed, and how the stroke is capped and joined.

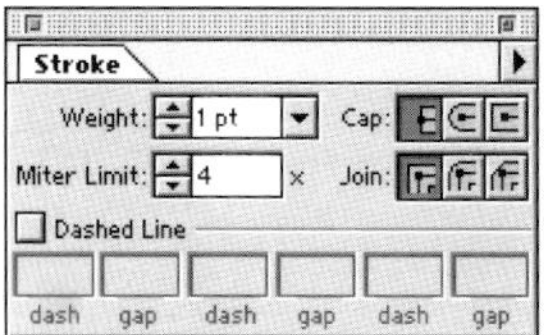

The Swatches palette Contains the colors, gradients, and patterns that are preloaded in Adobe Illustrator, as well as those you create and save for reuse. You can display swatches as a named list. To edit a swatch and globally update artwork painted with that swatch, double-click the swatch and edit the color in the Swatch Options dialog box. For gradient, spot color, or pattern swatches, hold down the Option and Command keys while dragging the new or edited version from the fill or stroke box over the old swatch to overwrite it. (For more information, see "Working with the Swatches palette" on page 166.)

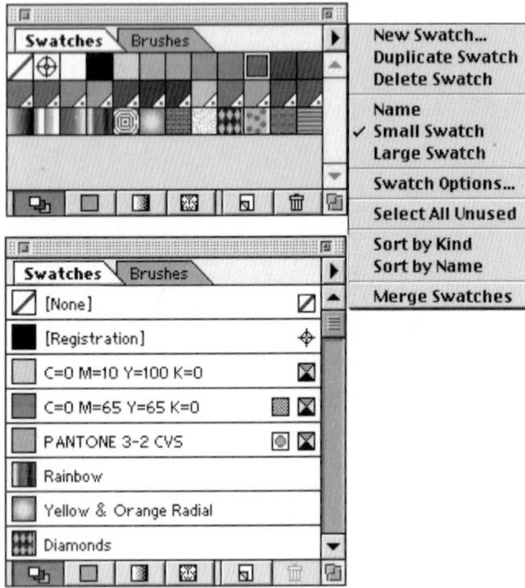

Note: Gradients, spot colors, and patterns are now stored in each piece of artwork, instead of globally for all open documents.

The Gradient palette Lets you create your own gradients. You can also use it with the Color and Swatches palettes to modify existing gradients. To update a gradient globally, select the swatch in the Swatches palette, edit the gradient using the Gradient and Color palettes, and then overwrite the original by holding down the Option and Command keys while dragging the new gradient from the fill box over the old swatch in the Swatches palette.

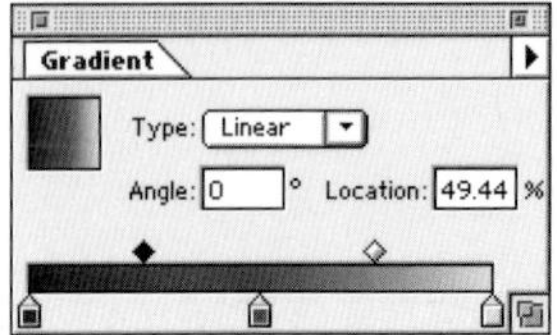

The Attributes palette Now contains Overprint settings. It also lets you validate a Web page URL assigned to an object by using the Launch Browser button.

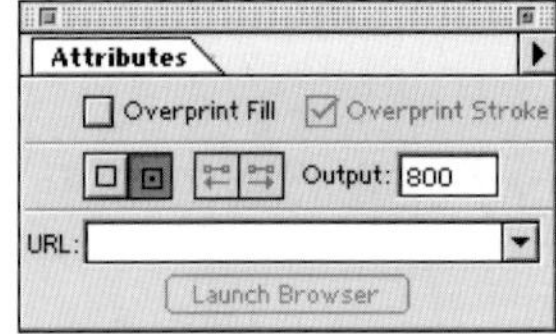

Toolbox changes

These illustrations highlight tools that have a new location or a new icon in Version 8.0. For more information on the 8.0 tools, see the Quick Reference Card or Chapter 2, "Looking at the Work Area."

For detailed information on individual tools, see online Help.

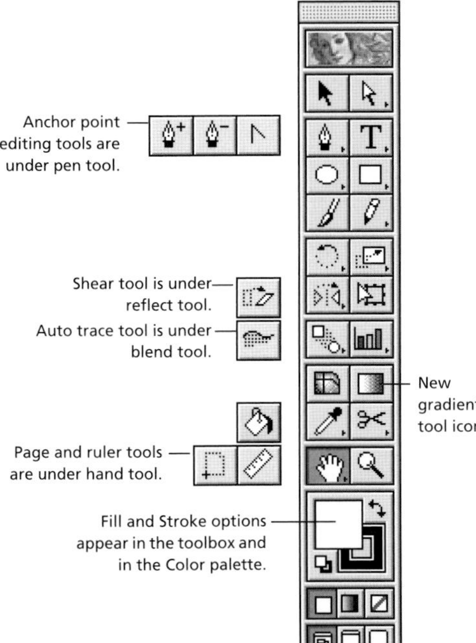

Palette changes

Some options in the Character and Paragraph palettes are now found in the options menu for these palettes.

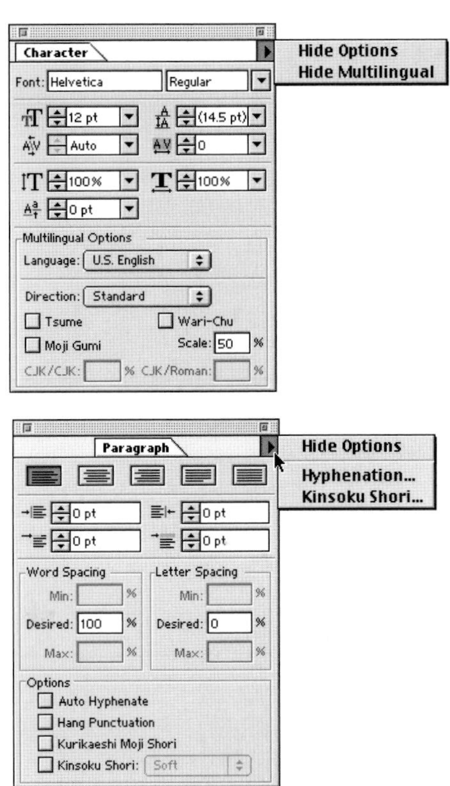

Appendix D: Moving to Illustrator from FreeHand or CorelDRAW

If you're familiar with either FreeHand or CorelDRAW, refer to this table to get up to speed quickly with Adobe Illustrator 8.0. This table compares commands or features that differ significantly in name or location between the three programs. (Subtle differences aren't listed. For example, for type-related commands, it's assumed that you'll look in the Type menu.)

The streamlined Illustrator 8.0 interface closely matches that in Adobe Photoshop and Adobe PageMaker in design, features, and keyboard shortcuts. Illustrator features a single menu bar, one toolbox, and 17 tabbed palettes. The menu bar lists options for setting up a file, editing and viewing objects and text, applying special effects, and customizing the workspace. The toolbox has keys for accessing tools using the keyboard, and tear-off menus for tool groups, like those in CorelDRAW. All palettes in Illustrator work in the same way—they can be collapsed, docked, or grouped.

FREEHAND	CORELDRAW	ILLUSTRATOR 8.0
Managing files		
Import	Import	File > Place
Report	Document Info or Properties	File > Selection or Document Info
Output Options	Print Preview	File > Document Setup
Viewing		
Panels, Inspectors	Roll-ups, Dockers	Palettes
Preview for Automatic or Manual Tiling	Printable Area	View > Show/Hide Page Tiling
Layers panel	Object Manager	Layers palette
Magnify tool	Zoom/pan tools	Zoom tool
Selecting objects		
Selected points are hollow.	Selected nodes are larger and solid.	Selected points are solid.
Unselected points are solid.	Unselected nodes are smaller and hollow.	Unselected points are hollow.
Pointer tool	Pick tool	Selection (arrow), direct-selection, or group-selection tool

FREEHAND	CORELDRAW	ILLUSTRATOR 8.0
Editing objects		
Fill Inspector	Interactive fill tool	See "Applying colors to artwork" on page 161.
Cut Contents/Paste Inside	Place Inside Container	Object > Masks > Make
Copy/Paste Attributes	Copy Properties From	Eyedropper/paint bucket tools
Duplicate	Repeat	Object > Transform > Transform Again (repeats last move, paste, and so on)
Transparency	Transparency	Object > Pathfinder > Soft/Hard
Remove Overlap	Weld	Object > Pathfinder > Unite
Expand Stroke	Contour > Outside	Object > Path > Outline Path
Inset Path	—	Object Path > Offset Path
Bend	Interactive Distort	Filters > Distort > Scribble and Tweak
Constrain	—	File > Preferences > General
—	Order	Object > Arrange
—	Intersection	Object > Pathfinder > Exclude
—	Separate	Object > Blends > Expand
—	Perspective	Filters > Distort
Skew	Shear (with pick tool)	Shear tool or free transform tool
—	Change to Line/Curve	Convert-direction-point or pen tool
—	Break Curve	Scissors tool
Drawing		
Freehand tool	Freehand tool	Pencil tool
Variable or Calligraphic Pen	Natural pen tool	Paintbrush tool > Calligraphic brush
Graphic Hose	—	Paintbrush tool > Scatter brush
Chart	—	Graph tool
Shift key constrains	Control key constrains	Shift key constrains

FREEHAND	CORELDRAW	ILLUSTRATOR 8.0
Text effects		
Shadow	Interactive drop shadow tool	Filter > Stylize > Drop Shadow
Run Around Selection	Wrap Paragraph Text	Type > Wrap
Flow Inside Path	Text tool	Area-type tool
Attach to Path	Text tool	Path-type tool
Detach from Path	Separate	Selection tool. (See "Creating type" on page 252.)
Convert to Paths	Convert to Curves	Type > Create Outlines

Index

C

D

H

N

O

P

S

X

Z

Production Notes

This book was created electronically using Adobe FrameMaker®. Art was produced using Adobe Illustrator and Adobe Photoshop. The Minion®, Frutiger™, and Granjon™ families of typefaces are used throughout this book.

Photography

Adobe Image Library (in Chapter 1; Endless Skies)

Adobe Image Library (in Chapter 10; Animal Life)